Bob Hall

Mon 10-12 GP1-9
Thurs 10-12 GP1-8
city PBG-13 Bob Hall
Ph 302 2237
for appointment.

QUANTITATIVE METHODS IN BUSINESS

North terrace   in @ 9¹⁰ for Text check.
       Exam   9²⁰   Sat   22 June 1996
A - Hi Bongethen Hall   Po - S   CB6-9 } centenary
Ho - Pi Brook man Hall   T - Z   CB5 -19 } Building

3 hr + 2 min

Q1-3 Scenario   28 % variables, 9 ea
Q4- 6 stats   48 % descriptive, Hyp, Estim
Q7-8 Fin - maths 24 % Interest Annuities

P₂4
Blue
Book

1995 sem 2 exam Exam sem2. doc Sol^n qmbus
Soln exam. doc in sol^n direc^t of QMBUS

QUANTITATIVE METHODS IN BUSINESS

**C. J. BRIEN, M. J. CORRELL, M. J. OLSSON,
R. E. HALL & D. J. SUTTON**

PRENTICE HALL
SYDNEY • NEW YORK • TORONTO • MEXICO • NEW DELHI
LONDON • TOKYO • SINGAPORE • RIO DE JANEIRO

Acquisitions Editor: Paul Petrulis
Production Editor: Elizabeth Thomas
Cover and text design: Jack Jagtenberg
Typeset by Monoset Typesetters, Queensland

Printed in Australia by Ligare Pty Ltd, Riverwood, NSW

1 2 3 4 5 00 99 98 97 96

ISBN 0 7248 1039 0

National Library of Australia
Cataloguing-in-Publication Data

Quantitative methods in business.

Bibliography
Includes index
ISBN 0 7248 1039 0

1. Business mathematics. 2. Commercial statistics.
I. Brien, Christopher J.

519.5024658

Prentice Hall of Australia Pty Ltd, *Sydney*
Prentice Hall, Inc., *Englewood Cliffs, New Jersey*
Prentice Hall Canada, Inc., *Toronto*
Prentice Hall Hispanoamericana, SA, *Mexico*
Prentice Hall of India Private Ltd, *New Delhi*
Prentice Hall International, Inc., *London*
Prentice Hall of Japan, Inc., *Tokyo*
Prentice Hall of Southeast Asia Pty Ltd, *Singapore*
Editora Prentice Hall do Brasil Ltds, *Rio de Janeiro*

 PRENTICE HALL

A Division of Simon & Schuster

C O N T E N T S

Chapter 21 Interest 642

Chapter 22 Annuities 657

PART VIII OPTIMISATION 679

Chapter 23 Linear programming 681

Appendix D Detailed instructions for Minitab menus 738

P R E F A C E

The aim of this book is to present the application of modern statistical and mathematical techniques, primarily in business and management. In spite of the elementary nature of the statistical and mathematical procedures presented, not all are commonly used in business and management today. We hope that the concentration on applications in this text will encourage their wider adoption.

We assume that, in practice, neither statistics nor mathematics will be used unless the burden of doing the calculations is taken over by a computer. Therefore, calculations are discussed only where they can be expected to help the reader to understand a procedure.

We are acutely aware that many tertiary students are overwhelmed by the number of procedures presented in their first courses in statistics. Because of this, we did not want to produce an encyclopaedic volume of statistical and mathematical procedures, so we cover only a limited set of procedures. In particular, we do not present special procedures for specific cases that are also covered by more general tests. For example, the two-sided z-test for a proportion is not presented because it is covered by the goodness-of-fit test, and in single sample cases a confidence interval is usually more appropriate than a hypothesis test.

Since probability is a common phobia for students in business and management, we confine our coverage of probability to using probability distributions as part of statistical inference procedures. This material is sufficient to explain the probabilistic basis of the statistical inference and is integrated with these procedures.

With the advent of modern computers, it has become customary to examine the assumptions underlying statistical inference procedures, and textbooks now include such material. However, the full set of conditions to meet the assumptions underlying all the procedures is seldom stated or investigated. We do this explicitly for all statistical inference procedures. The conditions are given in descriptive terms and are related to what should occur in practice if they are to be met. For example, the probability distribution that underlies a particular procedure is specified descriptively, rather than as mathematical formulae and properties. That is, words and diagrams are used to establish what is most likely to occur in a real situation.

We feel very strongly that most textbooks fail to give the students an outline of the subject so that they can work out how the many techniques fit together. To overcome this, we present overviews and scenarios. The overviews show how all the procedures fit together. The scenarios are real-life situations that involve questions that an investigator wants answered. The student selects the appropriate procedure from all the procedures presented, and selection guidelines are provided for this.

Central to each overview provided is the classification of the variables involved. In our experience, students have difficulty with the classifications currently in use as they do not directly indicate which procedure to use. For example, the one-way analysis of variance is used to analyse discrete data when the data consists of large counts. Yet, this procedure is based on a continuous distribution. There is also some controversy about choosing analyses according to the type of variable involved, a variable being a characteristic of the entities being observed. We believe that this is partly due to a failure to distinguish between the conceptual nature of the characteristic and the measurement obtained for the characteristic. Indeed, all measurements are discrete, strictly-speaking, yet some characteristics are inherently discrete while others are continuous. We have therefore taken the major step of using a nonstandard system to classify variables. We distinguish between limited and unrestricted variables on the basis of the likely number of different categories or values that are associated with the variable. That is, this system is based on the values recorded for a characteristic. We believe the choice of procedure can most often be based on this criterion.

The organisation and names of the chapters are based on the class of problem being solved, rather than on the historical names for procedures. The overviews can then be used as a basis for identifying the class of problem in a particular instance and the corresponding chapter consulted.

Student effort in the mathematics of finance and linear programming is directed to an overview of the usefulness of the techniques in business and management, and we have eliminated tedious hand calculation. Where possible, we have related this part of the book to the statistics work in the rest of the book. For example, we have indicated how information used in linear programming is collected by using statistical techniques.

The authors are indebted to Dr Michael Marinoff of the School of Information Systems at the University of South Australia for his many detailed comments on a draft version of this book and to the students of the University of South Australia for their feedback on the subjects in which the predecessors of this book were used. We also thank Ms Julie Catalano and Mr Paul Petrulis, Acquisitions Editors, Ms Elizabeth Thomas, Senior Production Editor and Mr David Weston, Publication Manager, from Prentice Hall of Australia for their invaluable assistance in getting this book into published form.

The data on real estate sales, given in Appendix A1, *Data sets*, has been kindly supplied by the South Australian Department of Environment and Natural Resources. We are grateful for their permission to use this data. We are also grateful for the support provided by Minitab Inc. in incorporating the use of Minitab in the book.

C. J. Brien
M. J. Correll
M. J. Olsson
R. E. Hall
D. J. Sutton

HOW TO USE THIS BOOK

There is sufficient material in this book for a one-semester course that covers either:

- all the material on the application of statistics; or
- most of the material on the applications of statistics and all the material on the applications of mathematics.

General material is given in standard size print, whereas examples that illustrate the application of this material are indented and set in a different typeface. It is recommended that you read the examples first to see the results of the procedures and then read the general material to extend your understanding of the topic.

For a particular procedure, the aspects that might be studied include:

- the purpose of the procedure;
- the steps to perform the procedure;
- the mathematical derivation of the procedure;
- the circumstances in which the procedure is appropriate;
- summarising the information yielded by the procedure.

In this book, we will concentrate on the first and last two of these aspects, as these are crucial to the use of statistics. Thus, even though statistics is a quantitative subject, our approach to the subject does not rely heavily on mathematical skills. The skills involved are arithmetic and formulae substitution, but not algebraic manipulation of formulae. In the past, courses in the application of statistics concentrated on the steps to perform the procedure. Great amounts of time were spent laboriously performing the statistical computations with pencil, paper and calculator. In this book, we outline the use of computers to minimise this aspect. The steps are discussed only where they help the student to understand the other aspects of the procedure.

Another characteristic of learning statistics is that many new terms and concepts are introduced. It will be important to distinguish between variance and variable, to realise that analysis of variance examines mean differences, not variance differences. You will need to use terminology carefully and make an effort to understand the precise technical meanings of terms. To help you with this, there is a Glossary at the end of the book. Key terms, which are defined in the Glossary, are in bold type where they first appear in a chapter, and are also listed at the end of each chapter.

The use of Minitab to perform the computations is described in a separate section towards the end of each chapter. Appendix B, *Summary of Minitab commands*, contains a summary of the Minitab commands used in the book. The menus and options used to access the Minitab commands are listed in the Minitab section towards the end of each chapter. The details for how to use the menus are in Appendix D, *Detailed instructions for Minitab menus*, explains how to use the menus. The data for many examples and exercises has been placed in Minitab files; the file names of those examples with files can be obtained from the output in the Minitab section and those for the exercises that have files are given with the exercises. The files are available from your instructor.

Reports on the examples are given as a separate section. They indicate how you should typically report the results of an analysis. These reports should include:

- a brief overview of how the data was collected;
- a statement of the problem that the analysis addressed;
- a concise statement of the results;
- supporting tables or figures referred to in the report.

Normally, the supporting tables and figures would accompany the report. However, to conserve space they are not repeated in the reports in this book.

The exercises include:

- Concept exercises that the students can use to check their understanding of the theory covered in the chapter.

- Exercises that students can use to practise the complete process of carrying out a particular procedure, including the performance of calculations, the drawing of conclusions from the results, and the writing of reports. For some of these exercises the Minitab computer output has been supplied so that the student can follow this example output, to familiarise themselves with the sequence of commands needed; they can also be attempted without having to use the computer.

About the Authors

Chris Brien   MScAgr, MAgrSc, PhD
Senior lecturer in Statistics,
School of Mathematics, Faculty of Applied Science and Technology
The University of South Australia

Margaret Correll   BSc, DipEd, BA, DipCompSci
Lecturer in Statistics,
School of Mathematics, Faculty of Applied Science and Technology
The University of South Australia

Marilyn Olsson   BA
Lecturer in Statistics,
School of Mathematics, Faculty of Applied Science and Technology
The University of South Australia

Bob Hall   BSc, MSc
Senior lecturer in Statistics,
School of Mathematics, Faculty of Applied Science and Technology
The University of South Australia

David Sutton   BMath(Hons), GDipBusAdmin, PhD
Lecturer in Information Systems,
School of Information Systems, Faculty of Business and Management
The University of South Australia

THE APPLICATION
OF STATISTICS

PART I

INTRODUCTION

In this part we aim to introduce you to what statistics is about and to the Minitab statistical package. In particular, we argue that statistics is a problem-solving tool useful in business decision making. We will formulate the precise problem that is to be solved for a particular example as the question to be investigated.

We also provide an overview of the statistical procedures covered in this book. While the reader may not understand the details at this stage, this summary shows the reader that there is a structure surrounding the statistical procedures covered in the book. As such it becomes a way for you to 'see the wood for the trees' and helps you in choosing how to analyse a particular set of data in order to answer the question being investigated. This latter skill will be required whenever you attempt to use statistical procedures in either your professional or private activities.

## CHAPTER 1

STATISTICS

INTRODUCTION

LEARNING OBJECTIVES

The learning objectives of this chapter are:
- to become familiar with the subject of statistics;
- to gain an insight into the usefulness of statistics;
- to obtain an overview of the statistical procedures presented here.

1.1 What is statistics?

1.1.1 History

The word statistics derives from the Greek and Latin words that mean 'of the state'. Statistics grew to mean 'arithmetic of the state'. Early examples of state arithmetic are the population censuses carried out by the Hebrews from the time of Moses, about 1500 BC, at least until the time of the Roman Empire, about 5 BC. These were carried out mostly for taxation and military service purposes. Other historical examples include the survey of the lands of England by William the Conqueror in the 11th century, also to determine taxation, and the records of births, deaths and marriages kept in the Middle Ages. Today a large array of such data is collected by the state; for example Gross National Product, Consumer Price Index, births, deaths, land use, employment, production figures and numbers of road accidents.

1.1.2 Dictionary definition

The Macquarie Dictionary (Delbridge et al., 1991) gives the following alternative definitions of **statistics**:
- the science that deals with the collection, classification, and use of numerical facts or data, bearing on a subject or matter;
- the numerical facts or data themselves.

Statistics therefore has two, possibly confusing, meanings: the first deals with the subject of statistics; the second concerns the objects themselves. The former seems to relate to the original usage of the word, while the latter seems to be a later development.

1.1.3 Common understanding

The common understanding of statistics has more to do with the second dictionary definition. That is, when people think of statistics, they think of the actual numbers. However, the first dictionary definition is the aspect most appropriate to the subject of this book.

1.1.4 Statistics today

Statistics has grown to be a science that is very widely used. Indeed, everyone is being constantly bombarded with statistical information: it is the warmest day on record; the rise in the major banks' interest rates over the past year has differed, with the total increase being between 2.75% and 3.65%; a particular sports team has had a 5-year winning streak. These are examples that affect us in our everyday lives. However, statistics is also widely used professionally. Just about every undergraduate course includes at least one statistics unit. The library shelves contain books on the application of statistics in business and management, economics, marketing research, law, libraries, agriculture, social sciences, physical sciences, engineering, chemistry and so on.

Statistics is one of the boom professions associated with the computer revolution. Much more data is being collected and requires analysis, and the analysis of such data is made much easier by computers. Statistics is now a science whose practitioners are concerned to help you obtain better information for better decision-making. An education in statistical methods will help you to cope with the great mass of statistical information that you will encounter in your private and professional life.

1.2 The role of statistics in business

In a nutshell, the role of statistics is to *help to answer questions* that arise in business, as well as more generally. So, statistics is a **problem-solving tool**: it provides you with procedures that solve the problem of answering **questions to be investigated**. Its great usefulness lies in the fact that it can help to answer a seemingly endless variety and number of questions. Statistics cannot help you solve all the problems that arise in business, but it is a tool that helps when you have to base decisions on hard evidence, that is, whenever you need to gather facts and summarise and interpret them. On the other hand, if you are prepared to base your decisions on 'gut-reaction', then you will have little need for statistics. However, in today's world, many decisions require justification with objective evidence; 'flying by the seat of your pants' is no longer good enough.

Statistics provides you with a set of procedures that allows you to assemble information that can be used as a basis for sound decision-making, but it is important to realise that statistics is only a tool in the decision-making process; it is not the whole process. Much business insight and acumen has to be used in formulating the question that is to be investigated, and in using the results of a statistical analysis.

The following examples illustrate the sort of question that you can expect to be able to solve once you are familiar with the material in this book.

EXAMPLE 1.1   SEX BALANCE AT A UNIVERSITY

The aim is to have an equal number of female and male students at universities. The equity and access officer of a large multicampus university wants to produce evidence of the balance of the sexes at the various campuses.

EXAMPLE 1.2   WORD PROCESSING SURVEY

A survey of an organisation's staff asks them all which word processing package they use. They are also asked to rate the package they used for ease of use, on a 5-point rating scale ranging from very easy to very difficult. The survey is designed to establish how the staff compare the different word processing packages for ease of use.

EXAMPLE 1.3   THE BEST-TASTING COLA

A marketing researcher wants to investigate why the best-selling cola is more popular than the others. Does it taste better or does it sell better for some other reason (such as the nature of its advertising program)?

EXAMPLE 1.4   ZONING PROPOSAL

The local government council is proposing to rezone a residential area as residential and light industrial. A member of council would like to know how many residents agree with this proposal. There are insufficient resources for all residents to be consulted.

EXAMPLE 1.5   CHRISTMAS WEATHER

Since Christmas day comes at the end of December, it occurs in the middle of summer in the southern hemisphere. Consequently, in many places it is expected to be rather warm. How often is the maximum temperature on Christmas day less than 20°C?

EXAMPLE 1.6   STRESS STUDY

A large corporation wants to determine whether the level of stress-related problems observed on the job for their employees is related to the time they take to get to work.

In each of these examples the investigator has posed a question and the answer to this question can be used as a basis for decision-making. The problem we will be confronting is how to answer such questions by using hard evidence.

Many of these questions might seem pretty straightforward. No doubt, even now, you could make an attempt to answer some of them. However, what is the best method of presenting the answer? By 'best' we mean how can the message be communicated most clearly to the intended audience? For example, it is easy to answer the question: how many male and female students are there at the university? From a list of students, count the numbers of each sex; then decide how best to present this information.

Perhaps it is not so straightforward to answer the question: does the best-selling cola also have the best taste? We must ensure that our conclusions apply to a wide group of people, such as all Australians; how can this be done? The question of the best method of presentation also arises here.

As far as determining how often the maximum temperature on Christmas day is less than 20°C, you might rely on your memory. You might guess that this would occur less than 1 in 10 times. Surely, a much better approach is to consult the weather records and find out exactly what proportion of Christmas days register lower than 20°C. This is the objective approach, mentioned above, that provides a much sounder basis for decision-making.

The following example gives you further insight into how statistics can contribute to sounder decision-making.

EXAMPLE 1.7   LOCAL CRIME RATE

An article in a local suburban newspaper, by Hider (1994), was headlined *Local crime rate slashed by 10pc*. The article quoted the local police inspector's claim that crime had fallen by an average of 10% compared with the same time last year. The data on the numbers of offences in two suburbs of Adelaide, contained in table 1.1, accompanied the article. The basic question is: what is the change in the crime rate in a particular part of the city?

The information must be presented in such a way that a valid, readily appreciated answer to the question is given. The first problem to be resolved is the method of computing the overall change in the rate, as it could be computed in at least two ways:

- the average of the decreases for each offence;
- the decrease in the yearly totals.

Both methods have been used and the results are presented in table 1.1. The answers differ by about 10%. Which is preferable? Whichever answer is preferred, it seems that the decrease in the crime rate is in fact more than the 10% claimed by the inspector.

Table 1.1   Numbers of offences in two areas of a city

Offence	Norwood			Unley		
	Oct 92– Mar 93	Oct 93– Mar 94	Decrease (%)	Oct 92– Mar 93	Oct 93– Mar 94	Decrease (%)
Breaks	865	651	24.7	1319	1049	20.5
Larceny/Illegal use	164	108	7.4	269	212	23.9
Illegal interference motor vehicle	117	59	15.0	151	76	18.5
Larceny motor vehicle	301	256	39.2	453	369	19.3
Other theft	527	488	34.1	800	609	21.2
Property damage	51	31	49.6	662	534	49.7
Offensive behaviour	48	24	50.0	92	41	55.4
Total	2073	1617	22.0	3746	2890	22.9
Average			31.4			29.8

Source: Abstracted from Hider (1994)

The data in table 1.1 also allows you to investigate differences in the decrease between offences and the areas. This information is more readily obtained from a diagram such as figure 1.1. It seems that theft and break-ins have decreased much less than other offences have, and that the decrease in the crime rate for the different offences is not the same for the two areas. For example, the decrease in property damage is much greater in Norwood than in Unley. However, a much smaller number of property damage offences were reported in Norwood.

This example has used statistical methods to collect the data, summarise it in tabular and/or diagrammatic form, and interpret the summaries.

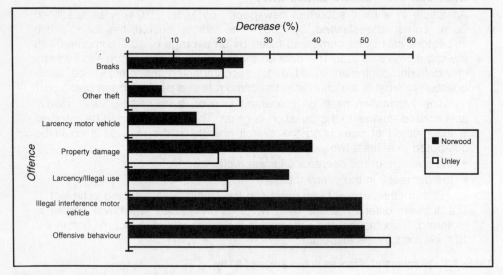

Figure 1.1   Crime rate in two areas of a city

Although example 1.7, *Local crime rate*, uses only very simple statistical techniques, it indicates the issues with which statistics is concerned: how to collect, analyse and present data so that questions are answered and sound business decisions are made. Put another way: statistics is about making the data talk!

1.3   Summary of procedures based on types of statistics

In summary, statistics helps answer questions by using different methods for different questions. A crucial problem that you are going to face is: what statistical procedure should I use to help answer my question? To help solve this problem:

- a summary of the statistical procedures covered in this book is provided here and in part VI, *Overview of statistical procedures*;

- a framework for and practice in choosing procedures to answer questions is given in chapter 13, *Overview of descriptive summaries*, and in part VI, *Overview of statistical procedures*.

The summaries in the book will help you to determine which class a question to be investigated belongs to, and what statistical procedure you should use to analyse it.

The summary of statistical procedures given here divides the techniques into four major categories of statistical procedures. The procedures available in each major category are then classified according to what type of statistic they are based on. The summary will not mean a lot to a reader who knows little about the material covered by the rest of the book, but it is presented here to show that there is an overall structure to the many procedures we cover. For each particular procedure the reader can refer to this summary to see how it fits into the overall structure. The summary given here is extended in chapter 13, *Overview of descriptive summaries*, and part VI, *Overview of statistical procedures*, to include combinations of variables. This extended summary is provided to help to determine which statistical procedure to employ.

The statistical methods described in this book can be classified into one of four **major categories of statistical procedures**:

A. **data collection procedures**: for collecting data so that the validity of the collected information is maximised;

B. **descriptive summaries**: for summarising aspects of the behaviour of just the data being analysed;

C. **estimation procedures**: for estimating population quantities using a sample;

D. **hypothesis tests**: for answering yes/no questions about the population using a sample.

The statistical procedures can then be summarised according to the types of statistics they represent. Figure 1.2 (on page 10) gives an overview of the general organisation of the statistical procedures.

In summary, the **types of statistics** covered, and their purposes, are:

- **distribution of variables**: to give an idea of how frequently values are observed;
- **single value**: to give the value of a single observational unit;
- **range of values**: to specify the range covered by a specified proportion of observational units;
- **measures of central tendency**: to give an idea of the value about which observations tend to cluster;
- **measures of dispersion**: to give an idea of how spread the values are;
- **measures of association**: to find out if there is an association between two unrestricted variables;
- **fitted lines**: to fit a straight line summarising the trend in the relationship between two unrestricted variables;
- **index numbers**: to examine changes over time or between different locations; and
- **time series**: to examine the history of a variable.

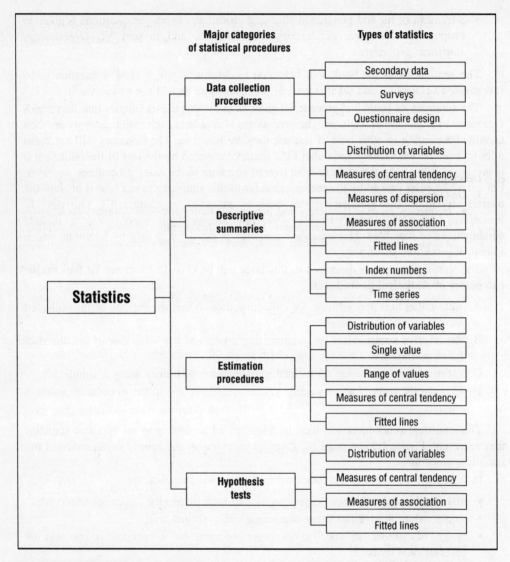

Figure 1.2   Organisation of statistical procedures according to major categories and types of statistics

The following summary explains how each particular statistical procedure fits into the structure in figure 1.2.

A. **Data collection procedures**
   1. *Observational data*
      Collection of data that reflects things as they are. Considerations are:
      • secondary data

- surveys — basic methods of sampling such as convenience sampling, judgement sampling, simple random sampling, systematic sampling; population subdivision for quota sampling, stratified random sampling, cluster sampling
- questionnaire design

2. *Experimental data**
Collection of data in which things have been manipulated

B.   Descriptive summaries

1. *Distribution of variables*
   - frequency, relative frequency and percentage table; one-way summary table; two-way and three-way contingency table — histogram, polygon, stem-and-leaf display, dotplot, bar or column chart; chart with bars or columns that are stacked or grouped

2. *Measures of central tendency*
   - mean, median, mode; one-way and two-way tables of a central tendency measure — bar chart, line diagram or boxplot

3. *Measures of dispersion*
   - range, interquartile range, standard deviation, coefficient of variation; one-way and two-way tables of a dispersion measure — boxplot

4. *Measures of association*
   - linear correlation coefficient and coefficient of determination — scatter diagram

5. *Fitted lines*
   - intercept and/or slope; mean response — scatter diagram

6. *Index numbers*
   - simple index numbers, unweighted aggregative and relatives index numbers and Laspeyres and Paasche weighted index numbers — line diagram

7. *Time series*
   - observed series; smoothed series using simple linear regression, moving averages or exponential smoothing; additively or multiplicatively deseasonalised series; forecast — line diagram

C.   Estimation procedures

1. *Distribution of variables*
   - confidence interval for the population proportion
   - can be used to determine sample size for given degree of confidence, sampling error and variability

2. *Single value*
   - prediction interval for a future observation

3. *Range of values*
   - tolerance interval for middle $100\pi\%$ of population values

4. *Measures of central tendency*
   - confidence interval for the population mean
   - can be used to determine sample size for given degree of confidence, sampling error and variability

5. *Fitted lines*
   - confidence intervals for the population intercept and the population slope; confidence interval for the population mean response at a particular X; prediction interval for a future observation at a particular X

D. **Hypothesis tests**

1. *Distribution of variables*
   - z-test for a proportion;* z-test for a proportion difference;* goodness-of-fit test; contingency table analysis

2. *Measures of central tendency*
   - unpaired t-test;* one-way analysis of variance

3. *Measures of association*
   - test for linear correlation*

4. *Fitted lines*
   - F-test for slope

* These methods have not been presented in this book.

1.4   Chapter summary

Statistics is the science that deals with the collection, classification, and use of numerical facts or data, bearing on a subject or matter. It has become a very widely used science. It can help to answer questions that arise in business, particularly decisions that must be based on hard evidence. As such, statistics gives you a set of procedures for assembling information that can be used as a basis for sound decision-making.

The statistical procedures covered in this book are classified into four major categories and according to the types of statistics on which they are based. A summary, using these classifications, has been provided to help you to identify which class of problem a particular statistical procedure can be used to solve. That is, the summary can help you decide which statistical procedure to use to answer the question you are investigating.

1.5   Key terms

- data collection procedures
- descriptive summaries
- distribution of variables
- estimation procedures
- fitted line
- hypothesis tests
- index number
- major category of statistical procedures
- measure of association
- measure of central tendency
- measure of dispersion
- problem-solving tool
- question to be investigated
- range of values
- single value
- statistics
- time series
- type of statistic

## CHAPTER 2

USING MINITAB

L E A R N I N G   O B J E C T I V E S

The learning objectives of this chapter are:
- to become familiar with the basic concepts required for using the statistical package, Minitab, on the computer;
- to become acquainted with the two modes of using the statistical package, Minitab, on the computer;
- to gain some practice with Minitab on the computer.

These days statistical procedures are carried out using computers. There are many statistical packages available and statistical procedures are now being incorporated with spreadsheet packages. In this book, **Minitab** is used for the computations. At the time of writing, Minitab covered a much wider range of statistical procedures than the spreadsheet packages did. Compared to other statistical packages, it is relatively easy to use; it is available on a wide range of computers, including minicomputers, IBM PC compatibles and Macintosh computers. This chapter outlines some of the basic concepts and features of Minitab.

When you want to use Minitab, the first thing you have to do is find a computer that contains the Minitab software. Then you have to carry out the operating system procedures that are necessary to prepare the computer for using Minitab. The instructions for this vary greatly so ask your instructor how to do it on the computer you want to use.

Once you have got Minitab started, the last line of output on your screen should contain the **Minitab prompt**:

```
MTB>
```

You are now ready to use Minitab. At this point Minitab has set up (in the computer's RAM memory, as opposed to a disk) an empty worksheet. You put information into this worksheet by entering numbers in columns. Each number in a column is thought of as occurring in a row of the worksheet, the first number in a column in the first row, the second number in the second row, and so on. In general, columns have different measurements, whereas rows are for different instances of the same measurement. For example, heights are stored in one column and weights in a second column; heights for different people are stored in different rows of the same column.

If you are using Release 8 of Minitab on the PC, the Minitab prompt will be contained in a screen such as the one shown in figure 2.1.

Note that although this screen was generated by the full version of Minitab, the student edition is sufficient for all the examples and exercises in this book. The main difference between the two versions is that the worksheet in the student edition is limited to 3500 cells and a maximum of 100 columns.

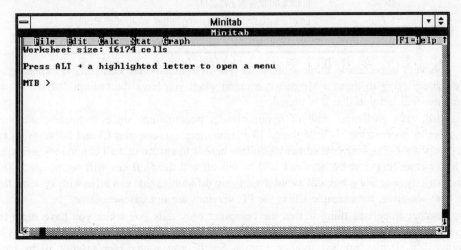

Figure 2.1   Opening Minitab window on a PC

2.1   General considerations

The normal sequence of operations in a Minitab session is as follows:

1. prepare for hardcopy;
2. enter or retrieve, display, check and, optionally, save data;
3. perform procedure;
4. stop Minitab.

These operations are performed with **Minitab commands**, a command being a line of information that begins with the name of the command. Sometimes Minitab subcommands are required. A **Minitab subcommand** is an additional line of information that begins with the name of the subcommand and specifies additional information that must be taken into account when carrying out the Minitab command.

Having stopped Minitab, use your computer's printout procedure to produce a hardcopy of any output that you have stored in an output listing file on a disk.

2.1.1   Entering commands

Now, as we mentioned above, the computer produces a prompt. A **computer prompt** is the set of characters at the lefthand edge of a line that a computer presents to indicate that it is waiting for your response. Prompts are very important in computing because they indicate not only that a response is required but the type of response you must give. The Minitab prompts are in table 2.1.

Table 2.1   Minitab prompts

Prompt	Expected response
MTB>	Enter Minitab command
DATA>	Enter a number or *end data*
SUBC>	Enter a subcommand supplying further information about command

It is very important to think about what type of command the computer is expecting. It is no good trying to input a Minitab command when you have the prompt *DATA>* — the computer will tell you that it is illegal.

Also, take particular note of a command's punctuation, since computers are very sensitive to punctuation — little things like semicolons (;), commas (,) and fullstops (.) are very important. The convention that we follow here is to ensure that all commands are typed in lower case; that is, the *Caps Lock* will be left off and the *Shift* key will not be used. This is not strictly necessary, but will avoid mystifying difficulties that can arise with systems that are case-sensitive, for example Unix; the PC versions are not case-sensitive.

Another important thing is that the computer only tells you when you have done the wrong thing. If you are correct, it produces the output requested; if no output is to be produced, it simply supplies another prompt. So the appearance of a prompt all by itself means that you have entered a legal command — enter the next command.

2.1.2   Subcommands

Many commands have optional subcommands. If there are several subcommands for a particular command, any one or any combination of them can be entered. To enter subcommands, a semicolon (;) must be entered at the end of the original command line and after each subcommand except the last. The last subcommand line must end in a fullstop (.).

If you get the message

$$**Subcommand \ does \ not \ end \ in \ . \ or \ ; \ (; \ assumed)$$

and you do not want to enter more subcommands, enter a fullstop (.) on a line by itself.

If you get the message

$$* \ ERROR \ * \ Subcommand \ in \ error \ — \ subcommand \ ignored.$$

work out what the problem is and proceed as if the line producing the message had never been entered. That is, enter a legal subcommand or a fullstop (.).

2.1.3   Windows, menus and screens

Windows, menus and screens are available on some versions of Minitab. This gives you the option of entering commands, as for any version of Minitab, or using the windows, menus and screens to help you execute commands. If it is available, the **session window** shown in figure 2.1 will be displayed when Minitab is started. This window is an area of the computer screen set up by Minitab to display the Minitab commands that have been executed, along with the output produced by these commands. Along the top of this Window is the **menu bar**, a list of the available pull-down menus: File, Edit, Calc, Stat, Graph and Help. Clicking on one of these produces the display of the associated **pull-down menu**, each pull-down menu consisting of a list of groups of related Minitab commands. You then select from the menu the group of commands to be executed.

The other window is the help window, and there are two screens: the data and graphics screens. The **data screen** is like a spreadsheet and is used to enter or modify data.

2.1.4   Files for permanent storage

Information on the screen is available only while it remains on the screen, and information stored in the worksheet disappears once Minitab is stopped. Files provide a more permanent store, on a computer's hard disk or a floppy disk, of information for input into or output from Minitab. Different three-letter extensions are added automatically to the files' names to indicate what type of information they contain. The following file extensions, and the contents of files with that extension, occur in this book:

.mtw   Minitab worksheet

.mtp   Minitab portable worksheet

.mtb   Minitab commands

.dat   data for input to Minitab

.lis   output listings

The differences between these file types' functions are important. The worksheet files, those with extensions *.mtw* and *.mtp*, are used to save all the information contained in the worksheet file between Minitab sessions. They contain the data, the names of columns and other such information, but not in a form suitable for printing on paper. They do not contain the output from analyses. Files with an *.mtw* extension can only be used on the type of computer on which they were created, whereas files with an *.mtp* extension can be moved between different types of computers; for example, *.mtp* files can be moved from Macintosh to PC computers, whereas *.mtw* files cannot.

Files with extension *.lis* contain the output from a Minitab session. They can be used to obtain hardcopy by printing them out. Generally, they cannot be used to re-enter the data into the worksheet. Files with extension *.dat* contain data ready for input into Minitab and are usually created with a text editor. They do not contain column names and other information stored in the worksheet. The data in them may not even be arranged in columns. These files can be printed out. Files with the *.mtb* extension contain sets of Minitab commands to be executed. They are usually created with a text editor and can be printed out.

2.2   An introductory example using commands

When using Minitab, you have to choose between typing in the commands directly or using pull-down menus to have the same commands executed. It is possible to execute some commands by typing in the commands and others by using pull-down menus. The method chosen is a matter of personal preference. However, for each command, *only one method needs to be used*.

EXAMPLE 2.1   PRICES OF COFFEE

In a survey of some local supermarkets, the prices of 100 g jars of instant coffee were obtained to gain some idea of the average price customers have to pay for this item. Suppose that table 2.2 presents the data that has been collected and that Minitab is to be used for the computations.

Table 2.2   Prices ($) for analysis

2.57	4.39	1.68	4.45	3.09	2.78	2.85	3.68
3.38	2.99	3.19	2.38	3.21	3.19	4.50	

The Minitab commands for this analysis are as follows:

```
MTB > outfile 'a:\example.lis'
MTB > set c1
DATA> end
MTB > name c1 'price'
MTB > print c1
MTB > save 'a:\example.mtp';
SUBC> portable.
MTB > mean 'price'
MTB > noout
MTB > stop
```

The following subsections set out the function of each of these commands.

2.2.1   Prepare for hardcopy

Before the material on the screen can be printed out on paper, the information has to be stored in a file that can then be printed after Minitab is stopped. To set up a file, use the *outfile* command:

```
MTB > outfile 'a:\example.lis'
```

In the example, the file to store what is displayed on the screen has been called *example.lis*. The drive specification *a:* has been supplied because the disk to hold the file is in drive a; note that the drive letter depends on which drive contains the disk you want to use. The name of the file, *example*, must contain no more than 8 characters; it could not, for instance, be *coffeeprice*. The extension *.lis* indicates that this file contains output listing. The complete drive and file name are enclosed in single quotation marks (').

All the output that appears on the screen *after* the *outfile* command until the *nooutfile* command is placed in the file *example.lis*. Note that the *outfile* command produces printed output. It stores the displayed output so that you can use your system's file print command to obtain a paper copy of the output.

2.2.2   Enter, display, check and save data

Commands can be used to enter, check and save the data. However, these operations are made much more easy by using the *data screen* and pull-down menus, as described in section 2.3.2, *Enter, display, check and save data*.

If you want to enter data and name the column by using commands, use the *set* and *name* commands. For example, if I have an *MTB>* prompt, the commands to put these numbers into column 1 of the worksheet and to name the column *price*, are as follows:

```
MTB > set c1
DATA> 2.57 4.39 1.68 4.45
DATA> 3.09 2.78 2.85 3.68 3.38 2.99 3.19 2.38 3.21
DATA> 3.19 4.50
DATA> end
MTB > name c1 'price'
```

Note that the data has been entered in what is called 'free format'. That is, each value on the same line is separated by at least one space. Also, the values are arbitrarily placed on lines — anywhere from one value per line to as many values as will fit on a line, as well as unequal numbers of values per line. In this example the data is placed in *c1*, but it might just as easily be placed in *c3*, *c9* or *c99*.

The *name* command gives the column its name, which is *price*. The names of columns must not exceed 8 characters, otherwise an error message will be issued. The name is surrounded by single quotation marks or apostrophes: 'price'. Once a column has been named, we can use either its number or its name in any succeeding commands. However, the name must always be enclosed in single quotation marks. In this case, the *name* command has been entered after the *set* command. This is not essential as the *name* command can be entered any time during the Minitab session, including before the *set* command.

The data is displayed, by using the *print* command, to check that the values stored in the column are correct and to have a copy of the data included in the outfile. Note that this print command displays data only on the screen, *not* on paper.

```
MTB > print c1

price
 2.57  4.39  1.68  4.45  3.09  2.78  2.85
 3.68  3.38  2.99  3.19  2.38  3.21  3.19
 4.50
```

The *save* command is used to save the contents of the worksheet in the file *example.mtp* on drive a. Again, the drive and file name are enclosed in single quotation marks (').

```
MTB > save 'a:\example.mtp';
SUBC> portable.

Worksheet saved into file: a:\example.mtp
```

It is most important to appreciate the difference between the files created by the *outfile* and *save* commands. The file created by the *outfile* command contains the commands and the output they produce; this file can be printed, but it cannot be used to reload the data into the worksheet. The file created by the *save* command contains only the data stored in the worksheet; this file can be used to reload the data into the worksheet, but it is not printable. The difference between the two files is emphasised by the use of different extensions: *lis* for files created by *outfile* and *mtp* for files created by *save*.

2.2.3 Perform procedure

For this example, the performance of the procedure is trivial. The mean is calculated with the *mean* command.

```
MTB > mean 'price'
 MEAN = 3.2220
```

2.2.4 Stop Minitab

The *nooutfile* command is issued to stop further recording, in the file, of output displayed on the screen. It is optional if it is to be followed immediately by the *stop* command, as the *stop* command also closes the file.

```
MTB > noout
MTB > stop
```

Finally, enter the *stop* command to finish the Minitab session.

To obtain a hardcopy of the information stored in *example.lis*, use your computer's procedure for obtaining a printout of a file. Note that if the *save* command had not been used, the contents of the worksheet would have permanently disappeared.

2.3   An introductory example using pull-down menus

Instead of entering the commands directly, you can use the pull-down menus. You have to choose which of the two alternative methods to use. It is possible to execute some commands by typing in the commands and execute others by using pull-down menus. The method chosen is a matter of personal preference. However, for each command, only one method is necessary.

EXAMPLE 2.1 PRICES OF COFFEE (repeated)
In a survey of some local supermarkets, the prices of 100 g jars of instant coffee were obtained to gain some idea of the average price customers have to pay for this item. Suppose that table 2.3 presents the data that has been collected and that Minitab is to be used for the computations.

Table 2.3   Prices ($) for analysis

2.57	4.39	1.68	4.45	3.09	2.78	2.85	3.68
3.38	2.99	3.19	2.38	3.21	3.19	4.50	

The commands for achieving the analysis in Minitab were given in section 2.2, *An introductory example using commands*. Table 2.4 outlines the menus and options that have to be selected for these commands to be executed. A detailed description of how to use the pull-down menus to execute these commands is given in the following subsections and in Appendix D, *Detailed instructions for Minitab menus*; the appendix is in alphabetical order for the commands.

Table 2.4   Menus and options for some Minitab commands

Minitab command	Menu	Option
outfile 'a:\example.lis'	File >	Other Files > Start Recording Session...
set c1	Edit >	Data Screen (Alt-D)
name c1 'price'		(use data screen)
print c1	Edit >	Display Data...
save ' a:\example.mtp';	File >	Save Worksheet As...
portable.		Minitab portable worksheet
mean 'price'	Calc >	Functions and Statistics > Column Statistics...
nooutfile	File >	Other Files > Stop Recording Session...
stop	File >	Exit

2.3.1   Prepare for hardcopy

Before the material on the screen can be printed out on paper, the information has to be stored in a file that can then be printed after Minitab is stopped. To set up a file, use the *outfile* command. To use the pull-down menus to execute this command, select the *Other Files* option of the *Files* menu as illustrated in figure 2.2.

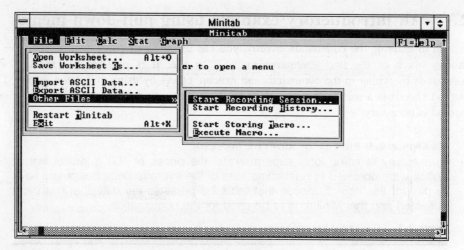

Figure 2.2   Menu to start recording displayed output

Click on the *Start Recording Session* option to display the dialog box in figure 2.3.

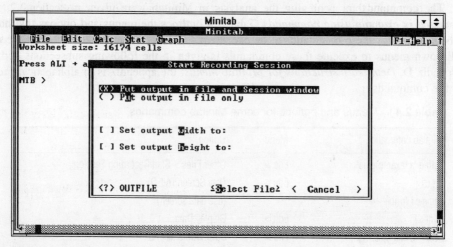

Figure 2.3   Dialog box to set options for saving displayed output

In this case, the defaults are suitable, so click on *Select file*. A dialog box will be displayed and this should be completed as shown in figure 2.4. That is, enter the file name as shown.

In the example, the file to store what is displayed on the screen has been called *example.lis*. The drive specification, *a:*, has been supplied as the disk to hold the file is in drive a; remember that the drive letter depends on which drive contains the disk you want to use. The name of the file, *example*, must contain no more than 8 characters; the name could not, for instance, be *coffeeprice*. The extension *.lis* indicates that this file contains output listing.

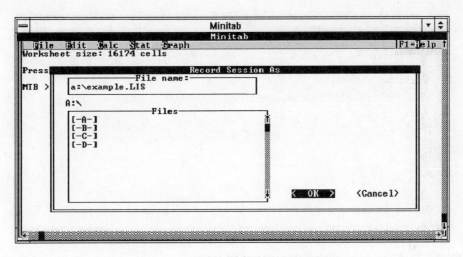

Figure 2.4   Dialog box to choose file for saving displayed output

All the output that appears on the screen *after* the *outfile* command until the *nooutfile* command is placed in the file *example.lis*. Note that the *outfile* command does not produce printed output. It stores the displayed output so that you can use your system's command to print out the file.

2.3.2   Enter, display, check and save data

To enter the data, use the spreadsheet-like data screen. To use the data screen, select the *Edit* menu as shown in figure 2.5 and click on *Data Screen*. Alternatively, press the *D* key while holding down the *Alt* key. This will display the data screen shown in figure 2.6.

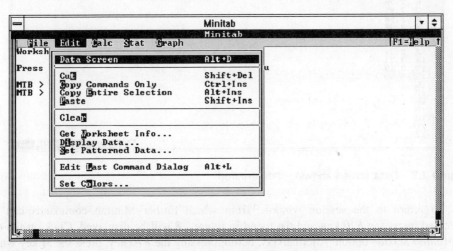

Figure 2.5   Menu containing option to switch to the data screen

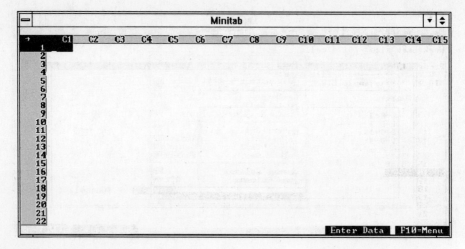

Figure 2.6   Data screen

Now enter the data by typing in the numbers and using arrow keys to move from cell to cell. To enter the name *price*, move the cursor up above the row containing the list of columns and enter the name, *without the single quotation marks*. The data screen should be as shown in figure 2.7. At this stage, check that the data you have entered is correct.

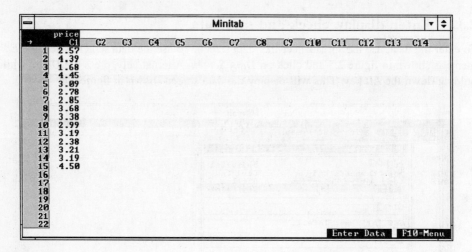

Figure 2.7   Data screen showing data entered

To return to the session window, from which further Minitab commands can be executed, press the *F10* key and the menu in figure 2.8 will be displayed. Click on the *Go to Minitab Session* option. Alternatively, before pressing the *F10* key, press the *M* key while holding down the *Alt* key.

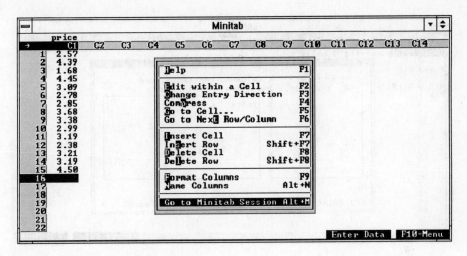

Figure 2.8   Menu to exit data screen

The following message will appear in the file created by *outfile*:

```
NOTE * The Data Screen was used to change the worksheet
```

To display the data, so that it can be included in the outfile, click on *Edit* to display the pull-down menu in figure 2.9. Select the *Display data* option.

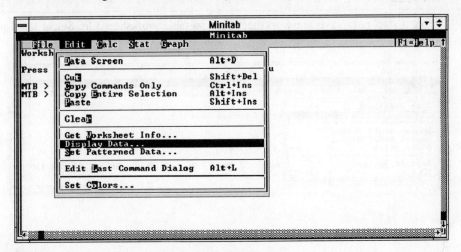

Figure 2.9   Menu containing option to display data

Now complete the dialog box given in figure 2.10 and select *OK* to execute the command.

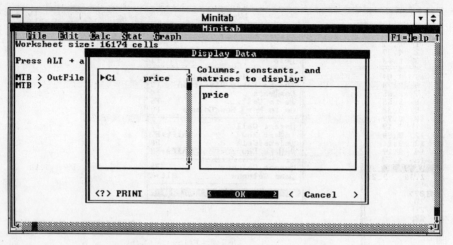

Figure 2.10   Dialog box for displaying a column

Note that this print command displays data only on the screen, *not* on paper. The file created by the *outfile* command will contain the following output:

```
MTB > Print 'price'.

price
   2.57    4.39    1.68    4.45    3.09    2.78    2.85    3.68    3.38
   2.99    3.19    2.38    3.21    3.19    4.50
```

The next step is to save the worksheet in a portable worksheet file. Select the *Save Worksheet As* option of the *File* menu, as shown in figure 2.11.

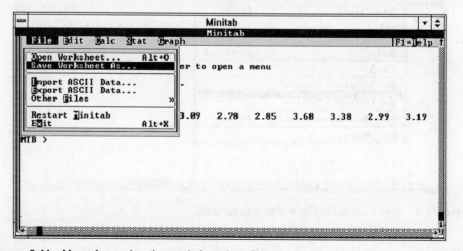

Figure 2.11   Menu for saving the worksheet in a file

If you choose the *Save Worksheet As* option, the dialog box in figure 2.12 will be displayed. Select *Minitab portable worksheet* and then click on *Select file*.

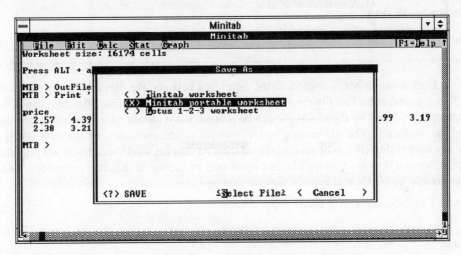

Figure 2.12   Dialog box for choosing type of file for saving worksheet

A dialog box will be displayed; complete this as shown in figure 2.13. That is, enter the file name as shown.

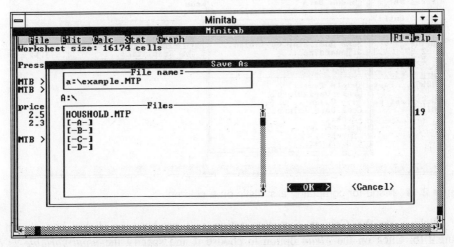

Figure 2.13   Dialog box to specify name of file in which to save worksheet

The file created by *outfile* will contain the following output:

```
MTB > Save 'a:\example.MTP';
SUBC> Portable.

Worksheet saved into file: a:\example.MTP
```

It is most important to appreciate the difference between the files created by the *outfile* and *save* commands. The file created by the *outfile* command contains the commands and the output produced by them; this file can be printed, but it cannot be used to reload the data into the worksheet. The file created by the *save* command contains only the data stored in the worksheet; this file can be used to reload the data into the worksheet, but is not printable. The difference between the two files is emphasised by the use of different extensions: *lis* for files created by *outfile* and *mtp* for files created by *save*.

2.3.3 Perform procedure

To compute the mean, select the *Function and Statistics* option of the *Calc* menu and the pull-down menu shown in figure 2.14 will be displayed.

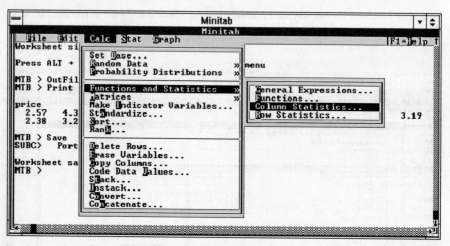

Figure 2.14 Menu for computing a statistic on a column

Clicking on the *Column Statistics* option will produce the dialog box shown in figure 2.15. Click on the *Mean* option to choose it and specify the *input variable* as *c1*. Finally, click on *OK* and the mean will be displayed.

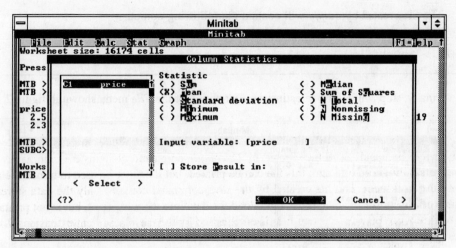

Figure 2.15   Dialog box for specifying a statistic to be computed on a column

The file created by *outfile* will contain the following output:

```
MTB > Mean 'price'.

  MEAN =  3.2220
```

2.3.4   Stop Minitab

Now that there is no more output to be produced, select the *Other Files* option of the *File* menu to produce the menu in figure 2.16. Click on *Stop Recording Session* and the *nooutfile* command will be issued. It is an optional command if it is to be followed immediately by the *stop* command, as the *stop* command also closes the file.

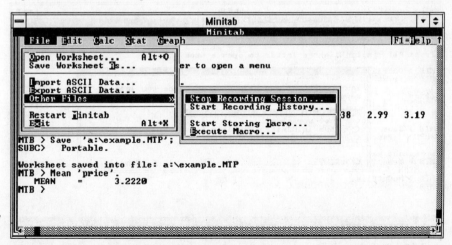

Figure 2.16   Menu to stop recording displayed output

The file created by *outfile* will contain the following output:

```
MTB > NoOutfile.
```

Finally, stop Minitab by selecting the *Exit* option of the *File* menu shown in figure 2.17.

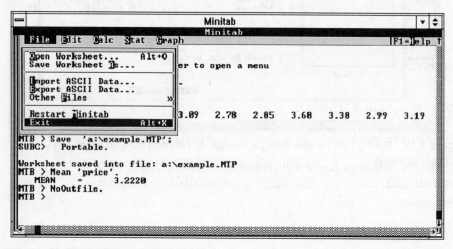

Figure 2.17   Menu to stop Minitab

The dialog box in figure 2.18 is presented. As the worksheet has just been saved, simply click on *OK* to stop Minitab without saving the worksheet. If you had not used the *save* command, the contents of the worksheet would have permanently disappeared.

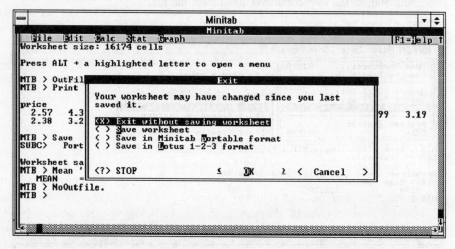

Figure 2.18   Dialog box to check worksheet saved before Minitab stopped

2.4   Chapter summary

This chapter has introduced you to the use of the statistical package Minitab. A Minitab session involves the following steps: preparing for hardcopy; enter or retrieving, displaying, checking and, optionally, saving data; performing procedures; stopping Minitab. After stopping Minitab, you need to arrange for the printing of any hardcopy that you have stored in a file. In using Minitab you have the option of typing in commands, and their subcommands, or using the pull-down menus to perform procedures. Whatever option you use, it is preferable to use the data screen to enter and modify data.

2.5   Key terms

- **computer prompt**
- **data screen**
- **menu bar**
- **Minitab**
- **Minitab command**

- **Minitab prompt**
- **Minitab subcommand**
- **pull-down menu**
- **session window**

2.6   Exercises

2.1 This exercise gives you some practice with the basic Minitab commands presented in sections 2.2, *An introductory example using commands*, and 2.3, *An introductory example using pull-down menus*. You will input a small set of data, display on the screen the data that has been put into the worksheet, do some computations on the data, save the data in a worksheet file for later use and obtain a printout of your results.

The first step is to get Minitab started on your computer. Once you have done this, the last line put on the screen by the computer should be the Minitab prompt:

```
MTB >
```

The next step is to decide whether you are going to type commands directly into Minitab or use Minitab's pull-down menus. If you are going to type in most of the commands, do part (a) and refer to section 2.2, *An introductory example using commands*, for a very similar example that includes the detailed commands. If you are going to use the menus, do part (b) and refer to section 2.3, *An introductory example using pull-down menus*, for a very similar example that includes the details for using the menus. Do *either* part (a) *or* part (b).

(a) Typing in the commands

- Prepare for hardcopy. Use the *outfile* command to arrange for everything that is displayed on the screen *from this point on* to be stored in a file called, say, *lengmean.lis*. Remember to enclose the drive and file name in single quotation marks (').

- Enter, display, check and save data. The data to be entered is as follows:

  4 18 11 7 7 10 5 33 9 12 3 11 10 6 26 37 15 18 10 21

  The *set* and *name* commands can be used to enter the data into *c1* and name the column. However, it is much simpler to use the data screen. To do this, click on *Edit* in the menu bar at the top of the screen and select *Data Screen*; or press the *D* key while the *Alt* key is held down.

  Now just enter the data into the cells in the first column, using the arrow keys to move after the number is entered.

  To give *c1* the name *length*, move the cursor into the line above *c1*. Type in *length* and press the *Enter* key.

  Check the data! Mistakes can be corrected as follows:
  - if the value in a cell is incorrect, move the cursor to the cell and type in the correct value;
  - if an extra value has been included, delete the cell by using the data screen menu that is displayed when the *F10* key is pressed;
  - if a value has been omitted, insert an extra cell by using the data screen menu that is displayed when the *F10* key is pressed; once the extra cell has been inserted, type in the value that was omitted.

  Once the data has been correctly entered, return to the Minitab session window. Press the *F10* key to display the data screen menu and select the *Goto Minitab session* option. You can do this without bringing up the menu by pressing the *M* key while holding down the *Alt* key.

  Use the *print* command to display the data, so that you will have a copy of it on paper for reference.

  Use the *save* command to save the Minitab worksheet in a Minitab portable worksheet file called, say *length.mtp*, for later use. Performing this command is also easier if you use the menus. Once again, if you are typing in the commands, do not forget to enclose the drive and file name in single quotation marks (').

- Perform procedure. Use the command *mean* to obtain the mean of the data.

- Stop Minitab. Use the *stop* command to stop Minitab.

  Now use your computer's commands for printing a file to obtain a paper copy of the output you have produced.

(b) Using pull-down menus

- Prepare for hardcopy. To arrange to have everything displayed on the screen *from this point on* stored in a file, access the *outfile* command from the menus as follows: *File > Other Files > Start Recording Session...* Call the output file, say, *lengmean.lis*.

- Enter, display, check and save data. The data to enter is as follows:

4 18 11 7 7 10 5 33 9 12 3 11 10 6 26 37 15 18 10 21

   Switch to the data screen to enter this data as follows: click on *Edit* in the menu bar at the top of the screen and select *Data Screen*; that is, it is accessed as *Edit > Data Screen*. Alternatively, press the *D* key while the *Alt* key is held down.

   Now just enter the data into the cells in the first column, using the arrow keys to move after the number is entered.

   To give *c1* the name *length*, move the cursor into the line above *c1*. Type in *length* and press the *Enter* key.

   Check the data! Mistakes can be corrected as follows:
   - if the value in a cell is incorrect, move the cursor to the cell and type in the correct value;
   - if an extra value has been included, delete the cell by using the data screen menu that is displayed when the *F10* key is pressed;
   - if a value has been omitted, insert an extra cell by using the data screen menu that is displayed when the *F10* key is pressed; once the extra cell has been inserted, type in the value that was omitted.

   Once the data has been correctly entered, return to the Minitab session window. Press the *F10* key to display the data screen menu and select the *Goto Minitab session* option. You can do this without getting up the menu by pressing the *M* key while holding down the *Alt* key.

   To display the data so that you will have a copy of it on paper for later reference, access the *print* command from the menus as follows: *Edit > Display Data*.

   To save the Minitab worksheet in a Minitab portable worksheet file for later use, access the *save* command from the menus as follows: *File > Save Worksheet As... > Minitab portable worksheet*. Call the file *length.mtp*.

- Perform procedure. To obtain the mean of the data, access the *mean* command from the menus as follows: *Calc > Functions and Statistics > Column Statistics...*

- Stop Minitab. To stop Minitab, access the *stop* command from the menus as follows: *File > Exit > Exit without saving worksheet*. It is not necessary to save the worksheet on exit this time as no change has been made to the worksheet since it was saved.

Now use your computer's commands for printing a file to obtain a paper copy of the output you have produced.

2.2   Statistical surveying often relies on randomly choosing individuals from a population. Minitab provides a computerised method of generating random numbers. Use the relevant parts of the first exercise, and the description below, to produce a column containing random numbers generated by Minitab.

(a)   Name a column *random*.

(b)   Use the following command, and associated subcommand, to store 20 numbers, randomly chosen from numbers 1 to 120, into the column named *random*:

```
MTB > random 20 'random';
SUBC> integer 1 120.
```

Note: if your version of Minitab has pull-down menus, you can execute this command from the menus using *Calc > Random data > Integer...*

(c)   Prepare for hardcopy.

(d)   Display your data on the screen.

(e)   Tally your data using the command:

```
MTB > tally 'random'
```

Note: if you have pull-down menus, you can execute this command from the menus using *Stat > Tables > Tally...*

(f)   Stop the Minitab session and obtain a hard copy.

2.3   In a survey of households from a city of 219 000 households, 200 households are selected. The number of children in each household is recorded. The raw data is given in table 2.5. However, this data has already been entered into Minitab and is available in the Minitab portable worksheet file *houshold.mtp*. Retrieve this file and use the *tally* command to find out the most frequently occurring number of children in a household. The *retrieve* command can be accessed from the menus by using *File > Open Worksheet... > Minitab portable worksheet*, and the tally command can be accessed by using *Stat > Tables > Tally*. If you are typing in the *retrieve* and *tally* commands and are not sure exactly what to enter for them, consult Appendix B, *Summary of Minitab commands*, to find out.

Table 2.5   *Number of children* for 200 surveyed households

0	1	0	2	2	2	2	2	0	3
0	2	2	3	3	2	3	2	3	2
2	2	1	0	2	1	3	2	2	2
2	2	1	2	2	0	1	3	2	2
0	2	3	2	2	0	2	1	2	3
2	2	1	2	1	1	2	0	2	2
3	2	2	2	2	2	1	2	0	2
3	2	2	0	1	2	1	2	2	2
1	2	2	1	2	2	3	1	2	2
1	0	1	2	1	3	2	2	1	2
2	2	2	2	2	2	1	1	2	2
0	2	1	3	2	0	2	2	1	1
1	2	2	1	2	1	2	2	2	1
1	2	2	1	2	2	2	2	0	1
2	0	0	2	1	2	2	3	2	2
2	2	2	2	2	0	2	2	2	1
1	2	2	3	2	0	2	1	1	3
2	2	3	2	2	1	2	3	2	2
2	2	2	1	2	2	2	3	2	1
0	2	1	2	2	2	2	2	2	2

PART II
DATA COLLECTION PROCEDURES

LEARNING OBJECTIVES

The learning objectives of this introduction to part II are:
- to understand the difference between a sample and a population;
- to know the different types of data.

Before you can analyse data, you have to collect it, so we begin by discussing the procedures for doing this. Although we spend much less time on these procedures than on analysing the data, the importance of the data collection phase of a study should not be underestimated. Indeed, the expression 'garbage in, garbage out' is particularly relevant to statistical analysis.

The data collection procedures to be covered are: obtaining secondary data, methods of sampling a population and questionnaire design. The principal aim of these procedures is to produce data from which valid conclusions can be drawn. However, before going on to cover them, we describe various types of data that might be obtained and the types of study that might be conducted.

Types of data

Observational versus experimental data

In looking at data collection, one can distinguish between two types of data based on the type of study from which it was collected.

Observational data is data that has been collected to examine things as they are. It is the classical data type, used at least as early as 1500 BC, and underlies the 'state arithmetic' from which the word *statistic* is derived. The Hebrews' census, mentioned in chapter 1, *Statistics*, is an example of a study producing observational data: data was collected to record things as they were. The other historical examples and the large amount of state data collected today, outlined in chapter 1, *Statistics*, are also examples of collecting observational data.

In a non-government context, you might want to examine average monthly sales figures, production figures or employee records for your company.

Experimental data is obtained when the investigator manipulates the situation and the response to the manipulations is observed. That is, the investigator intervenes. For example, two different advertising methods are used for different periods, and the sales made in the different periods are measured. To see if the advertising methods affect the sales, the investigator compares the sales periods for each of the two methods to see if manipulation has produced a different customer response and a difference in sales.

The use of statistical principles in this area began in the early 1900s. It revolutionised scientific experimentation, particularly in the biological sciences, then spread to the business and industrial areas. We are going to concentrate on observational studies.

Primary versus secondary data

Besides distinguishing between observational and experimental data, you can classify the data as either primary or secondary. It is called **primary data** when it is used by the investigator who made, or was responsible for, the original observations. **Secondary data**, on the other hand, is data that is being used by an investigator who did not make, nor was responsible for, the original observations; usually, the data is obtained from a publication.

In general, primary data tends to be **raw data** — the recorded values of the variables for the observational units; secondary data, however, tends to be **processed data**, in the form of tables and diagrams summarising the original raw data. However, there are exceptions to this rule. For example, the data used in example 6.5, *Residences sold in three localities*, is secondary data available in raw form.

Types of observational studies

Observational studies are merely studies made to collect observational data. However, an observational study might be a census or a survey.

A **census** is a study that observes every individual in the population — the population of the Roman empire, for instance, was determined by a census. Businesses continually monitor various aspects of their operations, and this amounts to collecting census data. As a simple example, the daily takings or number of customers of a retail store represent census data for that business. Employees' working hours also constitute census data. For a larger company, designing forms for collecting such data is an important task, since it involves a large amount of data.

A **survey** is a study that observes only a fraction of the population. The observed fraction is called a **sample**. Surveys are often conducted to obtain information about a specific question or issue.

Summary

Data has to be collected before it can be analysed. The most common type of study in business is the observational study, which collects observational data to examine what is going on in the world. Instead of conducting a census of the whole population, it is often more practical to conduct a survey in which a sample — a representative fraction of the whole population — is observed.

Key terms

- **census**
- **experimental data**
- **observational data**
- **observational study**
- **primary data**

- **processed data**
- **raw data**
- **sample**
- **secondary data**
- **survey**

CHAPTER 3

SECONDARY DATA

L E A R N I N G   O B J E C T I V E S

The learning objective of this chapter is:

- to know the various sources of secondary data.

3.1 Sources of secondary data

Secondary data can be very useful. If it is already collected, reliable and readily available, it is much more efficient to use secondary data than to collect primary data. A disadvantage of secondary data is that the investigator is not always aware of all the circumstances involved in collecting and processing the data. Sometimes a particular feature of the data, unknown to the investigators intending to use them, invalidates use of the data in that context.

However, a wealth of reliable secondary sources is available in Australia, including many printed resources. Several organisations now offer databases which are available electronically on media such as floppy disk and CD-ROM. Some of the secondary resources available for research in social science are discussed in Maher and Burke (1991).

An extremely important source of secondary data in Australia is the **Australian Bureau of Statistics**, which provides an enormous amount of statistical data through various media. As well as providing extensive information in printed form, the Bureau releases sets of financial indicators on floppy disk and census data for both 1986 and 1991 on CD-ROM. The Australian Bureau of Statistics (1994a) provides a catalogue of the information available.

Newspapers such as *The Australian* often publish information about share prices and interest rates, as well as regular features about financial matters with supporting statistics. Popular consumer journals such as *Choice* also provide well-researched articles on financial matters, and the Reserve Bank of Australia editorial committee publishes a monthly bulletin of economic information including financial market interest rates.

3.1.1   Australian Bureau of Statistics catalogue of secondary data

Using secondary data efficiently requires an understanding of what is available and how to access it. For example, to access the Australian Bureau of Statistics data, you need to know how it is catalogued. The products are catalogued by a 5-digit number, xxxx.x, as follows.

The first digit, 1–9, codes the main subject area:

1   General
2   Census of Population and Housing
3   Demography
4   Social Statistics
5   National Accounts, Foreign Trade and Finance
6   Labour Statistics and Prices
7   Agriculture
8   Secondary Industry and Distribution
9   Transport

The second digit, 0–9, codes a subgroup within the main subject, making a 2-digit subject code:

11   Catalogues/Guides
12   Classifications/Work Manuals
13   Multi-Subject Publications
14   Electronic Services
15   Consultancy Services

20   1981 Census
21   1986 Census
27   1991 Census

31   General Demography
32   Population Counts/Projections
33   Birth/Death Rates
34   Arrivals/Departures

41   General Social Statistics
42   Primary/Secondary/Tertiary Education
43   Hospitals/Health
44   Social Services/Welfare

51   General Finance
52   National Accounts
53   Foreign Investment/Balance of Payments
54   Overseas Trade
55   Public Sector Accounts
56   Finance

61   General Labour Statistics
62   Work Force
63   Employment Conditions
64   Prices/Indexes
65   Consumer Income/Expenditure

71   General Agriculture
72   Livestock
73   Crops/Pastures
74   Improvements and Practices
75   Agriculture Value
76   Fishing

81   General Industry
82   Manufacturing/Energy
83   Manufacturing Production
84   Mining
85   Service Industries
87   Building/Construction

91   General Transport
92   Services/Facilities
93   Registration Motor Vehicles
94   Accidents Motor Vehicles

The third and fourth digits are permanent serial numbers. The serial numbers do not change provided that the contents of the publication remain unchanged.

The fifth digit, 0–9, is a geographic indicator:

0   Australia
1   New South Wales
2   Victoria
3   Queensland
4   South Australia
5   Western Australia
6   Tasmania
7   Northern Territory
8   Australian Capital Territory
9   External Territories

This coding key can be used to identify the catalogue number for a particular subject, or to identify the nature of a publication from its catalogue number.

EXAMPLE 3.1   INFORMATION ON CONSUMER PRICE INDEX

Information is sought about the consumer price index in Australia. The publication has 64 as the first two digits and 0 as the last, so the catalogue number must be 64xx.0 even if the serial numbers are not known.

EXAMPLE 3.2   INTERPRETATION OF ABS CATALOGUE NUMBER

Since the ABS catalogue number is 6401.0, the publication is about the consumer price index in Australia because the coding identifies the following:

First digit: 6 = Labour Statistics and Prices
Second digit: 4 = Prices/Indexes
Third and fourth digit: 01 = Serial numbers
Fifth digit: 0 = Australia

3.2   Chapter summary

In this chapter we have considered some of the sources of secondary data available in Australia, particularly the sources of data available from the Australian Bureau of Statistics and its cataloguing method.

3.3   Key terms

- **secondary data**
- **Australian Bureau of Statistics**

3.4   Exercises

3.1   Locate the appropriate Australian Bureau of Statistics publication (Cat.No.6401.0) in a library and list the quarterly consumer price indexes for the last financial year for:
(a) the capital city in your state;
(b) Australia.

3.2   Using *The Weekend Australian* as your source:
(a) record the interest rate that you would get for:
(i) a savings account with an amount of $1000 at an ordinary savings bank;
(ii) a 3- to 12-month term deposit of $3000;
(iii) an at-call account at a permanent building society in this state;
(iv) a fixed account at a credit union in this state.
(b) record the interest rate that you would pay for:
(i) a credit card;
(ii) a housing loan through a savings bank;
(iii) a personal loan through a credit union.

3.3 Knowing the exchange rates between the currencies of different countries is useful for travellers and itinerant workers. Dealers in foreign exchange quote a price at which they are willing to buy a currency. Westpac Banking Corporation provides retail market exchange rates in the *Financial Review*. Use copies of this paper to find the buy/sell exchange rate prices for $1 Australian for the last five working days, for the following currencies:

(a) United States dollar;

(b) Japanese yen;

(c) United Kingdom pound;

(d) German Dmark.

3.4 Investors in residential real estate are interested in several factors relevant to their investment. In your state or territory, which organisations provide data about:

(a) sales of property;

(b) local government rates;

(c) land tax;

(d) occupancy rates;

(e) rental amounts?

CHAPTER 4

SURVEYS

LEARNING OBJECTIVES

The learning objectives of this chapter are:

- to understand the importance of sampling and to know how to use statistical principles in sampling;
- to know what the major sampling techniques are;
- to be able to select a sample.

4.1 Conducting a survey

Since it is seldom desirable to observe the whole population of interest (in a census), we usually make a **survey**, taking only a fraction or sample of the population, for the following reasons:

1. The resources required to conduct a survey on a smaller number of units obviously cost less.
2. With fewer units to observe, responses — and therefore results — are obtained more quickly.
3. A sample avoids eliminating the population in situations that involve destroying a unit; for example, testing ammunition or matches — a census would leave none to use again.

The overriding aim is to obtain a **representative sample** of the target population so that any conclusions drawn from the data will apply to the whole of that population. This will not happen if you systematically exclude from the sample segments of the population whose observation would alter the survey's conclusions. To improve the chances of obtaining a representative sample, consider the following items in planning the survey:

1. Specify the **aim** of the survey.
2. Define the **observational unit** — the unit to be observed as a single entity; for example, the responses might be obtained from a company, a household, or an individual.
3. Define **target population** — the set of all observational units about which the investigator aims to draw conclusions.
4. Decide on a **sampling method** — the strategy for choosing units.
5. Choose the **mode of response** — the method for obtaining the response.
6. Formulate the **variables** to be observed — a variable is a characteristic that varies from one observational unit to another; for example, the sex of the respondent, the number of defective items in batches of goods, the amount owed on a credit card, or the answer to a question in a **questionnaire**.
7. Determine **sample size** — the number of observational units to be observed. As a general principle, the more units the more precise your study will be, but this is offset by the cost of extra units. Indeed, the most precise information about a population would be obtained by observing each one of its units. However, this means a census, which would defeat our original intention of obtaining a sample to reduce time and costs.
8. Carry out a **pilot survey** — take a small sample to test your timing and questionnaire design before you take the main survey.

Of these items, only the aim, target population, observational unit, sampling method and mode of reponse are discussed in this chapter. Formulating the variables, in the case of questionnaires, is discussed in chapter 5, *Questionnaire design and data entry*. Determining the sample size is dealt with later, in part IV, *Estimation procedures*, as it requires techniques that are covered in that part.

The sampling methods are given in figure 4.1. They can be divided into probability and nonprobability sampling methods. **Probability sampling** means that the subjects in the sample are selected with known probability; **nonprobability sampling** means that they are not.

Definitions

Definitions of each of the sampling methods are given below. Of the methods described in figure 4.1, convenience, judgement, simple random and systematic sampling are the **basic sampling methods**. These methods select a sample of units from the whole population, whereas the other methods — quota, stratified random and cluster sampling — involve **subdividing the population** before sampling. The basic sampling methods of selection are then used for selecting units from each of the groups. Examples of each sampling method are given in section 4.2, *Basic sampling methods*, and section 4.3, *Subdividing the population before sampling*.

Convenience sampling occurs when units are selected from the population because they are the easiest or most convenient units to observe.

Judgement sampling occurs when certain units from the population are selected because the selector believes them to be the most representative.

Quota sampling occurs when the population is subdivided into groups before sampling; quotas — the numbers of units to be sampled from each group — are also specified. Units are then selected from the whole population by convenience sampling and units from a particular group are rejected once the quota for that group has been filled.

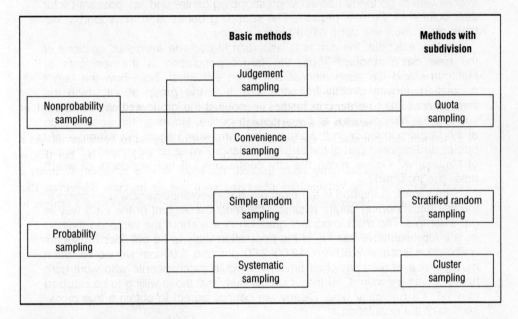

Figure 4.1   Sampling methods

Simple random sampling occurs when units are independently selected from a complete list of the entire population so that each unit has the same chance of being selected.

Systematic sampling occurs when units are selected from a complete list of the population and only the first unit is selected at random; then the other units are selected by taking every kth unit, where k is suitably chosen.

Stratified random sampling occurs when the population is subdivided into groups before sampling and units are randomly sampled from each group. Each unit in a group has the same chance of being selected.

Cluster sampling involves subdividing the population into groups before sampling and the groups are then randomly selected; all units in the selected clusters are observed. Each group, and therefore each unit in a group, has the same chance of being selected.

4.2   Basic sampling methods

4.2.1   Convenience sampling

In convenience sampling it is crucial for an element of expediency to be involved.

EXAMPLE 4.1 MARKET RESEARCH FOR A NEW DAIRY PRODUCT

Suppose a new dairy product is proposed for sale in Melbourne. A market researcher is engaged to find out what the residents of the Melbourne metropolitan area think about the product. The researcher arranges for interviewers to go to the nearest large shopping centre and ask passers-by for their opinion of the new product. The shopping centre is in the suburbs, but there are quite a few large office blocks nearby.

In this example, the aim is to ascertain Melbourne residents' opinions of the new dairy product. Thus, the target population is the residents of Melbourne and the observational unit is an individual. Note how the target population derives directly from the aim. It is the group about which the investigator aims to draw conclusions — not just the group actually sampled, such as the Melbournians at the shopping centre. However, the specification of the target population in the aim seems somewhat vague. For example, are babies and children part of the target population? What do we mean by the city of Melbourne? Do we mean the city centre only? If not, residents of which areas are included?

The sampling method in the example is convenience sampling — going to the nearest shopping centre is simply the most convenient or the easy way to get a sample. The most important question to ask about the sampling method is: is a representative fraction of the population likely to be obtained? It seems unlikely, because at 8.50 am, 12.00–2.00 pm and 5.00 pm we would catch mostly office workers; at other times, we would catch people who work from home or who are retired. Further, it seems likely that those willing to be stopped may be of a particular type. Clearly, we cannot expect to obtain a true cross-section of the population.

Telephone surveys are another form of convenience sampling. The disadvantage here is that they exclude those without a phone. Another form of convenience sampling is the **self-selected sample**, where an invitation to respond is widely broadcast and the respondents consist of those who volunteer to take part. For example, a newspaper publishes a questionnaire and asks readers to respond by post, or a television station asks viewers to answer a question by telephoning and saying 'yes' or 'no'. Problems with self-selected sampling include nonresponse by certain groups of viewers and individuals sometimes giving multiple responses, so that the responses are unlikely to be representative of those of the entire population.

It seems that convenience sampling is not usually representative; that is, the sample is usually biased.

4.2.2 Judgement sampling

In judgement sampling, a selector is appointed and the selector chooses from the population.

EXAMPLE 4.2 STUDENTS' OPINIONS

A university faculty wishes to survey its students on a particular issue but is unable to canvass them all. Someone in the faculty office selects several individuals whom they believe are representative of the students. In this example, the aim is to determine the attitudes of the students in a university faculty and so the target population is students in the university faculty. The observational unit is a student.

Again, we need to consider whether or not a representative fraction of the population is likely to be obtained. In this case, it seems that the answer is *Maybe!* If the selector knows the whole population and can select unbiasedly, the sample will be truly representative. It seems more likely that the selector will know only some of the students and will choose from this subgroup. These students may have opinions that are quite different to those unknown to the selector, who have no chance of being selected. Even a selector who does know the whole population still has to select unbiasedly.

The validity of this sampling method relies on the selector really knowing all the population and choosing units unbiasedly. Guaranteeing the achievement of these rather substantial conditions will be difficult.

4.2.3 Simple random sampling

The essential components of simple random sampling are the complete list of the population and independent selection from this list so that each unit has the same chance of selection. The complete list is called the **population frame**.

EXAMPLE 4.3 PURCHASER SURVEY WITH SIMPLE RANDOM SAMPLE

Suppose that the Real Estate Institute of South Australia wishes to survey everyone who has bought a residence in metropolitan Adelaide during the last 12 months, to gauge their opinion of the agent who sold them their residence. A complete list of all buyers in this area over the required period is obtained. There were 25 757 purchasers of residences and it is decided to survey 300 of these. Suppose our 300 purchasers are selected by the usual raffle technique. That is, 25 757 identically-shaped, numbered tickets, one for each purchaser, are placed in a large container. For the draw, 300 tickets are taken from the container one at a time — the tickets are thoroughly mixed before each ticket is selected.

In this case, the aim is to determine the opinions of purchasers of residences in metropolitan Adelaide over the previous 12 months. The target population is the purchasers of properties in metropolitan Adelaide over the prescribed 12-month period. The observational unit is the purchaser of a residence, which could mean an individual, a couple, several people in partnership, or a company.

Note that we have a complete list of all purchasers and the method of selection apparently gives each purchaser the same chance of selection. It seems likely that the sampled fraction will be representative of the target population, provided enough individuals have been selected. There is nothing in the selection procedure to indicate that some of the population has no chance of being selected and there is every chance that, by and large, all groups have been selected.

This method seems likely to result in a representative sample. There is, however, no absolute guarantee that it will; just that most often it will — you would have to be unlucky to obtain an unrepresentative sample.

4.2.4   Systematic sampling

In systematic sampling, first determine the distance, k, between consecutively selected observations by taking the integer part of N/n where N is the number of units in the population and n is the number of units to be sampled. The first unit is randomly selected from the first k units in the list, provided N is an exact multiple of n; otherwise it is randomly selected from the first $N - k \times (n - 1)$ units in the list. To select the other units, begin with the first selected unit and take every kth unit in the list.

> **EXAMPLE 4.4   PURCHASER SURVEY WITH SYSTEMATIC SAMPLE**
>
> Suppose that for the Real Estate Institute of South Australia survey I had decided to sample my list of purchasers systematically. As there are 25 757 purchasers in the population and 300 of them are to be selected, the distance between consecutively selected observations is the integer part of 25 757/300. That is, $k = 85$. Now 25 757 is not an exact multiple of 300 because 25 757/300 is not an integer. So, the first selected unit must be randomly selected from the first 342 (25 757 − 85 × (300 − 1)) purchasers in my list. Thereafter every 85th purchaser is selected.
>
> Note that every unit has the same chance of being selected, but that each unit is not selected independently of each other unit. Further, this kind of sampling presents a problem whenever there is periodicity in the list and this corresponds to the periodicity in the selection. For example, suppose there had been 85 local government areas and the list, because of a quirk in the way it was compiled, had one purchase from each local government area recorded in succession, and this pattern was repeated until all purchases were recorded. The proposed systematic selection procedure would mean that all purchases came from the same local government area. In this case, the selected sample would not be representative.

This sampling method relies on the list being effectively random, in which case the method is likely to yield a representative sample. It is employed when the investigator feels reasonably sure that there is no systematic pattern in the list and an easier or less time-consuming method than simple random sampling is needed.

Conclusions

From the discussion above, it seems that nonprobability sampling is easier to carry out, less costly, but seldom representative. On the other hand, probability sampling seems usually representative, but difficult, because it requires a complete list of the population.

Clearly, random sampling is not always practicable. But remember the limitations involved if you elect not to randomly sample: you run the risk of a biased sample, so your conclusions will not apply to some units. You must decide whether the method you propose to use will provide a representative fraction. It may be the best you can do and you should take the sample as only a rough guide.

You might go ahead with nonrandom sampling and decide that the sample is representative of some narrower population. For example, in the case of the student survey, you have opinions of only part of the student body, and the other part may hold quite different opinions. Your conclusions are then limited to the part of the student body you have sampled. Of course, if your target population is students known to the administration, there is no problem. If sampling is likely to be too biased to provide any worthwhile information, the survey should be abandoned.

4.3   Subdividing the population before sampling

The sampling methods not already discussed are those in which the population is subdivided before sampling, and one of the four methods just discussed is employed to select units from each group.

4.3.1   Methods of subdividing

Sometimes the population is subdivided into groups before the survey is made, and units are selected from the groups. For example:

- in a survey of a city, you might divide the city into groups according to its local government areas;
- in a survey of a state, you might divide the state into regions and regions into districts;
- in a survey of students at a university, you might divide the university students into faculties and years.

A group is called either a stratum or a cluster. It is called a **stratum** (plural strata) when units are observed from *all* groups. A group is called a **cluster** when *only some* groups are selected for observation.

In principle, sampling from a stratum or cluster and the sampling of clusters can be achieved by any one of the four basic methods outlined above. However, the three most commonly used methods are the methods with subdivision given in figure 4.1. Stratified random sampling occurs when units are selected at random from each stratum. Quota sampling involves selecting units from the population by convenience sampling, and the number observed from a stratum is prespecified by a quota. In cluster sampling, the clusters are selected at random and all units in the selected clusters observed.

EXAMPLE 4.5   PURCHASER SURVEY WITH SUBDIVIDED POPULATION
For our Real Estate Institute survey, you might subdivide metropolitan Adelaide according to local government areas. If you randomly sample purchasers from all local government areas in Adelaide, you will obtain a stratified random sample.

Quota sampling would involve establishing a quota for each local government area. Then you would select purchasers by convenience from the whole of Adelaide, checking their local government area in each case to ensure that you have not exceeded the quota. Once the quota for an area has been filled, exclude further purchasers from that area from the sample.

A cluster sample is obtained by making a simple random sample of local government areas and including all purchasers from the selected areas in the survey.

4.3.2   Reasons for subdividing

Efficiency

If the subdivision of the population uses existing population groups, then associated organisational structures can be used; for example, if a city's residents are subdivided according to the local government areas in which they live, the officers associated with each area can probably provide lists and knowledge about their area.

Schemes such as cluster sampling are sometimes more efficient because less of the population is involved. Only the sampled groups have to be listed, and it is necessary to negotiate with only the officers associated with the selected groups.

Comparison of groups

If samples have been taken from different groups, you can examine how the behaviours of the groups differ. For example, how differently do students in one school behave, compared with those in another?

Increased precision

For stratified random sampling, you can obtain more precise results if the units within each stratum are more homogeneous than the whole population. That is, the units in a group are relatively similar, compared to the whole population, for the variables being observed.

For cluster sampling, you can obtain more precise results if the units within a cluster are heterogeneous and, comparatively speaking, if the clusters exhibit the same degree of heterogeneity. That is, whenever differences between units in any one cluster are as great as in the whole population.

A very important consequence of increased precision is that you can sample fewer observational units and obtain the same information than you can with a less precise method. That is, the survey costs less.

EXAMPLE 4.5   PURCHASER SURVEY WITH SUBDIVIDED POPULATION
(continued)

We suggested that the Real Estate Institute of South Australia survey might employ either stratified random or cluster sampling, forming groups of purchased residences according to their local government areas.

Stratified random sampling will be more precise than simple random sampling only if the purchasers in any local government area have relatively similar opinions of the agents involved in their purchases.

On the other hand, cluster sampling will be more precise than simple random sampling if there is a wide range of opinions in each local government area and if different local government areas exhibit the same range. That is, each cluster should be representative of the whole population.

4.3.3   Numbers of units from the groups

At this stage, we are not in a position to discuss the absolute number of units to be observed from each group. However, we can outline the general principles for determining the relative numbers. At least three bases are available for deciding how many units should be sampled from each group.

Fixed numbers from the groups is the most arbitrary method of deciding how many units should be observed from each group of the population; in this case a predetermined, possibly unequal, number is taken from each group. This method is appealingly simple. However, it has drawbacks: it may result in unequal representation of the groups, and some of the calculations are more difficult than with other methods.

With **proportional numbers from the groups**, the proportion of units to be selected from the whole population is decided. This means that the proportion of units to be selected from each group is the same as for the whole population. The computations in this case are usually easier than for fixed numbers from each group. Also, it seems reasonable to take more units from larger groups. Usually, the quotas in quota sampling are determined in this way.

Optimal allocation of numbers from the groups is a method of choosing the number sampled from each group to obtain the most precise estimates. This method also reduces the cost of the survey. Optimal allocation involves providing detailed information about each group and using complicated formulae to calculate the required numbers, so its practical utility is limited.

EXAMPLE 4.6   HYPOTHETICAL SUBDIVIDED POPULATION

To illustrate the different methods of deciding how many units should be selected, here is a hypothetical example. Suppose the population to be sampled consists of 1000 units divided into 4 strata, as shown in table 4.1, and that the total number of units to be selected is 100. Table 4.1 gives an arbitrary set of fixed numbers that specify how many units are to be sampled from the strata. If proportional numbers from the groups are required, first note that the proportion to be sampled from the whole population is 100/1000 =
0.10. The proportion to be sampled from each stratum is therefore this proportion: 0.10. The corresponding numbers are given in table 4.1.

Table 4.1   Numbers of units for a hypothetical example

| Stratum | Population | Sampled | |
		Fixed	Proportional
A	500	30	50
B	100	30	10
C	150	20	15
D	250	20	25
Total	1000	100	100

4.3.4   Multistage samples

Multistage sampling involves more than a single subdivision of the population before sampling; it might involve combinations of stratified, cluster and quota sampling. The simplest form of multistage sampling is **two-stage cluster sampling**. In a two-stage cluster sampling, not only are the clusters randomly sampled, but units are randomly sampled from the selected clusters.

> **EXAMPLE 4.5   PURCHASER SURVEY WITH SUBDIVIDED POPULATION**
> (continued)
>
> The Real Estate Institute of South Australia survey will be a two-stage cluster sample if a simple random sample of local government areas is made and if purchasers are randomly sampled from the selected areas.

However, multistage sampling can be more complicated; the possibilities are seemingly endless. A more complicated example follows.

> **EXAMPLE 4.7   STATE SURVEY OF HOUSEHOLDS**
>
> In a survey of a state, the state is split into regions, a region is split into districts and each district is split into households. Suppose that all regions, and only some districts from each region and only some households from the selected districts, are to be sampled. One member of each household is interviewed. The sampling scheme is shown in figure 4.2 (opposite). As all regions are to be sampled they form strata, whereas the districts and households form clusters. The observational unit is a member of a household.

4.4   Mode of response

There are essentially three **modes of response**: personal interview, telephone interview and mail. Mail produces a lower response rate than the other two methods, but it is cheaper. Thus, mail may not be representative because some people do not bother to return the questionnaire.

4.5   Sources of bias in surveys

As we have indicated in the previous discussion, the sample may not truly reflect the whole population. There are evidently several reasons for this, which we now examine. In particular, we are concerned with bias in the conclusions drawn from a survey. Bias occurs when sample conclusions systematically deviate from the actual target population conclusions.

Selection bias arises from the systematic inclusion or exclusion of segments of the population when selecting the units to be observed. As a rule, the population *actually* sampled tends to differ from the target population. We dealt with this problem when

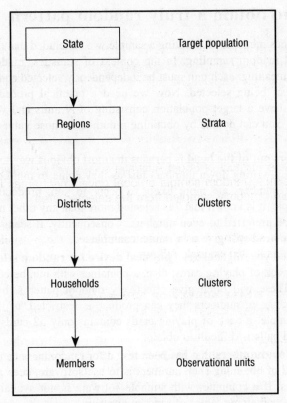

Figure 4.2 Multistage sample

describing the four basic sampling methods. For example, we concluded that our convenience sample of passersby at the shopping centre was not likely to be representative of the target population because certain segments of the population had no chance of being selected. Our sampling method resulted in selection bias. Similarly, we concluded that the judgement sample of students from the university faculty could suffer from selection bias.

Nonresponse bias occurs when selected units fail to provide a response. As mentioned above, mail surveys often have considerable nonresponse. Investigators tend to assume that the respondents and nonrespondents are equally representative of the population. If this were true, the nonresponse would not affect the conclusions and there would be no nonresponse bias. However, it seems that nonrespondents may well differ from respondents and so there will be nonresponse bias in the conclusions from the survey.

Response bias is a systematic error in the response given to a question. For example, the bias can result from the poor formulation of a question in a questionnaire. How such problems can arise will be discussed more fully in chapter 5, *Questionnaire design and data entry.*

4.6   How to obtain a truly random pattern

In examining various methods of selecting a sample, we concluded that the most satisfactory methods involved random sampling. In the context of statistics, random sampling has a precise, technical meaning: each unit must be independently selected and all units must have the same chance of being selected. Now we need a practical procedure for doing this. Suppose that you have a target population consisting of N units and you want to select a sample of n units. You can do this by obtaining n numbers whose values are between 1 and N.

Using **numbers out of the head** is perhaps the most obvious way to obtain the required numbers; that is, by writing down numbers just as they come to mind. However, favourite numbers or small numbers are more likely to occur to you, producing some degree of pattern. For example, it is known that 7 is selected more than any other number and that odd numbers tend to be preferred to even numbers. Consequently, it seems most unlikely that numbers out of the head will give us a random sample.

Another method you might use is a **physical device for random selection** such as coins that are tossed, a pack of playing cards, dice, a container with numbered tickets, or a set of numbered balls. These will often give effectively random patterns, but they are usually impractical. The range of numbers they can produce is restricted, or they are not readily available. For example, a pack of playing cards contains only 52 cards, and a set of 9000 uniquely identified balls is difficult to obtain.

A set of **random numbers** that has been tested for randomness can be used. The most convenient method of obtaining such numbers is to use software, such as spreadsheets and statistical packages. If a computer with suitable software is not available, there are many statistics textbooks containing tables of random numbers.

> **EXAMPLE 4.4   PURCHASER SURVEY WITH RANDOM SAMPLE** (continued)
>
> To determine the purchasers to be selected in the Real Estate Institute of South Australia's survey, the first task is to number the 25 757 listed purchasers from 1 to 25 757. To select the sample, you could then write down the first 300 numbers, between 1 and 25 757, that come to mind. However, there is no guarantee that everyone will have the same chance of selection. Alternatively, as previously suggested, you could number the registrants from 1 to 25 757 and put 25 757 pieces of paper in a hat from which we draw 300. Somewhat cumbersome! That leaves us with using random numbers from either a computer or tables.

4.7   Using Minitab to select the sample

Minitab can help us obtain our sample by generating a set of random numbers that can be used to determine which units are to be observed. Suppose we have a target population consisting of N observational units, and our task is to select a sample of size n. So each number we obtain must be between 1 and N. Unless we include all the numbers between 1 and N, some units will have no chance of being selected and the sample will not be random.

If we include numbers outside the range 1 to N we will be trying to observe nonexistent units.

The Minitab commands to produce n random numbers between 1 and N are:

```
MTB > random n c1;
SUBC> integer 1 to N.
MTB > print c1
```

where you substitute, into the *random* command, the particular values of n and N for our sample. In practice, it is a good idea to make Minitab calculate more than the required n, because some numbers might be repeated and we want to sample each unit only once. After generating a few more than n, we can then examine the first n for repeats. This is most easily done by using the *copy* command to transfer the first n to a new column and the *sort* command to put them into ascending order.

EXAMPLE 4.4   PURCHASER SURVEY WITH RANDOM SAMPLE (continued)
To determine which purchasers are to be selected in the Real Estate Institute of South Australia's survey, use the following commands in Minitab to generate 320 numbers between 1 and 25757 and to copy, sort and print the first 300. Note that we asked for 320 (not 300) numbers, to allow for repeats.

```
MTB > outfile 'a:\random.lis'
MTB > random 320 c1;
SUBC> integer 1 to 25757.
MTB > copy c1 c2;
SUBC> use 1:300.
MTB > sort c2 c2
MTB > print c2
```

If your version of Minitab has pull-down menus and you want to use them, table 4.2 lists the menus and options that access the required commands. Appendix D, *Detailed instructions for Minitab menus*, explains how to use the menus.

Table 4.2   Menus and options to generate random numbers

Minitab command	Menu	Option
outfile	File >	Other Files > Start Recording Session...
random	Calc >	Random Data...
integer		Integer...
copy	Calc >	Copy Columns...
use		Use Rows...
sort	Calc >	Sort...
print	Edit >	Display Data...

The output of the commands is as follows.

```
MTB > random 320 c1;
SUBC> integer 1 to 25757.
MTB > copy c1 c2;
SUBC> use 1:300.
MTB > sort c2 c2
MTB > print c2

C2
     39      259      648     1075     1089     1137     1414     1415
   1457     1741     1829     1857     1967     2006     2092     2128
   2151     2158     2372     2401     2482     2672     2905     3011
   3130     3224     3251     3526     3549     3661     3666     3754
   3958     4012     4023     4243     4247     4255     4446     4480
   4492     4709     4965     5045     5046     5056     5107     5118
   5200     5226     5282     5483     5603     5744     5792     5832
   5859     5943     5984     6020     6064     6078     6170     6290
   6342     6465     6474     6476     6520     6654     6919     7115
   7130     7209     7233     7374     7424     7480     7518     7725
   7736     7835     7918     7934     8003     8086     8122     8133
   8280     8285     8535     8906     9021     9314     9317     9323
   9424     9462     9503     9682     9703     9774     9866    10041
  10147    10151    10182    10296    10869    10932    10939    10960
  10981    11058    11356    11581    11582    11645    11693    11712
  11800    11807    11920    11960    12076    12077    12117    12264
  12295    12340    12368    12421    12421    12492    12519    12533
  12756    12765    12781    12928    12945    13076    13244    13259
  13318    13324    13371    13560    13615    13986    14038    14057
  14081    14183    14244    14271    14525    14542    14560    14570
  14620    14684    14809    14834    14960    15141    15224    15242
  15277    15435    15749    15966    16383    16397    16458    16583
  16770    16871    16888    16981    16993    17040    17042    17047
  17057    17072    17089    17158    17207    17257    17396    17410
  17426    17455    17536    17623    17725    17899    17901    18014
  18048    18125    18126    18160    18204    18385    18439    18513
  18562    18577    18591    18658    18974    19124    19403    19477
  19534    19559    19657    19684    19718    19841    19878    20007
  20043    20071    20120    20624    20691    20713    20843    20902
  20938    20983    20984    21107    21138    21293    21476    21584
  21876    22003    22016    22036    22078    22195    22226    22230
  22312    22318    22332    22506    22560    22674    22815    22892
  22898    22924    22968    22994    23119    23128    23181    23216
  23217    23289    23325    23412    23415    23492    23564    23568
  23571    23615    23626    23655    23685    23727    23740    23865
  23902    23918    23939    24049    24165    24355    24727    24733
  24763    24856    24909    24961    24994    25065    25188    25341
  25378    25465    25524    25747
```

On checking through the list, we see that only 12 421 is repeated. So we need to take another number from the original unsorted list of 320, making sure that this number is different from those in the first 300. The *print* command is used to display the unsorted list, so that the number can be selected.

```
MTB > print c1

C1
10960    18126     7518    12945    13324     2905    13244     8285
12421     6170    14542     3130     4255    23939    10296    12533
 6476    20843    18385    22016    10147     9682     2672    17899
 6520    22674    19477    23217     1075    18658    25747    22506
17257    15224    14560     6474     2158      648    23216    19841
22924    17623     9866     5483    22226    25188    19657    23615
10939     8122    18204    20984    17901    17455    19403    12117
 5200    18974    14183     2151    21876     6078    18125    23902
 6020    22036     2128     5056    23289     7130    24049    18439
16993    17207    16383    13076    12295     7934    11582    16871
 4243    14620     2482    11645     8535    24909    13371     7736
19878    13615    17072     8280    22003     3666    15966     4023
  259     4247    25378    23626    23564    24961    19684    19718
11800    17089    17410     2006     2401    18048     5107    17396
17042    15277     5045     2092     7374    11712    12264     7115
10981    15141     3011    23740    17725    21476    23415    13318
12519    23325    19534    11920     3754    10869    10041    12756
14057    22195     5118    11960    22898     4012    15242    23727
18014     3549    17057    12492    16397    14684    13986    11807
 5744    24856     7233    16981     1967    23685    14834    24165
19124     4709     5943     9021    18562     4492    16770    11581
20007     4446     6290    17426     3526    22968     1457     7835
16888    17158    12781    23571    14244    24763    12421    22560
20938    11058    22312    20043    21584     5859    12076     8133
11693    21138    14809    14570    22078    25341     5984     3661
15435     5792     5046     4965     5226     8906    22230    18160
12928     9314     1089     2372     7725    12765    23181    13560
11356    12077    23918    25524    22815    20713     7209    13259
22892     9317     7918    14525    22318    21293    17040     1415
 1414     9424    20120    24727    14081     4480     3224    25065
20691     3251    25465     5282     6064     6654     6342     9703
24355     7480    22332    12340     5832    23568    14038     9503
23412     1741     7424     6919     3958    23128     8003    16458
20071    17047     1829    10151    18591     6465    20624    23865
18513    14960     9462    23492    20902    14271    20983     9323
19559    21107    10932    22994    24733     1137    16583    17536
24994    23655    18577     1857     5603    15749    10182     8086
   39    23119    12368     9774     9667    17269    17802     9071
   26     1676    14271     8751    14778    23336    19130     9948
23397    18039    17709     9033     7246    23039    20599     5707
```

The next random number, in the unsorted list, is 9667 and this number does not occur in the first 300 numbers. That is, the complete list of purchasers to be selected is the same as the list of 300 sorted numbers except that a 12 421 is deleted and 9667 is inserted in the appropriate position.

4.8   Chapter summary

This chapter has discussed how to collect data by using surveys. Items to be considered in planning the survey have been listed. We have concentrated on sampling methods or strategies for selecting observational units from the target population, bearing in mind that our principal aim is to obtain a representative fraction of the target population. The methods we have presented are the basic sampling methods, as well as the methods that involve subdividing the population before sampling. The basic methods are convenience, judgement, simple random and systematic sampling; the methods that involve subdividing the population before sampling are quota, stratified random and cluster sampling. These methods were also classified as either probability or nonprobability sampling methods. We concluded that you should employ the probability sampling methods of simple random, systematic, stratified random and cluster sampling to ensure a representative sample. Selecting observational units with probability sampling methods is most conveniently done by using random numbers that are computer generated.

The advantages of subdividing the population before sampling include: efficiency; comparison of groups; increased precision. For deciding how many observational units should be selected from each group, there are at least three methods: fixed numbers from the groups; proportional numbers from the groups; optimal allocation of numbers from the groups. Of these, proportional numbers from the groups is probably the most practical.

More complicated methods of sampling, termed multistage samples, involve more than one subdivision of the population before sampling. The simplest form of multistage sampling is two-stage cluster sampling.

Three possible modes of response are personal interview, telephone interview and mail. The mail produces a lower response rate than the other two methods, but is cheaper.

Selection bias, nonresponse bias and response bias are different sources of bias that occur in surveys.

4.9   Key terms

- aim of survey
- basic sampling method
- bias
- cluster
- cluster sampling
- convenience sampling
- fixed numbers from the groups
- judgement sampling
- mode of response
- multistage sampling
- nonprobability sampling
- nonresponse bias
- numbers out of the head
- observational unit
- optimal allocation of numbers from the groups
- pilot survey
- physical device for random selection
- population frame

- probability sampling
- proportional numbers from the groups
- questionnaire
- quota sampling
- random number
- representative sample
- response bias
- sample size
- sampling method
- selection bias
- self-selected sample
- simple random sampling
- stratified random sampling
- stratum
- subdividing the population
- survey
- systematic sampling
- target population
- two-stage cluster sampling
- variable

4.10 Exercises

4.1 By definition the target population is the complete set of individuals or units about which the investigator aims to draw conclusions, while the sample consists of only a portion of the target population. Sometimes observing a portion of the population is more useful than observing the whole population. Give four examples from a business context when this statement is true.

4.2 Explain in your own words the difference between a census and a sample. Which of these two methods of collecting information would be most appropriate for the following situations? In your answer, identify the target population.

(a) The Childhood Services Department wishes to estimate the demand for preschools and childcare centres at Golden Grove, a new housing development area north of Adelaide.

(b) Irrigation is the lifeblood of the towns that depend on the income from rice and other crops, fresh and dried fruit, and dairy products along the banks of the Murray River, as it crosses three Australian states on the way to the sea at Goolwa in South Australia. Government analysts in these states are deeply concerned about the increasing salinity found in properties along the river and they wish to determine the extent of the problem.

(c) A Friendly Society is considering establishing a retirement village for its members. The board of the society requires an affirmative membership vote of 80% before this project can proceed.

(d) Each quarter the Australian Bureau of Statistics releases details of the Consumer Price Index, the latest unemployment figures and the balance of trade figures.

4.3 Large hotels often place a questionnaire in each of their rooms about the standard of their accommodation, facilities and service. The guests are requested to complete these forms and hand them into the reception desk at the end of their stay. The hotel management then examines the questionnaires and the points raised by the guests. Comment on the usefulness of the hotel management's method of obtaining the guests' opinions about the accommodation, facilities and service.

4.4 The owner of an engineering firm which has 720 employees wishes to introduce new technology. This will mean extensive changes to the firm's work practices and an increase in productivity, but it will also mean redeploying or retrenching some employees. The success of these changes depends on cooperation from the employees, so the manager decides to discuss the new scheme in person with a cross-section of the employees. He speaks to each section head about the new production techniques and suggests that they choose two employees from their section to take part in further discussions about the changes and their effect on the employment opportunities in the firm. Which sampling method is likely to be used to select these employees? Do you think that the manager's strategy will make the transition period less stressful for the employees?

4.5   In Australia, the costs of hospital and medical services are under scrutiny. At present, basic medical and hospital cover is funded by government through the Medicare levy raised by taxation. Some people pay for extra cover for these services out of their own pocket, or by subscribing to a private health insurance scheme, but so many rely solely on government funding that there are long waiting-lists for elective surgery in publicly funded hospitals. The government is under fire for this situation, which has received wide coverage in the media, with graphic stories of the stress that can arise from such lengthy delays. At the conclusion of a recent TV program on this subject, viewers were invited to take part in a survey. They were asked to ring selected telephone numbers to report how long they had been obliged to wait for elective surgery. Do you think that this method of data collection would provide a representative sample set of data? Can you suggest an alternative approach?

4.6   The continent of Australia is sparsely populated. Most of its population of 18 million people live and work in the six state capital cities dotted along the western, southern and eastern coastlines and in Canberra, the federal capital. The national parliament and the national headquarters of all the major corporations are located on the eastern seaboard. This means that business representatives, politicians and freight must be transported across vast distances, particularly from cities like Perth in Western Australia. An efficient airline network is essential if business is to remain viable.

In 1990 the national strike by airline pilots, who were seeking an increase in salary and a reduction in rostered hours on duty, brought the country to its knees. The strike continued for several months and was not resolved until the federal government intervened. The damage to business, manufacturing and tourism was enormous, and the public confidence in the airline companies was severely eroded. One of the companies involved decided to survey public opinion about the way it had handled the disruption caused by the prolonged strike. They sent a questionnaire by mail to a sample of 600 people. The sample was chosen by selecting at random 300 pages from each of the telephone directories for Sydney, New South Wales, and Melbourne, Victoria. A questionnaire was sent to the first private individual listed on each selected page.

(a)   What is the target population for this questionnaire?

(b)   Is it likely that any bias will result from this sampling method?

(c)   If the company had surveyed all the members of their 'frequent flyers club' would their opinions be more useful to the airline? Give reasons for your answer.

4.7   In a Budget presented to the Australian Federal Parliament in Canberra, the Australian Treasurer proposed including nominal increases in the value of share portfolios for assessing eligibility for the aged pension. This proposal caused widespread alarm among those senior citizens whose standard of living directly depends on the pension they receive.

A short time after this announcement was made a poll was taken of 1500 people, aged 18 years or older, to gauge the public reaction to this proposal. The people were selected at random from computerised lists of telephone numbers as outlined in table 4.3. The first person over 18 years old to come to the phone was asked if they approved of the proposal. Any number that was engaged or did not answer was called again up to three times with a minimum of two hours between calls.

Table 4.3   Numbers of adults polled in each state

State/Territory	Capital city	Outside capital city
Australian Capital Territory	50	—
Queensland	100	100
New South Wales	250	100
Northern Territory	50	50
South Australia	100	50
Tasmania	50	50
Victoria	250	100
Western Australia	100	100
Total	950	550

The results indicated that the Australian public strongly opposed these changes: 72% were against the move, 20% in favour and 8% undecided. Do you think that the results of this poll truly reflected the opinion of the adult Australian public? Give reasons for your answer.

4.8   A large store that supplies replacement parts for the motor industry is concerned that many of the account customers are delaying the payment of their accounts. This build-up in overdue accounts is seriously affecting the cashflow of the store. Management calls for an audit of the unpaid accounts to determine why so many accounts are in default. The auditor has to examine several hundred, say 400, accounts. He decides to select a sample of 20 unpaid accounts for examination. His aim is to select a sample that will reflect the population of all outstanding accounts. The numbers of accounts that remain unpaid for the month of March are listed in table 4.4.

(a) Obtain convenience, simple random and systematic samples of the accounts in default by employing, in turn, each of these basic sampling methods. Use Minitab to obtain your random numbers. For each sample:
  (i) list the account numbers to be sampled;
  (ii) discuss the suitability of the sampling method.
(b) Suggest how the accountant would select a judgement sample.

Table 4.4   Account numbers for accounts in default for March

	1	2	3	4	5	6	7	8	9	10
1	1150	709	4097	2910	1398	1479	185	2123	2892	377
2	3535	4202	2851	204	4467	3736	3528	597	1488	2341
3	2753	4388	1287	1876	4314	4226	535	661	162	3231
4	1615	1390	1883	2418	2172	1975	3017	4276	1816	4399
5	2463	459	1081	4030	1372	1751	750	3269	2536	3454
6	3066	3191	3893	1589	931	3832	1955	1449	623	1999
7	1185	1877	2521	4057	1108	2426	2970	2957	1196	3570
8	3386	2968	4131	3126	1720	1778	243	3045	795	218
9	1770	3339	4215	2084	4109	1709	3577	3907	4304	2030
10	2490	3144	2375	1860	1912	2648	2322	1730	1113	275
11	1621	1992	395	3098	2216	3563	2655	2286	3050	353
12	4329	917	3906	1727	3613	4374	3790	2356	3279	3998
13	3686	3836	1346	4465	4225	1029	273	2328	925	2289
14	3740	1415	3786	932	3058	3317	255	2319	398	1453
15	2793	1911	3792	560	3230	1061	3655	2075	1540	4303
16	4407	3667	1562	1295	2708	1792	1038	397	4002	1523
17	3294	2623	4098	522	1000	544	1097	4217	2196	905
18	3977	3840	3883	1510	1938	805	3245	341	1643	266
19	2975	2684	4043	136	131	3002	1512	4020	2935	4142
20	3406	722	3308	1042	3547	407	2385	4145	3352	4053
21	3598	1797	4130	672	144	507	3032	971	3463	3933
22	2996	3888	3119	197	779	1493	1516	912	3003	2304
23	645	1998	3510	2476	687	1737	2761	3741	2018	611
24	2572	3141	434	2039	4110	637	1214	3424	2057	2441
25	3811	3962	3643	141	4015	2704	3524	283	4177	1142
26	3488	862	712	4469	2046	2599	4364	1921	1726	4258
27	1215	3987	1820	3862	2291	3202	2080	3485	1742	339
28	3491	4261	227	2318	3227	2494	1514	1623	694	4320
29	2504	1972	2987	3776	3492	3215	2662	3367	1682	1414
30	4143	4353	3565	673	1271	1856	1565	2782	4317	4426
31	3390	2098	1350	3137	2262	1855	702	2273	2882	342
32	4223	1473	102	2646	834	1789	3152	1864	1717	318
33	2400	3323	4220	1886	2294	2237	2613	3629	4268	1575
34	3211	2937	1631	708	3545	2239	2279	1986	3281	3868
35	394	1008	1152	3682	988	3368	4475	3107	871	2803
36	1484	4255	3486	3145	4281	3381	1988	1407	245	146
37	3620	1186	3662	2754	3354	138	4305	2401	445	3088
38	3709	2732	2144	130	2040	2942	790	1640	2874	2598
39	2958	1086	3077	455	3121	3770	2117	2977	2101	3712
40	2980	1230	1781	1355	2114	4351	1789	2679	3794	3879

4.9 We have a list of addresses of the houses sold during a 12-month period in Campbelltown, a local government area in Adelaide, and 865 sales were made within this period. Suppose we have to survey these houses to investigate the saleability of all houses in the area, and we decide to select a simple random sample of just 60 houses for detailed examination.

(a) What is the target population for this survey?

(b) What is the observational unit ?

(c) Suppose the houses that sold are numbered from 1 to 865.

   (i) How many random numbers would you select, using Minitab, if you have to allow for repeated numbers?

   (ii) Give the full range from which the numbers have to be selected.

   (iii) List the Minitab commands you would use to create the random numbers you require.

   (iv) Use the Minitab commands in (iii) to obtain the random numbers.

   (v) Will this sample of 60 houses be representative of all the houses sold in the Campbelltown area during the 12 months? Give reasons for your answer.

(d) If a systematic sample of 60 was required instead, what Minitab commands would you use to make the selection? Make the selection, using Minitab to obtain any random numbers required.

(e) If a simple random sample is selected, each house sale has an equal chance of being included. Is this true for the systematic sample?

4.10 The University of South Australia has five campuses that cater for more than 23 000 students. In some areas facilities are not keeping pace with the demands of the new organisation. At a recent Council meeting, it was decided that extra funds would be spent on upgrading student facilities. The Student Union executive was invited to submit its priorities for spending the money to the next council meeting.

The Student Union executive decided to survey the students at the University for their opinions about the facilities to be upgraded. Since there was insufficient time to conduct a census of the student body, it was decided to conduct a survey of 100 students at each campus. Give a detailed account of how the executive should approach its task.

4.11 A building society that provides home loans, savings and investment facilities to its members has 40 branches, not only in the city centre but across the metropolitan area and in a few major country areas. The savings and investment account rates are very competitive and they change with movements in the money market. As the terms of investment expire, members move between accounts to take advantage of the best rate that is offered.

The manager of the society wishes to examine these movements to see which investment opportunities were most favoured by the members. There are 50 000 members and each member has one or more of the 21 accounts on offer. She decides to examine the movements between accounts made by a sample of 500 members and she is anxious to include a wide cross-section of membership in her final sample. Can you suggest a suitable sampling method for her to use?

4.12 A company that is about to release a new fireproof insulation product on the market has engaged a market research company to survey the people living in metropolitan Adelaide, to see how many homes are insulated. The results are needed in four weeks for presentation to a meeting of company representatives, and to save time the survey is to be conducted over the telephone. What type of sampling method or methods would you consider most suitable for this purpose?

4.13 The Riverland in South Australia is one of the main producers of citrus products in Australia for both the national and overseas markets. A recent freak hailstorm hit some of the orchards at Waikerie, just before the fruit had reached maturity. On some of the fruit blocks the hail had stripped the trees, while the fruit on others was so badly damaged it could not be packed for sale at the wholesale market.

Many of the growers carry crop damage insurance with a company recommended by their local cooperative, to cover losses incurred by natural disasters. An insurance assessor sent to the district is faced with the daunting task of assessing the extent of the loss for each individual claimant. Can you suggest an approach that will not only be acceptable to his company but also satisfy the growers?

4.14 The State Government Insurance Company (SGIC) has an increasing portfolio of claims for work-related accidents. The management monitors the demands on its funds and wants to see whether the continued increase in claims follows any particular pattern.

When claims are entered the claimant is asked to record the type of accident, the time of the day and the place where the accident occurred, the type of industry of the employer, the sex of the worker involved, whether safety regulations were in place, and the amount of the claim.

The management decides to examine a representative selection of claims chosen from the hundreds of outstanding claims awaiting settlement.

(a) What is the population from which the sample is to be drawn?

(b) What is the observational unit involved?

(c) Since the management is keen to identify any pattern in the claims, can you direct them to an area that will yield the most precise estimate of the demand for funds?

(d) Will the approach you have chosen guarantee that the sample will be representative?

4.15 Despite considerable improvements to the quality and availability of public transport the private motor vehicle still remains the most popular form of transport in South Australia. As a result, traffic control in built-up areas is a major concern. Even with laws governing speed restrictions, road closures, speed humps, and a greater police presence on the roads, serious road accidents are still on the increase, with the attendant high cost in lives and money. However, over recent months, with the introduction of hidden speed cameras and heavy speeding fines imposed by the state government, there has been a sharp decrease in the number of serious motor vehicle accidents.

Initially this response was enthusiastically welcomed by the public but the introduction of a more extensive network of these cameras has meant that the government is now being accused of revenue-raising. This adverse publicity has prompted the government to seek the help of a statistician to design a survey to gauge the general public's opinion about this issue.

The statistician suggests drawing a sample of 400 from all the adults who live within a radius of 50 km from the centre of Adelaide, the business centre and capital of South Australia. A map of the residential areas of South Australia is available and it shows 50 suburbs within the area. The selected adult residents will be interviewed by means of a short questionnaire on the use of hidden speed cameras to reduce the road accident toll.

Suggest a detailed plan for sampling the adult residents, bearing in mind its practical operation. In your plan list the advantages and disadvantages of the sampling methods you have employed.

CHAPTER 5

QUESTIONNAIRE DESIGN AND DATA ENTRY

LEARNING OBJECTIVES

The learning objectives of this chapter are:

* to become familiar with the different types of questions used in questionnaires;
* to be aware of problems with the wording and layout of questionnaires;
* to know the process for entering data into a statistical package.

It has often been said that 'no survey can be better than its questionnaire', a cliche that aptly expresses the truth that no matter how efficient the sample design or sophisticated the analysis, neither can make up for poor questions.

However, the design of **questionnaires** still relies heavily on commonsense and hunches, although there are several pitfalls you can identify and avoid. The main aim of this chapter is to outline the tools and pitfalls of questionnaire design. The material presented here is discussed in more detail in Oppenheim (1966), Moser and Kalton (1971) and Elliot and Christopher (1973).

In considering the pitfalls in questionnaire design, it is a good idea to remember that potential problems with a questionnaire often surface during the pilot survey.

5.1 Question content

There are two main types of questions in questionnaires: factual and opinion questions.

Factual questions

Leaving aside public opinion polls, most questions asked in surveys are **factual questions**, concerned with ascertaining facts. By 'fact' we mean information that can be verified by experience or observation. However, whether a particular fact can be determined accurately is another matter and does not bear on whether or not the question is factual. For example, a factual question is: how much did you pay for your house? Of course, at the time of the questionnaire, the answer to the question may not be known accurately or the respondent may not provide the true answer. Further examples of factual questions concern the means of travelling to work, location of residence, leisure pursuits and age.

A special but very common class of factual questions is **classification questions**. These are asked chiefly to classify a respondent, and they are asked more for comparative purposes than for reasons directly related to the aim of the survey itself. Examples of classification questions are those that ask for marital status, age, sex and income.

Classification questions are usually put at the end of the questionnaire because they ask the respondent for personal information and it is preferable to postpone asking for this kind of information until a relationship has been established with the respondent. Further, you are more likely to obtain satisfactory responses to classification questions if you first explain why you are asking for such information. That is, the interviewer should explain that answers to these questions are needed for comparing the views or facts for different kinds of people.

As an important exception, classification questions must be asked *before* any other questions when you are quota sampling. You, the interviewer, need to know the group to which the unit belongs so that you can decide whether to include the unit or whether it comes from a group whose quota has been exceeded.

Opinion questions

Opinion questions are concerned with obtaining information about peoples' opinions and attitudes. This is, in some ways, much more difficult than ascertaining factual information. For example, determining the price a respondent paid for a house is likely to be much easier than determining whether or not they are in favour of compulsory local government elections. Some reasons for this difficulty are:

- A person's opinion is usually many-sided; for example, civil liberties, political, financial and other aspects are involved in forming an opinion on compulsory local government elections. A person may be in favour on some grounds and not in favour on others so that there is no single correct answer to the survey question. On the other hand, there is a single answer to the house price question and it may even be possible to verify the information independently.
- Opinions are often ill-formed, whereas facts are not. Respondents will know, or be able to find out easily, what they paid for their house. Little thinking is required on their part. However, the respondents may not have reached an opinion on compulsory local government elections; they may have given it little thought so that a great deal of thought and self-analysis may be required before they can give an opinion. Further, there is no guarantee that they will reach a final conclusion; more information and argument may change their opinion.
- While it is necessary to ensure that the respondent understands the question when you are after factual information, it is well established that people answering opinion questions are more sensitive to changes in wording, emphasis, sequence and so on.

With this background, let's consider the forms of questions used in questionnaires. Questions can be divided into open questions and closed or precoded questions.

Open questions

Open questions place no restriction on a respondent's reply, except the space provided for it on the questionnaire. Examples are: How would you describe your residence? What improvements would you like to see in television programming?

The chief advantage of such questions lies in the freedom given to the respondent. The answer is not restricted to the choices provided in the questionnaire. However, while open questions are easy to ask, they are difficult to answer and still more difficult to analyse. It is not clear how to answer the question: how would you describe your residence? Should you describe it as a house as opposed to a flat? Should you use more descriptive categories such as bungalow, town villa and so on? Reconciling the respondents' different descriptions will make analysis difficult.

Sometimes **field-coded open questions** are used. That is, the interviewer asks an open question and records a code for the response; the interviewer determines the code from his or her private list.

Closed questions

Closed questions offer the respondent a set of possible answers from which to choose.

EXAMPLE 5.1   OCCUPATION
Would you classify your occupation as:
(1) Managerial   (2) Administrative   (3) Sales   (4) Production worker

EXAMPLE 5.2   LOCAL GOVERNMENT ELECTIONS
How do you feel about compulsory local government elections?

Strongly agree	Agree	Neither agree nor disagree	Disagree	Strongly disagree
☐	☐	☐	☐	☐

The advantages of the closed question are that it is easier and quicker to answer, requires no writing, and quantification and analysis is straightforward. Its major disadvantage is that it may lead the respondent in a certain direction, so it requires very careful formulation. Further, the alternatives it offers may force respondents to give answers that do not accurately reflect their opinion on the matter.

Sometimes both open and closed questions on the same issue are asked. Usually you begin with open questions to explore general facets of the issue, and proceed to closed questions for more specific information. Open questions are often used in pilot surveys and the answers are used to construct closed questions for the survey itself.

The basic types used to construct a single, closed question are multiple choice questions, rating scales and inventories.

Multiple choice questions

Multiple choice questions give respondents a set of possible answers and these answers are exhaustive. Sometimes the category *Other* is included to ensure that all possible answers have been covered. Clearly, it is undesirable to have many respondents select this category. Often, they are asked to select only one category and in such cases the answers must be mutually exclusive. Sometimes respondents are asked to select one or more answers. In some cases they are asked to rank either all or a specified number of the answers in some kind of order — for example, frequency of occurrence.

EXAMPLE 5.3   HOUSE PRICE
How much did you pay for your house?

$0–$50 000	☐
$50 000–$75 000	☐
$75 000–$100 000	☐
$100 000–$150 000	☐
$150 000–$200 000	☐
$200 000–$250 000	☐
more than $250 000	☐

EXAMPLE 5.4   TRANSPORT TO WORK
Which of the following are the three transport modes you most often use to travel to work? Rank them in the order of frequency of use.

car with driver only	☐
car with passengers	☐
motorbike/scooter	☐
bicycle	☐
walk	☐
bus	☐
train	☐
other	☐

The common property of these two questions is that the list of answers covers all possible answers.

Multiple choice questions are usually used with factual questions, where the set of possible answers can be reasonably determined. However, the order of the answers is important as it can greatly affect the results. For example, respondents tend to select the earlier and later answers.

Rating scale questions

Rating scale questions ask the respondent to give a rating for the subject of the question. They are thus opinion, rather than factual, questions. They are commonly set up as **category rating scales**, that is, as a set of ordered categories. Respondents must mark the category that best describes their opinion. That is, category rating scales are a special type of multiple choice question. Sometimes a **graphic rating scale** is used when a standard length line (say 10 cm) is provided for respondents to mark according to where they believe they fit between the two extremes at either end of the line. The answer is recorded as the numeric value obtained by measuring the distance from one end of the line to the respondent's mark.

EXAMPLE 5.5   STATISTICS IN COURSE

The following is an example of a question based on a category rating scale:

Is statistics an important subject in your course?

Strongly agree	Agree	Neither agree nor disagree	Disagree	Strongly disagree
☐	☐	☐	☐	☐

The question could be framed by using a graphic rating scale, as follows:

Is statistics an important subject in your course?

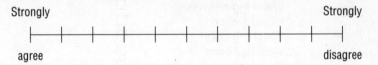

Strongly agree   Strongly disagree

Several points can be made about rating scales:

1. The number of categories is at the discretion of the questionnaire designer. Five is the most common, but seven and nine categories are also used. Sometimes dichotomies such as Yes/No and True/False are appropriate. However, remember that too few categories may result in only very broad information, whereas offering too many categories will mean that respondents will not be able to make a reliable choice of category. Further, the phenomenon of central tendency has to be taken into account. That is, respondents tend to avoid the extremes of a scale and usually cluster in the centre. Using extra categories initially and then ultimately combining extreme categories can sometimes overcome this.

2. You have to decide whether or not to include a neutral category. Without a neutral category the respondent may be forced to decide on an issue they are truly neutral about. On the other hand, including a neutral category invites a respondent to sit on the fence. The neutral category tends to be included more often than not.

3. The descriptors on the categories may vary: from positive to neutral to negative, as in the example above; from negative to positive to negative; from neutral to positive; or the inverse of any one of these. For example, *Importance* might be rated from unimportant to very important (neutral to positive); *Speed of lecturing* might be rated from too fast to too slow (negative to positive to negative).

   Be careful about the wording of the descriptors, particularly in factual questions, so that everyone has the same understanding of what they mean. For example, the use of *Frequently, Moderately, Often, Occasionally* is dangerous since these will be interpreted differently by the various respondents. One respondent might think that catching the bus once a week should be rated *Occasionally* whereas another respondent might think that this should be rated *Frequently*.

Inventory questions

An **inventory question** occurs when respondents are asked to check or mark a list in some way. The essential difference between an inventory question and other types of closed questions is that the list is not intended to be exhaustive. For this type of question, the respondents are generally asked to mark several responses.

EXAMPLE 5.6   INVENTORY QUESTIONS

Indicate which of the following activities you engage in at least once a week.

Reading   ☐
Watching television   ☐
Playing sport   ☐
Watching sport   ☐
Walking/hiking   ☐
Running/bicycle riding   ☐

In the following list rank the three attributes that you think most closely describe the real estate agent from whom you bought your house.

Trustworthy   ☐
Astute   ☐
Personable   ☐
Objective   ☐
Quiet   ☐
Sincere   ☐
Easygoing   ☐
Well-intentioned   ☐
Practical   ☐

5.2   Question wording

Some of the problems that can arise in the wording of questions include the following:

1. Questions that are not specific enough — do not ask general questions when specific information is required.
2. Difficult language and lengthy questions — use simple language and short questions.
3. Ambiguous questions — avoid these at all costs. For example: do you like travelling on trains and buses? This question will cause problems for respondents who like one and dislike the other.

4. Leading questions — these invite a particular response. A negative response is invited by questions of the form: you don't think ... do you? A positive response is invited by those of the form: shouldn't something be done about ...?

5. Questions that make false presumptions about the respondent — these lead to incorrect responses. For example: how did you vote in the last election? This question presumes that you did vote, and nonvoters might just make up a response.

6. Hypothetical questions — these are of dubious value. Consider the question: if fares on public transport decreased, would you use it more often? Most people like to keep their options open and make an idealistic appraisal of how they would react in such situations.

7. Embarrassing questions — these present a special problem for the questionnaire designer. Respondents are often reluctant to discuss private matters, give low-prestige answers or admit to socially unacceptable behaviour and attitudes. There are ways of formulating questions to overcome this.

8. Questions involving past events — peoples' memories are notoriously unreliable. Reliability depends on the time elapsed since the event and the importance of the event. It is important to help the respondent to recall information, so ask them to relate it to some personal event such as a birthday, holidays and so on.

9. Respondents are more likely give affirmative answers to statements. To avoid this risk, make some of your statements negative and others positive.

5.3   Question order and questionnaire layout

The questions making up your questionnaire are determined by the aim of the survey, as usual. However, resist the temptation to cover too much, to ask everything that might turn out to be interesting. The questionnaire should be no longer than is absolutely necessary for your purpose. Lengthy, rambling questionnaires are difficult for both the interviewer and the respondent. They encourage ill-considered responses and are often terminated prematurely, which means that you will miss out on some information. It seems preferable to obtain good information on a few specific matters than poor information on a large number of matters. In overcoming this problem, as with many other questionnaire problems, the pilot survey is very useful. Questions that provide little information can be weeded out and any problems of length will become apparent.

The general principles to follow for the ordering of questions are as follows:

1. Place related questions together.

2. Place easy questions before difficult questions and general questions before specific questions.

3. Delay sensitive and personal questions for as long as possible. As stated previously, classification questions should always be put at the end, unless quota sampling is being used.

4. Use **filter questions** to avoid asking irrelevant questions. For example, a question: '10. Do you...' is followed by: 'If the answer to question 10 was no, proceed to question...'.

This set of recommendations is based on the likelihood of getting a better response to difficult and sensitive questions after you have established a rapport with the respondent. If a sensitive question risks terminating the interview, it is better if this occurs after most of the questionnaire has been completed. Also, answering general questions before specific questions gives respondents a chance to develop their thoughts as they proceed through the questionnaire.

In some situations involving a series of related questions, an **attitude scale** is used. This is a score obtained from a series of questions designed to measure the respondent's attitude to a specific issue. Such a scale explores the many facets of an issue, and all the questions involved in obtaining the attitude scale are placed together.

A series of related questions can also be asked by replacing an inventory question with a set of single questions, each question corresponding to an item from the inventory. For example, the respondent might be asked to rate each item in the inventory for appropriateness.

A particular issue to take into account in laying out the questionnaire is the **halo effect** which occurs when the respondent gives a similar response to each of a series of questions without considering each question independently. A respondent in favour of conservation will tend to give positive answers to any questions on this subject, without considering the specific issue in each question separately. Also, a series of questions with rating scales all going in the same direction — for example, from positive to negative — tends to get a similar response for all questions. You can reduce this effect by randomising the direction of the rating scale although this may have the disadvantage of complicating the questionnaire's layout.

5.4   Data coding, entry and error-checking

Once the questionnaire is designed, the sample is selected and the questionnaire is administered. We then receive a pile of questionnaires containing information of interest to us. To find out what the respondents have said we have to analyse this information. This analysis may be quite simple, involving only tables of frequencies. Even so, it is often convenient to use a computer; we would analyse manually only very small, simple surveys. To prepare the data for entry into a computer, we usually convert it to a set of numeric codes; that is, we quantify it so that it can be entered efficiently.

So we are going to turn our attention to **data coding**. That is, assigning numeric values to each respondent's answers. However, before coding, it is a good idea to check over the completed questionnaires for any obvious problems. Have some respondents provided several answers to multiple choice questions where only a single response was required? Has a respondent failed to answer some questions? Is there a particular question that many respondents failed to answer? An incomplete questionnaire does not, in general, have to be abandoned. If it contains important, accurate answers, it would be wasteful to throw away such valuable information. A whole questionnaire is rejected only when the great majority of questions have not been answered. Otherwise, you record that there is a **missing value** for unanswered questions.

The set of codes for the answers to a particular question is called the **coding frame**. For closed questions in which a single response is expected this is straightforward and the coding consists of assigning a predetermined numeric value to each category, and a code for missing values is usually included. In fact, the questionnaire form could be **precoded**; that is, you can include on the form the numeric values to be assigned to the various categories. Often, a section down the side is separated off and marked *For office use only*, so that the codes can be entered by the interviewer or later by a coder. This makes the computer entry of the information easier.

Coding multiple answer questions (either multiple-choice or inventory questions) is not quite so simple. Take the question in example 5.4, *Transport to work*, where the respondents are asked to rank the three modes of transport they most frequently use, in order of frequency of use. That is, each respondent will nominate three modes and these could be any three of the eight listed. The simplest approach is to code each answer in the list as if it were a separate question. The coding frame for a particular mode of transport would then consist of codes 1, 2 and 3 for the different possible ranks, and a code such as 4 to indicate when that mode is unranked. This approach works well for a limited number of inventory items, as the number of codes to be entered equals the number of items. If you have many items, it is best to limit the number of answers, as in example 5.4, *Transport to work*. Then the code is recorded for each answer. For example 5.4, three codes would be recorded: one each for the modes ranked one, two, and three. This approach also causes problems in the analysis stage, although they are not impossible to overcome (Cody and Smith, 1985).

Coding open questions is the most difficult task of all. It is a matter of determining the basis of the code and deciding on how detailed a grouping you will allow. These depend on the range of answers you expect and the information you want to obtain. For example, consider the open question: how would you describe the residence you live in? This might be coded: 1 for a house, 2 for a flat; or 1 for a wholly-detached house, 2 for a semi-detached house, 3 for a single-storey flat, 4 for a multi-storey flat and 5 for some other type of residence. In general, it is better to err on the side of too much detail at this stage. Categories can be relatively easily combined during analysis, if necessary; it is much harder to split categories at this stage because you have to go back to the original questionnaires and recode. Too detailed a code can make allocating codes difficult and does not give you a useful summary of the data. Too few codes can be misleading.

After the data has been coded, the **data entry** phase begins; that is, the data is entered into the computer for analysis. The precise details for doing this depend on what package you use, although these days data is usually entered into a set of cells arranged in rows and columns, as for a spreadsheet. Most often the computer package expects all the values for one variable to be entered in one column, and the different variables put in different columns.

EXAMPLE 5.7   HOUSE SALES SURVEY

The data in table 5.1 are the responses from five houses in a survey of house sales. The table shows how the data would be entered into a computer package for analysis. The table presents, in one row, the selling price of a house, the area of the building, the number of rooms in the house, the estimated year of building, a rating of the condition of the house, and codes for the type of wall material, the type of roof material and the style of building. Note the two missing values, indicated by an asterisk (*) in the tables. Different packages use different conventions for missing values.

Table 5.1   Arrangement of the responses from 5 houses

Price ($)	Building area (ha)	No. of rooms	Year built	Condition	Wall type	Roof type	Style
165 000	133	5	1925	6	5	2	16
87 500	98	4	1966	6	1	1	30
86 000	98	4	1966	6	1	1	30
86 000	98	4	1966	6	1	1	30
55 000	*	*	1992	9	6	2	7

The final operation, before analysing the data, is **error checking**; in this phase, the data that has been stored in the computer is checked for errors in data coding and data entry. Even for very experienced coders and data entry personnel, mistakes are inevitable. With a lapse in concentration the wrong code can be assigned to an answer, the wrong key struck in entering a number, the code misread, numbers transposed, and so on. It is therefore essential that the information stored in the computer is checked as carefully as possible. If these errors are not removed, analyses will be incorrect and a large number of errors may lead to completely erroneous conclusions.

5.5   Entering the data into Minitab

The easiest way to enter data into Minitab, if you have a version with the pull-down menus, is to use the data screen, as described in Appendix D, *Detailed instructions for Minitab menus*. If you are not going to use the data screen, there are two commands in Minitab for entering data: *set* and *read*. The *set* command is used to enter all the values for one variable at a time. The *read* command is used to enter all the variables for each observational unit. It is generally easier with questionnaires to enter all the answers for each respondent together. So, you normally use the *read* command when commands are being used to input the data from questionnaires.

EXAMPLE 5.7   HOUSE SALES (continued)

To enter the data and names with the data screen, select the screen by using the *Edit > Data Screen* option or *Alt-D*. Enter the data and names into cells as shown in figure 5.1.

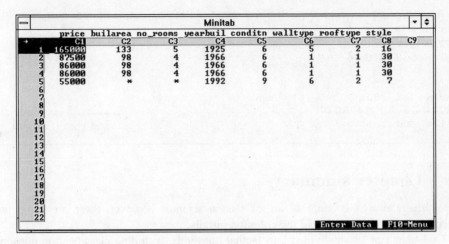

Figure 5.1   Data screen showing data entered

The Minitab *read* and *name* commands to input the data are used as follows:

```
MTB > outfile 'a:\housale1.lis'
MTB > name c1 'price' c2 'builarea' c3 'no_rooms'
MTB > name c4 'yearbuil' c5 'conditn' c6 'walltype'
MTB > name c7 'rooftype' c8 'style'
MTB > read c1-c8
DATA> 165000 133 5 1925 6 5 2 16
DATA> 87500 98 4 1966 6 1 1 30
DATA> 86000 98 4 1966 6 1 1 30
DATA> 86000 98 4 1966 6 1 1 30
DATA> 55000 * * 1992 9 6 2 7
DATA> end
 5 ROWS READ
```

The Minitab *set* and *name* commands to input the data are used as follows:

```
MTB > outfile 'a:\housale2.lis'
MTB > name c1 'price' c2 'builarea' c3 'no_rooms'
MTB > name c4 'yearbuil' c5 'conditn' c6 'walltype'
MTB > name c7 'rooftype' c8 'style'
MTB > set c1
DATA> 165000 87500 86000 86000 55000
DATA> set c2
DATA> 133 98 98 98 *
DATA> set c3
DATA> 5 4 4 4 *
DATA> set c4
DATA> 1925 1966 1966 1966 1992
```

continued . . .

79

```
DATA> set c5
DATA> 6 6 6 6 9
DATA> set c6
DATA> 5 1 1 1 6
DATA> set c7
DATA> 2 1 1 1 2
DATA> set c8
DATA> 16 30 30 30 7
DATA> end
```

5.6   Chapter summary

Questionnaire design is more of an art than a science; however, there are some basic principles that might help avoid the common pitfalls.

Questions can be subdivided into factual questions, including classification questions, and opinion questions. Generally, factual questions are more successful than opinion questions. Questions can also be categorised as open or closed questions. Open questions are easier to ask but more difficult to analyse than closed questions. Open questions are often used in pilot surveys and the answers are used to construct closed questions for the survey itself. The basic types used to construct a single, closed question are multiple choice, rating scale and inventory questions. Rating scale questions can be constructed by using category or graphic rating scales.

One of the most important aspects of creating a questionnaire is the wording of questions. Questions should be specific, simple, unambiguous and balanced with respect to whether respondents are likely to view them as positive or negative. Leading, presumptuous, hypothetical and memory-reliant questions should be avoided. Special consideration should be given to presenting potentially embarrassing questions.

It is very important to limit the length of the questionnaire. Generally, related questions should be placed together, and classification and more personal questions should be left until later in the questionnaire. Filter questions should be used to avoid irrelevant questions. Beware of the halo effect.

Once the questionnaire has been administered, the responses have to be coded. The codes are then entered into the computer and the entered data must be checked for the inevitable data entry errors. This is most important, as errors in the data will undermine the analyses.

5.7   Key terms

- attitude scale
- category rating scale
- classification question
- closed question
- coding frame
- data coding
- data entry
- error checking
- factual question
- field-coded open question
- filter question

- graphic rating scale
- halo effect
- inventory question
- missing value
- multiple choice question
- open question
- opinion question
- precoded questionnaire
- questionnaire
- rating scale question

5.8   Exercises

5.1   Questions can be: open or closed; opinion or factual/classification; multiple choice, inventory or rating scale. Use these terms to identify the type of the following questions.

(a) **A public transport survey**
When you complete your journey what is your destination? (Tick 1 box only)

☐ Home
☐ Work
☐ School, college, university
☐ Railway station

☐ Local shopping centre
☐ Professional (doctor, bank etc)
☐ Social sport, recreational
☐ City centre

(b) **A training course assessment questionnaire**
The training course material was:

Highly theoretical __ __ __ __ __ __ Highly practical
New to me   __ __ __ __ __ __ Previously known to me
Very useful   __ __ __ __ __ __ Of little value
Very relevant   __ __ __ __ __ __ Irrelevant

(c) **A student survey**

1. *Which course are you studying?* _____

2. *Please state your age group:*   Under 20   20 – 30 yrs   Over 30 yrs

3. *Are you attending university?*   Part-time   Full-time

4. *Do you have access to computer facilities*
   outside those available at the university?   Yes   No

   Where are these facilities available?   Home   Work

(d) **A survey of employees**

The management of this company wants to introduce flexitime into the current working fortnight, and is considering several options.

Which option do you favour?
Start at 8 am, 9-day fortnight, every other Friday on flexitime ☐
Start at 8 am, 9-day fortnight, choice of rostered day off   ☐
Late start or early finish, 10-day fortnight   ☐
Hours to remain unchanged   ☐

(e) **A survey of small business companies**

1. *What is the nature of your business?* _____

2. *How many employees does your company employ?* _____

3. *Are the premises:*   Owned by the company ☐ Leased ☐

4. *Is the company part of a chain of companies?*   Yes   No

5. *Where is the head office of this chain?*   Local   Interstate   Overseas

(f) **A bank customer service survey**

Please rate the location of this branch of the bank, as follows:

	Very good	Good	Satisfactory	Poor	Very poor
Proximity to shopping centre	5	4	3	2	1
Proximity to home/ office/workplace	5	4	3	2	1
Proximity to public transport	5	4	3	2	1
Car parking facilities	5	4	3	2	1

(g) **An inventory survey**

1. *How many individual inventory items do you stock?*_____

2. *Do you sell nonstocked items?*   ☐ Yes   ☐ No

3. *What is your inventory file growth?* _____

4. *What is the largest quantity (individual units) of inventory units on hand?*__

5. *Do you have multiple warehouses?* ☐ Yes ☐ No

6. *How many product classes do you have?* _____

7. *Do you have a inventory numbering system?* ☐ Yes ☐ No

8. *If yes, what is the maximum length of your inventory code number?*_____

9. *How comprehensive is your description of products?*_____

10. *Is more than one vendor involved when*
    you purchase any of your inventory items? ☐ Yes ☐ No

11. *Do you give quantity discounts or price breaks*
    to particular types of buyers (price matrix)? ☐ Yes ☐ No

12. *Do your prices change frequently?* ☐ Yes ☐ No

13. *How are price changes made?*
    On a percentage basis ☐ Yes ☐ No
    Individual items only ☐ Yes ☐ No
    By product class ☐ Yes ☐ No
    Other _____

14. *What is the costing method of your inventory?* _____

15. *What types of reports do you produce from your inventory?* _____

16. *Is there any other information that you believe is pertinent?* _____

    Source: Halper, S.D., Davis, G.C., O'Neil-Dunne, P.J., Pfau, P.R. (1985)

(h) **An environmental survey**
Do you agree with the following local government proposals?

	Strongly agree	Agree	Don't know	Disagree	Strongly disagree
Ban backyard burning	☐	☐	☐	☐	☐
Provide a recycling service	☐	☐	☐	☐	☐
Tighten controls on industrial sites	☐	☐	☐	☐	☐
Encourage the use of native plants	☐	☐	☐	☐	☐

(i) **A newspaper survey**
The federal government maintains that local industry should be more competitive and has proposed relaxing the current tariff restrictions on imported products, for example clothing.

Do you support this move? Yes No

Why? _____

_____

_____

5.2   Examine the following and rephrase if you feel it is necessary.

(a) *Which books from the recommended reading list have you read in the last semester?*

(b) *How often do you use the after-hours teller facility at your local bank?*
frequently ☐   occasionally ☐   never ☐

(c) Your firm is contemplating enterprise bargaining negotiations with the aim of entering into employment contracts for the next two years. It intends to abolish certain benefits, including the annual leave loading, and to improve productivity in return for some modest increase in the remuneration package for individual employees. Your firm decides to use a questionnaire to ascertain its employees' key priorities in terms of their current package.

If your annual leave loading was abolished but you were granted an immediate 5% financial increase, would you prefer to receive that increase in the form of:
Salary only
Superannuation
Fringe benefits

(d) *Do you agree with the recent excessive reductions in the number of state government public service employees?*

Yes ☐   No ☐

(e) *Does your company have an equal opportunity policy?*

Yes ☐   No ☐

*If not, why?*_____

(f) *If the government reduced the award rates for employees under the age of 18 years, would you employ more school-leavers?*

Yes ☐   No ☐

(g) *Of course, the union representative cannot back down and reject the latest pay rise offered by the employer. Do you agree?*

Yes ☐   No ☐

(h) *How many times in the last month has the photocopying machine broken down and caused delays?* _____

5.3   The data collected in the real estate survey in the Prospect area is ready for analysis. The variables recorded are price, settlement date, house area (in square metres), number of rooms, block size, estimate of the year when the house was built, rating of the condition of the house, type of wall material, type of roof material and style of the house.

Price	48000	48000	135000	130000	108000	110000	104000	123000	70000
Settlement date	290891	290891	271191	40592	110991	270592	271191	80791	40592
House area	*	*	132	121	81	77	63	125	74
No. rooms	*	*	5	6	4	4	4	4	4
Block size	0.03	0.03	0.0751	0.0751	*	*	*	0.0883	*
Year built	*	*	1950	1950	1984	1976	1974	1920	1970
Condition	*	*	7	6	8	8	8	7	7
Wall type	*	*	3	5	1	1	1	1	1
Roof type	*	*	1	1	1	1	1	2	1
Style	12	12	23	23	23	30	30	34	23

Enter the data with Minitab's data screen, if you have a version with pull-down menus, or by using Minitab's *read* command.

5.4   Exercise 5.8 involves a survey of the range of supermarket prices in metropolitan Adelaide for certain products. The survey form and coding sheet are provided with the exercise. The following are some results that have been collected and coded for entry into a computer.

4	5168	7	2.81	1	0.99	5	1.82	1	1.62	20	9	0.97	6	1.57	9	3.82
11	5085	10	3.77	7	0.93	3	1.74	2	1.05	20	1	0.76	3	1.35	5	2.29
10	5063	3	2.95	2	0.99	6	1.81	4	1.12	0	8	0.93	3	1.46	1	1.99
13	3124	7	3.25	1	1.07	5	1.92	2	1.25	20	3	0.95	6	1.63	11	4.06
7	*	11	3.95	1	1.30	5	1.95	2	1.25	20	7	1.16	6	1.95	2	3.99
5	5013	7	2.57	1	1.22	6	1.70	4	0.99	20	9	1.09	2	1.59	4	3.99
11	5037	12	4.39	1	1.09	3	1.77	3	.75	20	11	1.00	6	1.87	3	3.99
2	5032	1	1.68	1	1.08	5	1.80	4	2.74	5	9	1.93	6	1.88	2	4.58
10	*	12	44.5	1	1.09	5	1.75	4	1.17	20	99	1.07	6	1.88	9	3.39
11	*	11	3.09	1	1.08	5	1.75	2	1.47	20	11	1.27	3	1.58	13	2.58

(a)   A total of 284 students were involved in the data collection. Errors are bound to have been made in collection, data coding or data entry. Please help with identifying any errors or inconsistencies.

(b)   Enter the edited data with Minitab's data screen, if you have a version with pull-down menus, or by using Minitab's *read* command.

5.5   A leading supermarket chain has recently acquired an establishment in an outer suburban shopping centre and wishes to upgrade it. It intends to interview every 10th customer who passes through their checkout during one weekend trading period to find out whether they are satisfied with the present services. The following two questionnaires have been presented for the manager to consider. Consolidate the two into a final version, making your own improvements where necessary.

Questionnaire A

We are anxious to please you and invite your comments on our services. Please circle your answer.

Did you enjoy shopping at **Better Buy**?

Yes   No

Were the staff courteous and helpful?

Yes   No

Did we offer all the commodities you required?

Yes   No

How often do you shop at this supermarket?

once a week   twice a week
occasionally   this is my first visit

The new management intends to introduce new facilities, as follows; circle the two you think are most important.

Car parking
Home delivery
Coin-operated trolleys
Bakery on the premises
A clothing department
A fresh fruit & vegetable section
Other _____

Are you female or male?

Size of household:

Adults_____Children_____

Do you live close to this supermarket?

within 2 km   2–4 km
more than 4 km away

Thank you for your assistance.
Please place your completed questionnaire in the box provided as you leave the store.

Questionnaire B

Welcome to shopping at **Better Buy**. We welcome your comments on our facilities. Indicate your answer with a tick.

Are you male or female?

To which age-group do you belong?

0–15 yrs   25–50 yrs
15–25 yrs   50+ yrs

How often do you shop at this supermarket?

Are you shopping for a household?

Yes   No

If you are: No. of adults_____
No. of children_____

Are you shopping for a couple?

Yes   No

Are you shopping for one person?

Yes   No

How far is the supermarket from your normal residence?

1 km   2 km   3 km   >3 km

What new or improved facilities would you like the management to provide?

Home delivery
Paper / plastic shopping bags
Increased number of checkouts
Wider range of choice
A self-service refreshment area
Change in shopping hours
Car parking
Other comments_____
_____
_____

Thank you for your assistance.

5.6 The students' union has been invited to make a submission to the University Council about improvements to student facilities. Their representatives are anxious to hear students' opinions about how current facilities are used and whether any additions or changes are required. Prepare a draft questionnaire for this purpose.

5.7 The questionnaire on page 88 has been prepared for a survey at our university of students' attitudes to government spending.
  (a) Answer the questionnaire.
  (b) Complete the section down the lefthand edge headed *For Office Use*, entering the code for the answer given to each question. If there is no answer, enter an asterisk (*) to indicate a missing value. Code the answers to the first two questions 1–5 and code those for the third and fourth questions 1–4. Code the classification questions 1–3, 1–2, and 1–3, respectively.
  (c) Has the questionnaire achieved its purpose of making the students think carefully about the topic?
  (d) Suppose you combined your data with data from the other members of the class to form the results of the survey. What sampling method would you have used to obtain the students? Is the sample of students likely to be representative of the target population?

5.8 A survey is required to collect the prices of certain products commonly used in households so that prices in the city's metropolitan area can be analysed. A sample of the supermarkets in the metropolitan area is to be selected and the various products' prices recorded at each of these supermarkets.
  (a) What sampling method would you suggest for selecting the sample of supermarkets. Give reasons for choosing this method.
  (b) List the product brands that are likely to occur in the supermarkets in your sample and make a coding sheet based on these; use the coding sheet example on p. 91 as a guide. As a pilot exercise, fill out the *Supermarket price survey* form on p. 90, based on the information obtained from your local supermarket. Enter the price and code for each item, using your coding sheet to determine the codes.
  (c) Suppose you combined your data with data from the other members of the class to form the results of the survey. What sampling method would you have used to select supermarkets? Is the sample likely to be representative of the target population?

Government spending survey

For Office Use		Agree strongly	Agree	Not sure/ Don't know	Disagree	Disagree strongly
Code	**1. To what extent do you agree or disagree with the following statements?**					
1__	a. The economy is under control	☐	☐	☐	☐	☐
3__	b. The workforce is underpaid	☐	☐	☐	☐	☐
5__	c. Banks charge reasonable interest rates	☐	☐	☐	☐	☐
7__	d. Level of taxation is unfair	☐	☐	☐	☐	☐
9__	e. People expect life to be easy	☐	☐	☐	☐	☐
11__	f. Homes are too expensive	☐	☐	☐	☐	☐

2. To what extent do you think that the following are now problems in the Australian economy?

Code		Don't know	Very serious	Somewhat serious	Small problem	No problem
13__	High-risk investment	☐	☐	☐	☐	☐
15__	Government regulation	☐	☐	☐	☐	☐
17__	Unemployment	☐	☐	☐	☐	☐
19__	Productivity	☐	☐	☐	☐	☐
21__	Personal credit	☐	☐	☐	☐	☐
23__	Ageing population	☐	☐	☐	☐	☐
25__	Inflation (persistent increase in prices)	☐	☐	☐	☐	☐
27__	Business management	☐	☐	☐	☐	☐
29__	Wealth concentration	☐	☐	☐	☐	☐

continued . . .

3. What kinds of investment do you make in Australia?

		Often (once a month)	Occasionally (3–4 times a year)	Rarely (once a year)	Never
31__	a. Personal home	☐	☐	☐	☐
33__	b. Investment property	☐	☐	☐	☐
35__	c. Savings	☐	☐	☐	☐
37__	d. Shares	☐	☐	☐	☐
39__	e. Superannuation	☐	☐	☐	☐
41__	f. Collectibles	☐	☐	☐	☐
43__	g. Own business	☐	☐	☐	☐

4. Do you think that the Australian government should spend more or less money on the following:

		More	About the same	Less	Don't know
45__	Social welfare	☐	☐	☐	☐
47__	Trade	☐	☐	☐	☐
49__	Education	☐	☐	☐	☐
51__	Defence	☐	☐	☐	☐
53__	Leisure	☐	☐	☐	☐

For the following questions, circle the appropriate answer:

55__	Age	19 yrs or less	20–30 yrs	over 30 yrs
57__	Sex	Female	Male	
59__	Highest qualification	Tertiary	Secondary	Primary
61__	University school	_____

Supermarket price survey

This survey is designed to collect the prices of certain products commonly used in households so that price variation across a metropolitan area can be studied.

When you are collecting the brands and prices for the items requested below, please make sure that the items are the standard type. For example, exclude decaffeinated coffee, unsalted butter, low calorie lemonade, and so on. Also exclude any items on special.

	1 2
Supermarket name_____ Type	☐ ☐

	4 5 6 7
Location_____ Postcode	☐ ☐ ☐ ☐

Date of price collection_____

Item	Unit	Brand	Price	Deposit
		9 10	12 13 14 15	
Coffee (instant)	100 g	☐ ☐	☐ ▣ ☐ ☐	
		17	19 20 21 22	
Sugar (white)	1 kg	☐	☐ ▣ ☐ ☐	
		24	26 27 28 29	
Butter	500 g	☐	☐ ▣ ☐ ☐	
			(without deposit)	deposit
		31	33 34 35 36	38 39
Lemonade	1 litre (glass)	☐	☐ ▣ ☐ ☐	☐ ☐
		41 42	44 45 46 47	
Flour (plain white)	1 kg	☐ ☐	☐ ▣ ☐ ☐	
		49	51 52 53 54	
Dog food	1.2 kg can	☐	☐ ▣ ☐ ☐	
		56 57	59 60 61 62	
Soap powder	1 kg packet	☐ ☐	☐ ▣ ☐ ☐	

Collector's name_____   Collector's ID number_____

Collector's course_____

Supermarket price survey: coding sheet

Supermarket type
1. Archer
2. Low Price
3. Good Foods
4. Old World
5. Food Case
6. Another Case
7. 24 Hours
8. 007
9. Local area store
10. Super sales store
11. Other

Coffee brand
1. Low Price
2. Mountain View
3. Plantation
4. Plantation Roast
5. Dutch Cafe
6. Ourbrand
7. World Roast
8. Dutch Espresso
9. House of Max
10. Oldcafe
11. Oldcafe Blended
12. Oldcafe Bronze
13. Diablo
14. Other

Butter brand
1. Soft Spread
2. Low Price
3. Green Vale
4. Hillendale
5. All Farm
6. Eastern Star
7. Other

Sugar Brand
1. Sweet Crystal
2. Other

Flour brand
1. Cooks
2. Low Price
3. Red & Yellow
4. Shrubs
5. Freshland
6. Sulphur Crest
7. Supa Crust
8. Brownes
9. Tiger
10. Light Sifted
11. Silver Wings
12. Super sales store
13. Other

Soap powder brand
1. DirtBlaster
2. New Power
3. Overdrive
4. Supermo
5. El Supremo
6. Fantastic
7. Suntastic
8. FeastClean
9. BigSuds
10. Sudsomatic
11. Quickwash
12. Supreme
13. BlueWave
14. Silk
15. Other

Drink brand
1. Walls Drinks
2. Swept
3. Spirit
4. Woodlands
5. Other

Dog food brand
1. Low Price
2. Shrubs
3. Mates
4. Big Bites
5. Old World
6. Cobber
7. Other

Note: As an example, if your supermarket is part of the Another Case chain, its code is 6 and you should enter it in boxes 1 and 2 as follows:

<table>
<tr><td>1</td><td>2</td></tr>
<tr><td>□</td><td>6</td></tr>
</table>

PART III

DESCRIPTIVE SUMMARIES OF DATA

LEARNING OBJECTIVES

The learning objective of this introduction to Part III is:
- to know what a variable is and the different types that occur.

In this and subsequent parts of the book, we shall assume that you have completed the data collection stage and that the data is ready to be analysed. That is, as suggested in chapter 1, *Statistics*, statistical procedures are to be used as professional tools for helping to answer the investigator's questions.

In this part, we assume that the questions to be investigated concern just the observed units, so the answers will be confined to these units. The statistical procedures that do this are classified as **descriptive summaries**. These statistical procedures are primarily intended to summarise the data, and they include distribution tables, distribution diagrams, measures of central tendency, and measures of dispersion. That is, each summary will give us a picture of the data we have collected and it will be necessary to decide which summaries to use in each case. As will become clear, choosing the appropriate summaries depends on the questions to be investigated and the types of variables involved.

The two main types of variables are limited and unrestricted variables. A second, independent classification divides them into nominal, ordinal and interval/ratio variables. These variable types are discussed below. At this point, note that the summaries presented in this part cover situations involving the following combinations of limited and unrestricted variables:
- one limited variable
- two limited variables
- three limited variables
- one unrestricted variable
- one unrestricted and one limited variable
- one unrestricted and two limited variables
- two unrestricted variables

Variables

Chapter 4, *Surveys*, defined a **variable** as a characteristic of an observational unit that varies from unit to unit. The **value** of a variable is the number or category representing the amount or state of the characteristic associated with the variable. A set of raw data then consists of the values of the variables recorded from several units. An important consideration in determining the statistical procedure for a particular instance is the types of variables involved.

The prime distinction between limited and unrestricted variables is based on the number of values that are likely to be obtained. For **limited variables**, only a few (≤10, say) values are obtained. For **unrestricted variables**, many (>10, say) values are obtained. We have used 10 as the dividing line between limited and unrestricted values only as a rough guideline — this guideline will not always be followed. The crucial feature of limited variables is that you are likely to observe a particular value repeatedly, whereas with unrestricted variables a particular value does not recur very often.

Variables can also be classified according to the nature of the measurement obtained: nominal, ordinal or interval/ratio.

1. **Nominal variables** are variables whose values are names; they have no implicit order as far as the characteristic being observed is concerned.
2. **Ordinal variables** are variables whose values can be ordered, but it cannot be determined how far apart they are.
3. **Interval/ratio variables** are variables whose values can be ordered; also, numerically equal differences between the values represent the same difference in the characteristic being observed.

Although we stated that the two classifications of variables are independent, this is not entirely the case. Nominal variables are always limited, regardless of the number of values observed; ordinal and interval/ratio variables may be either limited or unrestricted. There are also other systems of classifying variables. For example, nominal and ordinal variables are sometimes referred to as **categorical variables**, because their values are thought of as a set of possible categories for describing units.

Variables are sometimes distinguished as qualitative or quantitative. A **quantitative variable** is one whose values measure the *quantity* of the characteristic on which the variable is based, whereas a **qualitative variable** is one whose values describe the *attributes* of the characteristic on which the variable is based. This classification of variables differs from our limited versus unrestricted classification. For example, some limited variables are qualitative, while others are quantitative. However, nominal and ordinal variables are qualitative variables and interval/ratio variables are quantitative variables.

Another classification distinguishes between continuous variables and discrete variables. A **continuous variable** is one for which the underlying variable measures a characteristic that, conceptually at least, varies continuously and so *potentially* the values form a continuum over the observed range. The values of a **discrete variable** are discontinuous; that is, they do not, even conceptually, form a continuous range. Again, this classification of variables is both similar to and different from others. For example, nominal variables are always discrete, and so are counts of items. However, discrete variables, such as counts, may be limited or unrestricted, depending on how many values are likely to be observed.

EXAMPLES

The following variables and their types illustrate the different systems of classifying variables, and the classification for each system described above is given; however, in this book, the limited versus unrestricted and nominal versus ordinal versus interval/ratio systems are the most important. Unless stated otherwise, assume that at least 30 observations have been taken in each case.

1. Suppose a questionnaire asks the respondent to indicate their sex. The variable *Sex* takes two values, *Female* and *Male*, that are merely names with no implicit ordering. It is thus a limited, nominal, qualitative, discrete variable.

2. The following question was asked in a survey:

   How do you feel about compulsory local government elections?

Strongly agree	Agree	Neither agree nor disagree	Disagree	Strongly disagree
☐	☐	☐	☐	☐

   This gives us a variable that has five values that can be ordered. That is, *Strongly agree* indicates more agreement than *Agree*. However, the difference in attitude to elections between the pair of consecutive values, *Strongly agree* and *Agree*, is not necessarily the same as the difference between any other pair of consecutive values, for example *Agree* and *Neither agree nor disagree*. The variable *Local government elections opinion* is a limited, ordinal, qualitative, discrete variable.

3. A survey of residents in a local government area obtains each respondent's taxable income, to the nearest dollar. The taxable incomes of two different residents is unlikely to be exactly the same, to the nearest dollar. Further, the incomes can be ordered and pairs of incomes differing by the same amount are equally different. For example, the incomes $25 186 and $25 286 differ by the same amount as the incomes $55 312 and $55 412. That is, the difference of $100 represents the same difference in amount of income. *Taxable income* is an unrestricted, interval/ratio, quantitative, continuous variable. Note that money is taken to be a continuous variable as it can, and sometimes is, expressed in parts of cents.

4. Suppose that students are ranked in order according to their results in an exam in an attempt to measure their knowledge of that

subject. The ranking will begin at one for the highest mark in the exam and finish close to the number of students in the class; the largest rank could well be in excess of 30. Clearly, someone with a smaller rank has more knowledge, but the difference between the two students' ranks gives us no idea of how different their knowledge is. The variable *Subject knowledge* is an unrestricted, ordinal, qualitative, continuous variable.

5. *Maximum daily temperatures*, to the nearest tenth of a degree (°C), are to be analysed. It is unlikely that any particular temperature value will recur often, and the same difference between pairs of temperature values represents the same difference in the maximum daily temperature. The variable is unrestricted, interval/ratio, quantitative and continuous.

6. A survey asks voters whether or not they agree with the Opposition policy to block a piece of government legislation. The variable, *Opinion on policy*, takes two values, *Agree* and *Disagree*, that have no implicit order. It is a limited, nominal, qualitative, discrete variable.

7. The ages, in years, of children in a school class are recorded. The range of ages of children in a school class tends to be about three years. The same difference in the values for the variable *Age* always represents the same difference in the children's ages, within the limits of the precision with which *Age* is measured. So we can determine how much children differ in age, although not very precisely. *Age* is a limited, interval/ratio, quantitative, continuous variable.

8. Boxes containing 24 cans of soft drink are being checked to determine how many cans in the box are below the specified volume. The variable is *Number cans below volume*. In this case, it is difficult to decide whether the variable is limited or unrestricted. If below-volume cans are unusual, the variable will be limited as it is likely to take only a few values such as 0–3. On the other hand, if the number of below-volume cans in a box may be any number between 0–24, it will be an unrestricted variable; it is also an interval/ratio, quantitative, discrete variable.

From these examples, you can see that neither the distinction between limited and unrestricted variables, nor the distinction between nominal, ordinal and interval/ratio variables is innate to the variables. It depends on how the values are recorded. For example, we suggested that *Income* measured to the nearest dollar is likely to be an unrestricted, interval/ratio variable. However, *Income* might be recorded as one of four nonoverlapping income ranges that cover the respondents' incomes. Then *Income* would be a limited variable. It would be ordinal if the respondents are ranked according to this.

On the other hand, the distinction between discrete and continuous variables is innate to the variables. That is, this classification fundamentally differs from the former classifications. The latter classification is intrinsic to the characteristic being observed, whereas the former reflect the values recorded. This is a most important difference.

Summary

A fundamental consideration in choosing a statistical procedure is the type of variable that has been observed. The primary distinction is made between limited and unrestricted variables. The crucial feature of limited variables is that a particular value is likely to be observed repeatedly, whereas with unrestricted variables a particular value does not recur often. A secondary classification of variables distinguishes them as nominal, ordinal and interval/ratio variables. These two classifications depend on what types of values have been recorded. They are not entirely independent. Nominal variables are always limited, no matter how many values have been observed. Ordinal and interval/ratio variables may be either limited or unrestricted.

There are other systems for categorising variables, apart from the two systems employed in this book.

Key terms

- **categorical variable**
- **continuous variable**
- **descriptive summaries**
- **discrete variable**
- **interval/ratio variable**
- **limited variable**
- **nominal variable**
- **ordinal variable**
- **qualitative variable**
- **quantitative variable**
- **unrestricted variable**
- **value**
- **variable**

## CHAPTER 6

DESCRIPTIVE SUMMARIES FOR LIMITED VARIABLES

L E A R N I N G   O B J E C T I V E S

The learning objectives of this chapter are:
- to be able to produce the following summaries of data that consist of limited variables:
  - one-way summary tables for one limited variable;
  - two-way and three-way contingency tables for two and three limited variables, respectively;
  - charts that consist of bars or columns that may be grouped or stacked;
- to be able to distinguish between situations in which the two or more limited variables are either dependent or independent;
- to be able to choose and interpret the appropriate summaries, depending on whether the limited variables are dependent or independent.

The following extract from the *Summary of procedures based on combinations of variable types* in part VI gives an overview of the descriptive summaries covered in this chapter.

1. *One limited variable*
   - **Distribution of variables**: frequency, relative frequency and percentage one-way summary tables — bar or column chart.
   - **Measures of central tendency**: mode (mean, median).
2. *Two limited variables*
   - **Distribution of variables**: two-way contingency table — chart with bars or columns that are grouped or stacked.
3. *Three limited variables*
   - **Distribution of variables**: three-way contingency table — chart with bars or columns that are grouped or stacked.

As outlined in the objectives, this chapter covers the use of distribution tables and distribution diagrams to examine the distribution of variables when one, two and three limited variables are involved. That is, the tables and diagrams summarise the pattern of observed values for a variable or observed combinations of several variables. They do this with frequency-based statistics such as frequencies, proportions and percentages. Each of sections 6.1, *One limited variable*, 6.2, *Two limited variables*, and 6.3, *Three limited variables*, describes a **distribution table** followed by the **distribution diagrams** that can be used to present the information in the table.

6.1   One limited variable

6.1.1   Distribution tables for one limited variable

Because the variable has only a limited set of values, the most obvious thing to do is to obtain the **frequency** with which each possible value occurs. You could also calculate the proportion or the percentage, both of which represent the proportion of times that each value occurs. The **proportion**, sometimes called the **relative frequency**, is computed by dividing the frequency by the total number of observations. The **percentage** is just the proportion multiplied by 100. These are gathered together in a one-way summary table, so that the **one-way summary table** contains **classes** corresponding to the values of the limited variable and, for each class, the frequency, relative frequency or percentage or some combination of these three. The one-way summary table summarises the distribution for a limited variable as it presents the pattern of observed values for the variable. It is much easier to see what values have occurred, and how often each occurred, in a one-way summary table than by scanning the original data. For summarising a limited variable, the proportions (or percentages) from the one-way summary table are particularly useful. They are more readily interpreted than the frequencies.

EXAMPLE 6.1   HOUSEHOLD SIZE

Suppose you survey households in a metropolitan area containing 219 000 households to obtain information about them. You select the households by obtaining a list of all the streets in the metropolitan area and randomly selecting 200 streets. You interview a resident of house number five in each selected street. One of the questions you ask is how many children there are in the household. Suppose that you have obtained the primary raw data in table 6.1 and that you want to know what numbers of children occur in the surveyed households.

Before analysing the data, you must identify the question to be investigated (including the group to which the conclusions are to apply) and the variables involved in this question. The question to be investigated in this case is: what are the sizes of the households surveyed in this metropolitan area? The variable involved is *Number of children* and this variable is limited, since only a few values will occur and each value will recur often. Further, it is an interval/ratio variable.

Quickly scanning the data reveals that the data contains, at least, the values 0, 1, 2 and 3. However, it is difficult to be sure that you have not missed some other value that occurs only infrequently, and it is also difficult to tell how often each of these values occurs. The one-way summary table for this example is presented in table 6.2, where the distribution for the *Number of children* is immediately apparent. For example, you can see that the most frequently occurring number of children in a household is two: it occurs in 60% of households. To say that 60% of households have two children seems to be more informative than saying that 120 households have two children.

Table 6.1 *Number of children* for 200 surveyed households

0	1	0	2	2	2	2	2	0	3
0	2	2	3	3	2	3	2	3	2
2	2	1	0	2	1	3	2	2	2
2	2	1	2	2	0	1	3	2	2
0	2	3	2	2	0	2	1	2	3
2	2	1	2	1	1	2	0	2	2
3	2	2	2	2	2	1	2	0	2
3	2	2	0	1	2	1	2	2	2
1	2	2	1	2	2	3	1	2	2
1	0	1	2	1	3	2	2	1	2
2	2	2	2	2	2	1	1	2	2
0	2	1	3	2	0	2	2	1	1
1	2	2	1	2	1	2	2	2	1
1	2	2	1	2	2	2	2	0	1
2	0	0	2	1	2	2	3	2	2
2	2	2	2	2	0	2	2	2	1
1	2	2	3	2	0	2	1	1	3
2	2	3	2	2	1	2	3	2	2
2	2	2	1	2	2	2	3	2	1
0	2	1	2	2	2	2	2	2	2

Table 6.2 One-way summary table for *Number of children*

Number of children	Frequency	Percentage
0	20	10
1	40	20
2	120	60
3	20	10
Total	200	($n = 200$)

6.1.2   Distribution diagrams for one limited variable

Bar or column charts are used to present the information from a one-way table in a diagram. In these charts, either a rectangle or line is plotted for each class. Also, they can be based on either the frequencies, proportions or percentages. For a **bar chart**, the rectangles or bars are plotted horizontally and their lengths correspond to the frequencies, proportions or percentages for the individual classes. For a **column chart**, the rectangles or bars are plotted vertically and their heights correspond to the frequencies, proportions or percentages for the individual classes. For both bar and column charts, the rectangles or lines are usually separated, because limited variables are often not continuous and the break signifies this.

In general, distribution diagrams display in a more readily absorbed form the information contained in a one-way summary table. However, the disadvantage is that a certain degree of accuracy is lost, so diagrams are used for an overall impression rather than an accurate record of the information.

Of the six possible distribution diagrams, those based on the bar chart are preferred. A bar chart makes it easy to compare at a glance the relative lengths of bars one above the other. When only one limited variable is involved there is little difference between the charts based on either frequencies, proportions or percentages. The only difference occurs in the scales on their axes. Note that the terms *bar chart* and *column chart* are not standardised. Some people refer to column charts as bar charts.

Another type of chart often used in the present context is the **pie chart**. In pie charts, a circle is divided into arcs, one for each class, so that the angle defining each arc is proportional to the percentage for that class. Pie charts are popular, especially now that computer programs can produce them. However, they are not the best way to present material because you cannot compare the frequencies or percentages as accurately as you can with bar charts.

EXAMPLE 6.1   HOUSEHOLD SIZE (continued)

The column chart for the household survey, based on frequencies, is shown in figure 6.1 and the bar chart, based on percentages, in figure 6.2. There is no difference in the basic shapes of the two charts. Note that the bars and columns are separated because the variable, *Number of children*, is not continuous. The pie chart for the example is given in figure 6.3.

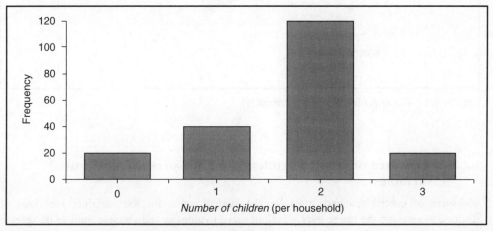

Figure 6.1   Column chart for *Number of children*

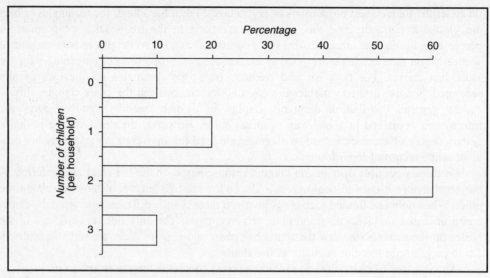

Figure 6.2   Bar chart for *Number of children*

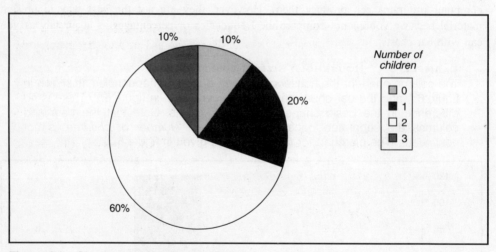

Figure 6.3   Pie chart for *Number of children*

6.1.3   Measures of central tendency and dispersion for limited variables

Measures of central tendency measure the typical value for the variable; measures of dispersion measure the range over which observed values of the variable tend to be spread. These measures are discussed in more detail in chapter 7, *Descriptive summaries for one unrestricted variable*. Generally, however, measures of central tendency and dispersion are not useful with limited variables. Usually, the complete distribution of values of the limited variable provides the best summary for limited variables.

On occasions when a measure of central tendency or dispersion seems necessary, the considerations that apply are the same as those outlined for unrestricted variables in chapter 7, *Descriptive summaries for one unrestricted variable*. However, if only a measure of central tendency is required, the mode may be the preferred measure, for reasons outlined below.

Mode

The **mode** is the value that occurs most frequently. It can be obtained from the one-way summary table.

EXAMPLE 6.1   HOUSEHOLD SIZE (continued)

The one-way summary in table 6.2 summarises the results of the survey. The mode for *Number of children* is 2, since this value has the highest frequency.

Notes

1. For nominal, limited variables such as *Sex*, the values of the variables are names. In these cases, the mode is the only measure that can be used as it is not possible to sum or rank names as is required to obtain the mean and median; determining the most frequently occurring name is all you can do.
2. For limited variables consisting of whole numbers, the mode is the most appropriate measure because it must be equal to a value of the variable. It gives an actual value: for example, the mode for *Number of children* in the household survey is 2 children, whereas the mean is 2.317 children.
3. The mode is unsuitable for nearly uniform or flat-topped distributions as there will be no clear mode for these distributions. In such cases, it is best to use the complete distribution and avoid measures of central tendency.
4. Extreme values have no effect on the mode.
5. The mode is easy to understand.
6. The range of statistical techniques based on the mode is not as large as it is for the mean.
7. For unrestricted data you need a large number of observations, so the mode is not usually used for such data. Further, the concept of the most frequent value is not natural for continuous data where nearly every value is unique. For example, consider *Management test score* from example 7.1, *Management capacity*. What is the mode? Does it make sense?

For limited variables, the preferred measure is often the mode, although for ordinal, limited variables the median is another strong contender. For example, the median rating for a question based on a rating scale would give you a useful summary of the typical response to the question.

6.2   Two limited variables

6.2.1   Distribution tables for two limited variables

Surveys often require you to look at two limited variables simultaneously, and a **two-way contingency table** makes this possible. A **contingency table** presents the frequencies, proportions or percentages for each possible combination of the values of the limited variables on which it is based. In this context, *contingency* means a possible combination of values, and a two-way contingency table is based on two limited variables.

In addition to the frequencies of the combinations of the limited variables, it is usual to include the **row totals** and **column totals** of these frequencies, as **margins** to the **main body** of the contingency table. The row totals are placed to the right, and the column totals are given below the body of the table. The **grand total**, or the total number of observations, is placed in the bottom righthand corner of the table. The frequencies in the main body of the table, the row totals and the column totals all sum to the grand total.

EXAMPLE 6.2   HOUSEHOLD SIZE AND STATUS

Suppose that the household survey (example 6.1, *Household size*) ascertained not only the number of children but the socioeconomic status of the household. Further, suppose that the question to be investigated is: how is *Number of children* related to *Socioeconomic status* for the households surveyed in the metropolitan area? We already know that there are either 0, 1, 2, or 3 children in the households surveyed. Since *Socioeconomic status* was graded as Low (1), Medium (2) or High (3), there are two limited variables involved in the question to be investigated: *Number of children* is an interval/ratio variable and *Socioeconomic status* is an ordinal variable. The coded data from a sample of 200 households, the raw data, may look something like that given in table 6.3.

This data involves $4 \times 3 = 12$ possible combinations of values of the limited variables; that is, there are 12 possible 'contingencies'. To form the contingency table we must compute the frequency for each possible combination. For example, how many 0 children, medium status households are there? That is, how many 0, 2 combinations are there?

Table 6.3   *Number of children* and *Socioeconomic status* for 200 surveyed households

H'hold	No. child.	Status	H'hold	No. child.	Status	H'hold	No. child.	Status	H'hold	No. child.	Status
1	0	1	9	0	2	17	3	3	25	2	1
2	1	3	10	3	3	18	2	1	26	1	2
3	0	1	11	0	3	19	3	3	27	3	2
4	2	1	12	2	1	20	2	2	28	2	1
5	2	3	13	2	1	21	2	3	29	2	1
6	2	3	14	3	1	22	2	2	30	2	2
7	2	1	15	3	1	23	1	2	31	2	3
8	2	1	16	2	1	24	0	3	32	2	1

continued . . .

Table 6.3   *continued*

H'hold	No. child.	Status	H'hold	No. child.	Status	H'hold	No. child.	Status	H'hold	No. child.	Status
33	1	3	71	3	3	109	2	1	147	2	2
34	2	2	72	2	2	110	2	2	148	3	3
35	2	3	73	2	1	111	0	2	149	2	2
36	0	3	74	0	2	112	2	1	150	2	3
37	1	2	75	1	3	113	1	2	151	2	1
38	3	3	76	2	1	114	3	1	152	2	2
39	2	3	77	1	3	115	2	3	153	2	1
40	2	1	78	2	2	116	0	3	154	2	2
41	0	2	79	2	2	117	2	1	155	2	2
42	2	1	80	2	2	118	2	2	156	0	3
43	3	2	81	1	2	119	1	1	157	2	2
44	2	1	82	2	3	120	1	3	158	2	3
45	2	1	83	2	1	121	1	1	159	2	1
46	0	2	84	1	2	122	2	3	160	1	3
47	2	1	85	2	1	123	2	1	161	1	1
48	1	1	86	2	1	124	1	3	162	2	2
49	2	1	87	3	1	125	2	2	163	2	1
50	3	3	88	1	1	126	1	3	164	3	3
51	2	1	89	2	1	127	2	2	165	2	1
52	2	1	90	2	3	128	2	1	166	0	3
53	1	2	91	1	1	129	2	2	167	2	2
54	2	1	92	0	3	130	1	3	168	1	1
55	1	3	93	1	3	131	1	1	169	1	1
56	1	3	94	2	3	132	2	2	170	3	1
57	2	1	95	1	2	133	2	1	171	2	3
58	0	3	96	3	1	134	1	2	172	2	1
59	2	1	97	2	2	135	2	2	173	3	3
60	2	1	98	2	3	136	2	1	174	2	2
61	3	3	99	1	2	137	2	2	175	2	3
62	2	2	100	2	2	138	2	1	176	1	2
63	2	2	101	2	2	139	0	3	177	2	3
64	2	3	102	2	1	140	1	3	178	3	1
65	2	2	103	2	1	141	2	1	179	2	1
66	2	1	104	2	1	142	0	3	180	2	2
67	1	2	105	2	3	143	0	3	181	2	1
68	2	3	106	2	3	144	2	1	182	2	1
69	0	2	107	1	3	145	1	1	183	2	3
70	2	2	108	1	1	146	2	2	184	1	1

continued . . .

Table 6.3   *continued*

H'hold	No. child.	Status	H'hold	No. child.	Status	H'hold	No. child.	Status	H'hold	No. child.	Status
185	2	1	189	2	3	193	1	1	197	2	2
186	2	3	190	1	1	194	2	1	198	2	1
187	2	2	191	0	3	195	2	2	199	2	2
188	3	1	192	2	2	196	2	1	200	2	2

The two-way contingency table in table 6.4 gives frequencies or total counts of all possible combinations of values of *Number of children* and *Socioeconomic status* and gives us a summary of the relationship between the variables. In particular, it tells us that there are six households that have 0 children and are of medium status. Notice that this table also has margins, consisting of row or column totals.

Table 6.4   Two-way contingency table for *Number of children* and *Socioeconomic status*

		Socioeconomic status			
		Low	Medium	High	Total
	0	2	6	12	20
Number of	1	14	12	14	40
children	2	56	40	24	120
	3	8	2	10	20
	Total	80	60	60	200

Now, to examine the relationship between the two limited variables, compare the trends in either the rows or the columns of the main body of the table. It is important that we compare either rows or columns, but not both. There is no point in looking at both as that amounts to looking at the same thing from two different points of view. In making these comparisons it is easier to use percentages, otherwise differences between the rows (or columns) in their numbers of observations obscure differences in the trends. In general, there are three possible percentages that can be calculated for a contingency table:

1. **row percentage**: cell frequency, divided by the total for the row in which the cell lies, and multiplied by 100;
2. **column percentage**: cell frequency, divided by the total for the column in which the cell lies and multiplied by 100;
3. **total percentage**: cell frequency, divided by the grand total and multiplied by 100.

Note that when you present tables of percentages you should include the numbers of observations on which each percentage is based, that is, the value of the denominator for each percentage. Including the denominator is important as smaller differences in percentages are of greater significance for a large number of observations than for a small number. For example, a 10% difference between two percentages means a difference of just one observation when the denominators are 10, whereas it means a difference of 10 observations when the denominators are 100; you can be surer that the difference is 10% when the denominators are 100.

EXAMPLE 6.2   HOUSEHOLD SIZE AND STATUS (continued)

In our household survey, we want to investigate the relationship between the *Number of children* in a household and its *Socioeconomic status*. The margin shows that, taken across all status groups, 60% of households have two children, as we concluded from the one-way summary table. Further, there are slightly more low-status households than those having medium or high status.

But this does not tell us about the relationship between the two variables. For example, is the trend in *Number of children* the same for all *Socioeconomic status* groups? Or is the trend in *Socioeconomic status* the same for households that differ in the *Number of children*? As suggested, investigating this question would be greatly assisted by computing row, column or total percentages. Tables 6.5, 6.6 and 6.7 contain these percentages, so we shall examine one of these tables.

Let's examine the table of column percentages, in table 6.5, to see if the trend in *Number of children* is the same for all *Socioeconomic status* groups. That is, is the pattern or trend the same in each column of the table? Each cell of the table is the number observed in that cell expressed as a percentage of the total number observed for that status; for example, the top left cell is 2.5 = 2/80*100. The table of column percentages is more useful here than the table of original frequencies, because the comparison of the different columns is unhindered by the different numbers of observations in each column. Note that the number of observations for each status is included in the last row of the table.

From table 6.5 it seems that low-status households have proportionally more two-children households and fewer no-children households compared with medium-status and high-status households. Medium-status households tend to have fewer three-children households than low-status and high-status households. High-status households tend to have more no-children and three-children and fewer two-children households compared with low-status and medium-status households.

Table 6.5 Column percentages for *Number of children* and Socioeconomic status

		Socioeconomic status			
		Low	Medium	High	Total
	0	2.5	10.0	20.0	10.0
Number of	1	17.5	20.0	23.3	20.0
children	2	70.0	66.7	40.0	60.0
	3	10.0	3.3	16.7	10.0
	n	80	60	60	200

Table 6.6   Row percentages for *Number of children* and Socioeconomic status

| | | Socioeconomic status | | | |
		Low	Medium	High	n
	0	10.0	30.0	60.0	20
Number of	1	35.0	30.0	35.0	40
children	2	46.7	33.3	20.0	120
	3	40.0	10.0	50.0	20
	Total	40.0	30.0	30.0	200

You may have chosen to examine the table of row percentages in table 6.6 instead of the column percentages in table 6.5. If so, you might conclude: no-children households occur most commonly in high-status households; one-child households are spread equally between the low-status, medium-status and high-status households; two-children households decrease as status increases; three-children households occur least frequently in medium-status households.

Table 6.7   Total percentages for *Number of children* and Socioeconomic status

| | | Socioeconomic status | | | |
		Low	Medium	High	Total
	0	1.0	3.0	6.0	10.0
Number of	1	7.0	6.0	7.0	20.0
children	2	28.0	20.0	12.0	60.0
	3	4.0	1.0	5.0	10.0
	Total	40.0	30.0	30.0	($n = 200$)

The third possibility is to use the table of total percentages in table 6.7 to examine the relationship between the variables. You might conclude that the most commonly surveyed type of household is a low-status household with two children; least common is a no-children, low-status household and both no-children and three-children in medium-status households.

Of the tables of percentages used above, the table of total percentages seems hardest to use. Which of the other two you use depends on your main interest. If your main interest is in comparing households of different status, then use the table of column percentages. However, use the table of row percentages if you have more interest in comparing households with different numbers of children. In this example, there is no clear-cut choice and it is up to the investigator to decide which table most suits the points they want to make. In other examples, it is more obvious which percentage table should be used.

EXAMPLE 6.3   COFFEE PREFERENCE

Consider a study of adults' preferences for three different coffee brands, in a city of over 1 million adults. The researcher goes to the local university canteen to obtain 60 females and 40 males to take part in the study. For each participant, the brand of coffee preferred and their sex is recorded. That is, two limited variables are recorded. In this case you will want to compare the male and female preferences; that is, the main interest is in how the different brands rate and how this differs between the surveyed male and female adults.

The question to be investigated here is the difference between the surveyed males' and females' preferences with respect to three brands of coffee. The two variables involved in this question — *Brand* and *Sex* — are nominal, limited variables.

The contingency table for answering the question to be investigated is given in table 6.8. It represents processed data that we want to analyse. As in example 6.2, *Household size and status*, it is better to examine one of the tables of percentages. Because the main interest is to compare different sexes, the percentages to be examined are those formed from the totals for each sex, as in table 6.9. The conclusion to be drawn from this table is that males prefer Dark Roast whereas there is no clear favourite for females.

Table 6.8   Two-way contingency table for *Brand* and *Sex*

| | Sex | | |
Brand	Female	Male	Total
Dark Roast	18	32	50
Min House	25	5	30
More Beans	17	3	20
Total	60	40	100

Table 6.9   Column percentages for *Brand* and *Sex*

| | Sex | | |
Brand	Female	Male	Total
Dark Roast	30.0	80.0	50.0
Min House	41.7	12.5	30.0
More Beans	28.3	7.5	20.0
n	60	40	100

6.2.2   Distribution diagrams for two limited variables

Information in two-way contingency tables can be presented in charts with either columns or bars that are either grouped or stacked. A **grouped chart** is a bar or column chart for two or more limited variables in which there is a rectangle for each combination of the values of the variables and the rectangles are grouped. A group of rectangles is formed by placing side-by-side those that have the same combination of values of all variables, except one; that is, one variable is selected to have its values differ between the rectangles in a group. A **stacked chart** is the same as a grouped chart except that the rectangles in a group are placed end to end. These charts can be based on frequencies, proportions or percentages. Probably the best form is stacked bar charts based on percentages.

EXAMPLE 6.2   HOUSEHOLD SIZE AND STATUS (continued)

Figures 6.4 and 6.5 show the grouped column and bar charts for the frequencies, respectively. Figures 6.6 and 6.7 give the stacked column and bar charts for the percentages, respectively.

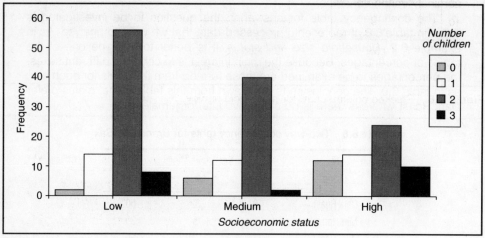

Figure 6.4   Grouped column chart for household survey

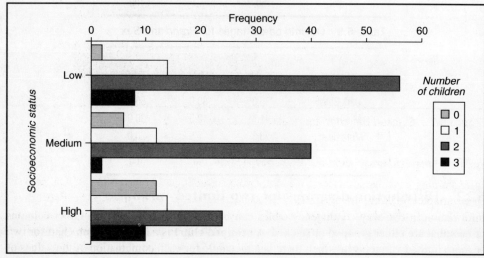

Figure 6.5   Grouped bar chart for household survey

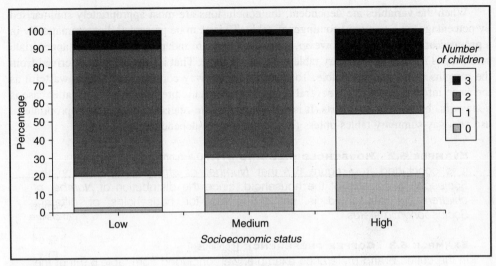

Figure 6.6   Stacked column chart for household survey

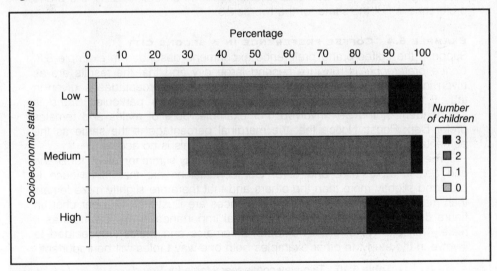

Figure 6.7   Stacked bar chart for household survey

6.2.3   Dependence versus independence

In examining contingency tables, it is important to distinguish between two situations: the two variables making up the table may be dependent or independent. The two limited variables are **dependent** if there is a difference between the column (row) percentages in different columns (rows) of the table. Otherwise, the two limited variables are **independent**; in this situation, the column (row) percentages in different columns (rows) of the table are the same.

111

When the variables are dependent, the conclusions are most appropriately summarised by percentages in a two-way contingency table. These can be presented diagrammatically in a grouped or stacked chart. However, if the variables are independent, the most appropriate summary is a one-way summary table for each variable. That is, use the tables derived from the margins of the two-way table. To present the two-way contingency table is wasteful as the same information is given several times. Diagrammatic presentation in this latter case is done with bar or column charts. It is most important to realise that it is *not* appropriate to use one-way summary tables unless the variables are independent.

EXAMPLE 6.2   HOUSEHOLD SIZE AND STATUS (continued)

It is concluded from figure 6.7 that *Number of children* depends on the *Socioeconomic status* of the household, since the distribution of *Number of children* per household is not the same for households of different *Socioeconomic status*.

EXAMPLE 6.3   COFFEE PREFERENCE (continued)

In the coffee-brand preference example, we concluded from table 6.9 that the percentage preferring a particular *Brand* depends on *Sex*. That is, the brand preference is not the same for the two sexes.

EXAMPLE 6.4   COFFEE PREFERENCE IN A SECOND CITY

Suppose the coffee-brand preference experiment, described in example 6.3, *Coffee preference*, is run in a second large city and that the results are as given in table 6.10. The corresponding table of sex percentages is given in table 6.11. In this case, the percentage preferring a particular *Brand* is independent of the *Sex* involved. For example, 30% of males and females prefer Dark Roast. Notice that the marginal percentage is the same as the percentage for both the females and the males. This is no accident.

The conclusions are summarised in the one-way summary tables for *Brand* and *Sex* in tables 6.12 and 6.13. Our conclusions are that Min House is preferred slightly more than the others and that there are slightly more female than male participants. The *Brand* differences are illustrated in a bar chart in figure 6.8. The *Sex* difference is of no real importance in this example as it merely reflects the different numbers of females and males we decided to involve in the study. In other examples both one-way tables will be important.

Table 6.10   Two-way contingency table for *Brand*
and *Sex* from a second city

| Brand | Sex | | |
	Female	Male	Total
Dark Roast	18	12	30
Min House	25	17	42
More Beans	17	11	28
Total	60	40	100

Table 6.11   Column percentages for *Brand* and *Sex* from a second city

	Sex		
Brand	Female	Male	Total
Dark Roast	30.0	30.0	30.0
Min House	41.7	42.5	42.0
More Beans	28.3	27.5	28.0
n	60	40	100

Table 6.12   One-way summary table for *Brand* from a second city

	Brand		
Dark Roast	Min House	More Beans	
30%	42%	28%	(n = 100)

Table 6.13   One-way summary table for *Sex* from a second city

	Sex	
Female	Male	
60%	40%	(n = 100)

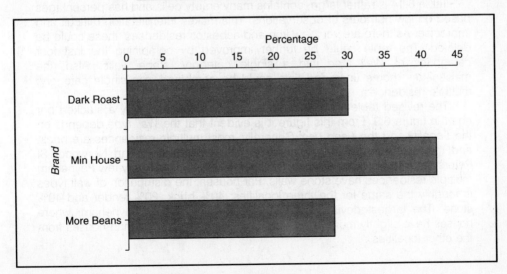

Figure 6.8   Bar chart for *Brand* from a second city

6.3   Three limited variables

To look at three limited variables, a **three-way contingency table** is used. An example is given to show how such tables are interpreted. The interpretation of the example is only a general indication, since statisticians can provide more thorough analyses. Also, the example shows what steps to take when a contingency table, two-way or three-way, has a small number of observations for particular values of a limited variable. That is, the table should be **collapsed** by performing the following actions:

1. omit from the analysis any observations having that value of a limited variable for which there is a small number of observations;
2. combine some of the categories of a limited variable to produce a category that has sufficient observations.

EXAMPLE 6.5   RESIDENCES SOLD IN THREE LOCALITIES

The raw data is available on all the residences sold over a 12-month period in three localities — three different local government areas. In particular, the land-use code and the type of wall are available. This data is available from the city's Lands Department and is secondary data.

   The question to be investigated is: does the type of wall vary with different land use and/or from locality to locality for the residences sold over a 12-month period in the three localities? Note that a census has been conducted for the population of interest. This question involves three nominal, limited variables: *Locality, Wall type* and *Land use*. For this combination of variables and the question, use the three-way contingency table of row percentages in table 6.14 (opposite) to answer the question.

   Table 6.14 is rather large, contains many empty cells and has percentages based on low numbers of observations. This makes interpretation difficult and imprecise. As there are very few iron and asbestos residences, these could be deleted. The table could be further improved by combining the last four categories of *Wall type* into a single category: stone walls. Also, the maisonettes, home units and flats could be combined in a single category: multiple residences.

   The revised table is given in table 6.15, and illustrated by a stacked bar chart in figure 6.9. From this figure it is evident that the *Wall type* depends on the *Locality* and the *Land use*. Generally, most multiple residences are brick, and the lowest proportion of these occurs in Kensington and Norwood. St Peters multiple residences do not have rendered walls and very few Payneham multiple residences have stone walls. For houses, the distribution of wall types is roughly the same for the three localities: 40% brick, 20% render and 40% stone. The largest deviation from this pattern occurs in Payneham, where houses have slightly more brick walls and fewer stone walls than houses from the other localities.

Table 6.14   Table of row percentages for *Localities, Wall types* and *Land use*

Kensington & Norwood	Wall types								n
	Brick	Iron	Render	Asbestos	Freestone	Bluestone	Basket Range	Block	
Land use									
House	38.2	—	19.5	—	28.5	13.0	0.8	—	123
Maisonette	39.1	—	21.7	—	21.7	17.4	—	—	23
Home unit	80.0	—	14.3	—	1.4	2.9	0.7	0.7	140
Flat	80.0	—	—	—	—	—	—	20.0	5

St Peters	Wall types								n
	Brick	Iron	Render	Asbestos	Freestone	Bluestone	Basket Range	Block	
Land use									
House	38.2	0.8	21.1	0.8	21.1	13.8	2.4	—	123
Maisonette	85.7	—	—	—	14.3	—	—	—	7
Home unit	87.8	—	—	—	10.2	—	2.0	—	49
Flat	100.0	—	—	—	—	—	—	—	2

Payneham	Wall types								n
	Brick	Iron	Render	Asbestos	Freestone	Bluestone	Basket Range	Block	
Land use									
House	47.4	—	16.5	2.1	28.4	3.6	0.5	1.6	194
Maisonette	100.0	—	—	—	—	—	—	—	5
Home unit	89.9	—	7.6	—	—	1.7	—	0.8	119
Flat	100.0	—	—	—	—	—	—	—	5

Table 6.15   Revised table of row percentages for *Localities, Wall types* and *Land use*

Kensington & Norwood	Wall types			n
	Brick	Render	Stone	
Land use				
House	38.21	19.51	42.28	123
Multiple residence	74.40	14.88	10.71	168

St Peters	Wall types			n
	Brick	Render	Stone	
Land use				
House	40.50	21.49	38.02	121
Multiple residence	87.93	--	12.07	58

continued . . .

Table 6.15   *continued*

Payneham	*Wall types*			*n*
	Brick	Render	Stone	
Land use				
House	48.42	16.84	34.74	190
Multiple residence	90.70	6.98	2.33	129

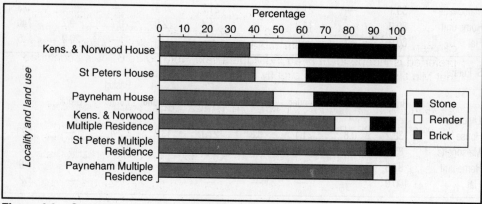

Figure 6.9   Stacked bar chart for *Localities*, *Wall types* and *Land use*

6.4   Reports on examples

The following reports, for the examples analysed in this chapter, indicate what material from a statistical analysis an investigator should include in a report. In general, the details of the statistical analysis are omitted so that the reader of the report can concentrate on the results.

EXAMPLE 6.1   HOUSEHOLD SIZE — REPORT

In a survey of households, the number of children was determined for 200 randomly selected households. Figure 6.2 shows that the surveyed households had between 0 and 3 children, inclusive, and that 60% of these households had 2 children.

EXAMPLE 6.2   HOUSEHOLD SIZE AND STATUS — REPORT

In a survey of households, the number of children and socioeconomic status was determined for 200 randomly selected households. From figure 6.7 it seems that for the surveyed households the number of children in a household depends on its socioeconomic status. In particular, it seems that low-status households have proportionally more two-children and fewer no-children households compared with other medium-status and high-status households. Medium-status households tend to have fewer three-children households than low-status and high-status households. High-status households tend to have more no-children and three-children and fewer two-children households compared with low-status and medium-status households.

EXAMPLE 6.3   COFFEE PREFERENCE — REPORT

To study adults' preference, in a city of over 1 million adults, for three different coffee brands, 60 females and 40 males at the local university canteen were observed. From table 6.9 it is concluded that, for the surveyed adults, the brand of coffee preferred depends on an individual's sex. It seems that males prefer Dark Roast whereas there is no clear favourite for females.

EXAMPLE 6.4   COFFEE PREFERENCE IN A SECOND CITY — REPORT

To study adults' preference, in a second city of over 1 million adults, for three different coffee brands, 60 females and 40 males at the local university canteen were observed. From table 6.11 it seems that the brand of coffee preferred is independent of an individual's sex. From figure 6.8 it is concluded that Min House is preferred slightly more than the others.

EXAMPLE 6.5   RESIDENCES SOLD IN THREE LOCALITIES — REPORT

We want to determine, for residences sold in the last 12 months, whether the type of wall varies with different land use and/or from locality to locality for the residences sold in three localities. From figure 6.9 it is concluded that the wall type depends on the locality and the land use for these residences. Generally, most multiple residences are brick; the lowest proportion of brick multiple residences occur in Kensington and Norwood. St Peters multiple residences do not have rendered walls and very few Payneham multiple residences have stone walls. For houses, the distribution of wall types is roughly the same for the three localities: 40% brick, 20% render and 40% stone. The largest deviation from this pattern occurs in Payneham, where there are slightly more brick-walled houses and fewer stone-walled houses.

6.5   Using Minitab to produce the tables

This section describes the Minitab commands to produce the one-way summary, and two-way and three-way contingency tables. It is not possible to produce the bar and column charts in release 8 of Minitab. These can be produced in a spreadsheet package that includes charting facilities.

6.5.1   One-way summary tables

To compute the one-way summary table in Minitab, use the *tally* command with *count* and *percent* subcommands.

EXAMPLE 6.1   HOUSEHOLD SIZE (continued)

The data from the household survey is contained in the Minitab portable worksheet file *houshold.mtp*. In this file, $c1$ contains the two hundred 0, 1, 2, and 3s for the *Number of children* in the household survey. The following commands will retrieve the portable worksheet file, check the contents of the worksheet, print out the data and produce the one-way summary table.

```
MTB > outfile 'a:\houshold.lis'
MTB > retrieve 'a:\houshold.mtp';
SUBC> portable.
MTB > info
MTB > print c1
MTB > tally c1;
SUBC> count;
SUBC> percent.
```

If your version of Minitab has pull-down menus and you want to use them, table 6.16 lists the menus and options that access the required commands. Appendix D, *Detailed instructions for Minitab menus*, explains how to use the menus. Note that the *Get Worksheet Info* option of the *Edit* menu is the equivalent of the *info* command. However, you can also use the data screen to examine the contents of the worksheet.

Table 6.16 Menus and options for Minitab commands to produce a one-way summary table

Minitab command	Menu	Option
outfile	File >	Other Files > Start Recording Session...
retrieve	File >	Open Worksheet...
port		Minitab portable worksheet
info	Edit >	Get Worksheet Info...
	(Edit >	Data Screen... [Alt-D])
print	Edit >	Display Data...
tally	Stat >	Tables > Tally...
count		Counts
percent		Percents

The output produced by these commands is:

```
MTB > retrieve 'a:\houshold.mtp';
SUBC> portable.
Worksheet retrieved from file: a:\houshold.mtp
MTB > info

COLUMN   NAME       COUNT
C1       no_child    200
C2       status      200

CONSTANTS USED: NONE
```

continued . . .

```
MTB > print 'no_child'.

no_child
   0    1    0    2    2    2    2    2    0    3    0    2    2    3    3
   2    3    2    3    2    2    2    1    0    2    1    3    2    2    2
   2    2    1    2    2    0    1    3    2    2    0    2    3    2    2
   0    2    1    2    3    2    2    1    2    1    1    2    0    2    2
   3    2    2    2    2    2    1    2    0    2    3    2    2    0    1
   2    1    2    2    2    1    2    2    1    2    2    3    1    2    2
   1    0    1    2    1    3    2    2    1    2    2    2    2    2    2
   2    1    1    2    2    0    2    1    3    2    0    2    2    1    1
   1    2    2    1    2    1    2    2    2    1    1    2    2    1    2
   2    2    2    0    1    2    0    0    2    1    2    2    3    2    2
   2    2    2    2    2    0    2    2    2    1    1    2    2    3    2
   0    2    1    1    3    2    2    3    2    2    1    2    3    2    2
   2    2    2    1    2    2    2    3    2    1    0    2    1    2    2
   2    2    2    2    2

MTB > tally 'no_child';
SUBC> counts;
SUBC> percents.

no_child   COUNT      PERCENT
   0         20        10.00
   1         40        20.00
   2        120        60.00
   3         20        10.00
  N=        200
```

Note that only output after the *outfile* command is shown because that is all that is stored in the output file *household.lis*.

6.5.2 Two-way contingency tables

To produce a two-way contingency table, containing frequencies only, use the Minitab *table* command. To produce tables that include the percentages, use the *colpercents*, *rowpercents* and *totpercents* subcommands.

EXAMPLE 6.2 HOUSEHOLD SIZE AND STATUS (continued)
The Minitab portable worksheet file *houshold.mtp* has, besides the *Number of children* stored in *c1*, the coded values for *Socioeconomic status* in *c2*. The coding for *Socioeconomic status* is described in table 6.17.

Table 6.17 Coding for *Socioeconomic status*

Socioeconomic status	Code
Low	1
Medium	2
High	3

The following summarises all the commands for producing the various two-way contingency tables that are used to examine the relationship between *Number of children* and *Socioeconomic status* in the household survey. It is assumed that the worksheet still has the contents of the file *houshold.mtp* loaded into it.

```
MTB > info
MTB > table c1  c2
MTB > table c2  c1
MTB > table c1  c2;
SUBC> colpercents.
MTB > table c1  c2;
SUBC> count;
SUBC> colpercents.
MTB > table c2  c1;
SUBC> count;
SUBC> rowpercents.
MTB > table c1  c2;
SUBC> rowpercents.
MTB > table c1  c2;
SUBC> colpercents.
MTB > table c1  c2;
SUBC> totpercents.
```

If your version of Minitab has pull-down menus and you want to use them, table 6.18 lists the menus and options that access the required commands. Appendix D, *Detailed instructions for Minitab menus*, explains how to use the menus.

Table 6.18   Menus and options for Minitab commands to produce a two-way contingency table

Minitab command	Menu	Option
info	Edit >	Get Worksheet Info...
	(Edit >	Data Screen [Alt-D])
table	Stat >	Tables > Cross Tabulation
count		Counts
rowpercents		Row Percents
colpercents		Column Percents
totpercents		Total Percents

The output of the commands summarised above, and comments, are given as follows. This output contains various two-way contingency tables to examine the relationship between *Number of children* and *Socioeconomic status* in the household survey.

```
MTB > info

COLUMN NAME      COUNT
C1       no_child  200
C2       status    200

CONSTANTS USED: NONE

MTB > table c1 c2

ROWS: no_child     COLUMNS: status

            1       2       3      ALL

    0       2       6      12       20
    1      14      12      14       40
    2      56      40      24      120
    3       8       2      10       20
  ALL      80      60      60      200

CELL CONTENTS --
              COUNT
```

The rows of this table contain the frequencies for each *Number of children* in a household, and the columns give the frequencies for each *Socioeconomic status*. Minitab tells you this in the heading above the table.

The previous table has the *Number of children* in the rows and the *Socioeconomic status* in the columns. This arrangement is determined by the order of the columns in the *table* command. To turn the table around, enter the columns in the opposite order. For example:

```
MTB > table c2 c1
ROWS: status    COLUMNS: no_child
              0       1       2       3      ALL
    1         2      14      56       8       80
    2         6      12      40       2       60
    3        12      14      24      10       60
  ALL        20      40     120      20      200

CELL CONTENTS --
              COUNT
```

To compute the table of column percentage for the original column order, with Minitab, use the following *table* command with the *colpercents* subcommand:

```
MTB > table c1 c2;
SUBC> colpercents.

ROWS:  no_child  COLUMNS:  status

                  1         2         3       ALL

    0          2.50     10.00     20.00     10.00
    1         17.50     20.00     23.33     20.00
    2         70.00     66.67     40.00     60.00
    3         10.00      3.33     16.67     10.00
  ALL        100.00    100.00    100.00    100.00

CELL  CONTENTS  --
              %  OF  COL
```

To obtain a table with both frequencies and column percentages, use the following *table* command with both the *count* and *colpercents* subcommands:

```
MTB > table c1 c2;
SUBC> count;
SUBC> colpercents.

ROWS:  no_child          COLUMNS:  status

                  1         2         3       ALL

    0             2         6        12        20
               2.50     10.00     20.00     10.00

    1            14        12        14        40
              17.50     20.00     23.33     20.00

    2            56        40        24       120
              70.00     66.67     40.00     60.00
    3             8         2        10        20
              10.00      3.33     16.67     10.00
  ALL            80        60        60       200
             100.00    100.00    100.00    100.00
CELL  CONTENTS  --
                  COUNT
                %  OF  COL
```

The contents of each cell of the table is specified at the bottom of the table produced by Minitab. That is, each cell consists of a count below which is the corresponding column percentage. Of course, if the columns are specified in the opposite order, you will want row percentages which can be obtained by using the *rowpercents* subcommand:

```
MTB > table c2 c1;
SUBC> count;
SUBC> rowpercents.

ROWS: status     COLUMNS: no_child

                0            1            2            3          ALL

   1            2           14           56            8           80
              2.50        17.50        70.00        10.00       100.00

   2            6           12           40            2           60
             10.00        20.00        66.67         3.33       100.00

   3           12           14           24           10           60
             20.00        23.33        40.00        16.67       100.00

  ALL          20           40          120           20          200
             10.00        20.00        60.00        10.00       100.00
CELL CONTENTS --
                   COUNT
                   % OF ROW
```

To compute the three different percentage tables, use the *rowpercents*, *colpercents* and *totpercents* subcommands of the *table* command. The three tables are as follows:

```
MTB > table c1 c2;
SUBC> rowpercents.
ROWS: no_child     COLUMNS: status
            1            2            3          ALL
  0       10.00        30.00        60.00       100.00
  1       35.00        30.00        35.00       100.00
  2       46.67        33.33        20.00       100.00
  3       40.00        10.00        50.00       100.00
 ALL      40.00        30.00        30.00       100.00
CELL CONTENTS --
              % OF ROW


MTB > table c1 c2;
SUBC> colpercents.
ROWS: no_child COLUMNS: status
            1            2            3          ALL
  0        2.50        10.00        20.00        10.00
  1       17.50        20.00        23.33        20.00
  2       70.00        66.67        40.00        60.00
  3       10.00         3.33        16.67        10.00
 ALL     100.00       100.00       100.00       100.00
CELL CONTENTS --
              % OF COL
```

continued . . .

123

```
MTB > table c1 c2;
SUBC> totpercents.
ROWS: no_child COLUMNS: status
                 1          2          3         ALL
   0           1.00       3.00       6.00       10.00
   1           7.00       6.00       7.00       20.00
   2          28.00      20.00      12.00       60.00
   3           4.00       1.00       5.00       10.00
ALL           40.00      30.00      30.00      100.00
CELL  CONTENTS  --
                    %  OF  TBL
```

6.5.3   Three-way contingency tables

To obtain the three-way contingency table in Minitab, the commands are exactly as described in section 6.5.2, *Two-way contingency tables*, except that three columns are specified in the *table* command.

EXAMPLE 6.5   RESIDENCES SOLD IN THREE LOCALITIES (continued)

The data from the residential sales census has been saved in a Minitab portable worksheet file named *vgsales.mtp*. The data is in coded form, and the codes for the three limited variables of interest are as described in table 6.19.

Table 6.19   Coding for limited variables in the residential sales survey

Locality	Code	Wall type	Code
Kensington & Norwood	15	Brick	1
St Peters	16	Iron	2
Payneham	19	Render	3
		Asbestos	4
Land use	Code	Freestone	5
House	11	Bluestone	6
Maisonette	12	Basket Range	7
Home unit	13	Block	8
Flat	14		

The commands to produce the three-way contingency table, computed from the residential sales census, follow:

```
MTB > retrieve 'a:\vgsales.mtp';
SUBC> portable.
MTB > info
MTB > table 'landuse' 'walltype' 'locality';
SUBC> rowpercents.
```

The output produced by these commands is:

```
MTB > retrieve 'a:\vgsales.mtp';
SUBC> portable.

Worksheet retrieved from file: a:\vgsales.mtp
MTB > info

COLUMN      NAME          COUNT       MISSING
C1          locality      841
C3          price         841            3
C8          no_rooms      841           20
C9          blocarea      841          349
C12         landuse       841
C15         walltype      841           46

CONSTANTS USED: NONE

MTB > table 'landuse' 'walltype' 'locality';
SUBC> rowpercents.

CONTROL: locality = 15
ROWS: landuse   COLUMNS: walltype

              1        2        3        4        5        6        7        8

11         38.21      --    19.51      --    28.46    13.01     0.81      --
12         39.13      --    21.74      --    21.74    17.39      --       --
13         80.00      --    14.29      --     1.43     2.86     0.71     0.71
14         80.00      --      --       --      --       --       --     20.00
17           --       --      --       --      --       --       --       --
ALL        59.11      --    16.84      --    14.43     8.25     0.69     0.69

              ALL

11        100.00
12        100.00
13        100.00
14        100.00
17           --
ALL       100.00

CONTROL: locality = 16
ROWS: landuse   COLUMNS: walltype

              1        2        3        4        5        6        7        8

11         39.84     0.81    21.14     0.81    21.14    13.82     2.44      --
12         85.71      --      --       --     14.29      --       --       --
13         87.76      --      --       --     10.20      --      2.04      --
14        100.00      --      --       --      --       --       --       --
17           --       --      --       --      --       --       --       --
ALL        55.25     0.55    14.36     0.55    17.68     9.39     2.21      --
```

continued . . .

```
            ALL

11          100.00
12          100.00
13          100.00
14          100.00
17            --
ALL         100.00


CONTROL: locality = 19
ROWS: landuse    COLUMNS: walltype

                1       2       3       4       5       6       7       8

11          47.42     --    16.49    2.06   28.35    3.61    0.52    1.55
12         100.00     --      --      --      --      --      --      --
13          89.92     --     7.56     --      --     1.68     --     0.84
14         100.00     --      --      --      --      --      --      --
17            --      --      --      --      --      --      --      --
ALL         64.71     --    12.69    1.24   17.03    2.79    0.31    1.24


            ALL

11          100.00
12          100.00
13          100.00
14          100.00
17            --
ALL         100.00


CELL  CONTENTS  --
                % OF ROW
```

The *table* command has the column named *locality* specified last, so that different two-way tables will be produced for each locality. The columns *landuse* and *walltype* are specified first and second, respectively, so that they will form the rows and columns of each of the two-way tables for each locality.

The output includes margins, labelled *ALL*, which were not included in table 6.14. The margins that correspond to the sums across the rows have all values equal to 100, as you would expect. In table 6.14 these have been replaced with the number of observations in that row. To obtain these, produce the three-way table of counts by executing the *table* command, either with no subcommands or including the *count* subcommand.

6.5.4 Combining and deleting rows and columns of contingency tables

In interpreting the three-way contingency table, we advised collapsing the contingency table either by omitting altogether some values of a limited variable or combining some values of a limited variable. Omitting values is achieved, in Minitab, by using the *copy* command in conjunction with either the *omit* or the *use* subcommand, depending on which is easier. Combining values is achieved, in Minitab, by using the *code* command.

To use the *copy* command to omit values, the source and destination columns have to be specified. The destination columns can, but do not have to, be the same as the source columns. The *copy* command should list the source columns, followed by the destination columns. As the number of source and destination columns must be equal, the copy command will contain twice the number of source columns. It is also very important to include *all* columns required for the analysis in the *copy* subcommand. Otherwise, you may get an error saying that there is an unequal number of values in columns. To check the lengths of columns enter the *info* command.

To specify which rows of the columns are to be retained or omitted, use the *use* and *omit* subcommands respectively. The rows to be operated on must be specified for these two subcommands and this is done in the same way for both. You can specify a series of rows, or you can specify rows that have values in a specified column equal to particular values.

To use the *code* command to combine values, you have to specify a set of source and destination columns. As for the *copy* command, the list of source columns should be followed by the list of destination columns and both lists must have the same number of columns. You have to determine, for those being combined, what value you will convert them to. Then you specify the old values, enclosed in parentheses, followed by the new value. You may have to convert each of several sets of values to a different new value.

EXAMPLE 6.5   RESIDENCES SOLD IN THREE LOCALITIES (continued)

A revised table was obtained by:

1. omitting iron and asbestos residences;
2. combining the last four categories of wall type into a single category of stone walls;
3. combining the maisonettes, home units and flats into a single multiple residences category.

The commands to do this are as follows:

```
MTB > copy 'locality' 'landuse' 'walltype' &
MTB >       'locality' 'landuse' 'walltype';
SUBC> omit 'walltype' = 24.
MTB > code (12 13 14) 12 'landuse' 'landuse'
MTB > code (5:8) 5 'walltype' 'walltype'
MTB > info
MTB > table 'landuse' 'walltype' 'locality';
SUBC> rowpercents.
```

Note the use of the ampersand (&) to continue the *copy* command onto a second line.

If your version of Minitab has pull-down menus and you want to use them, table 6.20 lists the menus and options that access the required commands. Appendix D, *Detailed instructions for Minitab menus*, explains how to use the menus.

Table 6.20 Menus and options for Minitab commands to combine and delete rows and columns of contingency tables

Minitab command	Menu	Option
copy	Calc >	Copy Columns...
omit		Omit Rows...
code	Calc >	Code Data Values...
info	Edit >	Get Worksheet Info...
	(Edit >	Data Screen [Alt-D])
table	Stat >	Tables > Cross Tabulation
rowpercents		Row Percents

First, the *copy* command, and associated subcommand, in the following output omits the two wall types. In this case, the source and destination columns are the same. That is, the original columns will be overwritten by those with the two wall types omitted. Three source columns are included in the command because all three are to be used to form the contingency table. If only one of these columns, say *walltype*, had been included, the table command would not work; there would have been an error message saying the columns are of unequal length. The *use* subcommand was not employed in this example because there were fewer values to be omitted than to be retained.

The two *code* commands combine the last three *Land use* categories and the last four *Wall types*, respectively. Again, the source column is overwritten by the column containing the combined values. In the case of the *Land use* categories, the last three categories are coded 12, 13 and 14. To combine these three categories, they must all be converted to the same code. They could all be converted to a completely new code, or the last two categories code could be converted to 12. The latter course was chosen. The *code* command will change all values 12, 13 and 14 in column *landuse* to 12. As the 12 remains the same, it could be left out of the set of old values to be converted to 12. In the second *code* command the codes 5, 6, 7 and 8 are converted to 5. Note the use of 5:8 to represent the numbers 5, 6, 7 and 8; 5:8 means all numbers obtained by starting at 5, and incrementing by 1 until 8 has been exceeded.

Finally, the *table* command, with *rowpercents* subcommand, is issued and the revised contingency table produced. Again, all rows sum to 100, as expected; the numbers of observations in each row are obtained from a table that contains the counts.

The output produced by the commands is as follows:

```
MTB > copy 'locality' 'landuse' 'walltype' &
MTB >       'locality' 'landuse' 'walltype';
SUBC> omit 'walltype' = 2 4.
MTB > code (12 13 24) 12 'landuse' 'landuse'
MTB > code (5:8) 5 'walltype' 'walltype'
MTB > info

COLUMN      NAME        COUNT      MISSING
C1          locality     835
C3          price        841           3
C8          no_rooms     841          20
C9          blocarea     841         349
C12         landuse      835
C15         walltype     835          46

CONSTANTS USED: NONE

MTB > table 'landuse' 'walltype' 'locality';
SUBC> rowpercents.

CONTROL: locality = 15
ROWS: landuse    COLUMNS: walltype

              1         3         5        ALL

11        38.21     19.51     42.28     100.00
12        74.40     14.88     10.71     100.00
17         --        --        --        --
ALL       59.11     16.84     24.05     100.00

CONTROL: locality = 16
ROWS: landuse    COLUMNS: walltype

              1         3         5        ALL

11        40.50     21.49     38.02     100.00
12        87.93      --       12.07     100.00
17         --        --        --        --
ALL       55.87     14.53     29.61     100.00

CONTROL: locality = 19
ROWS: landuse    COLUMNS: walltype

              1         3         5        ALL

11        48.42     16.84     34.74     100.00
12        90.70      6.98      2.33     100.00
17         --        --        --        --
ALL       65.52     12.85     21.63     100.00

CELL CONTENTS --
            % OF ROW
```

6.6   Chapter summary

To summarise a set of data consisting of the observed values of a single limited variable, a one-way summary table is used. This table may contain the frequencies, proportions (relative frequencies), percentages of the values of the variable or some combination of these three. The information in the one-way summary table can be presented diagrammatically in a bar or column chart based on either the frequencies, proportions or percentages. The most useful summary for limited variables is in terms of the proportions or percentages.

While the complete distribution of values of a limited variable usually gives the best summary for a limited variable, a measure of central tendency and/or dispersion is sometimes required. For limited variables, the preferred measure of central tendency is often the mode, although for ordinal, limited variables the median is also a strong contender.

When there are two limited variables, the descriptive summary is a two-way contingency table in which the frequencies, proportions or percentages are presented for each possible combination of the values of the limited variables on which the table is based. For interpretation, either the row, column or total percentages are preferred. In addition, row and column frequencies, or percentages computed from them, are added as margins to the table. Information in two-way contingency tables is presented diagrammatically by using charts with either columns or bars that are either grouped or stacked. These charts can be based on frequencies, proportions or percentages. Probably, the best form is stacked bar charts based on percentages.

The key issue to be investigated with two limited variables is whether they are dependent or independent. This is done with the contingency table and associated diagrams. When the variables are dependent, the conclusions are most appropriately summarised by percentages in a two-way contingency table. These can be presented diagrammatically in a grouped or stacked chart. However, if the variables are independent, the most appropriate summary is a one-way summary table for each variable. That is, the tables derived from the margins of the two-way table are used.

When three limited variables are of interest, a three-way contingency table and associated diagrams can be used to investigate the dependence between the variables.

When a contingency table, two-way or three-way, has only a few observations for particular values of a limited variable, the table should be collapsed by omitting or combining rows and/or columns of the table.

6.7   Key terms

- bar chart
- classes in a one-way summary table
- collapsed contingency table
- column chart
- column percentage
- column total
- contingency table
- dependent limited variables
- distribution diagram
- distribution of variables
- distribution table
- frequency
- grand total
- grouped chart
- independent limited variables
- main body of a contingency table
- margins of a contingency table
- measure of central tendency
- mode
- one-way summary table
- percentage
- pie chart
- proportion (*p*)
- relative frequency
- row percentage
- row total
- stacked chart
- three-way contingency table
- total percentage
- two-way contingency table

6.8   Exercises

6.1   In your own words explain what is meant by the term *variable*.

Variables may be classified either separately or by a combination of the following terms:

> *limited or unrestricted*
> *qualitative or quantitative*
> *nominal, ordinal or interval/ratio*
> *discrete or continuous*

What are the differences between these classifications?
Examine the statements (a)–(m) and answer the following questions:
  (i) What is the target population under discussion in each statement?
  (ii) What is the observational unit involved in the statement?
  (iii) What are the variable(s) and what type(s) are they?
  (a) More than 23,000 students are enrolled at the University of South Australia, making it the largest university in South Australia. Lectures are given at City, the Levels, Magill, Salisbury, Underdale and Whyalla campuses. Information on which campus each student mostly attends is to be collected.

(b) A recent survey of students recorded their country of birth. Countries of birth include Argentina, Australia, Brazil, China, Indonesia, Iraq, Japan, Lebanon, Malaysia, Taiwan, the United States and Vietnam.

(c) A census of first-year students in the Faculty of Business and Management is proposed, to determine what degree they are enrolled in. The degrees in which they might be enrolled include Accountancy, Business, Banking and Finance, Information Systems, Marketing or Real Estate.

(d) A survey of professional accountants aims to determine the highest qualification that they have obtained. The qualifications involved include Bachelor's, Honour's and Master's degrees, Graduate diploma and PhD.

(e) A large office with several secretaries has a computer network with a shared printer for producing correspondence and documents. This printer is to be replaced and the company's information technologist intends to survey the features of available printers. The following information is to be recorded for each printer:

- type of printer: laser, inkjet or dot matrix;
- production capacity: recommended pages per day;
- speed: pages per minute;
- clarity: rating on a 7-point scale;
- ability to handle graphics: yes or no;
- availability of service: rating into one of several classes;
- cost of service: dollars per hour.

(f) At the end of each month the sales representatives of a large insurance company have to submit a report on their activities. Each salesman is given a basic retainer that is supplemented by commissions. These commissions are determined according to the amount of new business they write up each month. Besides their sales report, they have to keep records for the taxation department of details of the allowances they have received from their employer for car, accommodation, meal and telephone expenses.

(g) The Cancer Society is concerned about the rapid increase in the number of reported cases of skin cancer in Australia. With summer approaching it is keen to promote a new range of sunblock creams as part of their prevention program, and the Society has engaged a market research company to assist in their campaign. Key areas to be researched are: the most common media observed (newspapers, magazines, billboards, TV and radio); type of promotion that most appeals (free samples, discount, two-for-one purchase) and range of product currently used (9+,12+,15+); age-group (<13, 13–18, 18–21, 21–30, 30–40, 40–50, over 50); sex (female, male).

(h) In South Australia, two pathology laboratories run a network of collection couriers, who visit the major hospitals and local medical practices to collect specimens for testing. Each courier has designated collection zones, and has to record the time of collection, the number of packages at each centre, and the urgency of the test.

(i) The Australian Red Cross Society relies on volunteers to maintain a blood bank for supplying blood to hospitals for many forms of surgery and emergency treatment. The blood is stored in batches according to the blood types A, AB, B and O. A further classification is Rh positive and Rh negative. It could cost lives if these types are not clearly and accurately marked.

(j) An efficient accounting system is essential to the success of any retail business. Information recorded on all dockets such as date of purchase, location of sale, type of sale (cash, card, store account), department, article purchased and the total amount paid are all essential for monitoring cashflow and stock replacement to keep up with demand.

(k) In a recent survey of absences in the State Public Service the following information was recorded for each employee: total number of days absent; longest single period of absence; whether or not ordinary sick leave, stress-related leave, accouchement leave or leave without pay has been taken.

(l) The Australian Bureau of Statistics is responsible for conducting the national census that records information about each household in Australia. This information is an invaluable resource for those planning community services such as housing developments, schools, hospitals, roads, public transport, recreation facilities, and family support services. Census questions included the size of the household, type of dwelling and size of mortgage, as well as the age, ethnicity, religion, level of education, income and type of employment for each household member.

(m) A state transport department, in a bid to decrease the expense of running its fleet of 200 vehicles, held an experiment to see which brand of tyre was most economical. Each vehicle was fitted with one of four brands of tyres, chosen at random, and then driven for 10 000 km. The department then measured the amount of tyre tread that was left.

6.2 In your own words, explain what is meant by the following terms:
   (a) distribution of a variable
   (b) relative frequency
   (c) proportion
   (d) one-way summary table
   (e) column chart
   (f) bar chart
   (g) contingency table
   (h) row, column and total percentage
   (i) grouped column chart
   (j) stacked bar chart
   (k) independent limited variables

6.3 For a survey investigating the variability of prices in supermarkets in a major city, a group of students was asked to collect details of the prices of certain items at their local supermarket. One of the items was a 100 g jar of coffee; each student selected a jar from the shelf and recorded its brand and price. The information provided by 84 students is given as follows. It is to be used to see which brands were selected by the students.

	Coffee brand	Brands selected in the survey					
1.	Low Price	10	11	11	12	1	7
2.	Mountain View	7	11	3	7	7	10
3.	Plantation	3	13	11	11	10	11
4.	Plantation Roast	10	11	7	7	11	11
5.	Dutch Cafe	5	11	11	11	11	11
6.	Ourbrand	11	11	10	7	11	11
7.	World Roast	12	12	11	11	11	9
8.	Dutch Espresso	11	8	11	7	12	12
9.	House of Max	10	8	9	11	12	12
10.	Oldcafe	11	12	11	7	11	11
11.	Oldcafe Blended	7	8	12	10	14	7
12.	Oldcafe Bronze	10	12	11	7	8	11
13.	Diablo	11	7	11	11	11	11
14.	Other	11	11	12	10	11	11

(a) What is the question to be investigated (including the group to which the conclusions apply)?

(b) What variable(s) are we concerned with here and what type(s) are they?

(c) Summarise the brands selected by the students.

6.4 This exercise is based on an article by Watson (1989) in *The Australian Computer Journal*. The frequency with which 10 industries are represented in the Top 200 Australian organisations is given in table 6.21.

Table 6.21   Frequencies of 10 industries in Top
200 Australian organisations

Industry	Frequency
Construction	4
Finance	43
Manufacturing	55
Mining	18
Primary	3
Public Service	7
Retail	8
Service	12
Transport	24
Wholesale	26
Total	200

In a recent mail survey, responses were received from organisations that reported the industries to which they belonged. The first two letters of the industries of the responding organisations are given in table 6.22. The distribution of responding organisations is to be examined.

Table 6.22   Industries of responding organisations

MA	MI	FI	RE	MA	TR	SE	MA	PU	MA	TR	TR	WH	WH	MA	FI
FI	MI	MA	SE	PU	MA	TR	PU	WH	MA	MI	FI	MA	PU	MA	WH
PR	SE	TR	MA	TR	MA	FI	MI	MA	FI	MA	MA	PU	WH	MA	WH

(a) What is the question to be investigated (including the group to which the conclusions apply)?
(b) What variable(s) are we concerned with here and what type(s) are they?
(c) Prepare a table, similar to table 6.21, listing the frequencies of *Industry* for the responding organisations.

(d) Convert the frequencies to percentages, and place them in your table. If you do this with Minitab you will need to identify the industries by number from 1 to 10. You can use this data to compare the distribution of *Industry* in the Top 200 with that for the responding organisations.

(e) What are the advantages of presenting the data in a table?

(f) What are the advantages of using percentages rather than frequencies?

(g) Which *Industry* has the highest representation? What is the name of the statistic you have calculated?

(h) What is the percentage of responding organisations from the transport industry?

(i) Determine whether the responding organisations are reasonably representative of the Top 200 organisations? Give reasons for your answer.

(j) Use a percentage chart to highlight the differences in the two sets of data.

6.5 Unemployment is a controversial topic in times of recession. Business leaders and politicians freely use unemployment figures to justify their policies and their efforts to reduce the hardship created by increasing levels of unemployment. In the early 1980s Australian unemployment rose to a high 10% for the first six months of 1983. After that it began to decrease.

Table 6.23 shows the employment status of the civilian population in South Australia in the late 1980s. These figures are to be used to determine whether the downward trend in South Australian unemployment has continued during 1986–92.

Table 6.23   Employment status of civilian population aged 15 and over

	Employment Status		
Time period	Unemployed ('000)	Employed ('000)	Total
1986–87	635.2	7044.3	7679.5
1987–88	610.5	7256.3	7866.8
1988–89	535.2	7551.2	8086.3
1989–90	515.0	7840.3	8355.2
1990–91	713.6	7808.8	8522.4
1991–92	888.9	7684.1	8572.9

Source: abstracted from Australian Bureau of Statistics (1994b)

(a) What is the question to be investigated (including the group to which the conclusions apply)?

(b) What variable(s) are we concerned with here and what type(s) are they?

(c) Convert the table of frequencies to a table of percentages by calculating the percentage unemployed and employed for each year.

(d) Has the downward trend continued?

6.6 The Graduate Destination Survey 1992 reported the destinations and occupations of the first-degree graduates who had completed Business Studies courses in Australian tertiary institutions. The destinations of graduates are listed in table 6.24 and we want to see whether the destination of these graduates is the same for both sexes.

Table 6.24   Percentages for destinations of male and female first-degree graduates

	Sex		
Destination	Males	Females	Total
Working full-time	56.2	51.8	54.0
Seeking full-time employment	18.8	22.2	20.4
Part-time employment	1.3	3.8	2.5
Unavailable	1.2	1.5	1.4
Study full-time	13.5	11.5	12.5
Overseas	9.1	9.1	9.1
Total number	1696	1620	3316

Source: abstracted from Graduate Careers Council of Australia (1993)

(a) What is the question to be investigated (including the group to which the conclusions apply)?

(b) What variable(s) are we concerned with here and what type(s) are they?

(c) Use a grouped column chart to show the different percentage levels for the two sexes.

(d) The main occupations for the same graduates are shown in table 6.25. Present a stacked bar chart to show the percentages for each sex.

Table 6.25   Percentages for occupations of male and female first-degree graduates

| | Sex | | |
Occupation	Males	Females	Total
Management/administration	28.7	17.0	23.3
Business professional	14.0	19.7	16.6
Sales, finance and related	15.1	13.8	14.5
Clerk	7.6	13.0	10.1
Accountant	10.6	6.9	8.9
Computer professional	6.2	3.8	5.1
Personnel	1.9	3.6	2.7
All others	15.9	22.2	18.8
Total number	953	839	1792

Source: abstracted from Graduate Careers Council of Australia (1993)

6.7   Information on the numbers of offenders for different ages for three categories of offence during a 12-month period is given in tables 6.26, 6.27 and 6.28. We need to investigate, for each category of offence, whether the extent to which the offences are committed depends on the age of the offender during the 12-month period.

Table 6.26   Numbers of drug and alcohol offences by offenders aged 10–19 years

| | Age | | | | | |
Offence	10–14 yrs	15 yrs	16 yrs	17 yrs	18 yrs	19 yrs
Possession/use	155	188	301	397	44	38
Selling/trading	19	14	16	14	25	20
Producing/manufacturing	4	15	47	57	7	14
Drink-driving	10	7	31	99	246	297
Other	81	175	277	396	19	11
Total	269	399	672	963	341	380

Source: South Australian Commissioner of Police (1993)

Table 6.27 Numbers of theft and damage offences by offenders aged 10–19 years

	Age					
Offence	10–14 yrs	15 yrs	16 yrs	17 yrs	18 yrs	19 yrs
Receiving/unlawful possession	183	157	172	178	171	138
Other theft	2183	1258	1130	936	762	596
Property damage	452	277	292	280	330	226
Break and enter	641	442	479	480	351	285
Total	3459	2134	2073	1874	1614	1245

Source: South Australian Commissioner of Police (1993)

Table 6.28 Numbers of violent and sexual offences by offenders aged 10–19 years

	Age					
Offence	10–14 yrs	15 yrs	16 yrs	17 yrs	18 yrs	19 yrs
Offences against the person	2	1	5	1	11	7
Assaults	264	202	213	250	278	279
Sex offences	41	20	15	12	26	28
Kidnapping/abduction	22	31	37	36	35	42
Robbery	80	70	50	50	36	34
Total	409	324	320	349	386	390

Source: South Australian Commissioner of Police (1993)

For each set of data, answer the following questions:

(a) What is the question to be investigated (including the group to which the conclusions apply)?

(b) What variable(s) are we concerned with here and what type(s) are they?

(c) What type of table has been used to present this data?

(d) Convert the frequencies in each table to percentages and use an appropriate distribution diagram to highlight the differences between the age-groups in that table.

6.8 A local government area was studied to ascertain residents' views on various waste collection issues. Two survey questions were concerned with the frequency of collection and the size of the bin and it is desired to see whether these two issues are related for the respondents to the survey. The results are given in table 6.29.

Table 6.29   Smaller bin and collection frequency for waste collection

	Collection frequency			
Smaller bin	Increase	Same	Decrease	Total
Agree	97	60	14	171
Neutral	12	71	3	86
Disagree	15	214	50	279
Total	124	345	67	536

(a) What is the question to be investigated (including the group to which the conclusions apply)?

(b) What variable(s) are we concerned with here and what type(s) are they?

(c) What are your conclusions from this study? Give reasons for your answer.

6.9 Does equal opportunity really exist in the State Public Service? The data from a recent survey of 100 randomly selected public servants was used to see whether their occupation varied according to their sex and marital status. The data is coded as shown in table 6.30.

Table 6.30   Coding for public servant survey

Sex	Marital status	Occupation
1 = male	1 = single	1 = professional
2 = female	2 = married	2 = managerial
		3 = sales
		4 = clerical and technical
		5 = other

The data from this survey is given in table 6.31 and is saved in a Minitab portable worksheet file called *pubserv.mtp*.

(a) What is the question to be investigated (including the group to which the conclusions apply)?

(b) Analyse the data to see whether *Occupation* varies with *Sex* and *Marital status* for this particular sample.

(c) What variable(s) are we concerned with here and what type(s) are they?

Table 6.31   Data from public servant survey

Obs. unit	Sex	Marital status	Occupation	Obs. unit	Sex	Marital status	Occupation	Obs. unit	Sex	Marital status	Occupation
1	1	2	4	35	1	2	2	68	1	2	2
2	1	2	3	36	1	2	2	69	1	2	2
3	1	1	4	37	1	2	5	70	1	2	2
4	1	2	2	38	1	2	4	71	1	1	5
5	1	2	4	39	1	1	5	72	1	2	2
6	1	1	3	40	1	2	3	73	1	2	4
7	1	2	5	41	2	2	3	74	1	2	2
8	1	2	4	42	2	1	2	75	1	2	2
9	1	2	4	43	1	2	4	76	1	2	2
10	1	2	4	44	2	1	2	77	1	2	4
11	1	2	2	45	1	2	3	78	1	2	3
12	1	2	3	46	1	2	4	79	1	1	5
13	1	2	2	47	2	2	4	80	1	1	5
14	1	2	3	48	1	2	4	81	1	2	5
15	1	2	2	49	1	1	3	82	1	2	5
16	1	2	4	50	1	2	2	83	1	1	3
17	2	2	1	51	1	2	3	84	1	1	4
18	1	2	2	52	1	2	3	85	1	2	4
19	2	1	2	53	2	1	3	86	1	2	4
20	1	2	2	54	2	2	3	87	1	2	4
21	1	2	4	55	1	2	2	88	1	1	3
22	1	2	2	56	2	2	4	89	1	2	1
23	1	2	4	57	1	2	3	90	1	2	2
24	1	2	4	58	1	2	4	91	1	2	4
25	2	2	5	59	1	2	4	92	1	2	4
26	1	2	4	60	2	1	2	93	1	1	5
27	1	2	3	61	1	2	4	94	1	2	3
28	1	2	4	62	1	1	3	95	1	1	5
29	1	2	3	63	1	2	5	96	1	2	2
30	1	2	5	64	1	2	4	97	2	2	4
31	1	2	2	65	2	2	1	98	1	2	2
32	1	2	4	66	1	2	5	99	1	2	3
33	1	2	4	67	2	1	2	100	2	2	3
34	1	2	4								

6.10 A selection of student statistics taken from the December 1994 issue of *New Outlook*, published by the University of South Australia, is presented in table 6.32.

Table 6.32   Total students by faculty, 1994

| | Sex | | | |
Faculty	Male	Female	Total	EFTSU*
Aboriginal and Islander Studies	221	449	670	427
Applied Science and Technology	1268	554	1822	1410
Art, Architecture and Design	552	643	1195	1105
Business and Management	2697	2136	4833	3478
Education	1456	3441	4897	3019
Engineering	2140	270	2410	1903
Health and Biomedical Sciences	418	960	1378	1037
Humanities and Social Sciences	679	2268	2947	2091
Nursing	287	2008	2295	1860
Whyalla Specific Courses	110	55	165	122
Miscellaneous Enrolments	79	97	176	48
Total	9907	12881	22788	16500

* EFTSU: effective full-time student units

(a) What variable(s) are we concerned with here and what type(s) are they?
(b) Examine this material and present a report which should include appropriate distribution diagrams to highlight the points of interest.

## CHAPTER 7

DESCRIPTIVE SUMMARIES FOR ONE UNRESTRICTED VARIABLE

L E A R N I N G   O B J E C T I V E S

The learning objectives of this chapter are:

- to be able to produce distribution tables and distribution diagrams for data involving one unrestricted variable: frequency, relative frequency and percentage tables; histograms; polygons; stem-and-leaf displays; dotplots;
- to know the features of the different distribution tables and distribution diagrams;
- to know what information such tables and diagrams provide and recognise patterns commonly occuring;
- to be able to produce and understand the purpose of the major measures of central tendency for data involving one unrestricted variable;
- to know the features of the measures of central tendency and when to use them;
- to be able to produce and understand the purpose of the major measures of dispersion for data involving a single unrestricted variable;
- to know the features of the measures of dispersion and know when to use them;
- to be able to recognise potential outliers in a set of data.

The following extract from the *Summary of procedures based on combination of variable types* in part VI gives and overview of the descriptive summaries covered in this and the previous chapter of part III, *Descriptive summaries of data*.

1. *One limited variable*
   - Distribution of variables: frequency, relative frequency and percentage one-way summary tables — bar or column chart.
   - Measures of central tendency: mode (mean, median).

2. *Two limited variables*
   - Distribution of variables: two-way contingency table — chart with bars or columns that are grouped or stacked.

3. *Three limited variables*
   - Distribution of variables: three-way contingency table — chart with bars or columns that are grouped or stacked.

4. *One unrestricted variable*
   - **Distribution of variables**: frequency, relative frequency and percentage tables — histogram, polygon, stem-and-leaf display, dotplot.
   - **Measures of central tendency**: mean, median — boxplot.
   - **Measures of dispersion**: range, interquartile range, standard deviation, coefficient of variation — boxplot.

As outlined in the objectives, this chapter covers the descriptive summaries under heading 4, *One unrestricted variable*.

7.1   Distribution of one unrestricted variable

A particular value of an unrestricted variable generally does not recur often. In a data set of 50 or so numbers a particular value might not recur at all or only once or twice at most. Consequently, it no longer makes sense to obtain the frequency of each value, as we did for limited variables in the one-way summary table. Methods for unrestricted variables are based on **class intervals**, a class interval being a continuous range of values of an unrestricted variable. Unlike classes in a one-way summary table which must correspond to the values of the limited variable, there is considerable freedom in choosing class intervals. Methods for unrestricted variables include **distribution tables** based on frequencies, proportions and percentages and **distribution diagrams** such as histograms and polygons, stem-and-leaf displays and dotplots. The aim of these procedures is to examine the distribution of values of the unrestricted variable. That is, to see the pattern in the observed values. Thus, answers are obtained to questions such as: how many people weigh between 100 and 120 kg? We will first cover distribution tables and then describe the diagrams that can be used to illustrate the distribution.

7.1.1   Distribution tables for one unrestricted variable

Frequency tables provide, for *unrestricted data*, a very simple intuitive method for examining the pattern in the observed values. As for the one-way summary table, a frequency table may contain either the frequencies, proportions or percentages, or some combination of these. A frequency table summarises information about a set of data in a form that is more readily assimilated than raw data. Constructing a frequency table requires the following steps:

1. divide the observed range into a set of nonoverlapping, preferably equal, class intervals;
2. proceed systematically through the observations, noting the class interval into which each observation falls;
3. record the number of observations that have occurred in the intervals;
4. compute and incorporate the proportions and percentages, if these are required.

Two factors to be taken into account for constructing a frequency table are: the number of class intervals and the sharing of a common boundary by consecutive intervals.

The number of class intervals

In practice, somewhere between 5 and 15 seems to be a satisfactory number of class intervals. The exact number depends on the number of observations; the more observations there are, the greater the number of class intervals. Too many intervals means that each interval will contain only a few observations, while too few intervals means that most intervals will have a similar number of observations.

Consecutive intervals sharing a common boundary

As noted previously, the class intervals should not overlap; however, for continuous variables, they should just touch so that consecutive intervals have a common boundary value. Consequently, *any* value that can occur conceptually can be assigned to some class interval, even when the value itself cannot be observed because the instrument making the measurements is not precise enough.

However, this creates the problem of what to do if an observed value should be exactly equal to a class interval boundary. The convention followed in this book is that a value exactly equal to the class interval boundary is placed in the larger of the two class intervals. Other conventions are also used.

EXAMPLE 7.1   MANAGEMENT CAPACITY

A company wants to assess the management capacity of 30 of its employees, and has acquired a management capacity test. The test involves several parts, administered separately, and a measure of an individual's capacity is provided by the mean of the scores from the different parts. This mean score must lie between 0 and 100.

The primary, or raw, data obtained from the 30 employees is presented in table 7.1. At this stage, the company wants an overall description of the results. The variable that has been measured is *Management test score* which is a continuous, unrestricted variable in that:

1. more than 10 values have been obtained and a value repeats infrequently;
2. management capacity is, conceptually, a continuously varying characteristic.

Looking at these we can see that the values range in the 60s, 70s and 80s, but little else. For example, it is difficult to determine whether they are evenly spread across this range or concentrated at particular values.

Table 7.1   Observed values of *Management test score*

81.3	80.1	74.3	75.3	63.6	68.5	68.7	83.0	76.9	64.3
74.2	69.8	76.8	74.3	79.2	61.1	98.8	66.2	74.8	76.1
83.0	68.5	66.6	64.5	63.5	66.3	76.7	59.7	73.8	70.3

The frequency table, including frequencies, proportions and percentages, has been computed for this data and is presented in table 7.2. What does it show? Most of the observations are around 75, with a smaller group around 65. Indeed, the proportion falling in the range 72.5–77.5 is 0.33 or 33% of the observations. This table tells us much more than we could learn by examining the original observations.

Note that class intervals of 5 points were used in constructing the frequency distribution table and that these intervals share a common boundary. According to the convention stated above, a value such as 72.5 would be placed in the class interval 72.5–77.5, rather than 67.5-72.5. Consequently, the class 72.5-77.5 could be designated *72.5 but less than 77.5*. Also, the frequencies add to 30, which is the total number of observations.

Table 7.2   Frequency table for *Management test scores*

Class intervals	Frequency	Proportion	Percentage
57.5–62.5	2	0.07	7
62.5–67.5	7	0.23	23
67.5–72.5	5	0.17	17
72.5–77.5	10	0.33	33
77.5–82.5	3	0.10	10
82.5–87.5	2	0.07	7
87.5–92.5	0	0.00	0
92.5–97.5	0	0.00	0
97.5–102.5	1	0.03	3
Total	30	1.00	100

Proportions and percentages are particularly useful for comparing distributions because they eliminate the differences between frequencies arising from different total numbers of observations. Further, they are more readily interpreted than the frequency.

7.1.2   Histograms and polygons for one unrestricted variable

Graphic presentation of the information in the frequency table is made in the form of a **histogram** or **polygon** based on either the frequency proportions or percentage. Note that a polygon is a line diagram. As far as the overall shape of the distribution is concerned, it does not matter which of the three quantities the distribution diagram is based on. The shape of the distribution will be the same for all three.

Both histograms and polygons involve plotting the frequency, proportion or percentage against the unrestricted variable. To this end, the axes should cover the observed range for the quantity to be plotted on them and, to help the plotting, regular marks are placed along each axis. In particular, the axis on which the unrestricted variable is to be plotted should not have a list of the class intervals along it.

Histograms consist of a set of joined boxes, each covering the part of the axis that corresponds with a class interval. For equal class intervals, the height of a box or length of a rectangular column is proportional to the frequency, proportion or percentage, whichever is being plotted. The boxes are joined to indicate that data are the values of a variable whose possible values are conceptually continuous across the observed range. For polygons, the frequency, proportion or percentage is plotted against the class midpoint as points that are joined with lines. The **class midpoint** is the mean of its two boundary values. At either end of the diagram, the line is taken down to the horizontal axis, reaching the axis at the midpoints of the class intervals immediately below and above the most extreme observed class intervals.

The more traditional way to present the histogram is with the measured variable on the horizontal axis, as shown in figure 7.1. However, it is also acceptable to present the histogram with the axes swapped around.

The information that can be obtained from these distribution diagrams is:

1. the general shape of the distribution;
2. where the observed values are concentrated;
3. the range of values;
4. the presence of extreme values or outliers.

However, be very careful in drawing conclusions from histograms as some patterns are merely artefacts of the particular set of class intervals used.

EXAMPLE 7.1   MANAGEMENT CAPACITY (continued)

For the 30 management test scores, the histogram based on the frequencies is presented in figure 7.1, and the histogram based on the percentages is shown in figure 7.2. The only difference between these two diagrams is in the values marked on the vertical scale; the basic shape remains the same. Note the scale-breaks included in the horizontal axis to indicate that the range from 0 to 57.5 has been omitted. The polygon, based on the percentages, is given in figure 7.3.

From these diagrams, it seems that the data has two peaks with values concentrated around 75 and to a lesser extent around 65. Overall, the scores cover the range 57.5–102.5, that is, about 40 points. However, there is a single extreme value or outlier corresponding to an employee who obtained a score of about 100 points.

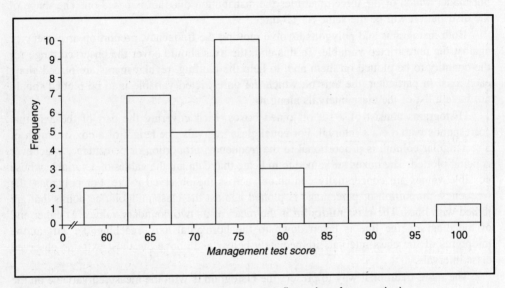

Figure 7.1   Histogram for *Management test score* (based on frequencies)

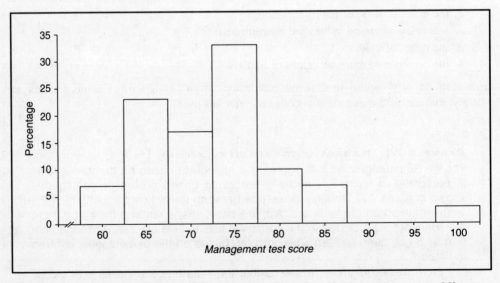

Figure 7.2   Histogram for *Management test score* (based on percentages — $n = 30$)

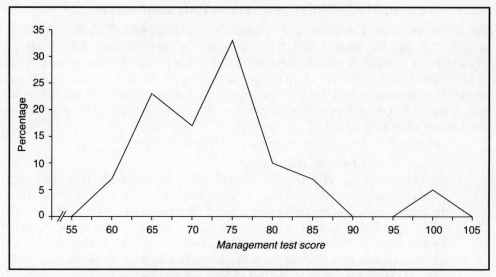

Figure 7.3   Polygon for *Management test score* (based on percentages — *n* = 30)

To see how the apparent shape is affected by the particular choice of class interval, consider the histogram obtained after changing the class intervals to 55–60, 60–65 and so on, as presented in figure 7.4. It has the advantage that the largest class interval, 95–100, does not exceed the maximum score possible from the test. From this histogram you could conclude that the scores are evenly spread from about 62.5 up to 82.5. Quite a different conclusion.

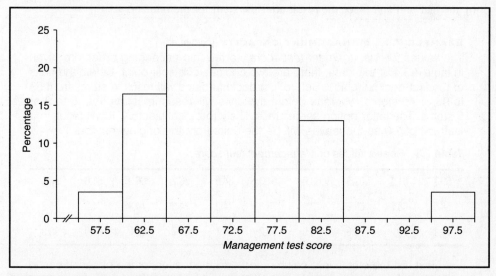

Figure 7.4   Revised histogram for *Management test score* (based on percentages — *n* = 30)

7.1.3   Stem-and-leaf displays for one unrestricted variable

An alternative to the histograms and polygons is the **stem-and-leaf display**. All these diagrams present the same information. However, the stem-and-leaf display has an advantage: for a single unrestricted variable it yields a more detailed record of the original observations. That is, it combines both the tabular and graphic displays into one display, and so has the advantages of both. Its chief disadvantage is that many people are still unfamiliar with it and, at first, it appears difficult to interpret. However, after only a little practice you can become adept at using it.

To construct the stem-and-leaf display, do the following steps:

1. Arrange the data into ascending order.
2. Decide whether the values are to be split before the hundreds, tens, units, first decimal place, second decimal place or some other point. The number formed from the digits to the left of the **split-point** is called the **stem** and the first digit to the right is called the **leaf**. If there is more than one digit to the right of the split-point, only the first is taken. The split-point should be chosen along lines similar to those for choosing class intervals for the frequency table. That is, there should be about 5–15 stems in the data and most stems should have several observations.
3. List, in a single column, all stems that can occur in the data, beginning with the stem for the smallest observation and ending with the stem for the largest observation.
4. Add the leaf for each observation alongside its stem so that leaves for the same stem form a row.
5. Specify the **leaf unit**: that is, whether the leaf represents a hundred, ten, unit, first-decimal place and so on.

Note that to reconstruct a number from the stem-and-leaf display, you take the leaf, multiply it by the leaf unit and place the result after the stem for the number.

> **EXAMPLE 7.1   MANAGEMENT CAPACITY** (continued)
> The values for *Management test score*, sorted into ascending order, are given in table 7.3. For this data, there are two choices of a split-point: before the units or the first decimal place. Before first decimal place will result in stems from 59 to 98 or 40 stems, whereas before the units will result in stems from 5 to 9 or 5 stems. The latter option seems most likely to be satisfactory. It will result in a leaf unit of 1.0 as the leaves will be the units from the original number.
>
> **Table 7.3**   Sorted values of *Management test score*
>
> | | | | | | | | | | |
> |------|------|------|------|------|------|------|------|------|------|
> | 59.7 | 61.1 | 63.5 | 63.6 | 64.3 | 64.5 | 66.2 | 66.3 | 66.6 | 68.5 |
> | 68.5 | 68.7 | 69.8 | 70.3 | 73.8 | 74.2 | 74.3 | 74.3 | 74.8 | 75.3 |
> | 76.1 | 76.7 | 76.8 | 76.9 | 79.2 | 80.1 | 81.3 | 83.0 | 83.0 | 98.8 |
>
> Next, list the stems in a column and add the leaves for the observations to yield the display given in table 7.4. That is, split the first observation 59.7 before the units, as in figure 7.5. The remaining observations are similarly split.

The leaf unit is 1.0 so that numbers are split before the units. Consequently, a leaf of, say, 8 represents $8 \times 1.0 = 8$. If the stem of the number with this leaf is 9, the original number must be 98, rounded down to the nearest unit.

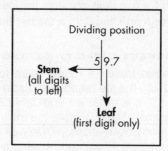

Figure 7.5 Dividing an observation into its stem and leaf

Table 7.4 Stem-and-leaf display for *Management test score*

Stem	Leaves
5	9
6	133446668889
7	034444566669
8	0133
9	8
Leaf unit = 1.0	

mainly used by hand.
can look at basic dis of num and a repeated value.

The stem-and-leaf display is in many ways equivalent to a histogram in which the class intervals correspond to those values that have the same stem. Of course, the stem-and-leaf display has the advantage that it retains more information about the values than the histogram does.

EXAMPLE 7.1   MANAGEMENT CAPACITY (continued)
The stem-and-leaf display in table 7.4 corresponds to a histogram with class intervals of 50–60, 60–70, 70–80, 80–90 and 90–100 formed according to the convention that values equal to a class boundary are placed in the larger class interval.

Multiple lines per stem

Sometimes putting all leaves on a single stem does not produce a good display of the distribution. There are either too few or too many stems so that there are too many or too few leaves on the stems. To overcome this problem, the leaves for a particular stem can be split over several lines. So that each line caters for the same number of possible leaf values, of which there are 10 altogether, the number of lines must be a factor of 10. Thus, you could have either two or five lines per stem. For two lines per stem, put the leaves 0,1,2,3,4 on one line, and 5,6,7,8,9 on the other; for five lines per stem put leaves 0,1 on one line, 2,3 on the next, 4,5 on the third, 6,7 on the fourth and 8,9 on the last line.

EXAMPLE 7.1   MANAGEMENT CAPACITY (continued)

The stem-and-leaf display in table 7.4 might seem too condensed. To get a better view of the distribution, the stem-and-leaf display with two lines per stem is produced, as in table 7.5. It is obtained from table 7.4 by splitting each row in that display between leaves 4 and 5. Note the inclusion of lines without any leaves, because there are no observations with leaves for that line. This is done so that all stems between the minimum and maximum values have two lines in the display. As a result it becomes obvious that there is an outlier corresponding to an observation of about 98. The stem-and-leaf display in table 7.5 seems to give a better picture of the distribution of this data than the display in table 7.4.

The information exhibited in the stem-and-leaf display in table 7.5 is similar to that in the histogram in figure 7.4. However, in addition to the information presented in the histogram, the stem-and-leaf display contains more precise information about the values. For example, 4 employees obtained a score of about 76.

Overall, the employees' scores range from about 59 to 98, with most values in the 60s and 70s. One employee achieved a somewhat higher score, of approximately 98.

Table 7.5   Stem-and-leaf display for *Management test score*

Stem	Leaves
5	9
6	13344
6	6668889
7	034444
7	566669
8	0133
8	
9	
9	8
Leaf unit = 1.0	

7.1.4   Dotplots for one unrestricted variable

Another diagram for displaying the distribution for unrestricted variables is the dotplot. It has the appeal of being an intuitively simple plot. It is the only satisfactory plot for a small set of observations from an unrestricted variable; that is, when there are not enough observations for histograms and stem-and-leaf displays. It can also be used for a large number of observations. Its chief disadvantage is that it tends to give a rather diffuse picture of the data.

A **dotplot** is constructed by drawing a line with a scale that covers the observed range of the data. Individual observations are plotted above this line as dots (or crosses), and coincident values have dots placed one above the other.

EXAMPLE 7.1   MANAGEMENT CAPACITY (continued)
The dotplot for *Management test score* is given in figure 7.6. The outlier is obvious. However, it does not give a good picture of the remaining features of the distribution of the data; the dots are spread out over the observed range.

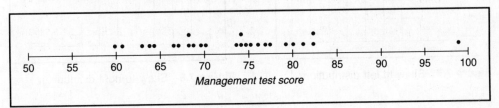

Figure 7.6   Dotplot for *Management test score*

7.1.5   Distribution attributes

In looking at the distribution diagrams for an unrestricted variable, we have encountered four **distribution attributes**:

1. **general shape**: the pattern in which the observed values are distributed across the observed range;
2. **central tendency**: the tendency for the values of a variable to cluster about a typical value;
3. **dispersion**: the range over which observed values of the variable tend to be spread;
4. **outliers**: extreme values of the variable that are either much smaller or much larger than nearly all the other observations.

The next section discusses shape in some detail and later sections discuss the measurement of central tendency and spread and the specification of outliers.

7.2   General shape

Some of the most common shapes are illustrated in figures 7.7–7.13. There are two skew distributions in figures 7.7 and 7.8. The **skew-to-the-left distribution** is characterised by a few values that are much smaller than most of the values. On the other hand, the **skew-to-the-right distribution** has a few values that are much larger than most of the values. It is important to note that the direction of the skew is the direction of the long tail of the distribution: that is, the position of the outliers relative to most of the values. The direction of the skew is *not* the relative position of the peak of the distribution. *Salaries* is an example of a variable that is skew-to-the-right, since there are usually a few individuals that get much higher salaries than the majority do.

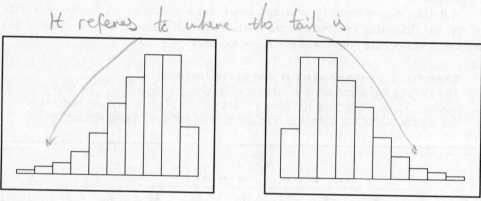

It referes to where the tail is

Figure 7.7 Skew to left distribution   **Figure 7.8** Skew to right distribution

Figures 7.9–7.11 illustrate several **symmetric distributions**. That is, for each distribution, the shape to the left of the peak is a mirror image of the shape to the right. Put another way, if you folded the distributions along the centre line, the left side would fit exactly onto the right side. The three distributions differ in the degree of peakedness. The **normal distribution** has a specific shape that is described as symmetric and bell-shaped. It was given this name because it was once thought that all variables must have a normal distribution. However, other shapes, such as those described here, are now acknowledged.

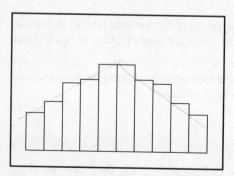

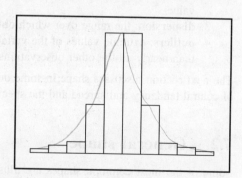

Figure 7.9 Flat, symmetric distribution   **Figure 7.10** Peaked, symmetric distribution

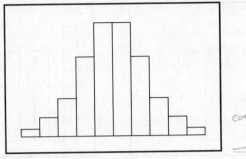

concave
concave
concave
change of slope

Figure 7.11 Normal distribution

All the distributions presented in figures 7.7–7.11 have a single peak, and so they are described as **unimodal**. A distribution with no peak is described as uniform; as in figure 7.12, all values of the variable occur equally frequently. The distribution in figure 7.13 has two peaks and is described as **bimodal**.

2 Peaks or 2 modes

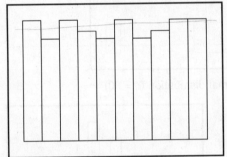

Plot

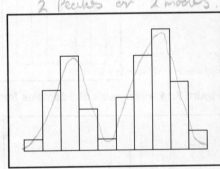

could be 2 sub groups

Figure 7.12 Uniform distribution   **Figure 7.13** Bimodal distribution

The diagrams in figures 7.7–7.13 are idealised. One has to be rather cautious in judging the shape of distributions. As mentioned previously, there is the problem of the apparent shape changing as the class intervals change. Another difficulty is that many observations are required to establish the shape of the distribution with any degree of certainty.

To demonstrate the latter problem, suppose I have at least 10 000 individuals on which I have measured an unrestricted variable, and suppose it has been confirmed that the distribution for this variable is normal. I now select three simple random samples of 30 individuals from the 10 000 available and produce a histogram for each sample (see figure 7.14). The histograms look anything but normal; all appear to have outliers and their shapes range from looking uniform to bimodal.

The exercise was repeated, with three samples of 100 selected. The corresponding histograms are shown in figure 7.15. While the shape suggests unimodality, the distributions still do not look particularly normal. It takes a sample of 500 individuals to make the distribution (in figure 7.16) look roughly normal. Clearly, you have to look at the very broad trend of the distribution. For distributions based on only a small number of observations, say less than 100, any conclusions about the general shape have to be broad and tentative.

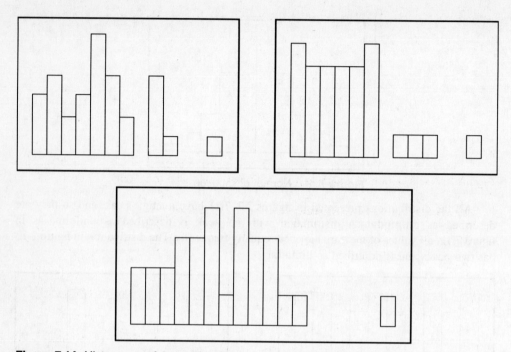

Figure 7.14 Histograms of 3 samples from a normal distribution ($n = 30$)

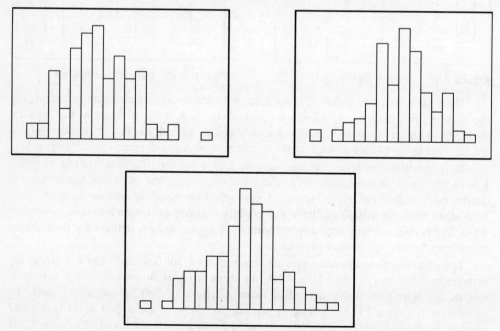

Figure 7.15 Histograms of 3 samples from a normal distribution ($n = 100$)

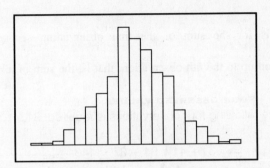

Figure 7.16 Histogram of a sample from a normal distribution ($n = 500$)

EXAMPLE 7.1   MANAGEMENT CAPACITY (continued)
The shape of the distribution of the 30 values of *Management test score*, as presented in figures 7.4 and 7.5, is probably best described as a flat, symmetric distribution.

7.3   Measures of central tendency for one unrestricted variable

Measures of central tendency or measures of location are used to obtain an estimate of the value about which observations tend to cluster. The two measures that we cover here are the mean and the median.

7.3.1   Mean

The **mean** can be described as the balance point of the data. That is, if we imagine that the dotplot for the observations consists of a weightless axis and that the dots are small balls of equal weight, the mean would correspond to the point at which the dotplot would balance.

The term *average* is often used synonymously for the *mean*. However, the mean is just one of several kinds of average and we will restrict ourselves to using the term *mean*. Strictly speaking, we should use the term *arithmetic mean* as there are several different means.

The mean is denoted by $\bar{y}$ and is calculated as

$$\bar{y} = \frac{\text{Sum of the observations}}{\text{Total number of observations}}$$

$$= \frac{\sum_{i=1}^{n} y_i}{n}$$

where $\sum_{i=1}^{n}$ stands for 'sum of the following with i going from 1 to n',

n stands for 'the total number of observations', and

y_i stands for 'the ith observation'.

Hence $\sum\limits_{i=1}^{n} y_i$ stands for the sum of the first observation, second observation, third observation and so on up to the nth observation; that is, the sum of all the observations.

EXAMPLE 7.2 FOUR OBSERVED VALUES

The mean of the following four observations is required: 31, 41, 34 and 37. The mean is:

$$\bar{y} = \frac{31 + 41 + 34 + 37}{4} = \frac{143}{4} = 35.75$$

EXAMPLE 7.1 MANAGEMENT CAPACITY (continued)

Suppose we want to determine the typical score of the 30 employees who took the management test. As before, one unrestricted variable, *Management test score*, is involved. The mean is a measure we can use to answer the question, and, using the values from table 7.1, the mean is 72.67.

Notes

1. The mean is easy to calculate and widely used, so people are generally familiar with it.
2. The mean is unduly influenced by outliers.
3. The mean has the advantage that a large number of statistical techniques are based on it.
4. The mean is most appropriately used for unrestricted variables whose distribution shape is symmetric.

7.3.2   Median

The **median** can be described as the middle value for the data; more precisely, the median (M) has as many values below it as above it. If n is the number of observations, the median will be the $\left(\frac{n+1}{2}\right)$th value in an ordered list of the data; the data can be arranged in ascending (or descending) order. Thus, to calculate the median, do the following:

1. Arrange the data in order.
2. Determine the position of the median, which is the $\left(\frac{n+1}{2}\right)$th value in the list of the ordered values.
3. If n is odd, $\left(\frac{n+1}{2}\right)$ is an integer and the median corresponds to an observed value; obtain the median by selecting the $\left(\frac{n+1}{2}\right)$th value from the ordered data.

   If n is even, $\left(\frac{n+1}{2}\right)$ is a number that ends in a half and the position of the median does not correspond to an observed value. Obtain the median by selecting, from the ordered list, the two observed values whose positions are closest to $\left(\frac{n+1}{2}\right)$ and computing the value halfway between them.

Note that $\left(\frac{n+1}{2}\right)$ is not the median itself, but merely the position of the median value. Also, since the stem-and-leaf display contains the data in ascending order, it might be used as the first step for calculating the median. However, this is possible only when the complete values can be reconstructed. That is, when the values are split so that there is only one digit to the right of the split-point.

EXAMPLE 7.2   FOUR OBSERVED VALUES (continued)

To obtain the median of 31, 41, 34, 37, reorder the observations into ascending order: 31, 34, 37, 41.

The position of the median in the ordered list is the $\left(\frac{4+1}{2}\right)$th = 2.5th value. Now, there is no actual observation corresponding to the middle value. To take the second value in the ordered list is not satisfactory as there is one value below it and two values above it. The third value is similarly inappropriate. It is the 2.5th value that is the middle value; there are two values below it and two values above it. To obtain the 2.5th value we must compute the value halfway between the second and third values. Thus the median is $34 + \frac{1}{2}(37 - 34) =$ 35.5. This can also be computed as the mean of the second and third values. That is, $(34 + 37)/2 = 35.5$.

EXAMPLE 7.1   MANAGEMENT CAPACITY (continued)

Obviously, the median can also be used to measure the typical score obtained by the company's employees. To compute the median of the 30 values of *Management test score*, the data must be arranged in ascending order, as in table 7.6. As 30 is an even number of observations, the median will be the mean of the values whose positions are closest to 15.5. It will be the mean of the 15th and 16th values. From table 7.6, the median is the mean of 73.8 and 74.2 = 74.

Table 7.6   Values of *Management test score* (in ascending order)

59.7	61.1	63.5	63.6	64.3	64.5	66.2	66.3	66.6	68.5
68.5	68.7	69.8	70.3	73.8	74.2	74.3	74.3	74.8	75.3
76.1	76.7	76.8	76.9	79.2	80.1	81.3	83.0	83.0	98.8

Note that the stem-and-leaf display cannot be used in this case because the complete values cannot be reconstructed from the display. There are two values to the right of the split-position and only one of these is taken to provide the leaf.

Notes

1. The median is not unbalanced by outliers.
2. The range of statistical techniques based on the median is not as large as that for the mean.
3. The median is most appropriately used for unrestricted variables whose distribution is skew in shape.

7.3.3   Choosing between the averages

Figure 7.17 illustrates the relationship between the mean and median for different distributions. That is, for symmetric distributions the mean and the median are equal; for a skew-to-the-left distribution the mean is less than the median; and the opposite is true for a skew to the right distribution. Of course, this reflects of the influence of outliers on the mean, but not the median, as noted previously.

Clearly, an unprincipled person might choose the measure that best suited their needs. For example, if the data is skew-to-the-right and as large a number as possible is required, the mean might be chosen. However, statisticians would suggest considering the points given in the notes when you choose an average. So for data that is skew-to-the-right, these points would lead you to reject the mean because it will not indicate accurately the typical value for the variable.

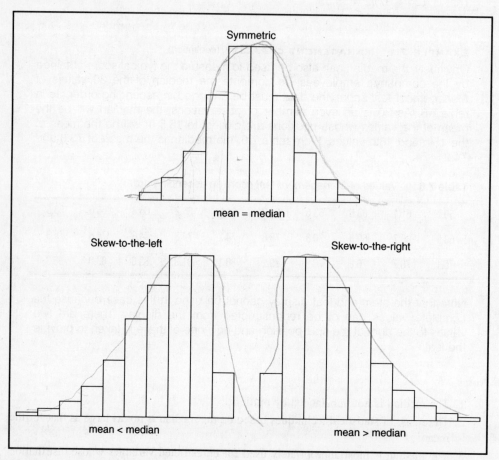

Figure 7.17 Relationship between averages for diffferent distributions

Indeed, you could argue that the median should be used always. After all, it is the preferred measure for skew distributions and gives the same answer as the mean does for symmetric distributions. However, it can be shown that for a symmetric distribution the mean is more precise than the median; for such distributions, the means for different samples vary less than the medians for the same samples do. Also, the measure of central tendency may be used as a basis for computing totals; the mean has the advantage of being directly related to the total. Consequently, we recommend that you use the mean when the distribution seems symmetric, and use the median when the distribution seems to be skew.

Sometimes it is difficult to decide if the distribution is skew or symmetric. As discussed in section 7.2, *Distribution attributes*, a large number of observations is generally required before you can be confident of describing a distribution's shape correctly. One rule that is sometimes suggested for deciding the distribution shape is to look at the difference between the mean and the median. However, this is not reliable as even for symmetric distributions the two are rarely exactly equal. So it becomes a matter of deciding how different they must be before you can conclude that the distribution is skew. We suggest that you take a very broad view of the distribution and do not become distracted by the aberrant behaviour of a very few observations.

An everyday example of where the median is usually preferred to the mean is house prices: their distribution tends to be skew-to-the-right because the number of more expensive homes tends to be lower.

EXAMPLE 7.1   MANAGEMENT CAPACITY (continued)

The question that has been investigated in this section is: what is the typical score obtained by the 30 employees who were given the management test? To answer this, the mean and median have been computed and the values obtained are in table 7.7. Which of these measures should be used in this case? From the distribution diagrams in section 7.1, *Distribution of one unrestricted variable*, the distribution seems essentially symmetric with a single value rather larger than the rest. However, contrary to what you might expect, the median is larger than the mean. The single large observation does not seem to have had sufficient effect on the mean to inflate it. Since the distribution is basically symmetric, the mean is the preferred measure of central tendency. That is, the typical score achieved by the employees is just under 73.

Table 7.7   Measures of central tendency for *Management test score*

Mean	72.67
Median	74.00

7.4   Measures of dispersion for one unrestricted variable

Measures of dispersion measure the spread exhibited by the data. The measures we will look at are:

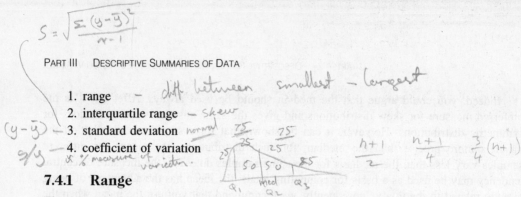

$$S = \sqrt{\frac{\sum (y - \bar{y})^2}{N - 1}}$$

1. range — *diff between smallest – largest*
2. interquartile range — *skew*
3. standard deviation — *normal*
4. coefficient of variation

$(y - \bar{y})$

$s/\bar{y}$ *% measure of variation.*

$\dfrac{n+1}{2}$ $\dfrac{n+1}{4}$ $\dfrac{3}{4}(n+1)$

7.4.1   Range

The **range** is simply the maximum value minus the minimum value.

> **EXAMPLE 7.1   MANAGEMENT CAPACITY** (continued)
>
> The minimum and maximum values for *Management test score* (from table 7.6) are 59.7 and 98.8, respectively. Hence,
>
> $$Range = 98.8 - 59.7 = 39.1$$
>
> That is, the scores cover a range of just under 40 points. However, note that the value of the range will be reduced to just 23.3 if the outlying maximum value is excluded.

Notes

1. The range is a simple, intuitively obvious measure.
2. It is affected badly by outliers since one outlier greatly increases the range, as shown by example 7.1, *Management capacity*.
3. It does not take into account the distribution of the data between the maximum and minimum values. The observed values may be evenly spread between maximum and minimum or be largely concentrated over only a small part of the whole range between the minimum and maximum. As long as the minimum and maximum are the same, the range will not change.
4. For the reasons outlined in 1–3, the range can be quite misleading, so it should be used only as a rough guide of the spread of the data.

7.4.2   Interquartile range

The **interquartile range** (IQR) is given by

$$IQR = Q3 - Q1$$

where $Q1$ is the **first quartile** or the value that has 25% of the observations below it; the position of the first quartile is half that of the median and so it is the $\left(\frac{n+1}{4}\right)$th value in an ordered list of the observed values;

$Q3$ is the **third quartile** or the value that has 75% of the observations below it; the position of the third quartile is half that of the median on from the median and so it is the $\left(\frac{3(n+1)}{4}\right)$th value in an ordered list of the observed values.

The quartiles resemble the median in that they all correspond to the value in a particular position in the ordered data, but they differ in their positions.The interquartile range gives the range covered by the middle 50% of the data. That is, any outliers at either end will be excluded.

EXAMPLE 7.1   MANAGEMENT CAPACITY (continued)

For *Management test score*, the position of the first quartile is $\left(\frac{30+1}{4}\right)$ = 7.75 and of the third quartile is $\left(\frac{3(30+1)}{4}\right)$ = 23.25. From table 7.6, the 7th and 8th values in an ordered list are 66.2 and 66.3. Hence, the first quartile is three-quarters of the distance from 66.2 to 66.3, which is 66.2 + $\frac{3}{4}$(66.3 − 66.2) = 66.275. Also, the 23rd and 24th values in an ordered list are 76.8 and 76.9. The third quartile is a quarter of the distance from 76.8 to 76.9 which is 76.8 + $\frac{1}{4}$(76.9 − 76.8) = 76.825. Thus, the interquartile range is 76.825 − 66.275 = 10.55. That is, the middle 50% of the scores cover a range of 10.55 points.

Notes

1. The interquartile range is a straightforward measure.
2. It is unaffected by outliers since these are in the excluded quartiles.
3. Few statistical techniques are based on the interquartile range.
4. It is the appropriate measure of dispersion when the median is used to measure central tendency; that is, when the data is skew.

7.4.3   Standard deviation and variance

To calculate the standard deviation, the **variance** is computed first. Then, the **standard deviation** is the square root of the variance. That is,

$$s = \text{standard deviation} = \sqrt{\text{variance}}$$

The variance is calculated from the following formula:

$$s^2 = \text{variance}$$

$$= \frac{\textbf{sum of squares of the deviations from the mean}}{\textbf{degrees of freedom}}$$

$$= \frac{\sum_{i=1}^{n}(y_1 - \bar{y})^2}{n - 1}$$

where $(y_i - \bar{y})$ means the deviation of an observation from the mean of all the observations;

degrees of freedom is the number of independent deviations (often, it equals $n - 1$ or the number of observations minus one).

The unit of the standard deviation is the same as for the original data; thus, if the original data is in grams then so is the standard deviation. This gives it an advantage over the variance whose unit is the square of that of the original data; so the variance is in grams² if the original data is in grams.

The standard deviation can be interpreted loosely as the 'average' absolute deviation from the mean; that is, the distance from the mean, regardless of whether the observations are above or below the mean. For symmetric distributions, the pattern of deviations below the mean will be the same as the pattern above the mean. However, for skew distributions, there will be more and smaller deviations on one side of the mean.

It can be proven that *at least* 75% of observations fall within two standard deviations of the mean, irrespective of the distribution of the data. More precise interpretations can be made for particular distributions. For example, for data whose distribution can be described as normal and for which sufficient observations are available, it is expected that:

1. $66\frac{2}{3}\%$ of observations will fall within the range covered by ±1 one standard deviation around the mean;
2. 95% of observations will fall within the range covered by ±2 standard deviations around the mean;
3. 99.7% of observations will fall within the range covered by ±3 standard deviations around the mean.

EXAMPLE 7.3   HOUSE SAMPLES FROM TWO LOCALITIES

For the selling prices of a simple random sample of 10 houses from each of two localities, we want to determine if the spread in the sampled prices is the same for each locality. The raw, primary data for the unrestricted variable, *Selling price*, appears in table 7.8, which also gives the computations for the standard deviations for the two localities.

First, examine the computations for locality A. The deviations of the observations from the mean are calculated by subtracting the mean from each of the observations. For the first observation, the deviation is $267\,000 - $201\,000 = $66\,000$. It can be mathematically proven that these deviations must sum to zero. Consequently, once you have nine deviations, you can work out the tenth. It must be minus the sum of the first nine. So there are only nine independent deviations.

The formula for the variance indicates that once the deviations are obtained, they have to be squared and then summed to yield the sum of squares of the deviations. The deviations are squared to remove the sign. The sum of squares of the deviations is divided by the number of independent deviations. This result might be loosely termed the 'average of the squared deviations'.

Finally, the standard deviation is obtained by taking the square root of the variance, thereby compensating for squaring the deviations. The standard deviation is now in the same units as the observations — that is, in dollars. The observed value of the standard deviation for locality A indicates that the observations in this locality are typically $74\,613 from the mean.

Turning to locality B, note that the means ($\bar{y}$ s) for the two localities are exactly equal. That is, overall the average selling prices of the houses are the same for the two localities. But is the spread in the prices the same? To get some idea, look at the deviations. The deviations for locality B seem to be generally smaller than those for locality A. That is, the observations seem to be less spread because they are generally closer to the mean. This is borne out by the value obtained for the standard deviation which turns out to be $30 598. That is, the prices in locality B are, on average, about half the distance from the mean compared to the prices from locality A.

Table 7.8   Computation of standard deviations for *Selling price* from two localities

Locality A		Locality B	
Selling price ($)	Deviation ($)	*Selling price* ($)	Deviation ($)
267 000	66 000	151 000	−50 000
155 000	−46 000	244 000	43 000
172 000	−29 000	181 000	−20 000
305 000	104 000	204 000	3 000
192 000	−9 000	190 000	−11 000
129 000	−72 000	199 000	−2 000
119 000	−82 000	214 000	13 000
332 000	131 000	230 000	29 000
149 000	−52 000	163 000	−38 000
190 000	−11 000	234 000	33 000
$\bar{y} = 201\,000$		$\bar{y} = 201\,000$	

$$s^2 = \frac{66\,000^2 + (-46\,000)^2 + \ldots + (-11\,000)^2}{10 - 1}$$

$$= \frac{50\,104\,000\,000}{9}$$

$$= 5\,567\,111\,111$$

$$s = \sqrt{5\,567\,111\,111}$$

$$= 74\,613$$

$$s^2 = \frac{(-50\,000)^2 + 43\,000^2 + \ldots + 33\,000^2}{10 - 1}$$

$$= \frac{8\,426\,000\,000}{9}$$

$$= 936\,222\,222$$

$$s = \sqrt{936\,222\,222}$$

$$= 30\,598$$

Locality B shows that a set of relatively similar values leads to a smaller standard deviation. Indeed if all observations were exactly equal, the mean would equal this value, the deviations would all be zero, and so the standard deviation would be zero.

In summary, the two sets of selling prices have the same level or mean but have a different spread.

EXAMPLE 7.1   MANAGEMENT CAPACITY (continued)

For *Management test score*, s = 8.18. That is, the scores are typically about 8.18 from the mean of 72.67. The range that covers two standard deviations either side of the mean is (56.31, 89.03). It includes all but one observation; that is, it includes 29/30 = 0.97 or 97% of the observations, which is not very different from the 95% expected for normally distributed data.

Notes

1. The standard deviation is more difficult to calculate than the range, but calculators and computers remove this disadvantage.
2. It is the most commonly used measure of dispersion.
3. All the observations are involved in calculating it.
4. The smallest value it can take is zero; it cannot be negative. It has the same units as the observations do.
5. It is affected by outliers, but not as badly as the range.
6. It is the appropriate measure to use when mean is used to measure central tendency. Like the mean, it has the advantage that many statistical techniques are based on it.
7. You need a reasonable number of values (say >10) to get a reliable value.
8. Be careful in computing the standard deviation when the mean of the data is very close to zero, as the value for the standard deviation may be computed as zero even though it cannot be, since the observations differ.

7.4.4   Coefficient of variation

The **coefficient of variation** (*CV*) measures the spread in a set of numbers, as a percentage of the mean. Its formula is

$$CV = \frac{s}{\bar{y}} \times 100$$

EXAMPLE 7.1   MANAGEMENT CAPACITY (continued)

For *Management test score*

$$CV = \frac{8.18}{72.67} \times 100$$
$$= 11.26\%$$

That is, the spread in the scores is about ±11.26% of the mean.

EXAMPLE 7.3   HOUSE SAMPLES FROM TWO LOCALITIES (continued)

The coefficients of variation for *Selling price* from localities A and B are 37.12% and 15.22%, respectively. The difference between the coefficients of variation exactly mirrors the difference in standard deviation in this case, because the means are exactly equal. That is, the coefficient of variation has no advantage over the standard deviation for this example.

Notes

1. The coefficient of variation is independent of the unit of measurement. Thus, converting measurements in inches to measurements in metres will not change the coefficient of variation.

2. It is related to the standard deviation but is easier to remember as it is a percentage.

3. When the standard deviation is proportional to the mean, the coefficient of variation gives a constant value. This usually happens when observations cover a wide range (say, maximum = 3 × minimum). That is, variances tend to be large for larger numbers and a comparison of standard deviations is not informative.

EXAMPLE 7.4   ANNUAL RATE OF RETURN ON INVESTMENT

A study is made of the return on investments of various types over a 5-year period. The mean and standard deviation of the return on investments over a 5-year period are determined for each type, and we want to compare the spread in returns for the different types to see how consistently the investment type can achieve its mean rate of return. In particular, the coefficient of variation is to be used because it measures this consistency in proportion to the magnitude of the rate of return. The data for four types of investment is in table 7.9; it is secondary data obtained from a published article.

The question to be investigated is: does the spread in investment return over a 5-year period differ between the investment types when this spread is being measured as a percentage of the mean level of return? The variables involved are *Annual rate of return* and *Investment type* — an unrestricted and a limited variable, respectively. With such a combination of variables, the example does not fit into this chapter, but is presented here to show you that the coefficient of variation can be constant.

The coefficients of variation in table 7.9 indicate that the variability in *Annual rate of return* on investments is about 90% of the mean *Annual rate of return*. This approximately constant value for the coefficient of variation occurs in spite of large differences in the means and standard deviations for *Annual rate of return*.

Table 7.9   Annual rate of return on investment over a
5-year period

Investment type	Mean *Annual rate of return* (%)	Standard deviation (%)	Coefficient of variation (%)
Art	20.7	16.9	82
Government bonds	10.8	9.4	87
S & P 500	13.2	11.9	90
Foreign bonds	15.4	16.3	106

Source: abstracted from Dilmore and Wilson (1992)

7.4.5   Choosing between measures of dispersion

The coefficient of variation is a specific purpose measure of dispersion. Since the range cannot be recommended, the choice of measures of dispersion for general use is between the interquartile range and standard deviation. The points outlined above indicate that you should use the interquartile range when you choose the median to measure central tendency; that is, when the distribution of the data is skew in shape. Similarly, use the standard deviation when the mean is more appropriate than the median; that is, when the distribution of the data is symmetric.

One implication of using only the standard deviation to measure dispersion for symmetric data is that the size of the deviations, used in computing it, would be approximately the same on both sides of the mean for this data.

EXAMPLE 7.1   MANAGEMENT CAPACITY (continued)

The question that has been investigated in this section is: what is the spread in the scores obtained by the 30 employees who were given the management test? The four competing measures of dispersion have been computed and the values obtained are in table 7.10. As with measures of central tendency, the issue here is: which of the four measures of dispersion should be used? Again, the data requires a general measure, rather than a specific one, so the coefficient of variation is not appropriate. Our choice is between the standard deviation and the interquartile range. In our consideration of measures of central tendency, we concluded that the distribution is essentially symmetric and that the mean should be used, so the measure of dispersion to use is the standard deviation. That is, the scores are typically about 8.18 points from the mean.

Table 7.10   Measures of dispersion for *Management test score*

Range	39.1
Interquartile range	10.55
Standard deviation	8.18
Coefficient of variation	11.26%

7.5   Diagram for illustrating central tendency and dispersion for one unrestricted variable

Box-and-whisker plot

The **box-and-whisker plot** is a particularly useful diagram for illustrating the central tendency and dispersion for unrestricted variables. It uses five measures that have now been covered: the minimum and maximum values, the first and third quartiles and the median. There is no commonly used equivalent to the box-and-whisker plot constructed using the mean and standard deviation. However, the boxplot can be used even if the distribution is symmetric, as the different measures of central tendency and dispersion lead to essentially the same conclusions.

The ends of the box correspond to the first and third quartiles, so that the width of the box is equal to the interquartile range or range that includes 50% of the observations; a '+' is placed in the box at a position corresponding to the middle of the data or median; the whiskers, on either side of the box, go from the end of the box to the minimum or maximum value obtained after outliers are excluded. The whiskers indicate the range covered by the 25% of the observations at either end. An observation is designated as a **possible outlier** if it is more than $1.5 \times IQR$ below the first quartile or above the third quartile. It is plotted with a '*'. If the observation is more than $3.0 \times IQR$ below the first quartile or above the third quartile, it is designated as a **probable outlier** and is plotted with an 'O'.

EXAMPLE 7.1   MANAGEMENT CAPACITY (continued)
The box-and-whisker plot for the values of *Management test score* is presented in figure 7.18, which shows that the median is about 74 and the interquartile range is about 10. There is a possible outlier corresponding to an individual who scored close to 100.

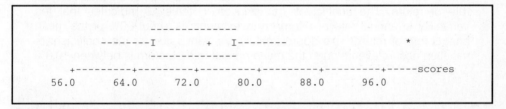

Figure 7.18   Box-and-whisker plot for *Management test score*

This diagram is most useful for indicating the point of central tendency, the spread in the data and whether or not there are outliers. Although some recommend using it to assess the general shape of a distribution, we advise against this because the rules used for determining the shape from it can be misleading, particularly if there are insufficient observations.

7.6   Reports on examples

The following reports for the examples analysed in this chapter indicate what material from a statistical analysis an investigator should include in a report. In general, the details of the statistical analysis are omitted so that the reader of the report can concentrate on the results.

EXAMPLE 7.1   MANAGEMENT CAPACITY — REPORT
A company assessed the management capacity of 30 of its employees with a test that yields a score between 0 and 100 for each employee. The 30 scores display an approximately symmetric distribution, as illustrated in figure 7.3. The

employees' mean score is 72.7, and the scores are typically 8.2 points above or below the mean. One employee obtained a score of 98.8 points, which is somewhat higher than the others.

EXAMPLE 7.2   FOUR OBSERVED VALUES — REPORT

The mean of the four observed values is 35.8 and the median is 35.5.

EXAMPLE 7.3   HOUSE SAMPLES FROM TWO LOCALITIES — REPORT

The selling prices for a simple random sample of 10 houses from each of two localities are obtained. Although the average selling price in both localities is $201 000, the prices from locality A are more spread than those from locality B; the observations from locality A are typically $74 613 from the mean whereas those from locality B are only $30 598 from the mean.

EXAMPLE 7.4   ANNUAL RATE OF RETURN ON INVESTMENT — REPORT

A study is made of the return made by various types of investment over a 5-year period. For four types of investment, the spread in the annual rate of return over a 5-year period was measured as a percentage of the mean annual rate of return. The coefficients of variation in table 7.9 indicates that the variability in annual rate of return on investments is about 90% of the mean annual rate of return. This approximately constant value for the coefficient of variation occurs even though the mean annual rate of return is between 10.8% and 20.7%.

7.7   Using Minitab to produce descriptive summaries for one unrestricted variable

This section describes the Minitab commands for producing the frequency table and histogram, stem-and-leaf display, dotplots, boxplots, and measures of central tendency and dispersion for one unrestricted variable. The polygons and high-resolution dotplots can be produced in a spreadsheet package.

7.7.1   Distribution tables and distribution diagrams

To produce the frequency table and histogram in Minitab, use the *histogram* command. This command produces just the frequencies for the class intervals and a histogram based on these frequencies; it does not produce the proportions or percentages in either the table or the diagram. The class intervals to be used in the frequency table and histogram can be specified by using the *start* and *increment* subcommands of the *histogram* command. The *start* subcommand specifies the midpoint of the first class interval and the *increment* subcommand specifies the size of the class interval.

To produce the stem-and-leaf display in Minitab, use the *stem* command. To modify the number of lines per stem, use the *increment* subcommand of the *stem* command. The *increment* subcommand specifies the difference between the smallest possible values on two consecutive lines of the stem-and-leaf display.

To produce the dotplot or boxplot in Minitab, use the *dotplot* or *boxplot* command, respectively.

EXAMPLE 7.1   MANAGEMENT CAPACITY (continued)

A Minitab worksheet contains the 30 management test scores in a column named *scores*. The set of commands producing the distributions and diagrams for this data is as follows:

```
MTB > outfile 'a:\manscore.lis'
MTB > retrieve 'a:\manscore.mtp';
SUBC> portable.          ᴗₒᵣ ꜰ:\
MTB > info
MTB > histogram 'scores'
MTB > histogram 'scores';
SUBC> start 57.5;        ── defines the axis
SUBC> increment 5.
MTB > stem 'scores'
MTB > stem 'scores';
SUBC> increment 10.
MTB > dotplot 'scores'
MTB > boxplot 'scores'
                          57.5  62.5
```

If your version of Minitab has pull-down menus and you want to use them, table 7.11 lists the menus and options that access the required commands. Appendix D, *Detailed instructions for Minitab menus*, explains how to use the menus.

Table 7.11   Menus and options for Minitab commands to produce diagrams for one unrestricted variable

Minitab command	Menu	Option
outfile	File >	Other Files > Start Recording Session...
retrieve	File >	Open Worksheet...
port		Minitab portable worksheet
info	Edit >	Get Worksheet Info...
	(Edit >	Data Screen [Alt-D])
histogram	Graph >	Histogram...
stem	Graph >	Stem and Leaf...
dotplot	Graph >	Dotplot...
boxplot	Graph >	Boxplot...

The output from the initial commands to retrieve the worksheet and check its contents is as follows:

```
MTB > retrieve 'a:\manscore.mtp';
SUBC> portable.

Worksheet retrieved from file: a:\manscore.mtp
MTB > info

COLUMN      NAME          COUNT
C1          scores           30
C2          scoreall         87
C3          branch           87


CONSTANTS USED: NONE
```

Frequency tables and distribution diagrams

EXAMPLE 7.1   MANAGEMENT CAPACITY (continued)

The command for producing the frequency table and histogram for *Management test score* (see table 7.2 and figure 7.1, respectively), and the associated output, are as follows. The data is in a column named *scores*.

```
MTB > histogram 'scores'

Histogram of scores    N = 30

Midpoint       Count
      60           2    **
      65           7    *******
      70           5    *****
      75          10    **********
      80           3    ***
      85           2    **
      90           0
      95           0
     100           1    *
```

The class interval size for this table and diagram is the difference between consecutive midpoints; that is, the class intervals are 5 points in width.

For this example, a second histogram was produced with different class intervals; the revised histogram is shown in figure 7.4. To produce this histogram, use the *start* and *increment* subcommands of the *histogram* command. To obtain a histogram with class intervals of 55–60, 60–65 and so on, specify a starting midpoint of 57.5 and an increment of 5. The commands, and resulting output, are as follows:

```
MTB > histogram 'scores';
SUBC> start 57.5;
SUBC> increment 5.

Histogram of scores    N = 30

Midpoint      Count
  57.50         1      *
  62.50         5      *****
  67.50         7      *******
  72.50         6      ******
  77.50         6      ******
  82.50         4      ****
  87.50         0
  92.50         0
  97.50         1      *
```

Stem-and-leaf displays

EXAMPLE 7.1   MANAGEMENT CAPACITY (continued)

The command to produce the stem-and-leaf display for *Management test score* (see table 7.5), and the associated output, are as follows. The data is in a column named *scores*.

```
MTB > stem 'scores'


Stem-and-leaf of scores    N = 30
Leaf Unit = 1.0


    1        5   9
    6        6   13344
   13        6   6668889
  (6)        7   034444
   11        7   566669
    5        8   0133
    1        8
    1        9
    1        9   8
```

Minitab has produced a column extra to those in table 7.5. This first column gives the cumulative number of leaves or observations on the lines of the display, beginning from both ends until the median line — that line with the middle value — is reached. The median line is indicated by enclosing in parentheses the number of leaves in that line. For the example, the median line is the first line of the stem 7 and it contains 6 observations as indicated by the (6). As indicated by the entries in the first column, there are 13 leaves on the lines above the median line and 11 leaves on those lines below the median line.

The stem-and-leaf produced by Minitab had two lines per stem. To produce a stem-and-leaf display with one line per stem, as in table 7.4, use the *increment* subcommand of the *stem* subcommand. Since the leaf unit is 1.0 on the stem-and-leaf display in the output above, an increment of 10 would be required for a display with one line per stem. The *stem* command with an *increment* subcommand of 10 and its associated output are as follows:

```
MTB > stem 'scores';
SUBC> increment 10.

Stem-and-leaf of scores    N = 30
Leaf Unit = 1.0

    1     5   9
   13     6   133446668889
  (12)    7   034444566669
    5     8   0133
    1     9   8
```

Dotplot and boxplot

EXAMPLE 7.1   MANAGEMENT CAPACITY (continued)
The commands to produce the dotplot and box-and-whisker plot for *Management test score* (see figures 7.6 and 7.18) values, and the associated output, are given as follows. The data is in a column named *scores*.

```
MTB > dotplot 'scores'

                       .   .          .  .
              ..  ... .   ...      .....  ..  .                          .
         +---------+---------+---------+---------+---------+-------scores
      56.0       64.0      72.0      80.0      88.0      96.0

MTB > boxplot 'scores'

                      --------------
             --------I         +   I--------                    *
                      --------------
         +---------+---------+---------+---------+---------+-----scores
      56.0       64.0      72.0      80.0      88.0      96.0
```

7.7.2   Measures of central tendency and dispersion

Many of the measures of central tendency and dispersion can be computed by using Minitab's *describe* and *let* commands. If you have a set of numbers and you require these statistics, put the numbers in a column of the Minitab worksheet. Then use the *describe* and *let* commands to compute the measures. You can also produce the box-and-whisker plot by using the *boxplot* command.

The measures produced by the *describe* command are the mean, median, standard deviation, minimum and maximum values and the quartiles. The range, interquartile range and coefficient of variation can be computed from quantities output by the *describe* command; this can be done with the *let* command or a calculator.

A particular point that arises with using the *let* command is that the results of *let* commands are stored by Minitab, so you must specify where they are to be stored. Further, in this instance, the *let* command is being used to compute a single value from a set of values. Minitab has available *constants* for storing single number results, and these are named *k1*, *k2* and so on up to *k100*. Minitab presets *k98* to the missing value code *, *k99* to the natural number $e = 2.718...$, and *k100* to $\pi = 3.14159...$

EXAMPLE 7.1   MANAGEMENT CAPACITY (continued)

Assume that the Minitab worksheet containing the 30 values of *Management test score* has been previously retrieved and that the data is stored in a column named *scores*. The commands (including the *describe* and *let* commands) for producing the measures of central tendency and dispersion for this data are as follows:

```
MTB > describe 'scores'
MTB > let k1=98.80-59.70
MTB > let k2=76.83-66.28
MTB > let k3=8.18/72.67*100
MTB > print k1-k3
```

If your version of Minitab has pull-down menus and you want to use them, table 7.12 lists the menus and options that access the required commands. Appendix D, *Detailed instructions for Minitab menus*, explains how to use the menus.

Table 7.12   Menus and options for Minitab commands to produce measures of central tendency and dispersion

Minitab command	Menu	Option
describe	Stat >	Basic Statistics > Descriptive Statistics...
let	Calc >	Functions and Statistics > General Expressions...
print	Edit >	Display Data...

The output produced by the commands outlined above is as follows:

```
MTB > describe 'scores'

               N     MEAN   MEDIAN   TRMEAN   STDEV   SEMEAN
scores        30    72.67    74.00    72.22    8.18     1.49

              MIN      MAX       Q1       Q3
scores      59.70    98.80    66.28    76.83

MTB > let k1=98.80-59.70
MTB > let k2=76.83-66.28
MTB > let k3=8.18/72.67*100
MTB > print k1-k3
K1          39.1000
K2          10.5500
K3          11.2564
```

In this output, the mean and median are given in the *describe* output, simply labelled as MEAN and MEDIAN. The standard deviation is the number under the heading STDEV, the minimum and maximum values are under the headings MIN and MAX, and the first and third quartiles are under the headings Q1 and Q3. The three *let* commands, following the *describe* output, produce the range, interquartile range and coefficient of variation, respectively; hence, these are stored in *k1, k2* and *k3*, respectively.

7.8   Chapter summary

A frequency table is used to examine the pattern in the observed values of an unrestricted variable. The table may contain either the frequencies, proportions or percentages, or some combination of these for the class intervals in the table. The information in the frequency table is presented graphically in the form of a histogram or polygon based on either the frequencies, proportions or percentages. Proportions or percentages are usually preferred to frequencies as they are more readily interpretable, particularly if distributions are to be compared.

The stem-and-leaf display is an alternative combined distribution table and diagram. It has the advantage that it retains more detail about the original data, and the disadvantage that it is based on frequencies. The dotplot is another distribution diagram, mainly used when there are too few observations to construct a meaningful frequency table and diagram.

In examining the distribution attributes for an unrestricted variable, the key aspects you should focus on are the general shape, central tendency, and dispersion of the distribution and the presence of outliers.

The most common shapes include the unimodal shapes of symmetric, skew-to-the-left and skew-to-the-right distributions; less frequently you might encounter a distribution with two peaks, called a bimodal distribution, or one with no peaks, called a uniform distribution. The normal distribution is a particular symmetric distribution that is described as bell-shaped. The only possible difference between two normal distributions is in their mean and standard deviation.

When judging the shape of the distribution, you have to look at the very broad trend in the distribution. For distributions based on only a few observations, say less than 100, your conclusions about the general shape can only be broad and tentative. Also, bear in mind that the apparent shape of the distribution can change if the class intervals are modified, particularly when only a few observations are available.

The measures of central tendency covered are the mean and median. We recommended using the mean when you think the distribution is symmetric, and the median if you believe the distribution is skew.

The measures of dispersion covered are the range, interquartile range, standard deviation and coefficient of variation. We suggested using the interquartile range when the median is appropriate for measuring central tendency; that is, when the distribution of the data is skew in shape. Similarly, use the standard deviation when the mean is more appropriate than the median; that is, when the distribution of the data is symmetric. We advised against using the range generally, and described the coefficient of variation as a specific purpose measure of dispersion.

The box-and-whisker plot is a diagram that is particularly useful for illustrating the central tendency and dispersion for unrestricted variables.

7.9   Key terms

- bimodal distribution
- box-and-whisker plot (or boxplot)
- central tendency
- class interval in a frequency table
- class midpoint in a frequency table
- coefficient of variation (CV)
- degrees of freedom
- deviation from the mean ($y_1 - \bar{y}$)
- dispersion
- distribution attributes
- distribution diagram
- distribution table
- dotplot
- first quartile ($Q1$)
- frequency table
- general shape
- histogram
- interquartile range (IQR)
- leaf
- leaf unit
- mean ($\bar{y}$)
- measure of central tendency
- measure of dispersion
- median (M)
- normal distribution
- outlier
- polygon
- possible outlier
- probable outlier
- range
- skew-to-the-left distribution
- skew-to-the-right distribution
- split-point
- standard deviation (s)
- stem
- stem-and-leaf display
- sum of squares
- symmetric distribution
- third quartile ($Q3$)
- unimodal distribution
- variance

7.10 Exercises

7.1 (a) In your own words explain the following terms: class interval in a frequency table; histogram; frequency polygon.

(b) What are the differences between a histogram and a frequency polygon?

(c) What information can be obtained from these distribution diagrams?

7.2 In your own words explain the following terms:

(a) general shape of a distribution
(b) measure of central tendency
(c) measure of dispersion
(d) standard deviation
(e) variance
(f) coefficient of variation

(g) outlier
(h) skewness of a distribution
(i) symmetric distribution
(j) normal distribution
(k) bimodal distribution

7.3 What shape would you expect to see in a distribution diagram showing the distribution of:

(a) the selling price of a house?
(b) the height of students studying accountancy at a university?
(c) the duration of transactions made by a teller in a savings bank?
(d) the number of shares held in an investment company?

7.4 At the end of each semester the results from several assessment items are combined to form a mark out of 100 for each student. This mark is converted to a grade by using the scheme in table 7.13. The final results for one group of Statistics students are summarised in figures 7.19 and 7.20. Use these distribution diagrams to examine the students' grade distribution.

Table 7.13 Scheme for converting marks to grades

Grade	Notation	%
High Distinction	HD	85 – 100
Distinction	D	75 – 84
Credit	C	65 – 74
Pass Level 1	P1	55 – 64
Pass Level 2	P2	50 – 54
Fail Level 1	F1	40 – 49
Fail Level 2	F2	Below 40

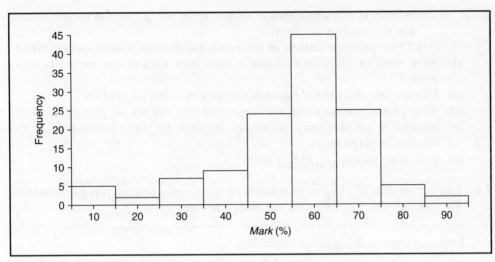

Figure 7.19   Distribution of *Marks* for a group of Statistics students

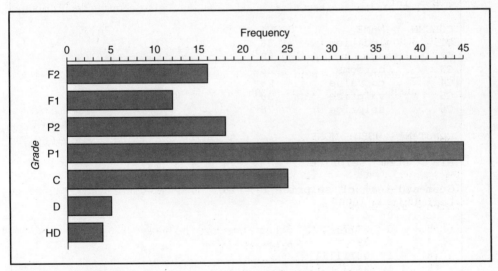

Figure 7.20   Distribution of *Grades* for a group of Statistics students

For each diagram:
(a) Answer the following questions:
   (i) What is the question to be investigated (including the group to which the conclusions apply)?
   (ii) What variable(s) are we concerned with here?
   (iii) What type of variable(s) are they?
   (iv) Which major category of statistical procedure applies here? Why?

      (v) What type of statistic should we use, given the question to be investigated and the variables involved?

      (vi) Which particular statistic or procedure, and diagram, should we use? Why?

(b) What types of distribution diagrams have been used to summarise the class results?

(c) Do these two distribution diagrams represent the same information?

(d) What general features of the distribution of *Marks* can you see in the histograms?

(e) Identify, if possible, any differences between the two distributions in the distribution diagrams.

(f) How many students received a credit?

7.5 Information on a set of home units has been stored in the Minitab portable worksheet file *homeunit.mtp*. Reproduce the following computer output.

```
MTB > retrieve 'a:\homeunit.mtp';
SUBC> portable.

Worksheet retrieved from file: a:\homeunit.mtp
MTB > info

COLUMN     NAME          COUNT
C1         location        28
C2         age             28
C3         norooms         28
C4         capvalue        28
C5         valprice        28
C6         selprice        28


CONSTANTS USED: NONE


MTB > stem 'selprice'

Stem-and-leaf of selprice  N = 28
Leaf Unit = 10000
     1     0  4
     5     0  6777
     7     0  89
    (8)    1  00111111
    13     1  2333
     9     1  4555
     5     1  777
     2     1
     2     2
     2     2  3
     1     2
     1     2
     1     2
     1     3  0
```

Examine the distribution of the *Selling price* for the set of home units and answer the following questions:

(a) What type of distribution diagram is used?

(b) What information can you obtain from this diagram?

(c) If you had to change the number of lines per stem in the display, how would you do this with Minitab? How would this affect the stem-and-leaf display?

(d) What does the column of figures on the lefthand side of the distribution diagram represent?

7.6 Table 7.14 contains the values of *Age* for the 28 home units whose *Selling price* was analysed in exercise 7.5. This data is also saved in the Minitab portable worksheet file *homeunit.mtp*.

Table 7.14   *Age* (years) of home units

32	9	9	22
24	94	24	14
16	25	20	19
28	19	22	19
26	108	20	69
29	22	21	24
33	20	21	17

Investigate the attributes of the *Age* distribution for these home units. Give a report, which includes an appropriate distribution diagram, to summarise the results of your investigation.

7.7 In an effort to minimise overhead costs, the State Cabinet decided to merge two government departments. The merger produced a surplus of administrative accounting staff in the payroll, finance and purchasing departments. To rationalise the staff quota, management offered special redundancy packages to encourage voluntary termination of employment.

The human resources manager had the task of advising management about what package to offer, and which types of employees to target. He advised reducing staff in the affected areas by 15%. To achieve this strategy, he directed his staff to prepare profiles of all employees who had service records of at least 10 years.

The records of *Length of service* in table 7.15 were obtained to examine the distribution of *Length of service*. The data has been saved in the Minitab portable worksheet file *lenserv.mtp*.

Table 7.15   *Length of service* (years)

33	41	11	15	42	33	30
37	39	20	41	15	15	44
14	23	35	10	22	32	36
32	13	30	22	12	26	27
23	22	10	14	13	37	15
45	16	31	11	15	11	32
11	10	12	19	23	33	19
24	24	11	28	39	28	15
12	23	24	39	20	14	16
28	11	23	17	28	23	13
17	34	12	21	25	20	39
10	17	16	19	40	11	25
27	23	10	26	10	23	39
36	18	34	17	17	41	17
10	16	26	38	26	10	16
20	21	15	12	37	19	22
26	15	23	27	10	22	33
34	11	35	32	17	19	14
28	13	10	11	30	13	19
16	20	15	14	36	22	21

(a) Answer the following questions:
  (i) What is the question to be investigated (including the group to which the conclusions apply)?
  (ii) What variable(s) are we concerned with here?
  (iii) What type of variable(s) are they?
  (iv) Which major category of statistical procedure applies? Why?
  (v) What type of statistic should we use, given the question to be investigated and the variables involved?
  (vi) Which particular statistic or procedure, and diagram, should we use? Why?
(b) Describe the distribution of *Length of service*.
(c) What is the typical value of the employees' *Length of service*?
(d) What percentage of staff have been employed by the government for more than 20 years?
(e) Prepare a summary of this data for the human resources manager.

7.8   The manager of a firm of accountants records the *Number of days absent* in the last year, for each of 25 employees, to characterise the numbers of days absent. The data is given in table 7.16.

Table 7.16   Number of days absent

2	3	6	2	6
5	2	5	0	5
0	7	5	5	7
2	2	4	5	4
2	4	4	3	3

(a) Answer the following questions:
   (i) What is the question to be investigated (including the group to which the conclusions apply)?
   (ii) What variable(s) are we concerned with here?
   (iii) What type of variable(s) are they?
   (iv) Which major category of statistical procedure applies here? Why?
   (v) What type of statistic should we use, given the question to be investigated and the variables involved?
   (vi) Which particular statistic or procedure, and diagram, should we use? Why?
(b) Find the mean and median for *Number of days absent.*
(c) What other measures of central tendency could you use for this data?
(d) Which seems to be the most suitable measure for the average *Number of days absent* for these employees? Why?

7.9 Examine the distribution diagrams in figures 7.21, 7.22 and 7.23. Each one is a graphical representation of a set of data. On the basis of the shape depicted in these distribution diagrams, which measures of location and spread would you choose to represent each set of data? Why?

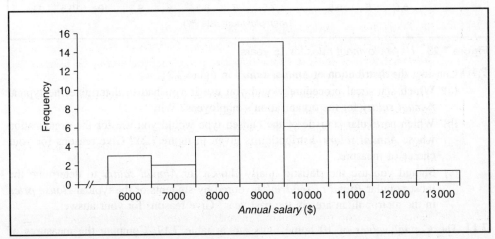

Figure 7.21   *Annual salaries* in an organisation

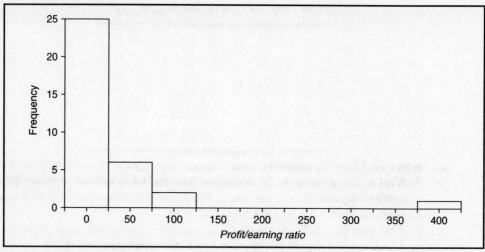

Figure 7.22 *Profit/earning ratios for listed companies*

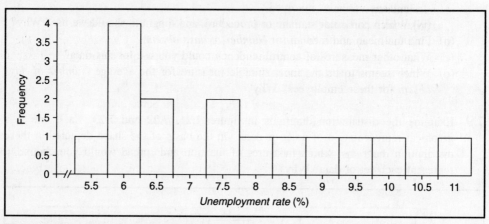

Figure 7.23 *Unemployment rates for 15 years*

7.10 Consider the distribution of *Annual salary* in figure 7.21.

    (a) Which statistical procedure would you use if you had to determine the typical *Annual salary* for the organisation's employees? Why?

    (b) Which particular statistic of the chosen type would you use for the organisation whose *Annual salary* distribution is given in figure 7.21? Give reasons for your choice of measure.

    (c) Should you use the statistic finally chosen for *Annual salary* to determine the most popular *Brand of softdrink* favoured by students or the typical *House price* in the metropolitan area in the past year? Give reasons for your answer.

7.11 The *Capital values* of 10 home units are in table 7.17. Compute the measures of central tendency and dispersion for the *Capital values* of these units.

Table 7.17   *Capital value ($) of 10 home units*

48 000	122 000
160 000	92 000
157 000	155 000
70 000	114 000
73 000	152 000

(a) With a calculator, compute the mean *Capital value* for the 10 home units.

(b) With a calculator, compute the deviations from the mean *Capital value* for each of the 10 home units. Guess the typical distance of a *Capital value* from the mean *Capital value*.

(c) Use the deviations from the mean to compute the standard deviation. How does the value for the standard deviation compare with your guess in (b)?

(d) Verify the results obtained in (a)–(c) by using the statistics functions on your calculator.

(e) Manually compute the median *Capital value* for the 10 home units.

(f) Manually compute the first and third quartiles of the *Capital value* for the 10 home units. Use these quartiles to compute the interquartile range, and explain what the interquartile range represents.

(g) Compare and contrast the values obtained in (a)–(f).

(h) What is the range of the *Capital value* for the 10 home units?

(i) From your answers for (a)–(h), draw the boxplot for this data.

7.12 Table 7.18 lists the data from a recent survey of *Annual income* for households in Statstown. This data is to be used to characterise the incomes of these households.

Table 7.18   *Annual income ($000) for Statstown*

93 000	82 000	102 000	90 000	95 000	93 000	76 000	86 000
72 000	75 000	75 000	77 000	92 000	84 000	97 000	71 000
98 000	114 000	86 000	82 000	92 000	80 000	95 000	96 000
86 000	92 000	93 000	89 000	80 000	93 000	91 000	104 000
87 000	92 000	83 000	101 000	84 000	71 000	95 000	103 000

(a) Answer the following questions:

  (i) What is the question to be investigated (including the group to which the conclusions apply)?

  (ii) What variable(s) are we concerned with here?

  (iii) What type of variable(s) are they?

  (iv) Which major category of statistical procedures applies here? Why?

(v) What type of statistic should we use, given the question to be investigated and the variables involved?

(vi) Which particular statistic or procedure, and diagram, should we use? Why?

(b) Answer the following questions as best as you can from table 7.18.

(i) What are the highest and lowest *Annual incomes* of the observed Statstown households?

(ii) Do all the observed Statstown households have approximately the same income?

(iii) What were the difficulties in obtaining the answers to these questions? Why?

(c) Suggest a method of presentation that would make your task much easier. If you have to make a choice between various methods, give reasons for your selection.

7.13 The data for *Annual income* in table 7.18 is saved in the Minitab portable worksheet file *inctown.mtp*. The following computer output gives three histograms for this data.

```
MTB > retrieve 'a:\inctown.mtp';
SUBC> portable.                          MTB > histogram 'Stattown';
                                         SUBC> start 65000;
Worksheet retrieved from file: a:\inctown.mtp   SUBC> increment 1000.
MTB > histogram 'Stattown'
                                         Histogram of Stattown n = 40
    Histogram of Stattown n = 40
                                         Midpoint  Count
Midpoint      Count                        65000     0
   70000        3  ***                      66000     0
   75000        4  ****                      67000     0
   80000        4  ****                      68000     0
   85000        7  *******                    69000     0
   90000        7  *******                    70000     0
   95000        9  *********                   71000     2  **
  100000        3  ***                       72000     1  *
  105000        2  **                        73000     0
  110000        0                            74000     0
  115000        1  *                         75000     2  **
                                            76000     1  *
MTB > histogram 'Stattown';               77000     1  *
SUBC> start 65000;                         78000     0
SUBC> increment 25000.                     79000     0
                                           80000     2  **
                                           81000     0
Histogram of Stattown n = 40              82000     2  **
Midpoint   Count                           83000     1  *
  65000      7  *******                     84000     2  **
  90000     30  ******************************   85000     0
 115000      3  ***                         86000     3  ***
                                           87000     1  *
                                           88000     0
                                           89000     1  *
```

continued . . .

```
                              90000        1  *
                              91000        1  *
                              92000        4  ****
                              93000        4  ****
                              94000        0
                              95000        3  ***
                              96000        1  *
                              97000        1  *
                              98000        1  *
                              99000        0
                             100000        0
                             101000        1  *
                             102000        1  *
                             103000        1  *
                             104000        1  *
                             105000        0
                             106000        0
                              10700        0
                             108000        0
                             109000        0
                             110000        0
                             111000        0
                             112000        0
                             113000        0
                             114000        1  *
```

(a) Reproduce this output.
(b) Which of the three histograms based on *Annual income* for Statstown do you think gives the clearest picture of the data? Give reasons for your choice.
(c) What is the shape of the distribution of *Annual income* for the observed Statstown households?
(d) Using the frequencies for each class in your selected histogram for Statstown, find the percentages of *Annual income* in each class.
   (i) Which classes have more than 15% of the observations for *Annual income*?
   (ii) Which classes have less than 10% of the observations for *Annual income*?
   (iii) Calculate the percentage of observed Statstown households whose *Annual incomes* fall in the range from $82 500 up to, but not including, $97 500.
   (iv) What percentage of observed Statstown households do have *Annual incomes* less than, but not including, $100 000?

7.14 Draw by hand the stem-and-leaf display for the Statstown *Annual income* data in table 7.18. Comment on the differences between this distribution diagram and the one you chose in exercise 7.13.

7.15 The Statstown *Annual income* data is given in table 7.18 and saved in the Minitab portable worksheet file *inctown.mtp*. The Minitab output to answer the questions in this exercise is as follows. Reproduce this output.

```
MTB > retrieve 'a:\inctown.mtp';
SUBC> port.

Worksheet retrieved from file: a:\inctown.mtp
MTB > info

COLUMN   NAME        COUNT
C1       Stattown      40
C2       Bustown       80

CONTSTANTS USED: NONE

MTB > describe 'Stattown'

                 N       MEAN     MEDIAN    TRMEAN     STDEV    SEMEAN
Stattown        40      88675     90500     88528      9846      1557
                MIN       MAX        Q1        Q3
Stattown      71000    114000     82000     95000
```

(a) What is the mean and median *Annual income* for the observed Statstown households? Which measure of central tendency would be appropriate for this data? Give reasons.

(b) What is the range, the interquartile range, the standard deviation and the coefficient of variation of *Annual income* for the observed Statstown households? Which measure of dispersion seems the most appropriate for the Statstown data? Why?

(c) Give the five measures, used in the boxplot, for the *Annual income* of the observed Statstown households. Use these to draw a boxplot for them. List some useful characteristics of boxplots.

(d) From your answers to this and previous exercises, write a report characterising the *Annual income* of the observed Statstown households.

7.16 The daily expenses of branch delegates to a statistical conference are listed in table 7.19 and saved in the Minitab portable worksheet file *confexp.mtp*. Use this data to determine the typical expense, and the spread in expenses, for these delegates.

Table 7.19   *Daily expenses ($) of delegates*

117.00	124.75	94.30	111.95	127.50	90.25
89.10	88.80	67.40	140.65	92.70	67.40
112.30	120.65	75.55	125.50	88.65	90.54
106.35	129.60	75.15	123.75	111.95	72.05
115.25	121.20	86.30	119.35	87.60	96.75
107.85	94.45	101.80	129.40	146.55	130.55
94.35	83.45	61.05	140.50	140.80	118.50
103.40	87.45	73.60	149.30	157.05	161.95
126.10	76.70	102.82	125.40	108.35	132.05
121.10	76.90	87.25	147.45	112.55	118.50

(a) Answer the following questions:
   (i) What is the question to be investigated (including the group to which the conclusions apply)?
   (ii) What variable(s) are we concerned with here?
   (iii) What type of variable(s) are they?
   (iv) Which major category of statistical procedures applies here? Why?
   (v) What type of statistic should we use, given the question to be investigated and the variables involved?
   (vi) Which particular statistic or procedure, and diagram, should we use? Why?
(b) What are the values of the mean and median for the branch delegates' *Daily expenses*? Of the mean and median, which is the most appropriate measure of central tendency for this data? Why?
(c) What are the values of the first and third quartiles for the branch delegates' *Daily expenses*? Find the interquartile range for this data.
(d) What is the standard deviation for the branch delegates' *Daily expenses*? Of the standard deviation and interquartile range, which is the most appropriate measure of dispersion for this data? Why?

7.17 A marketing consultant observed 60 consecutive customers at a local supermarket. One variable of interest was the amount spent there by each customer. Table 7.20 gives an ordered array of the amount spent by the customers. This information has been saved in the Minitab portable worksheet file *custsped.mtp*. It is to be used to characterise the amounts spent by these 60 customers.

Table 7.20 *Amount spent ($) by customers*

2.30	11.35	14.35	17.15	20.60	27.10	33.25	40.80	64.30	91.60
6.65	11.65	14.50	18.20	20.90	28.75	33.80	43.95	69.50	96.80
6.90	12.65	14.55	18.30	20.90	29.15	34.75	43.55	74.50	102.50
8.05	12.95	15.00	18.70	21.10	30.55	36.20	52.35	76.00	110.40
9.45	13.60	15.35	19.55	23.85	32.00	37.50	61.55	82.25	119.75
10.25	13.70	16.55	19.55	26.00	32.80	39.25	63.85	84.75	128.60

(a) Answer the following questions:
   (i) What is the question to be investigated (including the group to which the conclusions apply)?
   (ii) What variable(s) are we concerned with here?
   (iii) What type of variable(s) are they?
   (iv) Which major category of statistical procedures applies here? Why?
   (v) What type of statistic should we use, given the question to be investigated and the variables involved?
   (vi) Which particular statistic or procedure, and diagram, should we use? Why?

(b) Describe the distribution shape of *Amount spent* by the customers.

(c) Give an overall summary of this data.

7.18 For the branch delegates' *Daily expenses* (exercise 7.16), what percentages of these observations fall in the ranges covered by ±1, ±2 and ±3 standard deviations around the mean, respectively? Are these percentages consistent with those expected if *Daily expenses* is normally distributed?

7.19 The board of trustees of a company superannuation fund wants to develop a short-term strategy for future investments. The board secretary was asked to prepare information on the stocks of a cross-section of well-known national companies for the next board meeting. Table 7.21 lists the information for his selection of companies and it is saved in the Minitab portable worksheet file *indstock.mtp*.

For background information, the trustees are interested in a summary of the selected companies' current yields and popularity, the latter measured in terms of the current volume.

(a) Answer the following questions:

  (i) What is the question to be investigated (including the group to which the conclusions apply)?

  (ii) What variable(s) are we concerned with here?

  (iii) What type of variable(s) are they?

  (iv) Which major category of statistical procedures applies? Why?

  (v) What type of statistic should we use, given the question to be investigated and the variables involved?

  (vi) Which particular statistic or procedure, and diagram, should we use? Why?

(b) Prepare a report giving the required summary for their next board meeting.

Table 7.21   Performance of selected industrial stocks

Year High ($)	Year Low ($)	Stock	Volume	Close ($)	Move (%)	Yield (%)
448	249	ANZ	2 305 900	440	+9	4.55
210	137	ANI	1 826 000	196	+1	4.59
232	200	Adel Cement	319 100	220	+5	3.41
1026	729	Amcor	1 654 300	960	−8	3.23
1796	1018	BHP	1 446 500	1744	+12	2.32
338	221	BTR Nylex	1 274 100	311	+14	3.46
418	240	Boral	2 768 300	400	+10	4.50
460	200	Brash	8 100	244	+2	3.07
801	600	Bunnings	30 800	785	+15	3.06
452	332	Burns P	181 700	429	−1	3.96

continued . . .

Table 7.21   *continued*

Year High ($)	Year Low ($)	Stock	Volume	Close ($)	Move (%)	Yield (%)
1046	572	CCAmatl	137 400	1040	+30	1.38
492	330	CSR	1 553 400	467	+1	4.71
560	410	ColesMyer	1 767 800	522	+2	3.74
411	247	Comalco	2 491 500	328	−2	1.83
300	141	ConsPaper	1 000	285	+5	2.53
511	277	Email	734 300	510	+12	3.82
57	29	Equitlink	45 000	57	+1	5.26
135	70	FAI life	18 400	124	+3	5.85
910	509	Faulding	505 300	865	+10	1.62
910	378	Foodland	102 400	895	+5	3.02
160	109	Foster's	1 100 000	153	+4	3.92
279	205	Hardie J	119 300	232		5.17
660	492	Hills		660		2.65
900	446	ICI	63 200	890	+19	2.58
870	605	Mayne N	498 300	828	+1	3.62
195	124	Nat Foods	219 700	185		3.51
260	180	OPSM Pr	18 700	258	+3	4.26
552	400	Pac Dunlp	2 198 100	520	+3	2.89
330	80	SthCBroad	14 900	320	−5	3.75
295	198	Spicers	2 300	239	+1	5.44
365	181	Tubemaker	45 500	335		2.99
735	580	Wattyl	50 400	726	+1	2.62
795	515	Wesfarmers	16 700	795	+7	3.65
960	798	Weston G	1 600	950		1.74
332	260	Woolworths	936 300	310	+4	3.87

Source: abstracted from *The Advertiser* (1993a)

CHAPTER 8

DESCRIPTIVE SUMMARIES FOR ONE UNRESTRICTED VARIABLE AND SOME LIMITED VARIABLES

LEARNING OBJECTIVES

The learning objectives of this chapter are:
- to be able to produce and interpret distribution tables and distribution diagrams for data involving an unrestricted variable and a limited variable;
- to be able to produce and interpret one-way and two-way tables of measures of central tendency and dispersion;
- to be able to produce and interpret standardised scores;
- to know the uses of and be able to produce weighted means.

The following extract from the *Summary of procedures based on combinations of variable types* in part VI gives an overview of the descriptive summaries covered in this and the previous chapters of part III, *Descriptive summaries of data*.

1. *One limited variable*
   - Distribution of variables: frequency, relative frequency and percentage one-way summary tables — bar or column chart.
   - Measures of central tendency: mode (mean, median).
   - Measures of dispersion: range, interquartile range, (standard deviation, coefficient of variation).

2. *Two limited variables*
   - Distribution of variables: two-way contingency table — chart with bars or columns that are grouped or stacked.

3. *Three limited variables*
   - Distribution of variables: three-way contingency table — chart with bars or columns that are grouped or stacked.

4. *One unrestricted variable*
   - Distribution of variables: frequency, relative frequency and percentage tables — histogram, polygon, stem-and-leaf display, dotplot.
   - Measures of central tendency: mean, median — boxplot.
   - Measures of dispersion: range, interquartile range, standard deviation, coefficient of variation — boxplot.

5. *One unrestricted variable — one limited variable*
   - **Distribution of variables**: frequency, relative frequency and percentage tables for each value of limited variable — histogram, polygon, stem-and-leaf display, dotplot for each value of limited variable.
   - **Measures of central tendency**: one-way table of means or medians — boxplot for each value of limited variable, bar chart or line diagram.
   - **Measures of dispersion**: one-way table of ranges, interquartile ranges, standard deviations or coefficients of variation — boxplot for each value of limited variable.

6. *One unrestricted variable — two limited variables*
   - **Distribution of variables**: frequency, relative frequency and percentage tables for each combination of values of the limited variables — histogram, polygon, stem-and-leaf display, dotplot for each combination of values of the limited variables.
   - **Measures of central tendency**: two-way table of means or medians — boxplot for each combination of values of the limited variables, bar chart or line diagram.
   - **Measures of dispersion**: two-way table of ranges, interquartile ranges, standard deviations or coefficients of variation — boxplot for each combination of values of the limited variables.

As outlined in the objectives, this chapter covers the descriptive summaries under heading 5, *One unrestricted variable — one limited variable*, and heading 6, *One unrestricted variable — two limited variables*.

As discussed in chapter 7, *Descriptive summaries for one unrestricted variable*, when an unrestricted variable has been measured you can investigate the general shape of the distribution by using a distribution table and a distribution diagram, or obtain measures of central tendency and/or dispersion. In this chapter, the methods introduced in chapter 7 are extended to include an unrestricted variable *and* some limited variables. Basically, the methods used for just an unrestricted variable are applied to those values of the unrestricted variable that have the same value, or combination of values, of the limited variable(s).

8.1   Distributions for one unrestricted and one limited variable

In this case, the appropriate thing to use is a frequency table that has a set of frequencies for each value of the limited variable and to form a **distribution diagram** from the values of the unrestricted variable for each value of the limited variable. Thus, you could produce histograms, polygons, stem-and-leaf displays or dotplots from the values of the unrestricted variable for each value of the limited variable.

In general, there will not be the same number of observations for each value of the limited variable. Consequently, comparing raw frequencies is not satisfactory; it will be difficult to sort out whether differences between the frequencies for the same class interval occur because of differences in the number of observations or because of differences in the distributions for the various limited variables. This problem can be overcome by using proportions or percentages, rather than frequencies. That is, we adjust for the different total number of observations by dividing the frequencies by the total number. The diagram of choice in this situation would be percentage (or proportion) polygons superimposed on each other in the same diagram. Histograms cannot be easily superimposed to compare the distributions for the different values of the limited variable. Stem-and-leaf displays and dotplots have the disadvantage of being frequency-based distribution diagrams.

EXAMPLE 8.1   HOUSE PRICES IN THREE LOCALITIES

As in example 6.5, *Residences sold in three localities*, raw, secondary data is available on all the residences sold over a 12-month period in three different localities. In particular, the prices paid for the residences are available. The task is to compare the prices of houses in the three localities and so the question to be investigated involves an unrestricted variable, *House price*, and a limited variable, *Locality*. To compare prices, you could use a frequency table and a histogram or a polygon, or a stem-and-leaf display or a dotplot of *House price* for each *Locality*.

Table 8.1 is a frequency table containing frequencies and percentages for house prices in the three localities. From the frequencies we see that in all three localities there are many houses sold in the $100 000 to $175 000 price range. Whether there are differences within this range between the patterns for each locality is obscured by the fact that more houses were sold in Payneham than in the other two localities. However, the percentages show that there are relatively more houses in the $100 000 to $150 000 price range in Payneham than in the other two localities. The corresponding percentage polygons are given in figure 8.1.

The stem-and-leaf displays and dotplots of *House price* for the three localities are given in table 8.2 and figure 8.2 respectively. The percentage polygons seem the most satisfactory of the three types of distribution diagram, since the others have the disadvantage of being frequency-based distribution diagrams. However, note from table 8.2 that there are two very low house prices in Kensington and Norwood, and one of these is less than $10 000 as indicated by the 0 leaf on the first line of the stem-and-leaf display for Kensington and Norwood. One explanation for this is that the house was sold for a nominal price to a relative or friend.

From the percentage polygons in figure 8.1, it is evident that *House price* in all three localities is skew-to-the-right. The distributions for Kensington and Norwood and St Peters are very similar. Most of the house prices lie in the $60 000–$360 000 range, and are centred on $162 500. There are several houses in St Peters at about $562 500. Most house prices in Payneham fall in the $60 000–$237 500 price range, which is smaller than that of the other two localities. Further, house prices in Payneham are centred on $137 500, about $25 000 lower than the centre price of the other two areas.

Table 8.1   Frequency table for *House price* in three localities

House price Class Intervals ($000s)	Kensington		St Peters		Payneham	
	Frequency	Percentage	Frequency	Percentage	Frequency	Percentage
0–25	2	1.61	0	0.00	2	1.00
25–50	0	0.00	0	0.00	3	1.49
50–75	2	1.61	4	3.17	4	1.99
75–100	4	3.23	8	6.35	16	7.96
100–125	12	9.68	12	9.52	54	26.87
125–150	20	16.13	19	15.08	58	28.86
150–175	22	17.74	21	16.67	34	16.92
175–200	17	13.71	13	10.32	11	5.47
200–225	9	7.26	11	8.73	7	3.48
225–250	14	11.29	8	6.35	2	1.00
250–275	7	5.65	8	6.35	4	1.99
275–300	5	4.03	5	3.97	1	0.50
300–325	5	4.03	6	4.76	2	1.00
325–350	3	2.42	4	3.17	1	0.50
350–375	0	0.00	1	0.79	0	0.00
375–400	0	0.00	1	0.79	0	0.00
400–425	0	0.00	0	0.00	0	0.00
425–450	0	0.00	1	0.79	1	0.50
450–475	1	0.81	0	0.00	0	0.00
475–500	0	0.00	0	0.00	1	0.50
500–525	0	0.00	0	0.00	0	0.00
525–550	0	0.00	0	0.00	0	0.00
550–575	0	0.00	4	3.17	0	0.00
575–600	0	0.00	0	0.00	0	0.00
600–625	0	0.00	0	0.00	0	0.00
625–650	0	0.00	0	0.00	0	0.00
650–675	0	0.00	0	0.00	0	0.00
675–700	0	0.00	0	0.00	0	0.00
700–725	0	0.00	0	0.00	0	0.00
725–750	0	0.00	0	0.00	0	0.00
750–775	0	0.00	0	0.00	0	0.00
775–800	1	0.81	0	0.00	0	0.00
Total	124	100.00	126	100.00	201	100.00

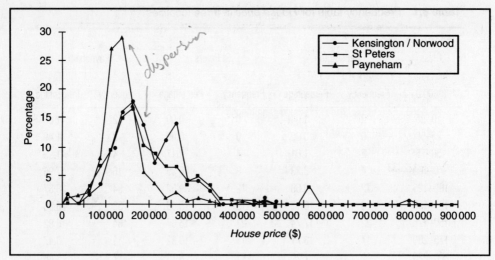

Figure 8.1   Percentage polygons for *House price* in three localities

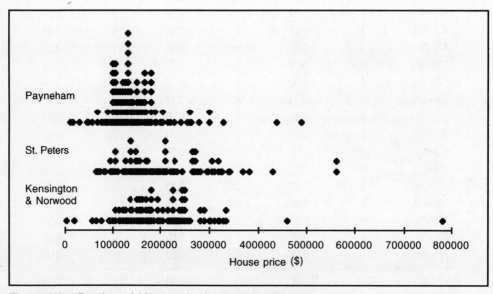

Figure 8.2   Dotplots of *House price* for three localities

Table 8.2   Stem-and-leaf displays of *House price* for three localities

Kensington and Norwood

0	02
0	567999
1	0000111112222222233333333333444
1	55555555555556666777777777778888889999
2	0001111222222233344444
2	555556688899
3	00122333
3	
4	
4	6
5	
5	
6	
6	
7	
7	8

St Peters

0	666788999999
1	000001122222222333333344444444444
1	555555556666666677777778889999999
2	0000011111122233344
2	6666677777899
3	0001222244
3	68
4	3
4	
5	
5	6666

continued ...

197

Table 8.2 *continued*

Payneham	
0	11244
0	55667788888888999999
1	00000000000000000000000000011111111111111111111122222222222222222222+
1	555555555555556666666666666666666667777788888888889
2	000012224
2	56667
3	003
3	
4	4
4	9

Leaf unit = 10 000

8.2   Measures for one unrestricted and one limited variable

When the questions to be answered involve one unrestricted and one limited variable, the measures to be used are the same as for one unrestricted variable, except that they are computed for each value of the limited variable.

8.2.1   Measures of central tendency

As for one unrestricted variable, the measures of central tendency for general use are the mean and the median. However, when you want to see if the values of the unrestricted variable depend on the limited variable, a one-way table of means or medians is appropriate. That is, as for the distribution diagrams, you calculate the measure from the values of the unrestricted variable for each value of the limited variable, and put these together in a **one-way table of a central tendency measure**. The table is called a *one-way table* because it contains data for the different values of only one limited variable. It is good practice to include, along with the measure of central tendency for each value of the limited variable, the number of observations used in calculating each value of the measure. This is because measures are more precise if they are based on more observations. Be particularly careful of means or medians based on only a few observations, as these are of little use.

EXAMPLE 8.1   HOUSE PRICES IN THREE LOCALITIES (continued)
Previously, the prices for the three localities were compared by using polygons. You may want to concentrate on the differences, between the three localities, in the typical selling price of houses, in which case a one-way table of means or medians of *House price* answers the question to be investigated. These tables are given in tables 8.3 and 8.4. Note that they include *n*, the number of observed houses, for each locality.

The medians are in every case lower than the means, which is to be expected since the distribution has been previously described as skew-to-the-right. Because the distribution has this shape, the median is the appropriate measure to use as it is not unbalanced by the extreme values. The medians indicate that house prices in Kensington and Norwood and St Peters are about the same — typically just over $170 000. On the other hand, prices in Payneham, at about $130 000, are generally a little over $40 000 less than in the other two localities. These conclusions are consistent with those based on the polygons in section 8.1, *Distributions for one unrestricted and one limited variable.*

Table 8.3   One-way table of *House price* means for three localities

Locality	Mean *House Price* ($)	n
Kensington & Norwood	188 502	124
St Peters	200 238	126
Payneham	139 779	201

reflects high prices.
Distorts the results.

Table 8.4   One-way table of *House price* medians for three localities

Locality	Median *House Price* ($)	n
Kensington & Norwood	174 000	124
St Peters	172 500	126
Payneham	130 000	201

The diagram for presenting the information in one-way tables of a central tendency measure is usually the bar chart, where a bar of length equal to the value of the measure is drawn for each value of the limited variable; the bars are separated by space. If the limited variable is continuous, as in example 8.2, *Yearly pattern in Queensland visitors for 1989–93,* a line diagram could be used. In a **line diagram**, a point is plotted for each value of the limited variable and a line is drawn between points with consecutive values for the limited variable.

EXAMPLE 8.1   HOUSE PRICES IN THREE LOCALITIES (continued)
The limited variable *Locality* is a nominal limited variable and so a bar chart is used to illustrate the differences between the *House price* medians for the different *Localities.* The diagram is given in figure 8.3.

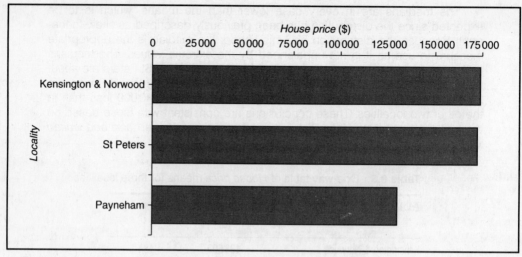

Figure 8.3   *House price* medians for three different localities

EXAMPLE 8.2   YEARLY PATTERN IN QUEENSLAND VISITORS FOR 1989–93

As part of planning a tourist business in Queensland, the operator wants to establish the annual pattern of visitors to Queensland over the past 5 years. The room occupancy rate of hotels, motels and guesthouses in Queensland for each month during the period 1989–93 have been obtained from the Australian Bureau of Statistics (1989–93).

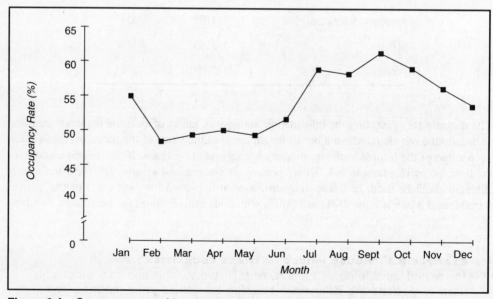

Figure 8.4   *Occupancy rate* of hotels, motels and guesthouses in Queensland

The question to be investigated is: what is the annual pattern of visitors to Queensland over the last five years as indicated by the occupancy rates? The variables involved are *Occupancy rate*, an unrestricted variable, and *Month*, a limited variable. *Month* is a limited variable, in spite of it having 12 values, as these values repeat over and over again with continued observation. *Month* is also continuous as it measures time since the beginning of the year; that is, conceptually, the possible values of the underlying variable form a continuum.

To examine the change in *Occupancy rate* with *Month*, the mean occupancy rate for each month has been determined and the results are illustrated in figure 8.4 with a line diagram, where the mean *Occupancy rate* is plotted against *Month*. *Occupancy rates* appear to peak in July, August, September and October.

8.2.2   Measures of dispersion

In this case a **one-way table of a dispersion measure** is appropriate; if the data is symmetric, the dispersion measure to use is the standard deviation, whereas if the data is skewed the interquartile range is used. Again, it is good practice to include the number of observations used in calculating each value of the measure.

EXAMPLE 8.1   HOUSE PRICES IN THREE LOCALITIES (continued)

As well as, or instead of, examining average price, you might be interested in comparing the spread of prices in the three localities. Then, the question to be investigated is: do prices vary more in one locality than in the others? If so, a one-way table of a dispersion measure is required. The one-way tables of standard deviations and interquartile ranges are given in tables 8.5 and 8.6, respectively. As the median was the appropriate measure of central tendency, the interquartile range is the appropriate measure of dispersion. The interquartile ranges in table 8.6 indicate that the middle 50% of house prices in Kensington and Norwood and St Peters cover a range of about $100 000, with Kensington and Norwood prices perhaps a little less variable than those in St Peters. Prices in Payneham are somewhat less variable than in the other two localities: the middle 50% of prices in Payneham cover a range of about $50 000.

Table 8.5   One-way table of standard deviations for *House price* from three localities

Locality	House price standard deviation ($)	n
Kensington & Norwood	88 320	124
St Peters	98 740	126
Payneham	56 981	201

Table 8.6 One-way table of interquartile ranges for *House price* from three localities

Locality	House price interquartile range ($)	n
Kensington & Norwood	95 250	124
St Peters	106 250	126
Payneham	51 250	201

8.2.3 Diagram for illustrating central tendency and dispersion

Again, the box-and-whisker plot illustrates both the central tendency and dispersion for situations where the median and interquartile range are used. Indeed, the diagram is ideally suited for situations involving an unrestricted variable and one or more limited variables. In this case, a box-and-whisker plot is produced from the values of the unrestricted variable for each value of the limited variable and these can be easily compared.

EXAMPLE 8.1 HOUSE PRICES IN THREE LOCALITIES (continued)

The box-and-whisker plot comparing the *House price* for the three localities is given in figure 8.5. The differences in central tendency and spread displayed in the plot are more obvious than in the tables: *House price* in Payneham is both lower and a little less spread than in the other two localities. Also, our attention is drawn to the presence of both possible and probable outliers in the three localities, although the most extreme prices are in the Kensington and Norwood area.

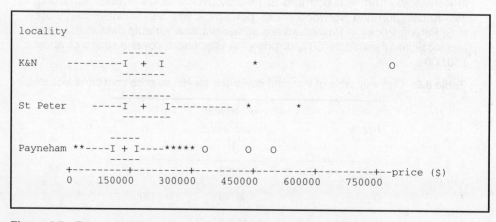

Figure 8.5 Box-and-whisker plot for *House price* in three localities

8.3   Standardising data

For comparing the values from two different sets of data, it is sometimes useful to **standardise** the values from each set, thus forming standardised scores. The **standardised score** is the number of standard deviations by which an observed value deviates from the mean. To obtain the standardised scores, compute the mean and standard deviation for a set of data and, for each observation in the set, subtract the mean to form the deviation and divide the deviation by the standard deviation. The formula to form the standardised score z_i for the observed value y_i is:

$$z_i = \frac{y_i - \bar{y}}{s}$$

A negative value is obtained for the standardised score if the original observation is below the mean; if the original observation is greater than the mean, a positive value is obtained. The standardised scores for a set of data have a mean of zero and a standard deviation of one. The general shape of the distribution of the standardised scores will be the same as the original data.

EXAMPLE 8.3   MANAGEMENT CAPACITY FOR TWO BRANCHES

In example 7.1, *Management capacity*, a company gave 30 of its employees a management test that resulted in a score between 0 and 100. These 30 employees were all from one branch of the company, and 57 employees from a second branch were also assessed. The company has the raw, primary data on file. Suppose I look up the scores for two individuals, one from each branch, and find that the employee from branch 1 scored 69.8 and the employee from branch 2 scored 68.7. Certainly, the branch 2 employee has scored a little lower than the branch 1 employee, but what is their relative standing in their respective branches?

The distributions for the two branches are in figure 8.6 and the table of means and standard deviations is in table 8.7. From the polygons, the scores from both branches appear to be symmetrically distributed. The means and standard deviations confirm the trend evident in the polygon; that is, the branch 2 scores tend to be lower and more spread out than those from branch 1. So to examine the relative standings of the two employees, we need to adjust for these differences in central tendency and dispersion by computing the standardised scores.

The standardised score for the branch 1 employee is:

$$z = \frac{69.8 - 72.67}{8.18} = -0.35$$

and for the branch 2 employee is:

$$z = \frac{68.7 - 66.19}{12.68} = 0.20$$

From the standardised scores, we conclude that the employee from branch 2 is slightly above average for their branch, 0.20 standard deviations above, whereas the employee from branch 1 is below average for their branch, 0.35 standard deviations below. That is, relatively speaking, the employee from branch 2 scored better than the employee from branch 1. The score of the branch 2 employee is 0.20 − (−0.35) = 0.55 standard deviations above that of the branch 1 employee.

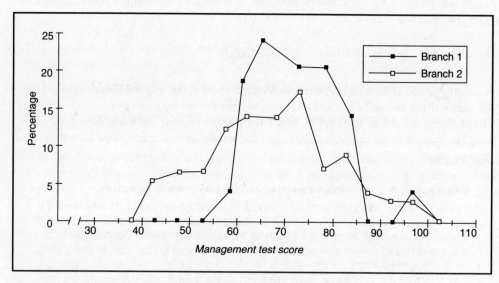

Figure 8.6   *Management test score* distributions for two branches

Table 8.7   Summary statistics for *Management test scores* from two branches

Branch	Mean	Standard deviation	n
1	72.67	8.18	30
2	66.19	12.68	57

8.4   Weighted means

In general, you use the weighted mean when you want to obtain the mean of a set of values, taking into account the relative importance of each value. The quantity measuring the relative importance of each value is called its **weight**. The formula for the **weighted mean** is:

$$\bar{y}_w = \frac{\textbf{sum of products} \text{ of weights and values}}{\text{sum of weights}}$$

$$= \frac{\sum\limits_{i=1}^{n} w_i y_i}{\sum\limits_{i=1}^{n} w_i}$$

$$\frac{\left(\bar{y}_A \times 30\right)\left(57 \times \bar{y}_B\right)}{87}$$

where y_i is the ith value;
      w_i is the weight for the ith value; $\text{or} \quad \frac{30}{87}\bar{y}_A + \frac{57}{87}\bar{y}_B$
      n is the number of values;

$\sum\limits_{i=1}^{n} w_i y_i$, the sum of products of the weights and values, is obtained by multiplying
a value by its corresponding weight and summing the resulting products.

Index numbers, covered in chapter 11, *Index numbers for unrestricted variables over time*, are examples of weighted means. Weighted means are also used to combine several means, each of which is based on a different number of observations. In this case, the weights are the numbers of observations on which the means are based so that the formula becomes:

$$\bar{y}_w = \frac{\text{sum of products of numbers of observations and means}}{\text{sum of numbers of observations}}$$

$$= \frac{\sum\limits_{i=1}^{m} n_i \bar{y}_i}{\sum\limits_{i=1}^{m} n_i}$$

where $\bar{y}_i$ is the ith mean;
      n_i is the number of observations for the ith mean;
      m is the number of means to be combined.

Careful contemplation of the formula for the weighted mean in this special case reveals that it can be re-expressed as

$$\bar{y}_w = \frac{\text{sum of all observations}}{\text{total number of observations}}$$

because $n_i \bar{y}_i$ is just the total of the observations for the ith mean and $\Sigma_{i=1}^{n} n_i$ is just the total number of observations involved in all means. One implication of this is that if the original raw data is available, the computation of the weighted mean can be avoided. Just compute the mean for all observations, ignoring the mean to which an observation contributed. However, it often happens that the original raw data is not available, particularly when the means represent secondary data, for example published data. In this case, the weighted mean must be computed.

EXAMPLE 8.3   MANAGEMENT CAPACITY FOR TWO BRANCHES (continued)

We want to obtain the combined mean of the two branches. We will act as if the raw data is not available and we have only the means for each branch, as given in table 8.7. To compute the combined mean, a weighted mean must be computed because the means are based on 30 and 57 observations, respectively. The combined mean is thus:

$$\bar{y}_w = \frac{(30 \times 72.67) + (57 \times 66.19)}{30 + 57} = \frac{2180.1 + 3772.83}{87} = 68.4$$

This value exactly equals the mean of all 87 observations. Note that the apparently obvious course — taking the mean of the two means — leads to 69.43. As with many 'obvious' procedures, this does not lead to the best answer. In combining two means you must take into account the differing numbers of observations. If you do this, the result has appeal because it corresponds to what would be obtained if all the data was available.

EXAMPLE 8.4   LOCAL CRIME RATE

Example 1.7, *Local crime rate*, presented some data on crime rates taken from a local suburban newspaper article and reproduced in table 8.8. Two ways of computing the overall crime rate were presented: the average of the decreases for each offence and the decrease in the yearly totals. They gave answers that differed by about 10% and we wondered which method should be used. We are now in a position to decide.

One problem in computing the mean of the individual decreases is that all decreases are treated equally; no account is taken of the difference between offences in the frequency with which they occur. This problem could be overcome by computing a weighted mean where the number of offences in the first year are used as weights. The calculations for the first year are as follows:

$$\bar{y}_w = \frac{(865 \times 24.7) + (164 \times 7.4) + \ldots + (48 \times 50.0)}{865 + 164 + \ldots + 48}$$
$$= 22.0$$

It is no accident that this is the same value as obtained by computing the percentage decrease using the totals. So, we conclude that this method is preferred because it is equivalent to a weighted mean that takes into account the different frequencies with which the offences occur. The weighted means indicate that the crime rate has decreased by about 22% in both areas.

Table 8.8 Numbers of offences in two areas of a city

	Norwood			Unley		
Offence	Oct 92– Mar 93	Oct 93– Mar 94	Decrease (%)	Oct 92– Mar 93	Oct 93– Mar 94	Decrease (%)
Breaks	865	651	24.7	1319	1049	20.5
Larceny/illegal use	164	108	7.4	269	212	23.9
Illegal interference motor vehicle	117	59	15.0	151	76	18.5
Larceny motor vehicle	301	256	39.2	453	369	19.3
Other theft	527	488	34.1	800	609	21.2
Property damage	51	31	49.6	662	534	49.7
Offensive behaviour	48	24	50.0	92	41	55.4
Total	2073	1617	22.0	3746	2890	22.9

Source: abstracted from Hider (1994)

8.5   Measures for one unrestricted variable and two limited variables

Again, when the questions to be answered involve one unrestricted and two limited variables, the measures to be used are the same as for one unrestricted variable, except that they are computed for each combination of the values of the two limited variables. This section concentrates on just the measures of central tendency; the treatment of measures of dispersion strongly parallels that for measures of central tendency.

8.5.1   Measures of central tendency

Once again, measures of central tendency for general use are the mean and the median. However, when you want to see how the values of the unrestricted variable differ for the different combinations of values of the limited variables, a two-way table of means or medians is appropriate. That is, as for the distribution diagrams, you calculate the measure for each combination of the values of the limited variables and put these together in the **main body** of a **two-way table of a central tendency measure**. The table is called a *two-way table* because it contains data for the different values of two limited variables. It is usual to include margins in such tables, to help you interpret the tables. Each margin corresponds to the one-way table of a central tendency measure for one of the limited variables. That is, they give the value of the measure of central tendency for the unrestricted variable computed for each value of one limited variable combined over the values of the other limited variable. Also, you should include the number of observations used in calculating each value of the measure of central tendency.

In examining two-way tables of a central tendency measure, it is important to distinguish between two situations: the two limited variables on which the table is based may be dependent or independent in their effect on the unrestricted variable. This is rather similar to the idea that two limited variables in contingency tables may be dependent or independent (see section 6.2.3, *Dependence versus independence*). However, there is the added qualification, in the case of two-way tables of a central tendency measure, that the two limited variables are dependent or independent *in their effect on the unrestricted variable*. That is, in the two-way tables of a central tendency measure, you examine the pattern in the values of the measure computed from the values of the unrestricted variable. On the other hand, in a contingency table you examine the pattern in the frequencies of the combinations of the two limited variables, or in percentages computed from the frequencies; the limited variables are the only variables involved in the contingency table.

To determine if the two limited variables are dependent or independent in their effect on the unrestricted variable, examine the values of the measure computed from the unrestricted variable for the combinations of the two limited variables. Compare either the rows or the columns of the table's main body, whichever you prefer — however, *only one is examined*. When the pattern in the differences between the values of the measure is not the same for all rows (columns), the two limited variables are said to be **dependent** (or to *interact*) in their effect on the unrestricted variable. If the pattern is the same, the two limited variables are said to be **independent** in their effect on the unrestricted variable. The two-way table of means or medians can be presented graphically in grouped bar charts or line diagrams. These greatly help you to make the comparisons required to determine whether or not the variables are dependent.

Of the two possible outcomes, the simplest is that the variables are independent, in which case the influence of each limited variable on the unrestricted variable can be examined separately. This is done by using the two one-way tables of the central tendency measure. If the variables are dependent, examine the information in the body of the two-way table to assess the joint influence of the two limited variables.

Table with dependent limited variables

EXAMPLE 8.4   HOUSE SALES IN TWO LOCALITIES

Example 8.1, *House prices in three localities*, examined the differences in *House price* for three different localities. We now want to make a more detailed investigation of two of the localities: Kensington and Norwood and Payneham local government areas. In particular, is the difference in the typical price for each of these two areas the same for all houses, irrespective of the number of rooms?

That is, the question to be investigated involves an unrestricted variable and two limited variables, the unrestricted variable being *House price* and the limited variables *Locality* and *Number of rooms*. For this question and the variables involved, a two-way table of a central tendency measure is required. As it has already been shown that *House price* is skew-to-the-right, medians are the appropriate measure of central tendency. Further, as shown in table 8.9, about 82% of all houses sold in these two localities have 4, 5 or 6 rooms, not including bathrooms, toilets and laundries. The houses with other than 4,

5, or 6 rooms are not sold often enough to provide reliable figures. So a two-way table of *House price* medians for houses with 4, 5 or 6 rooms in the two localities is given in table 8.10. The table includes two sets of margins, consisting of the *House price* medians for the two localities and for the different number of rooms, respectively. A grouped bar chart presenting the medians for the different combinations of number of rooms and localities is given in figure 8.7.

The *Locality* margin in table 8.10 indicates that *House price* in Kensington and Norwood is typically $32 000 more expensive than in Payneham. But can we conclude that, no matter what sized house, the typical difference will be $32 000? The answer is no, so we need to examine the *House price* medians in the main body of the table to check whether or not the difference is the same for all house sizes. That is, we have to determine whether or not *Locality* and *Number of rooms* are *dependent* in their effects on *House price*. To do this, we compare the *House price* medians for different localities or for houses with different numbers of rooms; that is, we compare the different rows or different columns of the main body, but not both the rows and the columns. We have chosen to compare the *House price* medians for houses from different localities. The price difference between localities is $21 000 for 4-roomed houses, $42 750 for 5-roomed houses and $61 250 for 6-roomed houses. The difference between the two localities increases with the number of rooms in the house, as is apparent in figure 8.7. *Locality* and *Number of rooms* are *dependent* in their effect on *House price*.

Thus, in this example, conclusions should be based on the medians in the main body of the table; the margins are misleading because they do not indicate how the differences in the two localities vary for houses with different numbers of rooms.

Table 8.9   One-way summary table for *Number of rooms*

Number of rooms	Frequency	Percentage
3	11	2.45
4	89	19.82
5	182	40.53
6	99	22.05
7	37	8.24
8	12	2.67
9	9	2.00
10	6	1.34
11	2	0.45
12	1	0.22
13	0	0.00
14	0	0.00
15	1	0.22

Table 8.10   Two-way table of *House price* medians ($) for different sized houses in two localities

| Locality | Number of rooms | | | |
	4	5	6	Total
Kensington & Norwood	129 000	170 000	211 250	160 000
	27	46	24	97
Payneham	108 000	127 250	150 000	128 000
	36	90	45	171
Total	112 500	136 000	158 000	137 000
	63	136	69	268

Each cell of the table contains the *House price* median ($) and the number of observations on which the median is based.

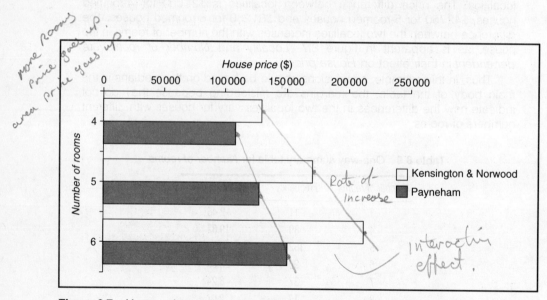

*more rooms →
price goes up.*

area price goes up?

Rate of Increase

Interaction effect.

Figure 8.7   *House price* medians for different sized houses in two localities

Table with independent limited variables

EXAMPLE 8.5   HOUSE SALES IN TWO LOCALITIES (continued)

We continue examining the differences between Kensington and Norwood and Payneham by determining how the area of the property or block changes with locality and number of rooms. Again, an unrestricted variable and two limited variables are involved: the unrestricted variable is *Block area* and the limited variables are *Locality* and *Number of rooms*. To decide whether to use a two-way table of means or medians to measure the central tendency of *Block area*, we require the distribution of *Block area* for each combination of *Locality* and *Number of rooms*. These are given in figure 8.8 and indicate that at least some of the distributions are skew-to-the-right. Consequently, the two-way table of medians is preferred to the two-way table of means.

The two-way table of *Block area* medians for this example is given in table 8.11 and illustrated in figure 8.9. The area difference between the two localities is 0.0413 ha for 4-roomed houses, 0.0326 ha for 5-roomed houses and 0.0339 ha for 6-roomed houses. The differences between the two localities are about the same, no matter how many rooms the house has. That is, *Locality* and *Number of rooms* are *independent* in their effect on *Block area*.

To investigate the influence of *Locality* and *Number of rooms* on *Block area*, we examine the two one-way tables of *Block area* medians for each of these limited variables in tables 8.12 and 8.13. From these tables we conclude that the block area in Kensington and Norwood is 0.0367 ha less than that in Payneham. Also, the block size increases with the number of rooms in the house: 6-room houses have a block size that is 0.0171 ha larger than 4-room houses.

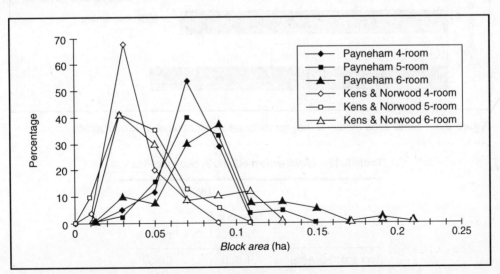

Figure 8.8   Polygons of *Block area* for each combination of *Locality* and *Number of rooms*

Table 8.11   Two-way table of *Block area* medians (ha) for different sized houses in two localities

	Number of rooms			
Locality	4	5	6	Total
Kensington & Norwood	0.0334 27	0.0404 46	0.0472 24	0.0383 97
Payneham	0.0747 36	0.0730 90	0.0811 45	0.0750 171
Total	0.0597 63	0.0655 136	0.0768 69	0.0665 268

Each cell of the table contains the *Block area* median (ha) and the number of observations on which the median is based.

[handwritten margin note: Use this because it is skewed. median]

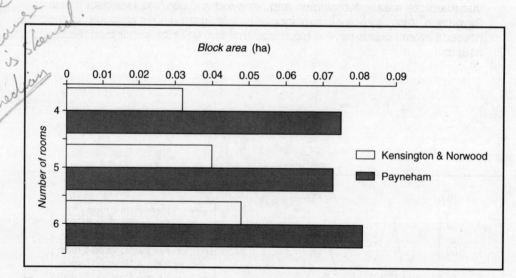

Figure 8.9   *Block area* medians (ha) for different sized houses in two localities

Table 8.12   *Block area* medians in two localities

	Locality	
	Kensington & Norwood	Payneham
Block area median (ha)	0.0383	0.0750
n	97	171

Table 8.13   *Block area* medians for different sized houses

	Number of rooms		
	4	5	6
Block area median (ha)	0.0597	0.0655	0.0768
n	63	136	69

8.6   Reports on examples

The following reports, for the examples analysed in this chapter, indicate what material from a statistical analysis an investigator should include in a report. In general, the details of the statistical analysis are omitted so that the reader of the report can concentrate on the results.

EXAMPLE 8.1   HOUSE PRICES IN THREE LOCALITIES — REPORT

An investigation was conducted to compare the prices of houses in three localities: the local government areas of Kensington and Norwood, St Peters and Payneham. Data is available for all the residences sold over a 12-month period in these localities. The percentage polygons in figure 8.1 show that the distribution of house prices in all three localities is skew-to-the-right. The distributions for Kensington and Norwood and St Peters are very similar. From the box-and-whisker plots in figure 8.5, we concluded that prices in Payneham are both lower and a little less spread than in the other two localities. Also, in all three areas several houses sold for very high prices. There are also two very low house prices for Kensington and Norwood, and an examination of the original data confirmed that these correspond to prices of $3880 and $4000.

The medians of prices from the three localities in figure 8.3 indicate that house prices in Kensington and Norwood and St Peters are typically just over $170 000. On the other hand, prices in Payneham, at about $130 000, are generally a little over $40 000 dollars less than in the other two localities. The interquartile ranges of prices from the three localities in table 8.6 indicate that the middle 50% of house prices in Kensington and Norwood and St Peters cover a range of about $100 000, with Kensington and Norwood prices perhaps a little less variable than those in St Peters. Prices in Payneham are somewhat less variable than in the other two localities: the middle 50% of prices in Payneham cover a range of about $50,000.

EXAMPLE 8.2   YEARLY PATTERN IN QUEENSLAND VISITORS FOR 1989–93 — REPORT

As part of planning a tourist business in Queensland, the operator wants to establish the annual pattern of visitors to Queensland over the past five years. The room occupancy rate of hotels, motels and guesthouses in Queensland for each month during the period 1989–1993 have been obtained from the Australian Bureau of Statistics (1989–1993).

The mean occupancy rate has been plotted against the month in figure 8.4. Occupancy rates appear to peak in July, August, September and October.

EXAMPLE 8.3   MANAGEMENT CAPACITY FOR TWO BRANCHES — REPORT

A company gave a management test with a score range of 0–100 to 30 of its employees from one branch and 57 from a second branch. The scores of two individuals, one from each branch, were compared, to evaluate their relative standings in their own branch. The branch 1 employee's score was 69.8 and the branch 2 employee's score was 68.7. However, their standardised scores are –0.35 and 0.20, respectively, so that the branch 1 employee is 0.35 standard deviations below average in his or her branch whereas the branch 2 employee is 0.20 standard deviations above the average in his or her branch. Overall, the score of the branch 2 employee is 0.20 – (–0.35) = 0.55 standard deviations better than the branch 1 employee.

EXAMPLE 8.4   LOCAL CRIME RATE — REPORT

The change in the crime rate between two periods separated by 12 months was examined in an article by Hider (1994) in a local suburban newspaper. The percentage decreases between the two periods for several offences have been computed for Unley and Norwood. Overall, the decrease in the crime rate was 22% for Unley and 22.9% for Norwood. However, as illustrated in figure 8.10, the decrease differed between offences and, for a particular offence, was not the same in Unley and Norwood. For example, offensive behaviour decreased more than larceny involving a motor vehicle. Also, the decrease in property damage is much greater in Norwood than in Unley.

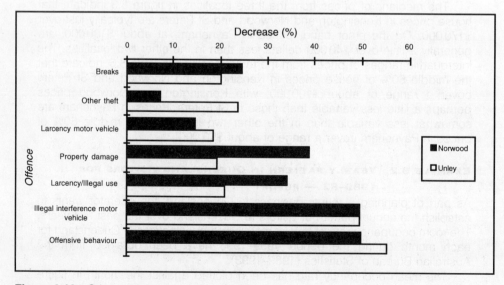

Figure 8.10 Crime rate in two areas of a city

EXAMPLE 8.5   HOUSE SALES IN TWO LOCALITIES — REPORT

Data was available on all the residences sold over a 12-month period in two localities: the Kensington and Norwood and Payneham local government areas. In a more detailed investigation of the differences between the two localities, the following questions were investigated:

1. the dependence of the typical house price on the number of rooms in the house and locality of the house;
2. the dependence of the typical block area on the number of rooms in the house and the locality of the house.

As far as the number of rooms in a house (not including bathrooms, toilets and laundries) is concerned, about 82% of all houses sold in these two localities have 4, 5 or 6 rooms. Only houses with these numbers of rooms are considered, because houses with other than 4, 5, or 6 rooms are not sold often enough to provide reliable figures. Also, since the distribution of both house price and block area is often skew-to-the-right for each locality and number of rooms, the medians have been used to measure the typical house price and block area.

The medians, computed from the house prices for the different combinations of number of rooms and localities, are presented in figure 8.7. Locality and number of rooms are dependent in their effects on house price because the difference in house price between the two localities is not the same for each number of rooms. The difference in house price between the two localities increases with the number of rooms in the house: $21 000 for 4-roomed houses, $42 750 for 5-roomed houses and $61 250 for 6-roomed houses.

Locality and number of rooms are independent in their effect on block area in that the difference in block area between the two localities is approximately the same for each number of rooms. The one-way tables of block area medians, for the different localities and for the different number of rooms in the houses, are given in tables 8.12 and 8.13 respectively. From these tables we conclude that the block area in Kensington and Norwood is 0.0367 ha less than that in Payneham. Also, the block size increases with the number of rooms in the house: 6-room houses have a block size that is 0.0171 ha larger than that of 4-room houses.

8.7   Using Minitab for one unrestricted variable and some limited variables

8.7.1   Distribution tables and distribution diagrams for one unrestricted and one limited variable

The commands for producing the distribution tables and distribution diagrams involving one unrestricted variable and one limited variable are the same as for those for producing them when just one unrestricted variable and no limited variable(s) are involved. The difference is that the *by* subcommand of the corresponding command has to be included. So, use the *histogram, stem, dotplot.* or *boxplot* commands with the *by* subcommand to obtain separate frequency tables and histograms, stem-and-leaf displays, dotplots or boxplots from the values of the unrestricted variable for each value of a limited variable.

EXAMPLE 8.1   HOUSE PRICES IN THREE LOCALITIES (continued)

In this example, distribution tables and distribution diagrams and measures of central tendency were produced for *House price* from three different localities. The data is contained in a Minitab portable worksheet file named *vgsales.mtp*, with the *House price* stored in *c3* and the *Locality* in *c1*, and the coding for *Locality* is given in table 8.14. However, the two columns contain the data not only for houses, but also for other types of residences. The type of residence was stored in *c12*, with houses coded as 11. So, before the analyses could be performed, the *copy* command had to be used to reduce the data in these columns to just that for the houses. This was done, as described in section 6.5.4, *Combining and deleting rows and columns of contingency tables*, with the *use* subcommand of the *copy* command.

Table 8.14   Coding for *Locality*

Locality	Code
Kensington & Norwood	15
St Peters	16
Payneham	19

The commands, and associated output, to retrieve the worksheet and reduce the data are given as follows:

```
MTB > outfile 'a:\vgdiags.lis'
MTB > retrieve 'a:\vgsales.mtp';
SUBC> portable.

Worksheet retrieved from file: a:\vgsales.mtp
MTB > info

COLUMN          NAME      COUNT    MISSING
C1           locality       841
C3              price       841          3
C8           no_rooms       841         20
C9           blocarea       841        349
C12           landuse       841
C15          walltype       841         46

CONSTANTS USED: NONE

MTB > copy c1 c3 c1 c3;
SUBC> use c12=11.
```

Having got the worksheet ready to perform the analyses, we used the following commands to produce the distribution tables and diagrams:

```
MTB > histogram c3;
SUBC> by c1;
SUBC> start 12500;
SUBC> increment 25000.
MTB > stem c3;
SUBC> by c1.
MTB > dotplot c3;
SUBC> by c1.
MTB > boxplot c3;
SUBC> by c1.
```

If your version of Minitab has pull-down menus and you want to use them, table 8.15 lists the menus and options that access the required commands. Appendix D, *Detailed instructions for Minitab menus*, explains how to use the menus.

Table 8.15   Menus and options for Minitab commands to produce diagrams for one unrestricted variable

Minitab command	Menu	Option
outfile	File >	Other Files > Start Recording Session...
retrieve	File >	Open Worksheet...
port		Minitab portable worksheet
info	Edit >	Get Worksheet Info...
	(Edit >	Data Screen [Alt-D])
copy	Calc >	Copy Columns...
use		Use Rows...
histogram	Graph >	Histogram...
stem	Graph >	Stem and Leaf...
dotplot	Graph >	Dotplot...
boxplot	Graph >	Boxplot...

Frequency tables and diagrams

EXAMPLE 8.1   HOUSE PRICES IN THREE LOCALITIES (continued)

In this example, frequency tables and polygons were produced for *House price* from three different localities (see table 8.1 and figure 8.1). The frequencies to produce them were obtained by using a *histogram* command that included the *start*, *increment* and *by* subcommands. The commands to do this, and associated output, are as follows:

```
MTB > histogram c3;
SUBC> by c1;
SUBC> start 12500;
SUBC> increment 25000.
Histogram of price   locality = 15   N = 124

Midpoint       Count
    12500        2   **
    37500        0
    62500        2   **
    87500        4   ****
   112500       12   ************
   137500       20   ********************
   162500       22   **********************
   187500       17   *****************
   212500        9   *********
   237500       14   **************
   262500        7   *******
   287500        5   *****
   312500        5   *****
   337500        3   ***
   362500        0
   387500        0
   412500        0
   437500        0
   462500        1   *
   487500        0
   512500        0
   537500        0
   562500        0
   587500        0
   612500        0
   637500        0
   662500        0
   687500        0
   712500        0
   737500        0
   762500        0
   787500        1   *
```

continued . . .

```
Histogram of price    locality = 16    N = 126 N* = 1


Midpoint          Count
   12500            0
   37500            0
   62500            4   ****
   87500            8   ********
  112500           12   ************
  137500           19   *******************
  162500           21   *********************
  187500           13   *************
  212500           11   ***********
  237500            8   ********
  262500            8   ********
  287500            5   *****
  312500            5   *****
  337500            3   ***
  362500            0
  387500            0
  412500            0
  437500            0
  462500            1   *
  487500            0
  512500            0
  537500            0
  562500            0
  587500            0
  612500            0
  637500            0
  662500            0
  687500            0
  712500            0
  737500            0
  762500            0
  787500            1   *
Histogram of price    locality = 19    N = 201 N* = 2
Each * represents 2 obs.


Midpoint          Count
   12500            2   *
   37500            3   **
   62500            4   **
   87500           16   ********
  112500           54   ***************************
  137500           58   *****************************
  162500           34   *****************
  187500           11   ******
  212500            7   ****
  237500            2   *
  262500            4   **
```

continued . . .

```
287500      1    *
312500      2    *
337500      1    *
362500      0
387500      0
412500      0
437500      1    *
462500      0
487500      1    *
512500      0
537500      0
562500      0
537500      0
537500      0
587500      0
612500      0
637500      0
662500      0
687500      0
712500      0
737500      0
762500      0
787500      0
```

Stem-and-leaf displays

EXAMPLE 8.1   HOUSE PRICES IN THREE LOCALITIES (continued)

In this example, stem-and-leaf displays were produced for *House price* from three different localities (see table 8.2). These displays were obtained with the *by* subcommand of the *stem* command. As with using the *histogram* command, the required prices are stored in *c3* and the *Locality* in *c1*. The stem command and associated output are as follows. Note the first line of the stem for 1 in the display for locality 19: there is a plus (+) at the end of the line indicating that not all the leaves could be fitted on the line.

```
MTB > stem c3;
SUBC> by c1.

Stem-and-leaf of price    locality = 15    N = 124
Leaf Unit = 10000

    2    0   02
    8    0   567999
   40    1   0000111112222222233333333333444
  (39)   1   5555555555555666677777777777788888899999
   45    2   0001111222222233344444
   22    2   555556688899
   10    3   00122333
    2    3
    2    4
    2    4   6
    1    5
    1    5
    1    6
    1    6
    1    7
    1    7   8

Stem-and-leaf of price    locality = 16    N  = 126
Leaf Unit = 10000                          N* = 1

   12    0   666788999999
   43    1   0000011222222223333334444444444
  (34)   1   5555555556666666677777777788889999999
   49    2   00000111111222333344
   30    2   6666677777899
   17    3   0001222244
    7    3   68
    5    4   3
    4    4
    4    5
    4    5   6666

Stem-and-leaf of price    locality = 19    N  = 201
Leaf Unit = 10000                          N* = 2

    5    0   11244
   25    0   55667788888888999999
 (112)   1   0000000000000000000000000000011111111111111111111222222222222222222+
   64    1   5555555555555666666666666666666677777
              888888889
   19    2   000012224
   10    2   56667
    5    3   003
    2    3
    2    4   4
    1    4   9
```

Dotplots

EXAMPLE 8.1   HOUSE PRICES IN THREE LOCALITIES (continued)

In this example, dotplots were produced for *House price* from three different
localities (see figure 8.2). Such diagrams can be produced by using the *by*
subcommand of the *dotplot* command. Again, the required prices are stored in
c3 and the *Locality* in *c1*. The *dotplot* command, and associated output, are
as follows:

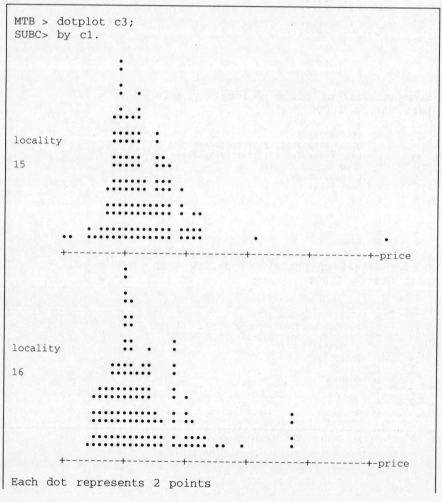

```
MTB > dotplot c3;
SUBC> by c1.
```

Each dot represents 2 points

continued . . .

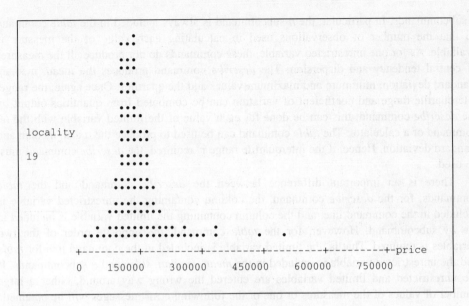

Boxplots

The box-and-whisker plot for *House price* from three localities (figure 8.5) is produced by using the *boxplot* command with the *by* subcommand. The *boxplot* command, and associated output, is as follows:

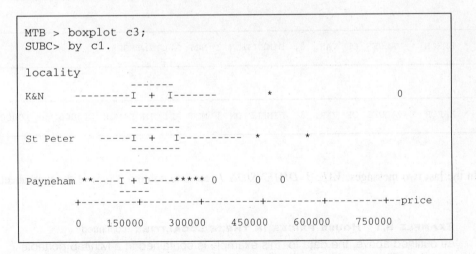

8.7.2   Measures of central tendency and dispersion for one unrestricted and one limited variable

The two commands you can use to produce the one-way tables of measures of central tendency and dispersion are the *describe* and *table* commands. For the *describe* command, use the *by* subcommand, whereas the *table* command requires the *mean, median, stdev* and *n* subcommands. In particular, the *n* subcommand is always included in the *table* command so that the number of observations used in calculating each value of the measure is available. As for one unrestricted variable, these commands do not produce all the measures of central tendency and dispersion. The *describe* command produces the mean, median, standard deviation, minimum and maximum values and the quartiles. Once again, the range, interquartile range and coefficient of variation can be computed from quantities output by the *describe* command; this can be done for each value of the limited variable with the *let* command or a calculator. The *table* command can be used to produce the mean, median and standard deviation. Hence, if the interquartile range is required, the *describe* command must be used.

There is an important difference between the *describe* command and the *table* commands: for the *describe* command, the column containing the unrestricted variable is included in the command line, and the column containing the limited variable is included in the *by* subcommand. However, for the *table* command, the opposite order of the two variables is required. That is, the limited variable is included in the command line for *table* and the unrestricted variable is included in the *mean, median, stdev* and *n* subcommands. If the unrestricted and limited variables are entered the wrong way around, either a large number of values of the measures or one of the following error messages will be obtained:

```
* ERROR * Non-integers in BY column
```

```
* ERROR * VALUES OF VAR.  3,  DIMENSION  1  NOT  ALL  INTEGER
```

```
* ERROR * VALUES OF VAR.  3,  DIMENSION  1  NOT  ALL  IN  RANGE  -10000 to 10000
```

In the last two messages, *VAR. 3, DIMENSION 1* refers to column 3 (*c3*) of the worksheet.

EXAMPLE 8.1   HOUSE PRICES IN THREE LOCALITIES (continued)

As outlined above, the data for this example is contained in a Minitab portable worksheet file, with *House price* stored in *c3* and *Locality* in *c1*, and the coding for *Locality* is given in table 8.14. However, the two columns contain the data not only for houses, but also for other types of residences. So, as described in section 8.7.1, *Distribution tables and distribution diagrams for one unrestricted and one limited variable*, the *copy* command is used to reduce the data in these columns to the data just for houses. Then the information for producing the one-way tables (tables 8.3 and 8.4) was obtained with the *describe* or *table* commands. The Minitab commands for producing the measures are as follows:

```
MTB > outfile 'a:\vg1way.lis'
MTB > retrieve 'a:\vgsales.mtp';
SUBC> portable.
MTB > info
MTB > copy c1 c3 c1 c3;
SUBC> use c12=11.
MTB > describe c3;
SUBC> by c1.
MTB > table c1;
SUBC> mean c3;
SUBC> n c3.
MTB > table c1;
SUBC> median c3;
SUBC> n c3.
MTB > table c1;
SUBC> mean c3;
SUBC> stdev c3;
SUBC> n c3.
```

If your version of Minitab has pull-down menus and you want to use them, table 8.16 lists the menus and options that access the required commands. Appendix D, *Detailed instructions for Minitab menus*, explains how to use the menus.

Table 8.16   Menus and options for Minitab commands to produce one-way tables of measures of central tendency and dispersion

Minitab command	Menu	Option
outfile	File >	Other Files > Start Recording Session...
retrieve	File >	Open Worksheet...
port		Minitab portable worksheet
info	Edit >	Get Worksheet Info...
	(Edit >	Data Screen [Alt-D])
copy	Calc >	Copy Columns...
use		Use Rows...
describe	Stat >	Basic Statistics > Descriptive Statistics...
table	Stat >	Tables > Cross Tabulation...
mean, median, stdev, n		Summaries...

The output for the *describe* and *table* commands is as follows:

```
MTB > describe c3;
SUBC> by c1.

  locality            N     N*    MEAN   MEDIAN   TRMEAN

price   15          124      0  188502   174000   183004
        16          126      1  200238   172500   190672
        19          201      2  139779   130000   135078


locality       STDEV  SEMEAN     MIN      MAX       Q1       Q3

price   15     88320    7931    3880   781000   135000   230250
        16     98740    8796   65000   560000   138000   244250
        19     56981    4019   12000   490000   108750   160000


MTB > table c1;
SUBC> mean c3;
SUBC> n c3.
 ROWS: locality


          price     price
          MEAN        N

 15      188502       124
 16      200238       126
 19      139779       201
ALL      170066       451


MTB > table c1;
SUBC> median c3;
SUBC> n c3.

ROWS: locality


          price     price
          MEDIAN      N

 15      174000       124
 16      172500       126
 19      130000       201
ALL        --         451
MTB > table c1;
SUBC> mean c3;
SUBC> stdev c3;
SUBC> n c3.

 ROWS: locality
```

continued . . .

	price MEAN	price STD DEV	price N
15	188502	88320	124
16	200238	98740	126
19	139779	56981	201
ALL	170066	83915	451

Note that all tables include the numbers of observations used in calculating each value of each measure.

8.7.3   Measures of central tendency and dispersion for one unrestricted variable and two limited variables

The *table* command, with *mean*, *median* and *n* subcommands, is used to produce two-way tables of means and medians. The limited variable is included in the *table* command and the unrestricted variable is included in the subcommands. If the variables are swapped around, the error messages given in section 8.7.2, *Measures of central tendency and dispersion for one unrestricted and one limited variable*, will result. Minitab does not produce the margins for the two-way table of medians, so you have to compute the two one-way tables for the margins separately. This is satisfactory unless the columns have different values missing from them. If tables of medians are to be computed and any of the columns involved contain missing values, it is safest to remove from all columns any rows that have a missing value in any one of the columns. This will ensure that the one-way tables correspond to the margins of the two-way tables.

EXAMPLE 8.5   HOUSE SALES IN TWO LOCALITIES (continued)

Table 8.10 contains a two-way table of *House price* medians for houses with 4, 5 or 6 rooms in the two localities Kensington and Norwood and Payneham. The commands to obtain the two-way tables of means and medians are as follows. The first three commands retrieve the worksheet from the portable worksheet file, check the contents of the worksheet and erase columns *c9* and *c15*. The columns are erased to leave enough room in the worksheet to execute the remaining commands. The next four commands are *copy* commands to ensure that the columns *c1*, *c3* and *c8* contain only the data from which the two-way table is to be produced and contain no missing values. The remaining commands are the *table* commands to produce the two-way tables of means and medians and the two one-way tables of medians.

```
MTB > outfile 'a:\vg2way.lis'
MTB > retrieve 'a:\vgsales.mtp';
SUBC> portable.
MTB > info
MTB > erase c9 c15
MTB > copy c1 c3 c8 c1 c3 c8;
SUBC> use c12=11.
MTB > copy c1 c3 c8 c1 c3 c8;
SUBC> omit c1=16 '*'.
MTB > copy c1 c3 c8 c1 c3 c8;
SUBC> use c8= 4 5 6;
SUBC> omit c8='*'.
MTB > copy c1 c3 c8 c1 c3 c8;
SUBC> omit c3='*'.
MTB > info
MTB > table c1 c8;
SUBC> mean c3;
SUBC> n c3.
MTB > table c1 c8;
SUBC> median c3;
SUBC> n c3.
MTB > table c1;
SUBC> median c3;
SUBC> n c3.
MTB > table c8;
SUBC> median c3;
SUBC> n c3.
```

If your version of Minitab has pull-down menus and you want to use them, table 8.17 lists the menus and options that access the required commands. Appendix D, *Detailed instructions for Minitab menus*, explains how to use the menus.

Table 8.17   Menus and options for Minitab commands to produce two-way tables of a central tendency measure

Minitab command	Menu	Option
outfile	File >	Other Files > Start Recording Session...
retrieve	File >	Open Worksheet...
port		Minitab portable worksheet
info	Edit >	Get Worksheet Info...
	(Edit >	Data Screen... [Alt-D])
erase	Calc >	Erase Variables...
copy	Calc >	Copy Columns...
use		Use Rows...
table	Stat >	Tables > Cross Tabulation...
mean, median, n		Summaries...

The output, from the commands outlined above, is as follows:

```
MTB > retrieve 'a:\vgsales.mtp';
SUBC> portable.

Worksheet retrieved from file: a:\vgsales.mtp
MTB > info

COLUMN    NAME        COUNT    MISSING
C1        locality     841
C3        price        841          3
C8        no_rooms     841         20
C9        blocarea     841        349
C12       landuse      841
C15       walltype     841         46

CONSTANTS USED: NONE

MTB > erase c9 c15
MTB > copy c1 c3 c8 c1 c3 c8;
SUBC> use c12=11.
MTB > copy c1 c3 c8 c1 c3 c8;
SUBC> omit c1=16 '*'.
MTB > copy c1 c3 c8 c1 c3 c8;
SUBC> use c8= 4 5 6;
SUBC> omit c8='*'.
MTB > copy c1 c3 c8 c1 c3 c8;
SUBC> omit c3='*'.
MTB > info

COLUMN    NAME        COUNT
C1        locality     268
C3        price        268
C8        no_rooms     268
C12       landuse      841

CONSTANTS USED: NONE

MTB > table c1 c8;
SUBC> mean c3;
SUBC> n c3.
ROWS: locality     COLUMNS: no_rooms

              4           5           6         ALL

15        126570      174905      199635      167570
              27          46          24          97

19        108607      124839      155622      129522
              36          90          45         171

ALL       116305      141773      170931      143293
              63         136          69         268
```

continued . . .

```
   CELL CONTENTS --
           price:MEAN
                  N
MTB > table c1 c8;
SUBC> median c3;
SUBC> n c3.
 ROWS: locality COLUMNS: no_rooms


             4            5            6        ALL

 15       129000       170000       211250       --
             27           46           24         97


 19       108000       127250       150000       --
             36           90           45        171


ALL          --           --           --         --
             63     13669268
   CELL CONTENTS --
           price:MEDIAN
                  N

MTB > table c1;
SUBC> median c3;
SUBC> n c3.


 ROWS: locality


           price      price
           MEDIAN         N

 15       160000          97
 19       128000         171
 ALL         --          268


MTB > table c8;
SUBC> median c3;
SUBC> n c3.
 ROWS: no_rooms


           price      price
           MEDIAN         N

 4        112500          63
 5        136000         136
 6        158000          69
 ALL         --          268
```

8.8   Chapter summary

This chapter describes how to use the procedures covered in the previous chapter for a single unrestricted variable when you have an unrestricted variable *and* some limited variables. Basically, the methods for just an unrestricted variable are applied to each value, or combination of values, of the limited variable(s).

If the question to be investigated involves one unrestricted and one limited variable, the available procedures are as follows:

1. To investigate the general shape, produce histograms, polygons, stem-and-leaf displays or dotplots from the values of the unrestricted variable for each value of the limited variable; the diagram of choice in this situation is percentage (or proportion) polygons superimposed on each other in the same diagram.
2. To describe central tendency, examine one-way tables of a central tendency measure; the measure of central tendency in the tables is the mean or the median.
3. To describe dispersion, examine one-way tables of a dispersion measure; the measure in the tables is usually the standard deviation or the interquartile range.

The box-and-whisker plot is ideally suited to represent both the central tendency and dispersion when there is an unrestricted variable and one or more limited variables. The usual diagram for presenting just the values of a measure of central tendency is the bar chart, unless the limited variable is continuous, in which case you could use a line diagram.

If the question to be investigated involves one unrestricted variable and two limited variables and central tendency is of interest, then two-way tables of a central tendency measure should be examined. From these, you can determine whether the two limited variables are dependent or independent in their effect on the unrestricted variable. The tables of a central tendency measure for presenting the results depend on whether they are dependent or independent.

A useful device for comparing the values from two different sets of data is to standardise the values, thus forming standardised scores. Standardised scores allow a relative comparison.

The weighted mean is used when a mean is to be computed and there are weights that reflect the importance of the values to be averaged.

8.9   Key terms

- dependent limited variables
- distribution diagram
- distribution of variables
- independent limited variables
- line diagram
- main body of a two-way table of a central tendency measure
- measure of central tendency
- measure of dispersion
- one-way table of a central tendency measure

- one-way table of a dispersion measures
- standardise
- standardised score (z)
- sum of products
- two-way table of a central tendency measure
- weight (w_i)
- weighted mean ($\bar{y}_w$)

8.10   Exercises

8.1   The results of a recent survey of *Annual income* for the households in two neighbouring towns, Statstown and Bustown, are presented in table 8.18. The incomes for the households in Statstown were examined in exercises 7.12–7.15. We want to compare the shape of the distributions of the *Annual income* for the observed households from the different towns.

Table 8.18   *Annual income* ($) for the households in two towns

Statstown

93 000	82 000	102 000	90 000	95 000	93 000	76 000	86 000
72 000	75 000	75 000	77 000	92 000	84 000	97 000	71 000
98 000	114 000	86 000	82 000	92 000	80 000	95 000	96 000
86 000	92 000	93 000	89 000	80 000	93 000	91 000	104 000
87 000	92 000	83 000	101 000	84 000	71 000	95 000	103 000

Bustown

107 000	125 000	102 000	146 000	99 000	125 000	127 000	109 000
129 000	113 000	102 000	102 000	112 000	153 000	103 000	111 000
139 000	109 000	116 000	136 000	137 000	106 000	133 000	106 000
123 000	112 000	123 000	90 000	115 000	102 000	112 000	138 000
122 000	106 000	117 000	123 000	122 000	135 000	136 000	132 000
109 000	114 000	140 000	156 000	105 000	121 000	148 000	101 000
147 000	93 000	143 000	127 000	133 000	111 000	127 000	113 000
108 000	151 000	111 000	118 000	158 000	162 000	111 000	144 000
122 000	144 000	159 000	88 000	115 000	154 000	101 000	148 000
143 000	110 000	97 000	119 000	153 000	101 000	146 000	127 000

(a) Answer the following questions:
   (i) What is the question to be investigated (including the group to which the conclusions apply)?
   (ii) What variable(s) are we concerned with here?
   (iii) What type of variable(s) are they?
   (iv) Which major category of statistical procedures applies here? Why?
   (v) What type of statistic should we use, given the question to be investigated and the variables involved?
   (vi) Which particular statistic or procedure, and diagram, should we use? Why?
(b) Answer the following questions as best as you can from table 8.18:
   (i) Are there any major differences between the samples from the two towns in the distribution of *Annual income*?
   (ii) What are the highest and lowest *Annual incomes* in the sample from Bustown?
   (iii) Do the households in the sample from Statstown have approximately the same *Annual income*?
   (iv) Are there any households more affluent than their neighbours in the sample from each town, using the *Annual income* as an indicator?
   (v) Do the households sampled from one town have a higher standard of living than the other?
(c) Did you have difficulty in answering the questions in part (b)? Give reasons for your answer.
(d) Can you suggest a method of presentation that would make your task much easier? If you have to make a choice between various methods, give reasons for your selection.

8.2 For the data from exercise 8.1, produce a distribution table of *Annual income* for each of the two towns. The data is saved in the Minitab portable worksheet file *inctown.mtp*, with the data from each town stored in separate columns. The following Minitab commands will put the annual incomes for the households from each town into one column and create a column containing a variable that identifies the town of each household.

```
MTB > outfile 'a:\inctown.lis'
MTB > retrieve 'a:\inctown.mtp';
SUBC> portable.
MTB > name c3 'town' c4 'income'
MTB > set c3
DATA> 40(1),80(2)
DATA> end
MTB > stack c1 c2 c4
MTB > info
```

If your version of Minitab has pull-down menus and you want to use them, table 8.18 lists the menus and options that access the required commands. Appendix D, *Detailed instructions for Minitab menus*, explains how to use the menus.

Table 8.19   Menus and options for Minitab commands to stack columns

Minitab command	Menu	Option
outfile	File >	Other Files > Start Recording Session...
retrieve	File >	Open Worksheet...
port		Minitab portable worksheet
info	Edit >	Get Worksheet Info...
	(Edit >	Data Screen [Alt-D])
name	Edit >	Data Screen
set		no equivalent
stack	Calc >	Stack...
info	Edit >	Get Worksheet Info...

(a) Use Minitab to obtain histograms on the same scale for each town.

(b) Draw the corresponding relative frequency polygons on the one diagram.

(c) What is the general shape of the *Annual income* for the households from Bustown? Does this shape differ from that of the households sampled from Statstown? If so, describe the differences.

8.3 Produce dotplots showing *Annual income* for the households sampled from Statstown and Bustown. This data is saved in the Minitab portable worksheet file *inctown.mtp*.

(a) What information is portrayed in these diagrams?

(b) Describe how the *Annual income* for the sampled households from one town differs from that for those from the other town.

8.4 An Australian university lecturer is preparing the marksheets for a first year Statistics course, which he has given during the semester to two different groups of students at the university. Group 2 has a stronger background in computing than Group 1 and the lecturer wishes to see whether the two sets of results reflect this difference in expertise. The students have been assessed with a mark out of 100. The results gained by the two sets of students are saved in the Minitab portable worksheet file *marks.mtp*.

(a) Answer the following questions:

(i) What is the question to be investigated (including the group to which the conclusions apply)?

(ii) What variable(s) are we concerned with here?

(iii) What type of variable(s) are they?

(iv) Which major category of statistical procedures applies here? Why?

(v) What type of statistic should we use, given the question to be investigated and the variables involved?

(vi) Which particular statistic or procedure, and diagram, should we use? Why?

(b) Reproduce the following computer output.

```
MTB > retrieve 'a:\marks.mtp';
SUBC> portable.

Worksheet retrieved from file: a:\marks.mtp

MTB > info

COLUMN   NAME    COUNT
C1       groups   261
C2       marks    261

CONSTANTS USED: NONE

MTB > stem c2;
SUBC> by c1.

Stem-and-leaf of marks    groups = 1    N = 118
Leaf Unit = 1.0

     4         1   6778
     4         2
     7         2   588
     8         3   3
    10         3   67
    14         4   1113
    28         4   55568888888889
    37         5   001223444
    47         5   6777889999
    56         6   022333444
   (15)        6   555666667778899
    47         7   11222233444
    36         7   55577778888899
    22         8   000122222334444
     7         8   6778899

Stem-and-leaf of marks    groups = 2    N = 143
Leaf Unit = 1.0

     1         1   6
     4         2   002
     4         2
     9         3   00111
    13         3   6789
    18         4   01123
    34         4   6667788888888889
    39         5   23344
    53         5   55556666677889
   (20)        6   00001222233333333444
```

continued . . .

```
70        6    55566666677777778888899999
43        7    00001111111122233444
24        7    5557777789999
11        8    01123
 6        8    55889
 1        9    0
```

```
MTB > dotplot c2;
SUBC> by c1.
```

```
                                        .
                                        :
                                        :
groups                                  :      .    :..    .   .. :
1                                       :    
                                .       :  .:.  ..  ..   ....  ::...: :: . :
                          .   . :  . . .:  .:.................................:
                        :.       . :. . . .:  .:.................................::
              ---+---------+---------+---------+---------+---------+--marks
```

```
                                                 :
                                               : .
                                        :   .     : .
groups                                  :   :    : : :
2                                       :   :    : : :
                                      .:   .   .:......  . ..
                                      ::  . .:...........:::  :           .
                        .   .       ::   .:. :   ...................: :::  : .
              ---+---------+---------+---------+---------+---------+--marks
                 15        30        45        60        75        90
```

```
MTB > describe c2;
SUBC> by c1.
```

	groups	N	MEAN	MEDIAN	TRMEAN	STDEV	SEMEAN
marks	1	118	62.91	65.50	63.91	17.37	1.60
	2	143	61.26	64.00	61.88	15.08	1.26

	groups	MIN	MAX	Q1	Q3
marks	1	16.00	89.00	50.00	77.25
	2	16.00	90.00	53.00	71.00

(c) Write a report, based on the computer output given in part (b), comparing the two
     groups of students.

8.5 Information collected from a class of students studying Statistics has been saved in the
     Minitab portable worksheet file *studhght.mtp*. Two of the columns in this file are *sex*
     and *height*. In the column named *sex*, the males are coded 1 and the females are coded
     2. We want to compare the two height distributions obtained for the observed students
     of each sex.

(a) Answer the following questions:
   (i) What is the question to be investigated (including the group to which the conclusions apply)?
   (ii) What variable(s) are we concerned with here?
   (iii) What type of variable(s) are they?
   (iv) Which major category of statistical procedures applies here? Why?
   (v) What type of statistic should we use, given the question to be investigated and the variables involved?
   (vi) Which particular statistic or procedure, and diagram, should we use? Why?
(b) Which distribution diagram is best for comparing the distributions of *Height* for male and female students? Why?
(c) Produce the distribution diagram chosen in (b) to compare the height distributions for the two sexes.
(d) Where do the two distributions differ?

8.6 A firm is investigating how two different *Methods of payment* affect the *Number of orders* taken by its sales force. For a certain period all orders have to be paid for in cash and the number of orders taken by 43 salespeople is recorded. For a second specified period all orders have to be paid for by cheque and the number of orders taken by 38 salespeople is recorded. We want to compare the number of orders taken by the 81 observed salespeople when the two different methods of payment were in operation. The data is saved in the Minitab portable worksheet file *orders.mtp*. The payments by cash are coded 1 and the payments by cheque are coded 2.
(a) Answer the following questions:
   (i) What is the question to be investigated (including the group to which the conclusions apply)?
   (ii) What variable(s) are we concerned with here?
   (iii) What type of variable(s) are they?
   (iv) Which major category of statistical procedures applies here? Why?
   (v) What type of statistic should we use, given the question to be investigated and the variables involved?
   (vi) Which particular statistic or procedure, and diagram, should we use? Why?
(b) Figure 8.11 contains frequency polygons giving the distributions of the *Number of orders* for the two *Methods of payment*. What information is summarised by the two polygons?
(c) The Minitab output opposite contains histograms showing the distributions of the *Number of orders* for the two *Methods of payment*. In these diagrams, cash payment is coded 1 and payment by cheque is coded 2.
   (i) Reproduce this output.
   (ii) Prepare a percentage frequency distribution table for this data and draw the corresponding percentage histograms.
   (iii) From the percentage histograms compare the shapes of the distributions of the *Number of orders* for each *Method of payment*.

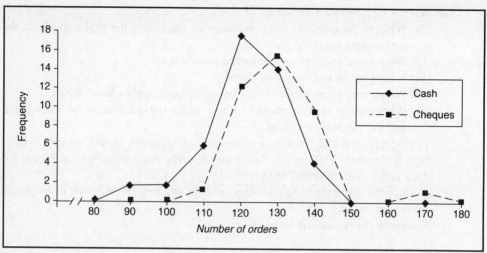

Figure 8.11 Distribution of *Number of orders* for two methods of payment

```
MTB > retrieve 'a:\orders.mtp';
SUBC> portable.
Worksheet retrieved from file: a:\orders.mtp
MTB > histogram 'no_order';
SUBC> by 'method'.

Histogram of no_order method = 1 N = 43

Midpoint      Count
      90          1    *
     100          1    *
     110          6    ******
     120         17    *****************
     130         14    **************
     140          4    ****
     150          0
     160          0
     170          0

Histogram of no_order method = 2 N = 38
Midpoint      Count
      90          0
     100          0
     110          1    *
     120         12    ************
     130         15    ***************
     140          9    *********
     150          0
     160          0
     170          1    *
```

(d) The following Minitab output contains dotplots showing the distributions of the *Number of orders* for the two *Methods of payment*. In these diagrams, cash payment is coded 1 and payment by cheque is coded 2.

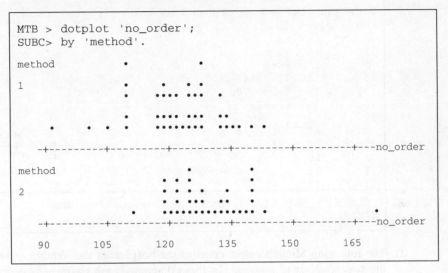

```
MTB > dotplot 'no_order';
SUBC> by 'method'.

method              •         •

1                   •     •   ••
                    •    ••••  •••   •
                    •         ••••  •••  ••
       •     •   •      ••••••••  ••••  •  •
    -+---------+---------+---------+---------+---------+---no_order

method                  •      •
                      • •  •   •
2                     • •  • •  •   •  •
                      • •  •••  ••   •
             •     ••••••••••••••••  •
    -+---------+---------+---------+---------+---------+---no_order
    90       105       120       135       150       165
```

   (i) Reproduce this output.

   (ii) What information is obtained from the dotplots?

   (iii) What difficulties did you encounter when using the dotplots?

   (iv) Compare the shape of the distributions by using the dotplots.

(e) The following Minitab output contains stem-and-leaf displays showing the distributions of the *Number of orders* for the two *Methods of payment*. In these diagrams, cash payment is coded 1 and payment by cheque is coded 2.

   (i) Reproduce this output.

   (ii) Compare the shape of the distributions by using the stem-and-leaf displays.

```
MTB > stem 'no_order';
SUBC> by 'method'.

Stem-and-leaf of no_order    method = 1    n = 43
Leaf Unit = 1.0

    1      9  1
    1   .  9
    2     10  0
    6     10  5999
    8     11  00
   15     11  7779999
  (10)    12  0001223444
   18     12  566677888
```

continued . . .

```
        9         13    22234
        4         13    569
        1         14    3

Stem-and-leaf of no_order     method = 2    n = 38
Leaf Unit = 1.0

        1         11    1
        5         11    8888
       13         12    01222344
       (9)        12    555667789
       16         13    122333
       10         13    578999
        4         14    002
        1         14
        1         15
        1         15
        1         16
        1         16
        1         17    0
```

(f) The following Minitab output contains the boxplots of the *Number of orders* for the two *Methods of payment*. In these diagrams, cash payment is coded 1 and payment by cheque is coded 2.

(i) Reproduce this output.

(ii) Identify any similarities and/or differences, evident from the boxplots, between the *Number of orders* obtained with the two *Methods of payment*.

```
MTB > boxplot 'no_order';
SUBC> by 'method'.

method
                          -------
1     *       *   ---------I  +  I----------
                          -------


                       ----------
2                ------- I   +    I-----                        *
                       ----------

   --+---------+---------+---------+---------+---------+---no_order
    90        105       120       135       150       165
```

(g) Which of the four distribution diagrams did you find the most useful in comparing the distributions of *Number of orders*, classified by *Method of payment*?

(h) The following output contains means and standard deviations of *Number of orders* for two *Methods of payment*. In this output, cash payment is coded 1 and payment by cheque is coded 2.

(i) Reproduce this output.

(ii) Compare the mean *Number of orders* by cash payment with the mean *Number of orders* paid by cheque.

(iii) Draw a bar chart to represent the mean *Number of orders* under each *Method of payment*.

(iv) Compare the standard deviations of the *Number of orders* for each *Method of payment*.

```
MTB > table 'method';
SUBC> mean 'no_order';
SUBC> stdev 'no_order';
SUBC> n 'no_order'.

 ROWS: method

          no_order    no_order    no_order
            MEAN      STD DEV           N

 1        122.02       10.40          43
 2        129.26       10.27          38
 ALL      125.42       10.90          81
```

(i)   The following output contains the medians and quartiles of *Number of orders* for two *Methods of payment*. In this output, cash payment is coded 1 and payment by cheque is coded 2.

(i) Reproduce this output.

(ii) Compare the median *Number of orders* for each *Method of payment*.

(iii) Draw a bar chart to represent the median *Number of orders* for each *Method of payment*.

(iv) Calculate the interquartile ranges for the *Number of orders* for each *Method of payment* and compare the results.

```
MTB > describe 'no_order';
SUBC> by 'method'.

          method       N     MEAN    MEDIAN   TRMEAN    STDEV   SEMEAN
               1      43   122.02    123.00   122.41    10.40     1.59
 no_order      2      38   129.26    127.00   128.56    10.27     1.67

          method               MIN       MAX      Q1       Q3
               1             91.00    143.00   117.00   128.00
 no_order      2            111.00    170.00   122.00   135.50
```

(j)   Which measures of central tendency and dispersion are the most appropriate to use with this data? Why?

8.7 Two members of the office staff, Ms Jones and Mr Smith, each operate a credit/debit account at the same building society branch. The balances of their individual accounts were recorded after each transaction over a 1-year period. The balances of the two accounts over this year are to be compared. The data is listed in table 8.20 and saved in the Minitab portable worksheet file *bankacc.mtp*.

Table 8.20   *Balance ($) for accounts of two staff members*

Ms Jones

−290	0	120	170	210	260	320	370	430	560
−240	10	120	180	220	260	330	390	440	560
−210	20	120	180	220	260	330	400	440	560
−180	30	130	180	220	260	330	400	450	580
−160	30	130	180	230	270	340	400	450	600
−150	60	130	190	230	270	340	400	460	630
−140	70	130	190	230	280	350	410	480	640
−130	90	130	200	240	280	350	410	490	600
−120	90	130	200	240	300	350	420	500	710
−70	100	140	200	240	300	360	420	510	730
−60	100	140	200	250	300	370	420	530	800
−20	110	150	210	250	310	370	420	530	820
0	110	170	210	180					

Mr Smith

−490	−110	−20	70	140	200	250	320	420	520
−370	−100	−10	70	140	200	270	320	420	530
−330	−100	0	90	150	210	270	330	440	560
−280	−90	10	90	150	210	270	340	450	580
−240	−90	10	90	160	230	280	350	460	590
−200	−80	20	100	180	230	280	380	460	690
−180	−60	30	110	180	240	290	380	470	740
−170	−40	40	110	190	240	290	390	480	810
−160	−40	50	130	190	240	310	390	490	830
−160	−30	70	140	190	250	320	400	510	−60

(a) Answer the following questions:
   (i) What is the question to be investigated (including the group to which the conclusions apply)?
   (ii) What variable(s) are we concerned with here?
   (iii) What type of variable(s) are they?
   (iv) Which major category of statistical procedures applies here? Why?
   (v) What type of statistic should we use, given the question to be investigated and the variables involved?
   (vi) Which particular statistic or procedure, and diagram, should we use? Why?

(b) Taken over the whole year, which account had more in it?

(c) If the bank imposes a fee on accounts involving more than 30 transactions per quarter, is either customer likely to incur this fee? Why?

(d) Write a brief report comparing the accounts of the two customers. If you had to grant one of these customers a loan, which one would you choose? Why?

8.8 The recession has meant a reduction in the number of positions available for young people, particularly in the public service. The government is under pressure to reverse its policy of freezing all new positions, and to create new opportunities for young people. As part of the campaign for this change of policy, all South Australian public service employees covered by the Government Management and Employment (GME) Act were surveyed and the age of each employee was recorded. We want to compare the age profile of South Australian public service employees with that of the whole Australian workforce. Table 8.21 lists the data.

Table 8.21 Age profile of the Australian workforce and South Australian public service employees at June 1992

Age (years)	Workforce	
	Whole Australian (%)	South Australian public service (%)
15-19	7.1	1.3
20-24	12.7	8.3
25-34	26.2	24.2
35-44	26.4	36.1
45-54	18.6	22.7
55-59	5.0	5.4
60+	4.1	2.0
	100.0	100.0

Source: abstracted from South Australian Department of Labour (1992)

(a) Answer the following questions:

(i) What is the question to be investigated (including the group to which the conclusions apply)?

(ii) What variable(s) are we concerned with here?

(iii) What type of variable(s) are they?

(iv) Which major category of statistical procedures applies here? Why?

(v) What type of statistic should we use, given the question to be investigated and the variables involved?

(vi) Which particular statistic or procedure, and diagram, should we use? Why?

(b) Is there any difference between the age profile of each group of employees?

8.9 Sometimes the original data from a survey is not available and all we have is secondary data similar to that given in table 8.22. This table gives age profiles of permanent male and female employees employed under the Government Management and Employment (GME) Act by the South Australian State Government for the year ended June 1992. The profiles of the two sexes are to be compared.

Table 8.22   Age profile of GME Act employees for each Sex, June 1992

	Sex	
Age group	Males	Females
15-19	32	73
20-24	358	760
25-29	553	824
30-34	987	1001
35-39	1648	948
40-44	1737	883
45-49	1371	621
50-54	992	365
55-59	626	201
60-64	223	65
Total	8531	5741

Source: abstracted from South Australian Department of Labour (1992)

(a) Answer the following questions:
  (i) What is the question to be investigated (including the group to which the conclusions apply)?
  (ii) What variable(s) are we concerned with here?
  (iii) What type of variable(s) are they?
  (iv) Which major category of statistical procedures applies here? Why?
  (v) What type of statistic should we use, given the question to be investigated and the variables involved?
  (vi) Which particular statistic or procedure, and diagram, should we use? Why?
(b) Prepare a percentage distribution table for the males and the females. Plot the percentages in polygons and describe the shape of the distributions.
(c) From the percentage polygons, what would you say is the typical age of males in the state public service? How does this compare with the typical age of females?
(d) Which distribution exhibits the greater dispersion?

8.10 Table 8.23 summarises workers' compensation claims in Administrative Units and other public sector organisations during 1990–92. This is an example of secondary data that we will use to examine the differences between the claims for the two years.

Table 8.23 Workers' compensation claims for 1990–92

Cause of injury (that resulted in a claim)	Number of new claims	
	1990–91	1991–92
Falls, trips, slips and stumbles of a person	1214	1177
Hitting objects with a part of body	696	654
Body stressing (for example, lifting, handling, over exertion)	1909	1881
Being hit by moving objects	1187	1235
Exposure to sound and pressure	215	261
Exposure to or contact with heat, radiation and electricity	91	76
Contact with chemicals and other substances	251	191
Contact with biological factors	47	55
Exposure to mentally stressing situations	509	550
Vehicle accident	451	391
Unspecified type of accident or disease	116	72
Total	6686	6543

Source: abstracted from South Australian Department of Labour (1992)

(a) Answer the following questions:
   (i) What is the question to be investigated (including the group to which the conclusions apply)?
   (ii) What variable(s) are we concerned with here?
   (iii) What type of variable(s) are they?
   (iv) Which major category of statistical procedures applies here? Why?
   (v) What type of statistic should we use, given the question to be investigated and the variables involved?
   (vi) Which particular statistic or procedure, and diagram, should we use? Why?
(b) What is the most common type of injury resulting in a claim?
(c) Has the pattern of claims shifted during the 2-year period?

8.11 The amount spent on food is a major item in the budget of every household. For a recent survey of the living expenses of an average Australian household, a simple random sample of 100 households was taken, and one section of the interview questionnaire asked how much money each household spent on food. The variables obtained are summarised in table 8.24. The information collected by the survey has been saved in the Minitab portable worksheet file *foodpur.mtp*. This data is to be used to investigate the effect of *Sex* and *Method of payment* on the typical *Amount spent weekly on food* for the 100 observed households.

Table 8.24   Variables from household survey

Variable	Coding
Amount spent weekly on food	—
Sex	1 = female; 2 = male
Method of payment	1 = cash; 2 = cheque
Number of people in household	—
Annual income	1 = 0 – <15 000; 2 = 15 000 – <25 000;
	3 = 25 000 – <30 000; 4 = >30 000

(a)   Answer the following questions:
   (i) What is the question to be investigated (including the group to which the conclusions apply)?
   (ii) What variable(s) are we concerned with here?
   (iii) What type of variable(s) are they?
   (iv) Which major category of statistical procedures applies here? Why?
   (v) What type of statistic should we use, given the question to be investigated and the variables involved?
   (vi) Which particular statistic or procedure, and diagram, should we use? Why?
(b)   The following computer output contains a histogram of *Amount spent on food* for each *Sex–Method* combination. To obtain this output the *Sex–Method* combinations were coded as shown in table 8.25. Reproduce this output. Describe the shapes of the distributions displayed in these histograms.

Table 8.25   Coding of *Sex–Method* combinations

Sex		Method		Sex-Method combination		calculation	code
female	[1]	cash	[1]	female/cash	[1,1]	(1–1)*2 + 1	1
female	[1]	cheque	[2]	female/cheque	[1,2]	(1–1)*2 + 2	2
male	[2]	cash	[1]	male/cash	[2,1]	(2–1)*2 + 1	3
male	[2]	cheque	[2]	male/cheque	[2,2]	(2–1)*2 + 2	4

```
MTB > retrieve 'a:\foodpur.mtp';
SUBC> portable.

Worksheet retrieved from file: a:\foodpur.mtp

MTB > info

COLUMN     NAME        COUNT
c1         amount        100
c2         sex           100
c3         method        100
c4         no_hhold      100
c5         income        100

CONSTANTS USED: NONE

MTB > name c6 'sex_meth'
MTB > let c6=('sex'-1)*2+'method'
MTB > hist c1;
SUBC> by c6;
SUBC> increment 15.

Histogram of amount    sex_meth = 1    N = 27

  Midpoint    Count
     15.0       0
     30.0       1   *
     45.0       2   **
     60.0       5   *****
     75.0       7   *******
     90.0       5   *****
    105.0       4   ****
    120.0       3   ***
    135.0       0
    150.0       0

Histogram of amount    sex_meth = 2    N = 19

  Midpoint    Count
     15.0       0
     30.0       1   *
     45.0       2   **
     60.0       3   ***
     75.0       5   *****
     90.0       3   ***
    105.0       2   **
    120.0       3   ***
    135.0       0
    150.0       0
```

continued . . .

```
Histogram of amount      sex_meth = 3     N = 30

Midpoint     Count
    15.0         0
    30.0         3    ***
    45.0         4    ****
    60.0         6    ******
    75.0         5    *****
    90.0         1    *
   105.0         7    *******
   120.0         3    ***
   135.0         1    *
   150.0         0

Histogram of amount      sex_meth = 4     N = 24

Midpoint     Count
    15.0         2    **
    30.0         1    *
    45.0         2    **
    60.0         5    *****
    75.0         9    *********
    90.0         1    *
   105.0         0
   120.0         2    **
   135.0         1    *
   150.0         1    *
```

(c) The computer output on page 249 contains a two-way table of means for *Amount spent on food* classified by *Sex* and *Method of payment*. Reproduce this output.
  (i) Are *Sex* and *Method of payment* dependent in their effect on the mean *Amount spent on food*? Give reasons.
  (ii) Which table(s) of means should you use to summarise the effects of *Sex* and *Method of payment* on the mean *Amount spent on food*?
  (iii) Summarise your conclusions about how *Sex* and *Method of payment* affect the mean *Amount spent on food*.
  (iv) Draw a grouped bar chart to illustrate your conclusions in (iii).
(d) The computer output on page 249 contains a two-way table of medians for *Amount spent on food* classified by *Sex* and *Method of payment*. Reproduce this output.
  (i) Are *Sex* and *Method of payment* dependent in their effect on the median *Amount spent on food*? Give reasons.
  (ii) Which table(s) of medians should you use to summarise the effects of *Sex* and *Method of payment* on the median *Amount spent on food*?
  (iii) Summarise your conclusions about how *Sex* and *Method of payment* affect the median *Amount spent on food*.
  (iv) Draw a grouped bar chart to illustrate your conclusions in (iii).

```
MTB > table c2 c3;
SUBC> mean c1;
SUBC> n c1.

  ROWS: sex    COLUMNS: method

                1           2          ALL

   1          80.19       81.38       80.68
               27          19          46

   2          76.67       71.62       74.43
               30          24          54

  ALL         78.34       75.94       77.31
               57          43          100
  CELL CONTENTS --
          amount:MEAN
                N
```

```
MTB > table c2 c3;
SUBC> median c1;
SUBC> n c1.
  ROWS: sex      COLUMNS: method
                1           2          ALL

   1          76.22       75.84        --
               27          19          46

   2          72.32       68.82        --
               30          24          54

  ALL          --          --          --
               57          43          100

  CELL CONTENTS --
          amount:MEDIAN
                N
```

(e) Now consider both the means and medians.
   (i) Is there any difference between the conclusions from the grouped bar charts produced from the means in (c) and those produced from the medians in (d)?
   (ii) From the histograms of the *Amount spent on food* for each *Sex–Method* combination given in (b), which measure of central tendency would you use? Why?

8.12 For the data introduced in exercise 8.11, the effect of *Number in household* and *Annual income* on the typical *Amount spent on food* is to be investigated.

(a) In this case, it is not possible to produce histograms of *Amount spent on food* for each combination of *Number in household* and *Annual income* because of the low numbers of observations for each combination. From your answers to exercise 8.11 (a), should you use a table of means or a table of medians to summarise the typical *Amount spent on food* when taking into consideration *Number in household* and *Annual income*? Give reasons for your answer.

(b) Obtain the table you chose in (a) and use it to summarise the effect of *Number in household* and *Annual income* on the typical *Amount spent on food*.

8.13 Minitab comes with a data set that is the result of a survey of 279 Wisconsin restaurants, undertaken for a study of the state's restaurant sector. Use the Minitab's *retrieve* command to retrieve the data from the Minitab portable worksheet file *restrnt.mtp*. Then use the *info* command to identify the columns of the worksheet used to store this data. Add this information to table 8.26.

Table 8.26   Variables observed in restaurant survey

Column	Variable	Description
	ID	*Identification number of restaurant*
	OUTLOOK	*Values 1,2,3,4,5,6 denoting very unfavourable to very favourable Outlook*
	SALES	*Gross 1979 sales* in $1000s
	NEWCAP	*New capital invested in 1979* in $1000s
	VALUE	*Estimated market value of the business* in $1000s
	COSTGOOD	*Cost of goods sold* as a percentage of sales
	WAGES	*Wages* as a percentage of sales
	ADS	*Advertising* as a percentage of sales
	TYPEFOOD	*Type of food restaurant.*
		1 = fast food, 2 = supper club, 3 = other
	SEATS	*Number of seats in dining area*
	OWNER	*Type of owner:*
		1 = sole proprietorship, 2 = partnership, 3 = corporation
	FT.EMPL	*Number of full-time employees*
	PT.EMPL	*Number of part-time employees*
	SIZE	*Size of restaurant.*
		1 = 1 to 9.5 full-time equivalent employees,
		2 = 10 to 20 full-time equivalent employees,
		3 = over 20 full-time equivalent employees,
		where full-time equivalent employees equals (number of full time) + $\frac{1}{2}$ (number of part-time).

(a) We want to see whether *Gross 1979 sales* of the observed 279 Wisconsin restaurants differ between *Types of owner*. Answer the following questions and use Minitab to perform the procedure(s) you select. Write a report summarising your conclusions.

   (i) What is the question to be investigated (including the group to which the conclusions apply)?

   (ii) What variable(s) are we concerned with here?

   (iii) What type of variable(s) are they?

   (iv) Which major category of statistical procedures applies here? Why?

   (v) What type of statistic should we use, given the question to be investigated and the variables involved?

   (vi) Which particular statistic or procedure, and diagram, should we use? Why?

(b) We want to code the number of seats as shown in table 8.27 and then, for the 279 observed restaurants, compare the typical *Gross 1979 sales* for the lowest and highest coded *Number of seats*, considering the smallest and largest *Number of full-time equivalent employees*.

Table 8.27   Coding *Number of Seats*

Code	Number of seats
1	<50
2	from 50 to <100
3	from 100 to <150
4	from 150 to <200
5	200 or more

   (i) Modify the data in the Minitab worksheet as follows:

     – Use the *code* command to put the coded values into c20.

     – Copy sales, size and coded number of seats for coded number of seats equal to 1 and 5. Put these values into c30, c31, c32. Now use the *copy* command to copy c30–c32 to c40–c42 for sizes 1 and 3.

   (ii) Answer the following questions and use Minitab to perform the procedure(s) you select. Write a report summarising your conclusions.

     – What is the question to be investigated (including the group to which the conclusions apply)?

     – What variable(s) are we concerned with here?

     – What type of variable(s) are they?

     – Which major category of statistical procedures applies here? Why?

     – What type of statistic should we use, given the question to be investigated and the variables involved?

     – Which particular statistic or procedure, and diagram, should we use? Why?

(c) Use Minitab to perform the statistical procedures to investigate the effect of *Type of owner* and *Size of restaurant* on the typical *Gross 1979 sales* of the 279 observed restaurants. Write a report summarising your conclusions.

## CHAPTER 9

MEASURES OF ASSOCIATION FOR TWO UNRESTRICTED VARIABLES

L E A R N I N G   O B J E C T I V E S

The learning objectives of this chapter are:

- to know when to use the linear correlation coefficient and the coefficient of determination;
- to be able to produce the scatter diagram, the linear correlation coefficient and the coefficient of determination for a set of data;
- to be able to interpret the scatter diagram, the linear correlation coefficient and the coefficient of determination for a set of data.

The following extract from the *Summary of procedures based on the combinations of variable type* in part VI gives an overview of the descriptive procedures covered in this and the previous chapters of part III, *Descriptive summaries of data*.

1. *One limited variable*

   - Distribution of variables: frequency, relative frequency and percentage one-way summary tables — bar or column chart.

   - Measures of central tendency: mode (mean, median).

   - Measures of dispersion: range, interquartile range, (standard deviation, coefficient of variation).

2. *Two limited variables*

   - Distribution of variables: two-way contingency table — chart with bars or columns that are grouped or stacked.

3. *Three limited variables*
   - Distribution of variables: three-way contingency table — chart with bars or columns that are grouped or stacked.

4. *One unrestricted variable*
   - Distribution of variables: frequency, relative frequency and percentage tables — histogram, polygon, stem-and-leaf display, dotplot.
   - Measures of central tendency: mean, median — boxplot.
   - Measures of dispersion: range, interquartile range, standard deviation, coefficient of variation — boxplot.

5. *One unrestricted variable — one limited variable*
   - Distribution of variables: frequency, relative frequency and percentage tables for each value of limited variable — histogram, polygon, stem-and-leaf display, dotplot for each value of limited variable.
   - Measures of central tendency: one-way table of means or medians — boxplot for each value of limited variable, bar chart or line diagram.
   - Measures of dispersion: one-way table of ranges, interquartile ranges, standard deviations or coefficients of variation — boxplot for each value of limited variable.

6. *One unrestricted variable — two limited variables*
   - Distribution of variables: frequency, relative frequency and percentage tables for each combination of values of the limited variables — histogram, polygon, stem-and-leaf display, dotplot for each combination of values of the limited variables.
   - Measures of central tendency: two-way table of means or medians — boxplot for each combination of values of the limited variables, bar chart or line diagram.
   - Measures of dispersion: two-way table of ranges, interquartile ranges, standard deviations or coefficients of variation — boxplot for each combination of values of the limited variables.

7. *Two unrestricted variables*
   - **Measures of association**: linear correlation coefficient and coefficient of determination — scatter diagram.

As outlined in the objectives, this chapter covers measures of association. So far we have dealt with measuring aspects of a single variable or the relationship between variables, at least one of which is a limited variable. In the case of limited variables only, the relationship between the variables was examined using a contingency table. For an unrestricted variable and one or more limited variables, the relationship was via the distributions or one-way and two-way tables of means. For example, dependence of *Number of children* on *Socioeconomic status* of household was examined with a two-way contingency table; dependence of *House price* on *Locality* was examined with a one-way table of means and dependence of *House price* on *Locality* and *Number of rooms* was examined with a two-way table of means.

This chapter is concerned with measuring the relationship between two unrestricted variables, that is, how the values of two unrestricted variables move in relation to each other.

For example, you might want to examine the prices and costs of a series of items to see whether there is a relationship between *Price* and *Cost*. The two variables are *Price* and *Cost* and the question to be investigated is: is price related to cost?

9.1   Diagram for association between two unrestricted variables

The relationship between two unrestricted variables is illustrated in a **scatter diagram**, in which you plot a point for each pair of values as shown in figure 9.1.

EXAMPLE 9.1   *PRICE* AND *BLOCK AREA* FOR HOUSES IN PAYNEHAM
The raw data for the prices and block areas for a simple random sample of 14 houses sold in the Payneham local government area is given in table 9.1. We want to see if there is a relationship between the selling price and the area of the block for the 14 observed houses. That is, are the prices for larger blocks higher than for smaller blocks? This question involves the two variables *Price* and *Block area* and these are both unrestricted variables.

Table 9.1   *Price* and *Block area* for 14 houses in Payneham

Price ($)	Block area (ha)
245 000	0.0539
185 500	0.0496
160 000	0.0601
290 000	0.1045
330 000	0.1137
135 000	0.0196
157 000	0.0465
170 000	0.0531
135 000	0.0349
178 000	0.0685
261 000	0.0528
175 000	0.0367
139 000	0.0353
106 500	0.0235

The scatter diagram for these two variables in figure 9.1 has 14 crosses, one for each house. The cross in the upper righthand corner of the diagram corresponds to the fifth house listed in table 9.1; this house has a price of $330 000 and an area of 0.1137 hectares. This diagram indicates that as *Block area* increases the *Price* also increases. Such a conclusion is justified because all the points are in the bottom lefthand and top righthand corners, and there are no points in either the top lefthand or bottom righthand corners. The bottom lefthand corner corresponds to smaller block areas and smaller prices, and the top righthand corner corresponds to larger block areas and larger prices. The top lefthand corner corresponds to smaller block areas and higher prices, and the bottom righthand corner corresponds to larger block areas and lower prices. Consequently, when one variable is small, so is the other, and when one variable is high, so is the other.

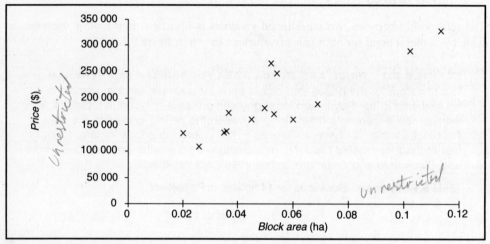

Figure 9.1   Scatter diagram for *Price* and *Block area* from Payneham

9.2   Measure of association between two unrestricted variables

The **linear relationship** between two unrestricted variables is measured by **Pearson's product moment correlation coefficient** or **linear correlation coefficient**, commonly denoted by r. The following facts will help you interpret the value of r:

1. r takes values from and including -1, through zero, and up to and including 1.
2. The closer to ±1 the stronger the linear association; that is, the points more closely lie on a straight line.
3. Call one variable X and the other variable Y:
   - r positive indicates that as X increases, so does Y.
   - r negative indicates that as X increases, Y decreases.

Figure 9.2 shows which values of r would be associated with different patterns of points. The first two diagrams show that if all the points lie exactly on a straight line the linear correlation coefficient will be exactly 1.0 or -1.0. The sign of the coefficient indicates whether the linear relationship between the two variables is **positive** or **negative**, that is, whether, as X increases, Y increases or decreases. The next two diagrams indicate that there are two 'degenerate' cases, exactly horizontal and vertical straight lines for which the linear correlation coefficient is exactly zero. In these two cases, there is clearly no relationship between the two variables. For the horizontal straight line, it does not matter what value of the X variable is observed, as the same value of the Y variable is obtained. For the vertical line, the values of the Y variable change and there is no possibility of a relationship with X as the values of the X variable do not change at all.

The second line of diagrams indicates that as the points become more scattered about a straight line the value of the linear correlation coefficient decreases. This continues until the point is reached in the last diagram on the second line where the points are scattered haphazardly all over the diagram. In this case, the linear correlation coefficient is approximately zero.

The last diagram is another degenerate case in which the linear correlation coefficient is exactly zero. It emphasises that the linear correlation coefficient measures the **linear association** *not* **curvilinear** or **nonlinear association**. Although the points follow a perfect curve, the linear association between them is zero. However, not all curvilinear trends have a linear correlation coefficient equal to zero. Consequently you must check linearity from the scatter diagram to ensure that data is linear and hence that r is appropriate.

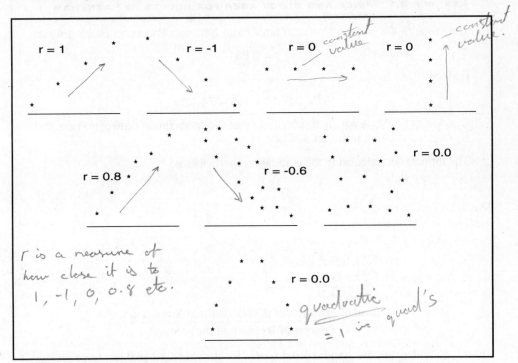

Figure 9.2 Scatter diagrams and values of the linear correlation coefficient

Finally, when assessing the strength of the linear relationship, the **coefficient of determination** is often used as it can be applied more generally than the linear correlation coefficient itself. The only practical difference between the linear correlation and the coefficient of determination, as far as this chapter is concerned, is that the direction of the relationship is eliminated from the coefficient of determination.

Coefficient of determination = R^2

$$= r^2 \times 100$$

So R^2 is closely related to r, but since it has been squared the direction of relationship is eliminated. A rule of thumb for deciding on strength of the relationship is:

R^2	Strength of relationship
0–25%	very little association
25–50%	weak association
50–75%	reasonable association
75–90%	strong association
90–100%	very strong association

EXAMPLE 9.1   PRICE AND BLOCK AREA FOR HOUSES IN PAYNEHAM
(continued)

The value of the linear correlation coefficient between *Price* and *Block area* is:

$$r = 0.861.$$

Further,

$$R^2 = 0.861^2 \times 100 = 74.13\%$$

Our rule of thumb leads us to conclude that the association between *Price* and *Block area* is close to being a strong one.

The formula for calculating the correlation coefficient is:

$$r = \frac{\displaystyle\sum_{i=1}^{n} z_{X_i} z_{Y_i}}{n-1}$$

$$= \frac{\displaystyle\sum_{i=1}^{n} \left(\frac{x_i - \bar{x}}{s_X}\right)\left(\frac{y_i - \bar{y}}{s_Y}\right)}{n-1}$$

$$= \frac{\textbf{Sum of products} \text{ of the standardised X and Y scores}}{\textbf{degrees of freedom} \text{ of the products}}$$

where z_{X_i} and z_{Y_i} are the **standardised scores** for the X and Y variables, respectively;
the degrees of freedom of the products is the number of independent products which is equal to $n-1$ where n is the number of pairs of observations;
$\bar{x}$ and $\bar{y}$ are the means for the X and Y variables, respectively;
s_X and s_Y are the standard deviations for the X and Y variables, respectively.

To calculate the correlation coefficient, the standardised scores are computed for both unrestricted variables as outlined in section 8.3, *Standardising data*. This puts the two possibly quite disparate variables on an equal footing as both sets of standardised scores have a mean of zero and a standard deviation of one. The full process of computing the correlation coefficient can be divided into two parts, outlined as follows: in the first part, the standardised scores are computed; in the second part, they are used to compute the coefficient.

1. *Calculating the standardised scores*:
   - compute the means and the deviations from the means;
   - obtain the standard deviations from these deviations;
   - divide the deviations by the standard deviations to produce the standardised scores;

2. *Forming the coefficient*:
   - multiply the pairs of standardised scores together to produce the products;
   - sum the products and divide by the degrees of freedom to yield the linear correlation coefficient.

EXAMPLE 9.1   *PRICE* AND *BLOCK AREA* FOR HOUSES IN PAYNEHAM
(continued)

The computation of linear correlation coefficient for the 14 houses from Payneham is outlined in table 9.2. First, the means, and deviations from them are computed for the prices and areas. From these, the standard deviations are calculated by squaring the deviations, adding them up, dividing the sum by $n - 1$ and taking the square root of the result. The standard deviations, at the bottom of the table, are used to produce the standardised scores by dividing the deviations by standard deviations. Notice that the relativities of the values for a variable are preserved in the standardised scores; for example, the highest and lowest values of one of the variables have the highest and lowest values for the corresponding standardised scores. These scores are plotted in figure 9.3. A comparison of figures 9.1 and 9.3 shows that the relationship between the standardised scores is the same as for the original values; the only difference between the two figures is in the scales on the two axes.

Now, the product of each pair of standardised scores is formed and placed in the column of the table headed *Product*. These products are summed and the result is given at the bottom of the table. Finally, the sum of products is divided by the degrees of freedom to yield the linear correlation coefficient:

$$r = \frac{11.19866}{13}$$

$$= 0.8613$$

Table 9.2 Computation of *r* for *Price* and *Block area* from Payneham

| House | Price (Y) ($) | Block area (X) (ha) | Deviations from mean | | Standardised scores | | |
			Price ($)	Block area ($)	Price ($)	Block area (ha)	Product
1	245 000	0.0539	54 500	0.0001357	0.8299	0.0050	0.00415
2	185 500	0.0496	−5 000	−0.0041643	−0.0761	−0.1535	0.01169
3	160 000	0.0601	−30 500	0.0063357	−0.4644	0.2336	−0.10847
4	290 000	0.1045	99 500	0.0507357	1.5151	1.8703	2.83378
5	330 000	0.1137	139 500	0.0599357	2.1242	2.2095	4.69342
6	135 000	0.0196	−55 500	−0.0341643	−0.8451	−1.2594	1.06438
7	157 000	0.0465	−33 500	−0.0072643	−0.5101	−0.2678	0.13661
8	170 000	0.0531	−20 500	−0.0006643	−0.3122	−0.0245	0.00764
9	135 000	0.0349	−55 500	−0.0188643	−0.8451	−0.6954	0.58771
10	178 000	0.0685	−12 500	0.0147357	−0.1903	0.5432	−0.10340
11	261 000	0.0528	70 500	−0.0009643	1.0735	−0.0356	−0.03816
12	175 000	0.0367	−15 500	−0.0170643	−0.2360	−0.6290	0.14847
13	139 000	0.0353	−51 500	−0.0184643	−0.7842	−0.6807	0.53379
14	106 500	0.0235	−84 000	−0.0302643	−1.2791	−1.1157	1.42705
Sum			0	0	0	0	11.19866
Mean	190 500	0.05376					
S	mean − Y = S		65 671	0.02713			

Figure 9.3 shows how the linear correlation coefficient measures linear association. It includes horizontal and vertical lines to show the quadrants in each of which all products have the same sign. The vertical line divides the diagram in half, so that points to its left have *Block area* values below the *Block area* mean, and so the standardised *Block area* values are negative; points to the right correspond to *Block area* values above the *Block area* mean. Similarly, the horizontal line divides the diagram in half so that points below it have *Price* values below the *Price* mean and so the standardised *Price* values are negative; points above correspond to *Price* values above the *Price* mean. The diagram shows the ensuing pattern of product signs. For example, points in the top left quadrant have negative *Block area* deviations and positive *Price* deviations, so the products must be negative.

In example 9.1, *Price and Block area for houses in Payneham*, most of the points lie in the two quadrants that yield positive products, which can be confirmed from the column of products in table 9.2. Hence, we get a large positive number for the sum of products and the value for *r* will be positive.

If you consider the various patterns of points in figure 9.2 and the likely values of the products, then it becomes clear why the suggested values of *r* are correct. For example, what values will be obtained for the products when the observations are spread all over the diagram? What values will be obtained for the products for a negative relationship?

Pearson form — Use mean.

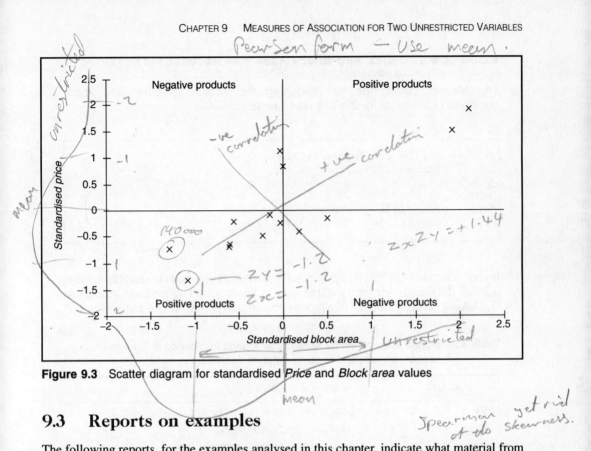

Figure 9.3 Scatter diagram for standardised *Price* and *Block* area values

9.3   Reports on examples

Spearman get rid of the skewness.

The following reports, for the examples analysed in this chapter, indicate what material from a statistical analysis an investigator should include in a report. In general, the details of the statistical analysis are omitted so that the reader of the report can concentrate on the results.

EXAMPLE 9.1 *PRICE* **AND** *BLOCK AREA* **FOR HOUSES IN PAYNEHAM —**
REPORT

The prices and block areas for a simple random sample of 14 houses sold in the Payneham area were analysed to see if there is a relationship between the selling price and the area of the block of these houses. The scatter diagram in figure 9.1 indicates that there is a linear relationship between the two variables. The linear correlation coefficient is 0.861 which leads to a coefficient of determination (R^2) of 74.13%, from which we conclude that the association between price and block area is close to being a strong one.

9.4   Using Minitab to examine association between two unrestricted variables

The Minitab commands for producing the scatter diagram and linear correlation coefficient are the *plot* and *correlation* commands, respectively.

EXAMPLE 9.1   *PRICE* AND *BLOCK AREA* FOR HOUSES IN PAYNEHAM
(continued)

The Minitab commands for producing the scatter diagram and linear correlation coefficient for the example are as follows:

```
MTB > outfile 'a:\housarea.lis'
MTB > retrieve 'a:\housarea.mtp';
SUBC> portable.
MTB > info
MTB > plot 'price' 'area'
MTB > correlation 'price' 'area'.
```

If your version of Minitab has pull-down menus and you want to use them, table 9.3 lists the menus and options that access the required commands. Appendix D, *Detailed instructions for Minitab menus*, explains how to use the menus.

Table 9.3   Menus and options for Minitab commands to produce a scatter diagram and linear correlation coefficient

Minitab command	Menu	Option
outfile	File >	Other Files > Start Recording Session...
retrieve	File >	Open Worksheet...
port		Minitab portable worksheet
info	Edit >	Get Worksheet Info...
	(Edit >	Data Screen [Alt-D])
plot	Graph >	Scatter Plot...
correlation	Stat >	Basic Statistics > Correlation...

The output produced by these commands is as follows:

```
MTB > retrieve 'a:\housarea.mtp';
SUBC> portable.
Worksheet retrieved from file: a:\housarea.mtp
MTB > info
COLUMN    NAME      COUNT
C1        price      14
C2        area       14
CONSTANTS USED: K1    K2    K3
MTB > plot 'price' 'area'
```

continued . . .

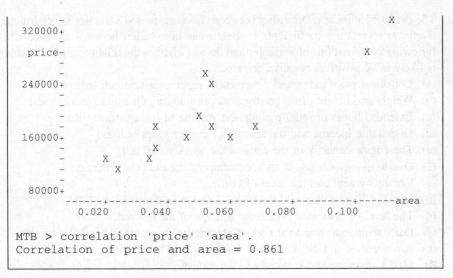

```
          -                                              X
320000+
  price-                                          X
          -
          -                        X
240000+                            X
          -
          -              X
          -         X          X       X
160000+                 X         X
          -        X
          -    X    X
          -      X
          -
 80000+
          ------+---------+---------+---------+---------+------area
          0.020     0.040     0.060     0.080     0.100

MTB > correlation 'price' 'area'.
Correlation of price and area = 0.861
```

9.5   Chapter summary

The scatter diagram, linear correlation coefficient and coefficient of determination have been introduced as procedures for examining the linear association between two unrestricted variables. We emphasised that the association must be linear, *not* curvilinear, for these procedures. We presented a rule of thumb, based on the coefficient of determination, for assessing the strength of the linear association between the two variables. The advantage of the coefficient of determination is that it eliminates the direction of the relationship.

9.6   Key terms

- coefficient of determination (R^2)
- curvilinear association
- degrees of freedom
- linear association
- linear correlation coefficient (r)
- linear relationship
- measure of association
- negative linear relationship
- nonlinear association
- Pearson's product moment correlation coefficient (r)
- positive linear relationship
- scatter diagram
- standardised scores (z)
- sum of products

9.7   Exercises

9.1   In your own words, explain the following terms:
   (a) deviation from the mean
   (b) linear association
   (c) scatter diagram
   (d) positive linear relationship
   (e) negative linear relationship
   (f) coefficient of determination
   (g) standardised scores

9.2 The extent of a linear relationship between two unrestricted variables is determined by the linear correlation coefficient, r, where r can take values between ± 1. Examine the following combinations of variables and decide whether the relationship between them is likely to be positive, negative or zero.

(a) Consumer price index and government superannuation entitlements.

(b) Weight and height of university students studying Quantitative Methods.

(c) Extended hours of retail trading and volume of merchandise sold.

(d) Disposable income and the amount of money spent on food.

(e) The engine capacity of the car and the weekly fuel bill.

(f) Overhead expenditure in an accountancy firm and profit margin.

(g) Unemployment and the level of crime.

(h) Level of import duty and the sales of cars manufactured overseas.

(i) The level of insurance premiums and age of the insured.

(j) Daily temperature and the cost of electricity for an office block.

(k) Absenteeism and the day of the week.

(l) Media coverage and sales of a new product.

9.3 There is a positive correlation between the profits recorded by a company and the amount of money appropriated to a sinking fund for improving the environmental aspects of the company site. Does this mean that more expenditure on environmental issues will increase company profit? Give reasons for your answer.

9.4 The linear correlation coefficient measures the linear relationship between two unrestricted variables. If one measurement did not vary, what would be the value of r?

9.5 A scatter diagram can be used to determine the direction of the linear relationship between two variables.

(a) Sketch the pattern of points you would expect to see in the following situations:

    (i) *Asking price* of used 2.8 litre Mercedes cars and *Year of manufacture*;

    (ii) *Length of service* and the *Number of house sales* made by real estate salespersons;

    (iii) *Number of hours speed traps used* and the *Number of motor-vehicle accidents*;

    (iv) *Sale price* and *Distance from the beach* for a simple random sample of houses sold in metropolitan Adelaide over the last 3 months;

    (v) *Sale price* and *Age* in years of houses in metropolitan Adelaide;

    (vi) *Size of company* and *Number of service offered* for the companies in a region;

    (vii) *Commission paid* for preparing a company tax return and *Company assets* for the companies in a city.

(b) Would it matter which variable you place on the vertical axis in each of these situations? Give reasons for your answer.

9.6 Examine the scatter diagrams in figures 9.4, 9.5, 9.6 and 9.7. Use the patterns of points given in figure 9.2 to suggest the level of correlation involved.

a) Positive slope r = 0.9

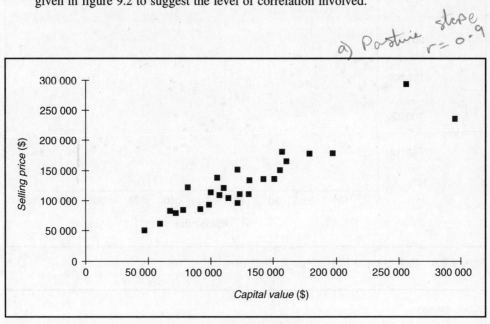

Figure 9.4 *Selling price* versus *Capital value* for home units

no linear relationship r = 0

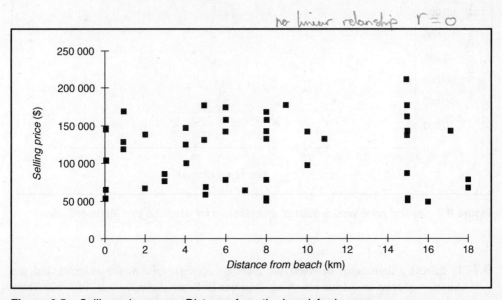

Figure 9.5 *Selling price* versus *Distance from the beach* for houses

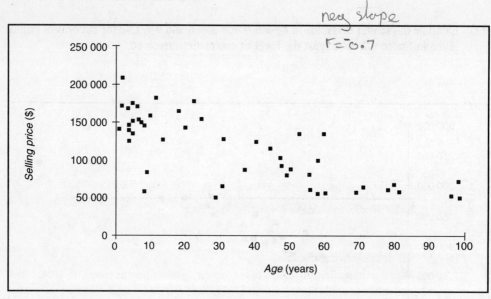

Figure 9.6   *Selling price* versus *Age* for houses

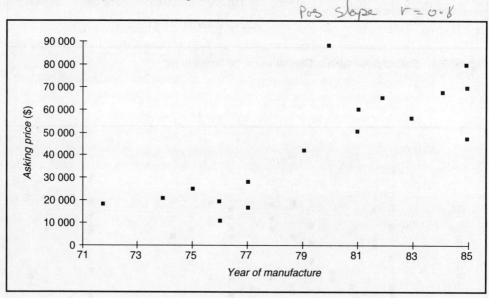

Figure 9.7   *Asking price* versus *Year of manufacture* for used 2.8 litre Mercedes cars

9.7 Is there a relationship between the *Number of registered motor vehicles* and the *Number of road accidents* involving fatalities in South Australia for 1987–92? Table 9.4 gives the secondary data for answering this question.

Table 9.4 Road traffic accidents involving fatalities in South Australia

Year	No. of road accidents	No. of registered motor vehicles (per 1000 population)
1987	226	575.5
1988	204	580.3
1989	201	584.9
1990	187	593.3
1991	166	569.2
1992	142	590.8

Source: abstracted from Australian Bureau of Statistics (1994b)

(a) Answer the following questions:
   (i) What is the question to be investigated (including the group to which the conclusions apply)?
   (ii) What variable(s) are we concerned with here?
   (iii) What type of variable(s) are they?
   (iv) Which major category of statistical procedures applies here? Why?
   (v) What type of statistic should we use, given the question to be investigated and the variables involved?
   (vi) Which particular statistic or procedure, and diagram, should we use? Why?

(b) Define the following terms and explain how they are calculated:
   (i) *Number of registered motor vehicles* standardised scores;
   (ii) *Number of road accidents* standardised scores;
   (iii) sum of products of the standardised scores.

(c) The following Minitab output contains the Minitab commands to compute the scatter diagram and standardised values for the data in table 9.4. Reproduce this output. Use a calculator and the means and standard deviations in the output to verify the standardised values for the first observation.

```
MTB > name c1 'accident' c2 'noregist'
MTB > set c1
DATA> 226 204 201 187 166 142
DATA> end data
MTB > set c2
DATA> 575.5 580.3 584.9 593.3 569.2 590.8
DATA> end data
MTB > plot c1 c2
```

continued . . .

```
accident-                    *
        -
        -
    210+
        -                         *           *
        -
        -
        -                                                              *
    180+
        -
        -    *
        -
        -
    150+
        -                                                          *
        -
        -
          ------+---------+---------+---------+---------+------noregist
             570.0     575.0     580.0     585.0     590.0     595.0

MTB > describe c1 c2

                N       MEAN     MEDIAN    TRMEAN    STDEV    SEMEAN
accident        6      187.7      194.0     187.7     29.9      12.2
noregist        6     582.33     582.60    582.33     9.19      3.75

              MIN        MAX         Q1        Q3
accident     42.0      226.0      160.0     209.5
noregist    569.20     593.30     573.92    591.42

MTB > name c3 'z_accid' c4 'z_regist'
MTB > let c3=(c1-mean(c1))/stdev(c1)
MTB > let c4=(c2-mean(c2))/stdev(c2)
MTB > print c1-c4

ROW     accident    noregist      z_accid      z_regist
1           226       575.5       1.28215      -0.74394
2           204       580.3       0.54631      -0.22137
3           201       584.9       0.44597       0.27944
4           187       593.3      -0.02230       1.19393
5           166       569.2      -0.72470      -1.42981
6           142       590.8      -1.52744       0.92176
```

$z = y_i - \bar{y} / s$

(d) Use a calculator to compute the products of the standardised scores given in the output in (c).

  (i) For each pair of observations, place a cross in the quadrant in figure 9.8 (opposite) in which the pair of observations would plot.

  (ii) Why are the signs of the products for the four quadrants as indicated in figure 9.8? How many positive and negative products are there for the example?

  (iii) Use this information to indicate whether the linear correlation coefficient between the *Number of registered motor vehicles* and the *Number of road accidents* is likely to be negative, positive or about zero.

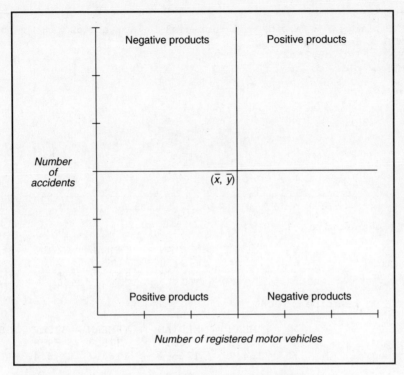

Figure 9.8   Quadrants containing products of deviations

(e)   What is the formula for the Pearson's product moment correlation coefficient?

    (i) Use this formula to calculate the correlation coefficient between the *Number of registered motor vehicles* and the *Number of road accidents*.

    (ii) Some calculators, such as the SHARP EL–735, allow two variables to be input for statistical calculations; these are often termed *bivariate statistics* functions. If you have such a calculator, use it to verify the value you obtained for the linear correlation coefficient.

(f)   The following Minitab output contains the commands to multiply the original observations by two and recompute the standardised scores. It also contains the scatter diagram. Reproduce this output. What effect did doubling the variables have on the standardised scores and the scatter diagram. Consequently, what effect will it have on the computed correlation coefficient?

```
MTB > name c5 'accid2'  c6 'noregis2'  c7 'z_accid2'  c8 'z_noreg2'
MTB > let  c5=2*c1
MTB > let  c6=2*c2
MTB > plot c5 c6

accid2   -                        *
         -
         -
    420+                                    *           *
         -
         -
         -                                                          *
    360+
         -
         -      *
         -
         -
    300+                                                      *
         -
         -
         -
         ------+---------+---------+---------+---------+------noregis2
            1140      1150      1160      1170      1180      1190

MTB > describe c5 c6

                  N      MEAN    MEDIAN    TRMEAN    STDEV   SEMEAN
accid2            6     375.3     388.0     375.3     59.8     24.4
noregis2          6    1164.7    1165.2    1164.7     18.4      7.5

                MIN       MAX        Q1        Q3
accid2        284.0     452.0     320.0     419.0
noregis2     1138.4    1186.6    1147.8    1182.8

MTB > let  c7=(c5-mean(c5))/stdev(c5)
MTB > let  c8=(c6-mean(c6))/stdev(c6)
MTB > print c5-c8

ROW      accid2    noregis2    z_accid2    z_noreg2

1           452      1151.0     1.28215    -0.74394
2           408      1160.6     0.54631    -0.22137
3           402      1169.8     0.44597     0.27944
4           374      1186.6    -0.02230     1.19393
5           332      1138.4    -0.72470    -1.42981
6           284      1181.6    -1.52744     0.92176
```

(g) What do you conclude about the relationship between the two variables.

9.8 You want to see how the *Asking price* of used 2.8 litre Mercedes cars changed with the *Year of manufacture*. The data in table 9.5 has been obtained over a 4-week period from local newspaper advertisements. You are going to investigate the relationship for the 21 observed cars.

Table 9.5 *Year of manufacture* and *Asking price* for used Mercedes cars

Car	Year of manufacture	Asking price ($)
1	85	47 000
2	85	69 950
3	74	21 950
4	79	44 000
5	79	44 000
6	80	89 950
7	76	20 000
8	76	19 990
9	74	21 950
10	75	24 950
11	81	49 000
12	77	16 900
13	72	17 750
14	76	12 000
15	82	63 000
16	77	27 750
17	84	69 000
18	85	79 995
19	83	54 995
20	81	59 950
21	81	59 995

(a) Answer the following questions:
   (i) What is the question to be investigated (including the group to which the conclusions apply)?
   (ii) What variable(s) are we concerned with here?
   (iii) What type of variable(s) are they?
   (iv) Which major category of statistical procedures applies here? Why?
   (v) What type of statistic should we use, given the question to be investigated and the variables involved?
   (vi) Which particular statistic or procedure, and diagram, should we use? Why?
(b) Perform the analysis you chose in (a). Note that the scatter diagram is given in figure 9.7.
(c) Explain how the linear relationship established in (b) would affect any decisions to purchase one of the cars in the collected sample.

9.9 Use the information about metropolitan Adelaide house sales (saved in a Minitab portable worksheet file called *housinfo.mtp*) to answer the following questions:

(a) Identify the columns, using Minitab *info* command.

(b) Which variables are unrestricted?

(c) For the *unrestricted variables only*, identify the variable that has the strongest linear relationship with *Sales price*.

(d) What is the value of the linear correlation coefficient for the variable identified in (c)? What is the strength of the linear relationship?

9.10 Table 9.6 contains the *Capital values* and *Selling prices* of a sample of home units. The data has been saved in the Minitab portable worksheet file *homeunit.mtp*. We want to see how closely the *Selling prices* reflect the *Capital values* for these home units.

(a) Answer the following questions:

(i) What is the question to be investigated (including the group to which the conclusions apply)?

(ii) What variable(s) are we concerned with here?

(iii) What type of variable(s) are they?

(iv) Which major category of statistical procedures applies here? Why?

(v) What type of statistic should we use, given the question to be investigated and the variables involved?

(vi) Which particular statistic or procedure, and diagram, should we use? Why?

(b) Compute the correlation coefficient and the coefficient of determination between *Capital value* and *Selling price*.

(c) Summarise your conclusions about the relationship between *Capital value* and *Selling price*. Note that the scatter diagram for the data is given in figure 9.4.

Table 9.6 *Capital value* and *Selling price* for a sample of home units

Capital value ($)	Selling price ($)	Capital value ($)	Selling price ($)
48 000	49 000	80 000	110 000
160 000	158 000	175 000	170 000
157 000	172 000	98 000	110 000
70 000	78 000	260 000	300 000
73 000	75 000	193 000	170 000
122 000	155 000	106 000	115 000
92 000	85 000	145 000	138 000
155 000	150 000	110 000	110 000
114 000	107 000	115 000	115 000
152 000	140 000	105 000	130 000
97 000	90 000	77 000	77 000
130 000	134 000	127 000	112 000
66 000	61 000	105 000	129 000
292 000	236 000	103 000	107 000

## CHAPTER 10

REGRESSION FOR TWO UNRESTRICTED VARIABLES

One limited variable eg sex (M/F)

two limited variables — no of child vs soc econ status.

Three limited variables — house price/location

one unrestricted

one unrestricted — one limited variable

one unrestricted — two limited variables

Two — unrestricted variables

L E A R N I N G   O B J E C T I V E S

The learning objectives of this chapter are:

- to be able to fit a straight line describing the linear relationship between two unrestricted variables, including the assessment of the strength of the relationship;
- to be able to interpret the intercept and slope of the fitted straight line;
- to be able to compute and interpret mean responses from the fitted straight line.

The following extract from the *Summary of procedures based on combinations of variable types* in part VI gives an overview of the descriptive summaries covered in this and the previous chapters of part III, *Descriptive summaries of data*.

1. *One limited variable*
   - Distribution of variables: frequency, relative frequency and percentage one-way summary tables — bar or column chart.
   - Measures of central tendency: mode (mean, median).
   - Measures of dispersion: range, interquartile range, (standard deviation, coefficient of variation).

2. *Two limited variables*
   - Distribution of variables: two-way contingency table — chart with bars or columns that are grouped or stacked.

3. *Three limited variables*
   - Distribution of variables: three-way contingency table — chart with bars or columns that are grouped or stacked.

4. *One unrestricted variable*
   - Distribution of variables: frequency, relative frequency and percentage tables — histogram, polygon, stem-and-leaf display, dotplot.
   - Measures of central tendency: mean, median — boxplot.
   - Measures of dispersion: range, interquartile range, standard deviation, coefficient of variation — boxplot.

5. *One unrestricted variable — one limited variable*
   - Distribution of variables: frequency, relative frequency and percentage tables for each value of limited variable — histogram, polygon, stem-and-leaf display, dotplot for each value of limited variable.
   - Measures of central tendency: one-way table of means or medians — boxplot for each value of limited variable, bar chart or line diagram.
   - Measures of dispersion: one-way table of ranges, interquartile ranges, standard deviations or coefficients of variation — boxplot for each value of limited variable.

6. *One unrestricted variable — two limited variables*
   - Distribution of variables: frequency, relative frequency and percentage tables for each combination of values of the limited variables — histogram, polygon, stem-and-leaf display, dotplot for each combination of values of the limited variables.
   - Measures of central tendency: two-way table of means or medians — boxplot for each combination of values of the limited variables, bar chart or line diagram.
   - Measures of dispersion: two-way table of ranges, interquartile ranges, standard deviations or coefficients of variation — boxplot for each combination of values of the limited variables.

7. *Two unrestricted variables*
   - Measures of association: linear correlation coefficient and coefficient of determination — scatter diagram.
   - **Fitted lines**: intercept and/or slope; mean response — scatter diagram.

As outlined in the objectives, this chapter covers the fitting of straight lines as a descriptive summary procedure. If there is a reasonable linear or curvilinear association between two unrestricted variables, you could consider fitting a straight line or curve to the points and using the coefficients from the equation, or mean responses computed from the equation, as summaries of aspects of the data. The process of fitting lines is called **regression**.

10.1   Descriptive simple linear regression

Simple linear regression is concerned with fitting a straight line to the data. In this section, regression is being used to provide a descriptive summary of the **linear relationship** exhibited by the data. That is, our conclusions are concerned only with the observed data,

$$Y = b_0 + b_1 x + b_2 x + b_3 x_3$$

and the fitted straight line or curve is used to describe the trend in this data. The first step is to plot a **scatter diagram**, as for the linear correlation coefficient, then the straight line is fitted. In general, the **equation for a straight** line can be written as:

$$Y = b_0 + b_1 X \quad mx \qquad c \qquad Y = mx + c$$

where Y and X are the names of the variables;

b_0 is the **intercept**; and

b_1 is the **slope**.

slope.

The intercept and slope are collectively known as the **regression coefficients**. To completely specify a straight line, you need only to provide values for the intercept and slope. The intercept is the position at which the line crosses the Y axis. The slope measures the rate of change in Y for each unit change in X. Lines with varying intercepts and slopes are shown in figure 10.1. Two lines have the same slope but different intercepts, whereas another pair of lines has the same intercept but different slopes.

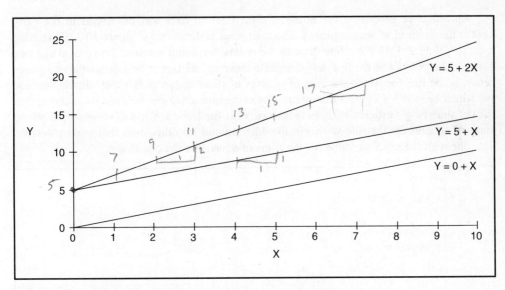

Figure 10.1   Straight lines with varying intercepts and slopes

Fitting a straight line amounts to finding suitable values of b_0 and b_1 for our data. An obvious method of fitting a line of best fit is to draw the line freehand. For example, suppose a straight line is to be fitted to the three points given in figure 10.2. Two possible lines, fitted freehand, are given in figure 10.2. Which is to be preferred? It is a matter of opinion. However, the choice is important because the values of b_0 and b_1 will not be the same for the two lines.

Handwritten note at top of page:

$\sum e^2$ is min implied

$e_1^2 + e_2^2 + e_3^2$ is sum $\to b_1$

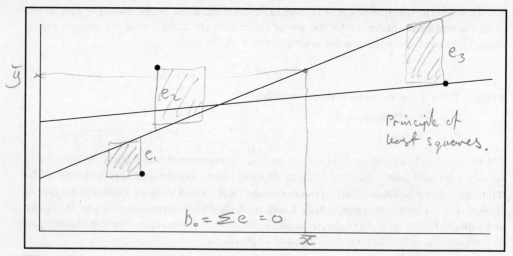

Handwritten annotations within figure:

$\bar{y}$

e_3

Principle of least squares.

$b_0 = \sum e = 0$

$\bar{x}$

Figure 10.2   Freehand fitting of straight lines

An objective procedure for fitting straight lines to data was developed in the early 1800s: the **method of least squares**. The main idea is illustrated in figure 10.3. If we have a set of points and we put a line through the points, we could measure the vertical distance between the points and the line, and designate these e_i. The line of best fit, in a least squares sense, is the line for which the sum of squares of these distances is least; that is, the line for which $e_1^2 + e_2^2 + e_2^3$ is a minimum. The same procedure can be used for a curve; the sum of squares of vertical distances from a curve is minimised. You can imagine computing sums of squares for the line shown in the diagram and for other lines that seem plausible. The line with the smallest value for the sums of squares is the one to use.

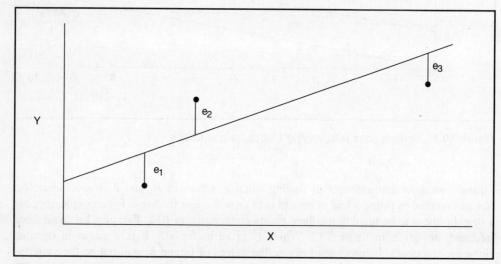

Figure 10.3   Least squares fitting of a straight line

However, you do not have to go to the trouble of computing lots of sums of squares. It can be proved, with calculus, that the formulae for the values of b_1 and b_0 of the straight line of best fit are:

Product of deviation $\qquad$ *slope* $= \dfrac{Y_2 - Y_1}{x_2 - x_1}$

where $m = $ *slope*

$$b_1 = \frac{\displaystyle\sum_{i-1}^{n}(x_i - \bar{x})(y_i - \bar{y})}{(n-1)s_X^2}$$

$$= \frac{\text{Sum of products of the } X \text{ and } Y \text{ deviations from their means}}{(\text{no. pairs} - 1) \times \text{variance of the } X \text{ values}}$$

$$b_0 = \bar{y} - b_1\bar{x}$$

Thus, the calculations are based on the deviations of the X and Y values from their respective means. The variance of the X values has to be calculated and this is done by using the deviations of the X values from their mean.

These two statistics represent summaries of the data. The slope describes the rate of change in Y for each unit change in X. The intercept represents the value of Y at which the line crosses the Y axis; that is, it is the value of Y when X is zero. Another summary that can be obtained by fitting a straight line is the mean response for a specified value of X. The **mean response**, for a specified value of X, is the typical or average value of Y for the specified value of X. It is the value of Y that lies on the fitted straight line at the position that corresponds to the specified value of X. This is illustrated in figure 10.4. The formula for the mean response is:

$$\bar{\bar{y}} = b_0 + b_1 x$$

where $\bar{\bar{y}}$ is the mean response;
$\quad$ x is the specified value of X.

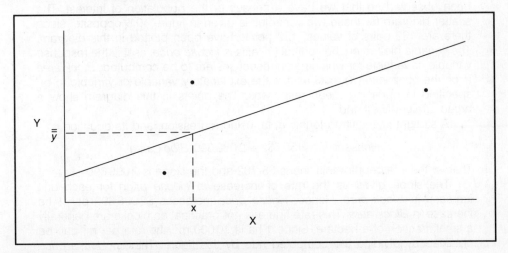

Figure 10.4 Mean response from a fitted straight line

Whereas in correlation there was no distinction between the two variables involved, this is not the case in regression. In regression, the variable whose values are to be specified in obtaining computed quantities is called the **explanatory variable**, denoted by X. On the other hand, the variable for which quantities are to be computed, for specified values of the explanatory variable, is called the **response variable**, denoted by Y. Quantities that might be computed are the mean response, the intercept, the slope or an interval estimate. In all of these, one variable's value is specified and the quantity is computed for the other variable.

The results depend on which you called the response variable (there is no such ordering and change in results in correlation). Thus, you speak of the regression of *response on explanatory*, that is, Y on X. For example, you might regress *Price* on *Cost*. It is important that you decide which variable is to be the explanatory variable according to the variable whose values are specified. The choice is *not* based on which variable causes the other. For example, you might think that *Cost* causes *Price* and that this is why *Price* has been designated the response variable; however, this is not the case. It is quite feasible to have *Cost* as the response variable and *Price* as the explanatory variable, if the *Price* is to be specified; for example, if you want to obtain the typical *Cost* for a *Price* that you specify.

EXAMPLE 10.1   *PRICES AND BLOCK AREAS IN ST PETERS*

As in examples 6.5, *Residences sold in three localities*, 8.1, *House prices in three localities* and 8.5, *House sales in two localities*, we have data for all the residences sold over a 12-month period in the St Peters local government area. The investigator wants to describe the relationship between *House price* and *Block area* to obtain two pieces of information about houses sold in this local government area during the 12-month period: the rate of increase in *House price* as *Block area* changes; and the typical *House price* for those houses with a *Block area* of 0.075 hectares.

That is, the questions under investigation involve two unrestricted variables: *House price* and *Block area*. Note that all sales in the area have been observed so that we have a census of the population of interest. The scatter diagram for these two variables is given in figure 10.5 opposite; since there are 122 pairs of values, 122 points have been plotted in this diagram. The variable plotted on the vertical (Y) axis is *House price,* as it is the response variable or variable for which mean responses are to be computed. *Block area* is on the horizontal (X) axis, as it is the explanatory variable or variable to be specified in obtaining mean responses. The points in this diagram show a broad straight-line trend.

A straight line is fitted to this data, using regression, and its equation is:

$$House\ price = 55\,762 + 2\,098\,690\ Block\ area$$

That is, the intercept for this line is 55 762 and the slope is 2 098 690.

The slope gives us the rate of increase in *House price* for each unit increase in *Block area*. Hence, *House price* increases \$2 098 690 per 1 ha increase in *Block area*. This rate figure is not practical as blocks are generally a small fraction of a hectare. Since 1 ha is 10 000 m², the rate per m² can be obtained by dividing the computed rate by this figure. That is, *House price* increases \$209.87 per m² increase in the *Block area*.

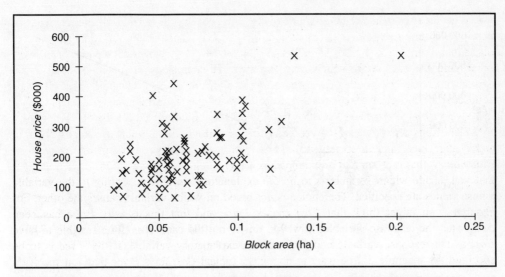

Figure 10.5   Scatter diagram for *House price* and *Block area* from St Peters

The intercept is the *House price* expected for a *Block area* of zero. This does not have a practical interpretation in this example. It is not sensible to think of a house on a block of zero area. In some instances, the intercept does have a practical interpretation. The mean response for a *Block area* of 0.075 ha is:

$$\bar{\bar{y}} = 55\,762 + 2\,098\,690 \times 0.075$$
$$= 213\,164$$

This indicates that the typical price of houses with a 0.075 ha block in St Peters during the 12-month period is $213 164.

`one price of houses of 0·075 ha in that area.`

Drawing the fitted straight line

The fitted straight line can be drawn by substituting two values of *X* into its equation, plotting the resulting two pairs of *X* and *Y* values, and joining the two plotted points.

EXAMPLE 10.1   *PRICES AND BLOCK AREAS IN ST PETERS* (continued)

For *Block area* = 0.05 ha, *House price* = 55 762 + 2 098 690 × 0.05 = 160 696
For *Block area* = 0.20 ha, *House price* = 55 762 + 2 098 690 × 0.20 = 475 500

This pair of points can also be used to draw the fitted straight line. They are plotted on the scatter diagram and joined up. The result of doing this is shown in figure 10.6.

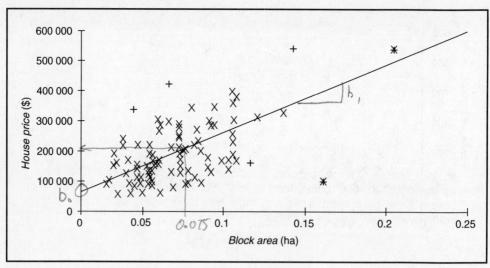

Figure 10.6   Scatter diagram, showing unusual observations and fitted straight line, for *House price* and *Block area* from St Peters

How good is the relationship?

To see how well the straight line fits, it is usual to use the **coefficient of determination**, R^2. In the context of regression, it can be interpreted as the percentage of the total variation in the response variable that can be explained by the explanatory variable. It is precisely the same R^2 that you would calculate from the correlation between the two variables; that is, $R^2 = r^2 \times 100$.

In regression, an **adjusted coefficient of determination**, R^2_{adj}, can also be calculated to take into account the sample size, n, and the number of explanatory variables, p. It is calculated by the following formula:

$$R^2_{adj} = \left[1 - (1 - r^2) \frac{n-1}{n-p-1} \right] \times 100$$

To assess the strength of the relationship, use the rule of thumb for R^2 given in section 9.2, *Measure of association between two unrestricted variables*.

> **EXAMPLE 10.1   PRICES AND BLOCK AREAS IN ST PETERS** (continued)
>
> The value of R^2 for the example is 45.5%. This indicates that 45.5% of the total variation in *House price* can be explained by differences in *Block area*. For the example, the adjusted R^2 is:
>
> $$R^2_{adj} = \left[1 - (1 - 0.455) \frac{121}{120} \right] \times 100$$
>
> $$= 45.0\%$$

The result is similar to that obtained for R^2. This is usually the case with simple linear regression. Both R^2s indicate that the relationship is weak, according to the rule of thumb given in section 9.2, *Measure of association between two unrestricted variables*.

Figure 10.6 reveals an important point about the relationship: there are some outliers, indicated by '+' and '*' as plotted in figure 10.6. The four '+'s correspond to observations that appear to be distant from the linear trend displayed by the rest of the data. In fact, these '+'s correspond to *five* observations, since the top '+' corresponds to two coincident points. The two '*'s correspond to observations that are a long way from the centre of most of the data; they will have a large effect on the value of the intercept and slope. In fact, these '*'s correspond to *three* observations, since the top '*' corresponds to two coincident points. You should check whether such observations are correct, since a mistake may have been made in recording or entering the data into the computer.

Which regression?

It is important to identify the response and explanatory variables correctly, because the equation for the fitted straight line depends on which of the two variables involved in the regression is specified as the response variable.

EXAMPLE 10.1 *PRICES AND BLOCK AREAS IN ST PETERS* (continued)

We have computed the regression for *House price* on *Block area* because we want to obtain mean responses for *House price*. The equation for the fitted straight line is:

$$House\ Price = 55\,762 + 2\,098\,690\ Block\ area$$

However, if *Block area* is regressed on *House price* the equation for the fitted straight line becomes:

$$Block\ area = 0.025911 + 0.00000022\ House\ price.$$

Since mean responses are required for *House price*, the first, not the second, equation is required.

10.2 Reports on examples

The following reports, for the examples analysed in this chapter, indicate what material from a statistical analysis an investigator should include in a report. In general, the details of the statistical analysis are omitted so that the reader of the report can concentrate on the results.

EXAMPLE 10.1 *PRICES AND BLOCK AREAS IN ST PETERS — REPORT*

Data is available on all the residences sold over a 12-month period in the St Peters local government area. We performed a simple linear regression analysis to determine: the rate of increase in house price as block area changes; the typical house price for those houses with a block area of 0.075 ha. The equation for the fitted straight line is:

$$House\ Price = 55\,762 + 2\,098\,690\ Block\ area$$

The slope from this equation indicates that house prices increase \$2 098 690 per hectare or \$209.87 per square metre. It was calculated that a block area of 0.075 ha typically sold for \$213 164. However, the coefficient of determination (R^2) is 45.5%. This indicates that only 45.5% of the total variation in house prices can be explained by differences in block area. Hence, house price has a weak relationship with block area.

10.3   Using Minitab for descriptive simple linear regression

In descriptive simple linear regression, the *plot* command is used to produce the scatter diagram and the *regress* command to compute the regression equation and R^2.

EXAMPLE 10.1   *PRICES AND BLOCK AREAS IN ST PETERS* (continued)

The commands to perform descriptive simple linear regression are as follows. The data is contained in a Minitab portable worksheet file that contains data for all types of dwellings and all local government areas. Consequently, use the *info* command to check the columns that have been retrieved, and use the *copy* command with *use* subcommand to reduce the data to just what is required for the analysis. Then use the *plot* command to produce the scatter diagram and the *regress* command to perform the simple linear regression analysis.

```
MTB > outfile 'a:\vgregn.lis'
MTB > retrieve 'a:\vgsales.mtp';
SUBC> portable.
MTB > info
MTB > erase c8 c15
MTB > copy c1 c3 c9 c12 c1 c3 c9 c12;
SUBC> use 'landuse' =11.
MTB > copy c1 c3 c9 c12 c1 c3 c9 c12;
SUBC> use 'locality'=16.
MTB > info
MTB > plot 'price' 'blocarea'
MTB > regress 'price' 1 explanatory 'blocarea'
```

If your version of Minitab has pull-down menus and you want to use them, table 10.1 lists the menus and options that access the required commands. Appendix D, *Detailed instructions for Minitab menus*, explains how to use the menus.

Table 10.1   Menus and options for Minitab commands to produce a
scatter diagram and linear regression analysis

Minitab command	Menu	Option
outfile	File >	Other Files > Start Recording Session...
retrieve	File >	Open Worksheet...
port		Minitab portable worksheet
info	Edit >	Get Worksheet Info...
	(Edit >	Data Screen [Alt-D])
erase	Calc >	Erase Variables...
copy	Calc >	Copy Columns...
use		Use Rows...
plot	Graph >	Scatter Plot...
regress	Stat >	Regression > Regression...

The output produced by these commands is as follows:

```
MTB > retrieve 'a:\vgsales.mtp';
SUBC> portable.

Worksheet retrieved from file: a:\vgsales.mtp

MTB > info

COLUMN     NAME         COUNT     MISSING
C1         locality      841
C3         price         841         3
C8         no_rooms      841        20
C9         blocarea      841       349
C12        landuse       841
C15        walltype      841        46


CONSTANTS USED: NONE
MTB > erase c8 c15
MTB > copy c1 c3 c9 c12 c1 c3 c9 c12;
SUBC> use 'landuse'=11.
MTB > copy c1 c3 c9 c12 c1 c3 c9 c12;
SUBC> use 'locality'=16.
MTB > info

COLUMN     NAME         COUNT     MISSING
C1         ocality       127
C3         price         127         1
C9         blocarea      127         4
C12        landuse       127
```

continued . . .

```
CONSTANTS USED: NONE

MTB > plot 'price' 'blocarea'

price  -
       -                                      2               2
       -
 480000+
       -
       -                  *
       -                              **
       -          *                   *
 320000+              *  *    *    *      2  *
       -            **        2       *
       -              4  2 **    2
       -      2   * * * 23 3
       -     *  *   22* 3* **  *2*
 160000+    2*  6322** 22* 2*   2  *
       -       2 3332    2 *              *
       -   2  *2 *22  *
       -    *  * * *
          ------+---------+---------+---------+---------+---------+blocarea

MTB > regress 'price' 1 explanatory 'blocarea'

The regression equation is
price = 55762 + 2098690 blocarea

122 cases used 5 cases contain missing values

Predictor          Coef        Stdev        t-ratio           p
Constant          55762        16041           3.48       0.001
blocarea        2098690       209699          10.01       0.000

s = 72936      R-sq = 45.5%     R-sq(adj) = 45.0%

Analysis of Variance

SOURCE          DF            SS              MS          F          p
Regression       1      5.32827E+11     5.32827E+11     100.16     0.000
Error          120      6.38358E+11     5319650304
Total          121      1.17119E+12

Unusual Observations
Obs.blocarea       price        Fit    Stdev.Fit     Residual   St.Resid
  43   0.159       120000      389874      19893       -269873    -3.85RX
  60   0.119       160000      305506      12264       -145506    -2.02R
  62   0.041       340000      140969       8993        199031     2.75R
  79   0.207       560000      490401      29556         69599     1.04 X
  80   0.207       560000      490401      29556         69599     1.04 X
  81   0.138       560000      345801      15807        214199     3.01R
  82   0.138       560000      345801      15807        214199     3.01R
 107   0.062       431347      185041       6819        246306     3.39R

R denotes an obs. with a large st. resid.
X denotes an obs. whose X value gives it large influence.
```

Note that at the end of the output produced by *regress*, Minitab has produced messages about outliers or unusual observations. It has identified the two types of outliers: influential and large-residual outliers.

10.4 Chapter summary

Simple linear regression is an objective procedure for fitting a straight line to two unrestricted variables, with the relationship between the two variables exhibited in a scatter diagram. It is important to correctly specify the response and explanatory variables. In general, the equation for a straight line can be written as:

$$Y = b_0 + b_1 X$$

In this equation, Y is the name of the response variable and X is the name of the explanatory variable. The intercept (b_0) is the position at which the line crosses the Y axis. The slope (b_1) measures the rate of change in Y for each unit change in X. Another summary, additional to the intercept and slope, is the mean response for a specified value of X. It is the typical or average value of Y for the specified value of X, and the formula for it is $\bar{\bar{y}} = b_0 + b_1 x$ where x is the specified value of X. So, it is the value of Y that lies on the fitted straight line at the position that corresponds to the specified value of X.

The strength of the relationship between the response and explanatory variables can be measured by using the coefficient of determination. In the context of regression, it can be interpreted as the percentage of the total variation in the response variable that can be explained by the explanatory variable. An adjusted coefficient of determination is also available, but in simple linear regression this is little different from the ordinary coefficient of determination.

10.5 Key terms

- adjusted coefficient of determination (R^2_{adj})
- coefficient of determination (R^2)
- equation for a straight line ($Y = b_0 + b_1 X$)
- explanatory variable (X)
- fitted line
- intercept (b_0)
- linear relationship
- mean response ($\bar{\bar{y}}$)
- method of least squares
- regression
- regression coefficients (b_0 and b_1)
- response variable (Y)
- simple linear regression
- scatter diagram
- slope (b_1)

10.6 Exercises

10.1 What type of diagram do we use to see whether two unrestricted variables have a linear relationship? If mean responses are to be computed, does it matter which variable is plotted on the vertical axis of our scatter diagram? Give reasons for your answer.

10.2 What are the advantages of fitting a straight line to the values of two unrestricted variables when the variables display a linear relationship?

10.3 In your own words define the following terms:
(a) explanatory or independent variable
(b) response or dependent variable
(c) method of least squares
(d) regression
(e) fitted line
(f) intercept
(g) slope of the fitted straight line
(h) coefficient of determination
(i) mean response
(j) extrapolation

10.4 For each of the following, identify the explanatory and response variables.
(a) The price of steel girders is to be computed from the manufacturing expenses in the steel industry.
(b) The value of a secondhand car is to be computed from the year of its manufacture.
(c) The outside temperature is to be computed from the cost of heating and cooling an office building.
(d) The amount of media publicity is to be used to obtain a restaurant's turnover.
(e) The weekly salary is to be used to calculate the amount of mortgage repayment.
(f) The cost of a car's fuel bill is to be computed from its engine capacity.
(g) Blood pressure levels are to be obtained for individuals of specified ages.
(h) For a particular share profit, the amount of dividend declared for the financial year is to be computed.
(i) The rate with which the performance of insurance salespersons increases with their length of experience is to be determined.

10.5 The coefficient of determination has different interpretations in the context of correlation and regression. What are they?

10.6 If the coefficient of determination between two variables is high, does this mean that one variable causes the other to vary? Give reasons for your answer.

10.7 What is the difference between the adjusted coefficient of determination and the coefficient of determination? Is it an advantage to make these adjustments when simple linear regression is involved? Give reasons for your answer.

10.8 You have obtained *Asking price* and *Year of manufacture* of 21 used 2.8 litre Mercedes cars advertised in a local newspaper over a four-week period. The data is given in table 10.2 and saved in the Minitab portable worksheet file *mercedes.mtp*. Linear regression is to be used to obtain the typical *Asking price* of a used 2.8 litre Mercedes car advertised in this four-week period for a specified *Year of manufacture*.

Table 10.2 *Year of manufacture* and *Asking price* for used 2.8 litre Mercedes cars

Car	Year of manufacture	Asking price ($)	Car	Year of manufacture	Asking price ($)	Car	Year of manufacture	Asking price ($)
1	85	47 000	8	76	19 990	15	82	63 000
2	85	69 950	9	74	21 950	16	77	27 750
3	74	21 950	10	75	24 950	17	84	69 000
4	79	44 000	11	81	49 000	18	85	79 995
5	79	44 000	12	77	16 900	19	83	54 995
6	80	89 950	13	72	17 750	20	81	59 950
7	76	20 000	14	76	12 000	21	81	59 995

(a) Answer the following questions:
   (i) What is the question to be investigated (including the group to which the conclusions apply)?
   (ii) What variable(s) are we concerned with here?
   (iii) What type of variable(s) are they?
   (iv) Which major category of statistical procedures applies here? Why?
   (v) What type of statistic should we use, given the question to be investigated and the variables involved?
   (vi) Which particular statistic or procedure, and diagram, should we use and why?
(b) Which variable is the response variable and which is the explanatory variable? Give reasons for your choice.
(c) Is it appropriate to fit a straight line to describe the relationship between the variables? Give reasons for your answer.
(d) Use linear regression to fit a straight line that describes the relationship between the *Asking price* for a used 2.8 litre Mercedes car and the *Year of manufacture*. State this line.
(e) What are the values of the intercept (b_0), and the slope (b_1)?
(f) Calculate the *Asking price* mean response for a used 2.8 litre Mercedes car registered in 1973.
(g) Calculate the *Asking price* mean response for a used 2.8 litre Mercedes car registered in 1984.

(h) Draw the fitted straight line on the scatter diagram for the original data.

(i) How strong is the relationship between *Asking price* and *Year of manufacture*?

10.9 Linear regression is to be used to obtain the typical *Closing price for the day* of the observed property trust share prices for a specified *Lowest price for the year*. The prices for these shares are in table 10.3 and saved in the Minitab portable worksheet file *proptrst.mtp*.

Table 10.3 *Closing price for the day* and *Lowest price for the year* of property trust shares

Closing price for the day (cents)	Lowest price for the year (cents)	Closing price for the day (cents)	Lowest price for the year (cents)
70	*	101	96
87	83	142	141
8	5	75	*
65	65	139	135
50	50	29	25
78	78	74	70
212	200	118	116
120	86	295	288
130	130	193	188
248	248	157	149

(a) Answer the following questions:
   (i) What is the question to be investigated (including the group to which the conclusions apply)?
   (ii) What variable(s) are we concerned with here?
   (iii) What type of variable(s) are they?
   (iv) Which major category of statistical procedures applies here? Why?
   (v) What type of statistic should we use, given the question to be investigated and the variables involved?
   (vi) Which particular statistic or procedure, and diagram, should we use? Why?
(b) Which variable is the response variable and which is the explanatory variable? Give reasons for your choice.
(c) Use the following Minitab output to answer the following:
   (i) Does there seem to be a linear relationship?
   (ii) What is the equation for the fitted straight line for this data?
   (iii) What is the value of the slope of this line? What does this slope mean?
   (iv) What is the value of the intercept? Interpret this result.
   (v) If the *Lowest price for the year* is 60 cents, what is the average *Closing price for the day* for the property trust shares?
   (vi) If the *Lowest price for the year* is 300 cents, what is the average *Closing price for the day* for the property trust shares?

(vii) Plot the fitted line on the scatter diagram in the Minitab output.

(viii) How strong is the relationship between *Closing price for the day* and *Lowest price for the year*?

```
MTB > retrieve 'a:\proptrst.mtp';
SUBC> portable.

Worksheet retrieved from file: a:\proptrst.mtp

MTB > info

COLUMN     NAME       COUNT       MISSING
C1         par          20
C2         close        20
C3         hiyear       20          2
C4         lowyear      20          2
C5         yield%       20
C6         fl/comp      20
C7         city         20

CONSTANTS USED: NONE

MTB > plot c2 c4
     -
  300+                                          *
     -
close -
     -                                    *
     -                               *
  200+                            *
     -                        *
     -                   ***
     -            *    *
  100+               *
     -          ***
     -      *   *
     -
     -    *
    0+  *
     +---------+---------+---------+---------+---------+-lowyear
     0        60       120       180       240       300
         N* = 2     response
                   number of explanatory var.
                 expl. var.
MTB > regress c2 1 c4

The regression equation is
close = 4.58 + 1.00 lowyear

18 cases used 2 cases contain missing values
```

continued . . .

```
Predictor          Coef        Stdev      t-ratio            p
Constant          4.576        3.695          24        0.233
lowyear         1.00494      0.02641       38.05        0.000
s = 8.132      R-sq = 98.9%      R-sq(adj)  =  98.8%
```

Analysis of Variance

```
SOURCE                DF           SS           MS           F            p
Regression             1        95731        95731      1447.47      0.000
Error                 16         1058           66
Total                 17        96789
```

Unusual Observations

```
Obs. lowyear    close        Fit   Stdev.Fit    Residual    St.Resid
8         86     120.00      91.00      2.11       29.00       3.69 R
18       288     295.00     294.00      4.84         .00       0.15 X
```

R denotes an obs. with a large st. resid.
X denotes an obs. whose X value gives it large influence.

10.10 A large supermarket chain has its own store brand for many grocery items. These tend to be priced lower than other brands. The management conducts a study over a 7-week period in which the weekly sales of the store brand of a particular item are recorded. During this period the only price change for the item is a weekly alteration of the major competing brand's price. The management wants to calculate the typical *Sales* of the store brand item during the seven-week period for specified *Prices* of the major competing brand. The results of this study are shown in table 10.4.

Table 10.4   *Sales* of store brand versus *Price* of competing brand

Price of competing brand ($)	Sales of the store brand
1.37	122
1.32	107
1.29	99
1.35	110
1.33	113
1.31	104
1.35	116

(a) Answer the following questions:
   (i) What is the question to be investigated (including the group to which the conclusions apply)?
   (ii) What variable(s) are we concerned with here?
   (iii) What type of variable(s) are they?

    (iv) Which major category of statistical procedures applies here? Why?

    (v) What type of statistic should we use, given the question to be investigated and the variables involved?

    (vi) Which particular statistic or procedure, and diagram, should we use? Why?

(b) Which variable is the response variable and which is the explanatory variable? Give reasons for your choice.

(c) Use linear regression to fit a straight line that represents the relationship between the two variables.

(d) What is the value of the slope of the fitted line? What does it mean in the context of this example?

(e) Do you consider that the fitted line will produce reliable mean responses? Explain how you reached your conclusion.

10.11 Minitab comes with a data set that is the result of a survey of 279 Wisconsin restaurants, for a study of the state's restaurant sector. Using the Minitab's *retrieve* command to retrieve the data from the Minitab portable worksheet file *restrnt.mtp*. Then use the *info* command to identify the columns of the worksheet used to store this data. You will see that *c3* is named *SALES* and *c8* is named *ADS*. These columns contain the variables *Gross 1979 sales* in $1000s and *Advertising expenditure* as a percentage of sales, respectively. You want to determine the rate of increase in *Advertising expenditure* for these restaurants as the *Gross 1979 sales* changes.

  (a) Answer the following questions:

    (i) What is the question to be investigated (including the group to which the conclusions apply)?

    (ii) What variable(s) are we concerned with here?

    (iii) What type of variable(s) are they?

    (iv) Which major category of statistical procedures applies here? Why?

    (v) What type of statistic should we use, given the question to be investigated and the variables involved?

    (vi) Which particular statistic or procedure, and diagram, should we use? Why?

  (b) Which variable is the response variable and which is the explanatory variable? Give reasons for your choice.

  (c) Use linear regression to fit a straight line that represents the linear relationship between the two variables.

  (d) What is the value of the slope of the fitted line? What does it mean in the context of this example?

  (e) Do you consider that the fitted line will produce reliable mean responses? Explain how you reached your conclusion.

## CHAPTER 11

INDEX NUMBERS FOR UNRESTRICTED VARIABLES OVER TIME

L E A R N I N G   O B J E C T I V E S

The learning objectives of this chapter are:

- to understand how index numbers monitor business and economic conditions;
- to be able to produce several types of index numbers: unweighted aggregative, unweighted relatives, Laspeyres and Paasche weighted index numbers;
- to know the features of each index number, and hence when to use it;
- to understand the purpose of an index number such as the consumer price index, and be able to interpret it.

The following extract from the *Summary of procedures based on combinations of variable types* in part VI gives an overview of the descriptive summaries covered in this and the previous chapters of part III, *Descriptive summaries of data*.

1. *One limited variable*
   - Distribution of variables: frequency, relative frequency and percentage one-way summary tables — bar or column chart.
   - Measures of central tendency: mode (mean, median).
   - Measures of dispersion: range, interquartile range, (standard deviation, coefficient of variation).

2. *Two limited variables*
   - Distribution of variables: two-way contingency table — chart with bars or columns that are grouped or stacked.

3. *Three limited variables*
   - Distribution of variables: three-way contingency table — chart with bars or columns that are grouped or stacked.

4. *One unrestricted variable*
   - Distribution of variables: frequency, relative frequency and percentage tables — histogram, polygon, stem-and-leaf display, dotplot.
   - Measures of central tendency: mean, median — boxplot.
   - Measures of dispersion: range, interquartile range, standard deviation, coefficient of variation — boxplot.

5. *One unrestricted variable — one limited variable*
   - Distribution of variables: frequency, relative frequency and percentage tables for each value of limited variable — histogram, polygon, stem-and-leaf display, dotplot for each value of limited variable.
   - Measures of central tendency: one-way table of means or medians — boxplot for each value of limited variable, bar chart or line diagram.
   - Measures of dispersion: one-way table of ranges, interquartile ranges, standard deviations or coefficients of variation — boxplot for each value of limited variable.

6. *One unrestricted variable — two limited variables*
   - Distribution of variables: frequency, relative frequency and percentage tables for each combination of values of the limited variables — histogram, polygon, stem-and-leaf display, dotplot for each combination of values of the limited variables.
   - Measures of central tendency: two-way table of means or medians — boxplot for each combination of values of the limited variables, bar chart or line diagram.
   - Measures of dispersion: two-way table of ranges, interquartile ranges, standard deviations or coefficients of variation — boxplot for each combination of values of the limited variables.

7. *Two unrestricted variables*
   - Measures of association: linear correlation coefficient and coefficient of determination — scatter diagram.
   - Fitted lines: intercept and/or slope; fitted values — scatter diagram.

8. *Unrestricted variables with measurements repeated over time or location*
   - **Index numbers**: simple index numbers, unweighted aggregative and relatives index numbers and Laspeyres and Paasche weighted index numbers — line diagram.

As outlined in the objectives, this chapter covers index numbers. Index numbers are a type of mean applied in specific circumstances. Their purpose is to measure the proportional change over time or location. They may measure monthly, quarterly or yearly changes or the change from one city to another. Our discussion here covers only index numbers that measure annual changes; however, the discussion applies equally when any other time interval or different locations are involved.

The categories of index numbers are:

price index numbers: measure changes in the **prices** of goods and services;
quantity index numbers: measure changes in the **quantities** of good and services produced or sold;
value index numbers: measure changes in **value** of goods and services.

Note that the distinction between price and value is that the price is the amount quoted as being needed to purchase an item whereas the value is the price × quantity.

Types of index numbers

There are different ways of computing index numbers to measure change over time. The different types of index numbers covered in this chapter are classified as follows:

1. Simple
2. Composite
   - Unweighted: aggregative; relatives.
   - Weighted: Laspeyres; Paasche.

11.1   Simple index numbers

Simple index numbers are index numbers calculated from a single item. In general, they can be calculated using a fixed or chain base.

In a **fixed-base index number**, the increase over time is expressed as a percentage of the period nominated as the **base period**. Thus, the formula for the simple fixed-base index number for the current year is:

$$Index\ number_{SF}^{current\ year} = \frac{Price_{current\ year}}{Price_{previous\ year}} \times 100$$

In a **chain-base index number**, the increase for one time is expressed as a percentage of the previous time. Thus, the simple chain-base index number is computed with the following formula:

$$Index\ number_{SC}^{current\ year} = \frac{Price_{current\ year}}{Price_{previous\ year}} \times 100$$

EXAMPLE 11.1   MEMBERSHIP OF A PROFESSIONAL SOCIETY

A professional society wants to report on the change in its membership fee from 1991 to 1993. So the question to be investigated is: what is the change in membership fee over a three-year period? The observed variables are *Membership fee* and *Year*, an unrestricted and a limited variable, respectively. The membership fee over the period 1991–93 is given in table 11.1. This data is primary data and represents a census for the question to be investigated.

To measure the change in membership fee over time, the fixed-base and chain-base index numbers are calculated as shown in table 11.1. The fixed-base index numbers show that the *Membership fee* in 1993 is 137.5% of what it was in the 1991, the base year. That is, *Membership fee* has risen by 37.5%

over the two-year period. The chain base, on the other hand, shows that *Membership fee* in 1993 is 125% of what it was in 1992. That is, *Membership fee* in 1993 increased 25% over that in 1992.

Table 11.1 Simple index numbers for *Membership fee* 1991–93

Year	Fee	Fixed-base	Chain-base
		Simple index numbers (%)	
1991	$40	$\frac{40}{40} \times 100 = 100.0$	
1992	$44	$\frac{44}{40} \times 100 = 110.0$	$\frac{44}{40} \times 100 = 110.0$
1993	$55	$\frac{55}{40} \times 100 = 137.5$	$\frac{55}{40} \times 100 = 125.0$

For the rest of the discussion on index numbers, we will deal with fixed-base index numbers, although the discussion applies equally to chain-base index numbers.

Selecting and shifting the base of an index number

The base year, for a fixed-base index number, is ideally as 'normal' as possible – not in a peak or trough of economic activity. However, as time progresses it is inevitable that the selected base year will become less appropriate and it will be necessary to move the base year. To convert previously calculated index numbers to the new base year the following formula is used:

$$Index\ number_{under\ new\ base}^{current\ year} = \frac{Index\ number_{under\ old\ base}^{current\ year}}{Index\ number_{under\ old\ base}^{new\ base\ year}} \times 100$$

This formula is appropriate for all fixed-base index numbers, not just simple index numbers.

EXAMPLE 11.1 MEMBERSHIP OF A PROFESSIONAL SOCIETY (continued)
If the base is to be shifted from 1991 to 1993,

$$Index\ number_{under\ base\ 1993}^{1992} = \frac{Index\ number_{under\ base\ 1991}^{1992}}{Index\ number_{under\ base\ 1991}^{1993}} \times 100$$

$$= \frac{110.0}{137.5} \times 100$$

$$= 80.0\%$$

Of course, in this case we have the original prices, so it is easy to confirm that:

$$Index\ number_{under\ base\ 1993}^{1992} = \frac{44}{55} \times 100$$

$$= 80.0\%$$

11.2   Composite index numbers

To be interested in the changes in price for a single commodity is somewhat unusual. More often we are interested in quantifying changes involving a number of items and this is the purpose of **composite index numbers**. The items in whose change one is interested is called the **basket of commodities**. For example, changes in food prices involve price changes in commodities such as bread, butter, milk and so on. Changes in car running costs involve price changes in items such as petrol, tyres and registration. Changes in farm production costs involve changes in machinery running costs, maintenance costs, and so on.

In the following sections we first consider two unweighted index numbers, then two weighted index numbers.

11.2.1   Unweighted index numbers

An **unweighted aggregative index number** represents the intuitively obvious approach to measuring the change in the prices of a set of commodities. That is, add up all the prices in a year and compare this to the sum of the prices in the base year.

$$Index\ number_{UA} = \frac{\sum\limits_{commodities}(Prices_{current\ year})}{\sum\limits_{commodities}(Prices_{base\ year})} \times 100$$

where $\sum\limits_{commodities}$ stands for 'sum over the commodities'.

EXAMPLE 11.2   FOOD PRICES OVER THREE YEARS

We want to measure the changes in the price of food for the years 1991–93, using the prices of four items — bread, milk, eggs and rump steak. We specified the precise details of the items, such as the type of milk and the brand and type of bread and we obtained the prices from the same local supermarket in the last week of each year. The question to be investigated is: what are the overall, or combined, changes in these food prices? The variables involved are the unrestricted variable *Price*, and the limited variables, *Year* and *Commodity*. The primary data for answering this question is in table 11.2.

In this example, our conclusions are restricted to just the collected data. This is at least partly due to the problems of making broader conclusions because of the way the data has been collected. For example, the sampling was convenience sampling, as the prices were obtained from a nearby supermarket, so this supermarket is unlikely to be representative of a broader group such as all supermarkets in the city or state. A second problem arises with the timing of the data collection. As prices have been collected for only a week, this will not be representative of price changes throughout the year; in particular, the price of rump steak varies with each season.

Table 11.2 *Price ($) for four food Commodities 1991–93*

			Year	
Commodity	Amount	1991	1992	1993
Bread	loaf	1.35	1.71	1.80
Milk	litre	0.75	0.90	1.03
Eggs	dozen	1.71	1.96	2.09
Rump steak	kilogram	4.95	7.63	9.11

The unweighted aggregative index number for 1992, with base year 1991, is:

$$Index\ number_{UA}^{1992} = \frac{1.71 + 0.90 + 1.96 + 7.63}{1.35 + 0.75 + 1.71 + 4.95} \times 100 = \frac{12.20}{8.76} \times 100 = 139.3\%$$

The computations for all three index numbers for this example are in table 11.3.

Table 11.3 Unweighted aggregative index numbers for four food *Commodities* 1991–93

		Year	
	1991	1992	1993
Total ($)	8.76	12.20	14.03
Index numbers$_{UA}$* (%)	100.0	139.3	160.2

*The base year is 1991.

Notes

1. Unweighted aggregative index numbers are simple, intuitively obvious measures.
2. They depend on the unit of measurement. For example, if you adjust the *Price* of milk to 2 litres instead of 1 litre and the *Price* of eggs to one egg rather than a dozen eggs, the unweighted aggregative index for 1992 becomes 142.3% and for 1993 becomes 165.5%.
3. The most expensive item can impose too much influence on the value of an unweighted aggregative index number.
4. They provide satisfactory index numbers if the prices for all the items are for the same amounts, for example, if you measure changes in the *Price* of coffee and all prices are for the same size of container. In this case, a uniform change in the unit for which the *Price* is quoted will not affect the index number values.

An **unweighted relatives index number** is calculated as the mean of the *price relatives*, multiplied by 100. That is,

$$Index\ number_{UR} = \bar{x}_{Price\ relatives_{current\ year}} \times 100$$

$$= \frac{\sum_{commodities}(Price\ relatives_{current\ year})}{n} \times 100$$

where n is the number of commodities.

The **price relatives** are calculated for each commodity in each year by taking the *Price* in that year over the *Price* in the base year. That is,

$$Price\ relative = \frac{Commodity's\ price_{current\ year}}{Commodity's\ price_{base\ year}}$$

The crucial property of a *price relative* is that it is unitless.

EXAMPLE 11.2   FOOD PRICES OVER THREE YEARS (continued)
The *price relative* for milk in 1992, with base year 1991, is:

$$\frac{0.90}{0.75} = 1.20$$

The *price relative* for milk in 1992 is unitless as it is the ratio of two milk *Prices*. Each of the milk prices are in units of dollars per litre and these cancel when the ratio is taken.

The complete set of *price relatives*, with base year 1991, for this example is given in table 11.4. Values for the unweighted relatives index numbers are also listed in table 11.4.

Table 11.4   *Price relatives* for four food *Commodities* 1991–93

| | | | Year | |
Commodity	Amount	1991	1992	1993
Bread	loaf	1.000	1.267	1.333
Milk	litre	1.000	1.200	1.373
Eggs	dozen	1.000	1.146	1.222
Rump steak	kilogram	1.000	1.541	1.840
Total		4.000	5.154	5.769
Index numbers$_{UR}$* (%)		100.0	128.9	144.2

* The base year is 1991.

Notes

1. The *price relatives* are unitless and so the unweighted relative index number values themselves are independent of the unit for which *Prices* are given.

2. The unweighted index numbers do not take into account differences in importance between the commodities. For example, rump steak had the largest increase and so it will make the value of the unweighted relatives index number larger than it would be if rump was not included. However, it may be the least important because people do not spend much of their food budget on it.

11.2.2 Weighted index numbers

In the discussion of unweighted index numbers, we noted that these index numbers do not take into account differences in importance between the commodities. In this section, we discuss the use of weights, and weighted index numbers, to reflect the relative importance of the commodities. Two **weighted index numbers** are covered: Laspeyres index numbers and Paasche index numbers. The difference between these two index numbers lies in the weights that are used. Laspeyres index numbers use base year weights and Paasche index numbers use current year weights.

So, computing weighted index numbers requires a set of weights. The **weights** should reflect the importance of the items. The most commonly used weights are the quantities sold. However, any numbers can be used, including subjectively derived numbers that are intended to reflect the relative importance of the items.

EXAMPLE 11.2   FOOD PRICES OVER THREE YEARS (continued)

A set of weights for this example is given in table 11.5. From these weights we see that eggs and rump steak are least important, milk and bread most important.

Table 11.5   Weights for four food *Commodities* 1991–93

	Total quantity sold (000 000s)		
Commodity	1991	1992	1993
Bread	20	22	29
Milk	23	28	35
Eggs	0.8	1.5	1.4
Rump steak	1.5	1.0	0.8

A **Laspeyres index number** is both a weighted and a prices index number that is computed using base year weights *when the weights are the quantities* of the commodities sold. A general formula for a weighted, prices index number using base year weights is:

$$Index\ number_{BW} = \frac{\sum_{commodities}(Weights_{base\ year} \times Prices_{current\ year})}{\sum_{commodities}(Weights_{base\ year} \times Prices_{base\ year})} \times 100$$

To calculate the index number, it is simplest to compute the **sum of products** for each year. This is done by summing the products of the base year weight and the price for a commodity in the year for which the sum is computed. The index number is then computed as the ratio of the sum of products in the current year and the sum of products for the base year, multiplied by 100.

But for a Laspeyres index number, the weights are specifically the quantities sold, so that the formula for it is obtained by substituting the *Quantities* for the *Weights*:

[handwritten: Total value @ new prices]

[handwritten: Laspeegres]

$$Index\ number_L = \frac{\sum_{commodities}(Quantities_{base\ year} \times Prices_{current\ year})}{\sum_{commodities}(Quantities_{base\ year} \times Prices_{base\ year})} \times 100$$

[handwritten: Total value @ old prices]

The index number is the ratio, expressed as a percentage, of the total cost of the quantities of the commodities sold in the base year, at current year prices, to the total cost of the quantities of the commodities sold in the base year, at base year prices.

EXAMPLE 11.2   FOOD PRICES OVER THREE YEARS (continued)

To calculate the Laspeyres index number for 1992, with base year 1991, requires the 1991 and 1992 *Prices*, from table 11.2, and 1991 Total *quantities sold*, from table 11.5, as follows:

$$Index\ number_L^{1992} = \frac{(20 \times 1.71) + (23 \times 0.90) + (0.8 \times 1.96) + (1.5 \times 7.63)}{(20 \times 1.35) + (23 \times 0.75) + (0.8 \times 1.71) + (1.5 \times 4.95)} \times 100$$

$$= 128.03\%$$

[handwritten: @ 1991]

The computation of Laspeyres index numbers for all years is summarised in table 11.6. The sums of products were first computed for each year. Then the index number was computed from these by taking the ratio of the sum of products for the current year and the sum of products for the base year, multiplied by 100.

Table 11.6 Laspeyres index for four food *Commodities* 1991–93

	Year		
	1991	1992	1993
Sums of products (base quantities × current prices)	53.043	67.913	75.027
Index numbers$_L$* (%)	100.0	128.0	141.4

* The base year is 1991.

A **Paasche index number** is both a weighted and a prices index number that is computed using current year weights *when the weights are the quantities* of the commodities sold. A general formula for a weighted, prices index number using current year weights is:

$$Index\ number_{CW} = \frac{\sum\limits_{commodities} (Weights_{current\ year} \times Prices_{current\ year})}{\sum\limits_{commodities} (Weights_{current\ year} \times Prices_{base\ year})} \times 100$$

Paasche index numbers, like Laspeyres, use the *Quantities* as the *Weights* so that the formula for a Paasche index number is:

$$Index\ number_P = \frac{\sum\limits_{commodities} (Quantities_{current\ year} \times Prices_{current\ year})}{\sum\limits_{commodities} (Quantities_{current\ year} \times Prices_{base\ year})} \times 100$$

This index number is the ratio, expressed as a percentage, of the total cost of the quantities of the commodities sold in the current year, at current year prices, to the total cost of the quantities of the commodities sold in the current year, at base year prices.

Again, the index number can be computed by first calculating, for each year, sums of products. In this case, two sums of products must be computed: the sum of products of the quantities and the prices in the current year, and the sum of products of the quantities in the current year and prices in the base year. The index number can then be calculated by taking the ratio of these two sums of products and multiplying them by 100.

EXAMPLE 11.2   FOOD PRICES OVER THREE YEARS (continued)

The computation of the Paasche index number for 1992, under a 1991 base year, uses the 1991 and 1992 *Prices*, from table 11.2, and 1992 *Total quantities sold*, from table 11.5. The computation proceeds as follows:

$$\begin{aligned}
Index\ number_P^{1992} &= \frac{(22 \times 1.71) + (28 \times 0.0) + (1.5 \times 1.96) + (1.0 \times 7.63)}{(22 \times 1.35) + (28 \times 0.75) + (1.5 \times 1.71) + (1.0 \times 4.95)} \times 100 \\
&= \frac{73.390}{58.215} \times 100 \\
&= 126.07\%
\end{aligned}$$

The computations of Paasche index numbers for all years are summarised in table 11.7. The sums of products are computed first, then the index numbers are then computed from these by taking the ratios of the two sums of products for the current year; finally, the result is multiplied by 100. Note the difference in the two sets of products presented in table 11.7. The first set is the total cost of the quantities of the goods sold in the current year at current prices; the second set is the total cost of the same quantities of goods, but at base year prices.

Table 11.7   Paasche index numbers for four food *Commodities* 1991–93

		Year	
	1991	1992	1993
Sums of products			
(current quantities × current prices)	53.043	73.390	98.464
(current quantities × base prices)	53.043	58.215	71.754
*Index numbers$_P$ (%)**	100.0	126.1	137.2

* The base year is 1991.

11.2.3 Summary

The values obtained for all four types of index numbers are given in table 11.8.

Table 11.8   Summary of index numbers (%) for four food *Commodities* 1991–93

		Year	
*Index number**	1991	1992	1993
Unweighted aggregative	100.0	139.3	160.2
Unweighted relatives	100.0	128.9	144.2
Laspeyres	100.0	128.0	141.4
Passche	100.0	126.1	137.2

* The base year is 1991.

Notes

1. The differences between the unweighted aggregative and unweighted relatives index numbers are due to their different methods of calculation. Unweighted relatives index numbers have the advantage of being unitless, whereas unweighted aggregative index numbers can be manipulated by changing the units for which prices are quoted.

2. Both Laspeyres and Paasche index numbers use quantities as weights to reflect differences between the items in their importance — Laspeyres and Paasche are somewhat lower than the unweighted relatives index numbers because of the lower importance of rump steak.

3. Neither Laspeyres nor Paasche index numbers are affected by a change in the amounts on which the prices are based, because the quantities also have to be modified by the same conversion factors.

4. Laspeyres and Paasche index numbers differ because of differences in the base-year and current-year weights.

5. Base-year weights have the problem of becoming outdated, so they may not reflect the current importance.

6. Current-year weights have to be collected each year, so it is more costly to obtain the information to compute Paasche index numbers.

7. Whether to use Laspeyres or Paasche index numbers depends on whether the importance of being current outweighs the cost.

11.3 Consumer price index

11.3.1 The Australian consumer price index

This is done every 5 YRS APPROX (Base yr)

The Australian **consumer price index** (CPI) is described in the Australian Bureau of Statistics (1993b) publication *A guide to the consumer price index*, which is summarised in this section. More detailed information can be obtained from the publication itself.

The consumer price index is a Laspeyres type index number, in that it has a fixed-base period and does not use current period weights. However, instead of using base period weights, the weights are updated about every five years. The base period is updated every ten years. So it is not a true Laspeyres index number. The index is calculated quarterly.

If done every yr, it is called a Paasch.

The Australian Bureau of Statistics (1988) defines the consumer price index to be:

'a measure of changes, over time, in retail prices of a constant basket of goods and services representative of consumption expenditure by resident employee households in Australian metropolitan areas'.

This definition is very specific — appropriately so, because it is used to determine what is included in the index and how it is collected. For instance, prices of goods and services are included, not just goods. Items are included if they represent a high proportion of the expenditure of a specific subset of households. They must be employee, as opposed to employer, households and must also be metropolitan, not country, households.

The index is based on altogether 100 000 individual prices from 8 cities on items divided into eight main groups:

1. Food
2. Clothing
3. Housing
4. Household equipment and operation
5. Transportation
6. Tobacco and alcohol
7. Health and personal care
8. Recreation and education

The items included in these groups were last reviewed in 1992.

The prices are collected by Australian Bureau of Statistics field staff from normal retail outlets, including supermarkets, department stores, footwear stores, restaurants, service stations, schools, airlines, plumbers and so on. Items such as fresh fruit and vegetables are collected weekly, fresh meat, bread and alcohol are collected monthly, and milk, electricity and gas, motor cars, magazines and education are collected quarterly. Average prices for the quarter are computed for each item.

As mentioned previously the weights are updated about every five years and this is done via the household expenditure survey, which measures the relative importance of each item in the total spending on all items. At the time of writing this book, the weights were based on the 1988–89 household expenditure survey. Also, the base period is updated about every ten years. At the time of writing, the base period is the 1988–89 period.

The reasons for reviewing the weights and base period of the consumer price index include:

> *Changed buying habits*: Consumers change the items they purchase; for example, they purchase video machines. This requires updating the list of items. Also, the relative importance of items change; for example, chicken rather than rump steak is purchased more often. This requires updating the weights.
> *Irrelevance of base period.*

11.3.2 Uses of the consumer price index

The consumer price index has two uses:

1. as an **adjuster for cost-of-living**;
2. as an economic indicator.

The consumer price index is used to make cost-of-living adjustments to items such as wages and taxes. This tends to escalate these items, as the cost-of-living is generally increasing. It is also used to adjust values for an item from different times so that they are comparable; that is, taking into account the difference in cost-of-living between the two times. It is also used as an economic indicator; for example, to indicate economic performance, especially the cost-of-living.

The consumer price index is often used as a cost-of-living index, which it is not. It is only a price index and it is based on a fixed set of goods and services. It does not take into account changing patterns in items purchased between revisions; nor does it take into account income and taxes, except sales tax, so it does not reflect changes in disposable income.

To use the consumer price index as an adjuster for cost-of-living, use the following formula to adjust a price to the base-year price level:

$$\text{Adjusted price} = \frac{\text{actual price}}{\text{consumer price index}} \times 100$$

EXAMPLE 11.3   GRADUATE'S SALARY

A graduate wants to determine how much her purchasing power, measured by net salary after tax, has increased since graduation in 1967. The question to be investigated is: what is the real increase in purchasing power? The variable involved is *Net salary,* which is an unrestricted variable.

Suppose that the graduate's 1988 *Net salary* was $52,000 and that her 1967 *Net salary* was $4000. Her purchasing power seems to have increased by:

$$\frac{52\,000 - 4000}{4000} \times 100 = 1200\%$$

However, this is clearly not the case as the effect of inflation has not been taken into account. Suppose the consumer price index, base year 1975, was 225% for 1988 and 68% for 1967. Then the adjusted salaries are:

$$\frac{52\,000}{225} \times 100 = 23\,111.11$$

$$\frac{4000}{68} \times 100 = 5882.35$$

The real increase in purchasing power is thus:

$$\frac{23\,111.11 - 5882.35}{5882.35} \times 100 = 292.9\%$$

That is, the graduate's purchasing power in 1988 has increased nearly 300% from what it was in 1967.

11.4 Reports on examples

The following reports, for the examples analysed in this chapter, indicate what material an investigator should include in a report. In general, the details of the statistical analysis are omitted so that the reader of the report can concentrate on the results.

EXAMPLE 11.1 MEMBERSHIP OF A PROFESSIONAL SOCIETY — REPORT

The membership fee of a certain professional society over the period 1991–93 is shown in table 11.9. Simple, fixed-base index numbers for the membership fee are also shown in table 11.9, and figure 11.1 shows the change in membership fee. The index numbers show that the membership fee in 1992 is 110% of what it was in 1991, the base year, and in 1993 is 137.5% of what it was in 1991. That is, membership fee rose by 10% in the first year and by 37.5% over the two-year period.

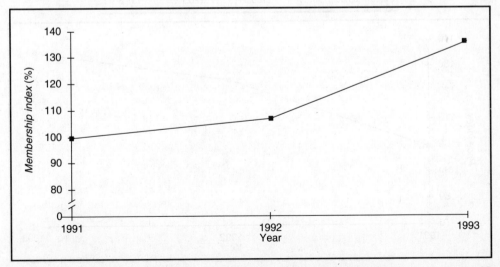

Figure 11.1 Change in a professional society's membership fee, 1991–93

Table 11.9   Simple, fixed-base index numbers for membership fees 1991–93

Year	Fee ($)	Index numbers (%)
1991	40	100.0
1992	44	110.0
1993	45	137.5

EXAMPLE 11.2   FOOD PRICES OVER THREE YEARS — REPORT

We want to measure the changes in the price of food for the years 1991–93, using the prices of four items — bread, milk, eggs and rump steak. We specified the precise details of the items, such as the type of milk and the brand and type of bread and we obtained the prices from the same local supermarket in the last week of each year.

Paasche index numbers for the three years for which prices were available are given in table 11.10 and illustrated in figure 11.2. Food prices increased by 26.1% in the first year and a further 11.1% in the second year so that over the two-year period they increased by 37.2%. These conclusions are restricted to just the data collected as they probably cannot be applied more widely — for instance, to all the supermarkets in the city and to price changes throughout the year.

Table 11.10   Paasche index numbers for four food *Commodities* 1991–93

	Year		
	1991	1992	1993
Index numbers (%)	100.0	126.1	137.2

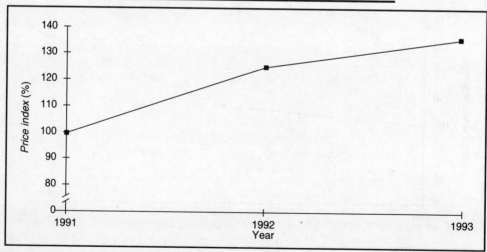

Figure 11.2   Changes in the prices of food commodities 1991–93

EXAMPLE 11.3 GRADUATE'S SALARY — REPORT

A graduate's 1988 net salary after tax was $52 000 and his 1967 net salary after tax was $4000. In 1975 dollars, the 1988 net salary is $23 111.11 and the 1967 net salary is $5882.35 so that the graduate's real increase in purchasing power is 292%.

11.5   Using Minitab to produce the index numbers

Use the *let* command, with *sum* and *mean* functions, to produce the index numbers.

EXAMPLE 11.2 FOOD PRICES OVER THREE YEARS (continued)

The complete set of commands to produce the index numbers for this example is as follows:

```
MTB > outfile 'a:\indx9193.lis'
MTB > retrieve 'a:\indx9193.mtp';
SUBC> portable.
MTB > info
MTB > print c1-c6
MTB > # compute unweighted aggregative index numbers
MTB > let k11=sum('price_91')      where k11 is a constant.
MTB > let k12=sum('price_92')
MTB > let k13=sum('price_93')
MTB > print k11-k13
MTB > let k1=k11/k11*100
MTB > let k2=k12/k11*100
MTB > let k3=k13/k11*100
MTB > print k1-k3
MTB > # compute unweighted relatives index numbers
MTB > let c7=c1/c1
MTB > let c8=c2/c1
MTB > let c9=c3/c1
MTB > name c7 'prel_91' c8 'prel_92' c9 'prel_93'
MTB > let k1=mean('prel_91')*100
MTB > let k2=mean('prel_92')*100
MTB > let k3=mean('prel_93')*100
MTB > print k1-k3
MTB > # compute Laspeyres index numbers
MTB > let k11=sum('quant_91'*'price_91')      value's
MTB > let k12=sum('quant_91'*'price_92')          "
MTB > let k13=sum('quant_91'*'price_93')          "
MTB > print k11-k13
MTB > let k1=k11/k11*100
MTB > let k2=k12/k11*100
MTB > let k3=k13/k11*100
MTB > print k1-k3
MTB > # compute Paasche index numbers
MTB > let k11=sum('quant_91'*'price_91')
```

continued . . .

```
MTB > let k12=sum('quant_92'*'price_92')
MTB > let k13=sum('quant_93'*'price_93')
MTB > print k11-k13
MTB > let k21=sum('quant_91'*'price_91')
MTB > let k22=sum('quant_92'*'price_91')
MTB > let k23=sum('quant_93'*'price_91')
MTB > print k21-k23
MTB > let k1=k11/k21*100
MTB > let k2=k12/k22*100
MTB > let k3=k13/k23*100
MTB > print k1-k3
```

If your version of Minitab has pull-down menus and you want to use them, table 11.11 lists the menus and options that access the required commands. Appendix D, *Detailed instructions for Minitab menus*, explains how to use the menus.

Table 11.11   Menus and options for Minitab commands to produce index numbers

Minitab command	Menu	Option
outfile	File >	Other Files > Start Recording Session...
retrieve	File >	Open Worksheet...
port		Minitab portable worksheet
info	Edit >	Get Worksheet Info...
	(Edit >	Data Screen [Alt-D])
print	Edit >	Display Data...
let	Calc >	Functions and Statistics > General Expressions...
name	Edit >	Data Screen

The output produced by the commands for retrieving and checking the contents of the file is as follows:

```
MTB > retrieve 'a:\indx9193.mtp';
SUBC> portable.

Worksheet retrieved from file: a:\indx9193.mtp
MTB > info

COLUMN    NAME          COUNT
C1        price_91        4
C2        price_92        4
C3        price_93        4
C4        quant_91        4
C5        quant_92        4
C6        quant_93        4

CONSTANTS USED: NONE
```

The relative values gives the Index.

continued . . .

Laspière: $\dfrac{Q_B \times P_C + - - -}{Q_B \times P_B + - - - - -}$

```
MTB > print c1-c6
```

(millions) $\times 10^6$

ROW	price_91	price_92	price_93	quant_91	quant_92	quant_93
1	1.35	1.71	1.80	20.0	22.0	29.0
2	0.75	0.90	1.03	23.0	28.0	35.0
3	1.71	1.96	2.09	0.8	1.5	1.4
4	4.95	7.63	9.11	1.5	1.0	0.8

Value 91 = quantity 91 × price 91

11.5.1 Unweighted aggregative index numbers

Value 92 = qu 91 × P92

EXAMPLE 11.2 FOOD PRICES OVER THREE YEARS (continued)

The commands, and associated output, for producing unweighted aggregative index numbers are as follows:

```
MTB > # compute unweighted aggregative index numbers
MTB > let k11=sum('price_91')
MTB > let k12=sum('price_92')
MTB > let k13=sum('price_93')
MTB > print k11-k13
K11        8.76000
K12        12.2000
K13        14.0300
MTB > let k1=k11/k11*100
MTB > let k2=k12/k11*100
MTB > let k3=k13/k11*100
MTB > print k1-k3
K1        100.000
K2        139.269
K3        160.160
```

11.5.2 Unweighted relatives index numbers

EXAMPLE 11.2 FOOD PRICES OVER THREE YEARS (continued)

The commands, and associated output, for producing unweighted relatives index numbers are as follows:

```
MTB > # compute unweighted relatives index numbers
MTB > let c7=c1/c1
MTB > let c8=c2/c1
MTB > let c9=c3/c1
MTB > name c7 'prel_91' c8 'prel_92' c9 'prel_93'
MTB > let k1=mean('prel_91')*100
MTB > let k2=mean('prel_92')*100
MTB > let k3=mean('prel_93')*100
MTB > print k1-k3
K1        100.000
K2        128.857
K3        144.232
```

11.5.3 Laspeyres index numbers

EXAMPLE 11.2   FOOD PRICES OVER THREE YEARS (continued)

The commands, and associated output, for producing Laspeyres index numbers are as follows:

```
MTB > # compute Laspeyres index numbers
MTB > let k11=sum('quant_91'*'price_91')
MTB > let k12=sum('quant_92'*'price_92')
MTB > let k13=sum('quant_93'*'price_93')
MTB > print k11-k13
K11        53.0430
K12        67.9130
K13        75.0270
MTB > let k1=k11/k11*100
MTB > let k2=k12/k11*100
MTB > let k3=k13/k11*100
MTB > print k1-k3
K1        100.000
K2        128.034
K3        141.446
```

All 91

11.5.4 Paasche index numbers

EXAMPLE 11.2   FOOD PRICES OVER THREE YEARS (continued)

The commands, and associated output, for producing Paasche index numbers are as follows:

```
MTB > # compute Paasche index numbers
MTB > let k11=sum('quant_91'*'price_91')
MTB > let k12=sum('quant_92'*'price_92')
MTB > let k13=sum('quant_93'*'price_93')
MTB > print k11-k13
K11        53.0430
K12        73.3900
K13        98.4640
MTB > let k21=sum('quant_91'*'price_91')
MTB > let k22=sum('quant_92'*'price_91')
MTB > let k23=sum('quant_93*'price_92')
MTB > print k21-k23
K21        53.0430
K22        58.2150
K23        71.7540
MTB > let k1=k11/k21*100
MTB > let k2=k12/k22*100
MTB > let k3=k13/k23*100
MTB > print k1-k3
K1        100.000
K2        126.067
K3        137.224
```

Present day quant

X

$$\frac{P_c \times q_c}{P_b \times q_c}$$

11.6   Chapter summary

Index numbers measure the proportional change in prices, quantities or values over time or location; this chapter has concentrated on price index numbers, and covered fixed-base index numbers more extensively than chain-base index numbers as the former are more commonly used.

Simple index numbers measure the change of a single item whereas composite index numbers measure the change in several items, known as the basket of commodities.

An unweighted aggregative index number, the simplest type of composite index number, is the ratio of the sum of the prices in the current year to the sum of the prices in the base year, multiplied by 100. It has the disadvantage of varying when you change the units for which the prices are quoted; this is not a problem if all commodities share the same unit.

An unweighted relatives index number measures the change in the prices of a set of commodities as the mean of the price relatives, multiplied by 100. The values obtained for it are independent of the units for which the prices of the commodities are quoted.

Neither unweighted index number takes into account the relative importance of the commodities; the commodity with the highest price or largest change will have most influence on their values. Weighted index numbers use weights to overcome this deficiency. Laspeyres and Paasche index numbers are weighted index numbers that measure changes in prices and use the quantities of the commodities sold as the weights. The difference between these two index numbers is that Laspeyres index numbers use base year weights and Paasche index numbers use current year weights. In deciding whether to use Laspeyres or Paasche index numbers, you have to balance the advantage of using the currently applicable weights against the cost of collecting them.

A Laspeyres index number is the ratio, expressed as a percentage, of the total cost of the quantities of the commodities sold in the base year, at current year prices, to the total cost of the quantities of the commodities sold in the base year, at base year prices.

A Paasche index number is the ratio, expressed as a percentage, of the total cost of the quantities of the commodities sold in the current year, at current year prices, to the total cost of the quantities of the commodities sold in the current year, at base year prices.

The Australian consumer price index is a Laspeyres type of index number designed to measure quarterly variation in the retail prices of goods and services to represent a high proportion of the expenditure of metropolitan employee households. The consumer price index is used to make cost-of-living adjustments to items such as wages and taxes. It is also used as an economic indicator of, in particular, trends in the cost-of-living.

Price Index : measures changes in the price of goods & services
quantity " : measures changes in the quantity

11.7   Key terms

- adjuster for cost-of-living
- base period
- basket of commodities
- chain-base index number
- composite index number
- consumer price index
- fixed-base index number
- index number
- Laspeyres index number (*Index number$_L$*)
- Paasche index number (*Index number$_P$*)
- price
- price index number
- price relative
- quantity
- quantity index number
- simple index number (*Index number$_S$*)
- sum of products
- unweighted aggregative index number (*Index number$_{UA}$*)
- unweighted relatives index number (*Index number$_{UR}$*)
- value
- value index number
- weight
- weighted index number

11.8   Exercises

11.1   What is the main role of index numbers?

11.2   A simple index number can be calculated using either a particular year as the base year or the chain-base method. In your own words explain the differences in the two methods.

11.3   The price of petrol is important in the Australian economy because of the vastness of the country. Changes in the price of petrol and associated products have a marked impact on the production and distribution of raw materials and manufactured goods. These price changes also affect the costs of running a car or using public transport. Which type of unweighted index number would you use if you had to adjust your budget to accommodate these price movements? Give reasons for your answer.

11.4   While it is often important to examine changes in the price of just one commodity, usually it is more appropriate to collect information on a group of goods or services. Laspeyres and Paasche index numbers are widely used for this purpose.

   (a) How do Laspeyres and Paasche index numbers differ from the unweighted aggregative index number?

   (b) There is one major difference between Laspeyres and Paasche index numbers in their application. What is it?

11.5   Describe in detail the differences between the terms *price, price relatives*, and *total value sold*.

11.6 Many types of index numbers are frequently quoted in the media, as follows. Describe their main features.

(a) Dow Jones average

(b) Retail price average

(c) Consumer price index

(d) Index of industrial production

(e) Gross domestic product

Although they rely on different data, they have one feature in common. What is it?

11.7 The consumer price index is widely used by politicians, the trade union movement, and the person in the street to support their points of view. Some of the uses commonly attributed to the consumer price index are as follows. Are these statements true or false? Why?

(a) It is a measure of inflation.

(b) It has a direct impact on the adjustment to rates of pay.

(c) It is used to escalate pensions and government superannuation payments.

(d) It is a cost-of-living allowance.

(e) It is used by the state and federal governments to make annual adjustments to fees and charges.

(f) It takes into account the cost of all goods and services.

(g) It is based on information gathered from everywhere in Australia.

(h) It can overstate the rate of inflation.

(i) All government charges are included in the calculations of this index.

(j) It can be used to compare prices in one capital city with another.

11.8 Index numbers have an important role to play in the application of quantitative methods to business. Table 11.12 contains an *Export price index* which classifies exports according to the Australian Standard Industrial Classification (ASIC). This index is constructed from *Prices* obtained for selected commodities from major exporters. We want to examine the difference in the price changes between the three *ASIC divisions* over the years 1987-92.

Table 11.12   *Export price index*(%) for three *ASIC divisions* 1987-92

	ASIC divisions		
Year	Agriculture	Mining	Manufacturing
1986–87	71.0	93.0	81.0
1987–88	93.0	84.0	89.0
1988–89	103.0	83.0	96.0
1989–90	100.0	100.0	100.0
1990–91	77.2	106.5	96.9
1991–92	72.9	103.5	89.8

* The base year is 1989–90.
Source: Australian Bureau of Statistics (1994b)

(a) Answer the following questions:

(i) What is the question to be investigated (including the group to which the conclusions apply)?

(ii) What variable(s) are we concerned with here?

(iii) What type of variable(s) are they?

(iv) Which major category of statistical procedures applies here? Why?

(v) What type of statistic should we use, given the question to be investigated and the variables involved?

(vi) Which particular statistic or procedure, and diagram, should we use? Why?

(b) Plot the index numbers for the three divisions against time. Comment on any differences in the trends between the divisions.

11.9 The *Consumer price index* is based on the prices of items in eight different *Groups*. As well as the overall index, an index is computed for each group. Group index numbers for the period 1983–92 are given in table 11.13. Use these to investigate the differences in the price changes between the groups for this period.

Table 11.13   *Consumer price index* (%) for eight groups 1983–92*

				Group				
Year	Food	Clothing	Housing†	Household equipment and operation	Transportation	Tobacco and alcohol	Health and personal care	Recreation and education
1982–83	61.5	61.7	53.8	64.4	59.4	54.8	76.7	62.6
1983–84	66.3	65.3	57.6	69.0	64.4	61.7	73.4	66.6
1984–85	69.7	69.4	62.0	72.3	68.5	66.8	61.0	69.1
1985–86	75.1	75.1	67.2	78.1	74.4	72.9	66.6	75.3
1986–87	81.1	82.4	72.2	83.9	82.7	80.6	77.3	82.2
1987–88	85.3	88.8	77.2	89.7	89.1	87.4	86.1	88.7
1988–89	93.4	95.1	86.9	94.8	92.5	92.4	93.3	94.2
1989–90	100.0	100.0	100.0	100.0	100.0	100.0	100.0	100.0
1990–91	103.3	104.6	103.5	105.1	106.9	108.8	109.6	105.0
1991–92	105.8	106.4	98.9	107.5	108.8	115.0	121.3	106.9

* The base year is 1989–90.
†This is affected by a change in the treatment of mortgage charges from March Quarter 1989
Source: Australian Bureau of Statistics (1994b)

(a) Answer the following questions:

(i) What is the question to be investigated (including the group to which the conclusions apply)?

(ii) What variable(s) are we concerned with here?

(iii) What type of variable(s) are they?

(iv) Which major category of statistical procedures applies here? Why?

(v) What type of statistic should we use, given the question to be investigated and the variables involved?

(vi) Which particular statistic or procedure, and diagram, should we use? Why?

(b) Write a report highlighting the changes in the consumer price index for the four *Groups*: Food, Clothing, Housing and Health and personal care.

11.10 The consumer price index for each of Australia's eight capital cities for the years 1980–92 is given in table 11.14. They are to be used to investigate the differences in the price changes between the capital cities for these years.

Table 11.14   *Consumer price index* (%): All groups index numbers for the *Capital cities* of Australia 1981–92

	Capital city							
Year	Sydney	Melbourne	Brisbane	Adelaide	Perth	Hobart	Canberra	Darwin
1980–81	49.3	49.1	50.2	49.7	49.6	50.4	50.0	52.7
1981–82	54.3	54.2	55.6	54.9	55.1	55.5	55.3	58.5
1982–83	60.8	60.3	61.7	61.4	60.7	61.5	61.9	64.8
1983–84	64.5	64.9	66.1	65.8	65.0	65.5	66.1	68.5
1984–85	67.0	67.8	69.2	68.9	67.5	68.6	69.3	71.1
1985–86	72.7	73.6	74.8	74.7	72.9	74.6	75.3	77.0
1986–87	79.5	80.5	81.2	81.5	80.2	81.9	81.6	83.9
1987–88	85.6	86.4	86.9	87.0	85.9	87.9	87.3	89.8
1988–89	92.5	92.3	93.0	93.3	92.3	93.4	93.1	94.2
1989–90	100.0	100.0	100.0	100.0	100.0	100.0	100.0	100.0
1990–91	104.9	105.8	104.9	106.2	105.1	104.9	105.1	105.7
1991–92	106.7	108.1	107.0	108.9	105.9	107.1	107.8	108.0

* The base year is 1989–90.
Source: Australian Bureau of Statistics (1994b)

(a) Answer the following questions:

(i) What is the question to be investigated (including the group to which the conclusions apply)?

(ii) What variable(s) are we concerned with here?

(iii) What type of variable(s) are they?

(iv) Which major category of statistical procedures applies here? Why?

(v) What type of statistic should we use, given the question to be investigated and the variables involved?

(vi) Which particular statistic or procedure, and diagram, should we use? Why?

(b) An investigator in Canberra wants to compare the trend in Canberra's consumer price index with that of the other cities. To keep things manageable, just two other cities are to be examined. Write a report outlining the differences in the consumer price index for the two cities of your choice and Canberra.

(c) Does your report support the claim that price levels are higher in Canberra? Give reasons for your answer.

11.11 Consider the *Price* means for the group of *Supermarket items* for five *Half-years* in table 11.15. This data is to be used to monitor changes in the *Prices* of these items over this two-and-a-half-year period.

Table 11.15 *Prices* means ($) for *Supermarket items* for five *Half-years*

Supermarket items	Amount	1	2	3	4	5
Coffee	100 g	3.18	3.24	3.35 1.05	3.50	3.99 +50% = 5.98
Sugar	1 kg	0.81	0.89	0.92 1.14	1.07	1.15 × 2 = 2.3
Butter	500 g	1.69	1.75	1.80 1.07	1.80	1.94
Lemonade	1 litre	1.10	1.11	1.13 1.03	1.12	1.19
Flour	1 kg	0.91	0.93	0.94 1.03	0.96	0.98
Dog food	1.2 kg	1.55	1.58	1.61 1.04	1.60	1.66
Soap powder	1 kg	3.12	3.36	3.57 1.14	3.79	4.06
Total		12.36	12.86	13.32 107	13.84	14.97

(handwritten annotations: Variable, limited, Variables, Half-year, limited, Unrestricted, limited)

(a) Answer the following questions:
   (i) What is the question to be investigated (including the group to which the conclusions apply)?
   (ii) What variable(s) are we concerned with here?
   (iii) What type of variable(s) are they?   *Descriptive Summaries*
   (iv) Which major category of statistical procedures applies here? Why?
   (v) What type of statistic should we use, given the question to be investigated and the variables involved?   *Index numbers*
   (vi) Which particular statistic or procedure, and diagram, should we use? Why?

(b) Calculate the simple fixed-base index number for soap powder, using half-year 1 as the base period.

(c) Calculate the simple index number for butter, using the chain-base method.

(d) Suppose you have only the index numbers calculated in (b) and you want to shift the base period to half-year 3. Use them to obtain the simple fixed-base index numbers for soap powder with base period half-year 3.

(e) The following Minitab output contains the commands to produce the unweighted aggregative index numbers for the whole table, using half-year 1 as the base period. Reproduce this output. Use a calculator to verify the result for half-year 5.

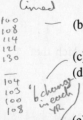

(handwritten margin notes:
limited: 100, 108, 114, 121, 130
104, 103, 100, 108 b change in each YR
88, 95, 100, 106, 114)

316

```
MTB > retrieve 'a:\indxsupa.mtp';
SUBC> portable.

Worksheet retrieved from file: a:\indxsupa.mtp
MTB > info

COLUMN   NAME      COUNT
C1       price_1      7
C2       price_2      7
C3       price_3      7
C4       price_4      7
C5       price_5      7
C6       quant_3      7
C7       quant_4      7
C8       quant_5      7

CONSTANTS USED: NONE

MTB > print c1-c8

ROW    price_1  price_2  price_3  price_4  price_5  quant_3  quant_4  quant_5
  1      3.18     3.24     3.35     3.50     3.99     13.1     12.2     14.5
  2      0.81     0.89     0.92     1.07     1.15      6.7      7.6      5.9
  3      1.69     1.75     1.80     1.80     1.94     10.3     10.4     10.6
  4      1.10     1.11     1.13     1.12     1.19      8.5      9.1      9.4
  5      0.91     0.93     0.94     0.96     0.98      7.7      8.0      8.1
  6      1.55     1.58     1.61     1.60     1.66     15.2     15.6     15.9
  7      3.12     3.36     3.57     3.79     4.06     20.0     20.0     19.5

MTB > # compute unweighted aggregative index numbers
MTB > let k11=sum('price_1')
MTB > let k12=sum('price_2')
MTB > let k13=sum('price_3')
MTB > let k14=sum('price_4')
MTB > let k15=sum('price_5')
MTB > print k11-k15
K11          12.3600
K12          12.8600
K13          13.3200
K14          13.8400
K15          14.9700
MTB > let k1=k11/k11*100
MTB > let k2=k12/k11*100
MTB > let k3=k13/k11*100
MTB > let k4=k14/k11*100
MTB > let k5=k15/k11*100
MTB > print k1-k5
K1           100.000
K2           104.045
K3           107.767
K4           111.974
K5           121.117
```

(f) The following Minitab output contains the commands, in addition to those given in part (e), for producing the price relatives and unweighted relatives index numbers for the supermarket items using half-year 1 as the base period. Reproduce this output. Use a calculator to verify the price relatives and unweighted relatives index for half-year 5.

```
MTB > # compute unweighted relatives index numbers
MTB > let c11=c1/c1
MTB > let c12=c2/c1
MTB > let c13=c3/c1
MTB > let c14=c4/c1
MTB > let c15=c5/c1
MTB > name c11 'prel_1' c12 'prel_2' c13 'prel_3'
MTB > name c14 'prel_4' c15 'prel_5'
MTB > print c11-c15

ROW    prel_1      prel_2      prel_3      prel_4      prel_5

 1          1     1.01887     1.05346     1.10063     1.25472
 2          1     1.09877     1.13580     1.32099     1.41975
 3          1     1.03550     1.06509     1.06509     1.14793
 4          1     1.00909     1.02727     1.01818     1.08182
 5          1     1.02198     1.03297     1.05494     1.07692
 6          1     1.01935     1.03871     1.03226     1.07097
 7          1     1.07692     1.14423     1.21474     1.30128

MTB > let k1=mean('prel_1')*100
MTB > let k2=mean('prel_2')*100
MTB > let k3=mean('prel_3')*100
MTB > let k4=mean('prel_4')*100
MTB > let k5=mean('prel_5')*100
MTB > print k1-k5
K1           100.000
K2           104.007
K3           107.108
K4           111.526
K5           119.334
```

(g) Suppose that coffee was bought in 150 g instead of 100 g jars, and sugar was bought in 2 kg instead of 1 kg bags, and assume that the new prices are in direct ratio to the old prices. Calculate the revised prices for supermarket items when bought in the large amounts.

(i) Calculate the unweighted aggregative index number for half-year 5, using the revised prices and half-year 1 as the base period.

(ii) Calculate the unweighted relatives index numbers for the half-year 5, using the revised prices and half-year 1 as the base period.

(iii) Compare your answers with the equivalent answers for parts (e) and (f). Comment on your results.

(h) In this exercise you have computed simple index numbers with a fixed and a chain base, unweighted aggregate index numbers and unweighted relatives index numbers. What are the advantages and disadvantages of these four index numbers?

11.12 Table 11.16 contains the mean prices for half-years 3, 4 and 5 from table 11.15, as well as the corresponding *Quantities*. This data is to be used to monitor changes in the *Prices* of the *Supermarket items* over this $1\frac{1}{2}$ year period, taking into account the relative importance of the items as measured by the *Quantities*.

Table 11.16   *Price* means and *Quantities* for *Supermarket items* for three *Half years*

Supermarket items	Half-year amount	Price means ($)			Quantities (000s)		
		3	4	5	3	4	5
Coffee	100 g	3.35	3.50	3.99	13.1	12.2	14.5
Sugar	1 kg	0.92	1.07	1.15	6.7	7.6	5.9
Butter	500 g	1.80	1.80	1.94	10.3	10.4	10.6
Lemonade	1 litre	1.13	1.12	1.19	8.5	9.1	9.4
Flour	1 kg	0.94	0.96	0.98	7.7	8.0	8.1
Dog food	1.2 kg	1.61	1.60	1.66	15.2	15.6	15.9
Soap powder	1 kg	3.57	3.79	4.06	20.0	20.0	19.5

(a) Answer the following questions:

(i) What is the question to be investigated (including the group to which the conclusions apply)?

(ii) What variable(s) are we concerned with here?

(iii) What type of variable(s) are they?

(iv) Which major category of statistical procedures applies here? Why?

(v) What type of statistic should we use, given the question to be investigated and the variables involved?

(vi) Which particular statistic or procedure, and diagram, should we use? Why?

(b) The following Minitab output contains the commands for computing the Laspeyres index numbers with time period half-year 3 as the base period. Reproduce this output. Use a calculator to verify the result for half-year 5.

```
MTB > retrieve 'a:\indxsupa.mtp';
SUBC> portable.

Worksheet retrieved from file: a:\indxsupa.mtp
MTB > print c3-c8

ROW      price_3    price_4    price_5     quant_3    quant_4    quant_5

  1        3.35       3.50       3.99        13.1       12.2       14.5
  2        0.92       1.07       1.15         6.7        7.6        5.9
  3        1.80       1.80       1.94        10.3       10.4       10.6
  4        1.13       1.12       1.19         8.5        9.1        9.4
  5        0.94       0.96       0.98         7.7        8.0        8.1
  6        1.61       1.60       1.66        15.2       15.6       15.9
  7        3.57       3.79       4.06        20.0       20.0       19.5

MTB > # compute Laspeyres index numbers
MTB > let k13=sum('quant_3'*'price_3')
MTB > let k14=sum('quant_3'*'price_4')
MTB > let k15=sum('quant_3'*'price_5')
MTB > print k13-k15
K13           181.304
K14           188.591
K15           204.049
MTB > let k3=k13/k13*100
MTB > let k4=k14/k13*100
MTB > let k5=k15/k13*100
MTB > print k3-k5
K3            100.000
K4            104.019
K5            112.545
```

(c) The following Minitab output contains the commands for computing the Paasche index numbers with time period half-year 3 as the base period. Reproduce this output. Use a calculator to verify the result for half-year 5.

```
MTB > # compute Paasche index numbers
MTB > let k13=sum('quant_3'*'price_3')
MTB > let k14=sum('quant_4'*'price_4')
MTB > let k15=sum('quant_5'*'price_5')
MTB > print k13-k15
K13           181.304
K14           188.184
K15           209.892
MTB > let k23=sum('price_3''quant_3'*)
MTB > let k24=sum('price_3''quant_4'*)
MTB > let k25=sum('price_3''quant_5'*)
```

continued . . .

```
MTB > print k23-k25
K23           181.304
K24           180.901
K25           186.533
MTB > let k3=k13/k23*100
MTB > let k4=k14/k24*100
MTB > let k5=k15/k25*100
MTB > print k3-k5
K3            100.000
K4            104.026
K5            112.523
```

(d) Write a short report comparing the Laspeyres and Paasche index numbers obtained in parts (b) and (c), giving reasons for your observations.

(e) What are the advantages or disadvantages of each of these index numbers?

11.13 Table 11.17 contains a record of some computer-traded property trust stocks for early February 1990. This data is to be used to monitor the daily change in the last sale price for computer-traded property trust stocks over the last 4 days, taking into account the relative importance of the different companies as measured by the volume of shares traded.

Table 11.17 *Property trust* records for 5-8 February 1990

					Date				
	5/2/90		6/2/90		7/2/90		8/2/90	
Property trust	Last sale ($)	Vol.	Last sale ($)	Vol.	Last sale ($)	Vol.	Last sale ($)	Vol.
Kern	0.35	152 300	0.35	52 500	0.36	36 500	0.35	300 000
Capital	2.10	10 200	2.10	12 900	2.10	6 700	2.11	17 300
NatMut	1.24	60 000	1.23	16 600	1.23	22 100	1.23	42 900

Source: abstracted from *The Advertiser* (1990)

(a) Answer the following questions:

(i) What is the question to be investigated (including the group to which the conclusions apply)?

(ii) What variable(s) are we concerned with here?

(iii) What type of variable(s) are they?

(iv) Which major category of statistical procedures applies? Why?

(v) What type of statistic should we use, given the question to be investigated and the variables involved?

(vi) Which particular statistic or procedure, and diagram, should we use? Why?

(b) Using 5/2/90 as the base period, compute the index numbers that represent the change in share prices, taking into account the relative importance of the different companies as measured by the volume of shares traded in the base period.

(c) Using 5/2/90 as the base period, compute the index numbers that represent the change in share prices, taking into account the relative importance of the different companies as measured by the volume of shares traded in the current year.

(d) What are the advantages or disadvantages of the methods you are using?

11.14 The prices of three agricultural products at the principal markets for 1962–92 in table 11.18 have been saved in the Minitab portable worksheet file *agrprice.mtp*. These prices are to be used to monitor the overall changes in the prices of these agricultural products during the period 1962–92.

Table 11.18   *Prices* of agricultural produce at principal markets 1962–92

| Year | Product | | |
	Wheat ($ per tonne)	Barley ($ per tonne)	Wool (cents per kg)
1962	55.70	49.43	91.69
1963	53.94	48.94	98.92
1964	52.65	49.12	119.53
1965	51.88	50.84	97.31
1966	55.15	51.85	102.98
1967	54.67	52.56	99.69
1968	58.86	52.47	82.87
1969	50.01	41.09	91.76
1970	51.88	36.82	75.02
1971	52.98	49.21	59.74
1972	55.26	40.96	72.21
1973	56.09	59.30	178.07
1974	103.20	87.59	176.54
1975	111.21	106.11	120.12
1976	104.46	98.14	134.46
1977	90.36	106.52	173.39
1978	102.20	88.37	179.03
1981	154.92	144.99	245.55

continued . . .

Table 11.18   *Continued*

		Product	
Year	Wheat ($ per tonne)	Barley ($ per tonne)	Wool (cents per kg)
1979	127.83	83.95	193.65
1980	153.24	126.84	224.56
1981	154.92	144.99	245.55
1982	159.61	139.47	262.85
1983	177.54	155.35	260.24
1984	164.86	153.95	281.10
1985	173.72	136.06	281.83
1986	170.63	122.58	304.92
1987	149.69	115.85	343.44
1988	169.07	123.36	493.03
1989	215.62	168.65	540.61
1990	199.39	167.63	469.60
1991	137.64	132.95	347.42
1992	203.58	144.81	308.58

Source: Australian Bureau of Statistics (1994b)

(a) Answer the following questions:
  (i) What is the question to be investigated (including the group to which the conclusions apply)?
  (ii) What variable(s) are we concerned with here?
  (iii) What type of variable(s) are they?
  (iv) Which major category of statistical procedures applies here? Why?
  (v) What type of statistic should we use, given the question to be investigated and the variables involved?
  (vi) Which particular statistic or procedure, and diagram, should we use? Why?
(b) Compute the unweighted aggregative index numbers for this data, using 1962 as the base year.
(c) Compute the unweighted relatives index numbers for this data, using 1962 as the base year.
(d) Compare the values obtained for the unweighted aggregative index numbers and the unweighted relatives index numbers. What do you conclude?

11.15 Use the information in the tables 11.19 and 11.20 to adjust for inflation the *Average weekly earnings* of full-time adult, Australian employees during 1987–92.

Table 11.19 *Average weekly earnings* for full-time adults 1987–92

Date on or before end of pay period	Average weekly earnings ($)
20 Feb 1987	455.10
19 Feb 1988	486.90
17 Feb 1989	524.30
16 Feb 1990	558.60
15 Feb 1991	597.80
21 Feb 1992	619.70

Source: Australian Bureau of Statistics (1994b)

Table 11.20 Consumer price index 1987–92: Weighted average of eight capital cities

Year	All groups consumer price index* (%)
1986–87	80.4
1987–88	86.3
1988–89	92.6
1989–90	100.0
1990–91	105.3
1991–92	107.3

* The base year is 1989–90.
Source: Australian Bureau of Statistics (1994b)

Describe the changes in the real *Average weekly earnings* between 1987–92 for full-time adult, Australian employees.

11.16 The price indexes of established houses and project homes in each Australian capital city 1988–92 are listed in table 11.21.

Table 11.21 *Price indexes** (%) of established houses and project homes in each Australian capital city 1988–92

Period	Sydney	Melbourne	Brisbane	Adelaide	Perth	Hobart	Darwin	Canberra
1988–89	95.2	91.4	86.2	91.3	89.0	93.1	98.8	93.9
1989–90	100.0	100.0	100.0	100.0	100.0	100.0	100.0	100.0
1990–91	100.5	95.2	114.3	106.2	94.8	106.3	109.3	107.3
1991–92	104.9	94.8	128.2	106.5	94.1	112.0	115.6	124.4

* The base year is 1989–90.
Source: Australian Bureau of Statistics(1994b)

For each capital city calculate a table of differences between index numbers from successive years. Report on the movements in house prices as depicted in the table you have calculated.

## CHAPTER 12

TIME SERIES ANALYSIS FOR UNRESTRICTED VARIABLES OVER TIME

L E A R N I N G   O B J E C T I V E S

The learning objectives of this chapter are:

- to understand the components of a classical time series model;
- to be able to deseasonalise a time series and interpret the results;
- to be able to smooth a time series and interpret the results;
- to understand the principles of forecasting.

The following extract from the *Summary of procedures based on combinations of variable types* in part VI gives an overview of the descriptive summaries covered in this and the previous chapters of part III, *Descriptive summaries of data*.

1. *One limited variable*
   - Distribution of variables: frequency, relative frequency and percentage one-way summary tables — bar or column chart.
   - Measures of central tendency: mode (mean, median).
   - Measures of dispersion: range, interquartile range, (standard deviation, coefficient of variation).

2. *Two limited variables*
   - Distribution of variables: two-way contingency table — chart with bars or columns that are grouped or stacked.

3. *Three limited variables*
   - Distribution of variables: three-way contingency table — chart with bars or columns that are grouped or stacked.

4. *One unrestricted variable*
   - Distribution of variables: frequency, relative frequency and percentage tables — histogram, polygon, stem-and-leaf display, dotplot.
   - Measures of central tendency: mean, median — boxplot.
   - Measures of dispersion: range, interquartile range, standard deviation, coefficient of variation — boxplot.

5. *One unrestricted variable — one limited variable*
   - Distribution of variables: frequency, relative frequency and percentage tables for each value of limited variable — histogram, polygon, stem-and-leaf display, dotplot for each value of limited variable.
   - Measures of central tendency: one-way table of means or medians — boxplot for each value of limited variable, bar chart or line diagram.
   - Measures of dispersion: one-way table of ranges, interquartile ranges, standard deviations or coefficients of variation — boxplot for each value of limited variable.

6. *One unrestricted variable — two limited variables*
   - Distribution of variables: frequency, relative frequency and percentage tables for each combination of values of the limited variables — histogram, polygon, stem-and-leaf display, dotplot for each combination of values of the limited variables.
   - Measures of central tendency: two-way table of means or medians — boxplot for each combination of values of the limited variables, bar chart or line diagram.
   - Measures of dispersion: two-way table of ranges, interquartile ranges, standard deviations or coefficients of variation — boxplot for each combination of values of the limited variables.

7. *Two unrestricted variables*
   - Measures of association: linear correlation coefficient and coefficient of determination — scatter diagram.
   - Fitted lines: intercept and/or slope; mean response — scatter diagram.

8. *Unrestricted variables with measurements repeated over time or location*
   - Index numbers: simple index numbers, unweighted aggregative and relatives index numbers and Laspeyres and Paasche weighted index numbers — line diagram.
   - **Time series:** observed series; smoothed series using simple linear regression, moving averages or exponential smoothing; additively or multiplicatively deseasonalised series; forecast — line diagram.

As outlined in the objectives, this chapter covers the analysis of time series. A time series is the history of a variable: that is, the recorded values of the variable over a particular period of time. A variable that is very commonly summarised as a time series is *Price*, where each value of the variable is the value of an index number computed for a basket of commodities as described in chapter 11, *Index numbers for unrestricted variables over time.*

Why do a time series analysis?

1. To explain what has happened in the past.
2. To understand what is happening now.
3. To forecast future values.

There are many methods of analysing time series data, and they vary greatly in complexity. Here we discuss the simplest methods available for smoothing and deseasonalisation. These methods are quite useful and widely used.

12.1   Classical time series analysis

Classical time series analysis depends on the identification of four **components** or types of movements in a time series:

1. Long-term trend (T)
2. Cyclic movements (C)
3. Seasonal movements (S)
4. Irregular or random movements (I)

12.1.1   Long-term or secular trend

The **long-term trend** is the general direction of the time series over a long period of time. Usually at least 30 observations are required for any persistent pattern to emerge. It may be a curve or a straight line. Figure 12.1 shows a time series displaying predominantly long-term trend; the trend is steadily increasing at first but rapidly increasing in the latter part of the series.

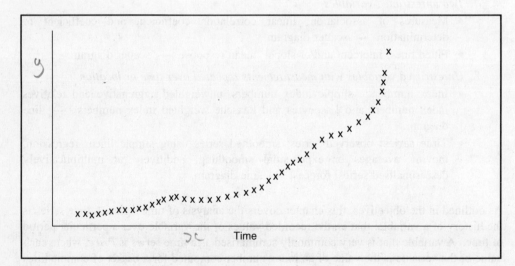

Figure 12.1   Long-term trend in a times series

12.1.2 Cyclic movements

Cyclic movements are the medium-term oscillations and swings whose lengths are unequal, such as booms and recessions in economic series; each swing usually takes several years. The time series in figure 12.2 displays predominantly cyclic movements.

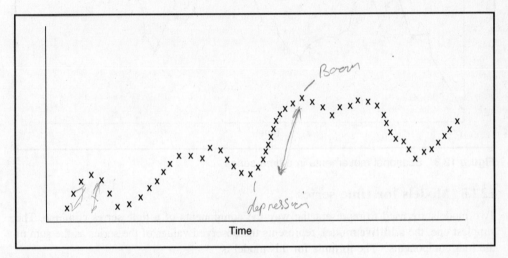

Figure 12.2   Cyclic movement in a time series

12.1.3 Seasonal movements

Seasonal movements are short-term patterns that recur repeatedly. The time period over which a complete pattern occurs is always the same and is usually no more than a year. For example, air-conditioner sales always increase in summer and decrease in winter; unemployment is usually highest around January. These particular patterns repeat every 12 months, but other patterns might repeat every day, week, month or year. For example, traffic patterns recur over a week, electricity consumption patterns recur over a day. The time series in figure 12.3 (on page 330) displays seasonal movements that recur every four observations.

12.1.4 Irregular movements

An **irregular movement** is a transitory movement, in a single observation, caused by chance events; that is, an irregular movement is the outcome of events that will not occur again. For example, in figure 12.3 the seasonal movements are not exactly equal over the entire period of the series because of irregular movements. Since irregular movements are random, they are generally of little interest and the aim of the analysis is to eliminate them.

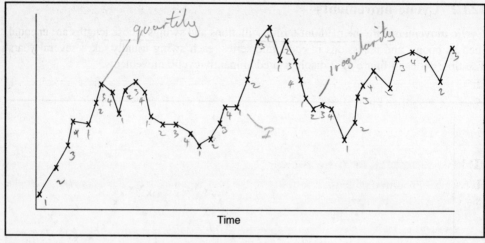

Figure 12.3   Seasonal movements in a time series

12.1.5   Models for time series

Two models are used to represent the way the components of a time series combine. The simplest one, the **additive model**, represents the observed values of the series as the sum of the four components. The formula for this model is:

$$y_i = T_i + C_i + S_i + I_i$$

where y_i is the observed value for the current time period;

T_i is the value of the long-term trend for the current time period, expressed in the same units as the observed value;

C_i is the value of the cyclic movement for the current time period, expressed as the deviation from T_i;

S_i is the value of the seasonal movement for the current time period, expressed as the deviation from $T_i + C_i$;

I_i is the value of the irregular movement for the current time period, expressed as the deviation from $T_i + C_i + S_i$.

In this model all the components have the same units as the observed values.

The other model, the **multiplicative model**, represents the observed values of the series as the product of the four components. The formula for this model is:

$$y_i = T_i \, C_i \, S_i \, I_i$$

where y_i is the observed value for the current time period;

T_i is the value of the long-term trend for the current time period, expressed in the same units as the observed value;

C_i is the value of the cyclic movement for the current time period, expressed as a proportion of T_i;

330

S_i is   the value of the seasonal movement for the current time period, expressed as a
proportion of T_iC_i;

I_i is   the value of the irregular movement for the current time period, expressed as
a proportion of $T_iC_iS_i$.

In addition, there are mixed time series models in which some terms add their effect and
others are multiplicative. These models are beyond the scope of this book.

How to decide whether to use the additive or multiplicative model in a particular
instance is explained in section 12.3, *Deseasonalisation*.

12.1.6 Examples of time series

Every series is different. Not all series have the four components. The following examples
show some possible situations.

EXAMPLE 12.1   CPI FOR INDONESIA 1981–89

In figure 12.4 the yearly consumer price index for Indonesia over the 1981–89
period displays only long-term trend and irregular movements.

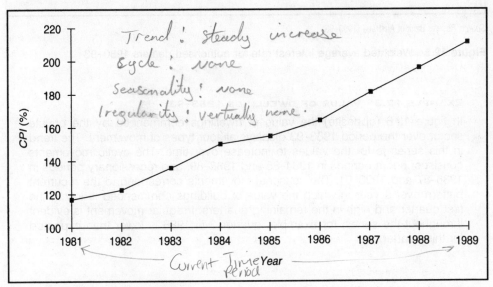

Source: Australian Bureau of Statistics (1983–92)

Figure 12.4   Consumer price index for Indonesia 1981–89

EXAMPLE 12.2   INTEREST RATES 1980–93

In figure 12.5 the weighted average interest rate for authorised short-term
money-market dealers displays cyclic and pronounced irregular movements.
Interest rates were relatively high in 1982, in April 1985 to mid-1987, and in
1989 to early 1990; they were low in early 1980, in late 1983 to early 1984, and
from mid-1991 onwards. Two examples of obvious irregular movements are
April 1982 and December 1983.

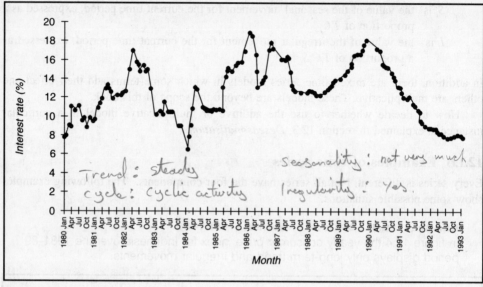

Source: Reserve Bank of Australia (1980–93)

Figure 12.5 Weighted average interest rate for authorised dealers 1980–93

EXAMPLE 12.3 VALUE OF DWELLINGS 1983–93

In figure 12.6 (opposite) the value of dwellings commenced by the private sector over the period 1983–93 displays all four types of movement. The trend in this series is for the values to increase over time. The cyclic movements consist of boom periods in 1984–85 and 1988–89, and recessionary periods in 1986–87 and 1990–91. The seasonal movements correspond to the recurrent pattern over a year in which the value of buildings commenced is low in the first quarter and high in the remaining quarters. Irregular movement is evident throughout the series; for example, quarter 2 in 1986 is lower than expected for this quarter.

EXAMPLE 12.4 PRODUCTION OF MEN'S JEANS 1983–92

In figure 12.7 (opposite) the production of men's jeans shows all four types of movements. The long-term trend is decreasing, although it differs from the other examples because there are two noticeable sudden shifts in the production level: one in July 1984 and the other in about October 1990. The shift in 1984 is explained by a change in the definition of the variable on which the series is based. Prior to July 1984 the production figures are for men's and youths' jeans, whereas only men's jeans are included from July 1984 onwards. The shift in 1990 appears to be a genuine change in the number of men's jeans produced in Australia.

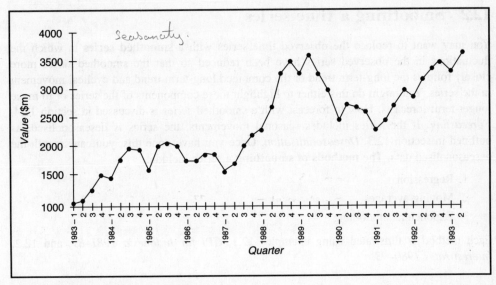

Source: Australian Bureau of Statistics (1983–92)

Figure 12.6   Value of dwellings commenced by the private sector in Australia 1983–93

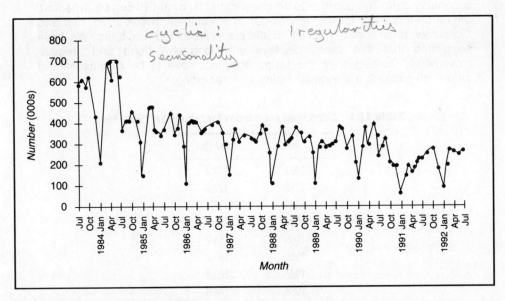

Source: Australian Bureau of Statistics (1983–92)

Figure 12.7   Production of men's jeans in Australia 1983–92

12.2   Smoothing a time series

You may want to replace the observed time series with a **smoothed series** in which the fluctuations in the observed series have been reduced so that the smoothed series more closely follows the long-term trend or the combined long-term trend and cyclical movement in the series. You might do this either to highlight these components of the series or to make longer-term forecasts. How to forecast with a smoothed series is discussed in section 12.4, *Forecasting*. If the series includes seasonal movements, the series is deseasonalised, as outlined in section 12.3, *Deseasonalisation*. Once you have done this, you can smooth the deseasonalised data. The **methods of smoothing** a series include:

1. Regression   – *non seasonal.*
2. Moving averages – *Seasonal – Smoothing + (most common)*
3. Exponential smoothing   *takes the easy way out*

Each method is illustrated using examples 12.1, *CPI for Indonesia 1981–89*, and 12.2, *Interest rates 1980–93*.

EXAMPLE 12.1   CPI FOR INDONESIA 1981–89 (continued)

The task is to forecast Indonesia's consumer price index for the year 2000. This index, whose base year is 1980, has been collected over the period 1981–89 and its values are given in table 12.1. The data in this table is processed, secondary data. The question to be investigated is: what CPI can be expected, based on this data, for the year 2000? The variables involved are *Year* and *Consumer price index*, both of which are unrestricted variables. We have suggested that this series displays only long-term trend and irregular movements. Consequently, the series does not have to be deseasonalised before we produce a smoothed series for forecasting.

Table 12.1   *Consumer price index* for Indonesia 1981–89

Year	Index (%)
1981	112.2
1982	122.9
1983	137.4
1984	151.7
1985	158.9
1986	168.2
1987	183.8
1988	198.6
1989	211.3

Source: Australian Bureau of Statistics (1983–92)

EXAMPLE 12.2   INTEREST RATES 1980–93 (continued)
We want to examine what has happened with interest rates over the period
1980–93. To do this, the weighted average interest rate on money outstanding
for authorised dealers in the short-term money market has been collected over
the period 1980–93. The processed, secondary data for this appears in table
12.2. This particular interest rate, also called the *official cash rate*, is the one
at which the Reserve Bank aims its operations in the short-term money market,
in its attempt to influence the amount of borrowing and lending in the economy
(Australian Bureau of Statistics, 1993a).

We have suggested that this series displays cyclic and pronounced
irregular movements. Consequently, the series does not have to be
deseasonalised before we smooth the series. The question to be investigated
in this case is: what are the trend and cyclical components for interest rates
over the period 1890–92? The variables involved are *Time* and *Interest rate*,
both of which are unrestricted variables.

Table 12.2   Weighted average interest rate (%) for authorised dealers 1980–93

Year	Jan	Feb	Mar	Apr	May	Jun	July	Aug	Sept	Oct	Nov	Dec
1980	7.92	8.20	9.25	8.98	10.74	10.34	10.91	9.58	9.81	8.92	9.83	9.43
1981	9.62	10.35	11.11	11.71	12.07	13.04	13.41	13.04	12.91	12.07	12.77	12.78
1982	13.25	13.41	14.85	17.05	15.40	14.88	13.12	15.12	13.12	13.28	12.42	10.87
1983	9.82	10.64	9.92	11.56	11.20	9.76	9.68	9.77	9.68	8.63	8.75	4.55
1984	7.05	8.75	11.19	13.39	13.30	11.42	11.18	10.81	10.56	10.57	10.82	10.98
1985	10.87	11.06	13.34	14.29	14.99	15.07	14.58	15.29	15.83	15.84	16.87	18.37
1986	18.32	18.16	16.74	15.06	12.31	13.20	13.43	16.42	17.13	16.63	16.21	15.40
1987	15.73	16.22	16.14	14.71	13.45	12.79	12.08	11.90	11.63	10.77	10.90	10.37
1988	10.23	10.25	10.33	10.36	11.2	11.79	12.02	12.39	12.65	13.20	14.03	14.34
1989	14.66	15.24	16.24	16.49	16.93	16.95	16.81	16.92	17.45	17.46	17.94	17.91
1990	17.67	16.65	16.31	15.09	14.96	14.98	14.91	13.98	13.94	13.35	12.97	12.57
1991	11.86	11.92	11.92	11.51	10.99	10.39	10.29	10.45	9.64	9.43	8.66	8.47
1992	7.83	7.43	7.40	7.43	6.68	6.41	5.97	5.61	5.54	5.59	5.69	5.73
1993	5.70	5.71	5.53	—	—	—	—	—	—	—	—	—

Source: Reserve Bank of Australia (1980–93)

12.2.1   Regression

Regression can be used to follow the long-term trend in a series, provided an equation can
be found that corresponds to the long-term trend. If the long-term trend follows a straight
line, then the linear regression techniques discussed in chapter 10, *Regression for two
unrestricted variables*, can be used. If the long-term trend follows a curve, then an equation
that follows the trend has to be identified and fitted with regression techniques. Regression
is generally not suitable for following the cyclic movement in a series.

When using regression, **coding the time period** is often convenient. For example, the first time period is given the value 1, the second time period 2, and so on. There are two reasons for this. First, the time periods may not be single numerical values measuring time; for example, to specify the time period for monthly data requires the year and the month. The second reason is that for yearly data the year is numerically large and this can cause numerical accuracy problems.

The smoothed series is obtained by substituting the observed times into the equation for the fitted line; if the time is coded, the coded values are substituted. Predictions can be obtained similarly for time periods that have not been observed. Note that for smoothing a time series, regression is used as a descriptive summary — in particular, to summarise the trend in the data and obtain the smoothed series. The statistical inference procedures for regression covered in chapter 16, *Estimation procedures for two unrestricted variables*, and chapter 20, *Test for relationship between two unrestricted variables*, do not apply here as the data is seldom independent.

The advantages of using regression to smooth a time series are as follows:

1. it can isolate the long-term trend from the other components of a series;
2. fitted values can be obtained for all observations.

The disadvantages of using regression to smooth a time series are as follows:

1. an equation that fits the long-term trend has to be specified;
2. the fitted trend cannot follow the nonregular cyclic movements, if that is what is required.

EXAMPLE 12.1   CPI FOR INDONESIA 1981–89 (continued)

The trend in this data appears to be linear and so linear regression can be used to fit a straight line trend to the data. In this case, the response variable is the *Consumer price index* and the explanatory variable is the *Year*. As 1980 is the base year for this index, it will be coded 0 and so the values used in the regression will be the number of years since 1980. The fitted straight line is given by

$$CPI = 99.489 + 12.2133\ Year$$

where *Year* is the number of years since 1980.

Note that the intercept is close to 100, which is what you would expect because the value of the consumer price index is 100 in the base year, the year for which the coded variable *Year* is zero.

Figure 12.8 gives the plot of the *Consumer price index*, with the fitted trend line. The fitted straight line appears to represent the trend. Now that the trend line has been added, some minor cyclical movement is apparent in the series; the *Consumer price index* rose slightly faster in 1983–84 and a little slower in 1986.

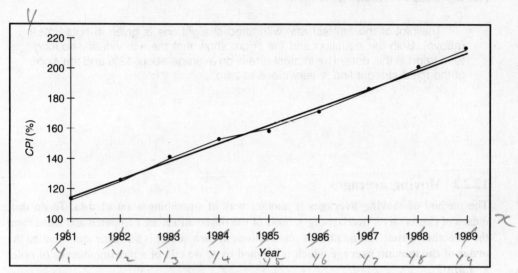

Figure 12.8 *Consumer price index* for Indonesia 1981–89, with fitted trend line

EXAMPLE 12.2 INTEREST RATES 1980–93 (continued)

In this case, the response variable is *Interest rate* and the explanatory variable is the *Time* of the observation where the first month in 1980 is numbered 1, the second month in 1980 is numbered 2, and so on up to the third month of 1993 which is numbered 159. The fitted straight line is given by

$$Interest\ rate = 12.1133 + 0.00645\ Time$$

where *Time* is the number of months from December 1979.

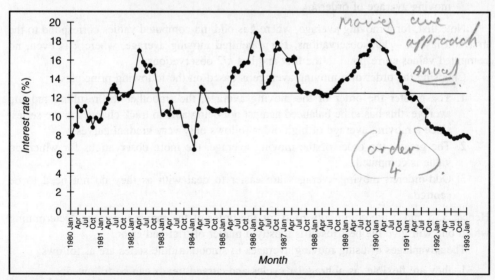

Figure 12.9 Weighted average interest rate for authorised dealers 1980–93, with fitted trend line

The plot of the *Interest rate* with fitted straight line is given in figure 12.9 (above). Both the equation and the figure show that there is virtually no long-term trend in this data. The interest rate is on average about 12% and the slope of the fitted straight line is very close to zero.

12.2.2 Moving averages

The method of **moving averages** is another way of smoothing a set of data. To do this, means of consecutive, overlapping subsets of the observations are computed and these form the smoothed series. The number of observations in each subset is the same and is called the **order of the moving average** which is denoted by k; we talk of a moving average of order k or $MA(k)$.

When moving averages are used to smooth time series data, moving averages for which the order is odd correspond to an observed time period. It is said that the values of the moving average are *centred* on the observed time periods. However, even-ordered moving averages are centred halfway between two observed time periods. To make even-ordered moving averages correspond to an observed time period, a **centred moving average of order k** [$CMA(k)$] is computed by:

1. computing a moving average of order k;
2. computing the arithmetic means of successive pairs of values from the even-ordered moving average of order k.

Note that, for a moving average, where k is odd, no computed values correspond to the first and last $(k - 1)/2$ observations. For a centred moving average, where k is even, no computed values correspond to the first and last $k/2$ observations.

Choosing the order of a moving average is based on the following principles:

1. The greater the order of the moving average, the smoother the resulting moving average; this has to be balanced against not being able to track changes in the series, since a moving average of high order follows only very gradual curves.
2. The greater the order of the moving average, the more observations for which no value is computed.
3. Odd-ordered moving averages are easier to deal with as they do not need to be centred.

Hence, 3, 5 and 7 are commonly used for the order of the moving average. Determining which one will give the best result is mostly a matter of trial-and-error.

The advantages of using moving averages to smooth a time series are as follows:

1. they are flexible, as nonregular cycles and curved trends can be followed;
2. they are not restricted to patterns for which an equation can be specified;
3. the computations are simple because only means have to be computed.

The disadvantages of using moving averages to smooth a time series are as follows:

1. the order of the moving average has to be specified;
2. values are not obtained for observations at the beginning and end of the observed time period;
3. for a series of completely random fluctuations, a series with false periodic movements is sometimes produced;
4. they have difficulty following rapidly but smoothly changing series;
5. since they are based on means, a particular value of a moving average is greatly affected by one or two large fluctuations in the series;
6. if you merely want to follow the long-term trend, cycles that are not regular in length and height are difficult to remove.

EXAMPLE 12.1   CPI FOR INDONESIA 1981–89 (continued)

As an example, the moving average of order 3 for the Indonesian consumer price index is given in table 12.3. To compute the moving average of order 3, the means of three consecutive observations are computed — that is, the mean of 1981, 1982 and 1983, followed by the mean of 1982, 1983 and 1984, and so on. The moving average of the year and the index is presented to emphasise that the first value of the moving average for the index corresponds to 1982; 124.17 is centred on 1982. Note that there is no value of the moving average for 1981 and 1989.

Table 12.3 Moving average of order 3 for the *Consumer price index* for Indonesia 1981–89

Observations		Moving average (3)	
Year	Index (%)	Year	Index (%)
1981	112.2	—	—
1982	122.9	1982	124.17
1983	137.4	1983	137.33
1984	151.7	1984	149.33
1985	158.9	1985	159.60
1986	168.2	1986	170.30
1987	183.8	1987	183.53
1988	198.6	1988	197.90
1989	211.3	—	—

The moving average of order 3 is plotted in figure 12.10. It closely follows the observed values of the consumer price index.

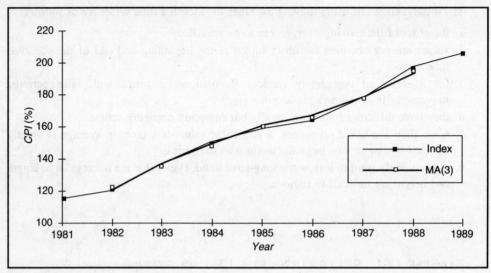

Figure 12.10   *Consumer price index* for Indonesia 1981–89, with moving average of order 3

The moving average of order 4 for the Indonesian consumer price index is given in table 12.4. Note that the moving average is centred on a half-year, rather than a year. To overcome this problem, the centred moving average of order 4 has been computed and is included in table 12.4; that is, arithmetic means of successive pairs of values from the moving average of order 4 are computed; the first value in the centred moving average is 136.887 and is the mean of 131.050 and 142.725, the first two values in the moving average of order 4.

Table 12.4   Moving average of order 4 for the *Consumer price index* for Indonesia 1981–89

Observations		Moving average (4)		Centred moving average(4)	
Year	Index (%)	Year	Index (%)	Year	Index (%)
1981	112.2	—	—	—	—
1982	122.9	—	—	—	—
1983	137.4	1982.5	131.050	1983	136.887
1984	151.7	1983.5	142.725	1984	148.387
1985	158.9	1984.5	154.050	1985	159.850
1986	168.2	1985.5	165.650	1986	171.512
1987	183.8	1986.5	177.375	1987	183.925
1988	198.6	1987.5	190.475	—	—
1989	211.3	—	—	—	—

EXAMPLE 12.2   INTEREST RATES 1980–93 (continued)

The moving averages of order 5 and 13 have been computed for the *Interest rate* and are plotted in figure 12.11. The moving average of order 5 has smoothed out the irregular movement and it follows the long-term trend and cyclical movement in the series. Note how the moving average of order 13 has smoothed out the peaks and troughs to a greater extent than the moving average of order 5. Perhaps a moving average of order 7 could be computed to check whether or not it is an improvement over the moving average of order 5.

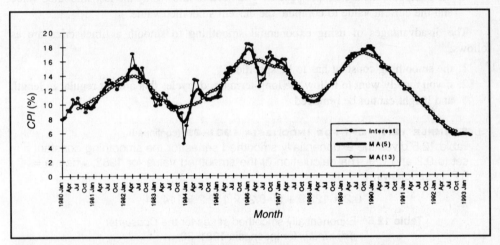

Figure 12.11   Weighted average interest rate for authorised dealers 1980–93, with moving averages of order 5 and 13

12.2.3   Exponential smoothing

Exponential smoothing determines the smoothed value at a particular time as the weighted average of all previous values in the series, and the weights decrease exponentially as you go back in the series. While this is a broad description of exponential smoothing, exponential smoothing is in fact achieved with the following formula:

$$E_i = \omega y_i + (1 - \omega)E_{i-1}$$

where E_i is the exponentially smoothed value at the current time period;

E_{i-1} is the exponentially smoothed value for the previous time period;

y_i is the observed value for the current time period;

ω is the **smoothing constant**.

This method involves choosing the smoothing constant. It should be between 0 and 1 and indicates what importance should be placed on the most recent value in the series. If there is a lot of irregular movement in the series, a low value of the smoothing constant should be used as this will give little weight to the current observation. On the other hand, if the series shows little variation the smoothing constant should be set close to one, to give the current observation a high weight. Again, it is a matter of trial-and-error to see which value gives the best result. Also, the smoothed value for the first time period should be set to the first observation; that is, $E_1 = y_1$ as there is no previous time period from which to obtain a smoothed value.

The advantages of using exponential smoothing to smooth a time series are as follows:

1. it is flexible, as nonregular cycles and curved trends can be followed;
2. it is not restricted to patterns for which an equation can be specified;
3. smoothed values are obtained for all observations;
4. the computations are simple because you need to know only the last smoothed value and the current value to compute the current smoothed value.

The disadvantages of using exponential smoothing to smooth a time series are as follows:

1. the smoothing constant has to be specified;
2. if you merely want to follow the long-term trend, cycles that are not regular in length and height cannot be removed.

EXAMPLE 12.1   CPI FOR INDONESIA 1981–89 (continued)
Table 12.5 gives the exponentially smoothed series for the smoothing constant set to 0.2 and 0.9. The calculation of the smoothed value for 1982, when $\omega = 0.2$, is as follows:

$$0.2 \times 122.9 + (1-0.2) \times 112.2 = 114.34.$$

Table 12.5   Exponentially smoothed series for the *Consumer price index* for Indonesia 1981–89

		Exponentially smoothed series	
Year	Index (%)	$\omega = 0.2$	$\omega = 0.9$
1981	112.2	112.2	112.2
1982	122.9	114.34	121.83
1983	137.4	118.952	135.843
1984	151.7	125.5016	150.1143
1985	158.9	132.1813	158.0214
1986	168.2	139.385	167.1821
1987	183.8	148.268	182.1382
1988	198.6	158.3344	196.9538
1989	211.3	168.9276	209.8654

The two exponentially smoothed series are plotted in figure 12.12. Clearly, for this series, the value of 0.2 for the time series does not give sufficient weight to the current observation, as the series persistently underestimates the value for the consumer price index. The value of the smoothing constant should be about 0.9 if the smoothed series is to follow the trend. That is, the smoothed value is just about equal to the observation for the current time period.

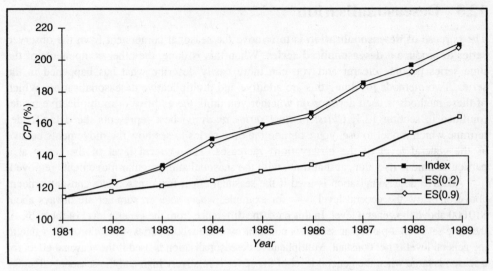

Figure 12.12   *Consumer price index* for Indonesia 1981–89, with exponentially smoothed
series for ω = 0.2 and 0.9

EXAMPLE 12.2   INTEREST RATES 1980–93 (continued)

Figure 12.13 gives the exponentially smoothed series, for the smoothing
constant set to 0.2 and 0.5. The smoothed series for ω = 0.2, which places low
weight on the current value, is smoother than that for ω = 0.5. However, the
smoothed series for ω = 0.2 tends to lag behind the observed series. On the
other hand, the smoothed series for ω = 0.5 closely follows the observed
series, perhaps a little too closely.

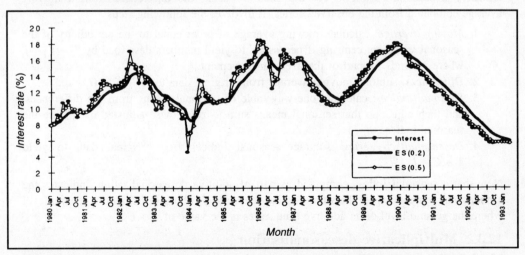

Figure 12.13   Weighted average interest rate for authorised dealers 1980–93, with
exponentially smoothed series for ω = 0.2 and 0.5

12.3   Deseasonalisation

The purpose of **deseasonalisation** is to remove the seasonal component from the observed series to produce a **deseasonalised series**. When this is done, the other components of the time series become clearer and you can more easily describe what has happened in the series. Two methods for doing this are additive and multiplicative deseasonalisation. Which of these methods is used depends on whether you think the additive or multiplicative model (outlined in section 12.1, *Classical time series analysis*) best represents the data. To determine which model to use, you examine the time series to see how the movements behave as the general level of the observations increases. The **general level** of the series at a particular time is its value, at that time, with the seasonal and irregular movements removed.

Additive deseasonalisation is used if the seasonal effect for a season is a constant amount above or below the general level — for example, where sales in summer are always about $10 000 above the general level. In this case, the difference from the general level of the value of the time series in a particular season is constant over the whole series; the ratio of the value to the general level is not constant. Multiplicative deseasonalisation is used if the seasonal effect for a season is large when the general level of the series is relatively high and the seasonal effect for that season is relatively small when the general level is relatively low. In this case, the seasonal effect should be a constant proportion of the general level — for example, sales are always twice the general level in summer. In this case, ratios are the appropriate way of measuring seasonal effect because they are constant whereas differences are not.

In both additive and multiplicative deseasonalisation, a **seasonal index** is calculated for each season; it measures the 'average' discrepancy between the general level and the values for that season.

12.3.1   Additive deseasonalisation

Additive deseasonalisation is accomplished by using the differences from a moving average computed from the observed series. It involves the following steps:

1. *Moving average*: calculate moving average of order equal to the periodicity of the seasonal variation, centring if necessary, to yield numbers described by $T_i + C_i + i_i$ where i_i stands for part of the irregular movement.
2. *Differences*: subtract moving average from original data to yield $S_i + (I_i - i_i)$.
3. *Seasonal indices*: calculate one-way table of seasonal means from the differences, and then adjust so that seasonal means sum to zero; these adjusted means are the seasonal indices, S_i.
4. *Deseasonalised series*: subtract seasonal indices from original data to yield $T_i + C_i + I_i$.

Note that a **seasonal index**, computed as part of additive deseasonalisation, indicates the amount that you can expect the value for that season to be above or below the general level where the general level of an additive time series is the value of $T_i + C_i$.

12.3.2   Multiplicative deseasonalisation

Multiplicative deseasonalisation is accomplished by taking the logarithms of the observed data and using the additive deseasonalisation method on them. It involves the following steps:

1. *Logarithms*: calculate the logarithms of the observed series.
2. *Deseasonalised logarithms*: use the additive deseasonalisation method on the logarithms to deseasonalise them.
3. *Seasonal indices*: backtransform the adjusted means formed in the previous step to obtain the seasonal indices.
4. *Deseasonalised series*: backtransform the deseasonalised logarithms, or else divide the observed data by the corresponding seasonal index found in the previous step.

This procedure relies on the fact that the logarithm of a product is the sum of the logarithms. Hence,

$$\log (T_i C_i S_i I_i) = \log T_i + \log C_i + \log S_i + \log I_i$$

Logarithms to any base can be used, usually either natural logarithms or logarithms to the base 10. With natural logarithms, backtransformation of a value is achieved by taking the exponential function of it. With logarithms to the base 10, backtransformation of a value is achieved by raising 10 to the power of that value.

Note that a seasonal index, computed as part of multiplicative deseasonalisation, indicates the proportion of the general level that you can expect for that season where the general level of a multiplicative time series is the value of $T_i C_i$. Sometimes the index is expressed as a percentage, by multiplying the proportion by 100.

EXAMPLE 12.5   TURNOVER OF ELECTRICAL STORES 1983–92

We want to examine the general pattern in sales of electrical stores. The quarterly figures for the turnover of electrical stores during the period 1983–92 (Australian Bureau of Statistics, 1983–92) are presented in table 12.6 and plotted in figure 12.14 this data is processed, secondary data. The plot reveals a seasonal pattern that is repeated over the four quarters of a year. It is decided to separate the seasonal from the other movements to investigate each component of the series. Hence, the question to be investigated is: what patterns, with respect to the different movements, has the series for turnover of electrical stores followed? The variables involved are *Turnover of electrical stores* and *Time*, both unrestricted variables.

The seasonal pattern is such that the difference between the highest and lowest season is about the same throughout the observed period, even when the general level has changed from about $900m in the early years to about $1300m in the latter years. Hence additive deseasonalisation should be used to deseasonalise this data, and a centred moving average of order 4 should be used to remove the seasonal pattern.

The quantities that are computed in deseasonalising the data are in table 12.6 and the deseasonalised series is plotted in figure 12.14. With the seasonal movements removed, the trend, cyclical and irregular movements of the series are easier to observe. It seems that, except for a dip in 1986–87, the *Turnover of electrical stores* has been steadily increasing since 1983.

Note also the means of the differences in table 12.7. The mean of these means was computed and subtracted from the original means to form the adjusted means. These adjusted means are the seasonal indices. From these indices we conclude that turnover is highest in the fourth quarter and lowest in the first quarter. Indeed, turnover will be $133 897 000 above the general level in quarter 4 and $72 625 000 below in quarter 1.

Table 12.6 Additive deseasonalisation of quarterly *Turnover* ($m) *of electrical stores* 1983–92

Year	Quarter	Turnover electrical stores ($m) $T_i + C_i + S_i + I_i$	Centred moving average (4) ($m) $T_i + C_i + i_i$	Difference ($m) $S_i + (I_i - i_i)$	Seasonal index ($m) S_i	Deseasonalised series ($m) $T_i + C_i + I_i$
1983	1	709.7	—	—	−72.625	782.325
	2	758.0	—	—	−18.865	776.865
	3	769.2	812.2875	−43.0875	−42.408	811.608
	4	991.9	820.7500	171.1500	133.897	858.003
1984	1	750.4	826.1125	−75.7125	−72.625	823.025
	2	785.0	831.0000	−46.0000	−18.865	803.865
	3	785.1	838.1625	−53.0625	−42.408	827.508
	4	1015.1	852.7750	162.3250	133.897	881.203
1985	1	784.5	872.7625	−88.2625	−72.625	857.125
	2	867.8	890.2250	−22.4250	−18.865	886.665
	3	862.2	899.9500	−37.7499	−42.408	904.608
	4	1077.7	908.3500	169.3500	133.897	943.8027
1986	1	799.7	900.4250	−100.7250	−72.625	872.325
	2	919.8	852.5875	67.2125	−18.865	938.665
	3	746.8	799.9750	−53.1750	−42.408	789.208
	4	810.4	757.0875	53.3125	133.897	676.503
1987	1	646.1	733.7250	−87.6250	−72.625	718.7247
	2	730.3	749.1750	−18.8750	−18.865	749.165
	3	749.4	804.0751	−54.6750	−42.408	791.808
	4	931.4	881.4625	49.9375	133.897	797.503
1988	1	964.3	953.5625	10.7375	−72.625	1036.925
	2	1031.2	1024.5750	6.6250	−18.865	1050.065
	3	1025.3	1069.5000	−44.2000	−42.408	1067.708
	4	1223.6	1095.9750	127.6249	133.897	1089.703
1989	1	1031.5	1138.7500	−107.2500	−72.625	1104.125
	2	1175.8	1190.4250	−14.6250	−18.865	1194.665
	3	1222.9	1236.1630	−13.2626	−42.408	1265.308
	4	1439.4	1264.4250	174.9750	133.897	1305.503
1990	1	1181.6	1272.6130	−91.0126	−72.625	1254.225
	2	1251.8	1270.0250	−18.2250	−18.865	1270.665
	3	1212.4	1273.2130	−60.8125	−42.408	1254.808
	4	1429.2	1275.1130	154.0874	133.897	1295.303
1991	1	1217.3	1278.5630	−61.2625	−72.625	1289.925
	2	1231.3	1284.2130	−52.9125	−18.865	1250.165
	3	1260.5	1285.8750	−25.3750	−42.408	1302.908
	4	1426.3	1287.7130	138.5875	133.897	1292.403
1992	1	1233.5	1289.7380	−56.2375	−72.625	1306.125
	2	1229.8	1304.0880	−74.2875	−18.865	125.665
	3	1278.2	—	—	−42.408	1320.608
	4	1523.4	—	—	133.897	1389.503

Table 12.7 Seasonal means of the differences for deseasonalising the *Turnover of electrical stores*

	Quarter				
	1	2	3	4	Mean
Means ($m)	−73.039	−19.279	−42.822	133.483	−0.414
Adjusted means ($m)	−72.625	−18.865	−42.408	133.897	

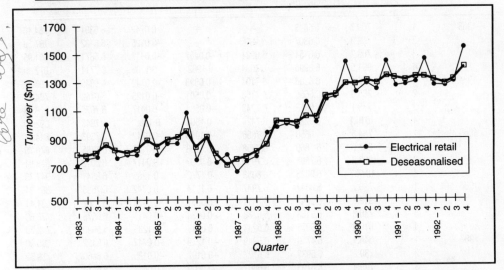

Figure 12.14 Observed and additively deseasonalised *Turnover of electrical stores* 1983–92

To illustrate multiplicative deseasonalisation, and what happens if the wrong method of deseasonalisation is used, the turnovers are multiplicatively deseasonalised. The quantities to be computed for this deseasonalisation are in table 12.8. Note that the natural logarithms of the original data are computed and deseasonalised; consequently, the exponential function is used to backtransform the deseasonalised logarithms. The deseasonalised series is plotted in figure 12.15. A close inspection of the plot for the multiplicatively deseasonalised series shows that the seasonal movement of the earlier, lower turnover values has not been completely removed. For the later, higher values of turnover seasonal movement is also apparent, but in a pattern that is the reverse of that at the start of the series, because too much movement or variation has been removed.

Table 12.9 gives the seasonal and adjusted seasonal means computed in multiplicatively deseasonalising the series, and these are on the logarithmic scales.   To obtain the seasonal indices, the adjusted means are back-transformed by using the exponential function. The seasonal index for the fourth quarter indicates that turnover in this quarter is 113.71% of the general level, whereas in the second quarter it is 92.84% of the general level.

Table 12.8 Multiplicative deseasonalisation of quarterly *Turnover* ($m) *of electrical stores*
1983–92

Year	Quarter	Turnover electrical stores ($m)	Logs of turnover	Centred moving average (4)	Difference	Adjusted seasonal mean	Logs of deseasonalised series	Deseasonalised series ($m)
		$T_iC_iS_iI_i$	$\log T_i + \log C_i + \log S_i + \log I_i$	$\log T_i + \log C_i + \log I_i$	$\log S_i + (\log I_i - \log I_j)$	$\log S_i$	$\log T_i + \log C_i + \log I_i$	$T_iC_iI_i$
1983	1	709.7	6.5648	—	—	−0.0742	6.6391	764.40
	2	758.0	6.6307	—	—	−0.0125	6.6432	767.56
	3	769.2	6.6454	6.6921	−0.0467	−0.0417	6.6871	801.95
	4	991.9	6.8996	6.7034	0.1962	0.1285	6.7711	872.30
1984	1	750.4	6.6206	6.7104	−0.0898	−0.0742	6.6949	808.24
	2	785.0	6.6656	6.7158	−0.0501	−0.0125	6.6782	794.91
	3	785.1	6.6658	6.7243	−0.0584	−0.0417	6.7075	818.53
	4	1015.1	6.9227	6.7424	0.1804	0.1285	6.7943	892.70
1985	1	784.5	6.6650	6.7666	−0.1016	−0.0742	6.7393	844.97
	2	867.8	6.7660	6.7858	−0.0198	−0.0125	6.7785	878.75
	3	862.2	6.7595	6.7957	−0.0362	−0.0417	6.8012	898.91
	4	1077.7	6.9826	6.8053	0.1772	0.1285	6.8541	947.75
1986	1	799.7	6.6842	6.7947	−0.1104	−0.0742	6.7585	861.34
	2	919.8	6.8242	6.7411	0.0831	−0.0125	6.8367	931.41
	3	746.8	6.6158	6.6788	−0.0630	−0.0417	6.6575	778.60
	4	810.4	6.6975	6.6233	0.0743	0.1285	6.5690	712.68
1987	1	646.1	6.4710	6.5949	−0.1239	−0.0742	6.5452	695.90
	2	730.3	6.5935	6.6127	−0.0192	−0.0125	6.6060	739.52
	3	749.4	6.6193	6.6801	−0.0609	−0.0417	6.6610	781.31
	4	931.4	6.8367	6.7733	0.0634	0.1285	6.7082	819.09
1988	1	964.3	6.8714	6.8556	0.0158	−0.0742	6.9457	1038.62
	2	1031.2	6.9385	6.9289	0.0095	−0.0125	6.9510	1044.21
	3	1025.3	6.9327	6.9715	−0.0387	−0.0417	6.9744	1068.96
	4	1223.6	7.1096	6.9963	0.1133	0.1285	6.9811	1076.06
1989	1	1031.5	6.9388	7.0347	−0.0960	−0.0742	7.0130	1111.00
	2	1175.8	7.0697	7.0771	−0.0074	−0.0125	7.0822	1190.64
	3	1222.9	7.1090	7.1143	−0.0054	−0.0417	7.1507	1274.98
	4	1439.4	7.2720	7.1392	0.1328	0.1285	7.1435	1265.84
1990	1	1181.6	7.0746	7.1459	−0.0713	−0.0742	7.1489	1272.67
	2	1251.8	7.1323	7.1439	−0.0116	−0.0125	7.1449	1267.60
	3	1212.4	7.1004	7.1468	−0.0464	−0.0417	7.1421	1264.03
	4	1429.2	7.2649	7.1484	0.1164	0.12 85	7.1364	1256.87
1991	1	1217.3	7.1044	7.1512	−0.0468	−0.0742	7.1786	1311.12
	2	1231.3	7.1158	7.1558	−0.0400	−0.0125	7.1284	1246.84
	3	1260.5	7.1393	7.1572	−0.0180	−0.0417	7.1810	1314.17
	4	1426.3	7.2628	7.1587	0.1041	0.12 85	7.1343	1254.32
1992	1	1233.5	7.1176	7.1603	−0.0427	−0.0742	7.1919	1328.57
	2	1229.8	7.1146	7.1703	−0.0557	−0.0125	7.1271	1245.32
	3	1278.2	7.1532	—	—	−0.0417	7.1949	1332.63
	4	1523.4	7.3287	—	—	0.12 85	7.2002	1339.71

Table 12.9   Seasonal means and indices for multiplicatively deseasonalised *Turnover of electrical stores*

	Quarter				
	1	2	3	4	Mean
Means	−0.07407	−0.01236	−0.04152	0.12867	0.00018
Adjusted means	−0.07425	−0.01254	−0.0417	0.12849	
Seasonal indices	0.9284	0.9875	0.9592	1.1371	

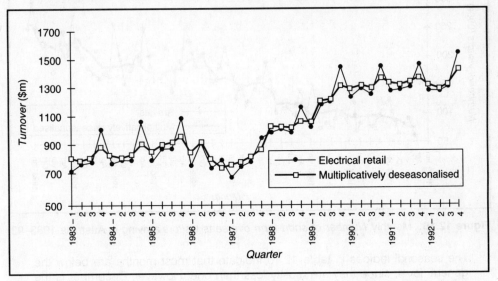

Figure 12.15   Observed and multiplicatively deseasonalised *Turnover of electrical stores* 1983–92

EXAMPLE 12.6   ARRIVALS IN AUSTRALIA 1983–92

We want to examine the general pattern in the arrival of visitors to Australia. The monthly numbers of short-term visitors arriving in Australia during the period 1983–92 (Australian Bureau of Statistics, 1983–92) are plotted in figure 12.16; this data is processed, secondary data. The plot reveals a seasonal pattern that is repeated over the 12 months of each year. It is decided to separate the seasonal from the other movements to investigate each component of the series. The question to be investigated is: what patterns, with respect to the different movements, has the series for visitor arrivals followed? The variables involved are *Numbers of short-term visitors* and *Time*, both unrestricted variables.

The seasonal pattern is such that the difference between the highest and lowest month increases as the number of visitors increases. Hence multiplicative deseasonalisation should be used to deseasonalise this data, and a centred moving average of order 12 should be used to remove the seasonal pattern. The plot of the deseasonalised series, along with the observed series (figure 12.16), shows that the number of visitors has been increasing steadily, but that periodically an unusually large number of arrivals occurs. For example, the deseasonalised series clearly indicates a substantial peak in arrivals around July 1988.

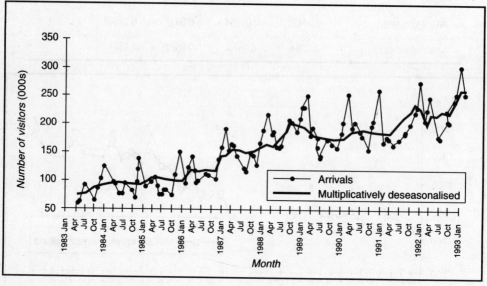

Figure 12.16   Monthly *Number of short-term overseas visitors* arriving in Australia 1983–93

The seasonal indices in table 12.10 indicate that most months are below the general level, since they are mostly less than one. However, December is the peak month for arrivals: 40% above the general level.

Table 12.10   Seasonal indices for the *Number of short-term overseas visitors* arriving in Australia

Month	Jan	Feb	Mar	Apr	May	Jun
	0.966	1.080	1.066	0.949	0.832	0.848
Month	Jul	Aug	Sep	Oct	Nov	Dec
	0.999	0.938	0.856	1.046	1.141	1.400

12.4   Forecasting

As stated at the outset, one of the purposes of analysing a time series is **forecasting**: the prediction of future values for the variable on which the series is based. The value produced is referred to as the **forecast**. Forecasting is notoriously unsuccessful. The fundamental premise of all forecasting techniques is that the past will continue into the future. Since this happens only to a limited extent, the chance of a correct forecast is quite low. However, in spite of the dangers, forecasting is often attempted as the only option available in planning for the future.

Generally, forecasting is based on the deseasonalised series and involves extrapolating the long-term trend. A series that displays seasonal movement must have that movement removed first. Then the long-term trend is determined. For forecasting some distance into the future, the most satisfactory method of ascertaining the trend is regression since as discussed in section 12.2, *Smoothing a time series*, regression is best at separating the long-term trend from the other components of a series. If regression is used to follow the long-term trend, then the (coded) time for which the forecast is required is merely substituted into the fitted equation.

EXAMPLE 12.1   CPI FOR INDONESIA 1981–89 (continued)
The following equation was established to describe the trend in the *Consumer price index* for Indonesia:

$$CPI = 99.489 + 12.2133\ Year \qquad \text{from MTB}$$

where Year is the number of years since 1980.
The forecast for the *Consumer price index* for Indonesia in the year 2000 is obtained by substituting (2000 – 1980) = 20 for the *Year* in this equation. That is,

$$99.489 + 12.2133 \times 20 = 343.8$$

The forecast is that the *Consumer price index* for Indonesia will be 343.8 in 2000.

12.5   Reports on examples

The following reports, for the examples analysed in this chapter, indicate what material from a statistical analysis an investigator should include in a report. In general, the details of the statistical analysis are omitted so that the reader of the report can concentrate on the results.

EXAMPLE 12.1   CPI FOR INDONESIA 1981–89 — REPORT
The consumer price index for Indonesia, base year 1980, has been collected over the period 1981–89 so that its value for the year 2000 can be forecast. This series displays a linear long-term trend and so simple linear regression was used to fit a straight line to follow the long-term trend. The original series and the fitted long-term trend line are shown in figure 12.8. The fitted straight line is given by

$$CPI = 99.489 + 12.2133\ Year$$

where *Year* is the number of years since 1980.
The forecast for the consumer price index for Indonesia in the year 2000, obtained from this equation, is 343.8.

EXAMPLE 12.2   INTEREST RATES 1980–93 — REPORT

The weighted average interest rate on money outstanding for authorised dealers in the short-term money market for the period 1980–92 has been obtained (Reserve Bank of Australia, 1980–93). This interest rate, also called the official cash rate, is the one at which the Reserve Bank aims its operations in the short-term money market in its attempt to influence the amount of borrowing and lending in the economy (Australian Bureau of Statistics, 1993a). The series, plotted in figure 12.17, seems to display cyclic and pronounced irregular movements, but little overall trend. The cyclic movement in the series has been emphasised by including the moving average of order 7 in figure 12.17.

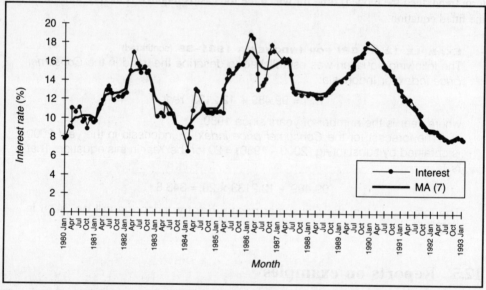

Figure 12.17   Weighted average interest rate for authorised dealers 1980–93, with a moving average of order 7

EXAMPLE 12.3   VALUE OF DWELLINGS 1983–93 — REPORT

The value of dwellings commenced in Australia by the private sector over the period 1983–93 is displayed in figure 12.6. The trend in this time series is for the values to increase over time. The cyclic movements consist of boom periods in 1984–85 and 1988–89 and recessionary periods in 1986–87 and 1990–91. The seasonal movements correspond to the recurrent pattern over a year in which the value of buildings comrnenced is low in the first quarter and high in the remaining quarters. Irregular movement is evident throughout the series; for example, quarter 2 in 1986 is lower than expected for this quarter.

EXAMPLE 12.4   PRODUCTION OF MEN'S JEANS 1983–92 — REPORT

Figure 12.7 shows the production of men's jeans over the period 1983–92. This series displays long-term trend, cyclical, seasonal and irregular movements.

The long-term trend is for production to decrease, although there are two noticeable sudden shifts in the level of production, one in July 1984 and the other in about October 1990. The shift in 1984 is explained by a change in the definition of the variable on which the series is based. Prior to July 1984 the production figures are for men's and youths' jeans, whereas only men's jeans are included from July 1984 onwards. The shift in 1990 appears to be a genuine change in the number of men's jeans produced in Australia.

EXAMPLE 12.5 TURNOVER OF ELECTRICAL STORES 1983–92 — REPORT

The quarterly turnover of electrical stores during the period 1983–92 (Australian Bureau of Statistics, 1983–92) is plotted in figure 12.14. The data exhibits a seasonal pattern that is repeated over the four quarters of a year. This was removed by using additive deseasonalisation and the deseasonalised series is also plotted in figure 12.14.

From the deseasonalised series it seems that, except for a dip in 1986–87, the turnover of electrical stores has been steadily increasing since 1983. We conclude from the seasonal indices computed in deseasonalising the data (table 12.11) that turnover is highest in the fourth quarter and lowest in the first quarter. Indeed, turnover will be $133 897 000 above the general level in quarter 4 and $72 625 000 below in quarter 1.

Table 12.11   Seasonal indices ($m) for turnover of electrical stores

from P. 346.

	Quarter		
1	2	3	4
−72.625	−18.865	−42.408	133.897

EXAMPLE 12.6 ARRIVALS IN AUSTRALIA 1983–92 — REPORT

The monthly numbers of short-term visitors arriving in Australia during 1983–92 (Australian Bureau of Statistics, 1983–92) are plotted in figure 12.16. This plot reveals a seasonal pattern that is repeated over the 12 months of each year. Multiplicative deseasonalisation was used to deseasonalise this data and the plot of the deseasonalised series is given in figure 12.18. Linear regression was used to fit a trend line to the deseasonalised series. The equation for the fitted trend line is:

response   *explanatory*

$$Arrivals = 66932 + 1367.24\,Time$$

where *Time* is the number of months since February 1983.

It is evident that the number of visitors has been increasing steadily, but that periodically an unusually large number of arrivals occurs. For example, the deseasonalised series clearly indicates a substantial peak in arrivals around July 1988.

The seasonal indices, computed in deseasonalising the data (table 12.10) indicate that most months are below the general level, since they are mostly less than one. However, December is the peak month for arrivals: 40% above the general level.

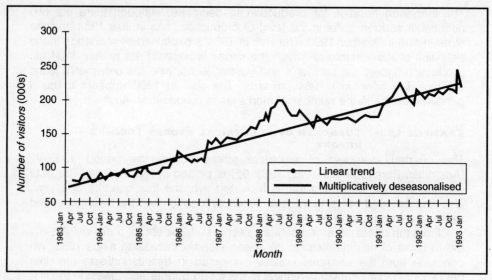

Figure 12.18   Deseasonalised and fitted linear trend for monthly number of short-term overseas visitors arriving in Australia 1983–93

12.6 Using Minitab to analyse time series

Minitab has no specific commands for performing classical time series analysis. However, you can use the sets of Minitab commands making up the macros *mvgavg* and *cmvgavg* to compute moving and centred-moving averages respectively, and the macro *expsmth* for doing exponential smoothing. Minitab does have the *regress* command for performing regression and the *tsplot* command for plotting time series. The use of the *regress* command for fitting straight lines is discussed in chapter 10, *Regression for two unrestricted variables*.

12.6.1 Moving averages

Before using the Minitab macros *mvgavg* and *cmvgavg* to compute moving and centred-moving averages, set the constants *k1–k3* as follows:

*k*1	number of the column containing the series
*k*2	number of the first of two consecutive columns to be used in computing the (centred) moving average, which will be stored in the first of the two columns
*k*3	the order of the (centred) moving average

Then use the Minitab *execute* command to execute the macro, which is stored in the file specified as part of the *execute* command. However, before executing the macro, you must change the directory to that containing the macros by using the Minitab *cd* command.

EXAMPLE 12.1   CPI FOR INDONESIA 1981–89 (continued)

The commands to compute the moving average of order 3 for the *Year* and the Indonesian *Consumer price index* and the centred moving average of order 4 for the Indonesian *Consumer price index* are as follows:

```
MTB > outfile 'a:\cpiindo.lis'
MTB > retrieve 'a:\cpiindo.mtp';
SUBC> portable.
MTB > info
MTB > let k1=1
MTB > let k2=4
MTB > let k3=3
MTB > cd a:\
MTB > execute 'mvgavg.mtb'
MTB > let k1=2
MTB > let k2=5
MTB > let k3=3
MTB > execute 'mvgavg.mtb'
MTB > let k1=2
MTB > let k2=6
MTB > let k3=4
MTB > execute 'cmvgavg.mtb'
MTB > name c4 'yr_ma3' c5 'cpi_ma3' c6 'cpi_cma4'
MTB > info
MTB > print c1-c6
```

If your version of Minitab has pull-down menus and you want to use them, table 12.12 lists the menus and options that access the required commands. Appendix D *Detailed instructions for Minitab menus*, explains how to use the menus.

Table 12.12   Menus and options for Minitab commands to produce moving averages and exponentially smoothed series

Minitab command	Menu	Option
outfile	File >	Other Files > Start Recording Session...
retrieve	File >	Open Worksheet...
port		Minitab portable worksheet
info	Edit >	Get Worksheet Info...
	(Edit >	Data Screen [Alt-D])
print	Edit >	Display Data...
let	Calc >	Functions and Statistics > General Expressions...
cd		no equivalent
execute	File >	Other Files > Execute Macro...
name	Edit >	Data Screen

The output produced by the commands outlined above is as follows. At the outset, columns containing the *Year* and the *Consumer price index* are set up in the Minitab worksheet. Then, to prepare for invoking them, you change to the directory containing the Minitab macros, and set the constants *k1–k3* as described above. Finally, use the *name* command to name the new columns, the *info* command to check that the columns have been created as expected, and the *print* command to display the results on the screen.

```
MTB > retrieve 'a:\cpiindo.mtp';
SUBC> portable.

Worksheet retrieved from file: a:\cpiindo.mtp
MTB > info

COLUMN      NAME         COUNT
C1          year             9
C2          index            9
C3          yearcode         9

CONSTANTS USED: NONE

MTB > let k1=1
MTB > let k2=4
MTB > let k3=3
MTB > cd a:\
MTB > execute 'mvgavg.mtb'
MTB > let k1=2
MTB > let k2=5
MTB > let k3=3
MTB > execute 'mvgavg.mtb'
MTB > let k1=2
MTB > let k2=6
MTB > let k3=4
MTB > execute 'cmvgavg.mtb'
MTB > name c4 'yr_ma3' c5 'cpi_ma3' c6 'cpi_cma4'
MTB > info

COLUMN      NAME         COUNT      MISSING
C1          year             9
C2          index            9
C3          yearcode         9
C4          yr_ma3           9           2
C5          cpi_ma3          9           2
C6          cpi_cma4         9           4

CONSTANTS USED: K1      K2      K3      K4      K5      K6

MTB > print c1-c6
```

continued . . .

ROW	year	index	yearcode	yr_ma3	cpi_ma3	cpi_cma4
1	1981	112.2	1	*	*	*
2	1982	122.9	2	1982	124.167	*
3	1983	137.4	3	1983	137.333	136.887
4	1984	151.7	4	1984	149.333	148.387
5	1985	158.9	5	1985	159.600	159.850
6	1986	168.2	6	1986	170.300	171.512
7	1987	183.8	7	1987	183.533	183.925
8	1988	198.6	8	1988	197.900	*
9	1989	211.3	9	*	*	*

12.6.2 Exponential smoothing

Before using the Minitab macro *expsmth* to compute the exponentially smoothed series, set the constants *k1–k3* as follows:

---

*k*1   number of the column containing the series

*k*2   number of the column in which to store the exponentially smoothed series

*k*3   the smoothing constant

Then use the Minitab *execute* command to execute the macro. However, before executing the macro, change the directory to that containing the macros by using the Minitab *cd* command.

EXAMPLE 12.1   CPI FOR INDONESIA 1981–89 (continued)

The commands to compute the exponentially smoothed series, with smoothing constant 0.9, for the Indonesian *Consumer price index* are as follows:

```
MTB > info
MTB > let k1=2
MTB > let k2=7
MTB > let k3=0.9
MTB > cd a:\
MTB > execute 'expsmth.mtb'
MTB > name c7 'cpi_es.9'
MTB > info
MTB > print c1 c2 c7
```

If your version of Minitab has pull-down menus and you want to use them, table 12.12 lists the menus and options that access the required commands. Appendix D, *Detailed instruction for Minitab menus*, explains how to use the menus.

The output produced by the commands outlined above is as follows. Use the same worksheet that you used to obtain the moving averages. The initial *info* command reveals that *c1* is the next free column, so set *k2* to 7. The *cd* command was not reissued as it is still in effect from computing the moving averages. After executing the macros, use the *info* and *print* commands to check the columns and display the results, respectively.

```
MTB > info

COLUMN      NAME           COUNT      MISSING
C1          year             9
C2          index            9
C3          yearcode         9
C4          yr_ma3           9              2
C5          cpi_ma3          9              2
C6          cpi_cma4         9              4

CONSTANTS USED:   K1   K2   K3   K4   K5   K6
MTB > let k1=2
MTB > let k2=7
MTB > let k3=0.9
MTB > cd a:\
MTB > execute 'expsmth.mtb'
MTB > name c7 'cpi_es.9'
MTB > info

COLUMN      NAME            COUNT       MISSING
C1          year              9
C2          index             9
C3          yearcode          9
C4          yr_ma3            9               2
C5          cpi_ma3           9               2
C6          cpi_cma4          9               4
C7          cpi_es.9          9               9

CONSTANTS USED:   K1     K2     K3     K4     K5     K6
MTB > print c1 c2 c7

ROW      year       index       cpi_es.9

 1       1981       112.2        112.200
 2       1982       122.9        121.830
 3       1983       137.4        135.843
 4       1984       151.7        150.114
 5       1985       158.9        158.021
 6       1986       168.2        167.182
 7       1987       183.8        182.138
 8       1988       198.6        196.954
 9       1989       211.3        209.865
```

12.6.3 Deseasonalisation

Deseasonalising a series involves using the Minitab commands *let, set, table* and *tsplot* and the macros *mvgavg* and *cmvgavg*. The new command here is the *tsplot* command. It has two arguments: the first specifies the number of periods over which the seasonal effect repeats, and the second specifies the column containing the series.

EXAMPLE 12.5   TURNOVER OF ELECTRICAL STORES 1983–92 (continued)
The commands to deseasonalise a series exhibiting seasonal variation that repeats every four time periods and is stored in *c3* are as follows. When you have established what columns are available by using the *info* command, perform the following steps to deseasonalise the series:

1. Make a plot of the time series by using the *tsplot* command, specifying the number of periods as 4 because the data is quarterly and there is likely to be a seasonal effect that repeats every four quarters.

2. Compute a centred moving average of order 4 with the Minitab macro *cmvgavg*.

3. Obtain the difference between the centred moving average of order 4 and the original data with the *let* command.

4. Compute the one-way table of quarterly seasonal means from the difference by using the *table* command.

5. Place the seasonal means in *c6* by using the *set* command. Note that as there are 10 years of data, the four quarterly means have to be repeated 10 times in *c6* so that there is the appropriate seasonal mean for each observation.

6. Adjust the seasonal means by using the *let* command with the *mean* function.

7. Subtract the adjusted seasonal means (the seasonal indices, in this case) from the original data to yield the deseasonalised series. Display this on the screen with the *print* command and plot it with the *tsplot* command.

```
MTB > outfile 'a:\electurn.lis'
MTB > retrieve 'a:\electurn.mtp';
SUBC> portable.
MTB > info
MTB > tsplot 4 c3
MTB > let k1=3
MTB > let k2=4
MTB > let k3=4
MTB > cd a:\
MTB > execute 'cmvgavg.mtb'
MTB > let c5=c3-c4
MTB > table c2;
SUBC> mean c5.
```

continued . . .

```
MTB > set c6
DATA> 10(-73.030 -19.279 -42.822 133.483)
DATA> end
MTB > let c6=c6-mean(c6)
MTB > let c7=c3-c6
MTB > name c4 'cma_4' c5 'diff' c6 'seas_ind' c7 'deseason'
MTB > print c1-c7
MTB > tsplot 4 c7
```

If your version of Minitab has pull-down menus and you want to use them, table 12.13 lists the menus and options that access the required commands. Appendix D, *Detailed instructions for Minitab menus*, explains how to use the menus.

Table 12.13   Menus and options for Minitab commands to deseasonalise a times series

Minitab command	Menu	Option
outfile	File >	Other Files > Start Recording Session...
retrieve	File >	Open Worksheet...
port		Minitab portable worksheet
info	Edit >	Get Worksheet Info...
tsplot	Graph >	Time Series Plot...
let	Calc >	Functions and Statistics > General Expressions...
cd		no equivalent
execute	File >	Other Files > Execute Macro...
table	Stat >	Tables > Cross Tabulation...
mean		Summaries...
set	Edit >	Set Patterned Data...
name	Edit >	Data Screen
print	Edit >	Display Data...

The output from these instructions is as follows:

```
MTB > retrieve 'a:\electurn.mtp';
SUBC> portable.

Worksheet retrieved from file: a:\electurn.mtp
MTB > info

COLUMN     NAME        COUNT
C1         year          40
C2         quarter       40
C3         elecsale      40

CONSTANTS USED: NONE
```

continued . . .

```
MTB > tsplot 4 c3

   1500+                                              4
      -                              4    4    4
elecsale-
      -
      -                                  2    23 1 3
   1200+                           4 23 1 3 1  2
      -
      -              4
      -     4    4                    23 1
      -                          41
    900+              2
      -           23     4
    - 23 123 1     1
    - 1                     3   23
      -                     1
    600+
        +---+---+---+---+---+---+---+---+---+---+
        0       8      16      24      32      40

MTB > let k1=3
MTB > let k2=4
MTB > let k3=4
MTB > cd a:\
MTB > execute 'cmvgavg.mtb'
MTB > let c5=c3-c4
MTB > table c2;
SUBC> mean c5.

ROWS: quarter

C5
           MEAN

     1     -73.039
     2     -19.279
     3     -42.822
     4     133.483
   ALL      -0.414

MTB > set c6
DATA> 10(-73.039 -19.279 -42.822 133.483)
DATA> end
MTB > let c6=c6-mean(c6)
MTB > let c7=c3-c6
MTB > name c4 'cma_4' c5 'diff' c6 'seas_ind' c7 'deseason'
MTB > print c1-c7
```

ROW	year	quarter	elecsale	cma_4	diff	seas_ind	deseason
1	1983	1	709.7	*	*	-72.625	782.32
2	1983	2	758.0	*	*	-18.865	776.86
3	1983	3	769.2	812.29	-43.087	-42.408	811.61
4	1983	4	991.9	820.75	171.150	133.897	858.00
5	1984	1	750.4	826.11	-75.712	-72.625	823.02
6	1984	2	785.0	831.00	-46.000	-18.865	803.86

continued . . .

```
 7  1984      3     785.1    838.16    -53.062    -42.408     827.51
 8  1984      4    1015.1    852.78    162.325    133.897     881.20
 9  1985      1     784.5    872.76    -88.263    -72.625     857.12
10  1985      2     867.8    890.22    -22.425    -18.865     886.66
11  1985      3     862.2    899.95    -37.750    -42.408     904.61
12  1985      4    1077.7    908.35    169.350    133.897     943.80
13  1986      1     799.7    900.42   -100.725    -72.625     872.32
14  1986      2     919.8    852.59     67.212    -18.865     938.66
15  1986      3     746.8    799.97    -53.175    -42.408     789.21
16  1986      4     810.4    757.09     53.312    133.897     676.50
17  1987      1     646.1    733.72    -87.625    -72.625     718.72
18  1987      2     730.3    749.17    -18.875    -18.865     749.16
19  1987      3     749.4    804.08    -54.675    -42.408     791.81
20  1987      4     931.4    881.46     49.937    133.897     797.50
21  1988      1     964.3    953.56     10.737    -72.625    1036.92
22  1988      2    1031.2   1024.57      6.625    -18.865    1050.06
23  1988      3    1025.3   1069.50    -44.200    -42.408    1067.71
24  1988      4    1223.6   1095.98    127.625    133.897    1089.70
25  1989      1    1031.5   1138.75   -107.250    -72.625    1104.12
26  1989      2    1175.8   1190.43    -14.625    -18.865    1194.66
27  1989      3    1222.9   1236.16    -13.263    -42.408    1265.31
28  1989      4    1439.4   1264.43    174.975    133.897    1305.50
29  1990      1    1181.6   1272.61    -91.013    -72.625    1254.22
30  1990      2    1251.8   1270.03    -18.225    -18.865    1270.66
31  1990      3    1212.4   1273.21    -60.812    -42.408    1254.81
32  1990      4    1429.2   1275.11    154.087    133.897    1295.30
33  1991      1    1217.3   1278.56    -61.262    -72.625    1289.92
34  1991      2    1231.3   1284.21    -52.912    -18.865    1250.16
35  1991      3    1260.5   1285.88    -25.375    -42.408    1302.91
36  1991      4    1426.3   1287.71    138.588    133.897    1292.40
37  1992      1    1233.5   1289.74    -56.238    -72.625    1306.12
38  1992      2    1229.8   1304.09    -74.287    -18.865    1248.66
39  1992      3    1278.2        *          *    -42.408    1320.61
40  1992      4    1523.4        *          *    133.895    1389.50
MTB > tsplot 4 c7

deseason-                                          4
       -
       -                              4    41 341 3
  1250+                                3 123  2    2
       -                                 2
       -
       -                          41
       -                      123
  1000+
       -                  4  2
       -              4  23
       -         4  3  1    1
       - 123 12              3    34
   750+                     2
       -                   41
       -
       -
       +---+---+---+---+---+---+---+---+---+---+
       0       8      16      24      32      40
```

12.7   Chapter summary

A time series is the history of a variable and is analysed to investigate the past, present and future behaviour of the series. Classical time series analysis, a relatively simple, widely used method of time series analysis, involves identifying and separating out the four components or types of movements in a time series: long-term trend; cyclic movements; seasonal movements; irregular or random movements.

A time series can be smoothed by using regression, moving averages or exponential smoothing. The smoothed series more closely follows the long-term trend or the combined long-term trend and cyclical movement in the series. You smooth a series to either highlight these components of the series or make longer-term forecasts. Regression is best if you want to separate the long-term trend from the other components, so long as you can find an equation that describes the trend. Moving averages or exponential smoothing have to be used if you want to follow the combined long-term trend and cyclical movement.

A time series is deseasonalised so that the other components of the time series are clearer and you can more easily describe what has happened in the series. Two methods for doing this are additive and multiplicative deseasonalisation; which method you use depends on whether the additive or multiplicative model seems the best one to represent the data. To determine which model to use, you must examine the time series to see how the movements behave as the general level of the observations increases. Additive deseasonalisation is used if the size of the seasonal movement for a season is constant; multiplicative deseasonalisation is used if the size of the seasonal movement for a season increases as the general level increases. During deseasonalisation, a seasonal index is computed and the index for a single season measures the 'average' discrepancy between the general level and the values for that season.

Forecasting is one of the important reasons for analysing a time series. It involves the prediction of future values for the variable on which the series is based. Generally, forecasting involves extrapolating the long-term trend. If a series displays seasonal movement, it must be deseasonalised before you determine the long-term trend. For forecasting some distance into the future, the most satisfactory method of ascertaining the trend is regression.

12.8   Key terms

- additive deseasonalisation
- additive model for a time series
- centred moving average of order k [$CMA(k)$]
- classical time series analysis
- coding the time period
- component of a time series
- cyclic movement (C)
- deseasonalisation
- deseasonalised series
- exponential smoothing
- forecast
- forecasting
- general level
- irregular movement (I)

- long-term trend (T)
- method of smoothing
- moving average [$MA(k)$]
- multiplicative deseasonalisation
- multiplicative model for a time series
- order of the moving average (k)
- regression
- seasonal index
- seasonal movement (S)
- smoothed series
- smoothing constant
- time series

12.9   Exercises

12.1   In your own words explain the following terms:
   (a) time series
   (b) long-term trend
   (c) cyclic movements
   (d) seasonal movements
   (e) irregular movements
   (f) deseasonalised series
   (g) additive model
   (h) multiplicative model
   (i)   coding the time period
   (j)   moving average
   (k) exponential smoothing

12.2   The apparent per capita *Tea and coffee consumption* in Australia during 1979–91 in table 12.14 has been saved in the Minitab portable worksheet file *consume.mtp*. This data is to be smoothed to remove the irregular movements from the series and to highlight the remaining movements.

Table 12.14   The apparent per capita *Tea and coffee consumption* in Australia 1979–91

Year	Tea consumption (kg)	Coffee consumption (kg)
1979	1.7	1.7
1980	1.6	1.7
1981	1.5	1.9
1982	1.6	1.9
1983	1.4	2.0
1984	1.5	2.1
1985	1.4	2.0
1986	1.4	1.6
1987	1.3	1.8
1988	1.2	2.1
1989	1.2	2.0
1990	1.1	2.0
1991	1.0	2.1

Source: Australian Bureau of Statistics (1984, 1986, 1991)

(a) Answer the following questions:
  (i) What is the question to be investigated (including the group to which the conclusions apply)?
  (ii) What variable(s) are we concerned with here?
  (iii) What type of variable(s) are they?
  (iv) Which major category of statistical procedures applies here? Why?
  (v) What type of statistic should we use, given the question to be investigated and the variables involved?
  (vi) Which particular statistic or procedure, and diagram, should we use? Why?
(b) The following Minitab output contains plots of both the *Tea and coffee consumption* series. Reproduce this output. Describe which components are present in these series.
(c) The Minitab commands and associated output for producing and plotting the moving averages of order 5 for both *Tea and coffee consumption* are as follows. Reproduce this output. Does the observed series show greater variability than the smoothed series? How well does the moving average follow the long-term trend?

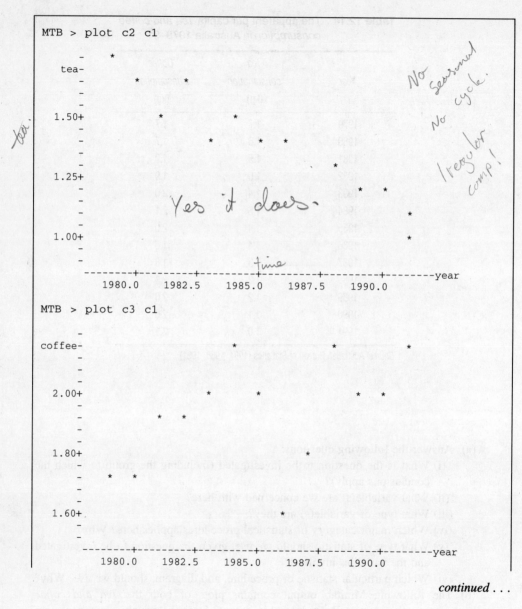

continued . . .

```
MTB > cd a:\
MTB > name c4 'tea_ma5'
MTB > let k1=2
MTB > let k2=4
MTB > let k3=5
MTB > exec 'a:\mvgavg.mtb'   — moving average,
MTB > name c5 'coff_ma5'
MTB > let k1=3
MTB > let k2=5
MTB > exec 'a:\mvgavg.mtb'
MTB > mplot c2 c1 c4 c1
```

```
       -    A                                              orig
       -                                                  smoothed
       -            A       A
       -                B
  1.50+            A   B   B    A                               Smoothed!
       -                          B
       -                    A      2    A
       -                            B
       -                                   2
  1.25+                                        B
       -                                        A   A
       -                                            B
       -                                               A                How
       -                                                              well
  1.00+                                                  A            does it
       -                                                              pick up
       -                                                             Trend.
       --------+---------+---------+---------+---------+---------+--------
            1980.0    1982.5    1985.0    1987.5    1990.0
       N* = 4
```

A = tea vs. year   B = tea_ma5 vs. year
```
MTB > mplot c3 c1 c5 c1
       -                        A           A        A
       -
       -
  2.00+                2       A           2   A
       -
       -            A   2     B   B   B   B   B
       -
       -            B
  1.80+                                A
       -
       -      A   A
       -
       -
  1.60+                            A
       -
       -
       --------+---------+---------+---------+---------+---------+--------
            1980.0    1982.5    1985.0    1987.5    1990.0
       N* = 4
```

    A = coffee vs. year   B = coff_ma5 vs. year

(d) The Minitab commands and associated output for producing and plotting the exponentially smoothed series using $\omega = 0.3$ for both *Tea and coffee consumption* are as follows. Reproduce this output. Does the observed series show greater variability than the smoothed series? How well does the exponentially smoothed series follow the long-term trend?

```
MTB > name c6 'tea_e.3' c7 'coff_e.3'
MTB > let k1=2
MTB > let k2=6
MTB > let k3=0.3
MTB > exec 'a:\expsmth.mtb'
MTB > let k1=3
MTB > let k2=7
MTB > exec 'a:\expsmth.mtb'
MTB > mplot c2 c1 c6 c1


        -      2
        -         B
        -         A   B   2
        -                   B   B
     1.50+              A         A   B
        -                              B
        -                  A       A   A   B
        -                                    B
        -                                  A       B
     1.25+                                           B
        -                                  A   A          B
        -                                               B
        -                                          A
     1.00+                                                   A
        -
        -
           --------+---------+---------+---------+---------+--------
            1980.0    1982.5    1985.0    1987.5    1990.0
            A = tea vs. year         B = tea_e.3 vs. year
MTB > mplot c3 c1 c7 c1


        -
        -                      A              A           A
        -
     2.00+              A      A                   A   A   B
        -                         B                       B
        -          A   A      B                 B   B
        -                  B
        -                              B   B
     1.80+              B                      A
        -          B
        -      2   2
        -
     1.60+                              A
        -
           --------+---------+---------+---------+---------+--------
            1980.0    1982.5    1985.0    1987.5    1990.0
            A = coffee vs. year      B = coff_e.3 vs. year
```

(e) The Minitab commands and associated output for producing and plotting the exponentially smoothed series using $\omega = 0.7$ for both *Tea and coffee consumption* are as follows. Reproduce this output. Does the observed series show greater variability than the smoothed series? How well does the exponentially smoothed series follow the trend?

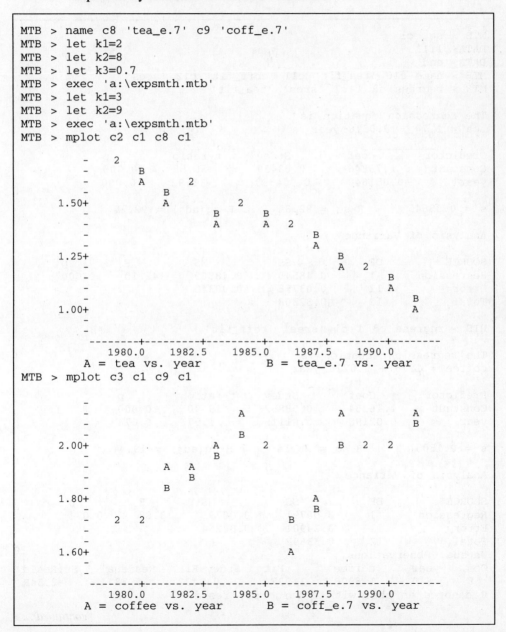

```
MTB > name c8 'tea_e.7' c9 'coff_e.7'
MTB > let k1=2
MTB > let k2=8
MTB > let k3=0.7
MTB > exec 'a:\expsmth.mtb'
MTB > let k1=3
MTB > let k2=9
MTB > exec 'a:\expsmth.mtb'
MTB > mplot c2 c1 c8 c1


        -     2
        -        B
        -        A      2
        -           B
    1.50+           A           2
        -             B      B
        -             A      A   2
        -                        B
        -                        A
    1.25+                          B
        -                          A   2
        -                               B
        -                               A
        -                                   B
    1.00+                                   A
        -
        -
          --------+---------+---------+---------+---------+--------
            1980.0    1982.5    1985.0    1987.5    1990.0
          A = tea vs. year          B = tea_e.7 vs. year
MTB > mplot c3 c1 c9 c1


        -
        -                      A              A            A
        -                                                  B
        -                         B
    2.00+                      A        2      B    2   2
        -                      B
        -            A    A
        -                 B
        -          B
    1.80+                                       A
        -                                       B
        -     2    2                       B
        -
        -
    1.60+                                   A
        -
        -
          --------+---------+---------+---------+---------+--------
            1980.0    1982.5    1985.0    1987.5    1990.0
          A = coffee vs. year         B = coff_e.7 vs. year
```

(f) **The Minitab commands and associated output for fitting a straight line to both series using regression and for plotting the fitted line are as follows. In fitting the straight line the *Year* was coded with 1979 coded as 1. Note that the column named 'sres' is included in the regression command only so that the fitted values can be obtained for plotting. Reproduce this output.**

```
MTB > set c1
DATA> 1:13
DATA> end
MTB > name c10 'tea_fit' c11 'coff_fit' c12 'sres'
MTB > regress c2 1 c1 'sres' 'tea_fit'

The regression equation is
tea = 1.74 - 0.0516 year

Predictor         Coef        Stdev      t-ratio          p
Constant       1.73846      0.03439        50.55      0.000
year          -0.051648     0.004333      -11.92      0.000

s = 0.05845      R-sq = 92.8%       R-sq(adj) = 92.2%

Analysis of Variance

SOURCE           DF          SS           MS          F          p
Regression        1        0.48549      0.48549     142.10     0.000
Error            11        0.03758      0.00342
Total            12        0.52308

MTB > regress c3 1 c1 'sres' 'coff_fit'

The regression equation is
coffee = 1.76 + 0.0220 year

Predictor         Coef        Stdev      t-ratio          p
Constant       1.76154      0.08852        19.90      0.000
year           0.02198      0.01115         1.97      0.074

s = 0.1505       R-sq = 26.1%       R-sq(adj) = 19.4%

Analysis of Variance

SOURCE           DF          SS           MS          F          p
Regression        1        0.08791      0.08791      3.88      0.074
Error            11        0.24901      0.02264
Total            12        0.33692
Unusual Observations
Obs.   year       coffee        Fit    Stdev.Fit    Residual    St.Resid
  8     8.0       1.6000     1.9374       0.0432     -0.3374      -2.34R
R denotes an obs. with a large st. resid.
```

continued . . .

regression

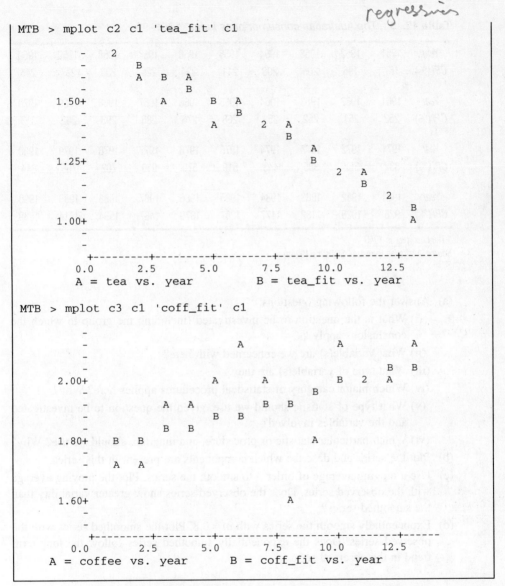

```
MTB > mplot c2 c1 'tea_fit' c1

        -    2
        -    B
        -    A   B   A
        -            B
  1.50+          A       B   A
        -                    B
        -            A       2   A
        -                        B
        -                            A
  1.25+  ·                       B
        -                            2   A
        -                                B
        -                                    2
        -                                        B
  1.00+                                          A
        -
        -

        +---------+---------+---------+---------+---------+------
       0.0       2.5       5.0       7.5      10.0      12.5
       A = tea vs. year          B = tea_fit vs. year


MTB > mplot c3 c1 'coff_fit' c1

        -
        -                    A           A           A
        -                                        B   B
  2.00+                  A       A       B   2   A
        -                            B
        -        A   A           B   B
        -            B   B
  1.80+  B   B                   A
        -    A   A
        -
        -
  1.60+                          A
        -
        +---------+---------+---------+---------+---------+------
       0.0       2.5       5.0       7.5      10.0      12.5
       A = coffee vs. year       B = coff_fit vs. year
```

(g) Which method best describes the long-term trend? Write a report, based on the method you chose, that summarises your conclusions about the long-term trend in the observed series.

12.3 Table 12.15 gives the *Australian consumer price index* for 1951-90. This data is to be smoothed to remove the irregular movements from the series and to highlight the remaining movements.

Table 12.15   *The Australian consumer price index* 1951–90*

Year	1951	1952	1953	1954	1955	1956	1957	1958	1959	1960
CPI (%)	167	196	205	206	211	224	229	233	237	245
Year	1961	1962	1963	1964	1965	1966	1967	1968	1969	1970
CPI (%)	252	251	252	258	268	276	286	293	302	313
Year	1971	1972	1973	1974	1975	1976	1977	1978	1979	1980
CPI (%)	332	352	385	443	510	579	650	702	766	844
Year	1981	1982	1983	1984	1985	1986	1987	1988	1989	1990
CPI (%)	926	1028	1132	1177	1257	1370	1487	1594	1714	1839

* The base year is 1945
Source: Australian Bureau of Statistics(1994b)

(a) Answer the following questions:
   (i) What is the question to be investigated (including the group to which the conclusions apply)?
   (ii) What variable(s) are we concerned with here?
   (iii) What type of variable(s) are they?
   (iv) Which major category of statistical procedures applies here? Why?
   (v) What type of statistic should we use, given the question to be investigated and the variables involved?
   (vi) Which particular statistic or procedure, and diagram, should we use? Why?
(b) Plot the series and describe which components are present in this series.
(c) Use a moving average of order 3 to smooth the series. Plot the moving average with the observed series. Does the observed series show greater variability than the smoothed series?
(d) Exponentially smooth the series with $\omega = 0.8$. Plot the smoothed series with the observed series. Does the exponentially smoothed series follow the long-term trend in the observed series?

12.4   The *Number of private dwellings commenced* in Australia during 1983–92 in table 12.16 are saved in the Minitab portable worksheet file *houstart.mtp*. This data is to be deseasonalised to separate the seasonal movements from the long-term trend and cyclic movements and smoothed to remove the irregular movements.

Table 12.16 *Number of private dwellings commenced* in Australia 1983–92

| Year | Quarter | | | |
	Mar	Jun	Sep	Dec
1983	22 750	25 420	28 970	33 330
1984	33 050	38 030	40 230	39 320
1985	33 980	39 190	39 720	36 210
1986	30 510	29 800	31 090	30 620
1987	27 010	27 770	30 960	33 420
1988	33 260	38 160	44 910	46 520
1989	40 430	43 100	38 530	35 450
1990	30 720	33 010	31 840	31 918
1991	27 393	30 195	33 791	35 236
1992	32 471	38 748	40 639	40 864

Source: Australian Bureau of Statistics(1983–92)

(a) Answer the following questions:
   (i) What is the question to be investigated (including the group to which the conclusions apply)?
   (ii) What variable(s) are we concerned with here?
   (iii) What type of variable(s) are they?
   (iv) Which major category of statistical procedures applies here? Why?
   (v) What type of statistic should we use, given the question to be investigated and the variables involved?
   (vi) Which particular statistic or procedure, and diagram, should we use? Why?
(b) The Minitab commands and associated output for plotting the observed series are on page 374. Reproduce this output.
   (i) Describe the movements present in the observed series.
   (ii) Which method of deseasonalisation should you use to deseasonalise this series?
   (iii) What order moving average would be involved in deseasonalising the data? Give reasons for your answer.
(c) The Minitab commands and associated output for additively deseasonalising the observed series and plotting the deseasonalised series begins on page 374. Reproduce this output.
   (i) What are the seasonal indices for this data?
   (ii) Describe in your own words the information the index gives for the first quarter.
   (iii) Describe how the *Number of dwellings commenced* varies through the course of a *Year*.
   (iv) What do you conclude about the long-term trend and the cyclic and irregular movements from the deseasonalised series?

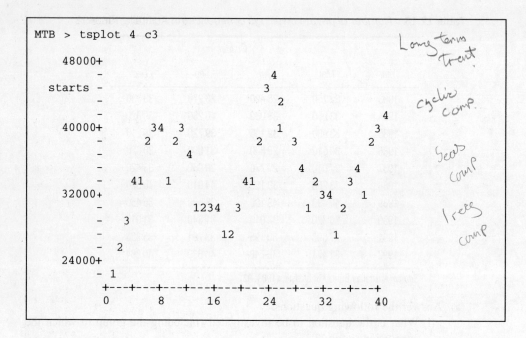

```
MTB > tsplot 4 c3

    48000+
         -                       4
  starts -                      3
         -                         2
         -                                      4
    40000+      34  3             1             3
         -     2   2           2    3          2
         -          4
         -                           4       4
         -   41   1          41        2    3
    32000+                              34    1
         -            1234  3         1    2
         -  3
         -                12              1
         - 2
    24000+
         -1
         +---+---+---+---+---+---+---+---+---+---+
         0       8      16      24      32      40
```

Long term trend
cyclic comp.
Seas comp
Irreg comp

```
MTB > cd a:\
MTB > let k1=3
MTB > let k2=4
MTB > let k3=4
MTB > execute 'a:\cmvgavg.mtb'
MTB > let c5=c3-c4

MTB > table c2;
SUBC> mean c5.

ROWS: quarter

             C5
           MEAN

  1     -2762.0
  2      2213.4
  3      1373.9
  4      1274.1
ALL        24.9

MTB > set c6
DATA> 10(-2762 213.4 1373.9 1274.1)
DATA> end
MTB > let c6=c6-mean(c6)
MTB > let c7=c3-c6
```

continued . . .

```
MTB > name c4 'cma_4' c5 'diff' c6 'seas_ind' c7 'deseason'
MTB > print c1-c7
```

ROW	year	quarter	starts	cma_4	diff	seas_ind	deseason
1	1983	1	22750	*	*	-2786.85	25536.8
2	1983	2	25420	*	*	188.55	25231.4
3	1983	3	28970	28905.0	65.00	1349.05	27620.9
4	1983	4	33330	31768.7	1561.25	1249.25	32080.7
5	1984	1	33050	34752.5	-1702.50	-2786.85	35836.9
6	1984	2	38030	36908.7	1121.25	188.55	37841.4
7	1984	3	40230	37773.7	2456.25	1349.05	38880.9
8	1984	4	39320	38035.0	1285.00	1249.25	38070.8
9	1985	1	33980	38116.2	-4136.25	-2786.85	36766.9
10	1985	2	39190	37663.7	1526.25	188.55	39001.4
11	1985	3	39720	36841.2	2878.75	1349.05	38370.9
12	1985	4	36210	35233.8	976.25	1249.25	34960.8
13	1986	1	30510	32981.2	-2471.25	-2786.85	33296.9
14	1986	2	29800	31203.7	-1403.75	188.55	29611.4
15	1986	3	31090	30067.5	1022.50	1349.05	29740.9
16	1986	4	30620	29376.3	1243.75	1249.25	29370.7
17	1987	1	27010	29106.3	-2096.25	-2786.85	29796.8
18	1987	2	27770	29440.0	-1670.00	188.55	27581.4
19	1987	3	30960	30571.2	388.75	1349.05	29610.9
20	1987	4	33420	32651.3	768.75	1249.25	32170.8
21	1988	1	33260	35693.7	-2433.75	-2786.85	36046.9
22	1988	2	38160	39075.0	-915.00	188.55	37971.4
23	1988	3	44910	41608.8	3301.25	1349.05	43560.9
24	1988	4	46520	43122.5	3397.50	1249.25	45270.7
25	1989	1	40430	42942.5	-2512.50	-2786.85	43216.9
26	1989	2	43100	40761.3	2338.75	188.55	42911.4
27	1989	3	38530	38163.7	366.25	1349.05	37180.9
28	1989	4	35450	35688.8	-238.75	1249.25	34200.8
29	1990	1	30720	33591.2	-2871.25	-2786.85	33506.9
30	1990	2	33010	32313.5	696.50	188.55	32821.4
31	1990	3	31840	31456.1	383.87	1349.05	30490.9
32	1990	4	31918	30688.4	1229.62	1249.25	30668.8
33	1991	1	27393	30580.4	-3187.38	-2786.85	30179.8
34	1991	2	30195	31239.0	-1044.00	188.55	30006.4
35	1991	3	33791	32288.5	1502.50	1349.05	32441.9
36	1991	4	35236	33992.4	1243.63	1249.25	33986.7
37	1992	1	32471	35917.5	-3446.50	-2786.85	35257.9
38	1992	2	38748	37477.0	1271.00	188.55	38559.4
39	1992	3	40639	*	*	1349.05	39289.9
40	1992	4	40864	*	*	1249.25	39614.7

continued . . .

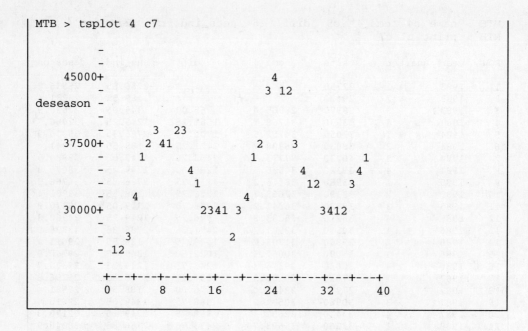

```
MTB > tsplot 4 c7

          -
          -
   45000+                              4
          -                          3 12
deseason  -
          -
          -            3   23
   37500+          2  41              2     3
          -       1                 1                      1
          -             4               4        4
          -            1               12      3
          -       4               4
   30000+             2341 3              3412
          -
          -    3              2
          - 12
          -
          +---+---+---+---+---+---+---+---+---+---+
          0       8      16      24      32      40
```

(d) The Minitab commands and associated output for producing and plotting the moving average of order 5 to smooth the deseasonalised data are as follows. Reproduce this output. How effective is the moving average in smoothing the data?

```
MTB > name c8 'time' c9 'dese_ma5'
MTB > set c8
DATA> 1:40
DATA> end
MTB > let k1=7
MTB > let k2=9
MTB > let k3=5
MTB > execute 'a:\mvgavg.mtb'
MTB > mplot c7 c8 c9 c8
```

continued . . .

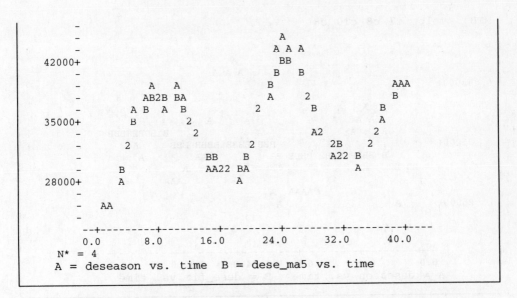

```
      -
      -                                              A
      -                                          A A A
 42000+                                           BB
      -                                           B    B
      -              A    A                     B                    AAA
      -           AB2B  BA                      A      2               B
      -         A  B  A   B                  2        B            B
 35000+         B           2                              A2          2
      -                   2                             A2           2
      -         2                   2                      2B      2
      -                         BB      B                 A22 B
      -         B              AA22  BA                       A
 28000+         A                     A
      -
      -     AA

        --+---------+---------+---------+---------+---------+----
        0.0       8.0      16.0      24.0      32.0      40.0
      N* = 4
      A = deseason vs. time   B = dese_ma5 vs. time
```

(e) The Minitab commands and associated output for fitting and plotting a regression line for the deseasonalised series are as follows. Does the fitted straight line adequately describe the long-term trend?

```
MTB > name c10 'dese_fit' c11 'sres'
MTB > regress c7 1 c8 'sres' c10

The regression equation is
deseason = 32434 + 99.0 time

Predictor    Coef    Stdev    t-ratio       p
Constant    32434     1600      20.27    0.000
time        99.02    68.01       1.46    0.154

s = 4965    R-sq = 5.3%    R-sq(adj) = 2.8%

Analysis of Variance
SOURCE        DF          SS            MS        F        p
Regression     1    52261408      52261408     2.12    0.154
Error         38   936850240      24653954
Total         39   989111680

Unusual Observations
Obs.    time    deseason      Fit   Stdev.Fit    Residual    St.Resid
 24     24.0       45271    34811         820       10460       2.14R

R denotes an obs. with a large st. resid.
```

continued . . .

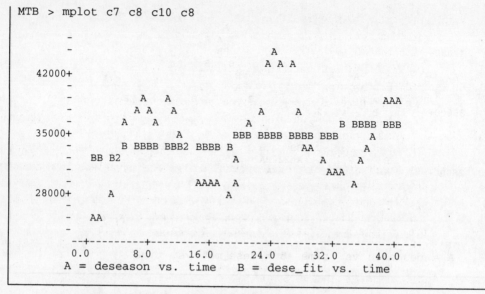

```
MTB > mplot c7 c8 c10 c8
```

(f) Compare the effect of moving averages and regression in smoothing the deseasonalised series in this case.

12.5 Table 12.17 gives the *Value of private dwellings commenced* in Australia during 1983–92. This data is to be deseasonalised to separate the seasonal movements from the long-term trend and cyclic movements and smoothed to remove the irregular movements.

Table 12.17   *Value ($m) of private dwellings commenced in Australia 1983–92*

	Quarter			
Year	Mar	Jun	Sep	Dec
1983	1042.8	1087.8	1270.4	1469.3
1984	1442.2	1733.6	1918.9	1884.0
1985	1659.6	1931.3	2020.8	1926.7
1986	1660.9	1658.9	1764.9	1759.4
1987	1563.7	1714.5	1910.7	2082.4
1988	2176.8	2582.3	3131.7	3349.9
1989	3163.7	3450.0	3091.0	2891.0
1990	2518.4	2775.6	2746.5	2644.2
1991	2323.8	2478.8	2768.7	2917.7
1992	2690.9	3207.4	3368.7	3402.8

Source: Australian Bureau of Statistics (1983–92)

(a) Answer the following questions:
  (i) What is the question to be investigated (including the group to which the conclusions apply)?
  (ii) What variable(s) are we concerned with here?
  (iii) What type of variable(s) are they?
  (iv) Which major category of statistical procedures applies here? Why?
  (v) What type of statistic should we use, given the question to be investigated and the variables involved?
  (vi) Which particular statistic or procedure, and diagram, should we use? Why?
(b) Plot the observed series. Which method of deseasonalisation should you use to deseasonalise this series?
(c) Use the appropriate method to deseasonalise this data. Plot the deseasonalised series. What do you conclude about the long-term trend and the cyclic and irregular movements from the deseasonalised series?
(d) Use a moving average of order 7 to smooth the deseasonalised series. Plot the moving average with the deseasonalised series. How effective is the moving average in smoothing the data?
(e) What value of the smoothing constant would you use to exponentially smooth the deseasonalised series? Obtain the exponentially smoothed series by using your proposed smoothing constant. Plot the exponentially smoothed series with the deseasonalised series and comment on the result.

12.6 Table 12.18 gives the *Room occupancy rates* for licensed hotels with facilities in Australia during 1988–93. This data is to be deseasonalised to separate the seasonal movements from the long-term trend and cyclic movements and smoothed to remove the irregular movements.

Table 12.18 *Room occupancy rates* (%) for licensed hotels with facilities in Australia 1988–93

						Month						
	Jan	Feb	Mar	Apr	May	Jun	Jul	Aug	Sep	Oct	Nov	Dec
Year												
1988	53.5	56.2	57.1	55.6	53.8	52.6	56.6	58.4	61.8	62.5	58.7	48.1
1989	50.6	54.1	54.9	52.2	48.5	48.3	50.9	49.9	52.1	52.3	53.8	44.9
1990	48.8	52.5	54.0	50.3	48.0	47.2	48.0	49.7	54.2	54.2	53.2	44.9
1991	47.2	47.8	49.2	47.5	45.4	47.0	49.4	50.7	55.3	56.4	56.1	46.2
1992	48.0	51.0	52.8	51.2	48.9	47.4	50.0	51.3	56.0	57.1	57.8	49.9
1993	54.0	55.0	57.1	53.7	52.6	50.5	52.7	55.2	60.4	63.3	64.7	55.2

Source: Australian Bureau of Statistics (1983–92)

(a) Answer the following questions:
  (i) What is the question to be investigated (including the group to which the conclusions apply)?
  (ii) What variable(s) are we concerned with here?
  (iii) What type of variable(s) are they?
  (iv) Which major category of statistical procedures applies here? Why?
  (v) What type of statistic should we use, given the question to be investigated and the variables involved?
  (vi) Which particular statistic or procedure, and diagram, should we use? Why?
(b) Plot the observed series. Which method of deseasonalisation should you use to deseasonalise this series?
(c) Use the appropriate method to deseasonalise this data. Plot the deseasonalised series. What do you conclude about the long-term trend and the cyclic and irregular movements from the deseasonalised series?
(d) Use a moving average of order 3 to smooth the deseasonalised series. Plot the moving average with the deseasonalised series. How effective is the moving average in smoothing the data?

12.7 Table 12.19 gives the *Production of men's jeans* in Australia during 1983–92. This data is to be deseasonalised to separate the seasonal movements from the other movements.

Table 12.19 *Production of men's jeans (000s) in Australia 1983–92*

						Month						
Year	Jan	Feb	Mar	Apr	May	Jun	July	Aug	Sept	Oct	Nov	Dec
1983	—	—	—	—	—	—	—	—	—	629	695	468
1984	220	696	706	602	720	635	371	410	410	467	418	342
1985	165	464	468	365	361	340	369	434	361	384	436	273
1986	109	373	376	365	354	322	342	335	373	390	348	293
1987	148	324	374	313	356	344	345	333	380	411	395	263
1988	110	266	360	251	269	292	296	355	327	271	303	230
1989	122	248	281	258	270	285	301	418	416	258	340	223
1990	129	265	373	293	395	344	227	266	292	196	197	205
1991	59	174	215	163	192	215	216	212	250	239	240	177
1992	81	196	246	222	200	226	241	225	240	—	—	—

Source: Australian Bureau of Statistics (1983–92)

(a) Answer the following questions:
  (i) What is the question to be investigated (including the group to which the conclusions apply)?
  (ii) What variable(s) are we concerned with here?

    (iii) What type of variable(s) are they?

    (iv) Which major category of statistical procedures applies here? Why?

    (v) What type of statistic should we use, given the question to be investigated and the variables involved?

    (vi) Which particular statistic or procedure, and diagram, should we use? Why?

(b) Plot the observed series. Which method of deseasonalisation should you use to deseasonalise this series?

(c) Use the appropriate method to deseasonalise this data. Plot the deseasonalised series. What do you conclude about the long-term trend and the cyclic and irregular movements from the deseasonalised series? Note that up until July 1984 the series included youths' as well as men's jeans.

CHAPTER 13

OVERVIEW OF DESCRIPTIVE
SUMMARIES

L E A R N I N G   O B J E C T I V E S

The learning objectives of this chapter are:

- to gain an overview of the descriptive summaries of data covered in this book;
- to be able to identify the appropriate descriptive summary for a specific situation.

As outlined in chapter 1, *Statistics*, the statistical methods covered in this book can be classified into one of four major categories of statistical procedures:

A. Data collection procedures: for collecting data so that the validity of the collected information is maximised;

B. Descriptive summaries: for summarising aspects of the behaviour of just the data being analysed;

C. Estimation procedures: for estimating population quantities using a sample;

D. Hypothesis tests: for answering yes/no questions about the population using a sample.

All the statistical techniques covered in this book were summarised in section 1.3, *Summary of procedures based on types of statistics*, and were grouped according to the following **types of statistics: distribution of variables, single value, range of values, measures of central tendency, measures of dispersion, measures of association, fitted lines, index numbers** and **time series**. This chapter gives an overview of the **descriptive summaries** that includes not only the types of statistics but also the various combinations of **variable** types covered in this book. Part VI, *Overview of statistical procedures*, gives an overview of all the statistical techniques and explains in detail the differences between the major categories of statistical procedures and between the various types of statistics.

The organisation of the summary in this chapter is illustrated in figure 13.1 on page 384, followed by the summary itself. Section 13.1, *Choosing a procedure*, describes how to use the summary to help to decide which procedure to utilise for a particular example. This involves identifying the major category of statistical procedures, the combination of variable types and the type of statistic for the example. The two most important variable types that you will need to distinguish between are the **limited** and **unrestricted variables**. The distinction between **nominal**, **ordinal** and **interval/ratio variables** is important to a lesser degree.

1. *One limited variable*
   - Distribution of variables: frequency, relative frequency and percentage one-way summary tables — bar or column chart.
   - Measures of central tendency: mode (mean, median).
   - Measures of dispersion: range, interquartile range, (standard deviation, coefficient of variation).

2. *Two limited variables*
   - Distribution of variables: two-way contingency table — chart with bars or columns that are grouped or stacked.

3. *Three limited variables*
   - Distribution of variables: three-way contingency table — chart with bars or columns that are grouped or stacked.

4. *One unrestricted variable*
   - Distribution of variables: frequency, relative frequency and percentage tables — histogram, polygon, stem-and-leaf display, dotplot.
   - Measures of central tendency: mean, median — boxplot.
   - Measures of dispersion: range, interquartile range, standard deviation, coefficient of variation — boxplot.

5. *One unrestricted variable — one limited variable*
   - Distribution of variables: frequency, relative frequency and percentage tables for each value of limited variable — histogram, polygon, stem-and-leaf display, dotplot for each value of limited variable.
   - Measures of central tendency: one-way table of means or medians — boxplot for each value of limited variable, bar chart or line diagram.
   - Measures of dispersion: one-way table of ranges, interquartile ranges, standard deviations or coefficients of variation — boxplot for each value of limited variable.

6. *One unrestricted variable — two limited variables*
   - Distribution of variables: frequency, relative frequency and percentage tables for each combination of values of the limited variables — histogram, polygon, stem-and-leaf display, dotplot for each combination of values of the limited variables.
   - Measures of central tendency: two-way table of means or medians — boxplot for each combination of values of the limited variables, bar chart or line diagram.

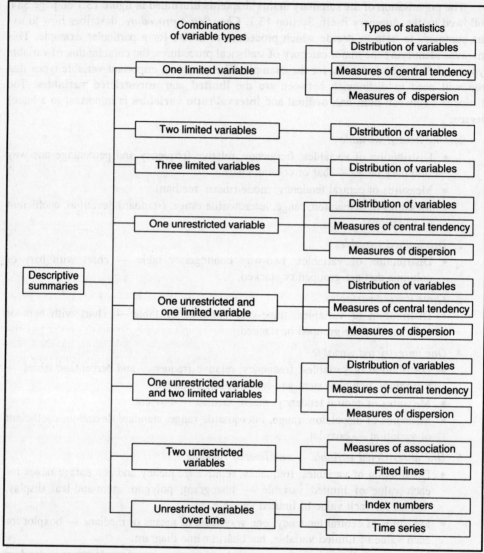

Figure 13.1 Organisation of descriptive summaries of data

- Measures of dispersion: two-way table of ranges, interquartile ranges, standard deviations or coefficients of variation — boxplot for each combination of values of the limited variables, bar chart or line diagram.

7. *Two unrestricted variables*
- Measures of association: linear correlation coefficient and coefficient of determination — scatter diagram.
- Fitted lines: intercept and/or slope; mean response — scatter diagram

8. *Unrestricted variables with measurements repeated over time or location*

- Index numbers: simple index numbers, unweighted aggregative and relatives index numbers and Laspeyres and Paasche weighted index numbers — line diagram.
- Time series: observed series; smoothed series using simple linear regression, moving averages or exponential smoothing; additively or multiplicatively deseasonalised series; forecast — line diagram.

13.1   Choosing a procedure

In section 1.3, *Summary of procedures based on types of statistics*, we suggested that a crucial problem you had to face is: what statistical procedure should I use to help answer the question that I have? By now you can probably more readily appreciate the difficulty of this problem. In the following examples, we investigate choosing descriptive summaries by asking a series of standard questions about the situation involved. By doing this you are using the **question to be investigated** and the variables involved to identify the procedure that will answer the question to be investigated. This is because the question to be investigated and the variables involved determine the major category of statistical procedures, the type of statistic and the combination of variable types — precisely the information used to categorise the various procedures in the summary. Having determined this information you should use it to identify the list in the summary that contains procedures you could apply to the example; the procedures are listed before the dash and diagrams that illustrate their results are after the dash. Choose, or at least indicate how you would choose, one of the procedures and, if available, a diagram.

EXAMPLE 13.1   STUDENT PREFERENCES FOR TEAMWORK

University students are asked to work on a subject in teams during tutorials. The subject coordinator wants to ascertain students' reactions to this arrangement, and conducts a survey of all those currently studying the subject; just 69% of students responded. The survey questionnaire asks students to rate their enjoyment of teamwork on a 5-point rating scale in which points range from *Like very much* to *Dislike very much*. The survey also asks them whether or not they have previously worked on a subject in teams. The coordinator wants to see if, for students currently studying the subject, the pattern of enjoyment differs between those students who have and those who have not had previous teamwork experience.

- What is the question to be investigated (including the group to which the conclusions apply)?
  Answer: The question to be investigated is: for students currently studying the subject, does the pattern of enjoyment of teamwork differ between those students of the subject who have and those who have not had previous teamwork experience?
- What variable(s) are we concerned with here?
  Answer: Teamwork enjoyment and *Teamwork experience*.

- What type of variable(s) are they?
  Answer: They are both limited variables.

- Which major category of statistical procedures applies here? Why?
  Answer: Descriptive summaries, because a census has been conducted.

- What type of statistic should we use, given the question to be investigated and the variables involved?
  Answer: Distribution of variables.

- Which particular statistic or procedure, and diagram, should we use? Why?
  Answer: Two-way contingency table with bar or column chart, that is grouped or stacked, since these allow an investigation of the dependence of *Teamwork enjoyment* on *Teamwork experience*. The particular percentage to be used has to be chosen. In this case, the most relevant percentages are those that are expressed as a percentage of the total number in the corresponding category of *Teamwork experience*. This will allow the comparison of the two distributions for those who have and those who have not had *Teamwork* experience.

EXAMPLE 13.2   PRICES MONITORING

A government agency responsible for monitoring prices for consumers is setting up a program to follow the price difference between the eight major supermarket chains in a large city. Four local government areas are selected and a supermarket is selected from each chain. At each supermarket the prices of 15 items are recorded each quarter.

At the outset the consumption per capita per quarter is obtained for the items from Australian Bureau of Statistics figures or from the committee's guesstimate. These initial figures will be used for the duration of the study.

What statistic should the agency use to follow the quarterly change in prices it obtains for one of the supermarket chains, the prices to be combined over the 15 items and the four supermarkets from a chain?

- What is the question to be investigated (including the group to which the conclusions apply)?
  Answer: The question to be investigated is: what has been the quarterly change in prices for one of the supermarket chains, the prices to be combined over the 15 items and the four supermarkets from a chain?

- What variable(s) are we concerned with here?
  Answer: The variables involved are *Price, Item, Consumption, Quarter* and *Local government area.*

- What type of variable(s) are they?
  Answer: All the variables are limited, except *Price* and *Consumption,* which are unrestricted. Note that the unrestricted variables are measured over time.

- Which major category of statistical procedures applies here? Why?
  Answer: Descriptive summaries, because only the collected data is of interest.

- What type of statistic should we use, given the question to be investigated and the variables involved?
  Answer: Index numbers.

- Which particular statistic or procedure, and diagram, should we use? Why?
  Answer: A weighted index number that uses base year weights with a line diagram, because this will allow price changes to be monitored over time. An index with base year weights is appropriate because the consumption figures can be used as weights to reflect the relative importance of the items and these weights are collected only at the outset. It cannot be a Laspeyres weighted index as the weights are not the total quantities sold for the period.

EXAMPLE 13.3   STAFF ADVANCEMENT

In a study of factors influencing the advancement of staff in a chain of large department stores, the salary increase over the period of employment and number of years of employment with the chain was extracted for virtually all the staff. The task is to measure the strength of the relationship between salary increase and number of years of employment.

- What is the question to be investigated (including the group to which the conclusions apply)?
  Answer: The question to be investigated is: what is the strength of the relationship between salary increase and number of years of employment for all the staff of a large department store?

- What variable(s) are we concerned with here?
  Answer: Salary increase and *Years of employment.*

- What type of variable(s) are they?
  Answer: They are both unrestricted variables.

- Which major category of statistical procedures applies here? Why?
  Answer: Descriptive summaries, because a census has been conducted.

- What type of statistic should we use, given the question to be investigated and the variables involved?
  Answer: Measure of association.

- Which particular statistic or procedure, and diagram, should we use? Why?
  Answer: Linear correlation coefficient and coefficient of determination with a scatter diagram, as these will measure the strength of the relationship between *Salary increase* and *Years of employment.*

EXAMPLE 13.3   STAFF ADVANCEMENT (continued)

Suppose that there is a moderate relationship between a staff member's salary increase and the number of years of their employment with the chain. Consequently the agency decides to determine the average increase in salary for each additional year of employment for staff employed by the company.

- What is the question to be investigated (including the group to which the conclusions apply)?
  Answer: The question to be investigated is: what is the average increase in salary for each additional year of employment for all the staff of a large department store?

- What variable(s) are we concerned with here?
  Answer: Salary increase and *Years of employment,* as before.

- What type of variable(s) are they?
  Answer: They are both unrestricted variables.

- Which major category of statistical procedures applies here? Why?
  Answer: Descriptive summaries, because a census has been conducted.

- What type of statistic should we use, given the question to be investigated and the variables involved?
  Answer: Fitted lines.

- Which particular statistic or procedure, and diagram, should we use? Why?
  Answer: Slope of the fitted line, as this measures the rate of increase in the dependent variable for each unit increase in the independent variable, and this is what is required. The diagram to illustrate the slope is the scatter diagram with the fitted line included; however, it is likely to be unnecessary.

EXAMPLE 13.4   EMPLOYEE AGE

A national insurance company wants to make a general comparison of the ages of its employees in the different states of Australia. It extracts the age, to the nearest year, of each employee, and the state in which they are employed.

- What is the question to be investigated (including the group to which the conclusions apply)?
  Answer: The question to be investigated is: how does the age of the employees of a national insurance company differ between the states of Australia?

- What variable(s) are we concerned with here?
  Answer: Age and *State.*

- What type of variable(s) are they?
  Answer: Age is an unrestricted variable and *State* is a limited variable.

- Which major category of statistical procedures applies here? Why?
  Answer: Descriptive summaries, because a census has been conducted.

- What type of statistic should we use, given the question to be investigated and the variables involved?
  Answer: Distribution of variables, measures of central tendency and measures of dispersion. As there is no specific aspect to be compared, all aspects will be compared.

- Which particular statistic or procedure, and diagram, should we use? Why?

  Answer: The statistics or procedures that might be used to compare the various aspects are as follows:

  1. *Distribution of variables*: relative frequency or percentage tables for each value of limited variable — relative frequency or percentage histogram, relative frequency or percentage polygon, stem-and-leaf display or dotplot for each value of limited variable.

  2. *Measures of central tendency*: one-way table of means or medians — boxplot for each value of limited variable, bar chart or line diagram.

  3. *Measures of dispersion*: one-way table of ranges, interquartile ranges, standard deviations or coefficients of variation — boxplot for each value of limited variable, bar chart or line diagram.

  The choice of a particular statistic or procedure will be required for each of the three different types of statistics to be used in the analysis of this example:

  1. *Distribution of variables.* The choice is between relative frequency and percentage tables and this is a matter of personal preference. We do not recommend using frequency tables because the number of staff is likely to differ between the states and so it will be difficult to compare frequencies for different states. The most useful distribution diagram for comparing distributions is likely to be a relative frequency (proportion) or percentage polygon for each value of the limited variable because this allows you to overlay the distributions for each state and thereby compare states. Distribution diagrams that present frequencies, such as stem-and-leaf displays and dotplots, make it difficult to compare the states.

  2. *Measures of central tendency.* Whether you use means or medians depends on whether the distribution of the data is symmetric or skew. A bar chart would be used to illustrate the differences because the limited variable is nominal.

  3. *Measures of dispersion.* Ranges are inappropriate as they have severe disadvantages. Coefficients of variation would not apply either, as they are a special purpose measure, mostly used when the largest observed value is at least 2 or 3 times the smallest observed value; this is unlikely in this example. Whether you use interquartile ranges or standard deviations depends on whether the data is symmetric or skew.

  Another option is to illustrate the measures of central tendency and dispersion using boxplots.

EXAMPLE 13.5   MONITORING AUTOMATIC TELLER MACHINE OPERATION

A bank division responsible for the operation of the bank's automatic teller machines maintains a record of the total amount of time that machines are inoperative each week. This data is to be used to monitor the ongoing performance of the bank's machines.

- What is the question to be investigated (including the group to which the conclusions apply)?
  Answer: The question to be investigated is: what pattern is evident, from week to week, in the total time that the bank's automatic teller machines are inoperative?

- What variable(s) are we concerned with here?
  Answer: Total time inoperative and *Week.*

- What type of variable(s) are they?
  Answer: They are both unrestricted variables.

- Which major category of statistical procedures applies here? Why?
  Answer: Descriptive summaries, because a census has been conducted.

- What type of statistic should we use, given the question to be investigated and the variables involved?
  Answer: Time series.

- Which particular statistic or procedure, and diagram, should we use? Why?
  Answer: The observed series with a line diagram, as this will serve to monitor the performance each week. However, you could also smooth the series to separate irregular movements from the other movements. There is unlikely to be seasonal movements so deseasonalisation is not required.

EXAMPLE 13.6   COMPUTER PRICES

A computer magazine wants to survey the retail price of computers at computer equipment retailers, electrical appliance retailers, electronics equipment retailers and department stores in a city. A list of all the retailers of the types to be surveyed is obtained from the city's business telephone book. A particular configuration of hardware and software is nominated as the standard system for an IBM personal computer, an IBM compatible personal computer and a Macintosh system. Each store in the list is to be contacted by telephone and asked to quote for the standard systems they sell. The magazine wants to investigate how the typical prices for the nominated systems are affected by the type of system and the type of store in the city surveyed.

- What is the question to be investigated (including the group to which the conclusions apply)?
  Answer: The question to be investigated is: how are the typical prices for the nominated systems affected by the type of system and the type of store in the city surveyed?

- What variable(s) are we concerned with here?
  Answer: Computer price, Type of computer and *Type of store.*

- What type of variable(s) are they?
  Answer: Computer price is an unrestricted variable and *Type of computer* and *Type of store* are both limited variables.

- Which major category of statistical procedures applies here? Why?
  Answer: Descriptive summaries, because a census is to be conducted.

- What type of statistic should you use, given the question to be investigated and the variables involved?
  Answer: Measure of central tendency.

- Which particular statistic or procedure, and diagram, should we use? Why?
  Answer: Two-way table of means or medians with a bar chart, as these measures of central tendency will reflect the differences in typical prices for the combinations of the two limited variables. Whether you use means or medians depends on whether the data is symmetric or skew. A bar chart would be used to illustrate the differences because both limited variables are nominal. Alternatively, the differences in typical price could be illustrated using a boxplot for each combination of values of the limited variables, although this would also include information on the dispersion of the prices.

EXAMPLE 13.6   COMPUTER PRICES (continued)

Suppose the magazine decided to examine another aspect of computer prices: how the variability of prices for the nominated systems is affected by the type of system and the type of store in the city surveyed. What technique would be appropriate for this? Note that the variables have not changed — they are still *Computer price, Type of computer* and *Type of store* and their types are as previously nominated. What has changed is the question to be investigated.

- What is the question to be investigated (including the group to which the conclusions apply)?
  Answer: The question to be investigated is: how is the variability of prices for the nominated systems affected by the type of system and the type of store in the city surveyed?

- What variable(s) are we concerned with here?
  Answer: See above.

- What type of variable(s) are they?
  Answer: See above.

- Which major category of statistical procedures applies here? Why?
  Answer: Descriptive summaries, because a census is to be conducted.

- What type of statistic should we use, given the question to be investigated and the variables involved?
  Answer: Measure of dispersion.

- Which particular statistic or procedure, and diagram, should you use? Why?
  Answer: A two-way table of ranges, interquartile ranges, standard deviations or coefficients of variation, because measures of dispersion are required to measure the variability in the *Computer price*. Of the measures available, ranges are inappropriate as they have severe disadvantages.

Coefficients of variation should not be used either as they are a special purpose measure, mostly used when the largest observed value is at least 2 or 3 times the smallest observed value; this is unlikely in this example. Whether you use interquartile ranges or standard deviations depends on whether the data is symmetric or skew. You could also use boxplots of *Computer price* for each combination of *Type of computer* and *Type of store* to illustrate the differences in price variability.

Example 13.6, *Computer prices,* demonstrates how the question to be investigated influences which type of statistic will be used. Comparing examples 13.1, *Student preferences for teamwork,* 13.3, *Staff advancement,* and 13.4, *Employee age,* will show how the type of variable influences which type of statistic will be used. All three of these examples are based on two variables and the basic problem is to examine the relationship between the values of the two variables. However, the type of variables differs for each example. Example 13.3, *Staff advancement,* is based on two unrestricted variables, example 13.4, *Employee age,* is based on an unrestricted and a limited variable, and example 13.1, *Student preferences for teamwork,* is based on two limited variables.

When choosing which descriptive summary to use for a particular situation, a table and a diagram are usually available for illustrating the conclusions drawn from the data. In the examples we specified both; however, you would usually present only one as either one conveys essentially the same information. The difference between tables and diagrams is that tables summarise the information in a detailed, precise form whereas diagrams give a more general, overall picture of the information. Whether you decide to use a table or a diagram depends on how important it is to provide detailed information, which means sacrificing the ease with which the overall results can be appreciated. In some instances, you may decide that both the detailed information (table) and the overall picture (diagram) are necessary. This should be the exception rather than the rule.

13.2 Chapter summary

Early in the chapter we presented a summary of the descriptive summaries, describing in detail the statistical procedures appropriate for the various combinations of variable types. The procedures appropriate for a particular combination are grouped according to the types of statistics they represent. The choice of a descriptive summary, using a series of standard questions, was demonstrated for a set of examples that require some descriptive summary for their analysis. The standard questions involve determining the question to be investigated and the variables involved. This information was used to identify the major category of statistical procedures, the type of statistic and the combination of variable types. Then the particular statistical procedure can be obtained from the summary, although you might have to consider the behaviour of the data before deciding exactly which procedure to follow.

13.3 Key terms

- descriptive summaries
- distribution of variables
- fitted line
- index number
- interval/ratio variable
- limited variable
- measures of association
- measure of central tendency
- measure of dispersion

- nominal variable
- ordinal variable
- question to be investigated
- range of values
- single value
- time series
- type of statistic
- unrestricted variable
- variable

13.4 Exercises

13.1 As a result of the increase in the number of regional shopping centres, many stores in the central business district of a large city have had greatly reduced turnovers. A large department store decided to increase its advertising to try to entice shoppers back to the area. The management decides to vary over several months the amount spent on advertising, recording this amount and the total amount of goods sold each week. The task is to see if advertising affects sales during this recorded period.

(a) What is the question to be investigated (including the group to which the conclusions apply)?

(b) What variable(s) are we concerned with here?

(c) What type of variable(s) are they?

(d) Which major category of statistical procedures applies here? Why?

(e) What type of statistic should we use, given the question to be investigated and the variables involved?

(f) Which particular statistic or procedure, and diagram, should we use? Why?

13.2 The manager of an electrical store believes that the cost of replacing the faulty parts of appliances that are still under guarantee has been rising at an accelerating rate. He delegates a staff member to determine the average cost of this customer service for each of the last 12 years. This data is then to be analysed to see if the manager's assessment is correct.

(a) What is the question to be investigated (including the group to which the conclusions apply)?

(b) What variable(s) are we concerned with here?

(c) What type of variable(s) are they?

(d) Which major category of statistical procedures applies here? Why?

(e) What type of statistic should we use, given the question to be investigated and the variables involved?

(f) Which particular statistic or procedure, and diagram, should we use? Why?

13.3 The Faculty of Business is investigating the employment record of its graduates from the last five years. One particular concern is to see whether the receipt of job offers depends on weighted average marks (WAM). The faculty surveyed as many of the last five years' graduates as possible to answer this question for these students. Each selected graduate was asked whether or not they received a job offer in the first three months of the year after graduating. Also, each student's WAM was classified as below 50, 50–70 or above 70.

    (a) What is the question to be investigated (including the group to which the conclusions apply)?

    (b) What variable(s) are we concerned with here?

    (c) What type of variable(s) are they?

    (d) Which major category of statistical procedures applies here? Why?

    (e) What type of statistic should we use, given the question to be investigated and the variables involved?

    (f) Which particular statistic or procedure, and diagram, should we use? Why?

13.4 As part of their quality assurance program the Quantitative Methods for Business lecturers used a survey to evaluate their current method of conducting tutorials in this course. Acting on their students' responses they decided to change the format for the coming semester. Students would be given a choice between a supervised tutorial in the PC pools, a traditional tutorial in a classroom, or a self-tested tutorial on a computer at a time that suited them. The options that resulted in the highest average percentage in the final examination would be offered in subsequent semesters.

    (a) What is the question to be investigated (including the group to which the conclusions apply)?

    (b) What variable(s) are we concerned with here?

    (c) What type of variable(s) are they?

    (d) Which major category of statistical procedures applies here? Why?

    (e) What type of statistic should we use, given the question to be investigated and the variables involved?

    (f) Which particular statistic or procedure, and diagram, should we use? Why?

13.5 A national accountancy firm is trying to decide whether to purchase a maintenance contract for its new laser printer. It believes that maintenance expense should be related to usage and the firm has collected information on weekly hours of use and annual maintenance expenses of its printers for the past year. It expects to operate the new printer for a minimum of 35 hours per week and wants to compute last year's typical annual maintenance for a printer used for 35 hours per week.

    (a) What is the question to be investigated (including the group to which the conclusions apply)?

    (b) What variable(s) are we concerned with here?

    (c) What type of variable(s) are they?

    (d) Which major category of statistical procedures applies here? Why?

(e) What type of statistic should we use, given the question to be investigated and the variables involved?

(f) Which particular statistic or procedure, and diagram, should we use? Why?

13.6 A new citrus alcoholic beverage has been launched in Adelaide as an alternative to beer. The product has been a runaway success and the company is preparing to expand into other markets. It wants to study the effectiveness of different ways of advertising its product, and surveys 400 hundred people who buy the beverage at the retail outlet selling the most product. Each customer is asked whether they have been introduced to the product: through a friend; by advertisements on television; by advertisements on radio; or in the printed media. Is there any evidence to suggest that, for these customers, the methods of advertising are equally effective?

(a) What is the question to be investigated (including the group to which the conclusions apply)?

(b) What variable(s) are we concerned with here?

(c) What type of variable(s) are they?

(d) Which major category of statistical procedures applies here? Why?

(e) What type of statistic should we use, given the question to be investigated and the variables involved?

(f) Which particular statistic or procedure, and diagram, should we use? Why?

13.7 A company that produces domestic heating and cooling systems wishes to anticipate next year's demands for their product. It examines the records of monthly sales to gauge the fluctuations in demand over a 5-year period.

(a) What is the question to be investigated (including the group to which the conclusions apply)?

(b) What variable(s) are we concerned with here?

(c) What type of variable(s) are they?

(d) Which major category of statistical procedures applies here? Why?

(e) What type of statistic should we use, given the question to be investigated and the variables involved?

(f) Which particular statistic or procedure, and diagram, should we use? Why?

13.8 A company makes a Workcover investigation and records for all claims made over the last three months, the amount of the claim, the sex of the person making the claim, and the classification of the employee. The task is to see if the amount of a claim differs between claimants of each sex and levels of classification, for this set of claims.

(a) What is the question to be investigated (including the group to which the conclusions apply)?

(b) What variable(s) are we concerned with here?

(c) What type of variable(s) are they?

(d) Which major category of statistical procedures applies here? Why?

(e) What type of statistic should we use, given the question to be investigated and the variables involved?

(f) Which particular statistic or procedure, and diagram, should we use? Why?

13.9   The owner of a small business is anxious to set up an investment fund to provide a regular income for his retirement. He examines the return of six companies for the past five years. While all the companies appear to have returned the same average amount in dividends, his final decision will depend on which share portfolio gave the most steady return.

(a) What is the question to be investigated (including the group to which the conclusions apply)?

(b) What variable(s) are we concerned with here?

(c) What type of variable(s) are they?

(d) Which major category of statistical procedures applies here? Why?

(e) What type of statistic should we use, given the question to be investigated and the variables involved?

(f) Which particular statistic or procedure, and diagram, should we use? Why?

13.10 The hours of retail trading are to be extended in metropolitan Adelaide to include Friday nights. Critics of this change maintain that the average weekly household expenditure will remain the same, and that people will simply change their shopping day. A major retailer decided to see if this claim held at three of its branches for the three weeks before and the three weeks after the introduction of the extended hours. The weekly sales of each branch were recorded for this period.

(a) What is the question to be investigated (including the group to which the conclusions apply)?

(b) What variable(s) are we concerned with here?

(c) What type of variable(s) are they?

(d) Which major category of statistical procedures applies here? Why?

(e) What type of statistic should we use, given the question to be investigated and the variables involved?

(f) Which particular statistic or procedure, and diagram, should we use? Why?

13.11 The managing partner of a large accountancy firm is preparing a report for the monthly partners' meeting where the budget for the next year will be decided. She is anxious to prepare a submission proposing that more funds be set aside for the firm's daily running costs. She makes a list of the annual expenses over the past five years for each of the following items: the lease of the premises; the purchase and depreciation of office furniture, computing and other office equipment; insurance; power; telephone; general consumables; postage; motor vehicle; and office cleaning. She also records costs incurred by staff salaries, superannuation, work cover levy, and hiring temporary staff.

Although the partner is concerned with the actual cost of these items, her main aim is to examine the overall cost changes during the past five years.

(a) What is the question to be investigated (including the group to which the conclusions apply)?
(b) What variable(s) are we concerned with here?
(c) What type of variable(s) are they?
(d) Which major category of statistical procedures applies here? Why?
(e) What type of statistic should be used, given the question to be investigated and the variables involved?
(f) Which particular statistic or procedure, and diagram, should we use? Why?

PART IV

ESTIMATION
PROCEDURES

LEARNING OBJECTIVES

The learning objectives of this introduction to Part IV are:
- to understand the process underlying statistical inference;
- to be aware of the basic terminology of statistical inference;
- to know the two branches of statistical inference and when they can be applied.

We now turn to the first branch of the very important topic of statistical inference. **Statistical inference** is concerned with using information obtained from a **sample** to draw conclusions about the **population**. Statistical inference is comprised of two branches:

1. **estimation procedures** for estimating population values from a sample of the population;
2. **hypothesis tests** for answering questions about the population by using a sample from it; the questions must have only two possible answers.

This is quite different from what was said about descriptive summaries, where we were interested in drawing conclusions only about the particular set of individuals measured. For descriptive summaries, the observations represent the whole population being investigated and we can be 100% certain of any conclusions we draw from them. If a census has been taken, then only descriptive summaries are appropriate, and statistical inference cannot be applied.

On the other hand, any inference drawn about the population from a sample inevitably involves some uncertainty because our information about the population is not complete — we have only the information provided by the sample. The role of statistical inference is to incorporate an assessment of this uncertainty with our conclusions. However, in performing statistical inference procedures, the first step is to obtain the corresponding descriptive summary to get an impression of the results indicated by the data.

EXAMPLE IV.1   SUPPORT FOR THE CURRENT MEMBER

Suppose the office of the Member of Parliament for a state electorate organised a survey to ascertain the level of support for that member, and takes a simple random sample of 200 voters from the electorate's 17 356 registered voters. Of the 200 sampled voters, 86 declare support for the current Member of Parliament; that is, 43% would vote for her. Note that this example involves one limited variable: *Vote for current member*, which takes two values, yes and no. The data represents primary data for the member's office, and some questions that might be investigated by using it are as follows:

- What proportion of voters interviewed would vote for the member?

- What proportion of voters in the electorate would vote for the member?

- Does the proportion of the electorate who would vote for the member differ from 52%?

The first question can be answered by using descriptive summaries — it is concerned with the particular set of people interviewed. As just one limited variable is involved here, we know from part III, *Descriptive summaries of data*, that the descriptive summary in this case is the one-way summary table containing the percentages of those who would and would not vote for the member. In this case, the information in the one-way summary table can be reduced to a single value, the proportion or percentage who would vote for the member. It is an unequivocal fact: 43% of those interviewed would vote for the member.

The second question should be answered by using a confidence interval — the question requires estimating from a sample of 200 the support for the member among the whole population of 17 356 voters. In this case, the quantity of interest is unknown. The sample is used to obtain some idea of the unknown population value.

The third question should be answered by applying a hypothesis test to the sample of 200. The question asked has only two possible answers and it concerns the population. Again, the sample is used to obtain some idea of the answer to the question about the population.

Suppose the second question is the one to be investigated in this example: what proportion of the voters in the electorate would vote for the current member? We found that 43% of the sampled voters supported the member. But what is the proportion in the population? We are uncertain about this. The information from our sample shows that the population value is likely to be about 43%, but not necessarily exactly that value. How close to 43% is the population value likely to be? The statistical inference procedure for this situation leads us to conclude that support in the population could in fact be between 36% and 50%. We can now see what degree of uncertainty we have about the population value. Consequently, we can make a more informed decision about the extent of the support for the current member because now we can take this uncertainty into account. Ignoring the uncertainty and assuming the population value is 43% may well lead us to make the wrong conclusion.

EXAMPLE IV.2   HOUSE PRICES IN THREE LOCALITIES
Example 8.1, *House prices in three localities*, involves the prices paid for all residences in three local government areas over a 12-month period. We want to compare the prices paid for these residences over that period. Because the data represents a census of the target population, the procedures of statistical inference do not apply. The differences in the average prices are precisely those reported in chapter 8, *Descriptive summaries for one unrestricted variable and some limited variables.*

Questions that involve estimation are the subject of this part; hypothesis tests are discussed in part V, *Hypothesis tests*. However, before dealing with particular inference procedures, we outline the general process of statistical inference, as follows.

The basis of statistical inference

The basic aim of statistical inference is to enable you to reach conclusions in uncertain circumstances — the uncertainty is due to the fact that only a partial observation of a population can be made with a sample. Statistical inference techniques help you to make appropriate business decisions in these conditions because the uncertainty is assessed, not just ignored.

Statistical inference involves the following process, which is illustrated in figure IV.1:

1. *Specify the parameter of interest:* the **parameter** is a numeric value calculated from the values of the observed variable for all members of the population.
2. *Set up a probability model for the situation:* the **probability model** is a *representation* of the relative frequencies with which the values of the variable occur in the population.
3. *Obtain a sample and compute a statistic related to the parameter:* the **statistic** is a numeric value calculated from the observed values of the variable for the members of the sample only.
4. *Derive the sampling distribution of the statistic:* The **sampling distribution** of a statistic gives the probability with which values of the statistic will occur when a population is repeatedly sampled; the statistic is computed, for each sample, from the values of the variable that is measured. In deriving the sampling distribution, one assumption we make is that the probability model adequately describes the population distribution of the values of the variable.

5. *Make inference about the parameter:* Use the sampling distribution of the statistic, under the probability model, to quantify the uncertainty in inferences or conclusions about the parameter.

So the key elements of this process are that we must rely on a sample of the population to draw our conclusions about the entire population and this imposes an element of uncertainty on our conclusions. The sampling distribution, which is based on a probability model, is used to assess this uncertainty.

The probability model is a model for the relative frequencies with which the values of the variable occur in the population. In this book, **probability** is used to mean the relative frequency of the values of a variable for a very large population. Consequently, the probability model specifies the probabilities or relative frequencies of all possible values of the variable. Just like any model, such as a wind tunnel for testing aircraft design, it is only a portrayal of a real situation — a portrayal close enough, we hope, to use as a basis for statistical inference.

Once the probability model and statistic have been nominated, the sampling distribution is derived mathematically; these mathematical derivations are outside the scope of this book, but note that they are well-established for the statistics we are concerned with.

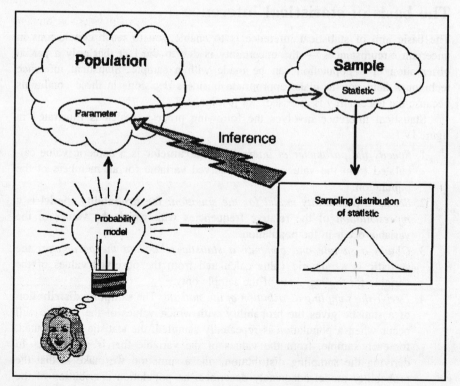

Figure IV.1 The process underlying statistical inference

The important feature of the sampling distribution of a statistic, for statistical inference, is that it allows us to quantify the probability with which values of the statistic will be obtained. For example, it enables us to determine which range will include most, say 95%, of the values of a statistic. But this will only be true if the sampling distribution describes the distribution of the nominated statistic, and this required that the **assumptions** made in deriving the sampling distribution be satisfied. These assumptions can be divided as follows:

1. a particular probability model represents the population distribution of the variable;
2. other validating assumptions made in deriving the sampling distribution of the nominated statistic.

For each inference procedure, we identify a set of **conditions** that specify the circumstances that must apply to a situation if these assumptions are to be met.

We now provide an overview of the parameters, statistics, probability models and sampling distributions presented in the following chapters.

Parameters versus statistics

For statistical inference it is important to distinguish between values computed from a sample and those from the population. This is done by using the two different terms introduced above: parameter and statistic. To distinguish further between parameters and statistics, we usually use Greek alphabet letters as symbols for parameters and Roman alphabet letters as symbols for statistics. Table IV.1 shows the symbols used for commonly occurring parameters and statistics.

Table IV.1   Symbols for parameters and statistics

Measure	Statistic	Parameter	
Proportion	p	π	(pi)
Mean	$\bar{y}$	μ	(mu)
Standard deviation	s	σ	(sigma)
Correlation coefficient	r	ρ	(rho)
Straight line intercept	b_0	β_0	(beta 0)
Straight line slope	b_1	β_1	(beta 1)

Probability models

As stated above, probability models are models for the relative frequencies of the values of the variable in the population. Many statistical inference procedures, including all those presented in this book, are based on one of the following two probability models:

Limited-variable probability model: The variable has k possible values, and the ith value occurs in the population with probability π_i with $0 \leq \pi_i \leq 1$ and

$$\sum_{i=1}^{k} \pi_i = 1.$$

Normal probability model: A continuous variable is measured; its values in the population follow the normal distribution.

These probability models can be expressed as mathematical equations known as **probability distribution functions**.

In general, the limited-variable probability model is used when limited variables have been observed. A special case of the limited-variable probability model occurs when the variable takes only two possible values, each occurring with probability π and $1 - \pi$, respectively.

On the other hand, the normal probability model is used when an unrestricted variable has been observed and the shape of the distribution for values of the variable for the whole population can be described as approximately symmetric and bell-shaped, as in figure IV.2. The peak of this distribution corresponds to the value of the population mean, μ, and the spread is specified by the population standard deviation, σ. If the distribution or pattern of the values in the population does not have this shape, the normal probability model cannot be used. There are other distributions for continuous variables which allow non-normal shapes — for example, distributions that are skew. These alternative distributions are outside the scope of this book.

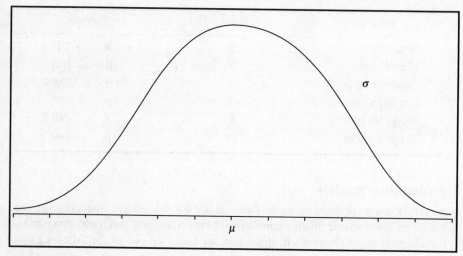

Figure IV.2 Normal probability model

The properties of all probability models for continuous variables are: all probabilities must be greater than or equal to zero; and the total area under the curve for a probability model must be one. The normal distribution has these properties. Generally, the probability model is not used directly but as a basis for obtaining the sampling distribution of a statistic.

EXAMPLE IV.3   PARTY SUPPORT

Suppose that at the last state election the only candidates who are standing in a particular electorate are from the Liberal, Labor and Democrat parties. A voter is selected and asked to nominate which party they support. The variable being measured is *Party of supported candidate*, a limited variable that takes three values.

A probability model appropriate for this variable is the following limited-variable probability model:

- the population proportion supporting the Liberal party is π_1;
- the population proportion supporting the Labor party is π_2;
- the population proportion supporting the Democrat party is π_3;
- each of π_1, π_2 and π_3 must be between zero and one, inclusive; and
- it must be that $\pi_1 + \pi_2 + \pi_3 = 1$.

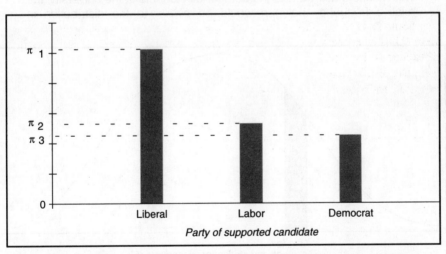

Figure IV.3   Limited-variable probability model for *party of supported candidate*

Figure IV.3 presents a diagram of this probability model; each column in the diagram has a height equal to the value of the corresponding parameter. This rather simple model represents the population relative frequencies of the values of the variable *Party of supported candidate*. If the values for the population were available, it could be used to predict the outcomes of observations. For example, how likely is it that our selected voter will support the Liberal party? The answer is π_1. Of course, when we use statistical inference procedures, the values for the population are not available, so the values of the parameters π_1, π_2 and π_3 are unknown. The aim of statistical inference is to obtain estimates of such parameters.

EXAMPLE IV.4 STUDENT EXPENDITURE

AusStudent, the government body that distributes tertiary student allowances, has decided to survey students at a major Australian university to determine how much students at the university typically spend on textbooks and stationery. AusStudent takes a simple random sample of 25 of the 11 200 students at the university, and at the end of the first month of the semester AusStudent asks the selected students to record how much they spent on textbooks and stationery during this period.

The question to be investigated is: what amount do students at a major Australian university typically spend on textbooks and stationery in the first month of the semester? The variable involved is *Textbook and stationery expenditure*, an unrestricted variable.

A probability model we could use for this variable is the normal probability model; that is, we will assume that the normal distribution approximately represents the population distribution of the variable. This means that if we had the data for all students at the university, the relative frequency polygon would be *similar* to the distribution in figure IV.4.

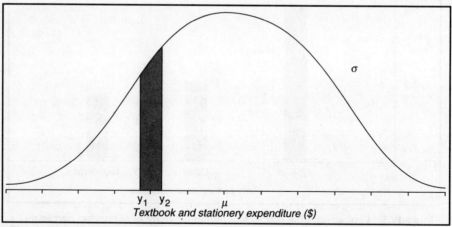

Figure IV.4   Normal probability model for *Textbook and stationery expenditure*

If the parameter values were available, we could use this distribution to ascertain the proportion of observational units in the population whose values for the variable fall in a specified range. For example, to obtain the proportion of students with *Textbook and stationery expenditure* between values y_1 and y_2, find the area under the curve above this range; that is, we require the area of the shaded region in figure IV.4. The computation of areas under the normal curve is very complicated, but can be conveniently done with computers.

However, when we use statistical inference procedures, the parameter values are not available, so the values of the population mean, μ, and the population standard deviation, σ, are unknown. Again, the aim of statistical inference is to obtain estimates of such parameters.

Sampling distributions

As discussed above, the sampling distribution shows the pattern or distribution of values of the statistic. It supplies the same information we would obtain from a relative frequency polygon based on values of the statistic from a very large number of samples. There are many sampling distributions in use, but the sampling distributions we are concerned with in this book are listed in table IV.2, together with the type of variable from which the statistics are calculated.

Table IV.2   Sampling distributions

Type of variable	Sampling distribution
Limited	Normal
	χ^2
Unrestricted	t
	F

Note the unusual dual role of the normal distribution. It is used as a probability model for unrestricted variables and will be used as the sampling distribution of statistics computed from limited variables.

EXAMPLE IV.3   PARTY SUPPORT (continued)
As already noted, the parameters of the probability model we used are unknown. If we want to gain some idea of the value of the population proportion, we have two options:
1. take a census of all voters in the electorate and determine the exact values of the parameters; or
2. take a sample of the voters and gain some indication of the values of the parameters.
If there are insufficient resources to take a census, we have no choice but to take a sample. What can be said about the proportions computed from a sample of, say, 200 voters? It is intuitively obvious that the sample proportions for each party are unlikely to be exactly equal to the population proportions. Further, a second sample of 200 voters, which is unlikely to include more than a few voters from the first sample, will almost certainly yield sample proportions that differ from the first sample.
More precisely, we can use mathematics to show that if many samples of the same size are taken and the proportions are computed from each, the sample proportion for any one of the parties will be

normally distributed with mean π_i and spread measured by the standard error $\sigma_p = \sqrt{\pi_i(1 - \pi_i)/n}$. The sampling distribution for one p_i, shown in figure IV.5, gives the relative frequencies of the various values of p_i in a large number of repeated samples.

If you noticed that the sampling distribution depends on the unknown π_i you may have concluded that this would prohibit its use. However, we can overcome this difficulty if we want to use the sampling distribution, and this is explained in chapter 14, *Estimation for limited variables*.

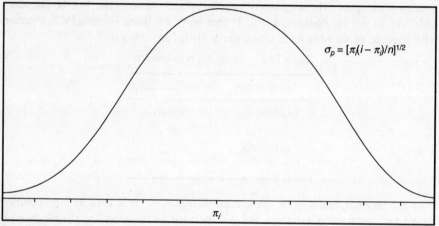

$$\sigma_p = [\pi_i(i - \pi_i)/n]^{1/2}$$

π_i

Figure IV.5 Sampling distribution of p_i

Interval and point estimates

For estimating a parameter, one obvious approach is to use the statistic as the 'best guess' for the population value. The statistic is called the **point estimate** of the corresponding parameter. This is satisfactory as far as it goes. However, as mentioned in the previous section, this does not incorporate any of the uncertainty in our estimate of the parameter. It seems reasonable to ask: what would be a feasible range of values for the population value? That is, rather than settle for a single, point estimate, an interval estimate is desirable and so this is what we propose to use. An **interval estimate** is a continuous range of feasible values for the population value of a quantity. There are very many interval estimates available, and these are comprehensively covered in Hahn and Meeker (1991). In this book we concentrate on those that are most useful.

Summary

The basic aim of statistical inference is to enable us to reach conclusions in the face of uncertain circumstances, the uncertainty due to the fact that a sample provides incomplete infrmation about the population.

Statistical inference techniques leads to more informed business decisions because the uncertainty is assessed, not ignored. Statistical inference involves the following steps:

1. Specify the parameter of interest.
2. Set up a probability model for the situation.
3. Obtain a sample and compute a statistic related to the parameter.
4. Derive the sampling distribution of the statistic.
5. Make inference about the parameter from the sampling distribution.

The probability model represents the population distribution of values of the observed variable. Many statistical inference procedures, including all those presented in this book, are based on either the limited-variable probability model or the normal probability model. The sampling distribution of the nominated statistic gives the probability with which values of the statistic will occur when the population is repeatedly sampled. In deriving this sampling distribution, assumptions have to be made and these can be divided as follows: the probability model represents the population distribution of the variable; and other validating assumptions. Consequently, all statistical inference procedures involve conditions that must be met if these assumptions are to hold and valid conclusions are to be obtained from them.

The two branches of statistical inference are estimation procedures and hypothesis tests. In estimation procedures, the value of a parameter is estimated. In hypothesis tests, a question is asked about the parameter and the answer to the question must be either yes or no.

In estimation procedures, interval estimates are preferred to point estimates because interval estimates incorporate an assessment of the uncertainty involved in observing only a sample of the population.

Key terms

- **assumptions**
- **conditions**
- **estimation procedures**
- **hypothesis tests**
- **interval estimate**
- **limited-variable probability model**
- **normal probability model**
- **parameter**
- **point estimate**
- **population**
- **probability**
- **probability distribution function**
- **probability model**
- **sample**
- **sampling distribution**
- **statistic**
- **statistical inference**

## CHAPTER 14

ESTIMATION FOR LIMITED VARIABLES

L E A R N I N G   O B J E C T I V E S

The learning objectives of this chapter are:

- to know when to apply, how to calculate and how to interpret the results of the confidence interval for the population proportion;
- to know the conditions required for the interval to be valid and how to determine when they are met;
- to be able to determine the sample size to give a prescribed level of precision in estimating the population proportion.

The following extract from the *Summary of procedures based on combinations of variable types* in part VI gives an overview of the estimation procedures covered in this chapter.

1. *One or two limited variable(s)*
   - **Distribution of variables**: confidence interval for the population proportion.
2. *One unrestricted variable or one unrestricted variable with one or two limited variable(s)*
3. *Two unrestricted variables*

As outlined in the objectives, this chapter covers the confidence interval for the population proportion. From the extract, it seems that the confidence interval technique applies when there are one or more limited variables and the results have been summarised in a **distribution table** containing **proportions**. This is true, although strictly speaking the technique applies to situations in which the measured variable is a limited variable with only two values. As explained in more detail in section 14.1.3, *Application to a multivalued,* *limited variable*, and 14.1.4, *Application to two limited variables*, applying the technique to a multivalued limited variable or to two limited variables involves taking just one proportion at a time. Then the remaining proportions are regarded as having been combined into a single proportion that equals one minus the single proportion. Further, since an inference procedure is involved, we must have taken a sample and the question to be investigated must be about the population and *not* confined to the sample.

In the case of a two-valued limited variable, the two values should be mutually exclusive and collectively exhaustive. By **mutually exclusive values** we mean that an observational unit can take only one of the two values. **Collectively exhaustive values** means that no more than the two values are possible. Taken together, the two conditions specify that the variable is a **well-defined limited variable**: each observational unit in the population can be unambiguously classified as taking one or the other of the only two possible values for the variable.

Since a limited variable with two values is the simplest variable possible, you might expect such variables to be rather uncommon. However, many questions involve a two-valued, limited variable: What proportion of rolls of a die will a five result in? What proportion of students are female? What proportion of children in a school become ill at least once during winter? What proportion of motor accidents involve drink-driving?

Note that for all these examples, each observed entity is classified into one of two categories that are mutually exclusive (one or the other) and collectively exhaustive (no other possibilities).

14.1 Confidence interval for the population proportion

Before we proceed to estimation procedures, we shall use descriptive summaries to make a preliminary examination of the data. The descriptive summary for data such as we are concerned with here is either a **one-way summary table** or a **contingency table** containing proportions or percentages.

EXAMPLE 14.1   SUPPORT FOR THE CURRENT MEMBER

In example IV.1, *Support for the current member*, a state Member of Parliament's office takes a simple random sample of 200 voters from its electorate of 17 356 registered voters. The survey was organised to assess the level of support for the electorate's member. The question to be investigated here is: what proportion of voters in the electorate would vote for the current member? As already noted, this example involves one limited variable: *Vote for current member* that takes two values, yes and no.

Of the 200 sampled voters, 86 say they would vote for the current Member of Parliament. That is, 43% would vote for her. These results are summarised in the one-way summary table in table 14.1 and, of the two proportions in this table, we are most interested in the proportion that would vote for the member.

Table 14.1   One-way summary table for voter survey

Vote for current member	Percentage
Yes	43
No	57
	(n = 200)

The most obvious approach to answering the question to be investigated is to use the sample statistic as an estimate of the population parameter. We can infer that the support for the member is 43%, taking $p = 0.43$ as our *point estimate* of the population value π; p provides us with a single value to estimate the population proportion. This is how such information is usually reported in Australia. However, an interval estimate gives us a more realistic assessment of support for the member. We should not assume that support in the whole electorate is exactly equal to the sample value.

The confidence interval for the population proportion is an interval estimate that provides us with a measure of the uncertainty of our estimate of the proportion. In calculating the confidence interval for the population proportion, we need to distinguish between two situations: (1) where the size of the population, N, is much larger than the sample size, n; (2) where it is not much larger. Statisticians describe the population as infinite or finite: a population is **infinite** if the population is very much larger than the sample.

14.1.1   Population much larger than sample ($N > 20n$)

A **confidence interval ($100\gamma\%$) for the population proportion** gives us the range that will include the population proportion $100\gamma\%$ of the time. This means that in $100\gamma\%$ of samples, the computed confidence interval will include the *population proportion, π*. $100\gamma\%$ is called the **confidence level**.

The confidence interval ($100\gamma\%$) for the population proportion is given by:

Confidence interval ($100\gamma\%$) for $\pi = (p - z_T \times s_p, p + z_T \times s_p)$

where p is the *sample proportion*;

z_T is the **theoretical value for the standard normal distribution** corresponding to $100\gamma\%$; $100\gamma\%$ of the values for a standard normal distribution occur between $-z_T$ and z_T (for further explanation see below);

s_p is called the **standard error** of the sample proportion (it measures the variability of the sample proportion) and it is equal to:

$$\sqrt{\frac{p(1 - p)}{n}}$$

Note that $z_T \times s_p$, the part of the formula to the right of the plus and minus signs, is called the **confidence interval bound**. The bound indicates the **precision** with which the proportion has been estimated. By incorporating the formula for the bound into that for the confidence interval, we obtain the following alternative expression for the confidence interval, involving quantities that have to be obtained directly:

$$\text{Confidence interval } (100\gamma\%) \text{ for } \pi = \left(p - z_T \times \sqrt{\frac{p(1-p)}{n}}, \quad p + z_T \times \sqrt{\frac{p(1-p)}{n}} \right)$$

A commonly used value for $100\gamma\%$ is 95%, in which case we can be 95% confident that the population proportion is in the computed range. Other values used for $100\gamma\%$ include 90%, 99% and 99.9%.

EXAMPLE 14.1   SUPPORT FOR THE CURRENT MEMBER (continued)

Having obtained our sample, we want to determine the range that we can be 95% confident will include the proportion of all voters in the electorate who support the current member. That is, the 95% confidence interval for the population proportion is appropriate. This requires n, p and z_T: the values for n and p for the sample are 200 and 0.43 respectively; the value of z_T for 95%, obtained by using a computer, is 1.96. So the calculation of the 95% confidence interval for the population proceeds as follows:

Confidence interval (95%) for π

$$= \left(0.43 - 1.96\sqrt{\frac{0.43 \times 0.57}{200}}, 0.43 + 1.96\sqrt{\frac{0.43 \times 0.57}{200}} \right)$$
$$= (0.43 - 0.0686, 0.43 + 0.0686)$$
$$= (0.36, 0.50)$$

Thus, our confidence interval tells us that we can be 95% confident that the true population proportion is somewhere between 0.36 and 0.50. Further, the precision with which the true population proportion is estimated is ±0.07.

Logic behind the confidence interval formula

This subsection explains why it can be said that the confidence interval will include the population mean $100\gamma\%$ of the time. The theoretical value, z_T, comes from the standard normal distribution. This is because, as discussed in the introduction to part IV, *Estimation procedures*, the normal distribution is the sampling distribution of the statistic p. The **standard normal distribution** is a normal distribution with mean zero and a standard deviation of one. This distribution is a special normal distribution that applies to a normally distributed variable that has been standardised according to the method described in section 8.3, *Standardising data*. The value of z_T used to calculate the confidence interval is the value of z_T such that $100\gamma\%$ of the values from a standard normal distribution fall in the range $(-z_T, z_T)$. Putting it another way, the area under the curve above the range $(-z_T, z_T)$ for the standard normal distribution is γ.

EXAMPLE 14.1   SUPPORT FOR THE CURRENT MEMBER (continued)
The value of z_T for 95%, as previously stated, is 1.96. That is, the range from –
1.96 to 1.96 includes 95% of the values for the standard normal distribution
(see figure 14.1). Consequently, the value of z_T for a 95% confidence interval
for the population proportion will always be 1.96.

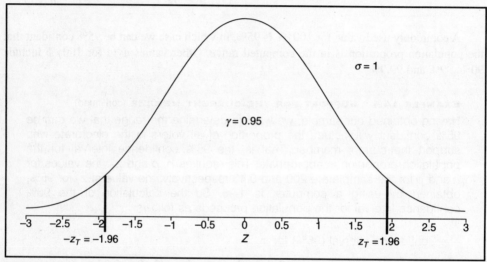

Figure 14.1   The range that includes 95% of values for the standard normal distribution

In fact z_T is the number of standard deviations above and below the mean that will
include $100\gamma\%$ of observations for any normal distribution, not just a standard normal
distribution. For example, because $z_T = 1.96$ for $\gamma = 0.95$, we can say that 95% of
observations will fall within ±1.96 (≈ ±2) standard deviations of the mean for any normal
distribution.

Now the **sampling distribution for the sample proportion** is the normal distribution
centred on π and with the standard deviation of this distribution $\sigma_p = \sqrt{\pi(1 - \pi)/n}$. So how
would you use this distribution to calculate the range that includes $100\gamma\%$ of sample
proportions? Since the sampling distribution is a normal distribution and $100\gamma\%$ of sample
proportions will be within $\pm z_T$ standard deviations of the mean for this distribution, the
range can be calculated by multiplying both $-z_T$ and z_T by σ_p and then adding π. The normal
distribution to the left in figure 14.2 illustrates this for $100\gamma\% = 95\%$, although very similar
diagrams could be presented for any other confidence level. For $100\gamma\% = 95\%$, $z_T = 1.96$
and so the range $(\pi - 1.96\sigma_p, \pi + 1.96\sigma_p)$ will include 95% of proportions when the
population is repeatedly sampled — we will refer to it as the 95% sampling range. The area
under the curve above this range is 0.95.

When it comes to calculating a confidence interval we do not know π and so we
substitute our sample value p and use $s_p = \sqrt{p(1 - p)/n}$ instead of σ_p. The confidence
interval is then obtained by multiplying both $-z_T$ and z_T by s_p and then adding p. The normal
distribution to the right in figure 14.2, which has mean p and spread s_p, illustrates this for
$100\gamma\% = 95\%$. We see that the shaded region under the righthand curve is above the range

corresponding to the computed confidence interval and its area is 0.95. Below the distributions are the confidence intervals (95%) for 20 different, random samples. The normal distribution to the right corresponds to the confidence interval for the third sample. We contend that we can be 95% confident that a confidence interval computed from a sample as just described will contain the population proportion.

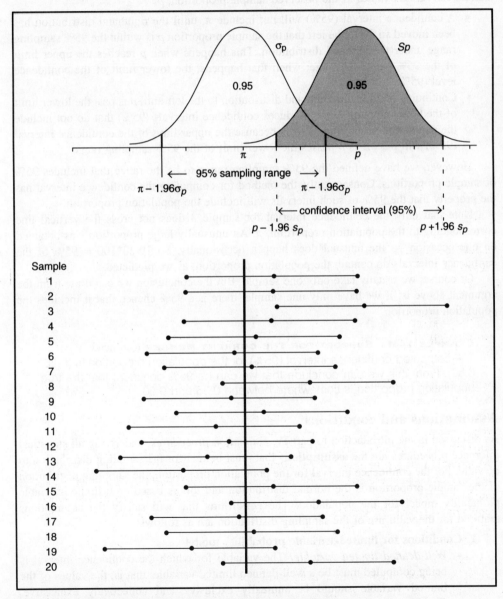

Figure 14.2 Sampling distribution and confidence intervals

To see why our claim is true we first note that, for practical purposes, s_p can be taken as equal to σ_p and so the widths of the two normal distributions are the same, as are those of the 95% sampling range and confidence interval (95%). The only difference between either the distribution or the ranges is that one is centred on π and the other on p. Now, sliding the righthand distribution horizontally demonstrates what happens to the confidence interval for various values of the observed sample proportion, p:

- A confidence interval (95%) will not include π, until the righthand distribution has been moved so far to the left that the sample proportion p is within the 95% sampling range under the lefthand distribution. This happens when p reaches the upper limit of the 95% sampling range; when that happens, the lower limit of the confidence level (95%) will be at π.
- Continuing to slide the righthand distribution to the left until p is past the lower limit of the 95% sampling range produces confidence intervals (95%) that do not include the population proportion. This is because the upper limit of the confidence interval (95%) will pass π as p passes the lower limit of the 95% sampling range.

However, we have defined the 95% sampling range to be the range that includes 95% of sample proportions. Consequently, the method for computing the confidence interval has the property that the 95% of such intervals will include the population proportion.

Note that only the confidence interval for sample 3 does not cross the vertical line corresponding to the population proportion, π. An unusually large proportion was obtained on one occasion — the unusual does happen occasionally. So $19/20*100 = 95\%$ of the confidence intervals do contain the population proportion, as we predicted.

Of course, we usually take only one sample. But the conclusion we can draw from the argument above is: if we have only one sample, there is a 95% chance that it includes the population proportion.

EXAMPLE 14.1   SUPPORT FOR THE CURRENT MEMBER (continued)
The computed confidence interval (95%) for the population proportion is (0.36, 0.50). From this we can conclude that we can be 95% confident that the true population proportion is somewhere between 0.36 and 0.50.

Assumptions and conditions

As discussed in the introduction to part IV, *Estimation procedures*, underlying all statistical inference procedures are the **assumptions** that must be met for the sampling distribution to be valid. For the confidence interval for the population proportion, the sampling distribution of the sample proportion is the normal distribution and this is based on a limited-variable probability model for the population. The **conditions** that will satisfy the assumptions required for the valid use of the sampling distribution are as follows:

1. **Conditions for limited-variable probability model**
   - *Well-defined limited variable:* The variable for which the confidence interval is being computed must be a well-defined limited variable: that is, the values of the limited variable should be mutually exclusive and collectively exhaustive. Checking that this condition is satisfied can be done by simply considering

whether the variable is limited and well-defined. Usually, there is no problem with this condition.

- *Stable population proportions:* The **stable population proportions condition** stipulates that the proportion of the population taking a particular value of the limited variable must remain stable or constant throughout the period to which the inferences are to apply. It will be met provided the population does not change during this period. So the data collection must be done quickly enough to ensure this and the inferences can be applied only while the population remains unchanged.

2. **Conditions for other validating assumptions**

- *Infinite population:* The sample should come from an effectively **infinite population**. The population can be regarded as effectively infinite if its number of individuals (N) is at least 20 times the number sampled (n); that is, if $N > 20n$.

- *Representative sample:* A **representative sample** is one that is an unbiased fraction of the original population. The methods that are likely to produce a representative sample were discussed in chapter 4, *Surveys*. We concluded that the probability sampling methods, such as simple random sampling, produce representative samples. So this condition will be met if a probability sampling method is used to select the sample. If not, one cannot guarantee that the condition will be met.

- *Independence:* The **independence condition** requires that the outcome of any observation is independent of the outcome of any other observation. This condition is difficult to check; in part, it involves ensuring that the study is conducted in such a way that each observation is made independently of the other observations.

- *Large number condition:* the **large number condition** stipulates that np is greater than or equal to five for all observed proportions. This can be checked by making sure that the number of observations for each value of the limited variable, np, is greater than or equal to five.

EXAMPLE 14.1   SUPPORT FOR THE CURRENT MEMBER (continued)

Assumptions and conditions

To assess whether our confidence interval for the proportion supporting the current member is likely to give us a true picture, we must check, as follows, the conditions under which the procedure is valid:

1. **Conditions for limited-variable probability model**

- *Well-defined limited variable:* The variable is *Vote for the current member*, which is clearly a two-valued, well-defined, limited variable, although we are not allowing for nonvoters.

- *Stable population proportions:* In this case, the proportions would not be stable if the survey was conducted over an extended period during which some voters changed their minds, because of issues that arose while the sample was being taken. There is no information indicating whether this occurred, so we will have to presume that the proportions are stable.

2. Conditions for normal other validating assumptions

- *Infinite population:* The population is effectively infinite: there are 17 356 voters in the population and this is greater than 20 × 200 = 4000.

- *Representative sample:* As the sample is random, there is no reason to expect that the sample is not representative of the population.

- *Independence:* The investigator must ensure that the observations were taken independently. Thus, we cannot allow for one person's coercion of another, which might occur if people are interviewed together. Again, we cannot tell whether or not this was the case, so we have to presume that the observations are independent.

- *Large number condition:* The large number condition is satisfied as, for the first proportion, $np = 200 \times 0.43 = 86$ and, for the second proportion, $np = 200 \times 0.57 = 114$. Note that 86 is just the number that would vote for the member and 114 is the number that would not vote for the member.

As all the conditions are met, it seems that the assumptions required to use the normal sampling distribution hold and we can validly use the confidence interval for the population proportion for this example.

14.1.2 Population not much larger than sample ($N \le 20n$)

In what has been presented so far, we have presumed that the size of the population is very large; $N > 20n$. What if the population is relatively small? This has to be taken into account in the confidence interval (and sample size) calculations. The formula for the confidence interval becomes:

Confidence interval ($100\gamma\%$) for π

$$= \left(p - z_T \times \sqrt{\frac{p(1-p)}{n}} \sqrt{\frac{N-n}{N-1}}, p + z_T \times \sqrt{\frac{p(1-p)}{n}} \sqrt{\frac{N-n}{N-1}} \right)$$

The difference between this and the previous formula is that the bound includes the **finite population correction factor**, which is equal to:

$$\sqrt{\frac{N-n}{N-1}}$$

This formula is equal to about 1 if the population size is considerably larger than the sample size. For example, for $N = 20n$ and N large enough, it can be shown that the finite population correction factor is approximately $\sqrt{19/20} = 0.9747$.

The conditions for this procedure are the same as for the infinite sample procedure, except that the infinite population condition changes to become a **finite population** condition. That is, the complete set of conditions are as follows:

1. **Conditions for limited-variable probability model**
   - *Well-defined limited variable*
   - *Stable population proportions*

2. **Conditions for other validating assumptions**
   - *Finite population*
   - *Representative sample*
   - *Independence*
   - *Large number condition*

For a population to be effectively finite, $N \leq 20n$.

14.1.3 Application to a multivalued, limited variable

The method can be applied to a multivalued (>2), well-defined, limited variable, summarised in a one-way summary table, by investigating questions that focus on only one value at a time.

EXAMPLE 14.2 HOUSEHOLD SIZE

In our survey of the *Number of children* in households, discussed in example 6, *Household size*, we summarised the data in the one-way summary table which is reproduced in table 14.2.

Table 14.2   One-way summary table for *Number of children*

Number of children	Frequency	Percentage
0	20	10
1	40	20
2	120	60
3	20	10
Total	200	($n = 200$)

Suppose we want to estimate the proportion of households in the surveyed area which have two children. That is, we focus on this one value of the limited variable. The 95% confidence interval for the population proportion is calculated as follows:

Confidence interval (95%) for π

$$= \left(0.6 - 1.96\sqrt{\frac{0.6 \times 0.4}{200}}, 0.6 + 1.96\sqrt{\frac{0.6 \times 0.4}{200}} \right)$$

$$= (0.6 - 0.0679, 0.6 + 0.0679)$$

$$= (0.53, 0.67)$$

As an exercise, check that the conditions required for the valid use of the confidence interval are met in this case.

Clearly, we could compute the confidence interval for each value of *Number of children* by concentrating on each value in turn.

14.1.4 Application to two limited variables

The method can also be applied when the data for two limited variables is summarised in a two-way contingency table.

EXAMPLE 14.3   HOUSEHOLD SIZE AND STATUS

The household survey described in example 6.2, *Household size and status*, determined not only the *Number of children* but also the *Socioeconomic status* of the household. The results of the survey were summarised in a two-way contingency table (reproduced in table 14.3) containing percentages, each of which is the percentage of all households with a particular combination of *Number of children* and *Socioeconomic status*, out of all households of that status.

Table 14.3   Column percentages for *Number of children* and *Socioeconomic status*

| Number of children | Socioeconomic status | | | |
	Low	Medium	High	Total
0	2.5	10.0	20.0	10
1	17.5	20.0	23.3	20
2	70.0	66.7	40.0	60
3	10.0	3.3	16.7	10
n	80	60	60	200

We might want to estimate, for each status, the proportion of households in the metropolitan area which have two children. The confidence interval for the low-status household is calculated as follows:

Confidence interval (95%) for π

$$= \left(0.7 - 1.96\sqrt{\frac{0.7 \times 0.3}{80}}, 0.7 + 1.96\sqrt{\frac{0.7 \times 0.3}{80}} \right)$$

$$= (0.7 - 0.1004, 0.7 + 0.1004)$$

$$= (0.60, 0.80)$$

When calculating this confidence interval, note that $n = 80$, as this is the number of observations on which the proportion is based. The confidence interval (95%) for the population proportion is 0.6667 ± 0.1193 for medium-status households and is 0.40 ± 0.1240 for high-status households. In computing these confidence intervals, $n = 60$ as this is the number of observations on which both these proportions are based.

The results, including confidence intervals (95%) for the population proportions, appear in figure 14.3. The percentage of high-status households with two children is considerably lower than for low-status and medium-status households; there is little difference between the last two status groups as far as the proportion with two children is concerned. We reach the conclusion by observing that most of the confidence intervals for low and medium status overlap.

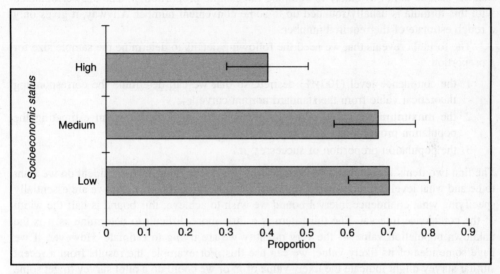

Note: the lines drawn on each bar correspond to the confidence interval (95%) for the population proportion corresponding to that bar.

Figure 14.3 Proportions of households with two children

However, a confidence interval cannot be computed for the proportion of low-status households with no children; nor can it be computed for medium-status households with three children. The problem is that the large number condition is not satisfied for these two combinations as there are only two observations for both of them.

14.2 Sample size determination for a proportion

The examples discussed so far have always included the sample size. However, as suggested in chapter 4, *Surveys*, the sample size must be determined when planning a survey. We now have the tools to calculate what sample size we need.

In practice, the sample size we choose is usually a trade-off between the desire for a result that is as precise as possible (take more observations) and the resources available (time and money). Sometimes people collect more observations than they need to reach the precision required, and this wastes resources. More often, not enough observations are taken for the sample, and this is also wasteful.

The formula for the **sample size** is:

$$n = \frac{z_T^2 \pi(1 - \pi)}{e^2}$$

To obtain this formula, we substitute π for p in the expression for the bound of the confidence interval, and the resulting expression is inverted. The reason for substituting π is that the sample is not available to compute the sample proportion, p. The answer obtained with this formula is usually rounded up to some convenient number. Anyway, it gives only a rough estimate of the required number.

The formula reveals that we need the following details to determine the sample size for a proportion:

1. the confidence level ($100\gamma\%$) desired, so that we can determine the corresponding theoretical value from the standard normal curve, z_T;
2. the **maximum tolerable error** or precision to be achieved, e, in estimating the population proportion;
3. the population proportion of successes, π.

The first two items in this list are determined by the investigator: how confident do we want to be and what level of precision do we want? By specifying the precision we are essentially specifying what confidence interval bound we wish to achieve; this bound is half the width of the confidence interval. The third item is a little more difficult to determine as it is the unknown population value — the very quantity we are trying to estimate. However, if we have some idea of its likely value, we can use this. For example, the results from a recent similar survey might indicate the likely value of π, or we could do a pilot survey to get some idea of π. If neither is possible, the most conservative thing to do is to put the largest possible value for $\pi(1 - \pi)$ into the formula, which occurs for a value of $\pi = 0.5$. This will let us determine the largest possible number of observations required, realising that we will have taken too many observations if π is very different from 0.5.

EXAMPLE 14.1   SUPPORT FOR THE CURRENT MEMBER (continued)

In our voting example, the proportion voting is only known to ±0.07. Suppose we wanted to know the proportion to ±0.03: how may people would we have to ask? Earlier, we obtained for $100\gamma\%$ = 95%, z_T = 1.96. Also, e = 0.03. But what about π? Suppose we plan to conduct the survey again, and, from our last one, we think π is about 0.45; thus we could use this value. However, if we have no idea, we could use π = 0.5. We might as well do this, as it is not much different to 0.45 and the value 0.5 is, as we said, the value that maximises $\pi(1 - \pi)$ and hence n:

$$n = \frac{1.96^2 \times 0.5 \times 0.5}{0.03^2}$$
$$= 1067.11$$

So take 1100 individuals. It makes sense to round up to a convenient number. It is pedantic to take exactly the computed number as it is only approximate. Also, rounding up is desirable as this will give us slightly more observations, rather than slightly less, than we need.

14.3 Reports on examples

The following reports, for the examples analysed in this chapter, indicate what material from a statistical analysis an investigator should include in a report. In general, the details of the statistical analysis are omitted so that the reader of the report can concentrate on the results.

EXAMPLE 14.1 SUPPORT FOR THE CURRENT MEMBER — REPORT

To assess the level of support for a state electorate's Member of Parliament, a survey of the electorate's 17 356 voters was made by interviewing 200 randomly selected voters. We can be 95% confident that 43% ± 6.9% of the electorates voters would support the member. To increase the precision of the percentage's estimate to ±3%, approximately 1100 voters would have to be surveyed.

EXAMPLE 14.2 HOUSEHOLD SIZE — REPORT

A survey of households in the metropolitan area of a city of 219 000 households determined the number of children for 200 randomly selected households. Table 14.4 shows that the surveyed households had between none and three children, inclusive, and that we can be confident that 60% ± 6.8% of all households in the metropolitan area had two children.

Table 14.4 *Number of children* in metropolitan households

Number of children	Percentage	Precision
0	10	±4.2
1	20	±5.5
2	60	±6.8
3	10	±4.2
Total	($n = 200$)	

EXAMPLE 14.3 HOUSEHOLD SIZE AND STATUS — REPORT

A survey of households in the metropolitan area of a city of 219 000 households established the number of children and socioeconomic status for 200 randomly selected households. The proportion of households with a particular number of children was computed for each status household and summarised in table 14.3.

The differences in the proportion of two-child households is investigated in more detail. The results are presented in figure 14.3. The percentage of high-status households with two children is considerably lower than for low-status and medium-status households; there is little difference between these last two status groups as far as the proportion with two-children households is concerned.

14.4 Using Minitab in estimation for limited variables

Minitab is used here mainly to obtain the theoretical value for the standard normal curve, z_T. To do this we use the *invcdf* command, with the *normal* subcommand. The *invcdf* command computes the inverse cumulative probability distribution function. The **inverse cumulative probability distribution function** yields the value of a quantity corresponding to a specified cumulative probability, where the quantity is distributed according to a nominated **probability distribution function,** such as the standard normal distribution function. The **cumulative probability** for a specified value of a particular quantity is the proportion of values below the specified value. For computing the confidence interval for the population proportion, the proportion supplied to the *invcdf* command is the proportion $(1 + \gamma)/2$; that is, the percentage $100(1 + \gamma)/2\%$ expressed as a proportion. The *let* command can also be used to compute the confidence interval and the sample size. However, there is little difference between using Minitab or a hand calculator to do these computations.

EXAMPLE 14.1   SUPPORT FOR THE CURRENT MEMBER (continued)

To obtain z_T for computing the 95% confidence interval, note that $(1 + 0.95)/2$ = 0.975. Then, z_T is obtained with the following Minitab commands:

```
MTB > outfile 'a:\ztheoret.lis'
MTB > invcdf 0.975;
SUBC> normal 0 1.
```

If your version of Minitab has pull-down menus and you want to use them, table 14.5 lists the menus and options that access the required commands. Appendix D, *Detailed instructions for Minitab menus,* explains how to use the menus.

Table 14.5   Menus and options for Minitab commands to produce normal theoretical values

Minitab command	Menu	Option
outfile	File >	Other Files > Start Recording Session...
invcdf	Calc >	Probability Distributions >
normal		Normal...

The output produced by the *invcdf* command is as follows:

```
MTB > invcdf 0.975;
SUBC> normal 0 1.
  0.9750 1.9600
```

The value of z_T is 1.96, the second value on the line of output after the command. To see why 0.975 is the value supplied to the *invcdf* command, consider the following points evident in figure 14.4:

- the range of values –1.96 to 1.96 includes 0.95 of the values for a standard normal distribution;
- as the distribution is symmetrical, the ranges less than –1.96 and greater than 1.96 contain the same proportion of values: 0.025;
- the three ranges include all possible values and so include 100% of the observations;
- the range less than 1.96 includes 0.95 + 0.025 = 0.975 of the values.

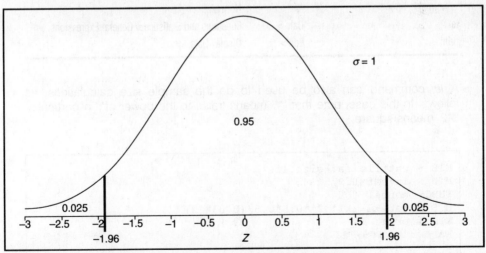

Figure 14.4   Ranges of values for the standard normal distribution

The *let* commands and associated output for computing the confidence interval (95%) are as follows:

```
MTB > outfile 'a:\cimean.lis'
MTB > invcdf 0.975 k1;
SUBC> normal 0 1.
MTB > let k2=k1*sqrt(0.43 * 0.57 / 200)
MTB > let k3=0.43-k2
MTB > let k4=0.43+k2
MTB > print k2-k4
K2        0.0686140
K3        0.361386
K4        0.498614
```

That is, the z_T is stored in $k1$ and then the bound is computed and stored in $k2$. Finally, the lower limit is stored in $k3$ and the upper limit in $k4$.

If your version of Minitab has pull-down menus and you want to use them, table 14.6 lists the menus and options that access the required commands. Appendix D, *Detailed instructions for Minitab menus*, explains how to use the menus.

Table 14.6   Menus and options for Minitab commands to produce confidence intervals and sample sizes

Minitab command	Menu	Option
outfile	File >	Other Files > Start Recording Session...
invcdf	Calc >	Probability Distributions >
normal		Normal...
let	Calc >	Functions and Statistics > General Expressions...
print	Edit >	Display Data...

A *let* command can also be used to do the sample size calculations, as follows. In this case, note that '**' means 'raise to the power of'; in particular, '**2' means square.

```
MTB > outfile 'a:\size.lis'
MTB > invcdf 0.975 k1;
SUBC> normal 0 1.
MTB > let k2=(k1**2)*0.5*0.5/(0.03**2)
MTB > print k2
K2        1067.11
```

14.5   Chapter summary

Suppose the following situation applies:

- a sample of an infinite population ($N > 20n$) has been taken;
- the value of a well-defined limited variable has been observed for each observational unit;
- the question to be investigated involves, for one of the values of the limited variable, the estimation of the population proportion from this sample.

In this case we should use the confidence interval ($100\gamma\%$) for the population proportion. It can also be applied when two limited variables have been observed. This interval has an advantage over the sample proportion which is a point estimate because it gives us an indication of the precision with which population proportion is estimated. The confidence interval ($100\gamma\%$) for the population proportion gives us the range that we can be $100\gamma\%$ confident will include the population proportion. This is because it can be demonstrated that if the population was repeatedly sampled and a confidence interval computed for each sample, $100\gamma\%$ of intervals would contain the population proportion.

You can be $100\gamma\%$ confident that the computed confidence interval will include the population proportion only if the assumptions made in deriving the sampling distribution are met. The sampling distribution of the sample proportion is the normal distribution and one of the assumptions made in deriving it is that a limited-variable probability model applies to population. It and the other assumptions will be met if the following conditions are satisfied:

1. **Conditions for limited-variable probability model**
   - *Well-defined limited variable*
   - *Stable population proportions*

2. **Conditions for other validating assumptions**
   - *Infinite population*
   - *Representative sample*
   - *Independence*
   - *Large number condition*

For a particular example, you must check whether these conditions are fulfilled. If they are not, the assumptions made in deriving the sampling distribution are not met and the procedure cannot be used for that example. You can also compute the confidence interval for the population proportion when the population is finite. The finite population correction factor must be employed.

In planning a survey, you have to decide on the sample size. You can calculate the sample size for a survey in which a population proportion is to be estimated, provided you specify what confidence level and what maximum tolerable error, or precision, you want to achieve.

14.6 Key terms

- assumptions
- collectively exhaustive values
- conditions
- confidence interval bound
- confidence interval (100γ%) for the population proportion
- confidence level
- contingency table
- cumulative probability
- distribution of variables
- distribution table
- finite population
- finite population correction factor
- independence condition
- infinite population
- inverse cumulative probability distribution function
- large number condition

- maximum tolerable error (e)
- mutually exclusive values
- one-way summary table
- precision
- probability distribution function
- proportion
- representative sample
- sample size
- sampling distribution for the sample proportion
- stable population proportions condition
- standard error (s_p)
- standard normal distribution
- theoretical value for the standard normal distribution (z_T)
- well-defined limited variable

14.7 Exercises

14.1 In your own words, explain the following terms:
- (a) point estimate
- (b) population
- (c) probability model
- (d) simple random sample
- (e) statistical inference
- (f) estimation
- (g) confidence level
- (h) population proportion
- (i) well-defined limited variable

14.2 When decisions are to be made about population values, what are some of the advantages gained by using a sample rather than the whole population in your determinations?

14.3 What is meant by the precision with which the population value is estimated?

14.4 What is the advantage of a probability sampling method such as simple random sampling?

14.5 What is meant by the term *sampling distribution of a statistic*?

14.6 Describe the sampling distribution of a sample proportion.

14.7 A point estimate of a population value does not give any information about how close this value lies to the population value it estimates. Comment on this statement.

14.8 If your sample came from a finite population, what formula would you use to estimate the population proportion?

14.9 Is it reasonable to expect that a confidence interval ($100\gamma\%$) will contain the population value 100% of the time? Give reasons for your answer.

14.10 As the size of the sample increases, the width of the interval estimated to contain the population proportion also increases. Is this true or false? Why?

14.11 A supermarket chain is considering changing the range of its store departments. For instance, the garden products section may be changed due to the uncertainty of demand and the perishability of some of the products. The management decides to survey customers over two weekends in one of its larger suburban stores to gauge customer demand for this section.
  (a) Answer the following questions.
    (i) What is the question to be investigated (including the group to which the conclusions apply)?
    (ii) What variable(s) are we concerned with here?
    (iii) What type of variable(s) are they?
    (iv) Which major category of statistical procedures applies here? Why?
    (v) What type of statistic should we use, given the question to be investigated and the variables involved?
    (vi) Which particular statistic or procedure, and diagram, should we use? Why?
  (b) How could the results of this survey help the management with its problem?

14.12 A survey of the smoking habits of students at a large university asked a random sample of 80 students if they regularly smoked cigarettes. Twenty-five, or 31%, of the students said that they smoked cigarettes on a regular basis. We want to determine the proportion of all students at the university who are regular cigarette smokers.
  (a) Answer the following questions:
    (i) What is the question to be investigated (including the group to which the conclusions apply)?
    (ii) What variable(s) are we concerned with here?
    (iii) What type of variable(s) are they?
    (iv) Which major category of statistical procedures applies here? Why?

(v) What type of statistic should we use, given the question to be investigated and the variables involved?

(vi) Which particular statistic or procedure, and diagram, should we use? Why?

(b) Is it true to say that 31% of all students at the university are regular cigarette smokers? Give reasons for your answer.

14.13 A local government area canvassed its residents' opinions on several environmental issues by way of a questionnaire. A pilot sample of 25 households was chosen from the 13 927 households in the area. One of the questions put to each selected household was whether or not they favoured a ban on backyard burning, and 19 households were in favour of this. How large a sample should be surveyed if we wish to be certain that the precision of our estimate is ±5% and have a confidence level of 90%?

14.14 The student union asked university council to introduce a third semester during the summer vacation, so that part-time students could complete their courses earlier. At a meeting the council decided to survey the university's 1103 academic staff to see how many staff were in favour of this program. A simple random sample of 50 academic staff members were interviewed, and 9 said they would support the program.

(a) Answer the following questions:

(i) What is the question to be investigated (including the group to which the conclusions apply)?

(ii) What variable(s) are we concerned with here?

(iii) What type of variable(s) are they?

(iv) Which major category of statistical procedures applies here? Why?

(v) What type of statistic should we use, given the question to be investigated and the variables involved?

(vi) Which particular statistic or procedure, and diagram, should we use? Why?

(b) What proportion of the staff interviewed agreed to support the program?

(c) How do we obtain the z_T value associated with the confidence interval (95%)?

(d) Compute the confidence interval (95%) for the proportion of academic staff at the university who would support the new program.

(e) What conditions are required for the confidence interval computed in (d) to be valid? Are they satisfied?

14.15 Forty thousand manufacturing companies in Australia were surveyed to see what proportion are involved in the food industry. In a simple random sample, 48 firms were selected and contacted. Six of these were involved in the food industry.

(a) Answer the following questions:

(i) What is the question to be investigated (including the group to which the conclusions apply)?

(ii) What variable(s) are we concerned with here?

    (iii) What type of variable(s) are they?

    (iv) Which major category of statistical procedures applies here? Why?

    (v) What type of statistic should we use, given the question to be investigated and the variables involved?

    (vi) Which particular statistic or procedure, and diagram, should we use? Why?

(b) What proportion of observed companies is involved in the food industry?

(c) Compute the confidence interval (95%) for the population proportion of companies involved in the food industry.

(d) A census reveals that the population proportion of manufacturing companies involved in the food industry is 0.977. Does your confidence interval actually contain this population value? Should you expect all such confidence intervals to contain the population proportion? Give reasons for your answer.

14.16 A survey is to be carried out to determine the proportion of households, in a particular local government area, with an *Annual income* of less than $25 000. A pilot survey of 100 households reveals that 63 households have an *Annual income* less than $25 000. From the values from the pilot survey, decide how large a sample you would need, in the main survey, to estimate the population proportion of households with *Annual incomes* less than $25 000. Suppose you have decided that the population proportion should be estimated with a precision of ±0.05 and with 95% confidence.

14.17 A caravan park at Port Macquarie, New South Wales, takes phone reservations for onsite accommodation. The management wants to estimate the proportion of no-shows they might expect generally. Of the past 275 phone reservations, 42 were no-shows.

(a) Answer the following questions:

    (i) What is the question to be investigated (including the group to which the conclusions apply)?

    (ii) What variable(s) are we concerned with here?

    (iii) What type of variable(s) are they?

    (iv) Which major category of statistical procedures applies here? Why?

    (v) What type of statistic should we use, given the question to be investigated and the variables involved?

    (vi) Which particular statistic or procedure, and diagram, should we use? Why?

(b) Construct a confidence interval (95%) for the population proportion of no-shows the management might expect generally.

(c) What do you conclude about the assumptions underlying the confidence interval for the population proportion for this example? Give reasons for your conclusions.

(d) What do you conclude from the confidence interval?

14.18 A market research company investigating student preference for different brands of soft drink took a simple random sample of 150 out of the 23 000 students, and found that 47 of the observed students preferred a particular brand of cola to any other soft drink. We want to determine the proportion of the 23 000 students who prefer the brand of cola.

(a) Answer the following questions:

(i) What is the question to be investigated (including the group to which the conclusions apply)?

(ii) What variable(s) are we concerned with here?

(iii) What type of variable(s) are they?

(iv) Which major category of statistical procedures applies here? Why?

(v) What type of statistic should we use, given the question to be investigated and the variables involved?

(vi) Which particular statistic or procedure, and diagram, should we use? Why?

(b) Calculate a confidence interval (95%) for the proportion of students in the population who prefer this brand of cola.

14.19 The proportion of women employed in the South Australian public service in the year ending June 1992 was 0.42. Can this value be used to estimate the proportion of all women who are in paid employment in South Australia in that same year? If so, how?

14.20 Opinion polls are often used to predict the outcome of government elections, the results of a referendum or success in sporting events. The opinions expressed may vary according to the sex or age of the person interviewed. A local daily newspaper took a poll to assess which party was likely to win the most seats in the next state election. The state has about one million registered voters. Voters were randomly selected from a computerised list of telephone numbers. The results are in table 14.7.

Table 14.7 Frequencies for *Party supported* by *Age*

Party supported	Age 18–24	25–39	40–54	55+
Labor	37	32	32	27
Liberal	41	43	54	58
Democrats	7	8	5	5
Independent/others	4	3	7	3
Undecided	11	14	12	7

Source: abstracted from *The Advertiser* (1993b)

(a) We want to use this information to determine how many people in this state aged 25–39 would vote for the Labor party. Answer the following questions:

(i) What is the question to be investigated (including the group to which the conclusions apply)?

(ii) What variable(s) are we concerned with here?

(iii) What type of variable(s) are they?

(iv) Which major category of statistical procedures applies here? Why?

(v) What type of statistic should we use, given the question to be investigated and the variables involved?

(vi) Which particular statistic or procedure, and diagram, should we use? Why?

(b) From table 14.7, estimate the proportion of those people aged 25–39 who would vote for the Labor party. Use a confidence level of 90%.

(c) Also estimate the proportion of people, aged 40–45 years, who would vote for the Liberal party. Is there any evidence that the population proportion differs from 54%? Give reasons for your answer.

14.21 In a survey, 129 male and 91 female students randomly chosen from those studying Quantitative Methods for Business were asked whether working as a member of a team enhanced their learning. The summary of their responses in table 14.8 is to be used to estimate the proportion of students of each sex that are studying the subject who thought their learning was enhanced by teamwork.

Table 14.8 Frequencies of *Enhanced learning* for each *Sex*

Enhanced learning	Sex		Total
	Male	Female	
Yes	79	66	145
No	50	25	75
Total	129	91	220

(a) Answer the following questions:

(i) What is the question to be investigated (including the group to which the conclusions apply)?

(ii) What variable(s) are we concerned with here?

(iii) What type of variable(s) are they?

(iii) Which major category of statistical procedures applies here? Why?

(iv) What type of statistic should we use, given the question to be investigated and the variables involved?

(v) Which particular statistic or procedure, and diagram, should we use? Why?

(b) Estimate the proportion of students of each sex that are studying the subject who thought their learning was enhanced by teamwork. Use a confidence level of 95%.

14.22 A committee is preparing a submission to the university council concerning the provision of student PC pools when the Faculty of Business and Management moves to a new campus. The committee surveyed 50 students chosen at random from the faculty to see how many of the students in the faculty were required to attend tutorials using the university PC pools. They found that 42 of the students attended at least one class a week that involved using a PC pool.

(a) Answer the following questions:

(i) What is the question to be investigated (including the group to which the conclusions apply)?

(ii) What variable(s) are we concerned with here?

(iii) What type of variable(s) are they?

(iv) Which major category of statistical procedures applies here? Why?

(v) What type of statistic should we use, given the question to be investigated and the variables involved?

(vi) Which particular statistic or procedure, and diagram, should we use? Why?

(b) Use this information to prepare a report in support of a request for computing equipment at the new campus, taking into account that the number of students from the faculty at the new campus is likely to be more than 3000 students.

14.23 The aim of this exercise is to investigate the sampling distribution of a two-valued limited variable. Samples of 50 will be selected from a population and a two-valued limited variable measured on each observational unit. The following limited-variable probability model will be used to represent the population: the population proportion for the value Yes is 0.63 and the population proportion for the value No is 0.37.

(a) What will be the sampling distribution for the sample proportion of those responding Yes? What will be the values of the measures of central tendency and spread of this distribution?

(b) Use the following Minitab commands to generate 10 000 observations, randomly selected from a population that has the limited-variable probability model specified above. The values will be stored in $c11–c60$.

```
MTB > outfile 'a:\sampdist.lis'
MTB > set c1
DATA> 1  0
DATA> set c2
DATA> 0.63  0.37
DATA> end
MTB > name c1 'value' c2 'pi'
MTB > print c1 c2
MTB > random 200 c11-c60;
SUBC> discrete c1 c2.
```

Regard each row of the columns $c11–c60$ as a sample of 50 from the population. Use the following commands to obtain the proportions for each sample and to summarise the attributes of these proportions.

```
MTB > rmean c11-c60 c61
MTB > name c61 'propn'
MTB > histogram c61
MTB > describe c61
```

If your version of Minitab has pull-down menus and you want to use them, table 14.9 lists the menus and options that access the required commands. Appendix D, *Detailed instructions for Minitab menus*, explains how to use the menus.

Table 14.9   Menus and options for Minitab commands to generate random values

Minitab command	Menu	Option
outfile	File >	Other Files > Start Recording Session...
set	Edit >	Data Screen
name	Edit >	Data Screen
print	Edit	Display Data...
random	Calc >	Random Data >
discrete		Discrete...
rmean	Calc >	Functions and Statistics > Row Statistics...
histogram	Graph >	Histogram...
describe	Stat >	Basic Statistics > Descriptive Statistics...

(c)   How do the results of (b) compare with what was predicted in part (a)? What do you conclude about the values that can be obtained for the sample proportion?

## CHAPTER 15

ESTIMATION FOR ONE UNRESTRICTED VARIABLE

L E A R N I N G   O B J E C T I V E S

The learning objectives of this chapter are:

- to know when to apply, how to calculate and how to interpret the results of the confidence interval for the population mean, the prediction interval for a future observation and a tolerance interval covering the middle $100\pi\%$ of population values;

- to know the conditions required for each of the intervals to be valid and how to determine when they are met;

- to be able to determine the sample size to give a prescribed level of precision in estimating the population mean.

The following extract from the *Summary of procedures based on combinations of variable types* in part VI gives an overview of the estimation procedures covered in this and the previous chapter of part IV, *Estimation procedures*.

1. *One or two limited variable(s)*
   - Distribution of variables: confidence interval for the population proportion.

2. *One unrestricted variable or one unrestricted variable with one or two limited variable(s)*
   - **Single value**: prediction interval for a single future observation.
   - **Range of values**: tolerance interval for middle $100\pi\%$ of population values.
   - **Measures of central tendency**: confidence interval for the population **mean**.

3. *Two unrestricted variables*

As outlined in the objectives, this chapter covers confidence, prediction and tolerance intervals for an unrestricted variable. Since these are inference procedures, to use them we must take a sample and the question to be investigated must be about the population and *not* confined to the sample. These intervals estimate different population quantities as follows:

- the *confidence interval* estimates the range that you can be confident will include the population mean;
- the *prediction interval* estimates the range that you can be confident will include a single future observation;
- the *tolerance interval* estimates a range that you can be confident will include a specified proportion of the values in the population.

The differences between the three intervals are as follows:

- the confidence interval is an interval estimate for the *mean* of a whole set of population values;
- the prediction interval is an interval estimate for a *single value* from the population;
- the tolerance interval is an interval estimate for the *range of values* that will include the specified proportion of values in the population.

Which interval is appropriate in a particular instance depends on the question to be investigated.

As described in the introduction to part IV, *Estimation procedures,* statistical inference procedures involving an unrestricted variable might well involve the assumption that the normal probability model applies to the unrestricted variables. Since this is often the case, the validity of conclusions from the procedures depends on whether or not the population distribution of the unrestricted variable is normal. The next section explains how to determine whether a variable can be described as normally distributed; subsequent sections cover the intervals. There are techniques to apply when the normality assumption is not met, but these are not covered in this book.

15.1   Normally distributed unrestricted variables

An unrestricted variable is a **normally distributed variable**, when the **normal probability model** applies to its values for all observational units from the population. For instance, if a histogram, such as a relative frequency histogram, of the values of the unrestricted variable *for the whole population* were obtained, this histogram would look like a **normal distribution**. In saying this, we have only specified that the shape of the population distribution of the variable is approximately symmetric and bell-shaped. The population mean, μ, and population standard deviation, σ, are allowed to vary. Figure 15.1 shows two normal distributions that differ in μ and σ.

In section 7.2, *Distribution attributes*, the normal distribution was suggested as a possible shape for a distribution diagram, and in chapter 14, *Estimation for limited variables*, the standard normal distribution was used in the confidence interval for the population proportion. A normally distributed variable standardised as described in section 8.3, *Standardising data*, will follow a standard normal distribution. The standard normal distribution is the particular normal distribution for which $\mu = 0$ and $\sigma = 1$.

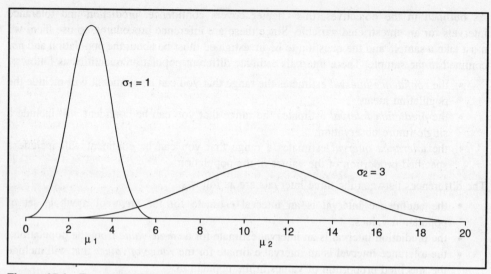

Figure 15.1   Two normal distributions differing in location and dispersion

So how can we check the assumption that the population distribution of a variable is normal? One possibility is to form a distribution diagram for the available data. From this we can assess whether the data indicates that the population distribution is normal. However, our sample is probably the only data that we have, and that is seldom large enough to form a distribution diagram for reliably assessing the shape of the distribution. In any case, assessing whether the distribution is bell-shaped is not easy. A better method is the **normal probability plot**.

In normal probability plots, a set of numbers is plotted against their normal scores. The **normal score** for the ith smallest number, from a set of n numbers, approximates the average value we could expect for the ith smallest observation in a sample of n observations of a variable whose population distribution is normal. For example, the normal score for the smallest of n numbers is the value expected for the smallest observation in a sample of n observations of a normally distributed variable. The normal score for the second smallest of n numbers is the value expected for the second smallest observation in a sample of n observations of a normally distributed variable. The normal score for the largest of n numbers is the value expected for the largest observation in a sample of n observations of a normally distributed variable. So the normal scores are the values you would expect for a sample of the same size from a variable whose population distribution is normal.

If the variable is normally distributed, the normal probability plot will display a *broad* straight line trend. To help you determine whether the line in a normal probability plot is straight enough, you can compute the observed **normal probability plot correlation coefficient**, r_N. It is the linear correlation coefficient from chapter 10, *Measures of association for two unrestricted variables*, that correlates the observed values and the normal scores. You then obtain a **theoretical value for the normal probability plot correlation coefficient**, r_T, such values depending on n, the number of observations, and α, the significance level. In this case, the significance level is the probability that you conclude the variable is normally distributed when in fact it is not. Some commonly used values for the significance levels are $\alpha = 0.10$, 0.05 and 0.01. A general discussion of significance levels is given in part V, *Hypothesis tests*. For a particular significance level, the value of r_T increases as n increases.

If the observed value, r_N, is less than or equal to the theoretical value, r_T, the hypothesis of normality should be rejected. Otherwise, retain the hypothesis of normality. Note that when the hypothesis of normality is retained, you cannot conclude that the variable is normally distributed; only that the available evidence does not suggest that it is nonnormal. This is equivalent to the outcome of a trial in which a defendant is declared innocent; in some cases it may be that the defendant is not innocent, but there is insufficient evidence to find them guilty. Of course, if more evidence comes to light, the verdict may change. In our case, we often have only weak evidence as the number of observations will generally be relatively small.

EXAMPLE 15.1   NORMAL VARIABLE

This example consists of ten observations. The normal probability plot, figure 15.2, appears to be satisfactory in that it shows a broad straight line trend. The normal probability plot correlation coefficient, r_N, is 0.982. For $n = 10$ and $\alpha = 0.05$, $r_T = 0.9179$. As 0.982 is greater than 0.9179, $r_N > r_T$ and the hypothesis of normality cannot be rejected. That is, the objective procedure based on r_N confirms the subjective conclusion drawn from the normal probability plot.

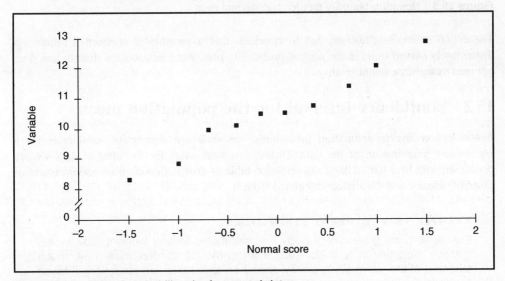

Figure 15.2 Normal probability plot for normal data

EXAMPLE 15.2   NON NORMAL VARIABLE

This example also consists of ten observations. Its normal probability plot, in figure 15.3, has a distinct curve which indicates that the variable is not normal.

Now, for this example, $r_N = 0.900$. As in the previous example, for $n = 10$ and $\alpha = 0.05$, $r_T = 0.9179$. As 0.900 is less than 0.9179, $r_N < r_T$ and the hypothesis of normality is rejected. Again, the objective procedure confirms the subjective conclusion we have drawn from the plot.

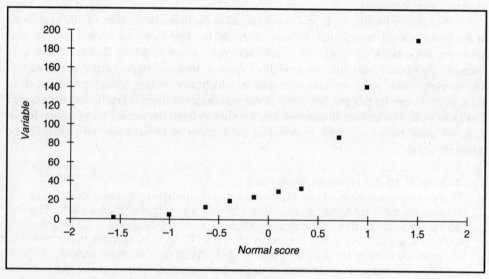

Figure 15.3   Normal probability plot for non normal data

These two examples illustrate that to conclude that a variable is nonnormal requires a distinctively curved trend in the normal probability plot. Waviness about a straight line does not usually indicate nonnormality.

15.2   Confidence interval for the population mean

Before proceeding to estimation procedures, we shall use descriptive summaries for a preliminary examination of the data. Descriptive summaries for the kind of data we are concerned with here would have a distribution table or distribution diagram and measures of central tendency and dispersion calculated from it.

EXAMPLE 15.3   STUDENT EXPENDITURE

AusStudent, the government body that distributes tertiary student allowances, surveys students at a major Australian university to determine how much students at the university typically spend on textbooks and stationery. It takes a simple random sample of 25 of the 11 200 students at the university. At the end of the first month of the semester the selected students were asked how much they had spent on textbooks and stationery during that period. The amounts they reported are in table 15.1; this data represents raw, primary data for AusStudent.

Table 15.1   *Textbook and stationery expenditure* ($) for selected students

213	134	266	225	274
316	96	84	272	211
296	321	181	125	197
310	168	271	79	101
221	243	192	213	332

The observed variable, *Textbook and stationery expenditure*, is an unrestricted variable. A dotplot for this data appears in figure 15.4. The mean for this data is $213.64 and the standard deviation is $77.93. The dotplot shows no particularly unusual observations and the data seems to be symmetrical about the mean value of $213.64. The standard deviation tells us that observations are, on average, $77.93 from the mean value.

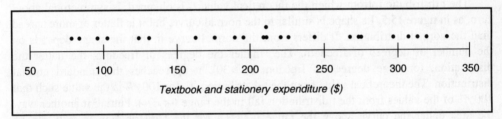

Figure 15.4   Dotplot for *Textbook and stationery expenditure*

Turning to the estimation of the *population mean*, you could employ a single point estimate of the population mean, μ. That is, use the *sample mean*, $\bar{y}$, as an estimate of μ. However, we know that the population mean is most unlikely to be exactly equal to the sample mean. It seems advisable, as in the case for a proportion, to incorporate some idea of the precision of our sample estimate into our conclusions. That is, we need an interval estimate and this is obtained from a confidence interval ($100\gamma\%$) for the population mean. This confidence interval ($100\gamma\%$) for the population mean gives us the range that will include the population mean $100\gamma\%$ of the time; that is, if we repeatedly sampled a population and calculated the confidence interval ($100\gamma\%$), in $100\gamma\%$ of samples, the confidence intervals would include the population mean, μ. The confidence interval ($100\gamma\%$) for the population mean is given by:

$$\text{Confidence interval } (100\gamma\%) \text{ for } \mu = (\bar{y} - t_T s_{\bar{y}}, \bar{y} + t_T s_{\bar{y}})$$

where $100\gamma\%$ is the **confidence level** desired by the investigator,

  t_T is the **theoretical value for the t distribution**, corresponding to $100\gamma\%$ and the degrees of freedom of $s_{\bar{y}}$ which are $n - 1$;

  $s_{\bar{y}}$ is the **standard error** of the sample mean (it measures the variability of the sample mean) and it is equal to $s/\sqrt{n}$.

That is,

$$\text{Confidence interval } (100\gamma\%) \text{ for } \mu = \left(\bar{y} - t_T \frac{s}{\sqrt{n}}, \bar{y} + t_T \frac{s}{\sqrt{n}}\right)$$

Again, the most commonly used value for $100\gamma\%$ is 95%, but if you want to be more certain of including the population mean you could obtain the confidence interval for $100\gamma\% = 99\%$ or even 99.9%. If you are happy to be less certain, you could obtain the confidence interval for $100\gamma\% = 90\%$. Also, note that the first formula for the confidence interval for the population mean is similar to the formula for the confidence interval for the population proportion. The general form of a confidence interval is:

(statistic − theoretical value × variability of statistic,

statistic + theoretical value × variability of statistic)

where the theoretical value is obtained from sampling distribution.

The t distribution, from which the theoretical value t_T is obtained, is symmetrical about zero, as in figure 15.5. Its shape is similar to the normal curve, but it is flatter or more spread than the normal distribution. It differs from the normal curve in that the shape depends on the number of degrees of freedom. The smaller the degrees of freedom, the flatter the distribution; for large degrees of freedom ($n > 30$), it approaches the standard normal distribution. The theoretical value from the t distribution, t_T, for $100\gamma\%$ is the value such that $100\gamma\%$ of the values from the t distribution fall in the range $(-t_T, t_T)$. Putting it another way, the area under the curve above the range $(-t_T, t_T)$ for the t distribution is γ. It can be mathematically proven that, if this value of t_T is used in calculating the confidence interval, the confidence interval will have the desired property that the population value of the mean, μ, will be included in $100\gamma\%$ of computed intervals.

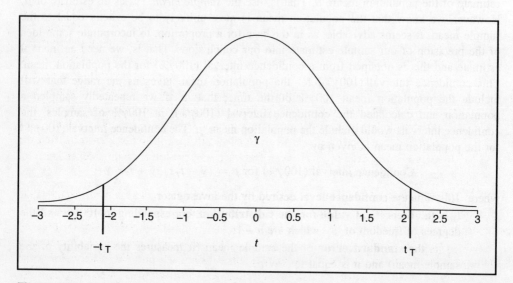

Figure 15.5   The theoretical value for the t distribution

Assumptions and conditions

As discussed in the introduction to part IV, *Estimation procedures*, underlying all statistical inference procedures are the **assumptions** made in deriving the sampling distribution and these must be met if the procedure's results are to be valid. For the confidence interval for the population mean, the sampling distribution is the t distribution and this is based on a normal probability model for the unrestricted variable. The **conditions** that will satisfy the assumptions required for the valid use of the sampling distribution are as follows:

1. **Conditions for normal probability model**
   - *Unrestricted variable*: The variable for which the confidence interval is being computed must be an unrestricted variable. Determining whether this condition is satisfied can be done simply by considering whether the variable is unrestricted. Usually, there is no problem with this condition.
   - *Normally distributed variable*: If we constructed a relative frequency distribution for the values of the variable for all observational units from the population, the shape of the distribution would be approximately symmetric and bell-shaped as required for the normal distribution. The distribution of the variable is checked by using the normal probability plot and the normal probability correlation coefficient, as outlined in section 15.1, *Normally distributed unrestricted variables*.

2. **Conditions for other validating assumptions**
   - *Infinite population*: The sample should come from an effectively **infinite population**. The population, from which the sample came, can be regarded as effectively infinite if the number of individuals in it (N) is at least 20 times the number sampled (n); that is, if $N > 20n$.
   - *Representative sample*: A **representative sample** is an unbiased fraction of the original population. The methods that are likely to produce a representative sample were discussed in chapter 4, *Surveys*. We concluded that the probability sampling methods, such as simple random sampling, produce representative samples. So this condition will be met if a probability sampling method is used to select the sample. If not, we cannot guarantee that the condition will be met.
   - *Independence*: The **independence condition** requires that the outcome of any observation is independent of the outcome of any other observation. This independence condition is difficult to check; in part, it involves ensuring that the study is conducted in such a way that each observation is made independently of the other observations.

While it is an assumption of this procedure that the variable is normally distributed, the conclusions will not be far wrong if there is some departure from normality. How much departure from normality can be tolerated depends on the number of observations. However, a general rule of thumb is that, for samples of 30 or more observations, the population distribution can be any shape. For samples of between 15 and 30 observations, the population distribution must be symmetric in shape. For samples with less than 15 observations, the population distribution must be approximately normal.

Sometimes the lower limit for a confidence interval, or a prediction or tolerance interval, is negative when negative values for the variable are impossible. For example, expenditure on books and stationery cannot be negative. It is not acceptable to solve this problem by setting the lower limit to zero. The problem can arise either because the assumption of normality is incorrect or because the number of observations is inadequate to estimate the interval precisely enough. Thus, to remove the negative lower limit you have to either modify the analysis to take into account the nonnormality or obtain a larger sample.

EXAMPLE 15.3   STUDENT EXPENDITURE (continued)

The question to be investigated is: What amount do students at a major Australian university typically spend on textbooks and stationery? The typical amount is to be determined from data obtained from a simple random sample of 25 of the 11 200 students at the university. That is, we want to estimate a population quantity from a sample. As the observed variable, *Textbook and stationery expenditure*, is an unrestricted variable, the question to be investigated can be answered by using a confidence interval for the population mean. Suppose that you are satisfied with being 95% confident that the computed range will include the population mean.

To compute the 95% confidence interval for the population mean requires n, $\bar{y}$, s, and t_T. Now, n, $\bar{y}$ and s are 25, \$213.64 and \$77.934, respectively. The value of t_T is obtained by using a computer and, for $100\gamma\% = 95\%$ and degrees of freedom $= 25 - 1 = 24$, is 2.0639. Figure 15.6 (opposite) shows that the range from -2.0639 to 2.0639 includes 95% of the values for the t distribution with 24 degrees of freedom.

Confidence interval (95%) for μ

$$= \left(213.64 - 2.0639 \frac{77.934}{\sqrt{25}}, 213.64 + 2.0639 \frac{77.934}{\sqrt{25}} \right)$$
$$= (213.64 - 32.17, 213.64 + 32.17)$$
$$= (181.47, 245.81)$$

That is, the population mean is estimated to within ±\$32.17 so that we are 95% confident the expenditure by the students is between \$181.47 and \$245.81. However, this interval is valid only if the assumptions underlying it are met; that is, if the listed conditions apply to this example. Checking these conditions proceeds as follows:

1. **Conditions for normal probability model**

   • *Unrestricted variable*: We have already stated that the observed variable, *Textbook and stationery expenditure*, can be classified as an unrestricted variable.

   • *Normally distributed variable*: The normal probability plot for *Textbook and stationery expenditure* is given in figure 15.7 (opposite). The associated correlation coefficient, r_N, is 0.981. For $n = 25$, $\alpha = 0.05$, r_T = 0.9582. As $r_N = 0.981$ is greater than r_T, there is no evidence to suggest that the variable is not normally distributed. We will presume that it is normally distributed.

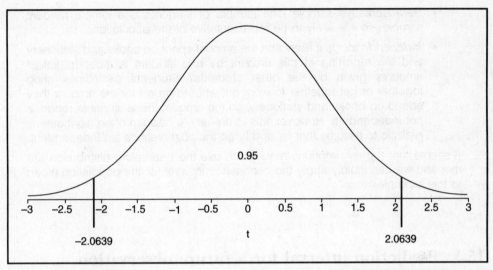

Figure 15.6   The range that includes 95% of values for the t distribution with 24 degrees of freedom

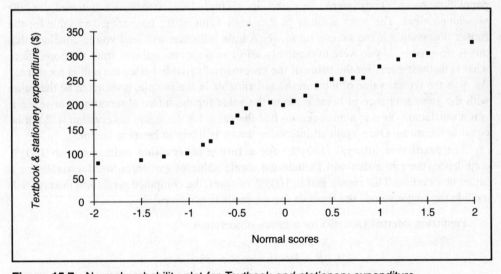

Figure 15.7   Normal probability plot for *Textbook and stationery expenditure*

2.   Conditions for other validating assumptions

- *Infinite population*: The number sampled is 25, so the population of students must be in excess of 20 × 25 = 500. There are altogether 11 200 students at the university, which is much greater than 500; thus, the population can be regarded as infinite.

445

- *Representative sample:* The sample of students is a simple random sample, so it is likely to be representative of the population.
- *Independence*: Is it likely that the amount spent on books and stationery and the reporting of this amount by one student is independent of amounts given by the other students? Students sometimes shop together or get together to work out what to report for the amount they spend on books and stationery, so the amount these students report is not independent. However, this is unlikely to happen often, so it seems realistic to assume that by and large the observations are independent.

It seems that the assumptions required to use the t sampling distribution are met and we can validly apply the confidence interval for the population mean to this example.

15.3 Prediction interval for a future observation

Descriptive summaries that might be used in a preliminary examination of the data, before the prediction interval is calculated, are the same as for the confidence interval for the population mean. They were discussed in section 15.2, *Confidence interval for the population mean*. The point estimate of the single value of the unrestricted variable for the further observation is the sample mean, $\bar{y}$. A little reflection will lead you to conclude that this is reasonable. If you were to randomly select an observational unit from the population, what is the best guess for the value of the unrestricted variable before the unit is measured? As $\bar{y}$ is the typical value of the unrestricted variable in the sample, it seems to be the value with the greatest chance of being close to the value for the future observation. However, it is not satisfactory as it is almost certain that the value for the future observation will not be equal to the mean. Once again an interval estimate is likely to be more useful.

The **prediction interval ($100\gamma\%$) for a future observation** estimates, with $100\gamma\%$ confidence, the range that will include the single value of the unrestricted variable for a future observation. This means that in $100\gamma\%$ of cases, the computed prediction interval will include the single value. The formula for the prediction interval is:

Prediction interval ($100\gamma\%$) for a future observation

$$= \left(\bar{y} - t_T s \sqrt{1 + \frac{1}{n}}, \bar{y} + t_T s \sqrt{1 + \frac{1}{n}} \right)$$

where $100\gamma\%$ is the confidence level desired by the investigator,

t_T is the theoretical value for the t distribution, corresponding to $100\gamma\%$ and the degrees of freedom of s which are $n - 1$;

s is the standard deviation.

That is, the prediction interval is based on the same set of statistics as the confidence interval; the formulae differ only in respect of the quantities under the square root symbol.

Assumptions and conditions

For the prediction interval for a future observation, the appropriate sampling distribution is the t distribution, and one of the assumptions made in deriving the sampling distribution is that a normal probability model applies to the variable. The conditions that will satisfy the assumptions required for the valid use of the prediction interval are as follows:

1. **Conditions for normal probability model**
   - *Unrestricted variable*
   - *Normally distributed variable*

2. **Conditions for other validating assumptions**
   - *Infinite population*
   - *Representative sample and future observation*
   - *Independence*

These conditions are exactly the same as the confidence interval for the population mean, with the extra condition that the future observation is representative of the population and independent of any other observations. Hence, checking the conditions for the prediction interval proceeds as for the confidence interval, except that we have to make some assessment of the conditions on the future observation. The conditions on the future observation are likely to be met if:

- the future observation is randomly selected from the same population as the original sample;
- the population has not changed between the time the original sample was taken and the future observation is obtained;
- the future observation is independent of any others in the population.

If all the conditions are not met, the range will not contain the future observation 95% of the time. You can calculate an interval but it will be meaningless. In particular, the condition that the variable is normally distributed is crucial to the validity of this method.

EXAMPLE 15.3   STUDENT EXPENDITURE (continued)

In the case of the student expenditure on textbooks and stationery, AusStudent might want to estimate the range that it can be 95% confident will include the amount spent on books and stationery if one more further student was randomly selected. This range is estimated by the prediction interval (95%) for a future observation. From our confidence interval calculations for this example, it is known that n, $\bar{y}$, s and t_T are 25, \$213.64, \$77.934 and 2.0639, respectively. Hence,

Prediction interval (95%) for a future observation

$$= \left(213.64 - 2.0639 \times 77.934\sqrt{1 + \frac{1}{25}}, 213.64 + 2.0639 \times 77.934\sqrt{1 + \frac{1}{25}}\right)$$

$$= (213.64 - 164.03, 213.64 + 164.03)$$

$$= (49.61, 377.67)$$

That is, it is estimated, with 95% confidence, that if we randomly selected another student, the amount the student spent on books and stationery in the first month of semester would be between $49.61 and $377.67.

We have already concluded that the assumptions underlying the confidence interval appear to be met for this example. Hence, the assumptions for the prediction interval will be met provided that the future observation is independent of all other observations, that it comes from the same population as the original population, and that the distribution of the population has not changed. This implies that the future observation involved book and stationery expenditure for a month equivalent to that for the original sample, and that the student can remember how much he or she spent on books and stationery just as accurately as those originally sampled. So provided the future observation fulfils these conditions, the assumptions underlying the prediction interval appear to be met.

15.4   Tolerance interval for the middle $100\pi\%$ of population values

Descriptive summaries that might be used in a preliminary examination of the data, before the tolerance interval is calculated, are the same as for the confidence interval for the population mean. They were discussed in section 15.2, *Confidence interval for the population mean*. The **tolerance interval ($100\pi\%$, $100\gamma\%$) for the middle $100\pi\%$ of population values** estimates, with $100\gamma\%$ confidence, the range of values containing the middle $100\pi\%$ of the values of the unrestricted variable in the population. The formula for this tolerance interval is:

Tolerance interval ($100\pi\%$, $100\gamma\%$) for the middle $100\pi\%$ of population values

$$= (\bar{y} - g_T s, \bar{y} + g_T s)$$

where $100\pi\%$ is the percentage, specified by the investigator, of population values to be covered by the range being estimated,

$100\gamma\%$ is the confidence level desired by the investigator,

g_T is the **theoretical value for computing the tolerance interval**, corresponding to $100\pi\%$, $100\gamma\%$ and n;

s is the standard deviation.

That is, the tolerance interval involves a theoretical value that differs from the confidence and prediction intervals.

Assumptions and conditions

In the case of the tolerance interval, the sampling distribution is unnamed. However, it is based on a normal probability model for the unrestricted variable. The conditions that will satisfy the assumptions required for the valid use of the sampling distribution are as follows:

1. **Conditions for normal probability model**
   - *Unrestricted variable*
   - *Normally distributed variable*

2. **Conditions for other validating assumptions**
   - *Infinite population*
   - *Representative sample*
   - *Independence*

These conditions are exactly the same as for the confidence interval for the population mean discussed in section 15.2, *Confidence interval for the population mean*. If any of the conditions are not met, the range containing $100\pi\%$ of the population values will not be the one estimated by the tolerance interval. As for the prediction interval, you can calculate an interval but it will be meaningless. In particular, the condition that the variable is normally distributed is crucial to the validity of the tolerance interval, whereas it was not for the confidence interval.

EXAMPLE 15.3   STUDENT EXPENDITURE (continued)

AusStudent might want to estimate the range of expenditures that covers what most students at the university spend on books and stationery in the first month. They decide to do this by obtaining the tolerance interval that estimates, with 95% confidence, the range containing the middle 95% of the amounts students spend.

By using the computer we find that for $100\pi\% = 95\%$, $100\gamma\% = 95\%$ and $n = 25$, $g_T = 2.6392$. Also, $\bar{y} = \$213.64$ and $s = \$77.934$. Hence:

Tolerance interval (95%, 95%) for the middle 95% of population values
$$= (213.64 - 2.6392 \times 77.934, 213.64 + 2.6392 \times 77.934)$$
$$= (213.64 - 205.68, 213.64 + 205.68)$$
$$= (7.96, 419.32)$$

That is, it is estimated, with 95% confidence, that 95% of students spend between \$7.96 and \$419.32. AusStudent might use this interval to decide whether the amount spent by a student is unusual. For example, a student who spent \$750 on books and stationery would seem to have spent an unusually high amount on books and stationery — only $2\frac{1}{2}\%$ of students spend more than \$419.32.

We examined the conditions for this data when the confidence interval was calculated, and concluded that the conditions were met, so we can assume that the unnamed sampling distribution applies and that the computed tolerance interval is valid.

15.5   Sample size determination for the mean

In planning a survey, the investigator has to determine how many observational units to sample. This section explains how to determine the **sample size** for surveys whose purpose is to estimate the population mean for an unrestricted variable, using a confidence interval for the population mean.

A formula that gives an approximate estimate, for $n > 30$, of the sample size is:

$$n = \frac{z_T^2 \sigma^2}{e^2}$$

Therefore, to determine the sample size, we must know:

1. the confidence level ($100\gamma\%$) desired so that we can determine the corresponding theoretical value from the standard normal curve, z_T;
2. the **maximum tolerable error** or precision, e, in estimating the population mean; and
3. the population standard deviation, σ.

The first two of these is under the control of the investigator — set these at the level you require. The third quantity is the most difficult to obtain as you will not know the population standard deviation when you are estimating the population mean — you will have to use a guesstimate. Data is sometimes available from similar situations and might give us an appropriate guide to the likely value of the population standard deviation. In other cases, we may need a pilot study to obtain a guide to the population standard deviation.

EXAMPLE 15.3   STUDENT EXPENDITURE (continued)

AusStudent may decide to run the survey at a second university. However, it has also decided that it requires the mean *Textbook and stationery expenditure* to be estimated to within about ±$10 — the precision of about $32 achieved with the first survey is inadequate. If the confidence level used previously, 95%, is to be retained, how many observations must be taken to achieve the desired precision?

Of the three quantities that have to be specified to use the formula for sample size, the population standard deviation is the unknown quantity. The only information available is the sample standard deviation from our first survey: $s = \$77.9$. To be conservative, we round up this value to provide a value of the population standard deviation for planning the survey. If we use the value $\sigma = 100$, we now have:

$$e = \$10$$
$$\sigma = \$100$$
$$z_T = 1.96$$

and

$$n = \frac{1.96^2 \times 100^2}{10^2}$$
$$= 384.16$$

Therefore, a sample of 400 should be taken. Note that the computed value is rounded up to slightly oversatisfy and hence be conservative. However, note that the critical premise underlying this prediction is that the population standard deviation is $100. If the standard deviation in the actual survey proves very different to this, then the actual precision will also be substantially different to what we want.

15.6   Reports on examples

The following reports, for the examples analysed in this chapter, indicate what material from a statistical analysis an investigator should include in a report. In general, the details of the statistical analysis are omitted so that the reader of the report can concentrate on the results.

> **EXAMPLE 15.3   STUDENT EXPENDITURE — REPORT**
>
> AusStudent took a simple random sample of 25 of the 11 200 students at a major Australian university. At the end of the first month of the semester it asked the selected students to record how much they spent on textbooks and stationery during that period. From the results, it is estimated with 95% confidence that the amount students at the university typically spend on textbooks and stationery in the first month is $213.64 ± $32.17. To improve the precision with which the mean is estimated to ±$10, it seems that 400 students have to be surveyed.
>
> Also, AusStudent wanted to estimate the range that would include 95% of the amounts spent by students. From the results, it was estimated with 95% confidence that the range $7.96 to $419.32 covers the expenditure amounts of the middle 95% of students.

15.7   Using Minitab in estimation for unrestricted variables

Minitab includes commands that enable you to check the assumption of a normally distributed variable, to obtain the theoretical values for the t distribution, and to compute the confidence interval for the population mean. Minitab commands are not available for prediction and tolerance intervals and r_T and g_T. However, Appendix C, *Minitab macros*, gives macros that compute these intervals and theoretical values. Generally, these macros require you to set constants, such as *k1*, before you invoke them with the Minitab *execute* command.

15.7.1   Checking normality

The three Minitab commands for checking normality are *nscores*, *plot* and *correlation*. The *nscores* command is used to compute the normal scores, the *plot* command is used to produce the normal probability plot, and the *correlation* command is used to produce the normal probability correlation coefficient.

Also, the Minitab macro *rtheoret* is used to obtain r_T. The macro computes r_T for $n = 3 \ldots 150$ and $\alpha = 0.10, 0.05$ and 0.01. Appendix C, *Minitab macros*, provides the macro *rtheoret* and associated macros. You must set the constants *k1* and *k2* as follows before invoking the procedure:

k1	n
k2	α

Then use the Minitab *execute* command to execute the macro. However, before executing the macro, you must change the directory to that containing the macros by using the Minitab *cd* command.

EXAMPLE 15.3   STUDENT EXPENDITURE (continued)
The Minitab commands for checking the assumption of a normally distributed variable for this example are as follows:

```
MTB > outfile 'a:\booksurv.lis'
MTB > retrieve 'a:\booksurv.mtp';
SUBC> portable.
MTB > info
MTB > name c2 'zscores'
MTB > nscores 'bookstat' 'zscores'
MTB > plot 'bookstat' 'zscores'
MTB > correlation 'bookstat' 'zscores'
MTB > let k1=25
MTB > let k2=0.05
MTB > cd a:\
MTB > execute 'rtheoret.mtb'
```

If your version of Minitab has pull-down menus and you want to use them, table 15.2 lists the menus and options that access the required commands. Appendix D, *Detailed instructions for Minitab menus*, explains how to use the menus.

Table 15.2   Menus and options for Minitab commands to check the normal distribution assumption

Minitab command	Menu	Option
outfile	File >	Other Files > Start Recording Session...
retrieve	File >	Open Worksheet...
port		Minitab portable worksheet
info	Edit >	Get Worksheet Info...
	(Edit >	Data Screen [Alt-D])
name	Edit >	Data Screen (Alt-D)
nscores	Calc >	Functions and Statistics > Functions...
plot	Graph >	Scatter Plot...
correlation	Stat >	Basic Statistics > Correlation...
let	Calc >	Functions and Statistics > General Expressions...
cd		not available
execute	File >	Other Files > Execute Macro...

The following output is produced by the Minitab commands listed above:

```
MTB > retrieve 'a:\booksurv.mtp';
SUB> portable.

Worksheet retrieved from file: a:\booksurv.mtp
MTB > info

COLUMN    NAME         COUNT
C1        bookstat       25
CONSTANTS USED: NONE
MTB > name c2 'zscores'
MTB > nscores 'bookstat' 'zscores'
MTB > plot 'bookstat' 'zscores'
  bookstat-
         -                                                    *
         -                                          *  *  *
     300+                                        *
         -                                  *  *  *
         -                                *
         -                              *
         -                   *2 **
     200+                  **
         -                *
         -             *
         -           *
         -          *
     100+        *    *
         -    *      *
         -
         -
         --------+---------+---------+---------+---------+----zscores
             -1.60     -0.80      0.00      0.80      1.60

MTB > correlation 'bookstat' 'zscores'

Correlation of bookstat and zscores = 0.981
MTB > let k1=25
MTB > let k2=0.05
MTB > cd a:\
MTB > execute 'rtheoret.mtb'
The Theoretical value for the normal probability plot r
has been computed for

the number of observations equal to
K6       25.0000
and significance level of
K7       0.0500000

The theoretical value is:
K3       0.958229
```

15.7.2 Confidence interval for the population mean

The Minitab command *tinterval* can be used to compute the confidence interval for a mean. This command is accessed, with the pull-down menus, by using *Stat > Basic Statistics > 1-Sample t....*

EXAMPLE 15.3 STUDENT EXPENDITURE (continued)

The Minitab command and associated output for producing the confidence interval for the population mean for this example are as follows:

```
MTB > info

COLUMN    NAME       COUNT
C1        bookstat      25

MTB > tinterval with confidence 95% on 'bookstat'

              N     MEAN    STDEV    SE MEAN    95.0 PERCENT C.I.
bookstat     25    213.6    77.9      15.6    ( 181.5,  245.8)
```

In computing the confidence interval, the Minitab command *tinterval* computes the required theoretical value, t_T. Although not necessary, you can obtain t_T separately by using the Minitab command *invcdf* with subcommand *t*. To obtain t_T, you have to supply the degrees of freedom of the standard error, $(n-1)$, and $(1+\gamma)/2$, which is $100(1+\gamma)/2\%$ expressed as a proportion. The general form of the Minitab command is:

```
MTB > invcdf (1 + γ)/2;
SUBC> t (n-1).
```

This command is accessed, with the pull-down menus, by using *Calc > Probability Distributions > T....*

EXAMPLE 15.3 STUDENT EXPENDITURE (continued)

For $100\gamma\% = 95\%$, $(1+\gamma)/2 = (1+0.95)/2 = 0.975$, and so the Minitab commands and associated output for obtaining t_T are as follows:

```
MTB > invcdf 0.975;
SUBC> t 24.
    0.9750    2.0639
```

15.7.3 Prediction interval for a future observation

There is no Minitab command to produce the prediction interval for a future observation. However, the macro *predint* provided in Appendix C *Minitab macros*, does the required computations. You must enter the data into a column and then set the constants *k1* and *k2* as follows before invoking the procedure:

k1	data column
k2	$100\gamma\%$

Note that if the value of *k2* is less than 1, it is multiplied by 100 as it is assumed that a proportion has been mistakenly supplied. Once you have set *k1* and *k2*, use the Minitab *execute* command to execute the macro.

EXAMPLE 15.3 STUDENT EXPENDITURE (continued)

The commands and associated output for computing the prediction interval for the example are as follows. The menus and options that access these commands are listed in table 15.2.

```
MTB > info

COLUMN       NAME       COUNT
C1           bookstat      25

MTB > let k1=1
MTB > let k2=95
MTB > cd a:\
MTB > execute 'predint.mtb'

 PREDICTION INTERVAL

The Prediction Interval has been computed for

 the confidence level (expressed as a percentage)
K3      95.0000
 from a sample whose descriptive statistics are:

                N       MEAN    MEDIAN    TRMEAN     STDEV    SEMEAN
bookstat       25      213.6     213.0     214.3      77.9      15.6

               MIN       MAX        Q1        Q3
bookstat      79.0     332.0     151.0     273.0

The upper and lower limits of the Prediction Interval are:
K4       49.6062
K5      377.674
```

15.7.4 Tolerance interval for the middle $100\pi\%$ of population values

Again, there is no Minitab command to produce the tolerance interval. However, the macro *tolerint* provided in Appendix C, *Minitab macros*, does the required computations. Before invoking the procedure, enter the data into a column and then set the constants *k1–k3* as follows:

k1	data column
k2	$100\gamma\%$
k3	$100\pi\%$

Note that if the values of *k2* or *k3* are less than 1, they are multiplied by 100 as it is assumed that proportions have been mistakenly supplied. Having set *k1–k3*, use the Minitab *execute* command to execute the macro.

EXAMPLE 15.3 STUDENT EXPENDITURE (continued)

The commands and associated output for computing the tolerance interval for the example are as follows. The menus and options that access these commands are listed in table 15.2.

```
MTB > info

COLUMN        NAME      COUNT
C1        bookstat        25

MTB > let k1=1
MTB > let k2=95
MTB > let k3=95
MTB > cd a:\
MTB > execute 'tolerint.mtb'

TOLERANCE INTERVAL

The Tolerance Interval has been computed for

  the percentage of the population values to be covered being
K13      95.0000
  and the required confidence level (as a percentage) being
K12      95.0000
  from a sample whose descriptive statistics are:
                N      MEAN    MEDIAN    TRMEAN      STDEV    SEMEAN
bookstat       25     213.6     213.0     214.3       77.9      15.6

               MIN       MAX        Q1        Q3
bookstat      79.0     332.0     151.0     273.0

The upper and lower limits of the Tolerance Interval are:
K5      7.95448
K6      419.326
```

In computing the tolerance interval, the macro *tolerint* computes the required theoretical value, g_T. Although not necessary, you can obtain g_T separately by using the macro *gtheoret*. To do this, set *k2* and *k3* as for *tolerint* and set *k4* to the sample size *n*.

EXAMPLE 15.3   STUDENT EXPENDITURE (continued)

The Minitab commands and associated output are as follows. The menus and options that access these commands are listed in table 15.2.

```
MTB > let k2=95
MTB > let k3=95
MTB > let k4=25
MTB > execute 'gtheoret.mtb'
 THEORETICAL VALUE FOR A TOLERANCE INTERVAL

The Theoretical value has been computed for

a sample of size
K4      25.0000
 and the percentage of the population values to be covered being
K13     95.0000
 and the required confidence level (as a percentage) being
K12     95.0000

The theoretical value is:
K5      2.63922
```

15.8   Chapter summary

We have covered three interval estimates for estimating different population quantities as follows:

- the confidence interval estimates the *mean* of the values of the whole population;
- the prediction interval estimates a *single value* from the population;
- the tolerance interval estimates the middle *range of values* that will include the specified proportion of values in the population.

Which interval is to be used depends on the question to be investigated.

The confidence interval ($100\gamma\%$) for the population mean gives us the range that we can be $100\gamma\%$ confident will include the population mean. Using this interval, rather than the sample mean as a point estimate, has the advantage of indicating the precision with which the population mean is estimated. The sampling distribution underlying this confidence interval is the t distribution and this is based on a normal probability model for the unrestricted variable. The conditions that will satisfy the assumptions required for the valid use of the sampling distribution are as follows:

1. Conditions for normal probability model
- *Unrestricted variable*
- *Normally distributed variable*

2. Conditions for other validating assumptions
- *Infinite population*
- *Representative sample*
- *Independence*

For a particular example, you must check whether these conditions are fulfilled. If they are not, the assumptions required to use the sampling distribution are not met and the procedure cannot be used for that example.

The prediction interval ($100\gamma\%$) for a future observation estimates, with $100\gamma\%$ confidence, the range that will include a single future observation from the same population as the sample. That is, we obtain an interval estimate of a single value. The sampling distribution for this prediction interval is the t distribution and this is based on a normal probability model for the unrestricted variable. The conditions that have to be satisfied are exactly the same as for the confidence interval for the population mean, with the extra condition that the future observation is representative of the population and independent of any other observations.

The tolerance interval ($100\pi\%$, $100\gamma\%$) for the middle $100\pi\%$ of population values estimates, with $100\gamma\%$ confidence, the range containing the middle $100\pi\%$ of the values, of the unrestricted variable, in the population. It is an interval estimate of a range of values. The sampling distribution for this tolerance interval is unnamed, but it is based on a normal probability model for the unrestricted variable. The conditions that have to be satisfied are exactly the same as for the confidence interval for the population mean.

A condition required by all three intervals is that the unrestricted variable is normally distributed, although this condition is not as crucial for the confidence interval as it is for the other two intervals. We presented a method for assessing whether the values of an unrestricted variable, for the observational units in a sample, come from a population whose values for this variable are normally distributed. This method involves plotting the observed data against their normal scores, producing what is termed a normal probability plot. This plot should show a broad straight line trend. To help us decide whether or not the line is straight enough, we compute the normal probability plot correlation coefficient, and a corresponding theoretical value. If the observed value, r_N, is less than or equal to the theoretical value, r_T, the hypothesis of normality should be rejected. Otherwise, retain the hypothesis of normality.

In planning a survey, you have to decide on the sample size. You can calculate the sample size for a survey in which a population mean is to be estimated provided you specify what confidence level and what maximum tolerable error, or precision, you want to achieve. You also require some idea of the value of the standard deviation for the unrestricted variable, and this may be obtained as a guesstimate from data gathered from similar situations or a pilot study.

15.9   Key terms

- assumptions
- conditions
- confidence interval (100γ%) for the population mean
- confidence level (100γ%)
- independence condition
- infinite population
- maximum tolerable error (e)
- mean ($\bar{y}$ or μ)
- measure of central tendency
- normal distribution
- normal probability model
- normal probability plot
- normal probability plot correlation coefficient (r_N)
- normal score
- normally distributed variable

- prediction interval (100γ%) for a future observation
- range of values
- representative sample
- sample size (n)
- single value
- standard error ($s_{\bar{y}}$)
- theoretical value for computing the tolerance interval (g_T)
- theoretical value for the normal probability plot correlation coefficient (r_T)
- theoretical value for the t distribution (t_T)
- tolerance interval (100π%, 100γ%) for the middle 100π% of population values

15.10 Exercises

15.1   Write down the formula for creating a confidence interval that will give a range of values likely to contain the population mean; then define in your own words the following terms:

  (a) sample mean
  (b) confidence level
  (c) degrees of freedom
  (d) t_T
  (e) standard error of the sample mean
  (f) standard deviation

15.2   What conditions are required for the confidence interval for the population mean to be valid? How can these conditions be checked? Does it matter if these conditions are not completely satisfied?

15.3   Will all confidence intervals for the population mean (each using the same level of confidence) based on samples of the same size from a specific population contain the population mean? Give reasons for your answer?

15.4   A confidence interval for the population mean estimates the population mean by obtaining the range of values that will include it 100γ% of the time.

(a) If you increase the sample size, what will happen to the interval and hence the precision of our estimate?

(b) Will the precision of our estimate of the population mean decrease or increase as the required confidence level increases? Give reasons for your answer.

(c) If we obtain confidence intervals ($100\gamma\%$) from several different samples of the same size from the same population, will the precision of our estimates be the same for all samples? Give reasons for your answer?

15.5 At the end of each quarter the Australian Bureau of Statistics publishes the latest consumer price index. This figure is derived from samples. What type of estimate has been used? Is this the most desirable estimate to use?

15.6 Exercise 8.1 presents the annual incomes for two simple random samples of households in Statstown and Bustown. Now the average income for households in each town is required. The populations of these towns are approximately 7500 and 9000.

(a) Answer the following questions:

(i) What is the question to be investigated (including the group to which the conclusions apply)?

(ii) What variable(s) are we concerned with here?

(iii) What type of variable(s) are they?

(iv) Which major category of statistical procedures applies here? Why?

(v) What type of statistic should we use, given the question to be investigated and the variables involved?

(vi) Which particular statistic or procedure, and diagram, should we use? Why?

(b) Reproduce the following Minitab output.

```
MTB > retrieve 'a:\inctown.mtp';
SUBC> portable.

Worksheet retrieved from file: a:\inctown.mtp
MTB > info

COLUMN     NAME      COUNT
C1      Stattown      40
C2      Bustown       80

CONSTANTS USED: NONE

MTB > describe c1 c2
```

	N	MEAN	MEDIAN	TRMEAN	STDEV	SEMEAN
Stattown	40	88675	90500	88528	9846	1557
Bustown	80	122913	121500	122639	18511	2070

continued . . .

```
                 MIN        MAX         Q1          Q3
Stattown        71000     114000      82000       95000
Bustown         88000     162000     109000      137750

MTB > invcdf 0.975;
SUBC> t 39.
    0.9750      2.0227
MTB > invcdf 0.975;
SUBC> t 79.
    0.9750      1.9905
MTB > name c3='zscore_S'
MTB > nscores c1 c3
MTB > plot c1 c3
```

(handwritten annotations: "95% conf", "t")

```
  Stattown-                                                      *
          -
          -
   105000+                                               *
          -                                          * * *
          -                                        *
          -                                 3 **
          -                           4   4
    90000+                         *2
          -                   3  *
          -                *2
          -            2 2
          -          *
    75000+      2   *
          -  2      *

          ------+---------+---------+---------+---------+----zscore_S
             -1.60     -0.80      0.00      0.80      1.60
MTB > corr c1 c3

Correlation of Stattown and zscore_S = 0.992

MTB > cd a:\
MTB > let k1=40
MTB > let k2=0.05
MTB > execute 'rtheoret.mtb'
The Theoretical value for the normal probability plot r
has been computed for

the number of observations equal to
K6      40.0000
and significance level of
K7       0.0500000

The theoretical value is:
K3       0.971484
MTB > name c4='zscore_B'
MTB > nscores c2 c4
```

continued . . .

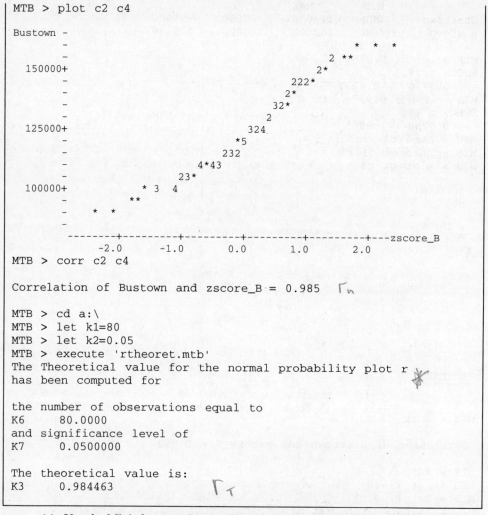

```
MTB > plot c2 c4

Bustown -
         -                                                    *   *   *
         -                                               2  **
  150000+                                             2*
         -                                      222*
         -                                    2*
         -                                   32*
         -                                  2
  125000+                           324
         -                       *5
         -                    232
         -                4*43
         -             23*
  100000+          *  3   4
         -          **
         -      *   *
         -

           --------+---------+---------+---------+---------+---zscore_B
              -2.0      -1.0      0.0       1.0       2.0
MTB > corr c2 c4

Correlation of Bustown and zscore_B = 0.985    ⌈n

MTB > cd a:\
MTB > let k1=80
MTB > let k2=0.05
MTB > execute 'rtheoret.mtb'
The Theoretical value for the normal probability plot r
has been computed for

the number of observations equal to
K6       80.0000
and significance level of
K7       0.0500000

The theoretical value is:
K3       0.984463              ⌈T
```

(c) Use the Minitab output in part (b) to determine the range that will include, with 95% confidence, the average income for households in each town.

(d) What conditions have to be met for the interval to be valid?

(e) Use the Minitab output in part (b) to decide whether the conditions have been met.

15.7 For each of the two towns in exercise 15.6, calculate the range that we can be 90% confident contains 95% of the population incomes.

(a) Answer the following questions:

(i) What is the question to be investigated (including the group to which the conclusions apply)?

(ii) What variable(s) are we concerned with here?

(iii) What type of variable(s) are they?

(iv) Which major category of statistical procedures applies here? Why?

(v) What type of statistic should we use, given the question to be investigated and the variables involved?

(vi) Which particular statistic or procedure, and diagram, should we use? Why?

(b) What is the formula for calculating the tolerance interval which estimates the range containing the middle $100\pi\%$ of the population values?

(c) What are the conditions under which this procedure is valid?

(d) In your own words explain the difference between the confidence interval for the population mean and the tolerance interval for the middle $100\pi\%$ of population values.

```
MTB > let k2=90
MTB > let k3=95
MTB > let k4=40
MTB > execute 'gtheoret.mtb'
 THEORETICAL VALUE FOR A TOLERANCE INTERVAL

The Theoretical value has been computed for

a sample of size
K4      40.0000
 and the percentage of the population to be covered being
K13     95.0000
 and the confidence level (expressed as a percentage) being
K12     90.0000

The theoretical value is:
K5      2.33678

MTB > let k4=80
MTB > execute 'gtheoret.mtb'
 THEORETICAL VALUE FOR A TOLERANCE INTERVAL

The Theoretical value has been computed for

a sample of size
K4      80.0000
 and the percentage of the population to be covered being
K13     95.0000
 and the confidence level (expressed as a percentage) being
K12     90.0000

The theoretical value is:
K5      2.20297
```

(e) From the Minitab output in exercise 15.6 and the above Minitab output, calculate the range that we can be 90% confident contains 95% of the population incomes for each town.

(f) Check your calculations for part (e) by using the *tolerint* macro.

15.8 A tertiary institution with 18 000 full-time students wishes to estimate the average number of hours per week that they study outside classes. It selected a simple random sample of 35 full-time students and asked them to record the number of hours they studied outside class in the last week. The results are given in table 15.3.

Table 15.3   *Study outside classes* (hours)

6.8	12.0	10.9	12.4	2.9
10.8	7.8	16.2	10.9	13.1
15.2	11.0	9.7	9.4	11.6
9.0	24.1	19.2	12.8	11.3
18.8	15.7	11.4	16.2	13.2
13.4	4.5	9.2	4.9	10.5
6.5	11.2	13.0	3.4	10.0

(a) Answer the following questions:
   (i) What is the question to be investigated (including the group to which the conclusions apply)?
   (ii) What variable(s) are we concerned with here?
   (iii) What type of variable(s) are they?
   (iv) Which major category of statistical procedures applies here? Why?
   (v) What type of statistic should we use, given the question to be investigated and the variables involved?
   (vi) Which particular statistic or procedure, and diagram, should we use? Why?
(b) What is the range that will include, with 95% confidence, the average number of hours that students at this university study outside classes?
(c) Suppose one more student is randomly selected from the same student body. Compute the range that you estimate, with 95% confidence, would include the number of hours studied by the student.
(d) What range of hours is it estimated, with 95% confidence, that 90% of students spend studying outside classes?
(e) Which interval gives the most useful information? Give reasons for your answer.

15.9 Table 15.4 records *Length of service* for all public service employees with service records of at least 10 years; this data was examined in exercise 7.7. The data has been saved in the Minitab portable worksheet file *lenserv.mtp*.

Table 15.4   *Length of service* (years)

33	41	11	15	42	33	30
37	39	20	41	15	15	44
14	23	35	10	22	32	36
32	13	30	22	12	26	27
23	22	10	14	13	37	15
45	16	31	11	15	11	32
11	10	12	19	23	33	19
24	24	11	28	39	28	15
12	23	24	39	20	14	16
28	11	23	17	28	23	13
17	34	12	21	25	20	39
10	17	16	19	40	11	25
27	23	10	26	10	23	39
36	18	34	17	17	41	17
10	16	26	38	26	10	16
20	21	15	12	37	19	22
26	15	23	27	10	22	33
34	11	35	32	17	19	14
28	13	10	11	30	13	19
16	20	15	14	36	22	21

(a) Use Minitab to obtain a histogram for this data. Describe the shape of the distribution for the complete set of data.

(b) Select two simple random samples and one systematic sample, each of size 8, from the population of 140 employees.

(c) For each sample, and for all employees, obtain the mean and median *Length of service* for the selected employees. What information do these values represent? Do these sample means and medians differ between themselves and from the population mean and median *Length of service*? What do you conclude from this comparison?

(d) Find the interquartile ranges and standard deviations of *Length of service* for all employees and for those in the selected samples. How closely do the sample values approximate to the population values?

(e) For each simple random sample, compute the confidence interval (95%) for the population mean.

(f) For each simple random sample, check the conditions for the confidence interval (95%) for the population mean to be valid. What do your conclusions about the conditions imply for the confidence interval computed in part (e)?

15.10 Bad debt percentage is defined as the dollar amount defaulted divided by the total amount loaned multiplied by 100. A bank wishes to establish the typical bad debt percentage for the 8000 personal loans it has made over the past year for the purchase of new cars. The files for the last 50 defaulted personal loans were examined and the recorded bad debt percentages extracted from them are given in table 15.5.

Table 15.5   *Bad debt percentage* for new car loans

4.58	3.52	4.75	4.75	4.47
3.44	5.35	4.53	4.94	4.57
5.73	4.42	4.82	6.13	5.09
4.18	4.45	4.95	3.51	4.47
4.64	4.88	3.94	6.21	5.49
4.31	4.60	3.98	4.11	5.41
5.24	3.89	6.08	4.72	4.55
3.97	4.22	3.72	4.08	5.96
4.53	5.15	4.43	3.26	5.03
5.09	3.79	4.33	3.37	3.86

(a) Answer the following questions:
   (i) What is the question to be investigated (including the group to which the conclusions apply)?
   (ii) What variable(s) are we concerned with here?
   (iii) What type of variable(s) are they?
   (iv) Which major category of statistical procedures applies here? Why?
   (v) What type of statistic should we use, given the question to be investigated and the variables involved?
   (vi) Which particular statistic or procedure, and diagram, should we use? Why?
(b) What is the shape of the distribution of *Bad debt percentage*?
(c) Calculate a confidence interval (99%) for the population mean *Bad debt percentage*.
(d) What is the range, estimated with 95% confidence, that will contain 95% of the population values for *Bad debt percentage*?
(e) What is the range, estimated with 95% confidence, that will include the value for the *Bad debt percentage* of a further randomly selected new car?
(f) Check the conditions required for the interval computed in part (e) to be valid. What do you conclude about the validity of this interval?

15.11 Table 15.6 presents the original data for *Monthly rental expenditure* from a pilot sample of independent realtors presented in table 15.6.

Table 15.6 *Monthly rental expenditure ($) from a pilot sample*

1047	573	576	655	808
1086	1159	655	665	805
958	1110	572	736	388
936	313	363	575	594
769	921	631	930	720

Use this data to decide what size sample you would need to estimate the population average *Monthly rental expenditure* to within ± $30 and with 95% confidence.

## CHAPTER 16

ESTIMATION FOR TWO UNRESTRICTED VARIABLES

L E A R N I N G   O B J E C T I V E S

The learning objectives of this chapter are:

- to know when to apply, how to calculate and how to interpret the results of the confidence intervals for the population intercept, population slope and population mean response and the prediction interval for a future observation;
- to know the conditions required for the confidence and prediction intervals to be valid;
- to be able to determine when the conditions for valid inference in linear regression are met;
- to understand the limitations of linear regression.

The following extract from the *Summary of procedures based on combinations of variable types* in part VI gives an overview of the estimation procedures covered in this and the previous chapters of part IV, *Estimation procedures*.

1. *One or two limited variable(s)*
    - Distribution of variables: confidence interval for the population proportion.
2. *One unrestricted variable or one unrestricted variable with one or two limited variable(s)*
    - Single value: prediction interval for a single future observation.
    - Range of values: tolerance interval for middle $100\pi\%$ of population values.
    - Measures of central tendency: confidence interval for the population mean.
3. *Two unrestricted variables*
    - **Fitted lines**: confidence intervals for population intercept, population slope and population mean response; prediction interval for a future observation.

As outlined in the objectives, this chapter covers the following estimation procedures:

- confidence interval for the population **intercept**;
- confidence interval for the population **slope**;
- confidence interval for the population **mean response**;
- prediction interval for a future observation.

Since these are statistical inference procedures, to use them we must have taken a sample and the question to be investigated must *not* confined to the sample but be about the population.

16.1   Probability model and inference questions in simple linear regression

This section introduces estimation procedures for simple linear regression. There are several estimation procedures designed to answer various questions you may wish to investigate in the context of simple linear regression. As outlined in chapter 10, *Regression for two unrestricted variables*, in regression you must distinguish between the response and explanatory variables. The **explanatory variable**, denoted by X, is the variable whose values are to be specified in obtaining computed quantities. The **response variable**, denoted by Y, is the variable for which quantities are to be computed for specified values of the explanatory variable. Quantities that might be computed are the mean response, the intercept, the slope or an interval estimate. In all these, one variable's value is specified and the quantity is computed for the other variable.

These estimation procedures are based on a **normal probability model with a linear relationship** for the response variable — the model has the following features:

1. Consider all observational units in the population that have the same value of the explanatory variable, X:
   - The response variable, Y, is normally distributed for these units with a particular mean, μ_Y, and standard deviation, σ_Y.

2. Compare normal distributions of the response variable, Y, for different values of the explanatory variable, X:
   - The population means of these distributions are linearly related to the explanatory variable.
   - The population standard deviations of these distributions are the same.

That is, in the setup we are now envisaging for regression we have an **equation for a straight line** that has been fitted to the values of the variables in the population. This equation is denoted by:

$$Y = \beta_0 + \beta_1 X$$

where Y is the name of the response variable;

X is the name of the explanatory variable;

β_0 is the population intercept;

β_1 is the population slope.

This line can be used to obtain the population mean for the response variable, called the population mean response, for a particular value of the explanatory variable, X. If x denotes the value of X for which the population mean response, μ_Y, is required, the equation tells us that:

$$\mu_Y = \beta_0 + \beta_1 x.$$

Figure 16.1 illustrates how the population relationship specifies the relationship between the population mean response and the value of the explanatory variable.

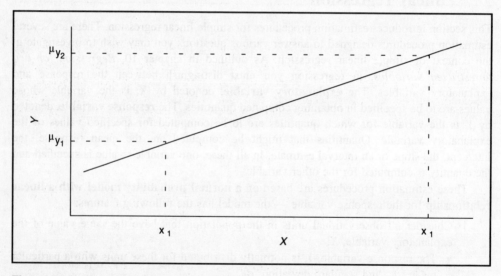

Figure 16.1 Population linear relationship

In addition to the linear relationship, the model specifies that the population distribution of the values of the response variable at each value of the explanatory variable is normal. Suppose you obtain the values of the response variable for all the observational units with a value of either x_1 or x_2 for the explanatory variable, as in figure 16.1; the model tells you that if a separate distribution of the values of the response variable is formed for each value of the explanatory variable, they should look more or less like figure 16.2 (opposite). That is, two normal distributions with the same population spread, σ_Y, but different population means, μ_{Y_1} and μ_{Y_2}.

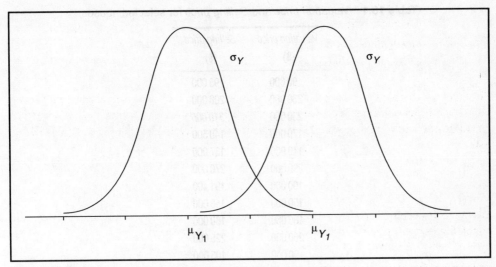

Figure 16.2   Population distributions for two different values of *X*

More generally, the population mean of the distribution of the response variable changes gradually as the value of the explanatory variable changes, and the rate of change is specified by the population linear relationship. As usual with statistical inference, the population parameters for this straight line, β_0 and β_1, are unknown. However, since we have data from a sample, this can be used to calculate the sample straight line. The equation for the sample straight line is:

$$Y = b_0 + b_1 X$$

and we do know the statistics b_0 and b_1 involved in this formula. We want to use these to draw conclusions about the population parameters.

EXAMPLE 16.1   ESTIMATING *SELLING PRICE* FROM *VALUATION PRICE*

A real estate agent wants to estimate the final selling price of a house from the valuation price agreed upon when the house was first put up for sale: that is, she wants to use the relationship between two unrestricted variables, *Valuation price* and *Selling price*. The agent has this information for houses sold in her area over a 12-month period. It is filed in alphabetical order according to the vendor's surname. The agent has information on 451 houses, but does not have time to extract the information for all of them, so she systematically samples 20 of these houses. Section 4.2.4, *Systematic sampling*, describes the procedure for this. It involves taking every 22nd (= integer part of 451/20) record. To determine where to start, randomly select one of the first 33 (= 451 – 22 × [20 – 1]) vendors. The valuation and selling prices in table 16.1 represent the agent's raw, primary data.

Table 16.1 *Valuation price* and *Selling price* for selected houses

Valuation price ($)	Selling price ($)
90 000	95 000
230 000	208 000
230 000	*310 000*
170 000	140 500
140 000	137 000
290 000	270 000
190 000	191 400
150 000	158 000
180 000	160 000
260 000	225 000
90 000	105 000
270 000	265 000
190 000	153 500
130 000	149 000
180 000	161 000
620 000	560 000
270 000	244 000
210 000	165 100
120 000	94 000
130 000	105 000

A preliminary examination of the data is now made, using descriptive summaries. Figure 16.3, a scatter diagram, illustrates the relationship between these two variables, which has an R^2 of 93.4%. It also includes the fitted straight line, whose equation is:

$$Selling\ price = 9745 + 0.89411\ Valuation\ price$$

Questions you might ask for this example are listed as follows. All these questions require statistical inference procedures as they are general questions that apply to the population; none are restricted to the sample observations.

1. What *Selling price* can I expect when the *Valuation price* is zero?
2. How much will *Selling price* change as a result of a $1 increase in the *Valuation price*?
3. What mean *Selling price* can I expect when the *Valuation price* is $135 000?
4. If I observed another house and it had a *Valuation price* of $215 000, what is its likely *Selling price*?

5.   Is the expected *Selling price* different from zero, when the *Valuation price* is zero?

6.   Is there a relationship between *Selling price* and *Valuation price*?

7.   Is the expected change in *Selling price* different from $1, when the *Valuation price* increases by $1?

For these questions, what are the response and explanatory variables? Why? *Answer: Valuation price* is the explanatory variable because its values are to be specified, whereas *Selling price* is the response variable because its values are to be computed.

Note that the first three questions would be answered by using confidence intervals, the last three by using hypothesis tests, and the fourth question requires a prediction interval. This example is used to illustrate the estimation procedures that answer the first four questions.

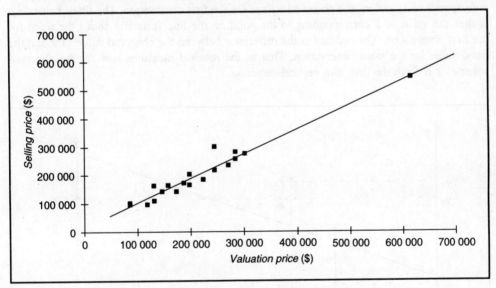

Figure 16.3   Scatter diagram for *Selling price* versus *Valuation price*

16.2   Conditions for valid inference in simple linear regression

All statistical inference procedures for regression involve checking essentially the same set of conditions. Consequently, the conditions, and the techniques for checking them, are outlined before the procedures themselves are described.

16.2.1   Residual analysis

Checking the conditions for valid inference in regression is done by examining the fitted values and the (standardised) residuals from the regression. The **fitted values** are the values of the response variable, Y, for the points on the fitted line corresponding to the observed values of the explanatory variable, X. The **residuals** are the differences between the observed values of the response variable, Y, and the fitted values. A residual reflects how far away the observed Y value is from the fitted line.

Let y_i be the observed value of Y for the ith observation,

x_i be the observed value of X for the ith observation,

$\hat{y}_i$ be the fitted value corresponding to the ith observation, and

e_i be the residual for the ith observation.

Then:

$$\hat{y}_i = b_0 + b_1 x_i \quad \text{and}$$
$$e_i = y_i - \hat{y}_i$$

The scatter diagram in figure 16.4 illustrates these quantities. The first plotted point corresponds to x_1 and y_1, the observed values for the first observation. The fitted value, $\hat{y}_1$, is then the value of Y corresponding to the point on the line vertically above the point for the first observation. The residual is the difference between the observed value of Y and the fitted value for the same observation. That is, the residual measures how far the observed value of Y is from the line, in a vertical direction.

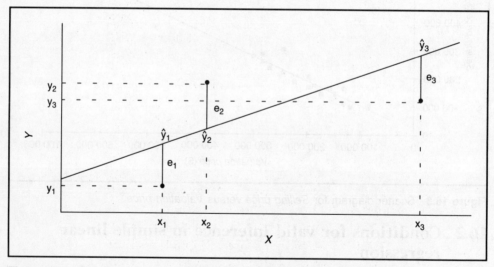

Figure 16.4 Fitted values and residuals in simple linear regression

Now it can be shown that the residuals do not have the same variance because they are computed from fitted values that also have different variances. The residuals are standardised by dividing each residual by its standard deviation producing the **standardised residuals**. That is, standardising the residuals removes the differences in variation between the residuals. It is the standardised residuals that are in fact used to make *standardised-residuals-versus-fitted-values* and *normal probability* plots for checking the conditions.

EXAMPLE 16.1   ESTIMATING *SELLING PRICE* FROM *VALUATION PRICE*

(continued)

The fitted values, residuals and standardised residuals are given in table 16.2. Note that the fitted values are obtained by substituting each of the *Valuation prices* into the equation for the fitted straight line. For example, for the first observation, the fitted value is calculated as 9745 + 0.89411 × 90 000 = 90 214.9; the value in the table, 90 214.3, is different in the first decimal place due to rounding. The residuals are then obtained by subtracting the fitted values from the selling prices. That is, 95 000 − 90 214.3 = 4785.7. Finally, the residuals are standardised to produce the standardised residuals.

Table 16.2   Fitted values, residuals and standardised residuals for *Selling price*

Valuation price ($)	Selling price ($)	Fitted values ($)	Residuals ($)	Standardised residuals
90 000	95 000	90 214.3	4 785.7	0.1812
230 000	208 000	215 389.5	−7 389.5	−0.2718
230 000	310 000	215 389.5	94 610.5	3.4796
170 000	140 500	161 743.0	−21 243.0	−0.7827
140 000	137 000	134 919.7	2 080.3	0.0772
290 000	270 000	269 036.0	964.0	0.0359
190 000	191 400	179 625.2	11 774.8	0.4328
150 000	158 000	143 860.8	14 139.2	0.5231
180 000	160 000	170 684.1	−10 684.1	−0.3931
260 000	225 000	242 212.7	−17 212.8	−0.6361
90 000	105 000	902 14.3	14 785.7	0.5597
270 000	265 000	251 153.8	13 846.2	0.5130
190 000	153 500	179 625.2	-26 125.2	−0.9603
130 000	149 000	125 978.6	23 021.4	0.8566
180 000	161 000	170 684.1	−9 684.1	−0.3563
620 000	560 000	564 091.8	−4 091.8	−0.2873
270 000	244 000	251 153.8	−7 153.8	−0.2651
210 000	165 100	197 507.3	ç32 407.3	−1.1905
120 000	94 000	117 037.6	−23 037.6	−0.8603
130 000	105 000	125 978.6	−20 978.6	−0.7806

Figure 16.5 gives an example of a *standardised-residuals-versus-fitted-values* plot.

16.2.2 Checking the conditions

As discussed in the introduction to part IV, *Estimation procedures*, underlying all statistical inference procedures are the **assumptions** made in deriving the sampling distribution and these must be met if the procedure's results are to be valid. For all the intervals computed from regression, the appropriate sampling distribution is the t distribution and this is based on a normal probability model, with a linear relationship between the response and explanatory variable, for the response variable. This model was described in section 16.1, *Probability model and inference questions in simple linear regression*. The **conditions** that will satisfy the assumptions required for the valid use of the sampling distribution are as follows:

1. **Conditions for normal probability model with linear relationship**
   - *Unrestricted variables*
   - *Normally distributed variable*
   - *Linear relationship*
   - *Homogeneity of variance*
   - *X is known without error*

2. **Conditions for other validating assumptions**
   - *Infinite population*
   - *Representative sample*
   - *Independence*

Further details of these conditions and the methods for checking them are described below.

Unrestricted variables

The response and explanatory variables must be unrestricted variables. Determining whether this condition is satisfied can be done simply by considering whether the variable is unrestricted. Usually, there is no problem with this condition.

Normally distributed variable

This condition requires that the population Y values at each value of X are **normally distributed**. You can check this by using the **normal probability plot**, along with the associated **normal probability plot correlation coefficient** r_N. In this plot, the standardised residuals are plotted against normal scores. You can use the normal probability plot correlation coefficient r_N, which is the correlation between the standardised residuals and normal scores, to assess objectively the normality of the variable. As outlined in section 15.1, *Normally distributed unrestricted variables*, which describes how to check for a normally distributed variable, the normal probability plot should display a broad straight line trend and r_N should be close to 1.

Regression analysis can withstand moderate departures from the normality condition. If there is serious departure from normality, there are techniques, beyond the scope of this book, for analysing nonnormal data.

Linear relationship

This condition requires that if there is any relationship between the response and explanatory variable, it should be a **linear relationship**, exhibiting no curvature. You can check it by examining the scatter diagram of Y against X, or by plotting the standardised residuals against the fitted values to produce the **standardised-residuals-versus-fitted-values plot**. The scatter diagram must exhibit either a straight line pattern or no pattern at all. In the standardised-residuals-versus-fitted-values plot, the standardised residuals should be symmetric about a horizontal line through zero. Patterns such as those shown in diagrams (a), (c), (d) and (f) of figure 16.5 indicate that the data is linear.

If the relationship is not linear, simple linear regression is not valid and an appropriate curve must be fitted. There are techniques for doing this but they are outside the scope of this book.

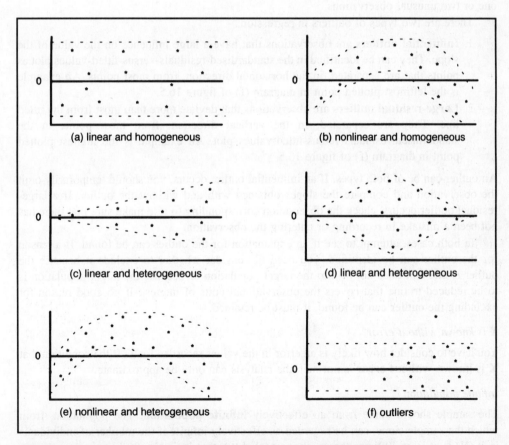

Figure 16.5   Examples of standardised-residuals-versus-fitted-values plots

Homogeneity of variance

For the data to be regarded as exhibiting **homogeneity of variance**, the variation of the population Y values at each value of X must be the same; that is, homogeneity of variance means equal variance. To meet this condition, the points in the standardised-residuals-versus-fitted-values plot should be contained between two bands that are the same vertical distance apart over the entire range. In figure 16.5, examples of such plots occur in diagrams (a), (b) and (f), whereas the patterns in diagrams (c), (d) and (e) indicate that the homogeneity of variance condition is violated. In diagrams (c) and (e) the variance increases as the size of the fitted values increases. In diagram (d), the variance peaks for midrange fitted values. This is an important condition and must be met if the analysis is to be valid. If the condition is not met, there are techniques for taking into account the heterogeneity of variance, but these are beyond the scope of this book.

A particular phenomenon highlighted by the standardised-residuals-versus-fitted-values plot is the occurrence of outliers, as in diagram (f) of figure 16.5. The presence of outliers should not be confused with heterogeneity of variance, since heterogeneity is not caused by one or two unusual observations.

There are two types of outliers in regression:

1. **Influential outliers** are observations that have a large influence on the value of the slope. They can be identified in the standardised-residuals-versus-fitted-values plot as points that are separated, in the horizontal direction, from most points. An example is the leftmost plotted point in diagram (f) of figure 16.5.
2. **Large-residual outliers** are observations that deviate more than most from the fitted line. They are separated, in the vertical direction, from most points in the standardised-residuals-versus-fitted-values plot. An example is the highest plotted point in diagram (f) of figure 16.5.

An outlier can be of both types. If an influential outlier occurs, you should temporarily omit the observation and compare the slopes obtained with and without the outlier. If a large-residual outlier occurs, check the observation corresponding to it to make sure that there has not been a mistake in recording or entering the observation.

In both cases, attempt to see if an explanation for the outlier can be found. If a reason for the outlier can be identified, you need to consider whether to exclude it because the outlier is one that does not fit into the target population or because the target population is to be reduced to one that covers the observational units of interest. If no good reason for excluding the outlier can be found, it must be retained.

X is known without error

You have to consider how likely is an error in the values recorded for X. If the condition that **X is known without error** is not met, the analysis can only be approximate.

Infinite population

The sample should come from an effectively **infinite population**. The population, from which the sample came, can be regarded as effectively infinite if the number of individuals in it (N) is at least 20 times the number sampled (n); that is, if $N > 20n$.

Representative sample

A **representative sample** is an unbiased fraction of the original population. The methods likely to produce a representative sample were discussed in chapter 4, *Surveys*. We concluded that the probability sampling methods, such as simple random sampling, produce representative samples, so this condition will be met if a probability sampling method is used to select the sample. If not, we cannot guarantee that the condition will be met.

Independence

The **independence condition** is that the value of the response variable for each observation is independent of that for other observations. In general, it is difficult to check this condition. In part, it involves ensuring that the data is collected in such a way that each observation is made independently of the other observations.

Regression is often applied to economic data taken consecutively in time. It is not possible to ensure that this data satisfies the independence condition, because in such situations, the observation made at one point in time may be affected by what happened at previous times. There are residual plots for checking whether consecutive observations are independent, but these are outside the scope of this book.

EXAMPLE 16.1   ESTIMATING *SELLING PRICE* FROM *VALUATION PRICE*
      (continued)

We now outline how to check the conditions that will satisfy the assumptions required for the valid use of statistical inference procedures to draw conclusions about the relationship between *Selling price* and *Valuation price*.

1.   Conditions for normal probability model with linear relationship

- *Unrestricted variables:* We have already stated that the response and explanatory variables, *Selling price* and *Valuation price*, respectively, can be classified as unrestricted variables.

- *Normally distributed variable:* The distribution of *Selling price* when *Valuation price* is $100 000 should be normal, as it should be for any other value of *Valuation price*. Thus, if you had a large number of observations for one value of *Valuation price*, the distribution of *Selling price* for this data should be normal. As there is not a large amount of data for each *Valuation price*, the normal probability plot in figure 16.6 is used to check the condition. Except for the point corresponding to the large-residual outlier in the top right corner, the trend seems approximately linear. The normal probability plot correlation coefficient, r_N, is 0.878. For $n = 20$ and $\alpha = 0.05$, the theoretical value for the normal probability plot correlation coefficient, r_T, is 0.9503. As $0.878 < 0.9503$, the normality hypothesis is rejected.

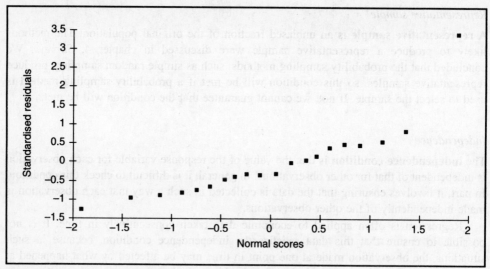

Figure 16.6   Normal probability plot for *Selling price* standardised residuals

- *Linear relationship:* The relationship between *Selling price* and *Valuation price* should be linear. In figure 16.3, the scatter diagram for *Selling price* and *Valuation price*, the trend seems to follow a straight line. In figure 16.7, the standardised-residuals-versus-fitted-values plot for *Selling price* and *Valuation price*, the points appear to be symmetrical about zero, except for a single high point. We conclude that the linear relationship condition is met.

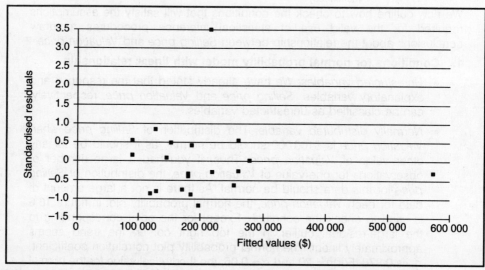

Figure 16.7   Standardised-residuals-versus-fitted-values plot for *Selling price* and *Valuation price*

- *Homogeneity of variance:* The variability in *Selling price* when *Valuation price* is $100 000 should be the same as when *Valuation price* is $200 000 or any other value of *Valuation price.* The standardised-residuals-versus-fitted-values plot for *Selling price* and *Valuation price,* in figure 16.7, indicates that the homogeneity of variance condition is met. For the range $90 000 to $300 000, where there is sufficient data to judge, the vertical spread in the data remains constant as one progresses from left to right across the plot. However, the standardised-residuals-versus-fitted-values plot draws attention to two outliers in this data, an influential and a large-residual outlier.

- *X is known without error:* The *Valuation price* should be known without error. There seems to be no problem in ascertaining and recording the *Valuation price* for each house, so there is no reason to assume that there is any error in an observed *Valuation price.* We can conclude that *X* is known without error.

2. Conditions for other validating assumptions

- *Infinite population:* The population is the 451 houses for which the agent has records, so $N = 451$. Further, $20n = 20 \times 200 = 400$, so $N > 20n$ and the population is effectively infinite.

- *Representative sample:* This condition requires that the sample of houses is representative of the population of 451 houses for which the agent has records. The sample is a systematic sample of the target population. Now this is not a random sample, but is likely to be representative, provided there is not some pattern in the way the records are filed. We will assume they are representative.

- *Independence:* For the independence condition to be met, the value of *Selling price* for one house must be independent of that for other houses. Since the observations are taken over a year, the selling price is influenced by factors outside the agent's control, and there appears to be a range of houses observed, it is likely that the selling prices are largely independent.

Summary

All the conditions checked, except the normality condition, appear to be met in the case of the regression of *Selling price* on *Valuation price.* The failure of the normality condition seems to be the result of a large-residual outlier. Checking the data reveals that the *Selling price* for the third house has been erroneously entered as $310 000; it should be $210 000. Correction of this value changes the equation for the fitted straight line to:

$$Selling \ price = 6670 + 0.88481 \ Valuation \ price$$

and R^2 becomes 97.7%, an increase of 4.3%.

Figure 16.8 gives the revised normal probability plot, and figure 16.9 gives the corrected standardised-residuals-versus-fitted-values plot. The revised normal probability plot looks satisfactory. The new value of r_N is 0.987 which is greater than $r_T = 0.9503$. The condition of normality is now apparently met.

The standardised-residuals-versus-fitted-values plot still indicates that the linear relationship and homogeneity of variance conditions are satisfied. There remains only the influential outlier, a rather more expensive house than most. The analysis has not been revised to exclude it. However, we may well decide that since such houses are sold so infrequently, the point should be omitted and our conclusions restricted to houses whose valuation prices have been anticipated to be less than $300 000.

Having corrected the mistaken observation, all conditions seem to be met in the case of the regression of *Selling price* on *Valuation price* and so statistical inference procedures for regression can be validly applied to this example.

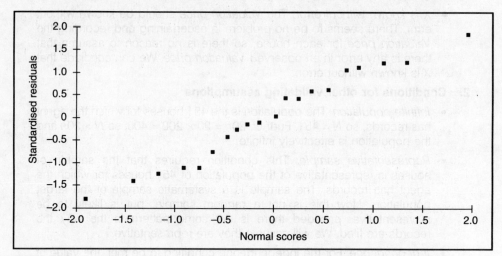

Figure 16.8   Revised normal probability plot for *Selling price* standardised residuals

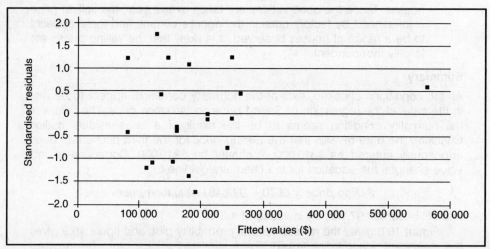

Figure 16.9   Revised standardised-residuals-versus-fitted-values plot for *Selling price* and *Valuation price*

16.3   Confidence interval for the population intercept

16.3.1   Calculating the confidence interval

The question investigated with this procedure is: what value for the response variable can be expected when the explanatory variable is zero? More formally, the question is: what is an estimate for the value of the population intercept β_0?

The formula for the **confidence interval ($100\gamma\%$) for the population intercept** is:

$$\text{Confidence interval } (100\gamma\%) \text{ for } \beta_0 = (b_0 - t_T s_{b_0}, \ b_0 + t_T s_{b_0})$$

where $100\gamma\%$ is the **confidence level** desired by the investigator,

t_T is the **theoretical value for the t distribution** corresponding to $100\gamma\%$ and the degrees of freedom of s_{b_0} which are $n - 2$;

s_{b_0} is the **standard error** of the sample intercept. It measures the variability of the sample intercept, b_0.

EXAMPLE 16.1   ESTIMATING *SELLING PRICE* FROM *VALUATION PRICE*
(continued)

The question investigated with this procedure is: what *Selling price* can be expected when the *Valuation price* is zero? We hope, in this example, that the expected *Selling price* is zero. Otherwise, *Selling price* is being under-estimated or overestimated by the same amount over the whole range of prices. Whether the *Selling price* is underestimated or overestimated by the *Valuation price* depends on whether the intercept is positive or negative, respectively.

For $n = 20$ and $100\gamma\% = 95\%$, $t_T = 2.1009$. For this example, $b_0 = 6670$ and $s_{b_0} = 7552$ so that:

Confidence interval (95%) for β_0
$= (6670 - 2.1009 \times 7552, \ 6670 + 2.1009 \times 7552)$
$= (6670 - 15\,866.00, \ 6670 + 15\,866.00)$
$= (-9196, 22\,536)$

That is, we can be 95% confident that the population intercept is between $-\$9196$ and $\$22\,536$. In particular, note that zero is a plausible value for the population intercept.

16.3.2   Assumptions and conditions

For the confidence interval for the population intercept, the sampling distribution is the t distribution. The conditions required for this confidence interval to be valid are as follows:

1. **Conditions for normal probability model with linear relationship**
   - *Unrestricted variables*
   - *Normally distributed variable*
   - *Linear relationship*
   - *Homogeneity of variance*
   - *X is known without error*

2. Conditions for other validating assumptions
- *Infinite population*
- *Representative sample*
- *Independence*

These conditions were checked in section 16.2.2, *Checking the conditions*, and after we corrected a mistaken value, we concluded that they appear to have been met.

16.4 Confidence interval for the population slope

16.4.1 Calculating the confidence interval

The question investigated with this procedure is: what change in the response variable can be expected when the explanatory variable changes by one unit? More formally: what is an estimate of the value of the population slope β_1?

The formula for the **confidence interval ($100\gamma\%$) for the population slope** is:

$$\text{Confidence interval } (100\gamma\%) \text{ for } \beta_1 = (b_1 - t_T s_{b_1}, \ b_1 + t_T s_{b_1})$$

where $100\gamma\%$ is the confidence level desired by the investigator,

t_T is the theoretical value for the t distribution, corresponding to $100\gamma\%$ and the degrees of freedom of s_{b_1} which are $n - 2$;

s_{b_1} is the standard error of the sample slope. It measures the variability of the sample slope, b_1.

EXAMPLE 16.1   ESTIMATING *SELLING PRICE* FROM *VALUATION PRICE*
(continued)

The question investigated with this procedure is: how much will *Selling price* change as a result of a $1 increase in the *Valuation price*? We hope, in this example, that the expected change in the *Selling price* will be $1 for each dollar increase in the *Valuation price*. If the slope is not 1, then the discrepancy between the two prices increases as the *Valuation price* increases. If the slope is greater than 1, the tendency for the *Valuation price* to be underestimated is greatest for the highest *Valuation prices*. On the other hand, a slope less than 1 indicates that overestimation is greatest for highest *Valuation prices*.

As with the previous interval, for $n = 20$ and $100\gamma\% = 95\%$, $t_T = 2.1009$.
For this example, $b_1 = 0.88481$ and $s_{b_1} = 0.03214$ so that:

Confidence interval (95%) for β_1
  $= (0.88481 - 2.1009 \times 0.03214, \ 0.88481 + 2.1009 \times 0.03214)$
  $= (0.88481 - 0.06752, \ 0.88481 + 0.06752)$
  $= (0.8173, 0.9523)$

That is, we can be 95% confident that the population slope is between $0.8173 and $0.9523 per dollar. In particular, note that $1 is not a plausible value for the slope.

16.4.2 Assumptions and conditions

For the confidence interval for the population slope, the sampling distribution is the t distribution. The conditions required for this confidence interval to be valid are the same as for the confidence interval for the population intercept; that is, the conditions are as follows:

1. **Conditions for normal probability model with linear relationship**
   - *Unrestricted variables*
   - *Normally distributed variable*
   - *Linear relationship*
   - *Homogeneity of variance*
   - *X is known without error*

2. **Conditions for other validating assumptions**
   - *Infinite population*
   - *Representative sample*
   - *Independence*

These conditions were checked in section 16.2.2, *Checking the conditions*, and after we corrected a mistaken value, we concluded that they appear to have been met.

16.5 Confidence interval for the population mean response

Having fitted a straight line, we may well wish to use its equation to estimate μ_Y, the population mean response for a particular value of the explanatory variable, X. We can obtain a point estimate of the population mean response for a specified value, x, of the explanatory variable by substituting x into the equation for the fitted line. That is,

$$\bar{\bar{y}} = b_0 + b_1 x$$

and the sample mean response, $\bar{\bar{y}}$, is a point estimate of μ_Y for $X = x$.

Now, as the fitted line is calculated from a sample set of observed Ys, it is obvious that our calculated values b_0 and b_1 are not exactly equal to the population values. Hence, the sample mean response of Y will not be exactly equal to the population mean response of Y. As for proportions and means previously, a confidence interval for the population mean response might be useful, since it would give us an interval estimate.

16.5.1 Calculating the confidence interval

The question investigated with this procedure is: what value can I expect for the mean of the response variable at a particular value of the explanatory variable? The formula for **the confidence interval (100γ%) for the population mean response** is:

$$\text{Confidence interval (100}\gamma\text{\%) for } \mu_Y = (\bar{\bar{y}} - t_T s_{\bar{\bar{y}}}, \bar{\bar{y}} + t_T s_{\bar{\bar{y}}})$$

where 100γ% is the confidence level desired by the investigator;

$\bar{\bar{y}}$ is the sample mean response;

t_T is the theoretical value for the t distribution, corresponding to $100\gamma\%$ and the degrees of freedom of $s_{\bar{\bar{y}}}$ which are $n-2$;

$s_{\bar{\bar{y}}}$ is the standard error of the sample mean response, $\bar{\bar{y}}$. It measures the variability of $\bar{\bar{y}}$ and depends on the value of the explanatory variable.

EXAMPLE 16.1   ESTIMATING *SELLING PRICE* FROM *VALUATION PRICE*
(continued)

The question investigated with this procedure is: what mean *Selling price* can I expect when the *Valuation price* is \$135 000? As with the previous interval, for $n = 20$ and $100\gamma\% = 95\%$, $t_T = 2.1009$.
  For $X = 135\,000$,

$$\bar{\bar{y}} = 6670 + 0.88481 \times 135\,000 = 126\,119.35 \text{ and } s_{\bar{\bar{y}}} = 4257$$

so that:

Confidence interval (05%) for μ_y
= $(126\,119.35 - 2.1009 \times 4257,\ 126\,119.35 + 2.1009 \times 4257)$
= $(126\,119.35 - 8943.5313,\ 126\,119.35 + 8943.5313)$
= $(117\,176,\ 135\,063)$

That is, we can be 95% confident that the population mean *Selling price*, when the *Valuation price* is \$135 000, is between \$117 176 and \$135 063.

16.5.2 Assumptions and conditions

For the confidence interval for the population mean response, the sampling distribution is the t distribution. The conditions required for this confidence interval to be valid are the same as for the confidence interval for the population intercept; that is, the conditions are as follows:

1. **Conditions for normal probability model with linear relationship**
   - *Unrestricted variables*
   - *Normally distributed variable*
   - *Linear relationship*
   - *Homogeneity of variance*
   - *X is known without error*

2. **Conditions for other validating assumptions**
   - *Infinite population*
   - *Representative sample*
   - *Independence*

These conditions were checked in section 16.2.2, *Checking the conditions*, and after we corrected a mistaken value, we concluded that they appear to have been met.

16.5.3 Notes on values of explanatory variable

It can be shown that the confidence interval will:
  - decrease as n increases;

- decrease as the range of X values increases; or
- increase with the distance of the value of X, for which the estimate is to be made, from the mean of the X values.

This clearly has implications for values of X for which observations should be obtained. If you know the X value(s) for which you are most interested in obtaining estimates, you should observe as wide a range as practicable, but with the X values for which you are most interested in obtaining estimates in the middle of this range.

Note that in estimating it is only safe to compute the mean response for values within the observed range of the explanatory variable; this is known as **interpolation**. Why? Because you have no information indicating whether the linear trend continues above or below the observed range of the explanatory variable. If it does not then **extrapolation**, or computation of mean response for values outside the observed range of the explanatory variable, may give a false estimate.

16.6 Prediction interval for a future observation

16.6.1 Calculating the prediction interval

The question investigated with this procedure is: what **single value** can I expect for the response variable if I take a further single observation for a particular value of the explanatory variable? The point estimate of the value of the response variable for a future observation with a particular value, x, of the explanatory variable is the sample mean response for x. As before, it can be obtained by substituting x into the equation for the fitted line. That is,

$$\bar{y} = b_0 + b_1 x.$$

As stated in section 15.3, *Prediction interval for a future observation*, the sample mean response represents the best guess that can be made at the value of the response variable before the unit is measured. However, the interval estimate for the value of a future observation is the prediction interval for a future observation, and this yields values that differ from the values derived by the confidence interval for the population mean response.

The formula for the **prediction interval ($100\gamma\%$) for a future observation** is as follows:

Prediction interval ($100\gamma\%$) for a future observation

$$= (\bar{\bar{y}} - t_T \sqrt{s_Y^2 + (s_{\bar{y}})^2}, \bar{\bar{y}} + t_T \sqrt{s_Y^2 + (s_{\bar{y}})^2}$$

where $100\gamma\%$ is the confidence level desired by the investigator;

$\bar{\bar{y}}$ is the sample mean response;

t_T is the theoretical value for the t distribution, corresponding to $100\gamma\%$ and the degrees of freedom of s_Y and s_{μ_Y} which are $n - 2$;

s_Y is called the **standard deviation about the regression line**. It measures the variability of the original observations around the fitted line;

$s_{\bar{y}}$ is the standard error of the sample mean response, $\bar{\bar{y}}$. It measures the variability of $\bar{\bar{y}}$ and depends on the value of the explanatory variable.

EXAMPLE 16.1   ESTIMATING *SELLING PRICE* FROM *VALUATION PRICE*
(continued)

The question investigated with this procedure is: what value for *Selling price* can I expect when another house comes onto the market and it has a *Valuation price* of $215,000? That is, we have to estimate the selling price of just one house that came onto the market after the 12-month period from which the original sample was selected.

As with the previous interval, for $n = 20$ and $100\gamma\% = 95\%$, $t_T = 2.1009$. For $X = 215\,000$,

$$\bar{\bar{y}} = 6670 + 0.88481 \times 215\,000 = 196\,904.15, \; s_Y = 15\,980 \text{ and } s_{\bar{\bar{y}}} = 3582$$

so that:

Prediction interval (95%) for a future observation

$$= (196\,904.35 - 2.1009 \times \sqrt{15\,980^2 + 3582^2} ,$$
$$196\,904.35 + 2.1009 \times \sqrt{15\,980^2 + 3582^2}$$
$$= (196\,904.35 - 34\,405.48, \; 196\,904.35 + 34\,405.48)$$
$$= (162\,498, \; 231\,310)$$

That is, we can be 95% confident that, if a further single observation is taken that has a *Valuation price* of $215\,000, the *Selling price* will be between $162\,498 and $231\,310.

Note that this is a rather wide interval; our estimated *Selling price* of $196\,904 could be out by as much as $34\,405. Since the strength of the relationship between *Selling price* and *Valuation price* is very good, with $R^2 = 97.7\%$, the only way to obtain a more precise estimate is to take a larger sample.

16.6.2 Assumptions and conditions

For the prediction interval for a future observation, the sampling distribution is the t distribution. The assumptions for this prediction interval to be valid are the same as for the confidence interval for the population intercept, with the extra assumption that the future observation comes from the same population as the original observations. That is, the conditions for all the assumptions to hold are as follows:

1. Conditions for normal probability model with linear relationship
   - *Unrestricted variables*
   - *Normally distributed variable*
   - *Linear relationship*
   - *Homogeneity of variance*
   - *X is known without error*

2. Conditions for other validating assumptions
   - *Infinite population*
   - *Representative sample and future observation*
   - *Independence*

That is, the conditions are the same as for the other intervals, but with the following extra conditions placed on the future observation:

- the future observation is representative of observational units with the prescribed value of X from the same population as the original sample;
- the population has not changed between the time the original sample was taken and the future observation is obtained;
- the future observation is independent of any others in the population.

EXAMPLE 16.1   ESTIMATING *SELLING PRICE* FROM *VALUATION PRICE*
(continued)

The conditions required for the prediction interval to be valid were checked in section 16.2.2, *Checking the conditions*, except for those conditions involving the future observation. The conditions involving the future observation are checked here. In this case the future observation is a house that came onto the market after the 12-month period from which the original sample was selected and it has a *Valuation price* of $215 000.

The first condition to be satisfied is that the house being sold is representative of houses valued at $215 000 from the same population as the 20 sampled houses. This would be the case if the house was randomly selected from all houses in the original population valued at $215 000; otherwise we cannot guarantee that it is representative. The house is one that came on to the market later. It has not been randomly selected so we cannot guarantee that it is representative. However, we will proceed on the presumption that the process that put it on the market later is effectively random and so the house is representative.

The distribution of the *Selling price* of houses valued at $215 000 must not have changed since the original sample was obtained. Thus, the average price or the spread in prices should still be the same when the extra house is observed. We presume that there has been little price movement between the original sample and the valuation of the further house.

The *Selling price* of the extra house must be independent of any other house. So, if the agent was playing the house off against another, the *Selling price* of the two houses would not be independent. We will presume that the house is being sold independently of other houses.

From the discussion above we conclude that, provided our presumptions are correct, the prediction interval for a future observation will be valid.

16.7   Report on example

The following report, for the example analysed in this chapter, indicates what material from a statistical analysis an investigator should include in a report. In general, the details of the statistical analysis are omitted so that the reader of the report can concentrate on the results.

EXAMPLE 16.1   ESTIMATING *SELLING PRICE* FROM *VALUATION PRICE*
— REPORT

A real estate agent investigated the relationship between the final selling price of a house and the valuation price agreed upon when the house was first put up for sale. The agent systematically sampled 20 of the 451 houses sold through the agency over a 12-month period. Simple linear regression was used to fit a straight line relationship. Figure 16.10 shows the relationship between selling and valuation price, along with the fitted straight line. The coefficient of determination (R^2) is 97.7%. The 95% confidence intervals for the population intercept, population slope and the population mean response for a valuation price of $135 000 were computed. Also, the 95% prediction interval for a valuation price of $215 000 was obtained.

We concluded from the confidence interval for the population intercept that we can be 95% confident that, when the valuation price is zero, the population mean selling price is between –$9196 and $22 536. A population intercept of zero is desirable in this situation, as a nonzero value would indicate that the selling price was consistently underestimated or overestimated. The confidence interval indicates that zero is a plausible value for the intercept.

From the confidence interval for the population slope, we can be 95% confident that in the population, the selling price will increase between $0.8173 and $0.9523 for each $1 increase in the valuation price. The value of the slope, being less than $1, indicates that the valuation price overestimates the selling price and that the extent of the overestimation is greatest for high valuation prices.

From the confidence interval for a population mean response, we estimated that the population mean selling price, when the valuation price is $135 000, is between $117 176 and $135 063. Notice that a correction is made for the overestimation, mentioned in discussing the slope, when the sample mean response is obtained.

From the prediction interval for a future single observation, we estimated that if a house came onto the market and its valuation price was $215 000, its selling price would be between $162 498 and $231 310. For this estimation to be correct, it has to be true that the house is representative of all houses with a valuation price of $215 000 sold in the area over the 12-month period.

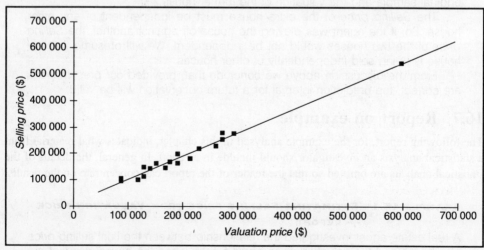

Figure 16.10   Relationship between *Selling price* and *Valuation price*

16.8 Using Minitab for estimation in regression

Minitab's *regress* command can be used to produce the various standard deviations and standard errors required for computing the intervals for estimation. You can compute the confidence interval for the population mean response and the prediction interval for a future observation, for $100\gamma\% = 95\%$, by using the *predict* subcommand of the *regress* command. You can also use the *invcdf* subcommand of the t command to obtain t_T for computing the confidence and prediction intervals. Some conditions can be checked by using the *nscores*, *plot* and *correlation* commands and the *rtheoret* macro. Use the *plot* command to produce the scatter diagram, and the *mplot* command to produce the scatter diagram including the fitted line.

> **EXAMPLE 16.1 ESTIMATING *SELLING PRICE* FROM *VALUATION PRICE***
> (continued)
>
> The commands to perform simple regression analysis, and associated condition checking, are as follows. The lines beginning with a hash (#) are explanatory comments. They are ignored by Minitab and can be omitted when you use these commands.

```
MTB > outfile 'a:\regnvalu.lis'
MTB > retrieve 'a:\regnvalu.mtp';
SUBC> portable.
MTB > info
MTB > name c3 'x'
MTB > set 'x'
DATA> 135000   215000
DATA> end
MTB > plot 'selprice' 'valprice'
MTB > name c4 'sres' c5 'fits'
MTB > info
MTB > regress 'selprice' explanatory 1 'valprice' 'sres' 'fits';
MTB > predict 'x'.
MTB > invcdf 0.975;
SUBC> t 18.
MTB > #Plot of fitted & original data to check linear relationship
MTB > mplot 'selprice' 'valprice' 'fits' 'valprice'
MTB > #Standardised-Residuals-versus-fitted-values plot to check
MTB > #   linear relationship and homogeneity
MTB > plot 'sres' 'fits'
MTB > #Normal Probability plot and correlation coefficient
MTB > #   to check normality
MTB > name c6 'zscores'
MTB > nscores 'sres' 'zscores'
MTB > plot 'sres' 'zscores'
MTB > correlation 'sres' 'zscores'
MTB > let k1=20
MTB > let k2=0.05
MTB > cd a:\
MTB > execute 'rtheoret.mtb'
```

First, use the *retrieve* command to get the data from the portable worksheet file. Then use the *info* command to check which columns contain the data. Next, name a column *x* and place the two values of *Valuation price* for which estimates are required, $135 000 and $215 000, in this column. Then use a *plot* command is produce the scatter diagram between the two variables.

Next, name two columns to store the results you produce during the analysis. When named, these columns have no data stored in them. At this point use an *info* command to check that the columns are set up correctly. Then use the *regress* command, in which you specify the names of four columns and the number of explanatory variables. On the command line, the order of the columns and the number of explanatory variables must be as follows:

1. the first column specifies the response variable;
2. the number of explanatory variables, 1, must be placed before the column containing the explanatory variable;
3. the second column specifies the explanatory variable;
4. the third column specifies a column into which the standardised residuals are to be put when the Minitab command is executed;
5. the fourth column specifies a column into which the fitted values are to be put when the Minitab command is executed.

The *regress* command also includes a *predict* subcommand to obtain the sample mean responses corresponding to the values of the explanatory variable stored in the nominated column.

The *invcdf* command produces the t_T value to be used for computing the intervals with a calculator. The value supplied in the command line of the *invcdf* command is $(1 + \gamma)/2 = (1 + 0.95)/2 = 0.975$ where $100\gamma\%$ is the confidence level required. The value supplied in the subcommand line is $n - 2 = 20 - 2 = 18$.

The *mplot* command produces a diagram that includes plots of both the response versus explanatory variables and the fitted values versus the explanatory variable. The columns in the *mplot* command are plotted in pairs, and the first column of each pair is plotted on the vertical axis.

The *plot* following the *mplot* command produces the residuals-versus-fitted-values plot. The remaining commands produce the normal probability plot, based on the standardised residuals, and the associated correlation coefficient and its theoretical value.

In section 16.2.2, *Checking the conditions*, the condition checking revealed that the third observation for *Selling price* is an error in the original file, so the analysis has to be run again with commands to correct the mistake. The simplest way to correct the mistake is to use the *data screen*. However, you can also use the following *print* and *let* commands to check the contents of the columns and make the correction.

```
MTB > print 'selprice' 'valprice'
MTB > # Command to correct 3rd observation
MTB > let c1(3)=210000
```

If your version of Minitab has pull-down menus and you want to use them, table 16.3 lists the menus and options that access the required commands. Appendix D, *Detailed instructions for Minitab menus*, explains how to use the menus. Note that if you use the menus to execute the *regress* command, you can omit the *name* command for naming columns for the standardised residuals and fits; Minitab automatically names these columns when the *regress* command is executed with menus.

Table 16.3   Menus and options for Minitab commands to perform a simple linear regression analysis

Minitab command	Menu	Option
outfile	File >	Other Files > Start Recording Session...
retrieve	File >	Open Worksteet...
port		Minitab portable worksheet
info	Edit >	Get Worksheet Info...
name	Edit >	Data Screen (Alt-D)
set	Edit >	Data Screen (Alt-D)
plot	Graph >	Scatter Plot...
regress	Stat >	Regression > Regression...
predict		Options...
invcdf	Calc >	Probability Distributions >
t		T...
mplot	Graph >	Multiple Scatter Plot...
nscores	Calc >	Functions and Statistics > Functions...
correlation	Stat >	Basic Statistics > Correlation...
let	Calc >	Functions and Statistics > General Expressions...
cd		not available
execute	File >	Other Files > Execute Macro...

The following output shows the complete analysis, including the correction of the mistaken observation:

```
MTB > retrieve 'a:\regnvalu.mtp';
SUBC> portable.

Worksheet retrieved from file: a:\regnvalu.mtp
MTB > info

COLUMN      NAME        COUNT
C1          selprice      20
C2          valprice      20

CONSTANTS USED: NONE


MTB > print 'selprice' 'valprice'

  ROW     selprice    valprice

    1        95000       90000
    2       208000      230000
    3       310000      230000
    4       140500      170000
    5       137000      140000
    6       270000      290000
    7       191400      190000
    8       158000      150000
    9       160000      180000
   10       225000      260000
   11       105000       90000
   12       265000      270000
   13       153500      190000
   14       149000      130000
   15       161000      180000
   16       560000      620000
   17       244000      270000
   18       165100      210000
   19        94000      120000
   20       105000      130000

MTB > #Command to correct third observation
MTB > let c1(3)=210000
MTB > name c3 'x'
MTB > set 'x'
DATA> 135000 215000
DATA> end
MTB > plot 'selprice' 'valprice'
```

continued . . .

```
           -                                                    *
selprice-

           -
           -
 450000+
           -
           -
           -
           -
 300000+
           -                            *  *
           -                             **
           -                    *  *
 150000+            ***  *2*
           -      *    *
           -      *   *
           -      *  *
           ----+---------+---------+---------+---------+---------+--valprice
            100000    200000    300000    400000    500000    600000
```

```
MTB > name c4 'sres' c5 'fits'
MTB > info

COLUMN      NAME        COUNT
C1          selprice       20
C2          valprice       20
C3          x               2
C4          sres            0
C5          fits            0
CONSTANTS USED: NONE

MTB > regress 'selprice' explanatory 1 'valprice' 'sres' 'fits';
SUBC> predict 'x'.

The regression equation is
selprice = 6670 + 0.885 valprice
Predictor          Coef         Stdev       t-ratio            p
Constant           6670          7552          0.88        0.389
valprice        0.88481       0.03214         27.53        0.000

s = 15980        R-sq = 97.7%       R-sq(adj) = 97.6%

Analysis of Variance

SOURCE          DF             SS              MS         F        p
Regression       1     1.93544E+11     1.93544E+11    757.96    0.000
Error           18      4596277760       255348768
Total           19     1.98140E+11

Unusual Observations
Obs.valprice     selprice    Fit Stdev.Fit    Residual    St.Resid
16    620000       560000          555250       13746    47500.58XX
denotes an obs. whose X value gives it large influence.
```

continued . . .

```
    Fit         Stdev.Fit                    95% C.I.                    95% P.I.
 126119              4257          ( 117173,  135065)      (   91368,  160870)
 196903              3582          ( 189375,  204432)      ( 162490,  231317)

MTB > invcdf 0.975;
SUBC> t 18.
     0.9750         2.1009
```

Table 16.4 lists the quantities required for statistical inference from the regression analysis, the labels Minitab gives them, and their values for this example. Note the confidence intervals (95%) for the population mean response and the prediction intervals (95%) for future observations in the last two lines of the regression output. The first of these last two lines corresponds to the first value of \$135 000 in the column named x; the second line corresponds to the second value of \$215 000 in this column.

Also, note the value of $t_T = 2.1009$ corresponding to $n = 20$ and $100\gamma\% = 95\%$.

Table 16.4   Quantities used in statistical inference

Item	Row label	Column label	Value
b_0	Constant	Coef	6670
b_1	valprice	Coef	0.88481
s_{b_0}	Constant	Stdev	7552
s_{b_1}	valprice	Stdev	0.03214
s_Y	S	—	15980
R^2	R-sq	—	97.7%
$\bar{y}$	—	Fit	126119
$s_{\bar{y}}$	—	Stdev.Fit	4257

The output from the commands to check some of the conditions required for the regression analysis is as follows:

```
MTB > #Plot of fitted & original data to check linear relationship
MTB > mplot 'selprice' 'valprice' 'fits' 'valprice'


           -                                                         A
           -                                                         B
           -
  480000+
           -
           -
           -
           -
  320000+
           -
           -                              4 2
           -                           4  2
           -              A B
 1600000+       A A B43 A
           -       B22B A
           -    4  AA
           -
           ----+---------+---------+---------+---------+---------+--
         100000    200000    300000    400000    500000    600000
        A = selprice vs. valprice  B = fits vs. valprice

MTB > #Standardised-residuals-versus-fitted-values plot to check
MTB > #  linear relationship and homogeneity
MTB > plot 'sres' 'fits'

   sres-
       -           *
       -
   1.2+      *   *        *
       -              *
       -
       -
       -        *    *           *
       -
   0.0+                *    *
       -             *   *
       -             *
       -
       -                   *
       -
       -          *
  -1.2+        **
       -             *
       -           *
       -
       ------+---------+---------+---------+---------+---------+fits
         100000    200000    300000    400000    500000    600000

MTB > #Normal Probability plot and correlation coefficient
MTB > #  to check normality
MTB > name c6 'zscores'
MTB > nscores 'sres' 'zscores'
MTB > plot 'sres' 'zscores'
```

continued . . .

```
sres   -
       -
       -                                                                  *
  1.2+                                                  *   *    *
       -                                            *
       -
       -                                   ** * *
       -
  0.0+                           * *
       -                     **
       -               *
       -            *
       -         *
 -1.2+        *   *
       -     *
       - *
       -
         --------+---------+---------+---------+---------+---------zscores
            -1.40      -0.70      0.00       0.70      1.40
```

MTB > correlation 'sres' 'zscores'

Correlation of sres and zscores = 0.987

MTB > let k1=20
MTB > let k2=0.05
MTB > cd a:\
MTB > execute 'rtheoret.mtb'
The Theoretical value for the normal probability plot r
has been computed for

the number of observations equal to
K6   20.0000
and significance level of
K7   0.0500000

The theoretical value is:
K3   0.950286

16.9 Chapter summary

The procedures covered in this chapter are based on quantities obtained when simple linear regression is employed. The basic setup here is an equation for a straight line, $Y = \beta_0 + \beta_1 X$, that has been fitted to the values of the variables in the population. The task is to draw conclusions about the parameters of this straight line from the statistics associated with the sample straight line, $Y = b_0 + b_1 X$.

The following estimation procedures have been covered:

- confidence interval for the population intercept
- confidence interval for the population slope
- confidence interval for the population mean response
- prediction interval for a future observation

Which interval to use in a particular case depends on the question to be investigated. However, all intervals incorporate an assessment of the precision with which a parameter is estimated by the corresponding statistic.

For all intervals, the sampling distribution is the t distribution and this is based on a normal probability model, with a linear relationship, for the response variable. The basic conditions that will satisfy the assumptions required for a particular interval to be valid are as follows:

1. **Conditions for normal probability model with linear relationship**
   - *Unrestricted variables*
   - *Normally distributed variable*
   - *Linear relationship*
   - *Homogeneity of variance*
   - *X is known without error*

2. **Conditions for other validating assumptions**
   - *Infinite population*
   - *Representative sample*
   - *Independence*

All intervals except the prediction interval have these conditions. The prediction interval has the further conditions: the future observation must be representative of the population and independent of any other observations. These conditions have to be checked for each example, and require an analysis of the residuals which is made by using the standardised-residuals-versus-fitted-values plot and the normal probability plot for the standardised residuals. If the conditions are not met the procedure cannot be used for the example.

16.10 Key terms

- assumptions
- conditions
- confidence interval (100γ%) for the population intercept
- confidence interval (100γ%) for the population mean response
- confidence interval (100γ%) for the population slope
- confidence level (100γ%)
- equation for a straight line ($Y = b_0 + b_1 X$ or $Y = \beta_0 + \beta_1 X$)
- explanatory variable (X)
- extrapolation
- fitted line
- fitted value ($\hat{y}_i$)
- homogeneity of variance
- independence condition
- infinite population
- influential outlier
- intercept (b_0 or β_0)
- interpolation
- large-residual outlier
- linear relationship

- mean response ($\bar{\bar{y}}$ or μ_Y)
- normal probability model with a linear relationship
- normal probability plot
- normal probability plot correlation coefficient (r_N)
- normally distributed variable
- prediction interval (100γ%) for a future observation
- representative sample
- residual (e_i)
- response variable (Y)
- single value
- slope (b_1 or β_1)
- standard deviation about the regression line (s_Y)
- standard error (s_{b_0}, s_{b_1} or $s_{\bar{\bar{y}}}$)
- standardised residual
- standardised-residuals-versus-fitted-values plot
- theoretical value for the t distribution (t_T)
- X is known without error

16.11 Exercises

16.1 A regression line fitted to past data may not provide reliable estimates of the population regression coefficients and the population mean response. Comment on this statement.

16.2 In planning the data collection, you have to decide on the range of values for the explanatory variable, taking into account the values for which estimates are to be made. What issues should you consider in choosing the range of values to be observed for the explanatory variable?

16.3   Inferential procedures for regression are based on certain assumptions which must be satisfied when applying them. What conditions are required for these assumptions to hold?

16.4   In regression, a residual is defined as the difference between an observed value of the response variable and a fitted value. The conditions required for inference procedures for regression to be valid are checked by analysing the behaviour of the standardised residuals.

(a)   What is a fitted value?

(b)   How are these standardised residuals calculated and why are they used in preference to an ordinary residual?

16.5   What effect would you expect a cluster of positive large-residual outliers to have on the fitted regression line?

16.6   The equation for the population straight line is denoted by $Y = \beta_0 + \beta_1 X$ where β_0 and β_1 are the parameters associated with the regression line. These parameters are usually unknown and we estimate them by using confidence intervals based on statistics obtained from a sample set of data. The confidence interval ($100\gamma\%$) for the population slope is:

$$\text{Confidence interval } (100\gamma\%) \text{ for } \beta_1 = (b_1 - t_T s_{b_1},\ b_1 + t_T s_{b_1})$$

What does s_{b_1} represent and how is it obtained?

16.7   The population average for a particular value of the explanatory variable can be estimated from a confidence interval ($100\gamma\%$) for the population mean response. However, we may want to obtain the range that we can be confident includes the value of the response variable if a further observation, with that particular value of the explanatory variable, is taken. Which estimation procedure applies in this case?

16.8   The Adelaide Real Estate Agents Association wants to estimate the typical *Selling price* of home units sold over the last 12 months in the Burnside and Unley local government areas from their *Valuation price*. It sends a letter to all agents in these areas, asking each agent to return information for one home unit randomly selected from those they have sold in these areas in the last 12 months. Altogether, about 600 home units were sold in these areas in this period.

The data for *Valuation price* and *Selling price* is in table 16.5 and saved in the Minitab portable worksheet file *homeunit.mtp*; the data for Burnside and Unley is saved along with the data for Kensington and Norwood and Payneham, and the data for Burnside and Unley has the column *location* equal to 2.

Table 16.5 *Valuation price* and *Selling price* for home units
in the Burnside and Unley local government areas

Valuation price ($)	Selling price ($)
100 000	90 000
147 000	134 000
65 000	61 000
250 000	236 000
128 500	110 000
180 000	170 000
122 000	110 000
330 000	300 000
193 000	170 000
115 000	115 000
140 000	138 000
125 000	110 000
115 000	115 000
138 000	130 000
95 000	77 000
120 000	112 000
129 000	129 000
127 000	107 000

(a) Answer the following questions:

(i) What is the question to be investigated (including the group to which the conclusions apply)?

(ii) What variable(s) are we concerned with here?

(iii) What type of variable(s) are they?

(iv) Which major category of statistical procedures applies here? Why?

(v) What type of statistic should we use, given the question to be investigated and the variable involved?

(vi) Which particular statistic or procedure, and diagram, should we use? Why?

(b) Reproduce the following Minitab output.

```
MTB > retrieve 'a:\homeunit.mtp';
SUBC> portable.

Worksheet retrieved from file: a:\homeunit.mtp
MTB > info
```

continued . . .

```
COLUMN      NAME              COUNT
C1          location            28
C2          age                 28
C3          norooms             28
C4          capvalue            28
C5          valprice            28
C6          selprice            28

CONSTANTS USED: NONE

MTB > copy c1-c6 c1-c6;
SUBC> use c1=2.

MTB > plot 'selprice' 'valprice'


          -                                                        *
selprice-
          -
          -
240000+                                              *
          -
          -
          -
          -                                  *    *
160000+
          -                      *
          -                   *  **
          -            222*
          -         *
80000+             *
          -      *
          -
          +---------+---------+---------+---------+---------+--valprice
        50000     100000    150000    200000    250000    300000

MTB > name c7 'sres' c8 'fits'
MTB > regress 'selprice' explanatory 1 'valprice' 'sres' 'fits';
SUBC> predict 123000.


The regression equation is
selprice = 443 + 0.919 valprice


Predictor            Coef      Stdev    t-ratio           p
Constant              443       4413       0.10       0.921
valprice          0.91851    0.02806      32.73       0.000


s = 7098          R-sq = 98.5%        R-sq(adj) = 98.4%
Analysis of Variance

SOURCE              DF           SS            MS         F        p
Regression           1   53979590656   53979590656   1071.31   0.000
Error               16     806188096      50386756
Total               17   54785777664
```

continued . . .

503

```
Unusual Observations
Obs.valprice    selprice       Fit    Stdev.Fit    Residual    St.Resid
  8    330000      300000    303550         5440       -3550    -0.78 X

X denotes an obs. whose X value gives it large influence.

   Fit      Stdev.Fit                95% C.I.                95% P.I.
113419           1789      ( 109627, 117212)    (  97897, 128941)


MTB > invcdf 0.95;
SUBC> t 16.
     0.9500      1.7459

MTB > mplot 'selprice' 'valprice' 'fits' 'valprice'
            -                                                              2
            -
            -
            -
            -
   240000+                                        A
            -                                      B
            -
            -
            -
            -                            A  2
   160000+                               B
            -                  A
            -                 A 32
            -              4443
            -        2
    80000+        2
            -    2
            -
            +---------+---------+---------+---------+---------+------
          50000    100000    150000    200000    250000    300000
             A = selprice vs. valprice B = fits vs. valprice
MTB > plot 'sres' 'fits'

   sres -
        -              2   *  *
        -
    1.0+                                    *
        -
        -
        -                         *
        -
        -    *        *
    0.0+
        -                    *
        -         *     *
        -
        -              *
   -1.0+
        -         *         *
        -
        -    *
        -
        --+---------+---------+---------+---------+---------+--fits
        50000    100000    150000    200000    250000    300000
```

continued . . .

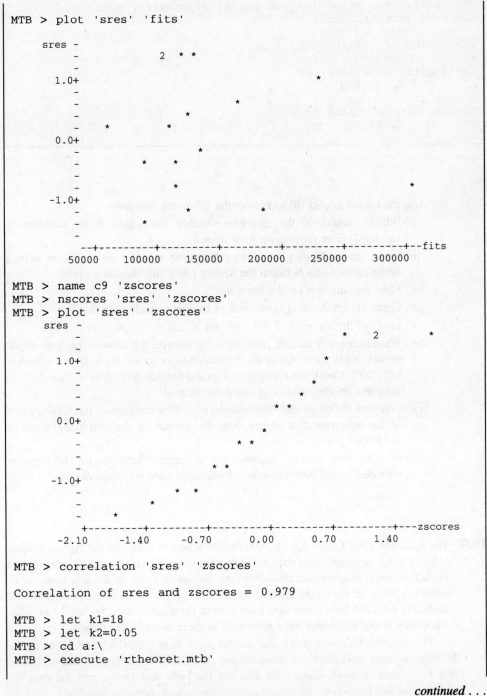

```
MTB > plot 'sres' 'fits'

    sres -
         -                     2    *  *
         -
    1.0+                                      *
         -
         -                              *
         -                        *
         -           *         *
    0.0+
         -                          *
         -              *      *
         -
         -                  *                            *
   -1.0+
         -
         -                    *
         -
         --+---------+---------+---------+---------+---------+---fits
        50000     100000    150000    200000    250000    300000

MTB > name c9 'zscores'
MTB > nscores 'sres' 'zscores'
MTB > plot 'sres' 'zscores'
    sres -
         -                                      *    2      *
    1.0+
         -                                    *
         -
         -                            *  *
    0.0+
         -                         *
         -                     *  *
         -
         -                 *  *
   -1.0+
         -             *   *
         -          *
         -       *
         +---------+---------+---------+---------+---------+---zscores
       -2.10     -1.40     -0.70     0.00      0.70      1.40

MTB > correlation 'sres' 'zscores'

Correlation of sres and zscores = 0.979

MTB > let k1=18
MTB > let k2=0.05
MTB > cd a:\
MTB > execute 'rtheoret.mtb'
```

continued . . .

```
The Theoretical value for the normal probability plot r
has been computed for

the number of observations equal to
K6          18.0000
and significance level of
K7          0.0500000

The theoretical value is:
K3          0.946121
```

(c) Use the output in part (b) to answer the following questions:

(i) Which variable is the response variable and which is the explanatory variable? Give reasons for your choice.

(ii) Use a scatter diagram to assess subjectively whether there appears to be a linear relationship between the *Selling price* and *Valuation price*.

(iii) State the equation for the fitted line.

(iv) Comment on the likely precision of estimates made with this line.

(v) Interpret the meaning of the intercept b_0 and the slope b_1 in this case.

(vi) What range will include, with 90% confidence, the amount that you would expect to pay for a unit in the Burnside/Unley area if the unit was valued at $123 000? Check the conditions required for this procedure to be valid and comment on the validity of using the interval.

(vii) Compute the range that will include, with 90% confidence, the *Selling price* of the next unit that comes onto the market, if the unit was valued at $123 000?

(viii) In your own words, describe the difference between the information provided by the two intervals calculated in parts (vi) and (vii).

16.9 The Adelaide Real Estate Agents Association wants to estimate the typical *Selling price* of home units sold over the last 12 months in the Kensington and Norwood and Payneham local government areas from the *Valuation price*. It sends a letter to all agents in these areas, asking each of them to return information for one home unit randomly selected from those they have sold in these areas over the last 12 months. Altogether about 450 home units were sold in these areas in this period.

The data for *Valuation price* and *Selling price* is in table 16.6 and saved in the Minitab portable worksheet file *homeunit.mtp*; the data for Kensington and Norwood and Payneham is saved along with data for Burnside and Unley, and the data for Kensington and Norwood and Payneham has the column *location* equal to 1.

Table 16.6 *Valuation price* and *Selling price* for home units in the Kensington and Norwood and Payneham local government areas

Valuation price ($)	Selling price ($)
53 950	49 000
167 000	158 000
189 500	172 000
79 950	78 000
79 500	75 000
165 000	155 000
95 000	85 000
160 000	150 000
115 000	107 000
150 000	140 000

(a) Answer the following questions:
  (i) What is the question to be investigated (including the group to which the conclusions apply)?
  (ii) What variable(s) are we concerned with here?
  (iii) What type of variable(s) are they?
  (iv) Which major category of statistical procedures applies here? Why?
  (v) What type of statistic should we use, given the question to be investigated and the variables involved?
  (vi) Which particular statistic or procedure, and diagram, should we use? Why?
(b) Which variable is the response variable and which is the explanatory variable? Give reasons for your choice.
(c) Use a scatter diagram to assess subjectively whether there appears to be a linear relationship between the *Selling price* and *Valuation price*.
(d) If there appears to be a linear relationship, use the least-squares method to find the regression coefficients b_0 and b_1.
(e) What range will include, with 95% confidence, the population value for the rate with which the *Selling price* changes as the *Valuation price* is increased? Check the conditions required for this procedure to be valid and comment on the validity of using the interval.

PART V

HYPOTHESIS TESTS

LEARNING OBJECTIVES

The learning objectives of this introduction to part V are:

- to understand the purpose of hypothesis tests;
- to gain an overview of the procedure for a hypothesis test;
- to understand the rationale underlying hypothesis tests.

The introduction to part IV, *Estimation procedures*, mentioned that estimation procedures form one branch of statistical inference, since they are concerned with estimating population quantities from a sample. Part V, *Hypothesis tests*, covers the other branch of statistical inference, **hypothesis tests**: procedures for answering questions about the population by using a sample — the questions must have only two possible answers.

EXAMPLE V.1 SUPPORT FOR THE CURRENT MEMBER

The introduction to part IV, *Estimation procedures*, gave an example including a simple random sample of 200 voters taken from a state electorate of 17 356 registered voters. Of the 200 sampled voters, 86 said they would vote for the current member of parliament; that is, 43% would vote for her. The question investigated in that part was: what proportion of voters in the electorate would vote for the member? However, suppose the question to be investigated is: in the electorate, does the current support for the member differ from support given at the time of the election? Further, it is known that 52% of voters in the electorate voted for the member at the last election. The question to be investigated becomes: does the proportion in the electorate that would vote for the member differ from 52%?

First, note that this is a question for which there are only two possible answers: the proportion either does or does not differ from 52%. Hypothesis tests are designed to provide answers to such two-answer questions. Second, the answer may seem obvious at first. That is, the current support for the member is 43% not 52%. However, 43%

is the sample percentage, not the population percentage, and our question concerns the population percentage. Our task is to decide whether a sample percentage of 43% is inconsistent with a population percentage of 52%.

Note that whether you use a confidence interval or a hypothesis test depends on the question to be investigated. If the question requires estimating the population value, a confidence interval is appropriate; however, if you wish to establish whether the population value could be equal to a particular value, a hypothesis test is appropriate.

Overview of hypothesis tests

This section presents several points that apply to all hypothesis tests:

- Hypothesis tests provide an *objective* procedure for deciding between two hypotheses.
- In this book, hypothesis tests consist of the following six steps:
  Step 1: Set up the hypotheses and nominate the significance level.
  Step 2: Specify and obtain the test statistic.
  Step 3: List and check conditions for the sampling distribution.
  Step 4: Obtain the probability of the test statistic.
  Step 5: State and apply the rule for rejecting the null hypothesis.
  Step 6: State the conclusion in terms of the question investigated.
- Crucial to every hypothesis test are the assumptions made in deriving the sampling distribution and that must be met if the procedure is to be valid. If they are not met, the test procedure must be abandoned, otherwise you will be drawing incorrect conclusions. However, there are usually alternative procedures that can be investigated; in particular, different probability models are available and it may be that they describe more accurately the behaviour in the data.
- Hypothesis tests do not prove or draw conclusions about which one can be 100% certain. They give us an indication of the most likely alternative.

Rationale for hypothesis tests

The logic of hypothesis tests is not intuitively obvious. However, it is exactly the same as that used in Australian trials to decide whether an individual is innocent or guilty of a crime. Bearing this in mind may help you understand hypothesis tests. This section explains the parallels between what happens in each step of the hypothesis test and what happens in a trial.

Step 1: Set up the hypotheses and nominate the significance level.

In this first step, the significance level, α, is nominated and the hypothesis to be tested is specified by putting forward two alternatives: the null and alternative hypotheses.

- The **null hypothesis**, denoted H_0, is generally the specific hypothesis that postulates specific conditions on the values of the parameters.
- The **alternative hypothesis**, denoted H_a, is the more general hypothesis; there is more freedom in the possible values of each parameter under it.

The purpose of every hypothesis test is to decide between these two hypotheses. Specifying the two hypotheses will make clear exactly what question the test is answering.

The **significance level**, α, specifies the probability that will be classified as unlikely enough to consider that the evidence against the null hypothesis is overwhelming.

This step is equivalent to the specification of the charge in a trial and the required strength of the evidence. The null hypothesis in the test is equivalent to the hypothesis that the defendant is innocent, and the alternative hypothesis is equivalent to the hypothesis that the defendant is guilty. As in the courtroom, the null hypothesis has a special status: it is the hypothesis that will be presumed to be true. In general, the required strength of evidence is not explicitly set to a nominated probability in a trial; the evidence against the defendant must always be considered overwhelming.

Step 2: Specify and obtain the test statistic.

The evidence against the null hypothesis is now amassed in the form of the test statistic. For all hypothesis tests, the **test statistic** measures how far the observed data is from what would be expected *if the null hypothesis were true*. That is, what evidence has been amassed against the presumption of the defendant's innocence?

Step 3: List and check conditions for the sampling distribution.

To assess the strength of the evidence against the null hypothesis, the probability of the observed value of the test statistic or more extreme values is computed using the sampling distribution of the test statistic. However, the valid use of this sampling distribution entails some **assumptions**. These assumptions hold under a set of **conditions** and so, before using the sampling distribution, the conditions are checked to ensure the validity of the computed probability.

In a trial, it is usual to make certain assumptions. For example, we can assume that fingerprints can be used to identify a person; and an accused person may establish that, when the crime was committed, they were nowhere near the scene, so it must be logically concluded that they did not commit the crime.

Step 4: Obtain the probability of the test statistic.

The **probability of the test statistic** and more extreme values is computed, *presuming the null hypothesis is true and the conditions are met*. The corresponding court room situation would be to compute the probability of the evidence given the presumption of innocence and some presumptions about the likelihood of events specified in evidence.

511

Step 5: State and apply the rule for rejecting the null hypothesis.

From the evidence and its probability, we decide whether the null hypothesis can be rejected. If the null hypothesis is rejected the result of the hypothesis test is said to be **significant**. Note that we cannot be 100% certain that our conclusion is correct.

The situation also has a courtroom parallel: it is decided whether the defendant is innocent or guilty. In reaching this conclusion the defendant is presumed innocent, and it is concluded that they are guilty only if the evidence establishes this *beyond reasonable doubt*. That is, we are never 100% certain that the defendant is either innocent or guilty. The phrase *beyond reasonable doubt* implies a degree of uncertainty.

Step 6: State the conclusion in terms of the question investigated.

Once we decide whether or not the hypothesis is to be rejected, we restate the conclusion in terms of the original question; this is equivalent to returning the verdict.   ■

The null hypothesis plays a pivotal role in an hypothesis test as follows:

- the test statistic measures how far the observed data departs from what is expected under the null hypothesis;
- the probability of the test statistic is computed assuming that it is true.

As discussed in step 5, your conclusion about the null hypothesis is not 100% certain to be correct. There is always the chance that you are wrong, although in some cases the chance is so small that you will be virtually 100% certain. Remember, however, that very unusual events do happen; for example, Baum and Scheuer (1976) report a case of the same person winning the same lottery twice, the chance of doing so being 500 million to 1. Two types of errors can be made in performing a hypothesis test. A **type I error** is made when the null hypothesis is true and it is rejected; this is the same as convicting an innocent person. A **type II error** is made when the null hypothesis is false and it is not rejected; this is the same as failing to convict a guilty person. The possible outcomes — the conclusion (or verdict) reached as a result of a hypothesis test — are illustrated in Table V.1.

Table V.1   Relationship between reality and verdict for H_0

H_0 verdict	H_0 reality	
	True	False
Not rejected	correct (innocent cleared)	Type II error (guilty cleared)
Rejected	Type I error (innocent convicted)	correct (guilty convicted)

The significance level, α, can also be interpreted as the level of risk we are prepared to take in making a type I error.

EXAMPLE V.1   SUPPORT FOR THE CURRENT MEMBER (continued)

Step 1: Set up the hypotheses and nominate the significance level.

The null hypothesis is that the population percentage is equal to 52% and the alternative is that it is not. The standard value of the significance level, α, is 0.05. That is, anything that occurs less than 1 in 20 times is said to be unlikely. Put another way, we are prepared to accept a 1 in 20 chance that we have rejected the null hypothesis when it is true.

Step 2: Specify and obtain the test statistic.

A test statistic is computed to measure the difference between the observed frequency supporting the current member and the expected frequency if support is 52%. We use the expected frequency for 52% support because that is the percentage hypothesised under the null hypothesis. Can you work out this frequency? The test statistic is computed from a sample; it is a single number that reflects how far the observed data departs from what is expected under the null hypothesis.

Step 3: List and check conditions for the sampling distribution.

The conditions that will satisfy the assumptions required for the valid use of the sampling distribution are checked.

Step 4: Obtain the probability of the test statistic.

From the sampling distribution, the probability of the test statistic is computed, assuming that the null hypothesis is true and the conditions are met. The probability of the test statistic is the chance of getting the observed value, and more extreme values, of the test statistic, *when the null hypothesis is true.*

Step 5: State and apply the rule for rejecting the null hypothesis.

The alternative hypothesis is rejected if the data is very unlikely when the null hypothesis is true. This is generally the case when the probability of the test statistic is less than or equal to α.

Step 6: State the conclusion in terms of the question investigated.

The evidence suggests that the support for the member has either changed or not changed.   ∎

At this point you might be thinking: Why bother with all this, just to decide whether or not the percentage support in the electorate differs from 52%? The answer is that the hypothesis test provides an objective procedure for making the decision. Without it, our decision becomes a subjective opinion. I might suggest that the support is not really different from 52% and you may disagree. Who is right? How do we resolve the difference?

Remember when you examined data by using descriptive summaries and you had to answer questions subjectively: Do these means differ? Are these two variables independent? It was often difficult to decide. Hypothesis tests provide an objective procedure for making these decisions.

Summary

Hypothesis tests are objective procedures for answering questions about the population by using a sample; the questions must have only two answers: yes or no. In this book, all hypothesis tests consist of the same six steps: (1) the null and alternative hypotheses are specified and the significance level is nominated; (2) the test statistic is computed to assess the evidence against the null hypothesis; (3) the validity of using the sampling distribution to compute the probability of the test statistic is assessed by checking whether a set of conditions are met; (4) the probability of the test statistic is computed; (5) the rule for rejecting the null hypothesis is stated and applied; (6) the conclusion is stated in terms of the question investigated.

The logic underlying hypothesis tests is not intuitively obvious. However, we drew a parallel between hypothesis tests and the courtroom trial to relate it to a more familiar setting.

Conclusions from hypothesis tests, like trial verdicts, can never be 100% certain. Two types of errors can be made when performing a hypothesis test: a type I error, which parallels convicting an innocent person, or a type II error, which parallels failing to convict a guilty person.

Key terms

- **assumptions**
- **alternative hypothesis (H_a)**
- **conditions**
- **hypothesis tests**
- **null hypothesis (H_0)**
- **probability of the test statistic (p_T)**

- **significance level (α)**
- **significant**
- **test statistic**
- **type I error**
- **type II error**

CHAPTER 17

GOODNESS-OF-FIT TEST FOR ONE LIMITED VARIABLE

L E A R N I N G   O B J E C T I V E S

The learning objectives of this chapter are:

- to know when to apply, how to calculate and how to interpret the results of the goodness-of-fit test;
- to consolidate your understanding of hypothesis tests;
- to know the conditions required for the goodness-of-fit test to be valid and how to determine when these are met.

The following extract from the *Summary of procedures based on combinations of variable types* in part VI gives an overview of the hypothesis test covered in this chapter.

1. *One limited variable*
   - **Distribution of variables**: z-test for a proportion; goodness-of-fit test.

2. *Two limited variables*

3. *One unrestricted variable — one limited variable*

4. *One unrestricted variable — two limited variables*

5. *Two unrestricted variables*

As outlined in the objectives, this chapter covers the hypothesis test known as the **goodness-of-fit test**. It applies when the data consists of the values of one limited variable and when the question to be investigated is: are the population **proportions** for the values of the limited variable different from those hypothesised? Further, since an inference procedure is

515

involved, we must have taken a sample and the question to be investigated must be about the population and *not* confined to the sample.

Other books present a special test for the case of a two-valued, limited variable: **z-test for a proportion.** This test is equivalent to the goodness-of-fit test: for the same hypotheses, the probabilities of the test statistics from the two tests are equal. Section 17.1.2, *One limited variable with two values*, gives an example of how the goodness-of-fit test is used for a two-valued limited variable.

17.1   Goodness-of-fit test

Before carrying out the hypothesis test, descriptive summaries are used for a preliminary examination of the data. The descriptive summaries that correspond to the goodness-of-fit test are the **one-way summary table** and the **bar** or **column chart**.

EXAMPLE 17.1   POLITICAL PARTY SUPPORT

Suppose that in example V.1, *Support for the current member,* we did not ask our simple random sample of voters whether they supported the member, but asked them to nominate which of the three major parties' candidates they would vote for at the next election. The question to be investigated is: has the electorate changed in its support of the parties since the last election?

The question to be investigated now concerns the population and there are only two possible answers, so a hypothesis test is required to answer the question. The variable involved, *Party of supported candidate*, is a limited variable, taking the three values *Liberal, Labor* and *Democrat*. Further, the question involves examining whether or not a sample is consistent with hypothesised values for the population proportions; the hypothesised values for the population proportions are those obtained at the last election. The *goodness-of-fit test* is therefore the appropriate procedure to use. However, before we apply this test, we make a preliminary examination of the descriptive summaries. The one-way summary table obtained from the responses is given in table 17.1.

Table 17.1   *Party of supported candidate* at the next election

Party of supported candidate	Frequency of votes	Percentage of votes
Liberal	86	43.0
Labor	55	27.5
Democrat	59	29.5
Total	200	

Suppose also that support for the parties at the last election was as given in table 17.2.

Table 17.2 *Party of supported candidate* at the last election

Party of supported candidate	Frequency of votes	Percentage of votes
Liberal	9 025	52.0
Labor	4 513	26.0
Democrat	3 818	22.0
Total	17 356	

The support seems to have changed. However, the goodness-of-fit test will give us an objective procedure for making this decision.

17.1.1 Steps for the goodness-of-fit test

The general steps to perform this hypothesis test are now outlined, followed by the analysis for the example.

Step 1: Set up the hypotheses and nominate the significance level.

The general form of the **null** and **alternative hypotheses** for the goodness-of-fit test are:

H_0: $\pi_i = \pi_{0i}$ for all i (The population proportion, π_i, is equal to the hypothesised value, π_{0i}, for all values of the limited variable.)

H_a: $\pi_i \neq \pi_{0i}$ for at least one i (At least one population proportion is not equal to its hypothesised value.)

The general form of these hypotheses is the same for every goodness-of-fit test. For any particular instance, you merely state the hypothesised proportions for each value of the limited variable. These proportions must sum to 1.

Also, the significance level, α, for the analysis must be chosen at this step. As stated in the introduction to part V, *Hypothesis tests*, the significance level is the probability that null hypothesis is rejected when it is true. The value for the significance level is then the value quantifying the risk of making this error that you are prepared to accept. Commonly used values are 0.10, 0.05, 0.01 and 0.001; 0.05 is probably suitable for most business applications.

Step 2: Specify and obtain the test statistic.

To calculate the **test statistic**, first calculate the frequency theoretically expected in each cell of the table when the null hypothesis is true. Then use the difference between the observed and expected frequencies to calculate the test statistic.

The test statistic $X^2_{(k-1)}$ is called **Pearson's chi-square statistic** with $(k-1)$ degrees of freedom. It is computed with the formula:

$$X^2_{(k-1)} = \sum_{i=1}^{k} \frac{(O_i - E_i)^2}{E_i}$$

where O_i is the **observed frequency** for a cell,

E_i is the theoretically **expected frequency** for a cell $(= n\pi_{0i})$,

k is the number of possible values for the limited variable, and

$(k - 1)$ is called the **degrees of freedom**.

This formula, expressed in words, is:

$$X^2_{\text{degrees of freedom}} = \text{Sum over all cells of} \left\{ \frac{[\text{observed frequency} - \text{expected frequency}]^2}{\text{expected frequency}} \right\}$$

The expected frequencies might not be whole numbers, and they must sum to n. If they are not whole numbers, they should *not* be rounded so that they always sum to n. Since the expected frequencies must sum to n, there are only $k - 1$ independent expected frequencies; the kth expected frequency is n minus the sum of the other $k - 1$ frequencies. Consequently, the degrees of freedom of the test statistic is $k - 1$.

Note that the test statistic measures the size of the difference between the observed and hypothesised frequencies. It can only be positive as it is the sum of the ratios of a squared quantity and a positive number. If the observed frequencies are exactly equal to those that would be expected under the null hypothesis, the test statistic would be zero.

Step 3: List and check conditions for the sampling distribution.

The **sampling distribution of the test statistic** for this hypothesis test is the **chi-square distribution** denoted χ^2 distribution. It is based on a **limited-variable probability model** for the population. The **conditions** that will satisfy the **assumptions** required for the valid use of the sampling distribution are as follows:

1. **Conditions for limited-variable probability model**
   - *Well-defined limited variable:* The variable on which the hypothesis test is being performed must be a **well-defined limited variable**: the values of the limited variable should be mutually exclusive and collectively exhaustive. Determining that this condition is satisfied can be done simply by considering whether the variable is limited and well-defined. Usually, there is no problem with this condition.
   - *Stable population proportions:* The **stable population proportions condition** stipulates that the proportion of the population taking a particular value of the limited variable must remain stable or constant throughout the period to which the inferences are to apply. It will be met provided the population does not change during this period. So the data collection must be done quickly enough and the inferences can be applied only while the population remains unchanged.

2. **Conditions for other validating assumptions**
   - *Infinite population:* The sample should come from an effectively **infinite population**. The population can be regarded as effectively infinite if the number of individuals in it (N) is at least 20 times the number sampled (n); that is, if $N > 20n$.

- *Representative sample:* A **representative sample** is an unbiased fraction of the original population. The methods that are likely to produce a representative sample were discussed in chapter 4, *Surveys*, where we concluded that the probability sampling methods, such as simple random sampling, produce representative samples. So this condition will be met if a probability sampling method is used to select the sample. If not, we cannot guarantee that the assumption will be met.
- *Independence:* The **independence condition** requires that the outcome of any observation is independent of the outcome of any other observation. This condition is difficult to check; it involves ensuring that the study is conducted in such a way that each observation is made independently of the other.
- *Large number condition:* The **large number condition** is that the expected frequencies must be greater than or equal to 5 for all values of the limited variable. This can be checked by making sure that the expected frequencies for all values of the limited variable are greater than or equal to 5; that is, $E_i = n\pi_{0i} \geq 5$ where π_{0i} are the hypothesised proportions for each value of the limited variable.

So the sampling distribution of the test statistic, *when H_0 is true and these conditions are met*, is the chi-square distribution, denoted χ^2 distribution. That is, when the population proportions are as hypothesised and the conditions are met, the distribution of values of the test statistic has the form shown in figure 17.1. The exact form of this distribution varies with its degrees of freedom, and the peak of the distribution is always less than its degrees of freedom.

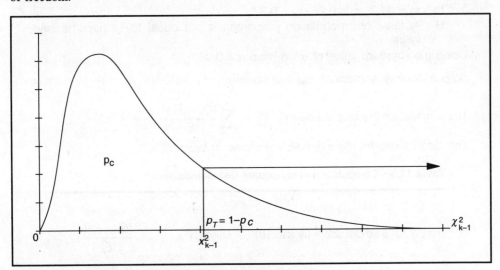

Figure 17.1   Chi-square distribution for the test statistic

Step 4: Obtain the probability of the test statistic.

We require the **probability of the test statistic**, p_T, which is the probability of getting the observed value, and more extreme values, of the test statistic. Because the test statistic measures how far the observed frequencies depart from the expected frequencies, the larger the test statistic then the more extreme the differences between these two sets of frequencies. So we can obtain the probability of the test statistic from the sampling distribution by determining the area, under the curve, above the range to the right of the observed value of the test statistic, as illustrated in figure 17.1.

Sometimes computer programs for computing the probabilities for the chi-square distribution provide the probability of being less than a nominated value. That is, they compute the **cumulative probability**, p_C. Then, $p_T = 1 - p_C$.

Step 5: State and apply the rule for rejecting the null hypothesis.

The general form of the rule for rejecting the null hypothesis is: if $p_T \leq \alpha$, reject H_0; otherwise, H_0 cannot be rejected.

Step 6: State the conclusion in terms of the question investigated.

Once you have decided whether or not the hypothesis is to be rejected, restate the conclusion in terms of the original question.   ∎

EXAMPLE 17.1   POLITICAL PARTY SUPPORT (continued)
The steps of the goodness-of-fit test are outlined as follows for the voting example.

Step 1: Set up the hypotheses and nominate the significance level.
   H_0: $\pi_1 = 0.52$, $\pi_2 = 0.26$, $\pi_3 = 0.22$
   H_a: At least one population proportion is not equal to its hypothesised value.
Using the standard value of α we have $\alpha = 0.05$.

Step 2: Specify and obtain the test statistic.

The formula for the test statistic is $X_2^2 = \sum_{i=1}^{3} \dfrac{(O_i - E_i)^2}{E_i}$.

The calculations for the example are shown in table 17.3.

Table 17.3 Computation of chi-square test statistic

Party of supported candidate	Frequencies		$\dfrac{(O_i - E_i)^2}{E_i}$
	Observed (O_i)	Expected (E_i)	
Liberal	86	104	$(86 - 104)^2/104 = 3.1154$
Labor	55	52	$(55 - 52)^2/52 = 0.1731$
Democrat	59	44	$(59 - 44)^2/44 = 5.1136$
Total	200	200	8.40215

The values of E_i in table 17.3 are the frequencies we would expect to obtain if the null hypothesis is true. That is, if the true population proportion that would vote for the Liberal candidate is 0.52, we can expect that in a sample of 200, 104 voters would indicate support for the Liberal candidate.

In computing the test statistic, the quantity $(O_i - E_i)^2/E_i$ is computed for each value of the limited variable. This quantity measures how far the frequency for each value departs from what is expected under the null hypothesis. Examining the values for this quantity in table 17.3 reveals that the observed frequency for the Democrat party is furthest away from its expected frequency. The test statistic itself is the sum of these quantities and so represents an overall measure of the size of the difference between the observed and hypothesised frequencies. Therefore, $X_2^2 = 8.4021$.

In some ways we do not appear to have got very far. We do have a test statistic that measures the size of the difference between the observed and expected frequencies. However, is 8.40 a big number indicating there is a big difference or a little number indicating little difference? To answer this question, we compute the probability of getting the observed value of the test statistic or more extreme values, when the null hypothesis is true. However, computing this probability entails some assumptions and so the conditions required for the assumptions to hold are checked before computing the probability to ensure its validity.

Step 3: List and check conditions for the sampling distribution.

The sampling distribution of the test statistic, X_2^2, is the chi-square distribution with two degrees of freedom. The sampling distribution, which is based on a limited-variable probability model, is shown in figure 17.2. It can be mathematically proven that, provided the assumptions required for its valid use are met, this is the distribution of the many statistics that would be obtained:

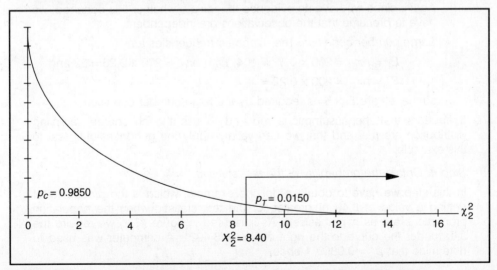

Figure 17.2 Chi-square distribution for test statistic with 2 degrees of freedom

- if we took many samples of 200 voters and calculated the test statistic for each; and

- if support for the candidates in the population is really 52%, 22% and 26%, respectively.

From the figure we see that we should expect values of X_2^2 of about 1 and 2 reasonably often when the null hypothesis is true and provided the assumptions are met. Checking the conditions that will satisfy the assumptions required for the valid use of the sampling distribution proceeds as follows:

1. Conditions for limited-variable probability model

- *Well-defined limited variable:* The variable is *Party of supported candidate*, which is clearly a three-valued, well-defined, limited variable, although we are not allowing for nonvoters.

- *Stable population proportions:* In this case, the proportions would not be stable if the survey is conducted over an extended period during which certain issues arise that cause some voters to change their minds. There is no evidence to indicate whether this was the case, so we have to presume that the proportions are stable.

2. Conditions for other validating assumptions

- *Infinite population:* The population is effectively infinite in that there are 17 356 voters in the population and this is greater than $20 \times 200 = 4000$.

- *Representative sample:* As the sample is random, there is no reason to expect that the sample is not representative of the population.

- *Independence:* You have to ensure that the observations were taken independently. For example, you should not interview people together because some are likely to be influenced by their fellow interviewees. Again, since we have no evidence to indicate whether this occurred, we have to presume that the observations are independent.

- *Large number condition:* The expected frequencies are:

$$E_1 = n\pi_{01} = 200 \times 0.52 = 104, \ E_2 = n\pi_{02} = 200 \times 0.26 = 52 \text{ and}$$
$$E_3 = n\pi_{03} = 200 \times 0.22 = 44$$

so that all are $E_i > 5$ as required by the large number condition.

It appears that the assumptions required to use the chi-square sampling distribution are met and that we can validly apply the goodness-of-fit test to this example.

Step 4: Obtain the probability of the test statistic.

In this step we have to obtain p_T for the example, which is the probability of getting a value of 8.40 or greater for the test statistic when the population proportions are as hypothesised. As illustrated in figure 17.2, we require the area under the curve to the right of $X_2^2 = 8.4021$. A computer was used to determine that $p_C = 0.9850$. Hence,

$$p_T = 1 - p_C = 1 - 0.9850 = 0.0150.$$

That is, the probability of getting values of the test statistic greater than or equal to 8.40 is 0.0150. Put another way, there is a chance of 15 in 1000 of the test statistic having a value of 8.40, or larger, when the null hypothesis is true. Not a very likely event!

To demonstrate how p_T measures the likelihood of the test statistic when the null hypothesis is true, consider p_T for the observed value of the test statistic, 8.40, and for a somewhat smaller value of the test statistic, 1.42 say. For $X_2^2 = 1.42$, $p_T = 0.4916$, whereas for $X_2^2 = 8.40$, $p_T = 0.0150$. That is, values of $X_2^2 = 1.42$ or larger have a probability of 0.4916 when the null hypothesis is true. Plenty of values more extreme than 1.42 will occur when the null hypothesis is true. However, our value of $X_2^2 = 8.40$ and larger values have a probability of 0.0150 when the null hypothesis is true. Very few values more extreme than 8.40 occur when the null hypothesis is true. That is, p_T measures how extreme the observed value of the test statistic is when the null hypothesis is true.

Step 5: State and apply the rule for rejecting the null hypothesis.

We have decided on $\alpha = 0.05$, so that our rule is: if $p_T \leq 0.05$, reject H_0; otherwise, H_0 cannot be rejected. As $p_T = 0.0150 < 0.05$, reject H_0.

Step 6: State the conclusion in terms of the question investigated.

The evidence suggests that the support for the candidates has changed.   ■

How would you test to see if there was any difference in support between the three candidates? You would use the goodness-of-fit test with H_0: $\pi_i = 1/3$ for $i = 1, 2, 3$.

17.1.2   One limited variable with two values

As stated at the beginning of this chapter, the goodness-of-fit test is equivalent to the z-test for a proportion when the limited variable has just two values: for the same hypotheses, the probability of the test statistics from the two tests are equal. An example of the use of the goodness-of-fit test for a two-valued limited variable follows.

EXAMPLE 17.2   SUPPORT FOR THE CURRENT MEMBER

Suppose the question in the voting survey had been left at: would you vote for the current member? This is the question posed in example V.1, *Support for the current member.* The observed variable is *Vote for current member* which is a two-valued, limited variable. Example 14.1, *Support for the current member*, reported that 86 of the 200 sampled said *yes* to the survey question. By comparison, 0.52 of the 17 356 voters in the electorate voted for the member in the recent election. It appears that support for the member has changed but, as discussed in the introduction to part V *Hypothesis tests*, the goodness-of-fit test provides an objective procedure for deciding if the evidence suggests that population proportion is different from 0.52.

The steps in the goodness-of-fit test for this example are given below. In performing this test, remember that there are two values for the limited variable, not just one. The second value is somewhat redundant, since the observed proportion for it is just 1 minus the observed proportion for the first value. Thus, the proportion of voters who said *no* is just $1 - 0.43 = 0.57$. However, we have to supply two hypothesised proportions and two observed frequencies to carry out the goodness-of-fit test.

Step 1: Set up the hypotheses and nominate the significance level.

H_0: $\pi_1 = 0.52$, $\pi_2 = 0.48$

H_a: At least one population proportion is not equal to its hypothesised value.

Using the standard value of α we have $\alpha = 0.05$.

Step 2: Specify and obtain the test statistic.

The formula for the test statistic is $X_1^2 = \sum_{i=1}^{2} \dfrac{(O_i - E_i)^2}{E_i}$.

The test statistic, computed from the values in table 17.4, is $X_1^2 = 6.4904$.

Table 17.4   Table of observed and expected frequencies for a two-valued limited variable

Vote for current member	Frequencies	
	Observed O_i	Expected E_i
Yes	86	104
No	114	96
Total	200	200

Step 3: List and check conditions for the sampling distribution.

The sampling distribution of the test statistic, X_1^2, is the chi-square distribution with one degree of freedom. Checking the conditions that will satisfy the assumptions required for the valid use of the sampling distribution proceeds as follows:

1. Conditions for limited-variable probability model

- *Well-defined limited variable:* The variable is *Vote for current member*, which is a two-valued, well-defined, limited variable.

- *Stable population proportions:* There is no information to indicate whether the survey was made quickly enough for the proportions to remain stable. We have to presume that they are stable.

2. Conditions for other validating assumptions.

- *Infinite population:* The population is effectively infinite: there are 17 356 voters in the population and this is greater than $20 \times 200 = 4000$.

- *Representative sample:* As the sample is random, there is no reason to expect that the sample is not representative of the population.

- *Independence:* Again, there is not sufficient information to indicate whether the observations were taken independently, so we have to presume that the observations are independent.
- *Large number condition:* The expected frequencies are:

$$E_1 = n\pi_{01} = 200 \times 0.52 = 104 \text{ and } E_2 = n\pi_{02} = 200 \times 0.48 = 96$$

so that both $E_i > 5$ as required by the large number condition.

It appears that the assumptions required to use the chi-square sampling distribution are met and that we can validly apply the goodness-of-fit test to this example.

Step 4: Obtain the probability of the test statistic.

Using the chi-square distribution with one degree of freedom it is found that $p_T = 0.0108$.

Step 5: State and apply the rule for rejecting the null hypothesis.

We have decided on $\alpha = 0.05$, so that our rule is: if $p_T \leq 0.05$, reject H_0; otherwise, H_0 cannot be rejected. As $p_T = 0.0108 < 0.05$, reject H_0.

Step 6: State the conclusion in terms of the question investigated.

The evidence suggests that the percentage of voters who would vote for the current member has changed since the last election.   ∎

17.2   Reports on examples

The following reports, for the examples analysed in this chapter, indicate what material from a statistical analysis an investigator should include in a report. In general, the details of the statistical analysis are omitted so that the reader of the report can concentrate on the results.

EXAMPLE 17.1   POLITICAL PARTY SUPPORT — REPORT

The electoral office of the current member of a state electorate, with 17 356 registered voters, interviewed 200 randomly selected voters to ascertain whether the support for the three major parties had changed since the last election. The results of the survey are summarised in table 17.1. The proportions of the vote obtained at the last election are given in table 17.2. A goodness-of-fit test indicated that the proportions of voters now voting for the three major parties is different ($p \leq 0.05$) from those obtained at the last election.

EXAMPLE 17.2   SUPPORT FOR THE CURRENT MEMBER — REPORT

The electoral office of the current member of a state electorate, with 17 356 registered voters, interviewed 200 randomly selected voters to ascertain whether the level of support for her had changed since the last election. The result was that 43% of voters interviewed would support the member and a goodness-of-fit test based on this result indicated that support in the electorate now differs ($p \leq 0.05$) from the 52% of votes she enjoyed at the election.

Rule: if P < 0.5 reject the null. [handwritten]

17.3 Using Minitab for the goodness-of-fit test

Minitab has no command for performing the goodness-of-fit test. However, the macro *goodfit* in Appendix C, *Minitab macros*, does the required computations. First, set up two columns: one named *o* that contains the observed frequencies, and the other named *e* that contains the expected frequencies. Then change the current directory to the one containing the macros and execute the macro with the *execute* command. For example, if the macro is stored in the file *goodfit.mtb* on a floppy disk in drive *a:*, the commands to execute the macro are as follows:

```
MTB > cd a:\
MTB > execute 'goodfit.mtb'
```

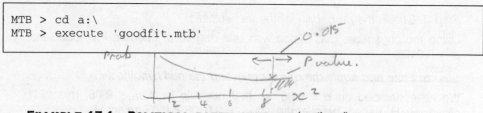

Prob [handwritten] *0.015* [handwritten] *→ P value.* [handwritten] *χ²* [handwritten]

EXAMPLE 17.1   POLITICAL PARTY SUPPORT (continued)

The commands, and associated output, for computing the goodness-of-fit test for the example are as follows:

```
MTB > outfile 'a:\support.lis'
MTB > name c1 'o' c2 'e'
MTB > set c1
DATA> 86 55 59
DATA> set c2
DATA> 104 52 44
DATA> end data
MTB > print c1 c2

ROW        o         e

  1       86       104
  2       55        52
  3       59        44

MTB > cd a:\
MTB > execute 'goodfit.mtb'

  Goodness of fit test

The chi-square test statistic is:
K1        8.40210
and its degrees of freedom is
K2        2.00000
The probability of the test statistic is
K3        0.0149798
```

[handwritten annotations around output:]

$\chi^2 = \sum \dfrac{(O-E)^2}{E}$

O − E   −18, +3, +15

observed / *expected*

52 %, *26 %*, *22 %*   *Take % and if 200 were same as before.*

200

Lib 1, *Lab* 2, *D* 3

← drive f.   *macro.*

$\dfrac{18^2}{104}$ $\dfrac{3^2}{52}$ $\dfrac{15^2}{44}$ *8.402*

[left margin handwritten, vertical:]
Degrees of freedom = n − 2
∴ x = n − 2
hence null hyp is true, diff is only due to sample.

if not x² > 2 − reject null hyp. [handwritten]

If your version of Minitab has pull-down menus and you want to use them, table 17.5 lists the menus and options that access the required commands. Appendix D *Detailed instructions for Minitab menus* explains how to use the menus.

Table 17.5   Menus and options for Minitab commands for performing the goodness-of-fit test

Minitab command	Menu	Option
outfile	File >	Other Files > Start Recording Session...
name	Edit >	Data Screen (Alt-D)
set	Edit >	Data Screen (Alt-D)
print	Edit >	Display Data...
cd		not available
execute	File >	Other Files > Execute Macro...

17.4   Chapter summary

The goodness-of-fit test is a hypothesis test that applies when the data consists of the values of one limited variable and when the question to be investigated is: do the population proportions for the values of the limited variable differ from those hypothesised? A preliminary examination of the data can be made by using the one-way summary table and the bar or column chart as descriptive summaries.

The test statistic for this test is called Pearson's chi-square statistic with $(k - 1)$ degrees of freedom and it measures the difference between the observed and expected frequencies. The expected frequencies are those that conform to the hypothesised proportions and, like the observed frequencies, sum to the number of observations.

The sampling distribution of the test statistic is the chi-square distribution with $(k - 1)$ degrees of freedom. This distribution is based on a limited-variable probability model for population. The conditions that will satisfy the assumptions required for the valid use of this sampling distribution are as follows:

1. **Conditions for limited-variable probability model**
   - *Well-defined limited variable*
   - *Stable population proportions*

2. **Conditions for other validating assumptions**
   - *Infinite population*
   - *Representative sample*
   - *Independence*
   - *Large number condition*

For a particular example, you must check whether these conditions are fulfilled. If the conditions are not met the procedure cannot be used for the example.

The probability of the test statistic p_T is obtained from the chi-square distribution by determining the area, under the curve, above the range to the right of observed value of the test statistic.

The goodness-of-fit test is equivalent to the z-test for a proportion when the limited variable has just two values in that, for the same hypotheses, the probabilities of the test statistics from the two tests are equal.

17.5   Key terms

- alternative hypothesis (Hₐ)
- assumptions
- bar chart
- chi-square distribution ($\chi^2_{\text{degrees of freedom}}$)
- column chart
- conditions
- cumulative probability (p_C)
- degrees of freedom
- distribution of variables
- expected frequency (E_{cell})
- goodness-of-fit test
- independence condition
- infinite population
- large number condition
- limited-variable probability model

- null hypothesis (H₀)
- observed frequency (O_{cell})
- one-way summary table
- Pearson's chi-square statistic ($\chi^2_{\text{degrees of freedom}}$)
- probability of the test statistic (p_T)
- proportion
- representative sample
- sampling distribution of a test statistic
- stable population proportions condition
- test statistic
- well-defined limited variable
- z-test for a proportion

17.6   Exercises

17.1   In your own words explain these terms:

(a) statistical inference
(b) subjective procedure
(c) objective procedure
(d) null hypothesis
(e) alternative hypothesis
(f) beyond reasonable doubt

(g) probability of the test statistic
(h) significance level
(i) significant
(j) type I error
(k) type II error

17.2 Examine the following problems and state the null hypothesis in each case:

    (a) In 1991, the proportion of overseas students at the University of South Australia who were born in Asia or the Middle East was 0.30. Using a simple random sample of first year students, determine whether this proportion has changed.

    (b) The introduction of speed cameras has changed the proportion of accidents on suburban roads that are fatal. Examine the police records of accidents occuring over one month to see whether this statement is true.

    (c) There are as many people in favour of the new legislation for extended retail trading hours as there are against. Is this statement endorsed by the opinion poll that claimed 60% of the general public want weekend trading?

    (d) A national campaign by an automobile manufacturer claims that its current small car is considered the best car on the market by 52% of Australians. Is this claim supported by the latest monthly car sales figures?

    (e) A market research company wishes to know whether support for a new product is equally divided between all age-groups. A recent survey of 500 customers in a city store showed that of those interested in the new product, 35% are under 25 years, 40% are aged between 25 and 50, and the rest were aged over 50. Is this a significant result?

17.3 Nonrejection of the null hypothesis implies that the null hypothesis is true. Comment on this statement?

17.4 Statistical inference uses information obtained from a sample to draw conclusions about the population. There are two categories:

    (a) confidence intervals, which use information from a sample to estimate parameters; and

    (b) hypothesis tests, which use information from a sample to answer a question about the population for which there is only a yes or no answer.

Which of these procedures provides more information about the population? Give reasons for your answer.

17.5 What conditions is the limited-variable probability model based on?

17.6 Identify the sampling distribution of the test statistic for the goodness-of-fit test.

17.7 One of the conditions that must be satisfied for the successful application of the goodness-of-fit test is the large number condition. What difficulties arise when this condition is not satisfied?

17.8 The finance manager of a department store believes that the company's cash flow problems are a direct result of the slow collection of accounts receivable. The accountant claims that 60% of the current accounts receivable are more than 60 days old. To see if the accountant's claim is justified, the manager takes a systematic sample of 120 of the 5000 accounts receivable — 79 of them are more than 60 days old.

(a) Answer the following questions:

   (i) What is the question to be investigated (including the group to which the conclusions apply)?

   (ii) What variable(s) are we concerned with here?

   (iii) What type of variable(s) are they?

   (iv) Which major category of statistical procedures applies here? Why?

   (v) What type of statistic should we use, given the question to be investigated and the variables involved?

   (vi) Which particular statistic or procedure, and diagram, should we use? Why?

(b) What is the observed proportion of overdue accounts?

(c) Use the following Minitab output to answer this part of the exercise:

   (i) Reproduce the output.

   (ii) Perform an objective test to see whether there is any evidence that the population proportion of accounts receivable over 60 days old is different from the accountant's claim. (Use a significance level of $\alpha = 0.05$.)

```
MTB > name c1 'o' c2 'e'
MTB > set c1
DATA> 79 41
DATA> set c2
DATA> 0.6 0.4
DATA> end data
MTB > let c2=c2*120
MTB > print c1 c2

ROW        o        e

  1       79       72
  2       41       48


MTB > cd a:\
MTB > execute 'goodfit.mtb'

 Goodness of fit test

The chi-square test statistic is:
K1      1.70139
and its degrees of freedom is
K2      1.00000
The probability of the test statistic is
K3      0.192106
```

17.9 Several accountancy companies have amalgamated as a single national company to capture a wider range of local and overseas business. The board of directors of the new company decides to commission a logo for the new company and is considering five design proposals (A, B, C, D, E). The selection is to be shown to all staff members (about 900), who will be asked to list their preferences. The managing director suggests that 40% of the staff will choose selection D and that the other designs will share the remaining votes equally. To see if the manager's claim can be supported, a simple random sample of 40 staff members was selected and their preferences for the designs are given in table 17.6.

Table 17.6   Preference for logo design

Design	A	B	C	D	E
Number preferring	5	9	8	14	4

(a) Answer the following questions:
  (i) What is the question to be investigated (including the group to which the conclusions apply)?
  (ii) What variable(s) are we concerned with here?
  (iii) What type of variable(s) are they?
  (iv) Which major category of statistical procedures applies here? Why?
  (v) What type of statistic should we use, given the question to be investigated and the variables involved?
  (vi) Which particular statistic or procedure, and diagram, should we use? Why?
(b) Use the goodness-of-fit test to determine whether this data supports the managing director's claim. (Use a significance level of $\alpha = 0.05$.)

17.10 This exercise is based on an article from *The Australian Computer Journal* by Watson (1989). The frequency with which 10 industries are represented in the Top 200 Australian organisations is given in table 17.7.

Table 17.7   Frequencies of 10 industries in Top 200 Australian organisations

Industry	Frequency
Construction	4
Finance	43
Manufacturing	55
Mining	18
Primary	3
Public Service	7
Retail	8
Service	12
Transport	24
Wholesale	26
Total	200

For a survey of all registered Australian companies (there are over 250 000 of them), a questionnaire was mailed to 300 selected companies. We want to see whether the distribution of the industries of all Australian companies is the same as that for the Top 200 organisations. The first two letters of the industries of the 96 responding organisations are listed as follows:

MA	MI	FI	RE	MA	TR	SE	MA	PU	MA	TR	TR	WH	WH	MA	FI
FI	MI	MA	SE	PU	MA	TR	PU	WH	MA	MI	FI	MA	PU	MA	WH
PR	SE	TR	MA	TR	MA	FI	MI	MA	FI	MA	MA	PU	WH	MA	WH
MI	WH	MA	PU	SE	MA	PU	MA	TR	WH	MI	FI	MA	PU	FI	MA
MI	FI	FI	MA	RE	MA	MA	TR	SE	PU	TR	TR	WH	WH	MA	MA
SE	WH	TR	MI	MA	FI	TR	MA	FI	MA	MA	MA	PU	WH	PR	MA

This data is saved in the Minitab portable worksheet file *industry.mtp* where the industries were coded as follows: Construction (1), Finance (2), Manufacturing (3), Mining (4), Primary (5), Public service (6), Retail (7), Service (8), Transport (9) and Wholesale (10).

(a) Answer the following questions:

    (i) What is the question to be investigated (including the group to which the conclusions apply)?

    (ii) What variable(s) are we concerned with here?

    (iii) What type of variable(s) are they?

    (iv) Which major category of statistical procedures applies here? Why?

    (v) What type of statistic should we use, given the question to be investigated and the variables involved?

    (vi) Which particular statistic or procedure, and diagram, should we use? Why?

(b) How many respondents were there?

(c) Use a diagram to summarise the information collected in the survey.

(d) How many respondents were involved in the manufacturing industry?

(e) Perform the hypothesis test to determine if the evidence suggests that the distribution of the industries of all Australian companies differs from that for the top 200 Australian organisations. (Use a significance level of $\alpha = 0.05$.) Note that you may have to combine industries to satisfy the large number condition. If so, you could form the following combinations: Construction and Manufacturing; Mining and Primary; Public service, Retail and Service.

17.11 In a simple random sample of 150 out of 23 000 students, 47 preferred a particular brand of cola to any other soft drink. Of the 23 000 students, does the proportion preferring the brand of cola differ from the traditional 25% share of the market? (Use a significance level of $\alpha = 0.05$.)

(a) Answer the following questions:

(i) What is the question to be investigated (including the group to which the conclusions apply)?

(ii) What variable(s) are we concerned with here?

(iii) What type of variable(s) are they?

(iv) Which major category of statistical procedures applies here? Why?

(v) What type of statistic should we use, given the question to be investigated and the variables involved?

(vi) Which particular statistic or procedure, and diagram, should we use? Why?

(b) Perform the appropriate test. (Use a significance level of $\alpha = 0.05$.)

## CHAPTER 18

TEST OF INDEPENDENCE FOR TWO LIMITED VARIABLES

LEARNING OBJECTIVES

The learning objectives of this chapter are:

- to know when to apply, how to calculate and how to interpret the results of the contingency table analysis;
- to know the conditions required for a contingency table analysis to be valid and how to determine when these are met;
- to be able to analyse, in detail, the trends exhibited by the data using appropriate tables of percentages and adjusted residuals as determined by a contingency table analysis.

The following extract from the *Summary of procedures based on combinations of variable types* in part VI gives an overview of the hypothesis tests covered in this and the previous chapter of part V, *Hypothesis tests*.

1. *One limited variable*
   - Distribution of variables: z-test for a proportion; goodness-of-fit test.

2. *Two limited variables*
   - **Distribution of variables**: z-test for a proportion difference; contingency table analysis.

3. *One unrestricted variable — one limited variable*

4. *One unrestricted variable — two limited variables*

5. *Two unrestricted variables*

As outlined in the objective, this chapter covers the hypothesis test known as **contingency table analysis**. It applies when the data consists of the values of two limited variables and when the question to be investigated is: are the two limited variables **dependent**? Further, since an inference procedure is involved, we must have taken a sample and the question to be investigated must be about the population and *not* confined to the sample.

Other books present a special test for the case of two two-valued, limited variables: **z-test for a proportion difference**. This test is equivalent to the contingency table analysis: for the same hypotheses, the probabilities of the test statistics from the two tests are equal. Section 18.2, *Summarising independence*, gives an example of how the contingency table analysis is used for two two-valued limited variables.

18.1   Contingency table analysis

Section 6.2, *Two limited variables*, presented contingency tables and charts with bars or columns that are grouped or stacked as descriptive summaries for data involving two limited variables. We examined these tables and diagrams to determine whether the variables were dependent or independent. However, the conclusion we made was a matter of opinion because it is not always obvious whether the differences between rows (or columns) of the table are sufficient to conclude that the variables are dependent. This chapter presents a hypothesis test as a means of deciding objectively whether or not two limited variables are dependent. However, before doing the contingency table analysis, we begin with a preliminary examination of the descriptive summaries.

EXAMPLE 18.1   HOUSEHOLD SIZE AND STATUS

Example 6.2, *Household size and status*, described a household survey in which we took a sample of 200 of the city's 219 000 households. To select the households, we obtained a list of all the streets in the metropolitan area and randomly selected 200 streets; a resident of house number five in each of these streets was interviewed. Amongst other information, the survey obtained the *Number of children* and *Socioeconomic status* of each of the 200 households. The primary, raw data was given in table 6.4. Suppose the question to be investigated is: are the two limited variables, *Number of children* and *Socioeconomic status*, related for all households from the metropolitan area of the city? This question is not confined to just the households surveyed. The descriptive summaries for a preliminary examination of the data are the table of column percentages, repeated in table 18.1, and the associated stacked bar chart in figure 18.1.

Table 18.1   Column percentages for *Number of children* and *Socioeconomic status*

		Socioeconomic status		
Number of children	Low	Medium	High	Total
0	2.5	10.0	20.0	10
1	17.5	20.0	23.3	20
2	70.0	66.7	40.0	60
3	10.0	3.3	16.7	10
n	80	60	60	200

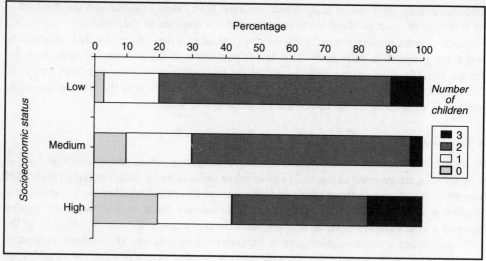

Figure 18.1 Stacked bar chart for household survey

From table 18.1 and figure 18.1 we concluded that it appears that high-status households have proportionally more no-children and three-children households compared with low-status and medium-status households. However, it is a matter of subjective opinion whether there is any difference between households of different status; we need a hypothesis test to determine objectively whether or not any relationship exists, and the appropriate test for this is a contingency table analysis.

The general steps for performing a contingency table analysis are now outlined, and the analysis for the example follows this general description.

Step 1: Set up the hypotheses and nominate the significance level.

The general form of the **null** and **alternative hypotheses** for this test are:

H_0: the two limited variables are independent
H_a: the two limited variables are dependent

The value of α to be used in the analysis must also be chosen at this step.

Step 2: Specify and obtain the test statistic.

To calculate the **test statistic**, first calculate the frequency theoretically expected in each cell of the table when the null hypothesis is true. The properties of such expected frequencies should be that:

- **row totals** and **column totals** are the same as those for the observed frequencies.
- the column proportions, computed from the expected frequencies, are the same for each column; similarly, the row proportions, computed from the expected frequencies, are the same for each row. That is, the expected frequencies display independence.

The formula for computing the expected frequencies with these properties is:

$$\text{Expected frequency for a cell} = \frac{\text{cell's row total} \times \text{cell's column total}}{\text{grand total}}$$

This formula may result in numbers that are not whole numbers. If this happens, the expected frequencies should *not* be rounded to whole numbers because, if they are rounded, they will not have the above properties.

The test statistic, $X^2_{(r-1)(c-1)}$, is called **Pearson's chi-square statistic** with $(r-1)(c-1)$ degrees of freedom. It is based on the goodness-of-fit formula and, in this case, its formula is:

$$X^2_{(r-1)(c-1)} = \sum_{i=1}^{r} \sum_{j=1}^{c} \frac{(O_{ij} - E_{ij})^2}{E_{ij}}$$

where O_{ij} is the **observed frequency** for a cell,
  E_{ij} is the theoretically **expected frequency** for a cell,
  r is the number of rows in the table, and
  c is the number of columns in the table.
  $(r-1)(c-1)$ is called the **degrees of freedom**.

This formula, expressed in words, is:

$$X^2_{\text{degrees of freedom}} = \text{Sum over all cells of} \left\{ \frac{[\text{observed frequency} - \text{expected frequency}]^2}{\text{expected frequency}} \right\}$$

This test statistic measures how far the observed frequencies are from displaying independence.

Step 3: List and check conditions for the sampling distribution.

The **sampling distribution of the test statistic** for this hypothesis test is the **chi-square distribution** (see figure 17.1) and this is based on a **limited-variable probability model**. The **conditions** that will satisfy the **assumptions** required for the valid use of the sampling distribution are as follows:

1. **Conditions for limited-variable probability model**
   - *Well-defined limited variables:* The variables on which the hypothesis test is being performed must be **well-defined limited variables**: the values of each limited variable should be mutually exclusive and collectively exhaustive.
   - *Stable population proportions:* The **stable population proportions condition** requires that the proportion of the population taking a particular combination of the values of the limited variables must remain stable or constant throughout the period to which the inferences are to apply.

2. Conditions for other validating assumptions

- *Infinite population:* The sample should come from an effectively **infinite population**.
- *Representative sample:* A **representative sample** is an unbiased fraction of the original population.
- *Independence:* The **independence condition** requires that the outcome of any observation is independent of the outcome of any other observation.
- *Large number condition:* The **large number condition** stipulates that the expected frequencies for most cells of the contingency table must be greater than or equal to 5. A general rule of thumb is that no cells should have an expected frequency less than one and that not more than 20% of cells should have expected frequencies less than 5. If this condition is not met, you should consider collapsing the table, as described in section 6.3, *Three limited variables* — rows or columns or both should be combined or deleted.

These conditions are the same as for the goodness-of-fit test, except that more than one limited variable is involved, there is a proportion for each combination of the limited variables, and the large number condition is a little different. Checking all the conditions proceeds in the same way as described for the goodness-of-fit test in section 17.1, *Goodness-of-fit test*.

Step 4: Obtain the probability of the test statistic.

The **probability of the test statistic**, p_T, has to be obtained from the χ^2 distribution by determining the area, under the curve, above the range to the right of the observed value of the test statistic.

Sometimes computer programs for computing the probabilities for the chi-square distribution provide the probability of being less than a nominated value. That is, they compute the **cumulative probability**, p_C. Then, $p_T = 1 - p_C$.

Step 5: State and apply the rule for rejecting the null hypothesis.

The general form of the rule for rejecting the null hypothesis is: if $p_T \leq \alpha$, reject H_0; otherwise, H_0 cannot be rejected.

Step 6: State the conclusion in terms of the question investigated.

Once you have decided whether or not the hypothesis is to be rejected, restate the conclusion in terms of the original question.   ∎

EXAMPLE 18.1   HOUSEHOLD SIZE AND STATUS (continued)

As already stated, the question to be investigated is whether, for a city's 219 000 households, the *Number of children* in the household is dependent on its *Socioeconomic status*. The question to be investigated involves two limited variables, concerns all households in the city, and has either a yes or a no answer. A hypothesis test is therefore appropriate and the contingency table analysis is the test that determines if the evidence suggests that the two variables are dependent.

Step 1: Set up the hypotheses and nominate the significance level.

H_0: *Number of children* and *Socioeconomic status* are independent
H_a: the two variables are dependent
Using the standard value of α we have $\alpha = 0.05$.

Step 2: Specify and obtain the test statistic.

The computation of the test statistic is based on the expected and observed frequencies in table 18.2.

Table 18.2   Expected and observed frequencies for *Number of children* and *Socioeconomic status*

Number of children	Low	Medium	High	Total
		Socioeconomic status		
0	8.00	6.00	6.00	20
	(2)	(6)	(12)	
1	16.00	12.00	12.00	40
	(14)	(12)	(14)	
2	48.00	36.00	36.00	120
	(56)	(40)	(24)	
3	8.00	6.00	6.00	20
	(8)	(2)	(10)	
Total	80	60	60	200

Note: observed frequencies are in brackets.

The properties of the expected frequencies are as follows:

1. Row and columns totals are the same as those for the observed frequencies.

2. The proportion of a particular status household is the same for each size household; also, the proportion of a certain size household is the same for each status. That is, the expected frequencies display independence; for example, the proportion of households with 0 children, irrespective of status, is:

$$0.10 = 8/80 = 6/60 = 20/200$$

This is what one would expect if the null hypothesis were true.

The formula for the test statistic is $X^2{}_{(r-1)(c-1)} = \displaystyle\sum_{i=1}^{r}\sum_{j=1}^{c}\frac{(O_{ij} - E_{ij})^2}{E_{ij}}$

Hence, the number of degrees of freedom is:

$$(r-1) \times (c-1) = (4-1) \times (3-1) = 3 \times 2 = 6$$

and the computation of the test statistic proceeds as follows:

$$X_6^2 = \frac{(2-8)^2}{8} + \frac{(6-6)^2}{6} + \frac{(12-6)^2}{6} + \ldots + \frac{(10-6)^2}{6}$$
$$= 22.194$$

This test statistic measures how far the observed frequencies depart from displaying independence since it measures the overall difference between the observed and expected frequencies.

Step 3: List and check conditions for the sampling distribution.

The sampling distribution of the test statistic, X_6^2, is the chi-square distribution with 6 degrees of freedom. This distribution is given in figure 18.2. Checking the conditions that will satisfy the assumptions required for the valid use of the sampling distribution proceeds as follows:

1. Conditions for limited-variable probability model

- *Well-defined limited variables:* The variables *Number of children* and *Socioeconomic status* are both well-defined, limited variables.
- *Stable population proportions:* There is no information indicating whether or not observations were made over a short enough time interval to ensure that the proportions are stable. We have to presume that the proportions are stable.

2. Conditions for other validating assumptions

- *Infinite population:* The population is effectively infinite: there are 219 100 households in the metropolitan area and this is greater than 20 × 200 = 4000.
- *Representative sample:* As the sample is random, there is no reason to expect that the sample is not representative of the population.
- *Independence:* Presumably, the survey was conducted so that the observation of each household is independent of the others and the number of children and socioeconomic status of each household is independent of the other households in the population.
- *Large number condition:* The large number condition is satisfied as all expected frequencies are greater than 5.

It appears that the assumptions required to use the chi-square sampling distribution are met and that we can validly perform a contingency table analysis on this example.

Step 4: Obtain the probability of the test statistic.

From figure 18.2 we can see that we can generally expect values of the test statistic to be about 5 when the two variables are independent and the assumptions are met. The probability of the observed value, and more extreme values, of the test statistic has been computed to be $p_T = 0.0011$. That is, the value of the test statistic, 22.194, and more extreme values would occur about 1 in 1000 times, when the null hypothesis is true and the conditions hold — a rather unusual value when the null hypothesis is true.

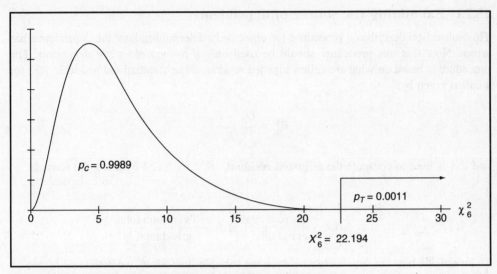

Figure 18.2   Chi-square distribution for 6 degrees of freedom

Step 5: State and apply the rule for rejecting the null hypothesis.

We have decided on $\alpha = 0.05$, so that our rule is: if $p_T \le 0.05$, reject H_0; otherwise, H_0 cannot be rejected. As $p_T = 0.0011 < 0.05$, reject H_0.

Step 6: State the conclusion in terms of the question investigated.

The evidence suggests that the number of children is dependent on the status of the household.
Our subjective conclusion has been confirmed with an objective hypothesis test.

18.2   Detailed examination of trends exhibited by data

The hypothesis test provides a procedure that helps us decide whether the variables are dependent or independent. However, this is not the end of the line in terms of interpreting the data. While this information is likely to be useful, usually we will be interested in more detailed conclusions about the patterns the data exhibits.

EXAMPLE 18.1   HOUSEHOLD SIZE AND STATUS (continued)

We concluded that *Number of children* and *Socioeconomic status* are dependent. That is, the pattern or trend in the number of children per household is not the same for each level of socioeconomic status; nor is the pattern in socioeconomic status the same for the different number of children per household.

However, we are interested in more details about the way they differ. For example, do low-status households have more or less no-child households than medium-status or high-status households?

18.2.1 Examining the source of dependence

This subsection describes a procedure for objectively determining how the dependence has arisen. Note that this procedure should be used *only if the variables are dependent*. The procedure is based on what are called adjusted residuals. The standardised residual, R_{ij}^S, for a cell is given by:

$$R_{ij}^S = \frac{O_{ij} - E_{ij}}{\sqrt{E_{ij}}}$$

and this is used to compute the **adjusted residual**, R_{ij}^A, for a cell by using the formula:

$$R_{ij}^A = \frac{R_{ij}^S}{\sqrt{1 - \dfrac{\text{cell's row total}}{\text{grand total}}}\sqrt{1 - \dfrac{\text{cell's column total}}{\text{grand total}}}}$$

To investigate how the dependence between the variables has arisen, we determine for which cells the observed frequencies deviate **significantly** from the expected frequencies. A cell deviates significantly whenever the absolute value of the adjusted residual is greater than the z_T for $1 - (\alpha/2)$. For example, for $\alpha = 0.05$, $z_T = 1.96$. Thus, any residual whose absolute value is above 1.96 represents a significant ($\alpha = 0.05$) departure from what is expected under the null hypothesis.

The point about this is that we are examining the *deviation from expectation*. But what is the expectation? The quick answer is the expected frequencies when the null hypothesis is true. However, as stated in section 6.2.1, *Distribution tables for two limited variables*, the data is best summarised in terms of column or row percentages. If the variables are independent we can expect that:

- for column percentages, the percentages in each column of the table are approximately equal to the percentages in the marginal column;
- for row percentages, the percentages in each row of the table are approximately equal to the percentages in the marginal row.

So a significant positive residual indicates that the percentage in that cell of the table is significantly greater than the corresponding percentage in the margin of the table. A significant negative residual indicates that the percentage in that cell of the table is significantly less than the corresponding percentage in the margin of the table.

EXAMPLE 18.1   HOUSEHOLD SIZE AND STATUS (continued)

The adjusted residuals, and column percentages, for the household survey are given in table 18.3. The computation is illustrated for the cell corresponding to households with three children and of medium socioeconomic status. From table 18.2, the observed and expected frequencies for this cell are 2 and 6 respectively. The standardised residual for this cell is:

$$R_{42}^S = \frac{O_{42} - E_{42}}{\sqrt{E_{42}}}$$

$$= \frac{2 - 6}{\sqrt{6}}$$

$$= -1.6330$$

and the adjusted residual is:

$$R_{42}^A = \frac{R_{42}^S}{\sqrt{1 - \dfrac{\text{row 4 total}}{\text{grand total}}}\sqrt{1 - \dfrac{\text{column 2 total}}{\text{grand total}}}}$$

$$= \frac{-1.6330}{\sqrt{1 - \dfrac{20}{200}}\sqrt{1 - \dfrac{60}{200}}}$$

$$= -2.0573$$

Table 18.3   Column percentages and adjusted residuals for *Number of children* and *Socioeconomic status*

| | Socioeconomic status | | | |
Number of children	Low	Medium	High	Total
0	2.5	10.0	20.0	10
	-2.89	0.00	**3.09**	
1	17.5	20.0	23.3	20
	-0.72	0.00	0.77	
2	70.0	66.7	40.0	60
	2.36	1.26	**-3.78**	
3	10.0	3.3	16.7	10
	0.00	**-2.06**	2.06	
n	80	60	60	n = 200

Note: the column percentages are above the adjusted residuals; the highlighted residuals deviate significantly from expectation.

There are 6 cells for which the observed frequencies deviate significantly from the expected frequencies. Since column percentages are used to summarise the trends in the data, we can expect, under the hypothesis of independence, each column to be approximately equal to the marginal column of percentages. So the adjusted residuals indicate the extent to which the percentages in the body of the table deviate from the marginal column of percentages.

The conclusions to be drawn, for each status, are as follows:

- low-status households had less than the expected 10% of no-children households and more than the expected 60% of two-children households;

- medium-status households had less than the expected 10% of three-children households;

- high-status households had more than the expected 10% of no-children and 10% of three-children households, and substantially less than the expected 60% of two-children households.

In summary, low-status households had a tendency to have fewer no-children and more two-children households than expected. Medium-status households tended to have fewer three-children households, and high-status households tended to have more no-children and three-children households and fewer two-children households than expected. These conclusions are in line with the subjective conclusions drawn in example 6.2, *Household size and status*.

18.2.2 Summarising independence

If the contingency table analysis indicates that the two variables are independent, then the effects of the two variables can be investigated independently. A **one-way summary table** for each variable is formed, each table corresponding to a margin of the two-way table. It is *not* appropriate to do this if the variables are dependent.

EXAMPLE 18.2   COFFEE PREFERENCE IN A SECOND CITY

Example 6.4, *Coffee preference in a second city*, reported the results of a survey to investigate the coffee-brand preferences of a city's 1 million or more adults. A convenience sample of males and a convenience sample of females were asked which of three brands of coffee they preferred. It was concluded, subjectively, that the percentage preferring a particular *Brand* is *independent* of the *Sex* involved. We might want to use a contingency table analysis to confirm this subjective conclusion. However, the convenience samples taken at the university canteen are unlikely to be representative of the adult population of the whole city: the condition of the sample being representative, required for the chi-square sampling distribution to be appropriate, is therefore unlikely to be met in this example.

We are left with the subjective assessment based on the descriptive summaries. From the two-way contingency table in table 6.11 we concluded that the percentage preferring a particular *Brand* was *independent* of the *Sex* involved. The one-way summary tables of percentages in tables 6.12 and 6.13 led to the conclusion that Min House was preferred slightly more than the others and that there were 50% more female than male participants.

EXAMPLE 18.3   COMPUTER SERVICE AT A UNIVERSITY

The information technology (IT) unit at a university surveyed the university's staff to determine their satisfaction with access to the unit's support team. The unit selected a sample of 50 of the 1124 academic staff and a sample of 50 of the 1218 general staff, thus obtaining a stratified random sample with two strata. A researcher, not from the IT unit, phoned each of the selected staff members and asked whether or not they felt that they had adequate access to the IT unit's support team. Fifty of each type of staff were selected to provide a precision of approximately ±0.1 for estimating the proportions of staff who felt that they had adequate access.

First we conduct an analysis to determine if the academic and general staff at the university differ in their opinions about access to the IT support team. The variables involved in the analysis are *Staff access*, with values adequate and inadequate, and *Staff type*, with values academic and general. These are both limited variables. The frequencies for the combinations of the two variables are summarised in the contingency table in table 18.4; the column percentages that allow us to compare the two *Staff types* are in table 18.5. The percentages indicate that the academic staff seem more satisfied with access to the IT support team than general staff are, but this is my opinion and you may not agree. Is the difference large enough?

Table 18.4   Two-way contingency table for *Staff access* and *Staff type*

Staff access	Staff type		
	Academic	General	Total
Adequate	31	24	55
Inadquate	19	26	45
Total	50	50	100

Table 18.5   Percentages of *Staff access* for different *Staff types*

Staff access	Staff type		
	Academic	General	Total
Adequate	62	48	55
Inadquate	38	52	45
n	50	50	100

The unit did a contingency table analysis of the frequencies and found that the conditions are met, the test statistic is 1.98, and the probability of this test statistic is 0.1594. Using a significance level of $\alpha = 0.05$, it concluded that there is not sufficient evidence to reject the null hypothesis. So the percentage who felt they had adequate *Staff access* is *independent* of the *Staff type* involved. That is, the two *Staff types* do not differ significantly in their satisfaction with access to the IT unit's support team. This is the opposite of the conclusion that was reached subjectively.

Thus, the best way to summarise the results is to use the one-way summary tables of percentages corresponding to the two margins, *Staff access* and *Staff type*. In this example, the *Staff type* margin is of little interest since all it contains is the numbers of academic and general staff that the unit decided to sample. Table 18.6 gives the one-way summary table for *Staff access*, and includes the bounds for the 95% confidence interval for the percentages. From this table we can conclude that about half the staff, irrespective of type, consider that they have adequate access to the IT unit's support team.

Table 18.6 One-way summary table of percentages for *Staff access*

Staff access		
Adequate	Inadequate	
55.0 ± 9.8*	45.0 ± 9.8*	($n = 100$)

* The bound for the 95% confidence interval.

18.2.3 Interpreting dependence

We have to be careful in interpreting dependence because it can occur between two variables that are not directly related. An infamous example is the controversy over the relationship between smoking and lung cancer. Initially, it was observed that many patients with lung cancer are smokers; that is, smoking and lung cancer are associated. Such association tempts many investigators to leap to the conclusion that there is a causal relationship, and indeed it was concluded that smoking causes lung cancer. However, there is an alternative explanation for the observed dependence: that is, the occurrence of smoking and of lung cancer are linked. For example, suppose something in their genotype makes certain people susceptible to lung cancer, and their smoking is also caused by a genotypic defect. If the inheritance of the two are linked because they are on the same chromosome, an association will be observed. What happens if this latter explanation is true and people give up smoking? Will lung cancer decrease? No, because lung cancer is not caused by smoking but by a genetic defect. So, to decide what action to take to reduce lung cancer, it is crucial to have the correct explanation. The observed association does not allow us to discriminate between the alternative explanations.

In the case of smoking and lung cancer, this problem prompted researchers to investigate further and establish that smoking directly caused lung cancer. The point is that the original evidence of dependence between the two was not sufficient to justify the conclusion of a causal relationship.

18.3 Reports on examples

The following reports, for the examples analysed in this chapter, indicate what material from a statistical analysis an investigator should include in a report. In general, the details of the statistical analysis are omitted so that the reader of the report can concentrate on the results.

EXAMPLE 18.1   HOUSEHOLD SIZE AND STATUS — REPORT

A survey of households determined the number of children and socioeconomic status for 200 randomly selected households. A contingency table analysis led to the conclusion that, in the city surveyed, the number of children and socioeconomic status are dependent ($p \leq 0.05$). The differences, in the number of children, between households of different status appear in figure 18.1. An analysis of adjusted residuals led to the conclusion that the low-status households tend to have fewer no-children and more two-children households, whereas medium-status households tend to have fewer three-children households, and high-status households tend to have more no-children and three-children households and fewer two-children households than expected.

EXAMPLE 18.2   COFFEE PREFERENCE IN A SECOND CITY — REPORT

For a survey of the coffee-brand preferences of adults in a large city, a convenience sample of males and a convenience sample of females were asked which of three brands of coffee they preferred. From table 6.11 it seems that the brand of coffee preferred is independent of the sex of the individual. From figure 6.8 we concluded that Min House is preferred slightly more than the others. As convenience samples, these samples are unlikely to be representative of the adults in the city. Consequently, a contingency table analysis was not attempted and the conclusions just outlined are only tentative and need confirmation from further studies.

EXAMPLE 18.3 COMPUTER SERVICE AT A UNIVERSITY — REPORT

The information technology unit (IT) at a university randomly sampled the academic and general staff there to determine their satisfaction with access to the unit's support team. A contingency table analysis of the results indicated that there was no difference ($p > 0.05$) between academic and general staff in their satisfaction with access to the IT unit's support team. From table 18.6 we concluded that about half the university's staff, irrespective of type, feel that they have adequate access.

18.4   Using Minitab for contingency table analysis

18.4.1   Computation for hypothesis test

The Minitab commands depend on whether you already have the contingency table or you have only the raw data.

Raw data

If you have only the raw data, you simply need to add the subcommand *chisq* 2 to the Minitab *table* command. The 2 in the *chisq* subcommand is an option value that tells

Minitab to include the expected frequencies in the table, and to produce the test statistic. This version of the subcommand cannot be executed by using menus.

The probability of the test statistic is not produced by the *chisq* subcommand but is computed as follows:

1. use the *cdf* command with the *chisq* subcommand to produces the cumulative probability, p_C;
2. Use the *let* command to compute $p_T = 1 - p_C$.

The general form of the commands are as follows:

```
MTB > cdf X2 k1;
SUBC> chisq df.
MTB > let k2=1-k1
MTB > print k2
```

Thus, the computed values of X^2 and the degrees of freedom (df) must be substituted into the *cdf* command and its *chisq* subcommand.

EXAMPLE 18.1   HOUSEHOLD SIZE AND STATUS (continued)

The data from the household survey is contained in the Minitab portable worksheet file *houshold.mtp*. In this file, *c1* contains the two hundred 0, 1, 2, and 3s for the *Number of children* and *c2* the two hundred 1, 2 and 3s that code for *Socioeconomic status* in the household survey. The following commands retrieve the portable worksheet file, check the contents of the worksheet, and produce the contingency table analysis.

```
MTB > outfile 'a:\houscont.lis'
MTB > retrieve 'a:\houshold.mtp';
SUBC> portable.
MTB > info
MTB > table c1 c2;
SUBC> colpercents;
SUBC> chisq 2.
MTB > cdf 22.194 k1;
SUBC> chisq 6.
MTB > let k2=1-k1
MTB > print k1 k2
```

If your version of Minitab has pull-down menus and you want to use them, table 18.7 lists the menus and options that access the required commands. Appendix D, *Detailed instructions for Minitab menus*, explains how to use the menus. Note that the *Get Worksheet Info* option of the *Edit* menu is the equivalent of the *info* command. However, you can also use the *data screen* to examine the contents of the worksheet.

Table 18.7 Menus and options for Minitab commands to produce a contingency table analysis from original data

Minitab command	Menu	Option
outfile	File >	Other Files > Start Recording Session...
retrieve	File >	Open Worksheet...
port		Minitab portable worksheet
info	Edit >	Get Worksheet Info...
	(Edit >	Data Screen [Alt-D])
table	Stat >	Tables > Cross Tabulation
colpercents		Column Percents
chisq 2		not available
cdf	Calc >	Probability Distributions >
chisq		Chisquare... > Cumulative probability
let	Calc >	Functions and Statistics > General Expressions...
print	Edit >	Display Data...

The following is the output of the commands to produce the two-way contingency table, test statistic and probability of the test statistic required to examine the relationship between *Number of children* and *Socioeconomic status* in the household survey. Note that the expected frequencies are included in the table produced by Minitab so that the large number condition can be checked.

```
MTB > retrieve 'a:\houshold.mtp';
SUBC> portable.

Worksheet retrieved from file: a:\houshold.mtp
MTB > info

COLUMN        NAME     COUNT
C1         no_child     200
C2           status     200

CONSTANTS USED: NONE

MTB > table c1 c2;
SUBC> colpercents;
SUBC> chisq 2.

ROWS: no_child       COLUMNS: status
```

continued . . .

	1	2	3	ALL
0	2.50	10.00	20.00	10.00
	2	6	12	20
	8.00	6.00	6.00	20.00
1	17.50	20.00	23.33	20.00
	14	12	14	40
	16.00	12.00	12.00	40.00
2	70.00	66.67	40.00	60.00
	56	40	24	120
	48.00	36.00	36.00	120.00
3	10.00	3.33	16.67	10.00
	8	2	10	20
	8.00	6.00	6.00	20.00
ALL	100.00	100.00	100.00	100.00
	80	60	60	200
	80.00	60.00	60.00	200.00

```
CHI-SQUARE =      22.194      WITH D.F. =       6

   CELL CONTENTS --
                      % OF COL
                      COUNT
                      EXP FREQ

MTB > cdf 22.194 k1;
SUBC> chisq 6.
MTB > let k2=1-k1
MTB > print k1 k2
K1          0.998887
K2          0.00111306
```

[Handwritten annotations in margin:] Null: columns are the same is independent of status · k_1 · 0.999 cdf · 0.00 · 6 · x^2 · (22.194) · $P = k_2 = 1-k_1$ · $P < 0.05$ reject null.

Contingency table

You will base the analysis on the contingency table itself if you have already produced the contingency table, or if only the contingency table is available. In these circumstances, you should create one column containing the counts from the contingency table and two columns containing indicator variables for the two limited variables. Then produce the contingency table and associated test statistic by adding the *frequencies* subcommand to the other subcommands of the *table* command you are using.

EXAMPLE 18.3 COMPUTER SERVICE AT A UNIVERSITY (continued)
The following commands enable you to input the two-way contingency table to examine the relationship between *Staff access* and *Staff type* in the university IT unit service survey. Put the observed frequencies in *c3*, and set c1 and *c2* to specify which combination of *Staff access* and *Staff type* each observed frequency corresponds to.

```
MTB > outfile 'a:\compserv.lis'
MTB > name c1 'access' c2 'type' c3 'obs_freq'
MTB > set c1
DATA> 1 2 1 2
DATA> end
MTB > set c2
DATA> 1 1 2 2
DATA> end
MTB > set c3
DATA> 31 19 24 26
DATA> end
MTB > print c1-c3
MTB > table c1 c2;
SUBC> freq c3;
SUBC> colpercents.
MTB > table c1 c2;
SUBC> freq c3;
SUBC> chisq 2.
MTB > cdf 1.98 k1;
SUBC> chisq 1.
MTB > let k2=1-k1
MTB > print k1 k2
```

If your version of Minitab has pull-down menus.i.Minitab: pull-down menus; and you want to use them, table 18.8 lists the menus and options that access the required commands. Appendix D, *Detailed instructions for Minitab menus*, explains how to use the menus.

Table 18.8 Menus and options for Minitab commands to produce a contingency table analysis from original data

Minitab command	Menu	Option
outfile	File >	Other Files > Start Recording Session...
name	Edit >	Data Screen [Alt-D]
set	Edit >	Data Screen [Alt-D]
print	Edit >	Display Data...
info	Edit >	Get Worksheet Info...
	(Edit >	Data Screen [Alt-D])
table	Stat >	Tables > Cross Tabulation
frequencies		Frequencies
colpercents		Column Percents
chisq 2		not available
cdf	Calc >	Probability Distributions >
chisq		Chisquare... > Cumulative probability
let	Calc >	Functions and Statistics > General Expressions...

The following output of the commands enables you to input the two-way contingency table and produce the test statistic and probability of the test statistic required for examining the relationship between *Staff access* and *Staff type* in the computer service survey.

```
MTB > name c1 'access' c2 'type' c3 'obs_freq'
MTB > set c1
DATA> 1 2 1 2
DATA> end
DATA> set c2
DATA> 1 1 2 2
DATA> end
MTB > set c3
DATA> 31 19 24 26
DATA> end
MTB > print c1-c3
 ROW     access     type     obs_freq

   1        1         1          31
   2        2         1          19
   3        1         2          24
   4        2         2          26


MTB > table c1 c2;
SUBC> freq c3;
SUBC> colpercents.

  ROWS: access         COLUMNS: type

                1         2       ALL

    1        62.00     48.00     55.00
    2        38.00     52.00     45.00
  ALL       100.00    100.00    100.00


   CELL CONTENTS --
                     % OF COL

MTB > table c1 c2;
SUBC> freq c3;
SUBC> chisq 2.
ROWS: access        COLUMNS: type

                1         2       ALL

    1           31        24        55
             27.50     27.50     55.00

    2           19        26        45
             22.50     22.50     45.00
```

continued . . .

```
  ALL          50        50       100
             50.00     50.00    100.00
  CHI-SQUARE =         1.980    WITH D.F. =      1

     CELL CONTENTS --
                        COUNT
                        EXP FREQ

MTB > cdf 1.98 k1;
SUBC> chisq 1.
MTB > let k2=1-k1
MTB > print k1 k2
K1         0.840610
K2         0.159390
```

18.4.2 Computation for summarising independence

Summarising independence requires the one-way summary tables for each limited variable. These can be obtained in several ways:

- from margins of two-way tables that contain row percentages *and* column percentages;
- by using the *totpercents* subcommand in two *table* commands, where only one variable is specified in each *table* command;
- from the tally command with the *percent* subcommand, provided you have the raw data to compute them from.

EXAMPLE 18.3   COMPUTER SERVICE AT A UNIVERSITY (continued)

To produce the two one-way summary tables for the computer service survey, use a *table* command with two limited variables, or two *table* commands with one limited variable. The *tally* command cannot be used because the raw data is not available for this example.

The *table* command with two limited variables, and associated output, are as follows. Both the *rowpercents* and *colpercents* subcommands are required to obtain both sets of marginal percentages.

```
MTB > table c1 c2;
SUBC> freq c3;
SUBC> rowpercents;
SUBC> colpercents.
ROWS: access       COLUMNS: type

             1         2        ALL

     1     56.36     43.64    100.00
           62.00     48.00     55.00
```

continued . . .

```
       2      42.22     57.78      100.00
              38.00     52.00       45.00
      ALL     50.00     50.00      100.00
             100.00    100.00      100.00


      CELL  CONTENTS  --
                               %  OF  ROW
                               %  OF  COL
```

The two *table* commands with one limited variable, and associated output, are as follows. These commands are an alternative to the previous command.

```
MTB > table c1;
SUBC> freq c3;
SUBC> totpercents.

 ROWS:  access


         %  OF  TBL

    1        55.00
    2        45.00
   ALL      100.00

MTB > table c2;
SUBC> freq c3;
SUBC> totpercents.
 ROWS:  type
          %  OF  TBL

    1        50.00
    2        50.00
   ALL      100.00
```

18.4.3 Computation for examining source of dependence

Minitab has no command or subcommand to produce the adjusted residuals. However, the macro *contares* in Appendix C, *Minitab macros*, does the required computations. Set up columns *c1* to *c3* so that each contains $r \times c$ entries corresponding to the cells of the table, as follows:

1. put the observed frequencies in *c3*;
2. specify, in either *c1* or *c2*, the rows of the table from which the observed frequencies come;

---

3. Specify in *c1* or *c2* (whichever you did not use for the rows) the columns from which the observed frequencies come.

Then use the Minitab *execute* command to execute the macro. If only raw data is available, you must first form the contingency table that includes the observed frequencies. Then enter the observed frequencies manually, as described above.

EXAMPLE 18.1   HOUSEHOLD SIZE AND STATUS (continued)

The commands for obtaining the contingency table, setting up the columns *c1* to *c3* to contain the contingency table, and obtaining the adjusted residuals for the household survey are as follows. For this example the two variables are dependent and the raw data was available in Minitab, so the following commands are designed to obtain the contingency table from the original data and then to set up three columns for the contingency table. If you already have the contingency table, omit the first step since you need only set up the columns for the contingency table. On the right of the hash (#) in the output are explanatory comments. These are ignored by Minitab and should be omitted when you use these commands.

```
MTB > outfile 'a:\housres.lis'
MTB > retrieve 'a:\houshold.mtp';
SUBC> portable.
MTB > info
MTB > table c1 c2
MTB > restart
MTB > name c1 'no_child' c2 'status' c3 'obs_freq'
MTB > set c1   # enter as: (values)c where c = no. cols
DATA> (0:3)3
DATA> end
MTB > set c2   # enter as: r(values) where r = no. rows
DATA> 4(1:3)
DATA> end
MTB > set 'obs_freq'   # enter row by row
DATA> 2 6 12 14 12 14 56 40 24 8 2 10
MTB > print c1-c3
MTB > cd a:\
MTB > execute 'contares.mtb'
```

If your version of Minitab has pull-down menus and you want to use them, table 18.9 lists the menus and options that access the required commands. Appendix D, *Detailed instructions for Minitab menus*, explains how to use the menus.

Table 18.9   Menus and options for Minitab commands to produce adjusted residuals from a contingency table analysis

Minitab command	Menu	Option
outfile	File >	Other Files > Start Recording Session...
retrieve	File >	Open Worksheet...
port		Minitab portable worksheet
info	Edit >	Get Worksheet Info...
	(Edit >)	Data Screen [Alt-D])
table	Stat >	Tables > Cross Tabulation
restart	File >	Restart Minitab
set	Edit >	Set Patterned Data...
print	Edit >	Display Data...
cd		not available
execute	File >	Other Files > Execute Macro...

The following is the output of the commands for producing the two-way contingency table, test statistic and probability of the test statistic required to examine the relationship between *Number of children* and *Socioeconomic status* in the household survey. Note that you use *restart* to clear the worksheet before you input $c1$ to $c3$. Also, when setting $c1$ and $c2$, you can either enter the six numbers into each column or use the Minitab abbreviations for what is termed *patterned data*. The three devices used are as follows:

1. a *number preceding a bracketed group* that specifies the number of times the whole group is to be repeated;

2. a *number following a bracketed group* that specifies how many times each element of the bracketed group is to be repeated;

3. *two numbers separated by a colon* that refers to the sequence of numbers you obtain by commencing with the first number and increasing the previous number by one to obtain the next number in the sequence. This is continued so that you include only numbers up to and including the second of the two specified numbers.

```
MTB > retrieve 'a:\houshold.mtp';
SUBC> portable.

Worksheet retrieved from file: a:\houshold.mtp
```

continued . . .

```
MTB > table c1 c2
ROWS: no_child        COLUMNS: status

                1          2          3        ALL

     0          2          6         12         20
     1         14         12         14         40
     2         56         40         24        120
     3          8          2         10         20
   ALL         80         60         60        200

   CELL  CONTENTS --
                        COUNT

MTB > restart
MTB > name c1 'no_child' c2 'status' c3 'obs_freq'
MTB > set c1   # enter as:   (values)c where c = no. cols
DATA> (0:3)3
DATA> end
MTB > set c2   # enter as:   r(values) where r = no. rows
DATA> 4(1:3)
DATA> end
MTB > set 'obs_freq'   # enter row by row
DATA> 2 6 12 14 12 14 56 40 24 8 2 10
DATA> print c1-c3

  ROW   no_child   status   obs_freq

    1          0        1          2
    2          0        2          6
    3          0        3         12
    4          1        1         14
    5          1        2         12
    6          1        3         14
    7          2        1         56
    8          2        2         40
    9          2        3         24
   10          3        1          8
   11          3        2          2
   12          3        3         10

MTB > cd a:\
MTB > execute 'contares.mtb'
Calculation of Adjusted Residuals for 2-way Contingency table
 - use to investigate source of dependence
 - use only when variables are dependent
 - a residual whose absolute value is > zT (= 1.96 for 0.05 alpha)
        is contributing to dependence
```

continued . . .

```
ROWS: no_child        COLUMNS: status

                1         2         3

  0    -2.8868    0.0000    3.0861
  1    -0.7217    0.0000    0.7715
  2     2.3570    1.2599   -3.7796
  3     0.0000   -2.0574    2.0574

  CELL  CONTENTS  --
              adj_res:MEAN
```

Having obtained the adjusted residuals you can form any tables you wish. For example, the table of column percentages could be obtained as follows:

```
MTB > table c1 c2;
SUBC> freq c3;
SUBC> colpercents.

 ROWS: no_child       COLUMNS: status

            1          2          3         ALL

  0       2.50      10.00      20.00      10.00
  1      17.50      20.00      23.33      20.00
  2      70.00      66.67      40.00      60.00
  3      10.00       3.33      16.67      10.00
 ALL    100.00     100.00     100.00     100.00

   CELL  CONTENTS  --
              % OF  COL
```

18.5 Chapter summary

Contingency table analysis is a hypothesis test applied when the data consists of the values of two limited variables and when the question to be investigated is: are the two limited variables dependent? A preliminary examination of the data can be made by using the two-way contingency tables and charts, with bars or columns that are grouped or stacked.

The test statistic for this test, Pearson's chi-square statistic with $(r - 1)(c - 1)$ degrees of freedom, measures the difference between the observed and expected frequencies in the main body of the contingency table. The expected frequencies are those that conform to the independence hypothesis and for which the row and column totals as the same as the observed frequencies.

The sampling distribution of the test statistic is the chi-square distribution with $(r - 1)(c - 1)$ degrees of freedom. This distribution is based on a limited variable probability model for the population. The conditions that will satisfy the assumptions required for the valid use of the sampling distribution are as follows:

1. **Conditions for limited-variable probability model**
   - *Well-defined limited variables*
   - *Stable population proportions*

2. **Conditions for other validating assumptions**
   - *Infinite population*
   - *Representative sample*
   - *Independence*
   - *Large number condition*

For a particular example, you must check whether these conditions are fulfilled. If the conditions are not met the procedure cannot be used for the example.

The probability of the test statistic, p_T, is obtained from the chi-square distribution by determining the area, under the curve, above the range to the right of observed value of the test statistic.

If the two variables are dependent, use the adjusted residuals to determine for which cells the observed frequencies deviate significantly from the expected frequencies. A significant positive residual indicates that the percentage in that cell of the table is significantly greater than the corresponding percentage in the margin of the table. A significant negative residual indicates that the percentage in that cell of the table is significantly less than the corresponding percentage in the margin of the table.

If the two variables are independent, you can investigate the effects of the two variables independently by forming a one-way summary table for each variable, with each table corresponding to a margin of the two-way table.

The contingency table analysis is equivalent to the z-test for a proportion difference when the two limited variables have just two values: for the same hypotheses, the probabilities of the test statistics from the two tests are equal.

Dependence must be interpreted carefully because it can occur between two variables that are not causally related.

18.6 Key terms

- adjusted residual (R_{ij}^A)
- alternative hypothesis (H$_a$)
- chi-square distribution ($\chi^2_{degrees\,of\,freedom}$)
- column total
- contingency table analysis
- cumulative probability (p_C)
- degrees of freedom
- dependent limited variables
- distribution of variables
- expected frequency (E_{cell})
- independence condition
- infinite population
- large number condition
- limited-variable probability model
- null hypothesis (H$_0$)

- observed frequency (O_{cell})
- one-way summary table
- Pearson's chi-square statistic ($\chi^2_{degrees\,of\,freedom}$)
- probability of the test statistic (p_T)
- representative sample
- row total
- sampling distribution of a test statistic
- significant
- stable population proportions condition
- test statistic
- well-defined limited variable
- z-test for a proportion difference

18.7 Exercises

18.1 Define in your own words the following terms:

    (a) dependent

    (b) independent

    (c) random

    (d) stratified random

    (e) representative sample

    (f) association

    (g) adjusted residuals

18.2 If you have a contingency table of observed frequencies for the combinations of two limited variables, how would you calculate the frequencies you would expect if the variables were independent?

18.3 What is the sampling distribution of the test statistic used in the contingency table analysis? State the conditions necessary for the valid use of this distribution.

18.4 Which conditions must be met for contingency table analysis to be valid? Is it vital to satisfy these conditions? Give reasons for your answer.

18.5 How do you calculate the test statistic for a contingency table analysis? What does the test statistic measure?

18.6 If the null hypothesis that the two variables are independent has been rejected, does this mean that the two variables have a causal relationship? Give reasons for your answer.

18.7 If a contingency table analysis indicates dependence between the two limited variables, how would you summarise this information? How would you detect the source of the dependence?

18.8 A supermarket manager wishes to investigate whether a customer's method of payment — cash or cheque — is dependent on her or his sex. He does this for a set day by taking a random sample from 2245 customers at the supermarket as follows: the day was divided into 15-minute intervals and all customers passing through a checkouts were observed; the checkout to be observed was randomly selected for each interval. The *Method of payment* and *Sex* of each customer were recorded, and this data is summarised in table 18.10.

Table 18.10   Observed frequencies for *Sex* and *Method of payment*

Sex	Method of payment		
	Cash	Cheque	Total
Female	33	19	52
Male	32	27	59
Total	65	46	111

(a) Answer the following questions:
  (i) What is the question to be investigated (including the group to which the conclusions apply)?
  (ii) What variable(s) are we concerned with here?
  (iii) What type of variable(s) are they?
  (iv) Which major category of statistical procedures applies here? Why?
  (v) What type of statistic should we use, given the question to be investigated and the variables involved?
  (vi) Which particular statistic or procedure, and diagram, should we use? Why?
(b) Calculate the expected frequencies necessary for an analysis to investigate whether the two variables, on which the table is based, are independent. Demonstrate that these expected frequencies display independence.
(c) The Minitab commands and associated output to answer this part of the exercise follows.
  (i) Reproduce this output.
  (ii) Provide evidence to objectively support the observation that *Method of payment* and *Sex* appear independent. (Use a significance level of $\alpha = 0.05$.)

```
MTB > name c1 'sex' c2 'method' c3 'obs_freq'
MTB > set c1
DATA> 2(1,2)
DATA> end
MTB > set c2
DATA> (1,2)2
DATA> set c3
DATA> 33 32 19 27
DATA> end
MTB > print c1-c3

 ROW     sex    method    obs_freq

  1       1       1          33
  2       2       1          32
  3       1       2          19
  4       2       2          27

MTB > table c1 c2;
SUBC> freq c3;
SUBC> chisq 2.

 ROWS: sex      COLUMNS: method

              1          2          ALL

    1        33         19          52
           30.45      21.55       52.00


    2        32         27          59
           34.55      24.45       59.00


  ALL        65         46          111
           65.00      46.00      111.00

CHI-SQUARE =      0.969    WITH D.F. =     1
CELL CONTENTS --
                           COUNT
                           EXP FREQ

MTB > cdf 0.969 k1;
SUBC> chisq 1.
MTB > let k2=1-k1
MTB > print k2
K2        0.324930
```

18.9 A simple random sample was taken from approximately 7500 couples in a community. The participation in the labour force was recorded for each partner to see whether male participation is related to female participation in this community. The results are summarised in table 18.11 and each number in the table is the number of couples whose partners exhibit the particular combination of labour force participation — for 104 couples, both the male and the female partner are employed, and for 59 couples, the male was employed and the female was not in the labour force.

Table 18.11   *Participation* in the labour force for couples

Male participation	Female participation		
	Employed	Unemployed	Not in labour force
Employed	104	2	59
Unemployed	0	0	0
Not in labour force	2	0	37

Note: Unemployed means registered as seeking employment, but currently unemployed. Not in labour force means not registered as seeking employment.

(a) Answer the following questions:
  (i) What is the question to be investigated (including the group to which the conclusions apply)?
  (ii) What variable(s) are we concerned with here?
  (iii) What type of variable(s) are they?
  (iv) Which major category of statistical procedures applies? Why?
  (v) What type of statistic should we use, given the question to be investigated and the variables involved?
  (vi) Which particular statistic or procedure, and diagram, should we use? Why?
(b) Use descriptive measures to examine the association between the variables.
(c) Calculate the frequencies expected when the two variables, on which the table is based, are independent and which have the same marginal totals as the observed frequencies. Demonstrate that these expected frequencies display independence.
(d) For this data, what problems arise with using the contingency table analysis to investigate the dependence between *Male participation* and *Female participation* in the labour force? How will you solve these problems?
(e) Perform the contingency table analysis to see whether, for couples in this community, *Female participation* and *Male participation* in the labour force are dependent. (Use a significance level of $\alpha = 0.05$.)

18.10 A metropolitan council conducted a survey, selecting 420 of the 38 379 residents in its area by using quota sampling to select 70 from each council ward. This sample may not be representative, but for the purpose of the analysis to be made here we shall presume that it is. This means that our conclusions must be regarded as tentative.

One of the survey questions was: do you agree or disagree that council should provide recycling services even if this would add about $3 to the average rates bill?

Respondents were also asked to indicate their age-group. The council wants to know whether the opinions of its residents on the *Recycling provision* depend on their *Age-group*. The responses of 415 of the respondents to these two questions are saved in the Minitab portable worksheet file *recycle.mtp*. Table 18.12 presents the observed frequencies for the combinations of the values of the two variables.

Table 18.12   Observed frequencies for *Recycling Provision* by *Age-group*

Recycling provision	Age-group					
	13–30	31–39	40–54	55–64	65+	Total
Agree	75	61	97	47	63	343
Neutral/don't know	4	0	3	3	6	16
Disagree	4	7	9	13	23	56
Total	83	68	109	63	92	415

(a) Answer the following questions:
  (i) What is the question to be investigated (including the group to which the conclusions apply)?
  (ii) What variable(s) are we concerned with here?
  (iii) What type of variable(s) are they?
  (iv) Which major category of statistical procedures applies here? Why?
  (v) What type of statistic should we use, given the question to be investigated and the variables involved?
  (vi) Which particular statistic or procedure, and diagram, should we use? Why?
(b) For the respondents, did their opinions on the *Recycling provision* depend on their *Age-group*? Give reasons for your answer.
(c) Use the following Minitab output to answer this part of the exercise.
  (i) Reproduce the output.
  (ii) Do an analysis that allows you to decide if residents' opinions in this local government area are dependent on their *Age-group*.

```
MTB > name c1 'recycle' c2 'age' c3 'obs_freq'
MTB > set c1
DATA> (1:3)5
DATA> end data
MTB > set c2
DATA> 3(1:5)
DATA> end data
MTB > set c3
DATA> 75 61 97 47 63
DATA>  4  0  3  3  6
DATA>  4  7  9 13 23
DATA> end data
MTB > info
```

continued . . .

```
COLUMN     NAME         COUNT
C1         recycle        15
C2         age            15
C3         obs_freq       15

CONSTANTS USED: NONE

MTB > print c1-c3

  ROW    recycle    age    obs_freq

   1        1         1        75
   2        1         2        61
   3        1         3        97
   4        1         4        47
   5        1         5        63
   6        2         1         4
   7        2         2         0
   8        2         3         3
   9        2         4         3
  10        2         5         6
  11        3         1         4
  12        3         2         7
  13        3         3         9
  14        3         4        13
  15        3         5        23

MTB > table c1 c2;
SUBC> freq c3;
SUBC> chisq 2.

  ROWS: recycle     COLUMNS: age

              1          2          3          4          5        ALL

  1          75         61         97         47         63        343
           68.60      56.20      90.09      52.07      76.04     343.00

  2           4          0          3          3          6         16
            3.20       2.62       4.20       2.43       3.55      16.00

  3           4          7          9         13         23         56
           11.20       9.18      14.71       8.50      12.41      56.00

  ALL        83         68        109         63         92        415
           83.00      68.00     109.00      63.00      92.00     415.00

CHI-SQUARE =     28.029    WITH D.F. =      8
```

continued . . .

```
 CELL  CONTENTS  --
                          COUNT
                          EXP  FREQ

MTB > cdf 28.029 k1;
SUBC> chisq 8.
MTB > let k2=1-k1
MTB > print k1 k2
K1          0.999532
K2          0.000467777
```

(d) The large number condition was not met for the analysis conducted in (c). We will combine the Neutral/don't know and Disagree categories and repeat the analysis, using the following Minitab output.

(i) Reproduce this output.

(ii) Perform the hypothesis test for this revised data.

```
MTB > name c1 'recycle' c2 'age' c3 'obs_freq'
MTB > set c1
DATA> (1:2)5
DATA> end data
MTB > set c2
DATA> 2(1:5)
DATA> end data
MTB > set c3
DATA> 75 61 97 47 63
DATA>  8   7 12 16 29
DATA> end data
MTB > info

COLUMN          NAME     COUNT
C1          recycle        10
C2              age        10
C3         obs_freq        10

CONSTANTS USED: NONE

MTB > print c1-c3

 ROW   recycle    age    obs_freq

   1         1      1          75
   2         1      2          61
   3         1      3          97
   4         1      4          47
   5         1      5          63
   6         2      1           8
   7         2      2           7
   8         2      3          12
```

continued . . .

```
    9           2       4           16
   10           2       5           29

MTB > table c1 c2;
SUBC> freq c3;
SUBC> chisq 2.

  ROWS: recycle        COLUMNS: age

              1             2             3             4             5           ALL

  1             75            61            97            47            63           343
              68.60         56.20         90.09         52.07         76.04        343.00

  2              8             7            12            16            29            72
              14.40         11.80         18.91         10.93         15.96         72.00

  ALL           83            68           109            63            92           415
              83.00         68.00        109.00         63.00         92.00        415.00

  CHI-SQUARE =        24.590     WITH D.F. =       4

    CELL CONTENTS --
                           COUNT
                           EXP FREQ

MTB > cdf 24.59 k1;
SUBC> chisq 4.
MTB > let k2=1-k1
MTB > print k1 k2
K1         0.999939
K2         0.000060856
```

(e) As the hypothesis test led to the conclusion that the variables are dependent, we will obtain and examine the adjusted residuals to reveal the source of the dependence between residents' opinions on *Recycling provision* and their *Age-group*. The Minitab output for doing this is as follows.

(i) Reproduce this output.

(ii) Report your conclusions about the relationship between residents' opinions on *Recycling provision* and their *Age-group*.

```
MTB > cd a:\
MTB > execute 'contares.mtb'
ADJUSTED RESIDUALS FOR 2-WAY CONTINGENCY TABLE
    - use to investigate source of dependence
    - use only when variables are dependent
    - a residual whose absolute value is > zT (= 1.96 for 0.05 alpha)
        is contributing to dependence
```

continued . . .

```
 ROWS: recycle        COLUMNS: age

              1          2          3          4          5

   1   2.0741     1.6802     2.0357    -1.8315    -4.0690
   2  -2.0741    -1.6802    -2.0357     1.8315     4.0691

   CELL CONTENTS --
            adj_res:MEAN

MTB > table c1 c2;
SUBC> freq c3;
SUBC> rowpercents.

 ROWS: recycle        COLUMNS: age

              1          2          3          4          5        ALL

   1     21.87      17.78      28.28      13.70      18.37     100.00
   2     11.11       9.72      16.67      22.22      40.28     100.00
 ALL     20.00      16.39      26.27      15.18      22.17     100.00

   CELL CONTENTS --
              % OF ROW
```

18.11 A sample of 129 male and 91 female students, randomly chosen from a quantitative methods subject, were asked whether working in a team enhanced their learning. We want to use the summary of their responses in table 18.13 to decide, for the students studying the subject, if there is a difference between the proportions of students of each sex who thought their learning was enhanced by team learning.

Table 18.13   Frequencies of *Enhanced learning* for each *Sex*

Enhanced learning	Sex		Total
	Male	Female	
Yes	79	66	145
No	50	25	75
Total	129	91	220

(a) Answer the following questions:

    (i) What is the question to be investigated (including the group to which the conclusions apply)?

    (ii) What variable(s) are we concerned with here?

    (iii) What type of variable(s) are they?

    (iv) Which major category of statistical procedures applies here? Why?

(v) What type of statistic should we use, given the question to be investigated and the variables involved?

(vi) Which particular statistic or procedure, and diagram, should we use? Why?

(b) Compute proportions for table 18.13 from which you can decide subjectively whether the proportion who thought their learning was enhanced by teams is the same for each sex. Draw a diagram of the proportions and report your conclusions from it.

(c) Perform an analysis to decide objectively whether the proportion who thought their learning was enhanced by teams is the same for each sex. Do your conclusions from that analysis agree with those arrived at subjectively?

CHAPTER 19

TEST FOR MEAN DIFFERENCES FOR AN UNRESTRICTED VARIABLE WITH A LIMITED VARIABLE

LEARNING OBJECTIVES

The learning objectives of this chapter are:

- to know when to apply, how to calculate and how to interpret the results of the one-way analysis of variance;
- to know the conditions required for the one-way analysis of variance to be valid, and how to determine when these are met;
- to be able to investigate differences between the population means when the one-way analysis of variance indicates that the differences are significant.

The following extract from the *Summary of procedures based on combinations of variable types* in part VI gives an overview of the hypothesis tests covered in this and the previous chapters of part V, *Hypothesis tests*.

1. *One limited variable*
   - Distribution of variables: z-test for a proportion; goodness-of-fit test.
2. *Two limited variables*
   - Distribution of variables: z-test for a proportion difference; contingency table analysis.
3. *One unrestricted variable — one limited variable*
   - **Measures of central tendency**: unpaired t-test; one-way analysis of variance.
4. *One unrestricted variable — two limited variables*
5. *Two unrestricted variables*

As outlined in the objectives, this chapter covers the hypothesis test known as the **one-way analysis of variance** or one-way ANOVA. It applies when the data consists of the values of one unrestricted and one limited variable and when the question to be investigated is: do the population **means** of the unrestricted variable differ for the different values of the limited variable? Further, since an inference procedure is involved, we must have taken a sample and the question to be investigated must be about the population and *not* confined to the sample.

When the limited variable has only two values, there is an alternative hypothesis test to the one-way analysis of variance: the **unpaired t-test**. This test is equivalent to the one-way analysis of variance, since for the same hypotheses the probabilities of the test statistics from the two tests are equal.

19.1   One-way analysis of variance

Before carrying out the hypothesis test, we use descriptive summaries for a preliminary examination of the data. The descriptive summary that corresponds to the one-way analysis of variance is the one-way table of means. However, the boxplot is a particularly effective summary for this situation as it provides a visual comparison of the different groups and flags outliers. Both summaries are examined. Of course, using the one-way table of means, instead of medians requires the distribution of the data to be symmetrical. So, if the data is symmetrical, the medians used in the boxplot will give the same impression as the means in the one-way table. We will leave further discussion of the distribution shape until the hypothesis test.

EXAMPLE 19.1   STUDENT EXPENDITURE IN THREE FACULTIES

As described in example 15.3, *Student expenditure*, AusStudent is the government body responsible for distributing the tertiary student allowance. It took a simple random sample of 25 of the 11 200 students at a major Australian university. At the end of the first month of the semester it asked these 25 students how much they spent on textbooks and stationery during that period. The mean and standard deviation of the amounts they reported were $213.64 and $77.93 respectively. From this AusStudent computed that you could be 95% confident that the mean amount spent was between $181.47 and $245.81.

AusStudent decided to run the survey again in the following year, to see whether there is a difference in the amount that students from three faculties typically spend on stationery and books. AusStudent randomly selected 15 students from each of the Applied Science, Business, and Medical Science faculties, the faculties having 1349, 982 and 377 students respectively. The amounts reported by the students, the raw data, are in table 19.1; as far as AusStudent is concerned this is primary data.

Table 19.1   *Textbook and stationery expenditure* ($) for 15 students from three faculties

	Faculty	
Applied Science	Business	Medical Science
207	197	199
143	43	298
162	224	253
174	244	261
281	196	185
195	233	254
272	161	282
315	231	337
199	196	158
174	158	226
71	227	383
87	219	276
176	225	210
123	228	241
78	237	276

The question to be investigated is: is there a difference in the amount that students from three faculties typically spend on stationery and books? The question concerns all students from all three faculties. Two variables are involved: *Faculty*, a limited variable, and *Textbook and stationery expenditure*, an unrestricted variable. For these variables and the question to be investigated, a hypothesis test is appropriate and the one-way analysis of variance is the correct test. It will test for differences between population *Textbook and stationery expenditure* means for the *Faculties*.

Before conducting the hypothesis test, we examine boxplots and a one-way table of means for a preliminary look at the data. The one-way table of means is in table 19.2 and the boxplot is in figure 19.1.

Table 19.2   One-way table of *Textbook and stationery expenditure* means by students from three faculties

	Faculty	
	Applied Science	Business	Medical Science
Mean ($)	177.13	201.27	255.93

This table can be used to answer the question: is there a difference between the amount spent by the observed students from three different faculties? Clearly, there is a difference: students from medical science spend over $50 more on textbooks and stationery than business students, and applied science students spend about $20 less than business students.

However, our original question concerned the whole population of students in each faculty. These sample differences may be just the result of chance fluctuations and, in the population, there may be no difference in the amount expended. I might suggest that there is little evidence of real difference. You might disagree. Who is right? Objectively deciding whether the differences are real or not is exactly what our hypothesis test, the one-way analysis of variance, is about.

Further insight can be gained from the boxplot. It appears that there is a distinct difference between the location of the boxes for applied and medical science. However, the difference between the box for business and the other two is not clear. There is a great deal of overlap. As well as differences in location, we can compare the spread of the observations from the three *Faculties*, and check the presence of outliers. The size of the three boxes is similar. There are potential outliers for two of the *Faculties* and a probable outlier for the third *Faculty*.

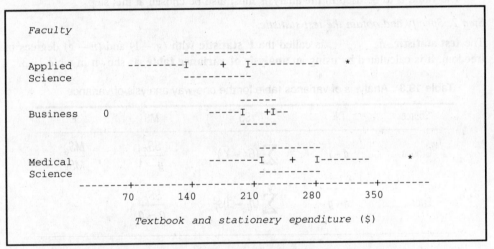

Figure 19.1 Boxplots for *Textbook and stationery expenditure* by students from three faculties

EXAMPLE 19.2 HOUSE PRICES IN THREE LOCALITIES

In example 8.1, *House prices in three localities*, differences between the three localities in the typical selling price of houses were investigated. The question investigated concerned all residences sold over a 12-month period in the three localities. It involved an unrestricted variable, *House price*, and a limited variable, *Locality*. It appears that we could use the one-way analysis of variance to determine objectively whether selling prices really differ between the three localities. However, since the data includes the prices for all houses sold during the period, it represents a census of the population of interest. It would therefore not be appropriate to use the one-way analysis of variance.

There is no need to conduct a hypothesis test to determine if there is a difference in the population means. Whatever differences occur between the average prices for the localities, these are the population differences. We simply have to assess the practical importance of the differences.

19.1.1 Hypothesis test

The role of the one-way analysis of variance is to provide an objective procedure for deciding if there are differences between means. We now outline the general steps for performing this hypothesis test, and the analysis for an example follows this general description. In outlining the one-way analysis of variance, the number of groups are denoted by g and the total number of observations by n.

Step 1: Set up the hypotheses and nominate the significance level.

The general form of the **null** and **alternative hypotheses** for this test are:

H_0: $\mu_1 = \mu_2 = \ldots = \mu_g$

H_a: at least one pair of population group means is different.

The value α to be used in the analysis must also be chosen at this step.

Step 2: Specify and obtain the test statistic.

The **test statistic**, $F_{g-1,\, n-g}$, is called the **F statistic** with $(g-1)$ and $(n-g)$ degrees of freedom. It is calculated by using an **analysis of variance table**, as shown in table 19.3.

Table 19.3   Analysis of variance table for the one-way analysis of variance

Source	DF	SS	MS	F
Groups	$g-1$	$\sum_{i=1}^{g}(\bar{G}_i - \bar{Y})^2$	$\dfrac{SS_G}{g-1}$	$\dfrac{MS_G}{MS_E}$
Error	$n-g$	$\sum_{i=1}^{g}(n_i - 1)s_i^2$	$\dfrac{SS_E}{n-g}$	
Total	$n-1$	$\sum_{i=1}^{g}\sum_{j=1}^{n_i}(y_{ij} - \bar{Y})^2$		

y_{ij}	the jth observation from the ith group
g	the number of groups
n_i	the number of observations in the ith group
n	the number of observations
$\bar{G}_i$	the sample mean for the ith group
$\bar{Y}$	the grand mean of all the observations
SS_G and MS_G	the sum of squares and mean square for groups
SS_E and MS_E	the sum of squares and mean square for error

Table 19.3 consists of rows for Groups, Error and Total and columns for source, **degrees of freedom** (DF), **sum of squares** (SS), **mean square** (MS) and the F statistic (F). The essence of the table is that the relative sizes of two variances, the group and error variances, are measured by taking their ratio. This ratio is the F statistic, and it measures the degree of difference between the sample means. That is, the larger the difference between the sample means, the larger the F statistic. As usual, the F statistic measures how far the data departs from what we would expect under the null hypothesis. It can be shown that, under the null hypothesis, the value of the F statistic is expected to be 1, so the more the F statistic exceeds 1, the greater the disparity between the data and the null hypothesis.

We mentioned that the F statistic, $F_{g-1, n-g}$, is the ratio of two variances, but there is no mention of variances in the table. However, recall from section 7.4.3, *Standard deviation and variance*, that:

$$\text{Variance} = \frac{\text{sum of squares}}{\text{degrees of freedom}} = \frac{SS}{df}$$

From the column headed MS in table 19.3, we calculate both mean squares from precisely the same quantities as for a variance. Indeed, the mean squares are variances; it is a quirk of history that the variances are called mean squares in the context of the analysis of variance. Further, from the column headed DF in table 19.3, we find that the variances in the F statistic have degrees of freedom $(g - 1)$ and $(n - g)$ respectively, and so we denote the test statistic $F_{g-1, n-g}$.

We will not deal with the details of computing the sums of squares in table 19.3 at this stage. However, there is an important relationship between quantities in the analysis of variance table: the sums of squares and degrees of freedom for the groups and error lines sum to the respective quantities for the total line. That is,

$$SS_T = SS_G + SS_E \text{ and } (n - 1) = (g - 1) + (n - g)$$

Step 3: List and check conditions for the sampling distribution.

The **sampling distribution of the test statistic** for this hypothesis test is the **F distribution** (see figure 19.2). The distribution is based on a **normal probability model**, possibly **with different group population means,** for the unrestricted variable. The **conditions** that will satisfy the assumptions required for the valid use of this sampling distribution are as follows:

1. **Conditions for normal probability model with possibly different group population means**
   - *Unrestricted and a limited variable:* The analysis of variance must be computed for one unrestricted and one limited variable. Determining if this condition is satisfied can be done simply by considering whether the variables are of the required type. Usually, there is no problem with this condition.

- *Normally distributed variable:* The unrestricted variable will be a **normally distributed variable** if a relative frequency distribution is constructed for the values of the variable from the population for each group and the shape of each distribution is approximately symmetric and bell-shaped as required for the normal distribution.

  The distribution of the variable is checked by using the **normal probability plot** and the **normal probability correlation coefficient**, as outlined in section 15.1, *Normally distributed unrestricted variables,* except that we use the residuals, not the original values. This plot should produce a rough straight line and r_N should be close to 1 if the variable is normally distributed with the same variance for each group. The **residuals** for this plot are computed by subtracting from each observation its group mean. That is,

  $$\text{residual} = \text{observation} - \text{group mean}$$

  or

  $$e_{ij} = y_{ij} - \overline{G}_i$$

  where e_{ij} is the residual for the jth observation from the ith group,

  y_{ij} is the jth observation from the ith group, and

  $\overline{G}_i$ is the mean for the ith group.

  The properties of these residuals are that those for each group sum to zero. Essentially, in computing the residuals we remove the mean differences between the groups. In particular, subtracting the group mean from the observations for that group does not affect the spread of the observations in that group. The group means themselves are called the **fitted values**.

- *Homogeneity of variance:* The data can be regarded as exhibiting **homogeneity of variance** only if the variation of the population Y values is the same for each group; that is, homogeneity of variance means equal variance. The homogeneity of variance assumption can be checked by examining the standard deviations for the groups and the residuals-versus-fitted-values plot.

  The standard deviation for a group can be computed from either the observations or the residuals for the group. The standard deviations for the g groups should be approximately equal if the assumption of homogeneity is to be met. To be more precise, we can examine the ratio of the maximum to the minimum standard deviation. A rule of thumb is: the assumption is not met when the mean number of observations in the groups is:

  (i) 10 or more, and the ratio is at least 2;

  (ii) 5 or more but less than 10, and the ratio is at least 3;

  (iii) less than 5, and the ratio is at least 6.

  Hence, if the ratio is less than 2, we can take it that the homogeneity assumption is met, irrespective of the number of observations per group.

The **residuals-versus-fitted-values plot** is obtained by plotting the residuals on the vertical (Y) axis and the fitted values on the horizontal (X) axis. This plot will have points arranged in vertical lines. These lines should be symmetrical about zero on the vertical (Y) axis and the spread of points along each line should be about the same for all lines. Large differences in the size of the lines indicate that the assumptions are not met. This means we need a model that better describes the behaviour of the data.

2. Conditions for other validating assumptions

- *Infinite population:* The sample for each group should come from an effectively **infinite population**. The population, from which the sample came, can be regarded as effectively infinite if the number of individuals in it (N_i) is at least 20 times the number sampled (n_i); that is, if $N_i > 20n_i$.
- *Representative sample:* A **representative sample** of each group population is required. The methods likely to produce a representative sample were discussed in chapter 4, *Surveys*. We concluded that the probability sampling methods, such as stratified random sampling, produce representative samples. So this condition will be met if a probability sampling method is used to select the sample from each group. If not, we cannot guarantee that the condition will be met.
- *Independence:* The outcome of any observation is independent of the outcome of any other observation. This **independence condition** is difficult to check; in part, it involves ensuring that the study is conducted in such a way that each observation is made independently of the other observations.

So the sampling distribution of the test statistic is an F distribution *when H_0 is true and these conditions are met*. That is, when there are no differences between the population means and the conditions are met, the distribution of values of the test statistic is of the form shown in figure 19.2. The exact form varies with the degrees of freedom of the two mean squares in the observed F statistic.

Note that the test will not be seriously wrong even when there are moderate departures from normality. Also note that if the assumption of normality holds, the distribution is symmetric and we can use the mean, as opposed to the median.

Step 4: Obtain the probability of the test statistic.

We require the **probability of the test statistic**, p_T, which is the probability of getting the observed value, and more extreme values, of the test statistic when the null hypothesis is true. We can obtain this by determining the area, under the curve for the sampling distribution, above the range to the right of the observed value of the test statistic as shown in figure 19.2. Usually computer packages give p_T, which they designate as either p or Prob.

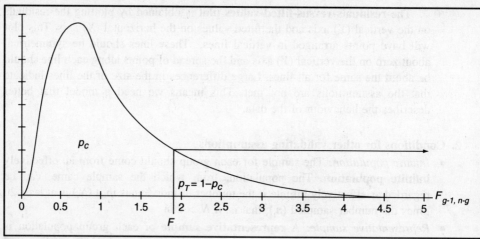

Figure 19.2   F distribution for test statistic

Step 5: State and apply the rule for rejecting the null hypothesis.
The general form of the rule for rejecting the null hypothesis is: if $p_T \leq \alpha$, reject H_0; otherwise, H_0 cannot be rejected.

Step 6: State the conclusion in terms of the question investigated.
Once you have decided whether or not the hypothesis is to be rejected, restate the conclusion in terms of the original question.   ∎

EXAMPLE 19.1   STUDENT EXPENDITURE IN THREE FACULTIES (continued)
Now we apply the one-way analysis of variance to this example to objectively confirm the conclusions that were subjectively arrived at from the descriptive summaries.

Step 1: Set up the hypotheses and nominate the significance level.
   H_0: $\mu_A = \mu_B = \mu_M$
   H_a: at least one pair of population *Faculty* means is different.
Using the standard value of α we have $\alpha = 0.05$.

Step 2: Specify and obtain the test statistic.

The test statistic is $F_{g-1,\, n-g} = \dfrac{MS_G}{MS_E}$

It is contained in the analysis of variance table in table 19.4. It is the value under the column headed F; that is, $F_{2,42} = 6.52$.

Table 19.4   One-way analysis of variance table for *Faculty* differences

Source	DF	SS	MS	F
Faculties	2	48 902	24 451	6.52
Error	42	157 530	3 751	
Total	44	206 431		

Step 3: List and check conditions for the sampling distribution.

The sampling distribution of the test statistic, $F_{2, 42}$, is the F distribution with two degrees of freedom for the numerator and 42 degrees of freedom for the denominator (see figure 19.6). The conditions that will satisfy the assumptions required for the valid use of the sampling distribution are as follows:

1. **Conditions for normal probability model with possibly different group population means.**

   - *Unrestricted and a limited variable*

   - *Normally distributed variable*

   - *Homogeneity of variance*

2. **Conditions for other validating assumptions**

   - *Infinite population*

   - *Representative sample*

   - *Independence*

The meaning of the assumption of a normal probability model with different group population means is illustrated in figure 19.3. We assume here that the population distribution of *Textbook and stationery expenditure*, for each *Faculty*, can be described by a normal distribution. The unknown population means may differ between the *Faculties,* but the unknown population standard deviations are assumed to be the same for all *Faculties*; that is, the spread of the three normal distributions are the same. Hence, the homogeneity of variance condition.

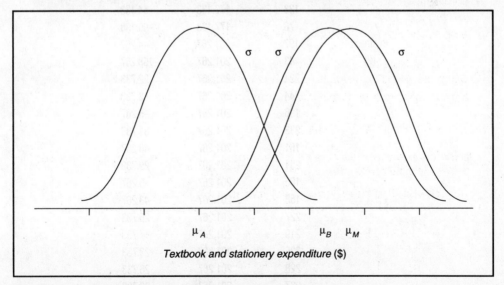

Figure 19.3 Population distributions for three groups

As previously noted, the residuals and fitted values are used to check the conditions. Their values for this example appear in table 19.5.

Table 19.5   Fitted values and residuals for *Textbook and stationery expenditure* by students from three faculties

Faculty	Textbook and stationery expenditure ($)	Fitted values ($)	Residuals ($)
Applied Science	207	177.133	29.867
(1)	143	177.133	−34.133
	162	177.133	−15.133
	174	177.133	−3.133
	281	177.133	103.867
	195	177.133	17.867
	272	177.133	94.867
	315	177.133	137.867
	199	177.133	21.867
	174	177.133	−3.133
	71	177.133	−106.133
	87	177.133	−90.133
	176	177.133	−1.133
	123	177.133	−54.133
	78	177.133	−99.133
Business	197	201.267	−4.267
(2)	43	201.267	−158.267
	224	201.267	22.733
	244	201.267	42.733
	196	201.267	−5.267
	233	201.267	31.733
	161	201.267	−40.267
	231	201.267	29.733
	196	201.267	−5.267
	158	201.267	−43.267
	227	201.267	25.733
	219	201.267	17.733
	225	201.267	23.733
	228	201.267	26.733
	237	201.267	35.733

Table 19.5   *(continued)*

Faculty	Textbook and stationery expenditure ($)	Fitted values ($)	Residuals ($)
Medical Science	199	255.933	−56.933
(3)	298	255.933	42.067
	253	255.933	−2.933
	261	255.933	5.067
	185	255.933	−70.933
	254	255.933	−1.933
	282	255.933	26.067
	337	255.933	81.067
	158	255.933	−97.933
	226	255.933	−29.933
	383	255.933	127.067
	276	255.933	20.067
	210	255.933	−45.933
	241	255.933	−14.933
	276	255.933	20.067

Checking these conditions proceeds as follows:

1. Conditions for normal probability model with possibly different group population means

- *Unrestricted and a limited variables:* We have already stated that the variables *Textbook and stationery expenditure* and *Faculty* can be classified as an unrestricted and a limited variable respectively.

- *Normally distributed variable:* The normal probability plot for the *Textbook and stationery expenditure* residuals is given in figure 19.4. The associated normal probability plot correlation coefficient, r_N, is 0.980. For $n = 45$ and $\alpha = 0.05$, $r_T = 0.9742$. The normal probability plot shows a roughly straight line pattern and r_N is greater than r_T. The assumption of normality appears to be met.

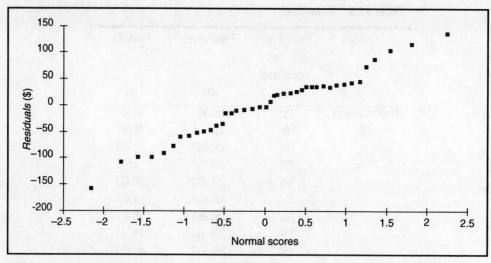

Figure 19.4   Normal probability plot for *Textbook and stationery expenditure* residuals

- *Homogeneity of variance:* The residuals-versus-fitted-values plot is in figure 19.5, where it appears that the middle faculty, Business, has a smaller variability. The range covered by the observations from that faculty appears smaller, particularly if we ignore the observation with the large negative residual (which means it is an unusually small value). However, the standard deviations for the three faculties are in table 19.6, and the ratio of the maximum to minimum standard deviation is 72.73/ 50.98 = 1.43. This is less than 2, indicating that the variances are homogeneous. Since our assessment of the plot is subjective, we base our decision on the standard deviations and conclude that the homogeneity of variance assumption appears to be met.

Table 19.6   One-way table of standard deviations for *Textbook and stationery expenditure* by students from three faculties

	Faculty		
	Applied Science	Business	Medical Science
Standard deviation ($)	72.73	50.98	58.00

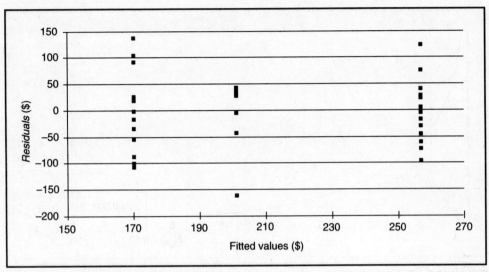

Figure 19.5   Residuals-versus-fitted-values plot for *Textbook and stationery expenditure* by students from three faculties

2. Conditions for other validating assumptions

- *Infinite population:* The numbers in each faculty are 1349, 982 and 377 and all of these are greater than $20 \times 15 = 300$. The faculties can be regarded as effectively infinite.

- *Representative sample:* The students from each faculty were randomly selected and so they are likely to be representative of the faculties.

- *Independence:* To be independent, the expenditure of each student must be independent of the others' expenditures. We assume that by and large each student decides how much to spend on books and stationery independently of other students, and that the survey is conducted in such a way that they report this amount independently.

It appears that the assumptions required to use the F sampling distribution are met for this example and we can validly apply a one-way analysis of variance to this example.

Step 4: Obtain the probability of the test statistic.

The probability of the observed value, and more extreme values, of the test statistic when there is no difference between the population means has been computed to be $p_T = 0.003$. Figure 19.6 gives the sampling distribution along with the test statistic and the probability of the test statistic.

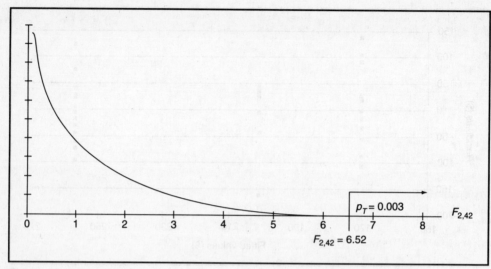

Figure 19.6 F distribution for test statistic with 2 and 42 degrees of freedom

Step 5: State and apply the rule for rejecting the null hypothesis.

We have decided on $\alpha = 0.05$, so that our rule is: if $p_T \leq 0.05$, reject H_0; otherwise, H_0 cannot be rejected. As $p_T = 0.003 < 0.05$, reject H_0.

Step 6: State the conclusion in terms of the question investigated.

The evidence suggests that at least one pair of faculty population means is different. Our subjective conclusion, that there is a difference between the students from different *Faculties* in the *Textbook and stationery expenditure*, is confirmed.   ∎

19.1.2 Explanations

Three aspects of the analysis of variance that are not obvious are:

1. Why is it called an analysis of variance when the aim of the procedure is to establish whether or not population means are different? This is paradoxical because we know from descriptive summaries that the mean is a measure of central tendency and the variance (= standard deviation^2) is a measure of dispersion or spread — two quite different attributes of a set of data.
2. Why is it necessary to assume that the variances of individual observations from the different groups are equal?
3. How does the test statistic assist us in deciding whether there are group differences?

Analysing variances

To tackle the first question, consider why the procedure is called an 'analysis of variance'. It is called this because it involves calculating and comparing the size of variances. As stated in the previous subsection, the test statistic measures the relative sizes of two variances, the group and error variances (mean squares), by taking their ratio.

It can be shown that the groups mean square measures the variance of the group means. So, as explained for the standard deviation, if the group means are all exactly equal the groups mean square would be zero. As the size of the difference between the group means increases, so does the size of the groups mean square. So it is clear that we use a variance, the groups mean square, to measure the spread in the group means; that is, we analyse a variance to measure how different some means are.

The other variance is the error variance or mean square. It is computed by averaging the variances for the groups. The formula for the error mean square is a weighted mean of the g group variances s_i^2 :

$$\text{Error MS} = \frac{\sum_{i=1}^{g} (n_i - 1)s_i^2}{\sum_{i=1}^{g} (n_i - 1)}$$

$$= \frac{\sum_{i=1}^{g} (n_i - 1)s_i^2}{n - g}$$

where s_i is the standard deviation of the observations from the ith group;
  $(n_i - 1)$ is the degrees of freedom of the variance for the ith group;

$$\sum_{i=1}^{g} (n_i - 1) = (n - g).$$

Since this error variance, or error mean square, measures the variability of individual observations from the same group, the test statistic measures the size of the spread in group means relative to individual variability. That is, the size of the *differences between means* is measured by *analysing variances*.

EXAMPLE 19.1   STUDENT EXPENDITURE IN THREE FACULTIES (continued)
The Faculties mean square is 24 451. The error mean square can be computed from the standard deviations in table 19.6, as follows:

$$\text{Error MS} = \frac{(15 - 1) \times 72.73^2 + (15 - 1) \times 50.98^2 + (15 - 1) \times 58.00^2}{(15 - 1) + (15 - 1) + (15 - 1)}$$

$$= \frac{157\,536.5862}{45 - 3} \left(= \frac{\text{Error SS}}{\text{Error DF}} \right)$$

$$= 3750.8711$$

Hence, the ratio of the variability in the faculty means to that of individual observations is:

$$F_{2,42} = \frac{24\,451.00}{3750.87} = 6.51.$$

Homogeneity of variance

Each group variance measures the spread of individuals within its group. These variances are pooled to form a single quantity, the error mean square. However, using this single value to estimate the variability of individuals in a group makes sense only if the variability is the same for all groups. Indeed, we obtain the **pooled standard deviation** by taking the square root of the error mean square.

EXAMPLE 19.1   STUDENT EXPENDITURE IN THREE FACULTIES (continued)

The error mean square measures the variability of *Textbook and stationery expenditure* by students from the same faculty. The pooled standard deviation is:

$$s_{pooled} = \sqrt{3750.87} = 61.24.$$

Thus, the expenditures will typically deviate ±61.24 from the mean expenditure. Further, since we concluded that the variable is normally distributed, we would expect about two-thirds of the observations to be within ±61.24 of the mean.

Test statistic

Finally, since the test statistic is the ratio of the group and error mean squares, either of the following will occur:

1. it will be about 1 if the variance of the group means is about the same as the variance of individuals from a group — that is, if the differences between the groups are no greater than can be expected from the fact that they consist of different individuals;
2. it will be large if the variance of the group means is larger than the variance of individuals from the same group — that is, if the differences between the groups are greater than can be expected from the fact that they consist of different individuals.

In the first situation we would conclude that on average there is no real difference between the groups; in the second situation we would conclude there are real group differences.

An equivalent, but more intuitive, approach than using the F statistic is to compare the boxplots for the different groups. Without the boxes it is difficult to decide if the differences are large enough to conclude that there are real differences between the groups. The boxes, whose width also measures how variable individuals from the same group are, give us a way of gauging the size of the differences between the medians. Of course, as the variable is normally distributed, the mean and the median will be approximately equal. The question of whether the F statistic is large enough to conclude that the group means are different can be regarded as equivalent to the question: are the boxes sufficiently separated to indicate a difference in the location of the boxes?

EXAMPLE 19.1   STUDENT EXPENDITURE IN THREE FACULTIES (continued)
From the boxplots for *Textbook and stationery expenditure* in figure 19.1 it
appears that there is a distinct difference between the location of the boxes for
applied science and medical science. However, the difference between the
box for business and the other two is not clear. There is a great deal of overlap.

19.1.3 Means testing

Having used the analysis of variance to establish that at least one pair of population means
is different, we still have to determine which of the means are different. To do this we use
a procedure based on the **least significant difference** (*LSD*); that is, the least difference
required to establish significance. This procedure applies only when a small number of
means is involved ($g < 6$). Also, it should only be used when the F statistic from the analysis
of variance is *significant*.

LSD(α) for two means

The procedure involves calculating the *LSD*(α) which is used to determine if pairs of means,
$\bar{x}_i$ and $\bar{x}_j$, are significantly different. The two means can be declared significantly different
if the absolute value of the difference between the two means, or difference with the sign
removed, is greater than the *LSD*(α); that is, if

$$\left| \bar{x}_i - \bar{x}_j \right| \geq LSD(\alpha)$$

The formula for the *LSD*(α) is

$$LSD(\alpha) = t_T s_{pooled} \sqrt{\frac{1}{n_i} + \frac{1}{n_j}}$$

where t_T is theoretical value for the t distribution, corresponding to α and the degrees of
freedom of s_{pooled} which are $n - g$;

$s_{pooled} = \sqrt{\text{Error MS}}$, and

n_i, n_j are the numbers of observations for each of the two means being compared.

Note that this formula is a general one that applies when the means being compared are not
based on equal numbers of observations. An *LSD*(α) must be computed for each of the
different combinations of numbers of observations. However, when the means are all based
on the same number of observations, only one *LSD*(α) has to be computed.

EXAMPLE 19.1   STUDENT EXPENDITURE IN THREE FACULTIES (continued)
For the student expenditure example, $g = 3$ so that the procedure can be used.
For this example, $s_{pooled} = \sqrt{3751} = 61.24$ and all the means are based on 15
observations. Further, for $\alpha = 0.05$ and $(n - g) = 42$, $t_T = 2.081$. Hence,

$$LSD(0.05) = 2.0181 \times 61.24 \sqrt{\frac{1}{15} + \frac{1}{15}}$$
$$= 45.13$$

Comparing a set of means

Generally, several means are compared, and the task is to determine the differences between them. This involves examining all pairwise differences which we can do in a table with both rows and columns corresponding to the groups — the rows and columns are ordered in ascending order of the values for the means. The body of this table should contain the differences between row means and column means — in particular, the row mean minus the column mean for entries below the diagonal. We can then determine which pairs of means are different by comparing the differences with the $LSD(\alpha)$.

EXAMPLE 19.1   STUDENT EXPENDITURE IN THREE FACULTIES (continued)
Table 19.7 contains the *Textbook and stationery expenditure* means for students from the three faculties, with the *Faculty* means in ascending order. The differences are computed for all pairs of the three means. The diagonal entries are empty because they are superfluous — they involve comparing a mean with itself. The entries above the diagonal are not included because they would be just the negatives of the entries below the diagonal.

Table 19.7   Differences between all pairs of *Faculty* means

Faculty		Applied Science	Business	Medical Science
	Mean ($)	177.13	201.27	255.93
Applied Science	177.13			
Business	201.27	24.14		
Medical Science	255.93	78.80	54.66	
	LSD(0.05)		45.13	

From table 19.7 we concluded that medical science students spend more on textbooks and stationery than both applied science and business students, and that there is no difference in the expenditure of students from the latter two faculties (since 24.14 < 45.13). Figure 19.7 demonstrates these differences by displaying the means with a bar chart.

When we examined the descriptive summaries, the difference between medical science and applied science students seemed clear-cut. However, it was difficult to determine exactly what other differences existed. Our hypothesis test, and associated mean testing procedure, have given us an objective procedure to sort out the differences between means.

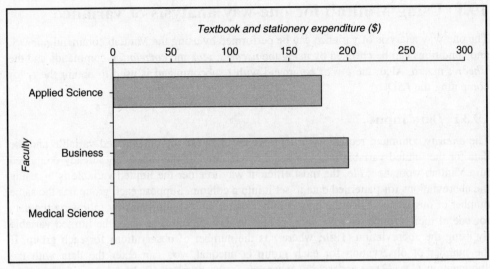

Figure 19.7   *Textbook and stationery expenditure* means for three faculties

19.2   Report on example

The following report, for the example analysed in this chapter, indicates what material from a statistical analysis an investigator should include in a report. In general, the details of the statistical analysis are omitted so that the reader of the report can concentrate on the results.

EXAMPLE 19.1   STUDENT EXPENDITURE IN THREE FACULTIES —

REPORT

AusStudent randomly selected 15 students from each of the Applied Science, Business and Medical Science faculties at a major Australian university; the faculties had 1349, 982 and 377 students respectively. At the end of the first month of the semester the selected students were asked how much they spent on textbooks and stationery during that period. The mean expenditures for each faculty are in table 19.8. An analysis of variance indicated that these means are significantly different ($p \leq 0.01$). By using the $LSD(0.05)$, we concluded that medical science students spend more on textbooks and stationery than both applied science and business students and that there is no expenditure difference between the latter two faculties.

Table 19.8   One-way table of *Textbook and stationery expenditure* means by students from 3 faculties

	Faculty			$LSD(0.05)$
	Applied Science	Business	Medical Science	
Mean ($)	177.13	201.27	255.93	45.13

19.3 Using Minitab for one-way analysis of variance

The one-way analysis of variance can be performed by using the Minitab command *oneway*, and conditions can be checked by using the *nscores*, *plot* and *correlation* commands and the *rtheoret* macro. Also, the *invcdf* command with *t* subcommand is used to obtain the t_T for computing the $LSD(\alpha)$.

19.3.1 Data input

The *oneway* command requires you to enter the data for the unrestricted variable and the data for the limited variable into two separate columns. If the data is not already contained in a Minitab worksheet file, the most efficient way to enter the limited variable is by using the abbreviations for patterned data to set it into a column. Suppose each group has the same number of observations and the data is to be entered into the columns by following the data for one of the *g* groups with the data for another group. You then enter the limited variable by using the abbreviation *(1:g)r*, where *r* is the number of observations for each group. If the number of observation for each group is unequal, you can enter the data with the abbreviation $(1)n_1,(2)n_2$, and so on, where n_1 is the number of observations for the first group and n_2 the number for the second group. Alternatively, you can always enter the values of the limited variable one at a time.

> **EXAMPLE 19.1 STUDENT EXPENDITURE IN THREE FACULTIES** (continued)
> The commands and associated output for entering the data for the example are as follows. The limited variable is put into a column named *faculty* and the unrestricted variable is put into a column named *expend*.

```
MTB > outfile 'a:\studexp.lis'
MTB > name c1 'faculty' c2 'expend'
MTB > set c1
DATA> (1:3)15
DATA> end
MTB > print c1

faculty
  1   1   1   1   1   1   1   1   1   1   1   1   1   1   1
  2   2   2   2   2   2   2   2   2   2   2   2   2   2   2
  3   3   3   3   3   3   3   3   3   3   3   3   3   3   3

MTB > set c2
DATA> 207 143 162 174 281 195 272 315 199 174
DATA>  71  87 176 123  78 197  43 224 244 196
DATA> 233 161 231 196 158 227 219 225 228 237
DATA> 199 298 253 261 185 254 282 337 158 226
DATA> 383 276 210 241 276
DATA> end
MTB > info
```

continued . . .

```
COLUMN      NAME          COUNT
C1          faculty         45
C2          expend          45
CONSTANTS USED: NONE

MTB > save 'a:\1waybook.mtp';
SUBC> portable.

Worksheet saved into file: a:\1waybook.mtp
```

These commands are most conveniently executed with the pull-down menus, if your version of Minitab has them. Table 19.9 lists the menus and options that access the required commands, and Appendix D, *Detailed instructions for Minitab menus*, explains how to use the menus.

Table 19.9 Menus and options for Minitab commands to enter data

Minitab command	Menu	Option
outfile	File >	Other Files > Start Recording Session...
name	Edit >	Data Screen
set c1	Edit >	Set Patterned Data...
print	Edit >	Display Data...
set c2	Edit >	Data Screen
info	Edit >	Get Worksheet Info...
	(Edit >	Data Screen [Alt-D])
save	File >	Save Worksheet As...
port		Minitab portable worksheet

19.3.2 Performing analysis and checking conditions

EXAMPLE 19.1   STUDENT EXPENDITURE IN THREE FACULTIES (continued)

The commands to perform the one-way analysis of variance, and to check the conditions, are as follows. First, name three columns — Minitab will use these to store results produced during the analysis, and at this stage they do not have data. Next, give a *oneway* command that includes the names of four columns, whose order determines their use as follows:

1. the first column specifies the unrestricted variable;

2. the second column specifies the limited variable;

3. the third column specifies a column into which the residuals are put when you execute the Minitab command;

4. the fourth column specifies a column into which the fitted values are put when you execute the Minitab command.

The first *plot* command produces the residuals-versus-fitted-values plot. The remaining commands produce the normal probability plot, based on the residuals, and the associated correlation coefficient and its theoretical value.

```
MTB > outfile 'a:\1waybook.lis'
MTB > retrieve 'a:\1waybook.mtp';
SUBC> portable.
MTB > name c3 'resi' c4 'fits' c5 'zscores'
MTB > info
MTB > oneway 'expend' 'faculty' 'resi' 'fits'
MTB > plot 'resi' 'fits'
MTB > nscore 'resi' 'zscores'
MTB > plot 'resi' 'zscores'
MTB > correlation 'resi' 'zscores'
MTB > let k1=45
MTB > let k2=0.05
MTB > cd a:\
MTB > execute 'rtheoret.mtb'
```

If your version of Minitab has pull-down menus and you want to use them, table 19.10 lists the menus and options that access the required commands. Appendix D, *Detailed instructions for Minitab menus*, explains how to use the menus.

Table 19.10 Menus and options for Minitab commands to produce the one-way analysis of variance

Minitab command	Menu	Option
outfile	File >	Other Files > Start Recording Session...
retrieve	File >	Open Worksheet...
port		Minitab portable worksheet
print	Edit >	Display Data...
name	Edit >	Data Screen
info	Edit	Get Worksheet Info...
	(Edit >	Data Screen [Alt-D])
oneway	Stat >	ANOVA > Oneway...
plot	Graph >	Scatter Plot...
correlation	Stat >	Basic Statistics > Correlation...
let	Calc >	Functions and Statistics > General Expressions...
cd		not available
execute	File >	Other Files > Execute Macro...

The output produced by the above commands is as follows:

```
MTB > retrieve 'a:\1waybook.mtp';
SUBC> portable.

Worksheet retrieved from file: a:\1waybook.mtp
MTB > print c1

faculty
   1  1  1  1  1  1  1  1  1  1  1  1  1  1  1
   2  2  2  2  2  2  2  2  2  2  2  2  2  2  2
   3  3  3  3  3  3  3  3  3  3  3  3  3  3  3

MTB > name c3 'resi' c4 'fits' c5 'zscores'
MTB > info

COLUMN        NAME          COUNT
C1            faculty        45
C2            expend         45
C3            resi            0
C4            fits            0
C5            zscores         0

CONSTANTS USED: NONE

MTB > oneway 'expend' 'faculty' 'resi' 'fits'

ANALYSIS OF VARIANCE ON expend
SOURCE        DF          SS          MS        F          p
faculty        2       48902       24451      6.52      0.003
ERROR         42      157530        3751
TOTAL         44      206431
                                       INDIVIDUAL 95 PCT CI'S FOR MEAN
                                       BASED ON POOLED STDEV
LEVEL        N        MEAN      STDEV  ----+---------+---------+---------+--
   1        15      177.13      72.73  (-------*-------)
   2        15      201.27      50.98      (-------*-------)
   3        15      255.93      58.00                     (-------*-------)
                                       ----+---------+---------+---------+--
POOLED STDEV =      61.24             160       200       240       280
```

continued . . .

```
MTB > plot 'resi' 'fits'


         -    *
         -
    100+  2                                                          *
         -
   resi-                                                             *
         -                            3                              *
         -  3                         6                              3
     0+  3                            3                              3
         -  *                                                        2
         -  *                         2                              *
         -  *                                                        *
         -                                                           *
   -100+  3                                                          *
         -
         -
         -                           *
         -
         ----+---------+---------+---------+---------+---------+--fits
            180       195       210       225       240       255


MTB > nscore 'resi' 'zscores'
MTB > plot 'resi' 'zscores'


         -                                                          *
         -
    100+                                                    *
         -
   resi-                                          * *
         -                                      *
         -                                  ****
         -                        **2**2****
     0+               2 *22**
         -              *2
         -            ****
         -          **
         -         *
   -100+    *  *  *  *
         -
         -
         -*
         -
         --------+---------+---------+---------+---------+--------zscores
             -1.60     -0.80     0.00      0.80      1.60


MTB > correlation 'resi' 'zscores'

Correlation of resi and zscores = 0.980

MTB > let k1=45
MTB > let k2=0.05
MTB > cd a:\
MTB > execute 'rtheoret.mtb'
```

continued . . .

```
The Theoretical value for the normal probability plot r
has been computed for

the number of observations equal to
K6          45.0000
and significance level of
K7           0.0500000

The theoretical value is:
K3           0.974171
```

19.3.3 Theoretical value for $LSD(\alpha)$

Computing the $LSD(\alpha)$ requires the theoretical value t_T. To obtain this theoretical value, use the Minitab command *invcdf* with subcommand t. To obtain t_T, you must supply the degrees of freedom of the pooled standard deviation, $(n - g)$, and $1 - (\alpha/2)$. The general form of the Minitab command is as follows:

```
MTB > invcdf 1 - (a/2);
SUBC> t (n-g).
```

If your version of Minitab has pull-down menus and you want to use them, the menu and options that accesses the *invcdf* commands is *Calc > Probability Distributions > T... > Inverse cumulative probability*. Appendix D, *Detailed instructions for Minitab menus*, explains how to use the menus.

EXAMPLE 19.1   STUDENT EXPENDITURE IN THREE FACULTIES (continued)
Now, for $\alpha = 0.05$, $1 - (\alpha/2) = 1 - (0.05/2) = 0.975$, so the Minitab commands and associated output for obtaining t_T are as follows:

```
MTB > invcdf 0.975;
SUBC> t 42.
     0.9750      2.0181
```

19.4 Chapter summary

The one-way analysis of variance (one-way ANOVA) is the hypothesis test that applies when the data consists of the values of one unrestricted and one limited variable and when the question to be investigated is: do the population means of the unrestricted variable differ for the different values of the limited variable? A preliminary examination of the data can be made by using a one-way table of means and a boxplot.

The test statistic is the F statistic with $(g - 1)$ and $(n - g)$ degrees of freedom and it is the ratio of the group and error mean squares from an analysis of variance table. The F statistic measures the degree of difference between the sample means, indicating how far the data departs from what you would expect under the null hypothesis that the population means are equal.

The sampling distribution of the test statistic is the F distribution with $(g - 1)$ and $(n - g)$ degrees of freedom. This distribution is based on a normal probability model, possibly with different group population means, for the unrestricted variable. The conditions that will satisfy the assumptions required for the valid use of this sampling distribution are as follows:

1. **Conditions for normal probability model with possibly different group population means**
   - *Unrestricted and a limited variable*
   - *Normally distributed variable*
   - *Homogeneity of variance*
2. **Conditions for other validating assumptions**
   - *Infinite population*
   - *Representative sample*
   - *Independence*

These conditions have to be checked for each example. Of central importance to this check are the residuals-versus-fitted-values plot and the normal probability plot based on the residuals. Also, the group standard deviations are examined and the differences between these are assessed by a rule of thumb. If the conditions are not met the procedure cannot be used for the example.

The probability of the test statistic, p_T, is obtained from the F distribution by determining the area, under the curve, above the range to the right of the observed value of the test statistic.

If it is established, using the analysis of variance, that at least one pair of population means is different, the least significant difference $[LSD(\alpha)]$ is used to determine which population means are different. This is done by comparing all pairs of differences between group sample means with the computed $LSD(\alpha)$. A pair of means whose absolute difference is greater than the $LSD(\alpha)$ is declared to be significantly different.

When the limited variable has just two values, the one-way analysis of variance is equivalent to an unpaired t-test; for the same hypotheses, the probabilities of the test statistics from the two tests are equal.

19.5 Key terms

- alternative hypothesis (H_a)
- analysis of variance table
- assumptions
- conditions
- degrees of freedom
- F distribution ($F_{degrees\ of\ freedom_1,\ degrees\ of\ freedom_2}$)
- F statistic ($F_{degrees\ of\ freedom_1,\ degrees\ of\ freedom_2}$)
- fitted value ($\overline{G}_i$)
- homogeneity of variance
- independence condition
- infinite population
- least significant difference [$LSD(\alpha)$]
- mean
- mean square
- measure of central tendency
- normal probability model with different group population means

- normal probability plot
- normal probability plot correlation coefficient (r_N)
- normally distributed variable
- null hypothesis (H_0)
- one-way analysis of variance (one-way ANOVA)
- pooled standard deviation (s_{pooled})
- probability of the test statistic (p_T)
- representative sample
- residual (e_{ij})
- residuals-versus-fitted-values plot
- sampling distribution of a test statistic
- sum of squares
- test statistic
- unpaired t-test

19.6 Exercises

19.1   The one-way analysis of variance (one-way ANOVA) is a statistical procedure to test whether there is a significant difference between two or more population means.

   (a) Why do we use the term *one-way*?

   (b) The test statistic follows which sampling distribution when the null hypothesis is true? Describe the shape of this sampling distribution.

   (c) The test statistic measures the relative sizes of two variances. In your own words describe what these two variances measure.

   (d) What are the conditions required for the valid use of the sampling distribution for this hypothesis test?

      (i) Why do we specify that the unrestricted variable involved must be normally distributed?

      (ii) Why must we assume that the variances of individual observations from the different groups are equal?

   (e) If we cannot reject the null hypothesis, what can we say about the population means?

(f) If the analysis of variance has established that at least one pair of population means is significantly different, we can determine which means are different by using a procedure based on the least significant difference [$LSD(\alpha)$].

    (i) State the formula for the $LSD(\alpha)$.

    (ii) If the numbers of observations used to calculate the sample means are unequal, what effect does this have on the calculation of the $LSD(\alpha)$?

19.2 The Adelaide Real Estate Agents Association wants to see whether the typical *Selling price* of home units sold over the last 12 months in the Burnside and Unley local government areas differs from that in the Kensington and Norwood and Payneham local government areas. To do this, they send a letter to all agents in those areas, asking each agent to return information for one home unit randomly selected from those they have sold in these areas in the last 12 months. Altogether about 600 home units were sold in the Burnside and Unley areas in this period; about 450 home units were sold in the Kensington and Norwood and Payneham areas during the same period.

The data for *Selling price* in table 19.11 is saved in the Minitab portable worksheet file *homeunit.mtp*. The data for the Kensington and Norwood and Payneham local government areas has the column *location* equal to 1, and the data for Burnside and Unley has the column *location* equal to 2.

Table 19.11   *Selling price* ($) for home units in the Burnside and Kensington and Norwood local government areas

Kensington and Norwood and Payneham	Burnside and Unley
158 000	134 000
49 000	90 000
172 000	61 000
78 000	236 000
75 000	110 000
155 000	170 000
85 000	110 000
150 000	300 000
107 000	170 000
140 000	115 000
	138 000
	110 000
	115 000
	130 000
	77 000
	112 000
	129 000
	107 000

Use the following Minitab output for this exercise. Reproduce this output.

```
MTB > retrieve 'a:\homeunit.mtp';
SUBC> portable.

Worksheet retrieved from file: a:\homeunit.mtp
MTB > info

COLUMN       NAME         COUNT
C1           location       28
C2           age            28
C3           norooms        28
C4           capvalue       28
C5           valprice       28
C6           selprice       28

CONSTANTS USED: NONE

MTB > boxplot 'selprice';
SUBC> by 'location'.

location

                 -----------------
1          ------I       +      I---
                 -----------------


                  -------
2         *   -------I+    I------            0              0
                  -------
        ----+---------+---------+---------+---------+---------+-selprice
        50000    100000    150000    200000    250000    300000

MTB > table 'location';
SUBC> mean 'selprice';
SUBC> n 'selprice'.

  ROWS: location

      selprice   selprice
        MEAN        N

   1    116900        10
   2    134111        18
  ALL   127964        28


MTB > name c7 'resi' c8 'fits' c9 'zscores'
MTB > oneway 'selprice' 'location' 'resi' 'fits'

ANALYSIS OF VARIANCE ON selprice
SOURCE      DF        SS           MS          F         p
location     1    1.904E+09    1.904E+09     0.69     0.413
ERROR       26    7.159E+10    2.753E+09
TOTAL       27    7.349E+10
```

continued . . .

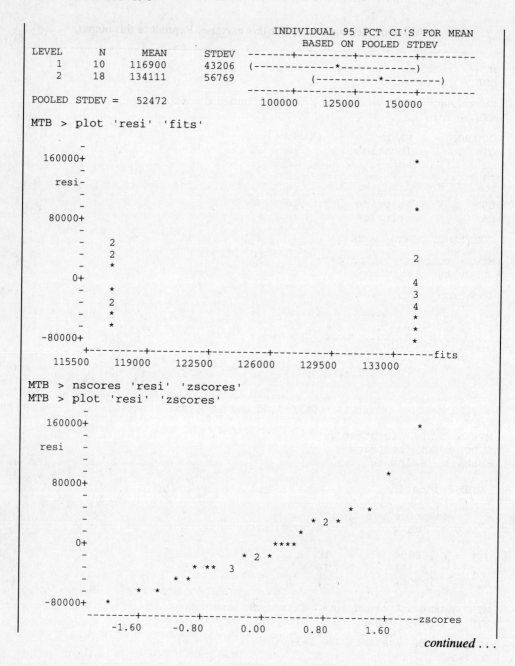

```
                                             INDIVIDUAL 95 PCT CI'S FOR MEAN
                                                  BASED ON POOLED STDEV
LEVEL      N      MEAN      STDEV  -------+---------+---------+---------
  1       10     116900     43206  (-------------*------------)
  2       18     134111     56769            (----------*---------)
                                   -------+---------+---------+---------
POOLED STDEV =   52472              100000    125000    150000

MTB > plot 'resi' 'fits'


          -
  160000+                                                      *
          -
   resi-
          -
          -                                                    *
   80000+
          -
          -       2
          -       2                                            2
          -       *
       0+                                                      4
          -       *                                            3
          -       2                                            4
          -       *                                            *
          -       *                                            *
  -80000+                                                      *
          +---------+---------+---------+---------+---------+------fits
        115500    119000    122500    126000    129500    133000

MTB > nscores 'resi' 'zscores'
MTB > plot 'resi' 'zscores'
          -
  160000+                                                *
          -
   resi  -
          -
          -                                         *
   80000+
          -
          -                                    *  *
          -                               * 2 *
          -                                *
       0+                            ****
          -                     * 2 *
          -           * ** 3
          -        * *
          -     *  *
  -80000+   *
          --------+---------+---------+---------+---------+-----zscores
              -1.60     -0.80      0.00      0.80      1.60
```

continued . . .

```
MTB > corr 'resi' 'zscores'

Correlation of resi and zscores = 0.941

MTB > let k1=28
MTB > let k2=0.05
MTB > cd a:\
MTB > execute 'rtheoret.mtb'
The Theoretical value for the normal probability plot r
has been computed for

the number of observations equal to
K6          28.0000
and significance level of
K7          0.0500000

The theoretical value is:
K3          0.961832
```

(a) Answer the following questions:
   (i) What is the question to be investigated (including the group to which the conclusions apply)?
   (ii) What variable(s) are we concerned with here?
   (iii) What type of variable(s) are they?
   (iv) Which major category of statistical procedures applies here? Why?
   (v) What type of statistic should we use, given the question to be investigated and the variables involved?
   (vi) Which particular statistic or procedure, and diagram, should we use? Why?
(b) Use the boxplots and the one-way table of means to summarise the data.
(c) Analyse the data in table 19.11 to see whether there is a significant difference in the mean *Selling price* between the *locations*. (Use a significance level of a = 0.05.)

19.3 At an International World Wide Web conference, delegates represented three different types of employer: 540 from government departments, 623 from tertiary institutions, 429 from private enterprise. A sample of 20 delegates was randomly selected from each group and each delegate's claim for *Daily expenditure* at the conference was recorded. We want to use this data to decide whether the *Daily expenditure* differs significantly between employees from each of the three *Types of employer*. The data from this sample is in table 19.12 and is saved in a Minitab portable worksheet file called *expenses.mtp*; the codes used in this file for *Types of employer* are 1 for government departments, 2 for tertiary institutions and 3 for private enterprise.

Table 19.12 *Daily expenditure* ($) by conference delegates

	Types of employer	
Government department	Tertiary institution	Private enterprise
117	94	147
89	83	141
112	87	157
106	77	108
115	77	113
108	90	112
94	67	141
103	91	126
126	72	124
121	97	119
127	94	129
93	67	141
89	76	149
112	75	125
88	86	147
125	102	131
89	61	119
121	74	162
129	103	132
122	87	118

(a) Answer the following questions:
   (i) What is the question to be investigated (including the group to which the conclusions apply)?
   (ii) What variable(s) are we concerned with here?
   (iii) What type of variable(s) are they?
   (iv) Which major category of statistical procedures applies here? Why?
   (v) What type of statistic should we use, given the question to be investigated and the variables involved?
   (vi) Which particular statistic or procedure, and diagram, should we use? Why?
(b) Use the boxplots and the one-way table of means to summarise the data.
(c) Analyse the data in table 19.12 to see whether there is a significant difference in the typical *Daily expenditure* between delegates from each of the three *Types of employer*. (Use a significance level of $\alpha = 0.05$.)

(d) If there is a significant difference, use the least significant difference [$LSD(\alpha)$] as follows to determine which *Types of employer* differ significantly in their mean *Daily expenditure*. (Use a significance level of $\alpha = 0.05$.)

(i) Determine the following: g; degrees of freedom of s_{pooled}; t_T; s_{pooled}; and number of observations in each group.

(ii) Calculate the least significant difference for $\alpha = 0.05$.

(iii) Examine all pairwise differences between the *Daily expenditure* means by using a table with both rows and columns corresponding to the values of the means arranged in ascending order.

(e) Write a report summarising your conclusions about the differences between *Types of employer* in their mean *Daily expenditure*.

19.4 A company has to choose a courier to deliver parcels to destinations in a large city. One important aspect is the time the courier takes to respond to a call. For a 4-week trial period the company tested each of four courier services to see if their typical response time differed during this period. The working hours for the trial period were divided into 5-minute intervals making a total of 1920 intervals. For each courier, 10 intervals were chosen at random and the time they took to respond to the calls were recorded. The results for the four couriers are in table 19.13 and are saved in the Minitab portable worksheet file called *delivery.mtp*.

Table 19.13   Courier *Response time* (mins)

	Courier		
A	B	C	D
13	3	37	28
19	6	10	26
15	3	28	9
4	3	22	30
19	24	30	3
28	8	24	26
19	29	22	19
28	22	16	29
19	16	31	35
35	17	29	28

(a) Answer the following questions:

(i) What is the question to be investigated (including the group to which the conclusions apply)?

(ii) What variable(s) are we concerned with here?

(iii) What type of variable(s) are they?

(iv) Which major category of statistical procedures applies here? Why?

(v) What type of statistic should we use, given the question to be investigated and the variables involved?

(vi) Which particular statistic or procedure, and diagram, should we use? Why?

(b) Use the boxplots and the one-way table of means to summarise the data.

(c) Carry out the six steps of the one-way analysis of variance to decide whether the mean *Response time* is the same for all *Couriers*. (Use a significance level of $\alpha = 0.05$.)

(d) Answer the following questions:

(i) What does the Courier MS measure?

(ii) Use the standard deviations to check the Error MS.

(iii) What does the Error MS measure?

(iv) Use the two mean squares to calculate the F statistic.

(v) What does the calculated F statistic tell us about *Response time* differences between *Couriers*?

19.5 In exercise 19.4 you discovered that at least one of the population mean *Response times* for a courier differs significantly from the time taken by at least one other courier. Use the least significant difference [*LSD*(α)] as follows to determine which couriers' population *Response time* means differ significantly. (Use a significance level of $\alpha = 0.05$.)

(a) Determine the following: g; degrees of freedom of s_{pooled}; t_T; s_{pooled}; number of observations in each group.

(b) Calculate the least significant difference for $\alpha = 0.05$.

(c) Examine all pairwise differences between the *Response time* means by using a table with both rows and columns corresponding to the values of the means arranged in ascending order.

(d) Write a report summarising your conclusions about the differences between the *Couriers* in their *Response time* means.

## CHAPTER 20

TEST FOR LINEAR RELATIONSHIP BETWEEN TWO UNRESTRICTED VARIABLES

LEARNING OBJECTIVES

The learning objectives of this chapter are:

- to know when to apply, how to calculate and how to interpret the results of the F-test for the slope;
- to know the conditions required for the F-test for the slope to be valid and how to determine when these are met;
- to understand the limitations of linear regression.

The following extract from the *Summary of procedures based on combinations of variable types* in part VI gives an overview of the hypothesis tests covered in this and the previous chapters of part V, *Hypothesis tests*.

1. *One limited variable*
   - Distribution of variables: z-test for a proportion; goodness-of-fit test.

2. *Two limited variables*
   - Distribution of variables: z-test for a proportion difference; contingency table analysis.

3. *One unrestricted variable — one limited variable*
   - Measures of central tendency: unpaired t-test; one-way analysis of variance.

4. *One unrestricted variable — two limited variables*

5. *Two unrestricted variables*
   - **Fitted lines**: F-test for slope.

20.1 Hypothesis tests in simple linear regression

As outlined in the objectives, this chapter covers the **F-test for the slope** which is a hypothesis test associated with simple linear regression. It applies when the data consists of the values of two unrestricted variables and when the question to be investigated is: is there a **linear relationship** between the two unrestricted variables? Further, since inference procedures are involved, we must have taken a sample and the question to be investigated must be about the population and *not* confined to the sample.

EXAMPLE 20.1   ESTIMATING *SELLING PRICE* FROM *VALUATION PRICE*

In example 16.1, *Estimating Selling price from Valuation price*, a real estate agent wanted to estimate the final selling price of a house from the valuation price agreed upon when the house was first put up for sale: that is, she wants to use the relationship between two unrestricted variables, *Valuation price* and *Selling price*. The agent has this information for houses sold in her area over a 12-month period, filed in alphabetical order according to the vendor's surname. The agent has information on 451 houses, but as she did not have time to extract the information for every house, she systematically sampled 20 of these houses. Section 4.2, *Systematic sampling*, describes the procedure for this: randomly select one of the first 33 (= 451 − 22 × [20–1]) vendors, and then take every 22nd (= integer part of 451/20) record. The valuation and selling prices in table 16.1 are presented again in table 20.1; this represents the agent's raw, primary data. In section 16.2, *Conditions for valid inference in simple linear regression*, we discovered that the third observation for *Selling price* is in error and should be $210\,000$. The corrected value will be used in subsequent analyses.

Table 20.1   *Valuation price* and *Selling price* for selected houses

Valuation price ($)	Selling price ($)
90 000	95 000
230 000	208 000
230 000	310 000
170 000	140 500
140 000	137 000
290 000	270 000
190 000	191 400
150 000	158 000
180 000	160 000
260 000	225 000
90 000	105 000
270 000	265 000
190 000	153 500

Table 20.1 *(continued)*

Valuation price ($)	Selling price ($)
130 000	149 000
180 000	161 000
620 000	560 000
270 000	244 000
210 000	165 100
120 000	94 000
130 000	105 000

Figure 20.1, a scatter diagram, illustrates the relationship between these two variables, with the third observation corrected. It also gives the fitted straight line. R^2 for this relationship is 97.7%. The equation for the straight line fitted to the corrected data is:

$$Selling\ price = 6670 + 0.88481\ Valuation\ price$$

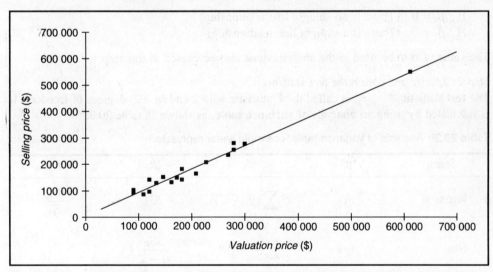

Figure 20.1 Scatter diagram for *Selling price* versus *Valuation price* (with corrected third observation)

Questions requiring hypothesis tests that you might ask for this example include the following:

- Does the expected *Selling price* differ from zero, when the *Valuation price* is zero?
- Is there a relationship between *Selling price* and *Valuation price*?
- Does the expected change in *Selling price* differ from $1 when the *Valuation price* increases by $1?

These questions require hypothesis tests because they involve questions about the population for which there are only two possible answers, yes or no. What are the response and explanatory variables for these questions? *Valuation price* is the explanatory variable because its values are to be specified, whereas *Selling price* is the response variable because its values are to be computed. This section describes the procedure for answering the second question for this example.

20.1.1   F-test for the slope

Sometimes we want to investigate the question: is there a relationship between the **response** and **explanatory variables**? The hypothesis test that answers this question is the F-test for the slope. Some books present an equivalent test, the t-test for the slope.

The general steps for this hypothesis test are now outlined, followed by the analysis for an example. In describing this analysis we use n to denote the number of pairs of observations.

Step 1: Set up the hypotheses and nominate the significance level.
The general form of the **null** and **alternative hypotheses** for this test are:

H_0: $\beta_1 = 0$ (There is no straight line relationship)
H_a: $\beta_1 \neq 0$ (There is a straight line relationship)

The value of α to be used in the analysis must also be chosen at this step.

Step 2: Specify and obtain the test statistic.
The **test statistic**, $F_{1, n-2}$, is called the **F statistic** with 1 and $(n-2)$ degrees of freedom. It is calculated by using an **analysis of variance table**, as shown in table 20.2.

Table 20.2   Analysis of variance table for simple linear regression

Source	DF	SS	MS	F
Regression	1	$r^2 \sum_{i=1}^{n} (y_i - \bar{y})^2$	SS_R	$\dfrac{MS_R}{MS_E}$
Error	$n-2$	$\sum_{i=1}^{n} (y_i - \hat{y}_i)^2$	$\dfrac{SS_E}{n-2}$	
Total	$n-1$	$\sum_{i=1}^{n} (y_i - \bar{y})^2$		

y_i	the ith observation for the response variable
n	the number of pairs of observations
$\hat{y}_i$	the fitted value for the ith observation $= b_0 + b_1 x_i$ where x_i is the ith observation for the explanatory variable
$\bar{y}$	the grand mean of the observations for the response variable
SS_R and MS_R	the sum of squares and mean square for regression
SS_E and MS_E	the sum of squares and mean square for error

Table 20.2 consists of rows for Regression, Error and Total and columns for source, **degrees of freedom** (DF), **sum of squares** (SS), **mean square** (MS) and the F statistic (F). Again, the essence of the table is that you measure the relative size of two variances, the regression and error variances, by taking their ratio. This ratio is the F statistic and it measures how close the pairs of observations are to lying on a straight line. That is, the closer the data are to lying on a straight line, the larger the F statistic. As usual, the F statistic measures how far the data departs from what you would expect under the null hypothesis.

$$\text{The test statistic is } F_{1,\, n-2} = \frac{\text{Regression MS}}{\text{Error MS}} = \frac{MS_R}{MS_E}$$

Again, there is an important relationship between quantities in the analysis of variance table: the sums of squares and degrees of freedom for the regression and error lines sum to the respective quantities for the total line. That is,

$$SS_T = SS_R + SS_E \text{ and } (n-1) = 1 + (n-2)$$

Step 3: List and check conditions for the sampling distribution.

The **sampling distribution of the test statistic** for this hypothesis test is the **F distribution** (see figure 20.2). The distribution is based on a **normal probability model**, possibly **with a linear relationship** between the response and explanatory variables. The **conditions** that will satisfy the **assumptions** required for the valid use of the sampling distribution are as follows:

1. **Conditions for normal probability model with linear relationship**
   - *Unrestricted variables*
   - *Normally distributed variable*
   - *Linear relationship*
   - *Homogeneity of variance*
   - *X is known without error*

2. **Conditions for other validating assumptions**
   - *Infinite population*
   - *Representative sample*
   - *Independence*

How to check these conditions was explained in section 16.2, *Conditions for valid inference in simple linear regression*. As in the one-way analysis of variance, the sampling distribution of the test statistic is an F distribution *when H_0 is true and these conditions are met*. That is, when there is no relationship between the two unrestricted variables and the conditions are met, the distribution of values of the test statistic takes the form given in figure 20.2. The exact form varies with the degrees of freedom of the two mean squares in the observed F statistic.

Step 4: Obtain the probability of the test statistic.

We require the **probability of the test statistic**, p_T, which is the probability of getting the observed value, and more extreme values, of the test statistic when the null hypothesis is true. We can obtain this by determining the area, under the curve, for the F distribution, above the range to the right of the observed value of the test statistic. Usually computer packages give p_T, which they designate as either p or Prob.

Step 5: State and apply the rule for rejecting the null hypothesis.

The general form of the rule for rejecting the null hypothesis is: if $p_T \le \alpha$, reject H_0; otherwise, H_0 cannot be rejected.

Step 6: State the conclusion in terms of the question investigated.

Once you have decided whether or not the hypothesis is to be rejected, restate the conclusion in terms of the original question. ∎

EXAMPLE 20.1 ESTIMATING *SELLING PRICE* FROM *VALUATION PRICE*
(continued)

The question to be investigated is whether there is a straight line relationship that can be used to estimate *Selling price* from the *Valuation price* for the 451 houses sold by the real estate agency in the 12-month period. That is, the question to be investigated involves two unrestricted variables, concerns all houses sold by the real estate agency, not just those in the sample, and has only a yes or no answer. Hence, a hypothesis test is appropriate and the F-test for the slope will show if there is a straight line relationship, in the population, between *Valuation price* and *Selling price*.

Step 1: Set up hypotheses and nominate the significance level.

H_0: $\beta_1 = 0$
H_a: $\beta_1 \ne 0$

Using the standard value of α we have $\alpha = 0.05$.

Step 2: Specify and obtain the test statistic.

The test statistic is $F_{1, n-2} = \dfrac{\text{Regression MS}}{\text{Error MS}}$

For the example, $F_{1, 18} = 253.38$

Step 3: List and check conditions for the sampling distribution.

The sampling distribution of the test statistic, $F_{1, 18}$, is the F distribution with 1 degree of freedom for the numerator and 18 degrees of freedom for the denominator (see figure 20.2). The conditions that will satisfy the assumptions required for the valid use of the sampling distribution are as follows:

1. Conditions for normal probability model with linear relationship
- *Unrestricted variables*
- *Normally distributed variable*
- *Linear relationship*
- *Homogeneity of variance*
- *X is known without error*

2. Conditions for other validating assumptions
- *Infinite population*
- *Representative sample*
- *Independence*

How to check these conditions for this example was explained in section 16.2, *Conditions for valid inference in simple linear regression*. It appears that all the assumptions required to use the F sampling distribution, that underlies the F-test for the slope, are met in the case of the regression of *Selling price* on *Valuation price*, once the third observation for *Selling price* has been corrected.

Step 4: Obtain the probability of the test statistic.

The probability of the observed value, and more extreme values, of the test statistic when there is no relationship between *Selling price* and *Valuation price* has been computed to be $p_T = 0.000$; figure 20.2 gives the sampling distribution along with the test statistic and the probability of the test statistic.

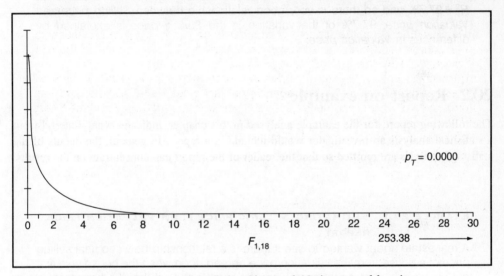

Figure 20.2   F distribution for test statistic with 1 and 18 degrees of freedom

Step 5: State and apply the rule for rejecting the null hypothesis.

We have decided on $\alpha = 0.05$, so that our rule is: if $p_T \leq 0.05$, reject H_0; otherwise, H_0 cannot be rejected. As $p_T = 0.000 < 0.05$, reject H_0.

Step 6: State the conclusion in terms of the question investigated.

The evidence suggests that there is a linear relationship between *Valuation price* and *Selling price*. ∎

20.1.2 Strength of the relationship

While we can use the above test to decide whether there is sufficient evidence of a linear relationship, it does not necessarily allow us to conclude that there is a strong relationship. For this we need to examine the **coefficient of determination**, R^2, as discussed in section 10.1, *Descriptive simple linear regression*.

In summary, investigating the relationship between two variables is a two-step process:

1. Determine whether there is a significant linear relationship by using the F-test for the slope.
2. *Only if* the F-test for the slope indicates that there is a linear relationship, examine R^2 to determine the strength of the relationship. This step is clearly unnecessary if you establish at the first step that there is no evidence of a relationship.

EXAMPLE 20.1   ESTIMATING *SELLING PRICE* FROM *VALUATION PRICE*
            (continued)

We concluded that there is a significant relationship between *Selling price* and *Valuation price* so that we should examine the strength of the relationship. $R^2 = 97.7\%$ and so there is very good relationship between *Selling price* and *Valuation price*: 97.7% of the variation in the *Selling price* is explained by differences in *Valuation price*.

20.2 Report on example

The following report, for the example analysed in this chapter, indicates what material from a statistical analysis an investigator would include in a report. In general, the details of the statistical analysis are omitted so that the reader of the report can concentrate on the results.

EXAMPLE 20.1   ESTIMATING *SELLING PRICE* FROM *VALUATION PRICE*
            REPORT

A real estate agent wanted to see if there is a relationship between final selling price of a house from the valuation price agreed upon when the house was first put up for sale. The agent systematically sampled 20 of the 451 houses sold through the agency over a 12-month period. Figure 20.1 shows the relationship between selling and valuation price, and includes the straight line fitted by using simple linear regression. An F-test of the slope was significant ($p < 0.001$), so we concluded that there is a straight line relationship between the selling and valuation price. The coefficient of determination (R^2) is 97.7%, which indicates a very good linear relationship.

20.3 Using Minitab for hypothesis testing in regression

Use Minitab's *regress* command to produce the analysis of variance for the F-test for the slope. The general use of this command and the commands for doing residual checking were explained in section 16.8, *Using Minitab for estimation in regression*. The test statistic and its probability are obtained from the analysis of variance table included in the output from the *regress* command, as outlined in table 20.3.

Table 20.3   Quantities used in the hypothesis test

Item	Row label	Column label	Value
F	Regression	F	757.96
p_T	Regression	p	0.000

EXAMPLE 20.1   ESTIMATING SELLING PRICE FROM VALUATION PRICE
(continued)

The commands to produce the complete analysis, including the correction of the third observation for selling price and the checking of conditions, are as follows:

```
MTB > outfile 'a:\regnvalu.lis'
MTB > retrieve 'a:\regnvalu.mtp';
SUBC> portable.
MTB > info
MTB > print 'selprice' 'valprice'
MTB > # Command to correct 3rd observation
MTB > let c1(3)=210000
MTB > name c3 'x'
MTB > set 'x'
DATA> 135000 215000
DATA> end
MTB > plot 'selprice' 'valprice'
MTB > name c4 'sres' c5 'fits'
MTB > info
MTB > regress 'selprice' explanatory 1 'valprice' 'sres' 'fits';
SUBC> predict 'x'.
MTB > #Plot of fitted & original data to check linear relationship
MTB > mplot 'selprice' 'valprice' 'fits' 'valprice'
MTB > #Standardised-Residuals-versus-fitted-values plot to check
MTB > #   linear relationship and homogeneity
MTB > plot 'sres' 'fits'
MTB > #Normal Probability plot and correlation coefficient
MTB > #   to check normality
MTB > name c6 'zscores'
MTB > nscores 'sres' 'zscores'
MTB > plot 'sres' 'zscores'
MTB > correlation 'sres' 'zscores'
MTB > let k1=20
MTB > let k2=0.05
MTB > cd a:\
MTB > execute 'rtheoret.mtb'
```

These commands, the output from them and the menus and options to execute them with pull-down menus were given in section 16.8, *Using Minitab for estimation in regression*. The part of the output that contains the analysis of variance table for the example is as follows. Note the values of the test statistic and its probability.

```
MTB > regress 'selprice' explanatory 1 'valprice' 'sres' 'fits';
SUBC> predict 'x'.

The regression equation is
selprice = 6670 + 0.885 valprice

Predictor        Coef         Stdev       t-ratio           p
Constant         6670          7552          0.88       0.389
valprice      0.88481       0.03214         27.53       0.000

s = 15980          R-sq = 97.7%        R-sq(adj) = 97.6%

Analysis of Variance

SOURCE          DF           SS            MS          F          p
Regression       1    1.93544E+11  1.93544E+11     757.96      0.000
Error           18     4596277760    255348768
Total           19    1.98140E+11

Unusual Observations
Obs.valprice  selprice     Fit   Stdev.Fit  Residual   St.Resid
16     620000     560000 555250      13746       4750      0.58 X

X denotes an obs. whose X value gives it large influence.

    Fit    Stdev.Fit            95% C.I.               95% P.I.
 126119        4257    ( 117173, 135065)    (  91368, 160870)
 196903        3582    ( 189375, 204432)    ( 162490, 231317)
```

20.4 Chapter summary

The F-test for the slope is the hypothesis test that is applied when the data consists of the values of two unrestricted variables and when the question to be investigated is: is there a linear relationship between the two unrestricted variables. A preliminary examination of the data can be made by using a scatter diagram and by fitting a straight line to the data.

The test statistic is the F statistic with 1 and $(n - 2)$ degrees of freedom and it is the ratio of the regression and error mean squares from an analysis of variance table. The F statistic measures how close the pairs of observations are to lying on a straight line.

The sampling distribution of the test statistic is the F distribution with 1 and $(n - 2)$ degrees of freedom. This distribution is based on a normal probability model, possibly with a linear relationship between the response and explanatory variable. These conditions have to be checked for each example, and this requires an analysis of the residuals by using the standardised-residuals-versus-fitted-values plot and the normal probability plot based on the standardised residuals. If the conditions are not met the procedure cannot be used for the example.

The probability of the test statistic, p_T, is obtained from the F distribution by determining the area, under the curve, above the range to the right of the observed value of the test statistic.

If the hypothesis test indicates that there is a linear relationship, the coefficient of determination is used to assess the strength of the relationship that has been established. A rule of thumb for doing this was given in section 10.1, *Descriptive simple linear regression*.

20.5 Key terms

- alternative hypothesis (H$_a$)
- analysis of variance table
- assumptions
- coefficient of determination (R^2)
- conditions
- degrees of freedom
- explanatory variable
- F distribution ($F_{degrees\ of\ freedom_1,\ degrees\ of\ freedom_2}$)
- F-test for the slope
- F statistic ($F_{degrees\ of\ freedom_1,\ degrees\ of\ freedom_2}$)

- fitted line
- linear relationship
- mean square
- normal probability model with a linear relationship
- null hypothesis (H$_0$)
- probability of the test statistic (p_T)
- response variable
- sampling distribution of a test statistic
- sum of squares
- test statistic

20.6 Exercises

20.1 What does the test statistic from the F-test for the slope measure?

20.2 Explain in your own words why the coefficient of determination (R^2) is ignored if the F-test for the slope is not significant.

20.3 Inferential procedures involve certain conditions that must be met for the use of the associated sampling distribution to be valid. What are the crucial conditions for the F-test for the slope?

20.4 What should you do when you observe (a) a large-residual outlier and (b) an influential outlier?

20.5 The Adelaide Real Estate Agents Association wants to see if there is a relationship that could be used in estimating *Selling price* quantities for home units sold over the last 12 months in the Burnside and Unley local government areas with a specified *Valuation price*. It sends a letter to all agents in these areas, asking each agent to return information for one home unit randomly selected from those they have sold in these areas in the last 12 months. Altogether about 600 home units were sold in these areas in this period.

The data for *Valuation price* and *Selling price* is in table 20.4 and is saved in the Minitab portable worksheet file *homeunit.mtp*; the data for Burnside and Unley is saved along with the data for Kensington and Norwood and Payneham, and the data for Burnside and Unley has the column *location* equal to 2.

Table 20.4   *Valuation price* and *Selling price* for home units in the Burnside and Unley local government areas

Valuation price ($)	Selling price ($)
100 000	90 000
147 000	134 000
65 000	61 000
250 000	236 000
128 500	110 000
180 000	170 000
122 000	110 000
330 000	300 000
193 000	170 000
115 000	115 000
140 000	138 000
125 000	110 000
115 000	115 000
138 000	130 000
95 000	77 000
120 000	112 000
129 000	129 000
127 000	107 000

(a) Answer the following questions:

(i) What is the question to be investigated (including the group to which the conclusions apply)?

(ii) What variable(s) are we concerned with here?

(iii) What type of variable(s) are they?

(iv) Which major category of statistical procedures applies here? Why?

(v) What type of statistic should we use, given the question to be investigated and the variables involved?

(vi) Which particular statistic or procedure, and diagram, should we use? Why?

(b) Which variable is the response variable and which is the explanatory variable? Give reasons for your choice.

(c) Reproduce the following Minitab output:

```
MTB > retrieve 'a:\homeunit.mtp';
SUBC> portable.

Worksheet retrieved from file: a:\homeunit.mtp
MTB > info

COLUMN      NAME         COUNT
C1          location        28
C2          age             28
C3          norooms         28
C4          capvalue        28
C5          valprice        28
C6          selprice        28


CONSTANTS USED: NONE

MTB > copy c1-c6 c1-c6;
SUBC> use c1=2.
MTB > plot 'selprice' 'valprice'

          -                                                    *
selprice-
          -
          -
  240000+                                          *
          -
          -                        *   *
  160000+
          -              *
          -           *  **
          -      222*
          -     *
   80000+     *
          -  *
          -

          +---------+---------+---------+---------+---------+--valprice
        50000    100000    150000    200000    250000    300000

MTB > name c7 'sres' c8 'fits'
MTB > regress 'selprice' explanatory 1 'valprice' 'sres' 'fits'
The regression equation is
selprice = 443 + 0.919 valprice

Predictor       Coef        Stdev       t-ratio         p
Constant         443         4413          0.10     0.921
valprice     0.91851      0.02806         32.73     0.000

s = 7098          R-sq = 98.5%        R-sq(adj) = 98.4%
```

continued . . .

```
Analysis of Variance

SOURCE        DF             SS            MS          F         p
Regression     1   53979590656   53979590656   1071.31     0.000
Error         16     806188096      50386756
Total         17   54785777664
Unusual Observations
Obs.valprice  selprice       Fit Stdev.Fit  Residual   St.Resid
 8      330000    300000  303550       5440     -3550     -0.78 X

X denotes an obs. whose X value gives it large influence.
```

(d) Use the output in (c) to answer the following questions:

(i) Use a scatter diagram to assess subjectively whether there appears to be a linear relationship between the *Selling price* and *Valuation price*.

(ii) What are the values of the regression coefficients b_0 and b_1.

(iii) Select two values for the *Valuation price* that lie within the range of observed data and calculate the mean response, using the equation for the fitted straight line. Plot the calculated mean responses onto the scatter diagram and draw the line of best fit.

(iv) Use the F-test for the slope to objectively determine whether there is a linear relationship. (Use a significance level of $\alpha = 0.05$.)

(v) What is the likely precision of the mean responses obtained using the sample straight line?

20.6 The Adelaide Real Estate Agents Association wants to see if there is a relationship that could be used in estimating *Selling price* quantities for home units sold over the last 12 months in the Kensington and Norwood and Payneham local government areas with a specified *Valuation price*. It sends a letter to all agents in these areas, asking each agent to return information for one home unit randomly selected from those they have sold in these areas in the last 12 months. Altogether about 450 home units were sold in these areas in this period.

The data for *Valuation price* and *Selling price* is in table 20.5 and is saved in the Minitab portable worksheet file *homeunit.mtp*; the data for Kensington and Norwood and Payneham is saved along with the data for Burnside and Unley, and the data for Kensington and Norwood and Payneham has the column *location* equal to 1.

Table 20.5 *Valuation price* and *Selling price* for home units in the Kensington & Norwood and Payneham local government areas

Valuation price ($)	Selling price ($)
53 950	49 000
167 000	158 000
189 500	172 000
79 950	78 000
79 500	75 000
165 000	155 000
95 000	85 000
160 000	150 000
115 000	107 000
150 000	140 000

(a) Answer the following questions:
   (i) What is the question to be investigated (including the group to which the conclusions apply)?
   (ii) What variable(s) are we concerned with here?
   (iii) What type of variable(s) are they?
   (iv) Which major category of statistical procedures applies here? Why?
   (v) What type of statistic should we use, given the question to be investigated and the variables involved?
   (vi) Which particular statistic or procedure, and diagram, should we use? Why?
(b) Which variable is the response variable and which is the explanatory variable? Give reasons for your choice.
(c) Use a scatter diagram to assess subjectively whether there appears to be a linear relationship between the *Selling price* and *Valuation price*.
(d) If there appears to be a linear relationship, use the least-squares method to find the regression coefficients b_0 and b_1.
(e) Use the F-test for the slope to objectively determine whether there is a linear relationship. (Use a significance level of $\alpha = 0.05$.)
(f) What is the likely precision of the mean responses obtained using the sample straight line?

PART VI

OVERVIEW OF STATISTICAL PROCEDURES

LEARNING OBJECTIVES

The learning objectives of this part are:

- to gain an overview of the statistical procedures covered in this book;
- to be able to identify the appropriate statistical procedure for a specific situation.

As outlined in chapter 1, *Statistics*, the statistical procedures covered in this book can be classified into one of the following four **major categories of statistical procedures**:

- A. **Data collection procedures**: for collecting data so that the validity of the collected information is maximised;
- B. **Descriptive summaries**: for summarising aspects of the behaviour of just the data being analysed;
- C. **Estimation procedures**: for estimating population quantities using a sample;
- D. **Hypothesis tests**: for answering yes/no questions about the population using a sample.

The different purposes of these four kinds of procedure are exemplified by the differences between the following questions that might be investigated for a study of support for the current member for a state electorate:

- What sampling method should I use to select voters to observe?
- In a sample of 100 voters, what proportion of voters would vote for the current member?
- What proportion of voters, registered to vote in the electorate, would vote for the current member?
- Does the proportion of registered voters who would support the current member differ from 52%?

Each of these questions is similar, yet they differ in particular aspects, so a different category of procedures is required to answer each one. Thus, the first stage of deciding which particular procedure to use involves determining the appropriate major category of statistical procedures. Next we have to decide which procedure to apply to answer the question. The procedures that might be applied in each case are summarised in the next section.

Summary of procedures based on combinations of variable types

Section 1.3, *Summary of procedures based on types of statistics*, summarised all the techniques covered in this book, and grouped them according to **types of statistics**. You can extend this summary also to classify statistical procedures in categories B, C and D according to the combination of variable types involved, as shown in figure VI.1 (opposite). Then you can identify the procedures available for a particular type of statistic and combination of variable types from the following summary. In the case of descriptive summaries, the procedures are listed before the dash and diagrams that illustrate their results are after the dash, as in chapter 13, *Overview of descriptive summaries*.

B. Descriptive summaries

1. *One limited variable*
   - Distribution of variables: frequency, relative frequency and percentage one-way summary tables — bar or column chart.
   - Measures of central tendency: mode (mean, median).
   - Measures of dispersion: range, interquartile range, (standard deviation, coefficient of variation).

2. *Two limited variables*
   - Distribution of variables: two-way contingency table — chart with bars or columns that are grouped or stacked.

3. *Three limited variables*
   - Distribution of variables: three-way contingency table — chart with bars or columns that are grouped or stacked.

4. *One unrestricted variable*
   - Distribution of variables: frequency, relative frequency and percentage tables — histogram, polygon, stem-and-leaf display, dotplot.
   - Measures of central tendency: mean, median — boxplot.
   - Measures of dispersion: range, interquartile range, standard deviation, coefficient of variation — boxplot.

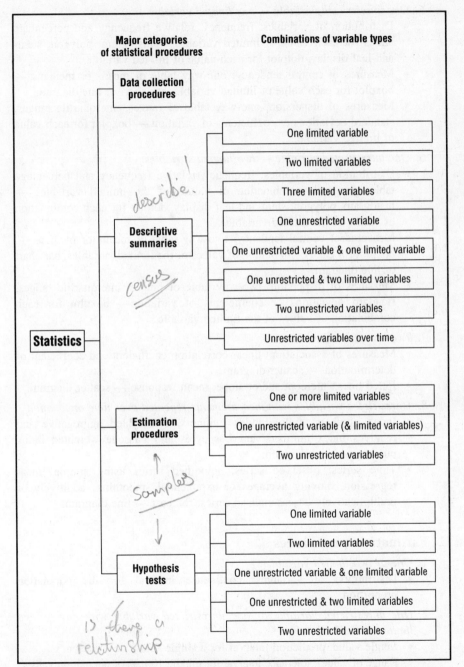

Figure VI.1   Organisation of statistical procedures according to major categories
and combinations of variable types

5. *One unrestricted variable — one limited variable*
   - Distribution of variables: frequency, relative frequency and percentage tables for each value of limited variable — histogram, polygon, stem-and-leaf display, dotplot for each value of limited variable.
   - Measures of central tendency: one-way table of means or medians — boxplot for each value of limited variable, bar chart or line diagram.
   - Measures of dispersion: one-way table of ranges, interquartile ranges, standard deviations or coefficients of variation — boxplot for each value of limited variable.

6. *One unrestricted variable — two limited variables*
   - Distribution of variables: frequency, relative frequency and percentage tables for each combination of values of the limited variables — histogram, polygon, stem-and-leaf display, dotplot for each combination of values of the limited variables.
   - Measures of central tendency: two-way table of means or medians — boxplot for each combination of values of the limited variables, bar chart or line diagram.
   - Measures of dispersion: two-way table of ranges, interquartile ranges, standard deviations or coefficients of variation— boxplot for each combination of values of the limited variable.

7. *Two unrestricted variables*
   - Measures of association: linear correlation coefficient and coefficient of determination — scatter diagram.
   - Fitted lines: intercept and/or slope; mean response — scatter diagram.

8. *Unrestricted variables with measurements repeated over time or location*
   - Index numbers: simple index numbers, unweighted aggregative and relatives index numbers and Laspeyres and Paasche weighted index numbers — line diagram.
   - Time series: observed series; smoothed series using simple linear regression, moving averages or exponential smoothing; additively or multiplicatively deseasonalised series; forecast — line diagram.

C. Estimation procedures

1. *One or two limited variable(s)*
   - Distribution of variables: confidence interval for the population proportion.

2. *One unrestricted variable or one unrestricted variable with one or two limited variable(s)*
   - Single value: prediction interval for a single future observation.
   - Range of values: tolerance interval for middle $100\pi\%$ of population values.
   - Measures of central tendency: confidence interval for the population mean.

3. *Two unrestricted variables*
   - Measures of association: confidence interval for the population linear correlation coefficient.*
   - Fitted lines: confidence intervals for population intercept, population slope and population mean response; prediction interval for a future observation.

D. Hypothesis tests

1. *One limited variable*
   - Distribution of variables: z-test for a proportion;* goodness-of-fit test.

2. *Two limited variables*
   - Distribution of variables: z-test for a proportion difference;* contingency table analysis.

3. *One unrestricted variable — one limited variable*
   - Measures of central tendency: unpaired t-test;* one-way analysis of variance.

4. *One unrestricted variable — two limited variables*
   - Measures of central tendency: two-way analysis of variance.*

5. *Two unrestricted variables*
   - Measures of association: test for linear correlation.*
   - Fitted lines: F-test for slope.

* These methods are not presented in this book.

Choosing a procedure

Earlier in the book we presented a crucial problem you were yet to face: what statistical procedure should I use to help answer the question that I have? In this section, we attempt to overcome this problem by developing a strategy for choosing statistical procedures. This strategy is an extension of the one outlined in chapter 13, *Overview of descriptive summaries*.

Choosing which procedure to use for a particular situation depends on:

- the **question to be investigated**;
- the combination of **variable** types involved (**limited** or **unrestricted**; **nominal**, **ordinal** or **interval/ratio**);
- the behaviour of the data (skew, symmetric and so on).

So, in choosing a procedure, we first identify the question to be investigated and the variables involved, along with their types. Then you use this information to make your choice; to make this process easier, it is broken down to involve specifying:

- the major category of statistical procedures;
- the type of statistic involved; and
- the procedure among those available for that type of statistic and major category.

The last step of this process is best carried out by referring to the summary, as it lists the statistical procedures according to the major category of statistical procedures, type of statistic and combinations of variable types. The whole process is dealt with as a series of standard questions that must be answered to determine which particular procedure to use for an example.

The major categories of statistical procedures we have covered are:

A. Data collection procedures
B. Descriptive summaries
C. Estimation procedures
D. Hypothesis tests

Choosing between the last three categories depends on the general nature of the question to be investigated. Is it about the available data only? Does it require estimating a population parameter, or does it ask a yes/no question about the population? The first thing to do is to decide whether the results are to apply to just the data that has been collected. If so, descriptive summaries is the major category of statistical procedures to use. Otherwise, you have to establish that you have a sample of the whole population and decide whether a quantity is to be estimated or a yes/no question is being asked. The outcome of this deliberation will lead you to decide whether you require an estimation procedure or a hypothesis test. Note that broad questions — those that do not restrict the conclusions to just the available data — should be taken to apply to the whole population.

The types of statistics we have covered in this book, and their purposes, are:

- **distribution of variables**: to give an idea of how frequently values are observed;
- **single value**: to give the value of a single observational unit;
- **range of values**: to specify the range covered by a specified proportion of observational units;
- **measures of central tendency**: to give an idea of the value about which observations tend to cluster;
- **measures of dispersion**: to give an idea of how spread the values are;
- **measures of association**: to find out whether there is an association between two unrestricted variables;
- **fitted lines**: to fit a straight line summarising the trend in the relationship between two unrestricted variables;
- **index numbers**: to examine changes over time or between different locations;
- **time series**: to examine the history of a variable.

Which of these types are of interest in a particular situation depends on the question to be investigated — for example, a measure of central tendency and/or dispersion may be required.

In the following examples, we investigate the process of choosing statistical procedures by asking a series of standard questions about the situation involved. In each case, choose, or at least indicate how you would choose, a procedure and, if available, a diagram; for estimation procedures and hypothesis tests refer to the corresponding type of statistic in descriptive summaries for the diagrams available. The examples do not involve the first category, *Data collection procedures*.

EXAMPLE VI.1   WORD PROCESSING SURVEY

A survey of an organisation's staff asks them all which word processing package they use, to determine which package the staff most commonly use.

- What is the question to be investigated (including the group to which the conclusions apply)?

  Answer: The question to be investigated is: what word processing package is most commonly used by the organisation's staff?

- What variable(s) are we concerned with here?

  Answer: Word processing package used.

- What type of variable(s) are they?

  Answer: A nominal limited variable.

- Which major category of statistical procedures applies here? Why?

  Answer: Descriptive summaries, because a census has been conducted.

- What type of statistic should we use, given the question to be investigated and the variables involved?

  Answer: Measure of central tendency.

- Which particular statistic or procedure, and diagram, should we use? Why?

  Answer: The mode, because it is the most frequently occurring value, as required, and it is the most appropriate measure for nominal data. A diagram is unecessary in this case.

EXAMPLE VI.1   WORD PROCESSING SURVEY (continued)

Besides indicating which word processing package they used, the staff rated it for ease of use on a 5-point scale ranging from very easy to very difficult. The task is to establish how the staff compared the different word processing packages for their ease of use.

- What is the question to be investigated (including the group to which the conclusions apply)?

  Answer: The question to be investigated is: what is the opinion of the organisation's staff about the ease of use of the different word processing packages?

- What variable(s) are we concerned with here?

  Answer: Word processing package used and *Ease of use.*

- What type of variable(s) are they?

  Answer: Both are limited variables.

- Which major category of statistical procedures applies here? Why?

  Answer: Descriptive summaries, because a census was conducted.

- What type of statistic should we use, given the question to be investigated and the variables involved?

  Answer: Distribution of variables.

- Which particular statistic or procedure, and diagram, should we use? Why?

  Answer: Two-way contingency table with stacked bar chart, because they allow the investigation of the relationship between the two limited variables *Word processing package used* and *Ease of use*. The appropriate percentage has to be chosen. In this case, the most relevant percentages will be those that are expressed as a percentage of the total number in the corresponding category of *Word processing package used*. This will allow us to compare the distributions for the different packages.

EXAMPLE VI.2   MARKETING CORN CHIPS

The marketing manager of a large supermarket chain would like to know if it can be generally said, for that chain, that there is a relationship between shelf space devoted to a particular brand of corn chips and the sales of corn chips. The shelf space and sales of the brand of corn chips in a sample of 12 supermarkets in the chain are obtained for a specific week.

- What is the question to be investigated (including the group to which the conclusions apply)?

  Answer: The question to be investigated is: is the shelf space devoted to the particular brand of corn chips related to the sales of these corn chips for this chain's supermarkets?

- What variable(s) are we concerned with here?

  Answer: Shelf space and *Sales* of the brand of corn chips.

- What type of variable(s) are they?

  Answer: Both are unrestricted variables.

- Which major category of statistical procedures applies here?

  Answer: Hypothesis test, because we want to use a sample to answer a question about the population, and the question has only two possible answers.

- What type of statistic should we use, given the question to be investigated and the variables involved?

  Answer: Measures of association, as we only want to see if the two are related.

- Which particular statistic or procedure, and diagram, should we use? Why?

  Answer: Test for linear correlation, as this will test for a linear relationship between *Shelf space* and *Sales* of the brand of corn chips. The relationship can be illustrated with a scatter diagram.

EXAMPLE VI.3   STUDENT EXPENDITURE

AusStudent wants to determine the proportion of tertiary students in Australia who spend more than $100 on textbooks and stationery. AusStudent organises student union representatives at each Australian university to ask a sample of five fellow students whether they spent more than $100 on textbooks and stationery. The results are collated by the president of each union and sent to AusStudent.

- What is the question to be investigated (including the group to which the conclusions apply)?

  Answer: The question to be investigated is: what proportion of Australian tertiary students spend more than $100 on textbooks and stationery?

- What variable(s) are we concerned with here?

  Answer: Textbook and stationery expenditure.

- What type of variable(s) are they?

  Answer: A limited variable with two values only: less than or equal to $100 and more than $100.

- Which major category of statistical procedures applies here? Why?

  Answer: Estimation procedure, because we want to use a sample to estimate some population quantity.

- What type of statistic should we use, given the question to be investigated and the variables involved?

  Answer: Distribution of variables.

- Which particular statistic or procedure, and diagram, should we use? Why?

  Answer: Confidence interval for the population proportion, as this provides an estimate of the population proportion that indicates the precision with which it is estimated. You could use a bar or column chart to illustrate the proportion spending more and the proportion spending less than $100 on textbooks and stationery.

EXAMPLE VI.4   PRODUCTION TIMES

For a particular product, a company runs the production line to fill an order as soon as it is received. Generally, it receives orders of between 50 and 500 units. To estimate the production time per unit of product, over the last 12 months the company randomly sampled orders for the product in this period. The number of units ordered and the time taken to produce them were determined from the factory's operations record.

- What is the question to be investigated (including the group to which the conclusions apply)?

  Answer: The question to be investigated is: what increase in production time is required for each extra unit of a company's particular product?

- What variable(s) are we concerned with here?

  Answer: Production time and *Order size.*

- What type of variable(s) are they?

  Answer: Both are unrestricted variables.

- Which major category of statistical procedures applies here? Why?

  Answer: Estimation procedure, because we want to use a sample to estimate some population quantity.

- What type of statistic should we use, given the question to be investigated and the variables involved?

  Answer: Fitted lines.

- Which particular statistic or procedure, and diagram, should we use? Why?

  Answer: Confidence interval for the population slope, because that will estimate the population rate of increase in the production time. The diagram to illustrate the slope is the scatter diagram, with the fitted line included; however, it is likely to be unecessary.

EXAMPLE VI.5   SALES STAFF QUALIFICATIONS

The personnel officer of a large retail store wants to know if there is a difference in the amounts sold by different categories of the store's salespeople. The categories of people are: not completed high-school; no tertiary education; holder of a business degree; and holder of a nonbusiness degree. A random sample of ten individuals from each category is selected and the total value of their sales over a month is obtained.

- What is the question to be investigated (including the group to which the conclusions apply)?

  Answer: The question to be investigated is: for the salespeople of a large retail store, do the amounts sold by different categories of people differ?

- What variable(s) are we concerned with here?

  Answer: Category of person and *Value of sales.*

- What type of variable(s) are they?

  Answer: One limited and one unrestricted variable.

- Which major category of statistical procedures applies here? Why?

  Answer: Hypothesis test, because we want to use a sample to answer a question about the population, and the question has only two possible answers.

- What type of statistic should we use, given the question to be investigated and the variables involved?

  Answer: Measure of central tendency.

- Which particular statistic or procedure, and diagram, should we use? Why?

  Answer: One-way analysis of variance, as this will let us investigate the differences between the *Value of sales* population means for each *Category of persons*. The diagrams that could be used to illustrate the results are boxplots, one for each value of the limited variable, a bar chart or a line diagram. As the limited variable is a nominal variable, a bar chart would be used rather than a line diagram. The choice between a bar chart and boxplots is a matter of personal preference.

Summary

We have presented a summary of the statistical procedures to apply for the various combinations of variable types. The procedures appropriate to a particular combination are grouped according to the types of statistics they represent. The choice of a particular procedure, using a series of standard questions, was illustrated for a set of examples. The standard questions involve determining the question to be investigated and the variables involved. This information was used to identify the major category of statistical procedures, the type of statistic and the combination of variable types. The particular statistical procedure can then be obtained from the summary, although sometimes the behaviour of the data must be considered to decide exactly which procedure to employ.

Key terms

- data collection procedures
- descriptive summaries
- distribution of variables
- estimation procedures
- fitted line
- hypothesis tests
- index number
- interval/ratio variable
- limited variable
- major category of statistical procedures
- measure of association
- measure of central tendency
- measure of dispersion
- nominal variable
- ordinal variable
- question to be investigated
- range of values
- single value
- time series
- type of statistic
- unrestricted variable

Exercises

VI.1 A building contractor has built a large number of houses about the same size and value. A real estate appraiser takes a sample of them and assesses the value of each to estimate the typical or average value of all houses of this size and value built by the contractor.

(a) What is the question to be investigated (including the group to which the conclusions apply)?

(b) What variable(s) are we concerned with here?

(c) What type of variable(s) are they?

(d) Which major category of statistical procedures applies here? Why?

(e) What type of statistic should we use, given the question to be investigated and the variables involved?

(f) Which particular statistic or procedure, and diagram, should we use? Why?

VI.2 The purchase decisions made by three stock portfolio managers were studied to see if the purchases that made profits differed between the managers. Purchases made by each manager were randomly sampled and whether or not each purchase showed a profit was recorded.

(a) What is the question to be investigated (including the group to which the conclusions apply)?

(b) What variable(s) are we concerned with here?

(c) What type of variable(s) are they?

(d) Which major category of statistical procedures applies here? Why?

(e) What type of statistic should we use, given the question to be investigated and the variables involved?

(f) Which particular statistic or procedure, and diagram, should we use? Why?

VI.3 A banking group wishes to investigate its customers' use of credit cards to upgrade customer services. The group commissioned a study to see if the average monthly amount ($) owed on credit cards differed between customers who held a Visa card only, those who held only a Bankcard, and those who held both, while taking account of their employment status (professional, nonprofessional, not in labour force and so on). As not all customer records could be examined, a simple random sample of customers was selected and the amount owed at the end of the last month recorded.

(a) What is the question to be investigated (including the group to which the conclusions apply)?

(b) What variable(s) are we concerned with here?

(c) What type of variable(s) are they?

(d) Which major category of statistical procedures applies here? Why?

(e) What type of statistic should we use, given the question to be investigated and the variables involved?

(f) Which particular statistic or procedure, and diagram, should we use? Why?

VI.4 A manufacturer claims that at least 25% of the public prefers her product to others on the market. To check her claim, a simple random sample of individuals is drawn and their preference for the manufacturer's product recorded.

(a) What is the question to be investigated (including the group to which the conclusions apply)?

(b) What variable(s) are we concerned with here?

(c) What type of variable(s) are they?

(d) Which major category of statistical procedures applies here? Why?

(e) What type of statistic should we use, given the question to be investigated and the variables involved?

(f) Which particular statistic or procedure, and diagram, should we use? Why?

VI.5 A life insurance company has introduced a term life insurance policy for its current whole-life policyholders, to compensate for the loss in whole life coverage caused by an inflationary economy. The company examined a sample of its whole-life policyholders to estimate, for all of them, how much whole-life insurance coverage increases as a result of a $1 increase in annual income.

(a) What is the question to be investigated (including the group to which the conclusions apply)?

(b) What variable(s) are we concerned with here?

(c) What type of variable(s) are they?

(d) Which major category of statistical procedures applies here? Why?

(e) What type of statistic should we use, given the question to be investigated and the variables involved?

(f) Which particular statistic or procedure, and diagram, should we use? Why?

VI.6 The manager of a motel knows what proportion of nights she can expect a particular number of rooms in her motel to be vacant. After a new motel was built near hers, she recorded the number of vacant rooms in her motel. Does this data indicate that her pattern of vacancies has changed since the new motel was built? (Note: there are never more than 10 vacant rooms on any one night.)

(a) What is the question to be investigated (including the group to which the conclusions apply)?

(b) What variable(s) are we concerned with here?

    (c) What type of variable(s) are they?

    (d) Which major category of statistical procedures applies here? Why?

    (e) What type of statistic should we use, given the question to be investigated and the variables involved?

    (f) Which particular statistic or procedure, and diagram, should we use? Why?

VI.7 A social scientist wants to know if there is a relationship between a household's disposable monthly income and how much it spends monthly on food. He took a simple random sample of 20 households with two adults and two children and recorded the disposable income and the amount spent on food for the last month for each household.

    (a) What is the question to be investigated (including the group to which the conclusions apply)?

    (b) What variable(s) are we concerned with here?

    (c) What type of variable(s) are they?

    (d) Which major category of statistical procedures applies here? Why?

    (e) What type of statistic should we use, given the question to be investigated and the variables involved?

    (f) Which particular statistic or procedure, and diagram, should we use? Why?

VI.8 A corporation wanted to determine whether the level of its employees' stress-related problems observed on the job was related to the time they took to get to work. The stress and travel times were recorded for a simple random sample of 133 employees. Stress was recorded as high, moderate or low by their supervisor; time taken to get to work was recorded as less than 30 minutes, 30–60 minutes and greater than 60 minutes.

    (a) What is the question to be investigated (including the group to which the conclusions apply)?

    (b) What variable(s) are we concerned with here?

    (c) What type of variable(s) are they?

    (d) Which major category of statistical procedures applies here? Why?

    (e) What type of statistic should we use, given the question to be investigated and the variables involved?

    (f) Which particular statistic or procedure, and diagram, should we use? Why?

VI.9 The Traffic Services division is continually reviewing methods of traffic law enforcement to help reduce the risk of accident and injury to the motorist and pedestrian alike. Compulsory seat belts, random breath testing and speed cameras are just a few of the programs that the division has adopted. The Traffice Services' most recent report presented the number of road crash fatalities for the years 1962–92, along with the date when each program was introduced. Use this information to determine whether the programs have been successful.

(a) What is the question to be investigated (including the group to which the conclusions apply)?

(b) What variable(s) are we concerned with here?

(c) What type of variable(s) are they?

(d) Which major category of statistical procedures applies here? Why?

(e) What type of statistic should we use, given the question to be investigated and the variables involved?

(f) Which particular statistic or procedure, and diagram, should we use? Why?

VI.10 A national supermarket chain has opened several new stores at various locations in metropolitan Adelaide over the past two years. One of the special services these new stores offer is that customers may pay for their purchases with Bankcard, Visa or MasterCard credit cards, cash or an approved cheque. The management selected a simple random sample of 100 customers over a seven-day period and recorded how much each customer spent and what method of payment was used. The managment wished to see whether the typical amount spent by customers differed according to method of payment.

(a) What is the question to be investigated (including the group to which the conclusions apply)?

(b) What variable(s) are we concerned with here?

(c) What type of variable(s) are they?

(d) Which major category of statistical procedures applies here? Why?

(e) What type of statistic should we use, given the question to be investigated and the variables involved?

(f) Which particular statistic or procedure, and diagram, should we use? Why?

VI.11 When the Department of Transport minister announced the privatisation of the State Transport Authority, the move received widespread publicity. A local newspaper took a poll to see what proportion of the general public were in favour of this change in control of the transport facility.

(a) What is the question to be investigated (including the group to which the conclusions apply)?

(b) What variable(s) are we concerned with here?

(c) What type of variable(s) are they?

(d) Which major category of statistical procedures applies here? Why?

(e) What type of statistic should we use, given the question to be investigated and the variables involved?

(f) Which particular statistic or procedure, and diagram, should we use? Why?

VI.12 A domestic air carrier offered a special advanced booking rate to business class passengers flying between Adelaide and the other capital cities. The airline estimated that at least 30% of their business class passengers would take up this offer. During the first three months of operation, they recorded the fares chosen by business class passengers. Does the data show that the policy attracted a substantial increase in business class passengers making advanced bookings during this period?

    (a) What is the question to be investigated (including the group to which the conclusions apply)?

    (b) What variable(s) are we concerned with here?

    (c) What type of variable(s) are they?

    (d) Which major category of statistical procedures applies here? Why?

    (e) What type of statistic should we use, given the question to be investigated and the variables involved?

    (f) Which particular statistic or procedure, and diagram, should we use? Why?

VI.13 Engineers at a city's powerstation want to ensure that adequate supplies are available in sustained periods of above average temperatures. The heavy demands of air-conditioning units must be anticipated so that backup generators can be brought on line to meet peak loads.

    To gain some idea of future requirements in heatwave conditions, they examined their January to March records for the past three years and extracted the daily figures for power demand and temperature. Use this data to estimate the typical power demand for each temperature (as a whole degree), in the range 30–40°C.

    (a) What is the question to be investigated (including the group to which the conclusions apply)?

    (b) What variable(s) are we concerned with here?

    (c) What type of variable(s) are they?

    (d) Which major category of statistical procedures applies here? Why?

    (e) What type of statistic should we use, given the question to be investigated and the variables involved?

    (f) Which particular statistic or procedure, and diagram, should we use? Why?

THE APPLICATION
OF MATHEMATICS

PART VII

INTRODUCTION TO FINANCIAL MATHEMATICS

LEARNING OBJECTIVES

The learning objectives of this introduction to part VII are:

- to gain an overview of the applications of financial mathematics covered in this book;
- to know how to use the Sharp EL-735 when performing financial calculations.

Elementary mathematical techniques can be applied to all kinds of business and personal situations to make optimal use of available resources. For example, individuals and businesses are challenged to find answers to questions demanding the **optimisation** of money.

This part introduces financial mathematics, a set of very useful tools for dealing with questions about how best to manage a single amount of money over a period of time. More complicated problems that involve the balancing of several factors are solved with the operations research technique of **linear programming**, explained in part VIII, *Optimisation*.

EXAMPLE VII.1   OPTIMAL USE OF MONEY

Examples of questions solved using financial mathematics are as follows:

- What is an optimal savings regime?
- What is the best way to obtain finance?
- Should the property mortgage be refinanced when interest rates change?
- What is the best way to pay a fixed expense account?
- Does buying the largest size of a supermarket product ultimately give the best value?

Financial mathematics is a set of rules used by financial organisations, and understanding them allows companies and individuals to organise their financial affairs for optimal results. Central to financial mathematics is the concept of value of money over time. Note that mathematical techniques alone may not be sufficient for problem-solving as they often require statistically collected data. Statistics and mathematics may have to be combined with flair and imagination to provide a realistic solution for a specific problem.

Conventionally, money *received* by a person or entity is regarded as a **positive cashflow**. The money received may be payment for services, the return of a loan or a borrowed amount. In each of these cases, the cashflow amount is given a positive sign. For example, if I borrow $5000, then the cashflow amount is +$5000.

Conversely, money *paid out* by a person or entity is regarded as a **negative cashflow**. The money paid out may be a payment for services, a loan or the repayment of an amount borrowed. In each case, the cashflow amount is assigned a negative sign. For example, if I pay back an amount of $5050, then the cashflow amount is −$5050.

It is important to enter the cashflow amounts correctly into a financial calculator.

Much of the tedium in performing financial calculations manually has been removed with the use of sophisticated calculators and computers. In particular, financial calculators are powerful devices for performing financial calculations and the next section introduces you to one such calculator: the Sharp EL-735.

Introduction to the Sharp EL-735 calculator

The calculator recommended for part VII, *Introduction to financial mathematics*, is the Sharp EL-735. It was chosen because it can be used for statistical calculations with one-variable and two-variable data, and also for financial mathematical calculations.

The calculator is turned on by pressing the $\boxed{\text{ON}}$ key, and turned off by pressing the $\boxed{\text{OFF}}$ key. It has two modes of operation:

1. the **finance mode**, which is the default mode and is used for financial calculations;
2. the **statistics mode**, which is used for statistics calculations.

To change mode, press $\boxed{\text{2nd F}}$ then $\boxed{\text{STAT}}$. This key **toggles** between statistics and finance mode: pressing it will make the calculator change from one to the other.

To set the number of decimal places, press $\boxed{\text{2nd F}}$ $\boxed{\text{TAB}}$, then the number of decimals required; for example, if you need two decimals, press $\boxed{\text{2nd F}}$ $\boxed{\text{TAB}}$ $\boxed{2}$.

The **registers** of the calculator are the memories for storing numbers in calculations for finance and statistics modes. They are cleared by $\boxed{\text{2nd F}}$ $\boxed{\text{CA}}$. (*Note:* As the registers of the calculator are not cleared by turning off the calculator, it is essential that you *press this key combination at the start of every calculation.*)

The **financial mathematics keys** are used for:

- number of time periods $\qquad\qquad\qquad\qquad$ $\boxed{\text{n}}$

- interest rate per time period $\qquad\qquad\qquad$ $\boxed{\text{i}}$

- present value or the amount at the beginning $\quad$ $\boxed{\text{PV}}$

- future value or the amount at the end $\qquad\quad$ $\boxed{\text{FV}}$

- periodic payment made in each time period $\quad$ $\boxed{\text{PMT}}$

Summary

The introduction to this part has given some examples of how mathematics may be applied to find optimal solutions to problems in business. Also, the following useful features of the Sharp EL-735 have been described: important operational steps such as how to turn the calculator on and off; how to obtain either the finance or the statistics mode of operation; how to clear the registers; and commonly used financial mathematics keys.

Key terms

- **finance mode**
- **financial mathematics**
- **financial mathematics key**
- **linear programming**
- **negative cashflow**

- **optimisation**
- **positive cashflow**
- **registers**
- **statistics mode**
- **toggling**

## CHAPTER 21

INTEREST

LEARNING OBJECTIVES

The learning objectives of this chapter are:

- to be able to perform interest calculations when either simple or compound interest rates are involved;
- to be able to convert compound interest rates to effective annual interest rates.

Interest is a financial reward for lending money or the price paid for borrowing money over a length of time. **Nominal interest rate** is usually stated on an annual basis (per annum) but is often calculated over periods shorter than a year, for example, quarterly. Interest accrued may be paid to the account over a different period from the one on which the interest is calculated; for example interest calculated daily but paid monthly. Variations in the interest rate offered, the timespan of such offers, and how **accrued interest** is paid into accounts all provide fertile ground for financial mathematics techniques.

Interest rates vary from one financial institution to another. Although questions about how these interest rates are set and who decides on the rates are beyond the scope of this book, we recommend you read the discussion on who sets interest rates in *Choice* (1991).

21.1 Simple interest

Simple interest is calculated for an agreed **time period** and paid on the original sum of money borrowed or invested. It is not concerned with the speed at which the money is returned within that agreed period. Simple interest is the basic unit for all financial mathematical calculations.

21.1.1 Notation

The following notation is used for simple interest calculations, with the corresponding keys of the calculator shown:

P is the **principal**, **present value** or original amount that is lent or borrowed;

$\boxed{\text{PV}}$

t is the total time of the loan expressed as whole numbers and/or decimal parts of a year — for a year t is 1; for 2 years t is 2; for 6 months t is 0.5;

n is the total number of time periods for which interest accrues on the loan — n is 1 for simple interest;

$\boxed{\text{n}}$

j is the nominal annual interest rate;

i is the **interest rate for the time period** ($i = j \times t$);

$\boxed{\text{i}}$

I_n is the interest accrued during time period n. l_1 is the total interest for simple interest;

S_n is the total amount, including interest accrued, called **future value**, at the end of the nth time period.

$\boxed{\text{FV}}$

21.1.2 Calculations

When making simple interest calculations, we obtain the interest rate for the time period by multiplying the nominal interest rate by the length of the loan in years: $i = j \times t$.

The interest amount, at the end of that time period, is calculated by multiplying the interest rate for the period by the amount borrowed: $I_1 = P \times i$.

Total owed is calculated by adding the interest to the original amount:

$$\begin{aligned} S_1 &= P + I_1 \\ &= P + Pi \\ &= P(1 + i) \end{aligned}$$

EXAMPLE 21.1   CALCULATING AMOUNT TO BE REPAID ON A LOAN

A business owner borrows from relatives $15000 for 6 months to finance repairs to the computers in an accountancy consulting business. The relatives are happy to lend the money with no security, but all agree to an interest rate of the current credit union rate of 7.75% per annum plus 2% per annum to cover costs and inconvenience. How much would be repaid?

Collecting the information together:

$$P = \$15000$$
$$j = 9.75\% \text{ per annum} = 0.0975$$
$$t = 6 \text{ months} = 0.5 \text{ year}$$

Calculating the interest rate for the time period:

$$\begin{aligned} i &= j \times t \\ &= 0.0975 \times 0.5 \\ &= 0.04875 \end{aligned}$$

Calculating the interest amount for the time period:

$$I_i = P \times i$$
$$= 15\,000 \times 0.04875$$
$$= \$731.25$$

How much does the business owner repay to the relatives?

$$S_1 = P + I_1$$
$$= 15\,000 + 731.25$$
$$= \$15\,731.25$$

Using the calculator

The amount to be repaid can be calculated in the financial mode of the calculator by using the following entry sequence:

1. Toggle the calculator so that payment is made at the end of the time period.

2. Clear the registers.

3. Enter the amount of 15 000 as PV (put it in as a positive, that is, money paid in).

4. Enter the 6 months interest, as a percentage, i .

5. Enter the number of time periods as 1, into n .

6. Compute the total amount with FV (which will be negative, that is, money paid out).

Using Sharp EL-735:

2nd F BGN/END so that BGN does not appear on the display

2nd F CA

15 000 PV 9.75 × .5 = i 1 n COMP FV

Answer: –$15 731.25. The business owner will repay $15 731.25.

The interest paid, I_1, can be calculated from the amount repaid with the following entry sequence, where RCL means recall.

Using Sharp EL-735:

RCL FV + RCL FV =

Answer: –$731.25. That is, $731.25 interest will be paid out.

Notes

- If calculating with a formula, enter interest in decimal form.

- If using the Sharp EL-735, enter interest into $\boxed{i}$ as a percentage.

21.1.3 Rearranging formulae

As long as only one variable is unknown in a formula, rearranging the formula will allow you to calculate the missing variable. If I_1 and P are known, then rearranging the formula $I_1 = P \times i$ leads to one for the interest rate for the time period $i = I_1 \div P$.

EXAMPLE 21.2   CALCULATING THE GROSS ANNUAL RATE OF RETURN

Real estate agents often quote the annual rental received for an investment property as a percentage of the asking price of the property. This provides a **gross annual rate of return**: it is the amount of return on the investment, not taking into account expenses incurred in obtaining the return.

A unit was advertised for $75 000. The advertisement also stated that the unit was rented for $125 per week. The real estate agent claimed that the unit was returning nearly 9%. Is this correct?

Collecting the information together:

$75 000 is paid out

$125 per week is equivalent to $125 \times 52 = $6500 per year received

So
$$i = I_1 \div P$$
$$= 6500 \div 75\,000$$
$$= 0.0867 \text{ (as a percentage} = 8.67\%)$$

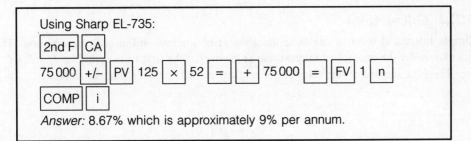

Using Sharp EL-735:

$\boxed{\text{2nd F}}\ \boxed{\text{CA}}$

$\boxed{75\,000}\ \boxed{+/-}\ \boxed{\text{PV}}\ \boxed{125}\ \boxed{\times}\ \boxed{52}\ \boxed{=}\ \boxed{+}\ \boxed{75\,000}\ \boxed{=}\ \boxed{\text{FV}}\ \boxed{1}\ \boxed{n}$

$\boxed{\text{COMP}}\ \boxed{i}$

Answer: 8.67% which is approximately 9% per annum.

The formula $S_1 = P(1 + i)$ can also be rearranged to yield expressions for the quantities P and i, as follows:

$$P = \frac{S_1}{1 + i}$$

$$i = \frac{S_1 - P}{P}$$

21.2   Compound interest

Compound interest is a refinement of basic simple interest. The total time of the loan is divided into time periods, and for each of these interest is calculated and added to the original amount in the account, usually at the end of each time period. This means that interest is calculated for both the original amount and the interest that has accrued to that time. The result is that more interest is accrued by compound interest than simple interest. Most financial institutions calculate long-term interest this way. Important factors are the original amount loaned or borrowed, the size of the interest rate, the length of time period for interest calculations, and when the interest is added to the account.

21.2.1   Notation

The following notation used with compound interest is similar to that used for simple interest calculations, but each time period for calculation must be clearly defined:

P is the principal, present value or original amount lent or borrowed; $\boxed{\text{PV}}$

t is the total time of the loan expressed as whole numbers and/or decimal parts of a year — for a year t is 1, for 2 years t is 2, for 6 months t is 0.5;

y is the number of time periods in which interest is calculated, accumulated or accrues in *one* year — one year has 2 six-months, 4 quarters, 12 months;

n is the number of time periods for the loan ($n = t \times y$); $\boxed{\text{n}}$

j is the nominal annual interest rate;

i is the interest rate for the time period ($i = j \div y$); $\boxed{\text{i}}$

I_n is the interest accrued during time period n;

I_T is the total interest accumulated over the total time;

S_n is the total amount, including interest accrued, called future value, at the end of the nth time period. $\boxed{\text{FV}}$

21.2.2   Calculations

Simple interest is used to calculate the amount of interest within each time period. The calculation for the amount of interest due at the end of the first time period is: $I_1 = P \times i$.

The sum accrued at this stage is the original amount plus the interest amount:

$$\begin{aligned} S_1 &= P + I_1 \\ &= P + Pi \\ &= P(1 + i) \end{aligned}$$

At the end of the second time period, similar calculations are made but the amount is now S_1:

$$\begin{aligned} I_2 &= S_1 \times i \\ &= P(1+i)i \qquad \text{since } S_1 = P(1+i) \text{ from before} \\ S_2 &= S_1 + I_2 \\ &= P(1+i) + P(1+i)i \\ &= P(1+i)^2 \end{aligned}$$

Similarly,
$$I_3 = P(1 + i)^2 i$$
$$S_3 = P(1 + i)^3$$

Expressions could be written down for I_4, S_4 and so on. However, the above expressions lead us to conclude that the general pattern is:
$$I_n = P(1 + i)^{(n - 1)} i$$
$$S_n = P(1 + i)^n$$

S_n is the total amount received at the end, called the future value (FV), and it follows an exponential growth.

The **total interest** received is the difference between the final amount and the original amount. That is, $I_T = S_n - P$.

EXAMPLE 21.3   AMOUNT IN THE ACCOUNT AT THE END OF THE TOTAL TIME

Term deposits are often used by people wishing to store money they do not need for the present.

An inheritance of $30 000 was put in a term deposit for 2 years, where interest of 5.15% per annum was accrued monthly. What amount was in the account at the end of 2 years?

Collecting the information together:

The time period used here is a month.

$P = \$30\,000$

$j = 5.15\%$ per annum $= 0.0515$

$i = 0.4292\%$ per month (5.15% per annum ÷ 12)

$\quad = 0.004292$

$n = 24$ months (2 years × 12)

Now $\quad S_{24} = P(1 + i)^{24}$

$\quad\quad = 30\,000(1 + 0.004292)^{24}$

$\quad\quad = \$33\,247.41$

Using Sharp EL-735:

2nd F | CA

(30 000 is paid out)

30 000 | +/– | PV | 5.15 | 2nd F | i | 2 | 2nd F | n | COMP | FV

Answer: $33 247.41

Monthly calculations occur so often that the calculator has two special functions:

2nd F | i | divides the annual interest by 12 to give monthly interest;

2nd F | n | multiplies years by 12 to give the number of months.

21.2.3 Comparing simple and compound interest

Simple interest calculation on an initial amount P, with interest i in each time period and n time periods, results in an overall $S_n = P + P \times i \times n = P(1 + in)$. This is a relationship where S_n is proportional to i. *Compound* interest under the same conditions results in $S_n = P(1 + i)^n$. This is an exponential relationship.

The final amount under compound interest will exceed that under simple interest for $n > 1$. However, the gap between them depends on the sizes of P, i and n. The differences resulting from simple versus compound interest are greater if the amounts are larger, the interest rates higher and the number of time periods greater.

EXAMPLE 21.4   COMPARING THE AMOUNTS RESULTING FROM SIMPLE AND COMPOUND INTEREST CALCULATIONS

This example is based on an account amount of \$100 000, where interest of 20% per annum is accrued monthly. What amount will be in the account at the end of 2 years, if (1) simple and (2) compound interest methods are used to accrue interest?

The formulae to compute the total amount in the account at the end of each time period are:

1. *for simple interest:* $S_n = P(1 + in) = 100\,000(1 + 0.20n)$
2. *for compound interest:* $S_n = P(1 + i)^n = 100\,000(1 + 0.20)^n$

The results of using these formulae for each of the 24 time periods are in table 21.1 and plotted in figure 21.1. Initially, the total amount in the account is very similar for the simple and compound interest. However, the total amount gradually becomes greater for compound interest. After 24 months, compounding gives \$8691 more interest than the simple method of calculation.

Table 21.1   The total amount accrued under simple and compound interest

Time period (month)	Total amount (\$)	
	Simple interest	Compound interest
1	101 666.67	101 666.67
2	103 333.33	103 361.11
3	105 000.00	105 083.80
4	106 666.67	106 835.19
5	108 333.33	108 615.78
6	110 000.00	110 426.04
7	111 666.67	112 266.48
8	113 333.33	114 137.58
9	115 000.00	116 039.88
10	116 666.67	117 973.88
11	118 333.33	119 940.11
12	120 000.00	121 939.11

Table 21.1   (*continued*)

Time period (month)	Total amount ($)	
	Simple interest	Compound interest
13	121 666.67	123 971.43
14	123 333.33	126 037.62
15	125 000.00	128 138.24
16	126 666.67	130 273.88
17	128 333.33	132 445.11
18	130 000.00	134 652.53
19	131 666.67	136 896.74
20	133 333.33	139 178.35
21	135 000.00	141 497.99
22	136 666.67	143 856.29
23	138 333.33	146 253.90
24	140 000.00	148 691.46

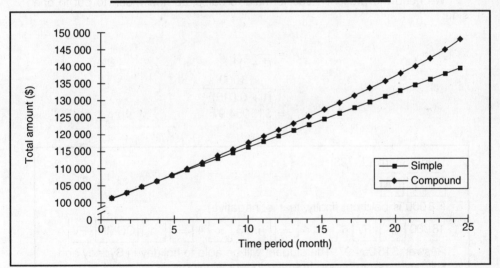

Figure 21.1   The total amount accrued under simple and compound interest

21.2.4 Rearranging the formula

Provided at least three of the variables are known, the formula $S_n = P(1 + i)^n$ can be rearranged to find the remaining variable. There are three rearrangements of the formula. While each version can be calculated with the formula and a calculator that has exponential and logarithmic functions, calculation is much easier with the Sharp EL-735. The three known values are entered into the registers and the fourth is computed by the calculator.

Present value

This version of the formula is useful for calculating how much lump sum to put aside now, as the present value, to meet a future lump sum commitment. We assume that the interest rate will continue over the time of the investment and that compound interest applies.

$$P = \frac{S_n}{(1 + i)^n}$$

EXAMPLE 21.5   PRESENT VALUE OF A FUTURE NEED

A hard-working part-time student won $20 000 in a lottery. She would like to take a holiday with some of the proceeds, but will need a new car in 3 years' time for an estimated cost of $18 000. She decides to set aside a lump sum with a credit union that pays an annual rate of 6% with interest added into the account on a quarterly basis. How much should she put away now?

Collecting the information together:

$$i = 1.5\% \text{ per quarter } (6\% \div 4) = 0.015$$
$$n = 12 \text{ quarters } (3 \times 4)$$
$$S_{12} = \$18\,000$$

We need the present value formula to calculate how much to put to one side:

$$P = \frac{S_n}{(1 + i)^n}$$
$$= \frac{18\,000}{(1 + 0.015)^{12}}$$
$$= \$15\,054.97$$

Using Sharp EL-735:

| 2nd F | CA |

(18 000 is paid out finally, that is, negative)

18 000 | +/− | FV | 6 | ÷ | 4 | = | i | 3 | × | 4 | = | n | COMP | PV

Answer: $15 054.97. The student will be able to holiday in Sydney and still have some change from the lottery winnings!

Number of time periods

This version of the formula is useful for calculating how long we need to achieve a goal with a specific lump sum available and knowledge of the interest rates.

$$n = \frac{\ell n[S_n/P]}{\ell n[1 + i]} \quad \text{where } \ell n \text{ means logarithm to the base } e.$$

Interest rate for the time period

This version of the formula is useful for calculating interest rate for the time period we need in order to achieve a goal over a set time, with a specific lump sum that can be put to one side now.

$$i = (S_n/P)^{1/n} - 1$$

21.3 Effective annual interest rate

Compound interest for several time periods yields a higher payout than simple interest yields for the same nominal interest rate. The compound interest calculation could be restated as a simple interest calculation with a higher annual interest rate. This interest rate is called the **effective annual interest rate** (r).

The amount in the account after one year, using simple interest with a nominal annual interest rate of r, is given by $S_1 = P + Pr$. The amount in the account after the y time periods in one year, using compound interest with an interest for each time period of i, is given by $S_y = P(1 + i)^y$. These will give the same amount if:

$$P + Pr = P(1 + i)^y$$
$$1 + r = (1 + i)^y$$
$$r = (1 + i)^y - 1$$

where r is called the effective annual interest rate.

This is very useful for comparing different compounding interest systems when there are no other factors such as account fees and risk of investment to be considered.

EXAMPLE 21.6 COMPARING EFFECTIVE ANNUAL INTEREST RATES FOR BUILDING SOCIETY AND CREDIT UNION SAVINGS ACCOUNTS

Consider the following possibilities for savings accounts: a permanent building society offers 4.75% per annum compounded monthly; and a credit union offers 5.25% per annum compounded six-monthly. What is the effective interest rate in each case and which is the more profitable account?

Collecting the information together:

Building society	Credit union
$i = 0.0475 \div 12 = 0.00396$	$i = 0.0525 \div 2 = 0.02625$
$y = 12$	$y = 2$

Computing the effective annual interest rates:

Building society
$r = (1 + i)^y - 1$
$\quad = (1 + 0.000396)^{12} - 1$
$\quad = 0.0485$ or 4.85%

Credit union
$r = (1 + i)^y - 1$
$\quad = (1 + 0.02625)^2 - 1$
$\quad = 0.0532$ or 5.32%

These calculations are easy when the calculator is used.

Using Sharp EL-735:

| 2nd F | CA |

Building society

12 | 2nd F | | ->EFF | 4.75 | = |

Answer: 4.85% effective annual interest rate.

Credit union

2 | 2nd F | | ->EFF | 5.25 | = |

Answer: 5.32% effective annual interest rate.
The credit union is still the best option but the gap is not as much as for the quoted rates.

21.4 Chapter summary

This chapter has shown us how to perform simple financial mathematics calculations under different conditions and we have encountered new terminology such as present and future values and effective annual interest rates. Both formula and financial calculator methods of calculation have been shown.

21.5 Key terms

- accrued interest
- compound interest
- effective annual interest rate (r)
- future value (S_n or FV)
- gross annual rate of return
- interest
- interest rate for the time period

- nominal interest rate (j)
- present value (P or PV)
- principal (P or PV)
- simple interest
- term deposit
- time period
- total interest (I_T)

21.6   Exercises

21.1

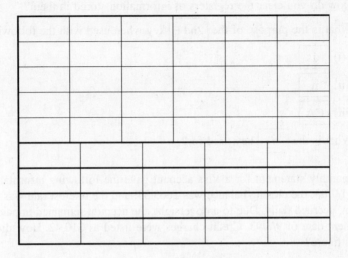

Use the grid above to indicate the position of the following keys on the Sharp EL-735 calculator. Also describe what the key is used for.

(a) $\boxed{+/-}$ (h) $\boxed{\text{STAT}}$ toggle key

(b) $\boxed{\text{2nd F}}$ (i) $\boxed{\text{OFF}}$

(c) $\boxed{\text{CA}}$ (j) $\boxed{\text{ON}}$

(d) $\boxed{\text{COMP}}$ (k) $\boxed{\text{PMT}}$

(e) $\boxed{\text{FV}}$ (l) $\boxed{\text{PV}}$

(f) $\boxed{\text{i}}$ (m) $\boxed{\text{RCL}}$

(g) $\boxed{\text{n}}$ (n) $\boxed{\text{BGN/END}}$ toggle key

21.2 Use your Sharp EL-735 to perform the following steps. Record the answer in each case.

(a) 9.5 $\boxed{\text{i}}$ (e) $\boxed{\text{RCL}}$ $\boxed{\text{i}}$

(b) 9.5 $\boxed{\text{2nd F}}$ $\boxed{\text{i}}$ (f) $\boxed{\text{RCL}}$ $\boxed{\text{n}}$

(c) 2 $\boxed{\text{n}}$ (g) 100 000 $\boxed{+/-}$ $\boxed{\text{PV}}$

(d) 2 $\boxed{\text{2nd F}}$ $\boxed{\text{n}}$

21.3   Answer the following questions about the Sharp EL-735 calculator.

(a) How do you toggle between financial mode and statistics mode?

(b) How do you clear the registers of information stored in them?

(c) What is the purpose of the ⎡2nd F⎤ key when used with the following keys:

(i) ⎡ i ⎤

(ii) ⎡ n ⎤

(iii) ⎡ CA ⎤

(d) What is the ⎡ +/− ⎤ key used for?

21.4   The monthly statement for a Visa account gave the following information: the date was 11/7/93; the closing balance was $663.33; and the interest rate was 19.750% per annum, accrued daily. Due to an oversight, the account remained unpaid by the next statement date of 9/8/93. Credit charges were listed as $10.42. How did Visa arrive at this figure?

21.5   A house is advertised for sale for $520 000 with 12% rental guaranteed in the first year. What amount must be charged for the weekly rent?

21.6   Local government rates are usually paid annually. A rates assessment claims that $722.05 must be paid immediately. The householder would otherwise have placed the money in a 12-month term deposit at an interest rate of 4.25% per annum, calculated and accrued annually. Under these conditions, what would the rates money be worth to the householder in 12 months' time?

21.7   A home unit in a desirable location is offered for sale at $125 000 and rent of equivalent units is $135 per week.

(a) What would a real estate agent claim as the annual rate of return of the property?

(b) What assumption(s) have been made in making this claim?

(c) What other factors should be taken into account to give a more realistic picture of the return to the investor?

21.8   A department store advertises 6 months interest-free terms on the purchase of a phone/fax machine costing $999. What is a reasonable cash offer to make for the item, given that finance company interest rates were 6% per annum at the time of the sale, calculated and accrued monthly?

21.9   A student in the last year of a university course needs to borrow $500 to buy some textbooks. The funds will be needed for three months until some part-time work brings a cashflow. A relative offers to lend the money as long as the return is the same as bank interest for their account. How much should be repaid if their account is:

(a) a high performance passbook (deeming account) which pays 4% per annum accrued quarterly?

(b) with a permanent building society which pays 4.75% per annum accrued monthly?

21.10 Private school fees of $1150 must be paid in three months' time. What lump sum do I need to set aside now:

(a) in my ordinary bank account which is returning 3.75% per annum accrued monthly?

(b) in my permanent building society account which is returning 4% per annum accrued monthly?

21.11 Many retired people use the interest from a lump sum investment for their living expenses. In recent years there have been many complaints about the reduced income of retirees because the interest rates are lower than they were. Consider the following situations:

- A retired couple have invested $250 000 for one year at 13% per annum, calculated and accrued monthly, and inflation is 9.4% over the year.
- A retired couple have invested $250 000 for one year at 5.2% per annum, calculated and accrued monthly, and inflation is 1.2% over the year.

(a) Which couple is better off after one year? Give reasons for your answer.

(b) What other factors should be taken into account as the couple continue their retirement?

21.12 Income and growth bonds give debentures, which are considered one of the safest fixed interest investments. The investors usually have first call on a company's assets. An investor has $5000 to invest for 2 years and has decided to place the money in income and growth bond debentures. The options for interest per annum and time period for interest payments are given in table 21.2. Calculate the effective annual interest rate for each option.

Table 21.2 Interest rates for income and growth debentures

Interest per annum (%)	Frequency of interest payment	Effective annual interest rate (%)
5.75	Annual	
5.6	Quarterly	
5.6	Monthly	

Source: abstracted from Australian Guarantee Corporation Limited (1993)

21.13 In 1989 an industrial warehouse was purchased for $61 500 with a tenant paying $700 per month.
(a) What was the gross annual rate of return for the property?
(b) Calculate the value and rental of the property for 1990–2, assuming that they have kept up with inflation; use the values of the Australian consumer price index in table 21.3 as a measure of inflation from 1989 to 1992.

Table 21.3   Australian CPI, values and rents for 1989–92

	Year			
	1989	1990	1991	1992
Australian CPI (%)	100.0	107.3	110.7	111.8
Value ($000s)	61.5			
Rent ($ per month)	700			

Source: abstracted from Australian Bureau of Statistics (1994b; 1992; 1983–92)

(c) If the rent in 1992 was actually $860 per month:
   (i) what was the gross rate of return on the investment?
   (ii) how did the gross annual rate of return change?
(d) In 1993, after negotiation with the long-term tenant, the monthly rental was renegotiated to $800.
   (i) What information do you need so that you can comment on the gross rate of return this time?
   (ii) Obtain the information you require from appropriate sources.
   (iii) Calculate the gross annual rate of return for 1993.
   (iv) Compare the gross annual rates of return for the years 1989, 1992 and 1993.
(e) If the original purchase amount had been placed in a well-managed cash trust for the five years from 1989 to 1993, the average return would have been 10.69% per year. Would the investor have been better off placing the money in the property purchased or putting the amount in a well-managed cash trust?

CHAPTER 22

ANNUITIES

LEARNING OBJECTIVES

The learning objectives of this chapter are:
- to understand the term annuity;
- to understand the difference between ordinary annuity and annuity due;
- to be able to compute the present value, future value or periodic payment for an ordinary annuity and for an annuity due;
- to understand the amortisation of a debt;
- to be able to calculate the present value, periodic payment or number of time periods for the amortisation of a debt.

Chapter 21, *Interest*, showed that the simple interest calculation is basic to all interest payments. Compound interest was shown as a refinement of simple interest where interest is calculated from both the original amount and the interest accrued up to that point. Calculations thus far have involved a single amount, either loaned or borrowed, repaid with a single amount. Many financial situations are more dynamic than this.

Savings in an account could involve one or more of the following kinds of savings:
- one initial deposit;
- regular periodic savings;
- variable deposits made irregularly.

Withdrawals from the savings account could take equivalent forms. Borrowing and repaying have possibilities similar to those of saving and withdrawing.

A sequence of equal **periodic payments** occurs so commonly in finance that it has been given the special name **annuity**. The time between payments is referred to as the **time period**. Further, it is usually agreed that **interest** will be accrued for each of these time periods. Annuities are used for several purposes:

- saving for a special purpose — for example, buying a new car, taking a trip overseas;
- financing a regular source of income from savings — for example, retirement;
- borrowing regularly in anticipation of future repayment — for example, reverse mortgage;
- repaying a mortgage — for example, business, investment, family home.

The mathematical calculations for annuities are used widely by business organisations and individuals. There are two types of annuities, for which the calculations are different:

1. an **ordinary annuity** for which payments are made at the end of the time period;
2. an **annuity due** for which the payments are made at the beginning of the time period.

Using Sharp EL-735:

Set annuity type in the Sharp EL-735 by pressing $\boxed{\text{2nd F}}$ $\boxed{\text{BGN/END}}$.

These keys toggle between the two types of annuities. The calculator display shows either:

1. nothing for payment at the end — ordinary annuity; or
2. BGN for payment at the beginning — annuity due.

Notation

The following notation is used for annuity calculations, with the corresponding keys of the calculator shown:

p is the regular, equal payment called the periodic payment; $\boxed{\text{PMT}}$

i is the interest rate for the time period; $\boxed{\text{i}}$

P is the **principal, present value** or original amount that is lent or borrowed; $\boxed{\text{PV}}$

n is the total number of time periods for which interest accrues on the loan; $\boxed{\text{n}}$

S_n is the total amount, including interest accrued, called **future value**, at the
end of the nth time period. $\boxed{\text{FV}}$

22.1   Ordinary annuity

This type of annuity has payments *at the end of each time period*, as shown on the time-line diagram in figure 22.1. It is commonly used for repaying mortgages.

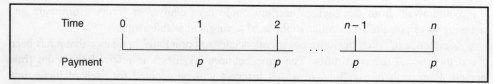

Figure 22.1   Payments for an ordinary annuity

The basic steps involved in an ordinary annuity are as follows:

1. periodic payment is made at the end of each time period;
2. simple interest is paid on the total amount in the account at the beginning of the time period, using the interest rate for the time period;
3. the interest calculated is added to the total amount in the account.

These steps are shown in figure 22.2. Note that the previous balance, plus the interest on it, is obtained by multiplying the previous balance by $(1 + i)$.

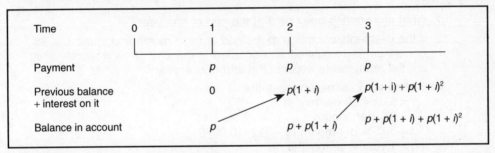

Figure 22.2 Steps in an ordinary annuity

The pattern for the amount in the account at the end of time period n is:

$$S_n = p + p(1 + i) + p(1 + i)^2 + p(1 + i)^3 + \ldots + p(1 + i)^{n-1}$$

This is called a geometric series. It has the property that the sum is $S_n = \dfrac{p[(1 + i)^n - 1]}{i}$.

Although this formula appears complex, the Sharp EL-735 is very easy to use for the calculation. How the geometric series equals the formula is explained as follows:

$$S_n = p + p(1 + i) + p(1 + i)^2 + p(1 + i)^3 + \ldots + p(1 + i)^{n-1}$$

Multiplying S_n by $(1 + i)$ makes each term one power higher than before:

$$(1 + i)S_n = p(1 + i) + p(1 + i)^2 + p(1 + i)^3 + \ldots + p(1 + i)^{n-1} + p(1 + i)^n$$

Taking the difference between the two series will make most of the terms disappear, leaving only the last term of $(1 + i)S_n$ and the first term of S_n on the righthand side:

$$(1 + i)S_n - S_n = p(1 + i)^n - p$$

Multiplying out the lefthand side:

$$S_n + iS_n - S_n = p(1 + i)^n - p$$

Collecting terms on the lefthand side:

$$iS_n = p(1 + i)^n - p$$
$$iS_n = p[(1 + i)^n - 1]$$
$$S_n = \frac{p[(1 + i)^n - 1]}{i}$$

The total interest paid is the difference between the future value and the present value:

$$I_T = S_n - P$$

EXAMPLE 22.1   COMPARING THE APPARENT PAYMENT TOWARDS A LOAN WITH THE ACCRUED VALUE UNDER AN ORDINARY ANNUITY

A family is paying off a loan from a financial institution by monthly payments of $1354.29.

1. What amount has been paid at the end of one year?

2. If the payments are made at the end of each month and interest of 9% per annum is calculated and accrued at the end of each month, what are the repayments worth at the end of one year?

Collecting the information together:

p = $1354.29 per month

j = 9% per annum

i = 0.75% per month (9 ÷ 12) = 0.0075

n = 1 year = 12 months

1. After 1 year:

$p \times n$ = 1354.29 × 12

= $16 251.48

2. After 1 year, but taking into account the interest:

$$S_n = \frac{p[(1 + i)^n - 1]}{i}$$

$$= \frac{1354.29[(l + 0.0075)^{12} - 1]}{0.0075}$$

= $16 938.90

When interest is taken into account, the actual value of the repayments exceeds the apparent value by $687.42.

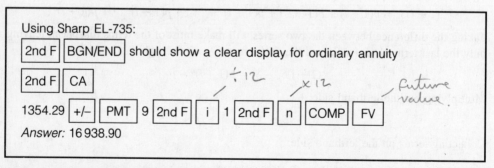

Using Sharp EL-735:

2nd F BGN/END should show a clear display for ordinary annuity

2nd F CA

1354.29 +/− PMT 9 2nd F i 1 2nd F n COMP FV

Answer: 16 938.90

22.2   Periodic payment

As shown in section 22.1, *Ordinary annuity*, the equation for the amount saved for an ordinary annuity is:

$$S_n = \frac{p[(1 + i)^n - 1]}{i}$$

The periodic payment can be found if S_n, i and n are all known by rearranging the above formula to yield:

$$p = \frac{S_n \times i}{(1 + i)^n - 1}$$

This relationship is particularly useful in the case of a sinking fund.

Sinking fund

A **sinking fund** is a special fund, set aside by annuity payments, for large budget items such as replacing business computer equipment, buying a car or painting the house. The future cost of such items is estimated first. Equal periodic deposits are then made into an account at the end of each time period, accruing interest in each time period so that the fund reaches the required amount with the final deposit.

EXAMPLE 22.2   CALCULATING THE SINKING FUND FOR BUYING A CAR

Find the amount we should put aside each quarter to accommodate a fund of $40 000 to buy a car in 5 years' time. Assume that interest will continue at the nominal rate of 3.75% per annum accruing quarterly.

Collecting the information together:

$S_n = \$40\,000$ *Final. amount*
$j = 3.75\%$ per annum
$i = 0.9375\%$ per quarter $(3.75 \div 4) = 0.009375$
$n = 20$ quarters (5×4)

The amount to be set aside each quarter is calculated as follows:

$$p = \frac{S_n \times i}{(1 + i)^n - 1}$$
$$= \frac{40\,000 \times 0.009\,375}{(1 + 0.009\,375)^{20} - 1}$$
$$= \$1827.69 \text{ each quarter.}$$

Using Sharp EL-735:

2nd F BGN/END should show a clear display for ordinary annuity

2nd F CA

40 000 +/− FV 3.75 ÷ 4 = i 5 × 4 = n COMP PMT

Answer: 1827.69

22.3   Amortisation under an ordinary annuity

In section 21.2, *Compound interest*, the sum (future value) S_n of a principal amount (present value) P, using compound interest at the rate of i per time period, for n time periods, was shown to be:

$$S_n = P(1 + i)^n$$

In section 22.1, *Ordinary annuity*, the sum (future value) of an ordinary annuity of p periodic payments, paid at the end of each of n time periods, where interest is accruing at the rate of i per time period, was found to be:

$$S_n = \frac{p[(1 + i)^n - 1]}{i}$$

In many personal and business situations, such as a property mortgage, financing a loan involves agreement that the borrowed principal plus accrued interest will be paid in full to the lender, with a series of equal payments under an ordinary annuity approach by the borrower.

A debt is said to be **amortised** when the amount borrowed, plus the interest accrued, is paid in full, usually by means of equal periodic payments. This occurs when the compound interest sum (future value) equals the annuity sum (future value). The compound interest sum represents the amount the lender would *expect* to be the future value of the amount borrowed after n periods. The annuity sum represents the *actual* value to the lender of the payments received from the borrower. When these are equal the debt has been paid in full. That is,

$$S_n = P(1 + i)^n = \frac{p[(1 + i)^n - 1]}{i}$$

Provided three of P, p, i and n are known, these formulae can be rearranged to give information about the fourth.

EXAMPLE 22.3   AMORTISATION OF A HOUSE LOAN

The sum of $100 000 was borrowed to finance the purchase of a house, with interest at 9% per annum calculated and accrued monthly. The financial institution requires repayment of $899.73 at the end of each month. What is the compound future value and the annuity future value for this loan after 20 years?

1.   What is the expected value of the loan to the financial institution after 20 years?

Collecting the information together:

$P = \$100\,000$

$j = 9\%$ per annum

$i = 0.75\%$ per month $(9 \div 12) = 0.0075$

$n = 240$ months (20×12)

The expected value is a compound interest calculation:

$$S_n = P(1 + i)^n$$
$$= 100\,000(1 + 0.0075)^{240}$$
$$= \$600\,915.15$$

Using Sharp EL-735:

2nd F	CA

100 000 | +/− | PV | 9 | 2nd F | i | 20 | 2nd F | n | COMP | FV

Answer: 600 915.15

---

2. What is the actual value of the repayments received from the borrower over 20 years?

Collecting the information together:

p = \$899.73
j = 9% per annum
i = 0.75% per month = 0.0075
n = 240 months

The actual value is an annuity calculation:

$$S_n = \frac{p[(1 + i)^n - 1]}{i}$$
$$= \frac{899.73[(1 + 0.0075)^{240} - 1]}{0.0075}$$
$$= \$600\,917.85$$

Using Sharp EL-735:

2nd F	BGN/END	should show a clear display for ordinary annuity

2nd F	CA

899.73 | +/− | PMT | 9 | 2nd F | i | 20 | 2nd F | n | COMP | FV

Answer: 600 917.85

---

3. Has the loan been discharged after 20 years?

Yes, the total amount repaid is \$600 915.15 for an original loan of \$100 000. (There is a slight rounding error.)

22.4 Present value when amortising under an ordinary annuity

As pointed out in section 22.3, *Amortisation under an ordinary annuity*, the future value can be determined by

$$S_n = P(1 + i)^n \text{ (compound interest)}$$

Future value of current money.

and

Future value of annuity

$$S_n = \frac{p[(1 + i)^n - 1]}{i} \text{ (ordinary annuity).}$$

These two expressions are equated to yield:

$$P(1 + i)^n = \frac{p[(1 + i)^n - 1]}{i}$$

and then rearranged to find an expression for the present value P, in terms of p, i and n:

$$P = \frac{p}{i}[1 - (1 + i)^{-n}]$$

EXAMPLE 22.4   EXAMINING PRIZE ALTERNATIVES TO DECIDE WHICH IS BETTER

The sum of $100 000 is the prize offered by a lottery. An alternative to this prize is the offer of $2000 a month for 5 years. Are these prize options equivalent now, if interest rates are likely to continue at 3.75% over the 5 years and interest is accrued monthly? In the context of this section, the question can be answered by computing the present value of the alternative; further, the periodic payment, interest and number of time periods are known.

Collecting the information together:

$p = \$2000$
$j = 3.75\%$ per annum
$i = 0.3125\%$ per month $(3.75 \div 12) = 0.003125$
$n = 60$ months (5×12)

Using the formula for present value:

$$P = \frac{p}{i}[1 - (1 + i)^{-n}]$$

$$= \frac{2000}{0.003125}[1 - (1 + 0.003125)^{-60}]$$

$$= \$109\,266.22$$

Thus the alternative has better value. Note, however, that with cash in hand you may be able to negotiate a more favourable interest rate.

Using Sharp EL-735:

| 2nd F | BGN/END | should show a clear display for ordinary annuity

| 2nd F | CA |

2000 | +/– | PMT | 3.75 | 2nd F | i | 5 | 2nd F | n | COMP | PV

Answer: 109 266.22

22.5   Periodic payment when amortising under an ordinary annuity

The calculation to find the periodic payment to amortise a specified present value involves rearranging the present value formula given in section 22.4, *Present value when amortising under an ordinary annuity*:

$$p = \frac{Pi}{1 - (1 + i)^{-n}}$$

EXAMPLE 22.5   MONTHLY PAYMENTS ON A CAR

A small car is purchased for $18 000 with a deposit of 10% and the balance to be borrowed for 5 years at 11.5% accrued monthly.

1. What is the amount to be borrowed?
    The amount to be borrowed is found by reducing $18 000 by 10%:

$$P = 18000 - \frac{10}{100}18000$$
$$= 18000 - 1800$$
$$= \$16\,200$$

Using Sharp EL-735:

18 000 | – | 10 | 2nd F | % |

Answer: 16 200

2. What is the regular monthly payment amount?
    Collecting the information together:

    $P = \$16\,200$
    $j = 11.5\%$ per annum
    $i = 0.9583\%$ per month $(11.5 \div 12) = 0.009583$
    $n = 60$ months (5×12)

    Using the formula for periodic payment:

$$p = \frac{Pi}{1 - (1 + i)^{-n}}$$

$$= \frac{16\,200 \times 0.009\,583}{1 - (1 + 0.009\,583)^{-60}}$$

$$= \$356.28 \text{ per month}$$

Using Sharp EL-735:

| 2nd F | | BGN/END | should show a clear display for ordinary annuity

| 2nd F | | CA |

| 16 200 | | +/– | | PV | 11.5 | 2nd F | | i | 5 | 2nd F | | n | | COMP | | PMT |

Answer: 356.28

---

3. What is the sum of the monthly payments?
    The sum of the monthly payments:
    Total payments = $p \times n$ = 356.28 x 60 = $21\,376.80
4. What is the total amount paid when the deposit is included?
    Total amount paid for the car, including the deposit:
    Total paid = 1800 + 21 376.80 = $23 176.80

Using Sharp EL-735:

| 21 376.81 | | + | | 1800 | | = |

Answer: 23 176.81

22.6 Number of time periods when amortising under an ordinary annuity

Sometimes a borrower is interested in amortising the debt at a faster rate than that proposed by the lending institution. If this is to be accomplished by higher regular repayments, we can calculate the time needed to repay the debt in terms of the number of time periods. To obtain the formula, we rearrange the formula for the periodic payment $p = Pi/[1 - (1 + i)^{-n}]$ to get n by itself, using logarithms to base e, called ℓn, in the process. The rearranged formula is:

$$n = \frac{\ell n(p) - \ell n(p - Pi)}{\ell n(1 + i)}$$

EXAMPLE 22.6   TIME TO AMORTISE A HOME UNIT MORTGAGE
The purchase of a 2-bedroom home unit involved borrowing $89 000 for 10 years when the interest rate was 9.5% per annum, accruing monthly. After

monthly repayments were set at $1151.64, the investors found they could make regular monthly repayments of $2000. How long did the mortgage amortisation take?

Collecting the information together:

$P = \$89\,000$
$j = 9.5\%$ per annum
$i = 0.7917\%$ per month $(9.5 \div 12) = 0.007917$
$p = \$2000$

Using the formula for the number of time periods:

$$n = \frac{\ell n(p) - \ell n(p - Pi)}{\ell n(1 + i)}$$

$$= \frac{\ell n(2000) - \ell n(2000 - 89\,000 \times 0.007917)}{\ell n(1 + 0.007917)}$$

$$= 55.08 \text{ months}$$

That is, it took 4 years and 7 months paying $2000 and one smaller payment in the final month.

Using Sharp EL-735:

$\boxed{\text{2nd F}}$ $\boxed{\text{BGN/END}}$ should show a clear display for ordinary annuity

$\boxed{\text{2nd F}}$ $\boxed{\text{CA}}$

$89\,000$ $\boxed{+/-}$ $\boxed{\text{PV}}$ 9.5 $\boxed{\text{2nd F}}$ $\boxed{i}$ 2000 $\boxed{\text{PMT}}$ $\boxed{\text{COMP}}$ $\boxed{n}$

Answer: 55.08

22.7   Principal remaining during an annuity

As each periodic payment is made for an annuity, part of the payment meets the interest accruing on the principal and only part goes to paying off the principal itself. A common problem in annuities is determining how much of the principal remains unpaid partway through the total time of the loan. This is done by comparing compound interest sum with the annuity sum as described in section 22.3, *Amortisation under an ordinary annuity*. The difference represents the difference between the expected value of the loan and the actual value of what has been received. It is what the lender regards as owing to them. Hence, it is the amount that would discharge the debt and also, therefore, the amount that the lender still has on loan to you. It is the unpaid principal.

EXAMPLE 22.3 AMORTISATION OF A HOUSE LOAN (CONTINUED)

The sum of $100,000 was borrowed to finance the purchase of a house, with interest at 9% per annum calculated and accrued monthly. The financial institution requires repayment of $899.73 per month. We worked out that the debt will be amortised over 20 years. How much of the principal will remain unpaid after 10 years?

1. What is the expected value of the loan to the financial institution after 10 years?
    Collecting the information together:

    > $P = \$100\,000$
    > $j = 9\%$ per annum
    > $i = 0.75\%$ per month $(9 \div 12) = 0.0075$
    > $n = 120$ months (10×12)

    The expected value is a compound interest calculation:

    $$S_n = P(1 + i)^n$$
    $$= 100\,000(1 + 0.0075)^{120}$$
    $$= \$245\,135.71$$

Using Sharp EL-735:

$\boxed{\text{2nd F}}\ \boxed{\text{CA}}$

$100\,000\ \boxed{+/-}\ \boxed{\text{PV}}\ 9\ \boxed{\text{2nd F}}\ \boxed{i}\ 10\ \boxed{\text{2nd F}}\ \boxed{n}\ \boxed{\text{COMP}}\ \boxed{\text{FV}}$

Answer: 245 135.71

---

2. What is the actual value of the repayments received from the borrower over 10 years?
    Collecting the information together:

    > $p = \$899.73$
    > $j = 9\%$ per annum
    > $i = 0.75\%$ per month $= 0.0075$
    > $n = 120$ months

    The actual value is an annuity calculation:

    $$S_n = \frac{p[(1 + i)^n - 1]}{i}$$
    $$= \frac{899.73[(1 + 0.0075)^{120} - 1]}{0.0075}$$
    $$= \$174\,110.60$$

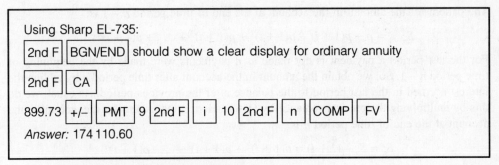

Using Sharp EL-735:

[2nd F] [BGN/END] should show a clear display for ordinary annuity

[2nd F] [CA]

899.73 [+/–] [PMT] [9] [2nd F] [i] [10] [2nd F] [n] [COMP] [FV]

Answer: 174 110.60

3. How much is still owed on the loan?
    Amount still owing on the loan is:
        $245 135.71 – $174 110.60 = $71 025.11
    After half the time (10 years) nearly three quarters of the loan remains
    unpaid.

22.8   Annuity due

This type of annuity has *payments at the beginning of each time period*, as the time-line diagram in figure 22.3 shows. Notice that n payments are made after $n - 1$ time periods. Annuity due is the type of annuity commonly used for payment of leases.

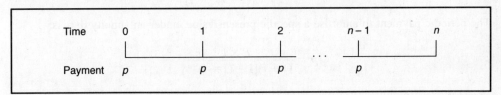

Figure 22.3   Payments for an ordinary annuity

The formulae for annuity due are a little more complicated than for the ordinary annuity but similarities can be observed. The steps for the first two periods are given in figure 22.4. Note that, as for an ordinary annuity, we obtain the previous balance plus the interest on it by multiplying the previous balance by $(1 + i)$.

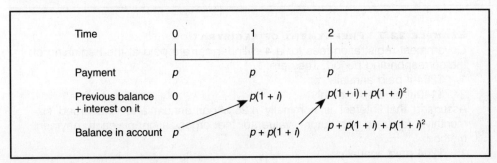

Figure 22.4   Steps in an annuity due

The pattern for the amount in the account at the end of time period $n - 1$ is:

$$S_{n-1} = p + p(1 + i) + p(1 + i)^2 + p(1 + i)^3 + \ldots + p(1 + i)^{n-1}$$

For the last period a payment is not made as n payments were made by the beginning of time period $n - 1$. So, we obtain the amount in the account after time period n by adding the interest accrued in the last period to the balance after the previous period. As usual, we do this by multiplying the previous balance by $(1 + i)$. Hence, the pattern for the amount in the account at the end of time period n is:

$$S_n = S_{n-1}(1 + i) = p(1 + i)^2 + p(1 + i)^3 + \ldots p(1 + i)^n$$

This is another geometric series and so can re-expressed as explained for the ordinary annuity.

S_n is the amount accumulated at the end of the total time available. It is also called the **future value** (*FV*) for an annuity due. It is calculated as:

$$S_n = \frac{p(1 + i)[(1 + i)^n - 1]}{i}$$

The periodic payment for an annuity due when the future value is known is:

$$p = \frac{S_n \times i}{(1 + i)[(1 + i)^n - 1]}$$

The periodic payment to amortise a specific present value, under an annuity due, is:

$$p = \frac{P \times i}{(1 + i)[1 - (1 + i)^{-n}]}$$

Using Sharp EL-735:

Remember to toggle the $\boxed{\text{BGN/END}}$ button by pressing $\boxed{\text{2nd F}}$ first, so that BGN appears on the calculator display, for annuity due.

EXAMPLE 22.7   PREPAYMENT OF REGISTRATION

Government registration fees for a 4 cylinder car are paid at the beginning of the corresponding period. They are:
1. $264 if paid annually; or
2. $140 if paid six-monthly.

Assuming that interest is nominally 4.25% per annum and is accrued six-monthly, calculate the future value to the organisation of each payment method.
1. $264 paid annually.
    Collecting the information together:

$P = \$264$

$j = 4.25\%$ per annum $= 0.0425$

$i = 2.125\%$ per six months $(4.25 \div 2) = 0.02125$

$n = 2$ time periods of six months (1×2)

The future value of the payment is a compound interest calculation:

$S_1 = P(1 + i)^n$

$= 264(1 + 0.0425)^2$

$= \$275.34$

Using Sharp EL-735:

| 2nd F | CA |

| 264 | +/− | PV | 4.25 | × | .5 | = | i | 2 | n | COMP | FV |

Answer: 275.34

---

2. $140 paid six monthly.

Collecting the information together:

$p = \$140$

$j = 4.25\%$ per annum $= 0.0425$

$i = 2.125\%$ per six months $(4.25 \div 2) = 0.02125$

$n = 2$ time periods of six months (1×2)

As two payments are made and these have to be paid at the beginning of each time period, the future value of the payments is an annuity due calculation:

$$S_n = \frac{p(1 + i)[(1 + i)^n - 1]}{i}$$

$$= \frac{140(1 + 0.02125)[(1 + 0.02125)^2 - 1]}{0.02125}$$

$$= \$288.99$$

which is $13.65 more than the first option, probably to cover the extra processing costs.

Using Sharp EL-735:

| 2nd F | BGN/END | until BGN appears on the display |

| 2nd F | CA |

| 140 | +/− | PMT | 4.25 | × | .5 | = | i | 2 | n | COMP | FV |

Answer: 288.99

22.9 Choosing financial mathematics procedures

The financial mathematics material covered in this book may be classified into one of four **major categories of financial mathematics**:

A. Simple interest: single payment with interest computed for the total time;

B. Compound interest: single payment with interest computed for each period;

C. Ordinary annuity: multiple payments at end of each period and interest computed for each period;

D. Annuity due: multiple payments at beginning of each period and interest computed for each period.

The differences between these categories may be identified by asking the following questions:

1. How often are payments made?
2. When are the payments made?
3. When is the interest calculated?
4. What is the major category of financial mathematics?

In the context of the work covered in the preceding sections, the following answers are possible. The process is illustrated in figure 22.5 (opposite).

1. How frequently are the payments made?
   - once in the total time
   - every time period

2. When are the payments made?
   - at the beginning of each time period
   - at the end of each time period

3. When is the interest calculated?
   - at the end of the total time
   - at the end of each time period

4. What is the major category of financial mathematics?
   A. Simple interest
   B. Compound interest
   C. Ordinary annuity
   D. Annuity due

22.10 Chapter summary

In this chapter we defined the terms ordinary annuity, annuity due, periodic payment and amortisation. We showed how to calculate present value, future value, periodic payment and the time needed to amortise a debt. We also presented a strategy for choosing the major category of procedure for solving a financial problem.

$(Q7 - Q8) \, 24\,\%$

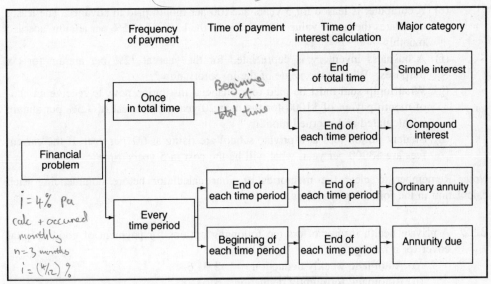

Figure 22.5   Choosing the major category for a financial problem

22.11 Key terms

- amortisation
- annuity
- annuity due
- future value (S_n or FV)
- interest
- major category of financial mathematics

- ordinary annuity
- periodic payment (*p* or PMT)
- present value (*P* or PV)
- principal (P or Pr)
- sinking fund
- time period

22.12 Exercises

22.1 Determine the major category of financial mathematics involved in each of the following situations. No calculations are required.

(a) The sum of $10 000 is lent to a relative for a year at 10% interest per annum, with the interest calculated and accrued at the end of the year.

(b) The sum of $10 000 is put into a term deposit account for 18 months at 10% interest per annum, with the interest calculated and accrued every six months.

(c) The sum of $10 000 is put into an account at the end of every six months for 18 months at 10% per annum interest, with the interest calculated and accrued six-monthly.

(d) The sum of $10 000 is put into an account at the beginning of every six months for 18 months at 10% per annum interest, with the interest calculated and accrued six-monthly.

(e) A computer is leased for 3 years at $100 per month paid in advance. The lessor calculates the future value of the lease on the basis of 13.5% per annum, accrued monthly.

(f) A business inventory is depreciated for the year at 12% per annum for tax purposes. What is the value of the inventory now?

(g) What lump sum must be paid to a financial institution now, to receive an end-of-month payout of $1000 for the next 20 years, if interest of 7.5% per annum is calculated and accrued monthly?

(h) Student tuition fees at a private school are rising at 6% per year. If the current fees are $3000 per year, what will be the cost in 5 years' time?

Note: Remember to clear the memories of your calculator before commencing each calculation in the following exercises.

22.2 A private health insurer offers the following options for payment of good hospital cover for a family:

(i) Automatic weekly deduction	$ 31.64
(ii) Automatic fortnightly deduction	$ 63.28
(iii) Automatic monthly deduction	$137.10
(iv) Direct monthly payment	$143.50
(v) Quarterly payment	$411.30
(vi) Six-monthly payment	$809.40
(vii) Annual payment	$1584.20

Assume that payments are made and interest accrued at the end of each time period for the three automatic deductions (i)–(iii) and at the beginning of each time period for (iv)–(vii).

(a) Calculate the future value to the organisation of each payment method if interest is nominally 4.25% per annum.

(b) Why do you think the organisation requests different amounts of payment under (iii) and (iv)?

(c) What is the relationship between an ordinary annuity and an annuity due?

22.3 Local government rates can be paid, in advance, by annual payment of $722.05 or by quarterly instalments of $184.21. Assuming that interest is nominally 4.25% per annum, calculate the annual value to the organisation of each payment method. (Consider that the year runs from the time of one due rate to the next — *not* one financial year to the next.)

22.4 Government registration fees, paid in advance, for cars vary depending on the number of cylinders and length of time of registration.

(a) Registration for a 6-cylinder car costs:
 (i) $322 if paid annually;
 (ii) $172 if paid six-monthly.

(b) Registration for an 8-cylinder car costs:
   (i) $376 if paid annually;
   (ii) $201 if paid six-monthly.

Assuming that interest is nominally 4.25% per annum, accrued for each time period, calculate the annual value to the organisation of each payment method. Discuss the advantages and disadvantages to the car owner of each type of payment.

22.5 As the winner of first prize in a competition you are offered the options: $20 000 a year for life; or $4000 a month for 5 years.

(a) Assuming that you will invest the money in managed share trusts that return 11.36% per annum paid monthly, and that you live for only 5 years, which of these options would give better return? (Assume annuity due and calculate the future value.)

(b) If you were to live for the next 20 years, which option would give you a better return?

(c) Which Australian Bureau of Statistics publication helps people estimate life expectancy?

22.6 A person planning to travel to Europe in two years' time would like to have $10 000 at the start of the trip. How much should be put into a savings account at the end of each month if the interest at 3.75% per annum is paid monthly?

22.7 A middle-aged couple wants to set aside a nest egg worth $250 000 for their retirement in 10 years' time. They decide to achieve their goal by regular fortnightly saving. If interest is 4% compounded at the end of each fortnight, how much should they save per fortnight?

22.8 The biggest personal financial transaction for most people is the purchase of a house. A buyer takes out a house mortgage for $120 000. If interest is 8.75% per annum accrued monthly and the loan is for 20 years, what monthly repayment must be made to amortise this debt? What assumption has been made in this exercise? Is the assumption realistic?

An index for estimating the affordability of housing is that annual repayments are no more than 25% of annual gross income.

(a) How much annual income is needed to support the repayments?

(b) How large would the monthly repayment be, if the home mortgage interest rate was 14.5% per annum for 20 years?

(c) What level of income is needed to sustain the repayments under these conditions?

(d) Historically, interest rates rise and fall. Discuss the factors, including interest rates, which would place a household at risk in terms of meeting house mortgage repayments.

22.9 A couple has a combined income of $51 000.
   (a) What level of monthly repayments can they afford for a house mortgage, under the 25% of gross annual income rule?
   (b) If the house mortgage rate is currently 8.75% per annum, accrued monthly, and the loan is taken for 25 years, what maximum amount can they afford to borrow?

22.10 A business borrows $50 000 to purchase equipment to increase its long-term profitability. The loan is taken over 5 years, with interest of 9.75% per annum compounded monthly.
   (a) If the debt is to be amortised in 5 years, what repayment amount does the lending institution require?
   (b) What is the total interest received by the institution?
   (c) Management decides to make repayments of $1200 monthly.
      (i) For how long will the loan run under these circumstances?
      (ii) What interest is paid?
      (iii) What expenses could be incurred as a result of accelerated payments?

22.11 A business leases a new luxury car priced at $48 500. It pays a deposit of 10% and borrows the balance from the car company's financial arm at 13.67% per annum accrued monthly for a term of 3 years. Repayments are made at the beginning of each month.
   (a) How much is borrowed from the finance company?
   (b) What is the size of the monthly repayment?
   (c) How much is paid over the 3 years?
   (d) How much interest is paid over the 3 years?

22.12 A company leases a popular brand car for $30 000, without deposit, under a 36-month lease agreement. Payments of $575 are paid per month. At the end of the leasing period, the leasing company expects to sell the car for $16 000. What is the interest rate paid under this lease, assuming that payments are made at the beginning of each time period?

22.13 Refer to Mellor and Best's newspaper article on a leasing package for private buyers. (For details, see references at the end of the book.) What is the interest rate for Smart Buy if the car is bought (valued) for $12 220 at the end of 3 years?

22.14 Many elderly people are asset-rich but income-poor. In recent times reverse mortgages have been suggested as a means of solving this problem. Find out how reverse mortgages operate and explain why safeguards should be built in.

22.15 State whether the following are usually paid at the beginning or at the end of the time period, and what options are available for paying each:

    (a) private health insurance?

    (b) water and sewerage?

    (c) council rates?

    (d) electricity?

    (e) telephone?

    (f) car registration?

22.16 Bankers Trust Australia Group (1993) ran an advertisement: 'This is Perhaps the Most Infuriating Ad You Will Ever Read. Unless You are 21'. Guthrie (1993) and Farr (1993) wrote letters to the editor discussing this advertisement. Locate the advertisement and letters (from newspaper or library sources) and study them. Then use the financial mathematical methods covered in this course to make the suggested calculations. Next, summarise the material.

PART VIII

OPTIMISATION

L E A R N I N G   O B J E C T I V E S

The learning objective of this introduction to part VIII is:

- to gain a general introduction to linear programming.

Linear programming finds the optimum solution when several variables have to be balanced simultaneously.

EXAMPLE VIII.1   OPTIMISING WITH SEVERAL VARIABLES

Examples of such questions follow:

- What is the most profitable allocation of a group of portfolio investments when each investment involves certain risks?
- What combinations of different media advertisements, reaching various audience types, will minimise advertising costs for a business?

Researchers in South Australia have recently developed linear programming models which helped Penfolds Wines schedule its production of 'transfer method champagne' and reduced the amount of champagne held in stock (Hruby and Panton, 1993). These developments were achieved by taking into account the uncertainties of consumer demand and constraints on the production process.

Linear programming techniques are used in many different environments and their application is often very complex, involving thousands of variables. We recommend that you consult management science journals, operational research journals such as *Interfaces*, and research journals relevant to your particular discipline to find out about these applications.

The aim of this part is to introduce you briefly to the use of linear programming as an optimisation tool. Our main emphasis here is on modelling the problem and examining how changes affect current information. The problem will be solved graphically or by computer. The simplex tableau algorithm is the main tool for the work, but the algebra is not explicitly developed here.

As with financial mathematics, numbers used in this type of work are assumed to have been collected by statistical methodology where necessary. It is a time-consuming process. To show this, some questions ask you to collect the data you need to solve a particular problem.

CHAPTER 23

LINEAR PROGRAMMING

L E A R N I N G   O B J E C T I V E S

The learning objectives of this chapter are:

- to understand the general concept of modelling business decisions with mathematical models;
- to understand that a linear program is a special case of a mathematical model;
- to be able to formulate appropriate problems as simple linear programming models;
- to be able to graph the feasible solution region of a linear program involving two variables so as to find the optimal solution to the problem;
- to be able to conduct a sensitivity analysis to examine how changes in the defined coefficients and constants in a linear programming model affect the optimal solution.

Many situations involve several factors at the same time, with a requirement of **optimisation** within constraints. For example, a company wishing to maximise profit, minimise cost and achieve maximum contact with interested people may also need to take into account such factors as finance, people or material available.

Linear programming is a tool you can use to solve problems where:
1. the objective is clear;
2. there are several alternatives;
3. resources are limited

EXAMPLE 23.1   OPTIMISING THE PROFIT FROM SUBMISSIONS AND TENDERS

A small company funded by government and private business sources wishes to organise work for its staff. Each submission drafted for government funding takes 2 person days and is likely to result in a grant with an expected value of $3000. Each tender for a specific business takes 3 person days and is likely to result in a contract with an expected value of $4000. In any week no more than 12 person days are available for drafting documents and the company can produce no more than 5 documents because it depends on library research and secretarial support. How many submissions and tenders should be organised to maximise the company's funds? What maximum weekly amount of money can the company expect to receive?

This example shows that the company's objective is to maximise the amount of money coming in. There are several alternatives: it can submit for government funding or tender for private work.

Certain constraints make the solution less than obvious to the decision-maker: the limit on the number of days available to draft the documents (12 person days), and the limit on the number of documents the company can produce (5 documents). To come to the best solution, these matters must be taken into account.

23.1   Formulating the linear programming model

Bringing together the various aspects of a problem to be solved requires a mathematical mechanism: the **linear programming model**. The steps for constructing it are as follows:

1. define the decision variables;
2. represent the objective;
3. represent the constraints controlling the system.

The **decision variables** define the alternatives you must choose from. The objective is represented in terms of the **objective function** that defines profit (cost) in terms of decision variables. A **constraint** is a restriction on the solution of the problem imposed by limited **resources**. The **lefthand side of a constraint** contains the algebraic statement about the resources required. The **righthand side of a constraint** usually contains the amount of the resource available.

EXAMPLE 23.1   OPTIMISING THE PROFIT FROM SUBMISSIONS AND TENDERS (continued)

The first step is to define, with algebraic representation, the alternatives available.

Let x_1 = the number of submissions to government

x_2 = the number of tenders to business

x_1 and x_2 are called decision variables because they describe all the decisions that could be made.

The second step is to represent the objective. If each submission to government yields the company \$3000 then x_1 submissions would bring $3000x_1$ dollars. Similarly, if each tender for private business yields the company \$4000 then x_2 tenders would bring in $4000x_2$ dollars. The total received by the company would be $3000x_1 + 4000x_2$. This general form is called the objective function. The objective is to maximise the objective function; that is, maximise $3000x_1 + 4000x_2$.

The third step involves the resources available. Two resources are constraining the solution. One deals with time — the amount needed and the amount available; the other deals with the number of documents the company can produce in the time available.

- The time available for drafting documents is 12 person days. Submissions take 2 days and tenders take 3 days. x_1 submissions will take $2x_1$ days and x_2 tenders will take $3x_2$ days. In total these will need $2x_1 + 3x_2$ days. However, there is a limit of 12 on the number of days available. The constraint can be expressed as an inequality $2x_1 + 3x_2 \leq 12$.

- The total number of documents the company can produce is $x_1 + x_2$ but it can only produce a maximum of 5 documents; that is, $x_1 + x_2 \leq 5$.

- Most linear programming models assume that the alternatives are not negative; that is, $x_1, x_2 \geq 0$.

All these algebraic statements together form a group called the linear programming model for the problem.

Model

Let x_1 = the number of submissions to government

x_2 = the number of tenders to business

Maximise	$3000x_1 + 4000x_2$	objective function
such that	$2x_1 + 3x_2 \leq 12$	time constraint
	$x_1 + x_2 \leq 5$	documents constraint
	$x_1, x_2 \geq 0$	non-negative constraint

Notice how the objective function and constraints take the form of a constant (or value) times an algebraic variable (unknown value): $2x_1 + 3x_2$. This is called a **linear form**. There are no terms with powers like $2x^2$ or products of variables like $3x_1x_2$. The constants in the objective function are called **objective function coefficients**; each of these is the profit (cost) for one unit of a decision variable.

The linear programming conditions listed previously can now be extended to include one about linearity.

> Linear programming is a tool you can use to solve problems where:
> 1. the objective is clear;
> 2. there are several alternatives;
> 3. resources are limited;
> 4. the objective function and constraint inequalities are linear.

How can the **optimal solution** be found from the model, when the optimal solution consists of the values of the decision variables that give the maximum (or minimum) value of the objective function?

23.2   Methods to find the optimal solution

23.2.1   Trial-and-error method

In the **trial-and-error method** you substitute values for x_1 and x_2 that satisfy the constraints into the objective function. You continue this until you think you have the best value of the objective function; the corresponding values of x_1 and x_2 are declared to be the optimal solution. Unfortunately, this method is not only tedious but could miss the optimal solution.

23.2.2   Graphical method

The **graphical method** provides a display of the constraints and is suitable where there are only two variables, x_1 and x_2. The method involves the following steps:

1. Graph the constraints as equalities — don't forget that two points are needed to plot each straight line.
2. Find the feasible region where all the constraints are satisfied. It may not be possible to satisfy all the constraints, in which case the region is called unfeasible and there is no solution.
3. Find the points of intersection on the edge of the feasible region — these are called the **extreme points**. Mathematicians have shown that the optimal solution is usually found at an extreme point, and the point corresponding to the optimal solution is called the **optimal point**.
4. Find the **optimal value** using one of the following two procedures:
   - Evaluate the objective function at all the extreme points and choose those with the optimal value, for example highest profit, lowest cost and so on.
   - Use the **iso-profit** (or **iso-cost**) **method** to find the optimal point and evaluate the objective function for the optimal point to find the optimal value.

> **EXAMPLE 23.1   OPTIMISING THE PROFIT FROM SUBMISSIONS AND**
> **TENDERS** (continued)
>
> **Model**
>
> Let x_1 = the number of submissions to government
> x_2 = the number of tenders to business

Maximise $3000x_1 + 4000x_2$ objective function
such that $2x_1 + 3x_2 \le 12$ time constraint
                      $x_1 + x_2 \le 5$ documents constraint
                      $x_1, x_2 \ge 0$ nonnegative constraint

Graph the first constraint as an equality

Change the first constraint $2x_1 + 3x_2 \le 12$ to an equality $2x_1 + 3x_2 = 12$.
Find two points on the straight line $2x_1 + 3x_2 = 12$. Identifying where the line
cuts the axes is usually the easiest method.

Let $x_1 = 0$ Let $x_2 = 0$
That is, $3x_2 = 12$ That is, $2x_1 = 12$
                  $x_2 = 4$ $x_1 = 6$
Point   (0, 4)   Point   (6, 0)

Plot points (0, 4) and (6, 0) and join the two points together as in figure 23.1.

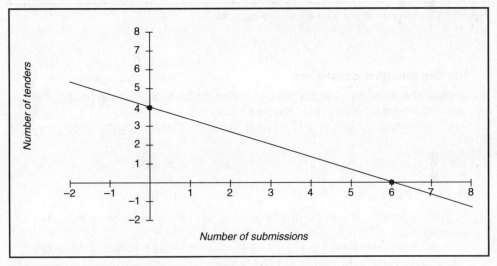

Figure 23.1   Graph of line for time constraint

Find where the time constraint (inequality) is satisfied

On which side of line $2x_1 + 3x_2 = 12$ is $2x_1 + 3x_2 \le 12$ true? Pick a point on
either side of the line. Usually (0, 0) makes the calculation simple. If the
inequality is true for the point chosen, shade the other side of the line on the
diagram; if it is false, shade the side of the line which contains the chosen
point:

$2x_1 + 3x_2 \le 12$
$0 + 0 \le 12$ *true!*

Shade the diagram where it is not true, as shown in figure 23.2.

685

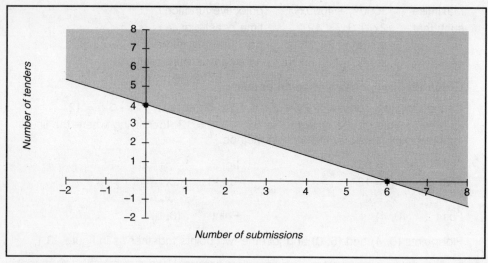

Figure 23.2   Region where time constraint is untrue

Plotting the other constraints

Repeat the shading method for the other constraints, superimposing the shading for each constraint on the same diagram.

The second constraint is $x_1 + x_2 \leq 5$. This becomes the straight line $x_1 + x_2 = 5$.

Let	$x_1 = 0$	Let	$x_2 = 0$
That is,	$x_2 = 5$	That is,	$x_1 = 5$
Point	$(0, 5)$	Point	$(5, 0)$

Plot points $(0, 5)$ and $(5, 0)$ and join the two points together as illustrated in figure 23.3.

On which side of the line $x_1 + x_2 = 5$ is $x_1 + x_2 \leq 5$ true? To find out evaluate the inequality at $(0, 0)$. That is, $0 + 0 \leq 5$ *true!*

Shade the region in figure 23.3 where this inequality is not true, on the opposite side of the line from $(0, 0)$.

The third constraint is $x_1 \geq 0$. Shade the region in figure 23.3 where it is not true.

The fourth constraint is $x_2 \geq 0$. Shade the region in figure 23.3 where it is not true.

Once you have shaded these four regions, the part of the diagram that remains unshaded is called the **feasible solution region**.

The next step is to find the extreme points, which are the points of intersection on the edge of the feasible solution region. Clearly $(0, 0)$, $(0, 4)$ and $(5, 0)$ are extreme points but there is also one at the intersection of $2x_1 + 3x_2 = 12$ and $x_1 + x_2 = 5$.

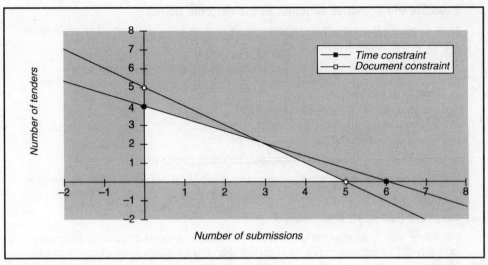

Figure 23.3   Time and documents constraints

Solving for the unknown point of intersection

A coefficient is defined as the number in front of an x-variable term. For example, in the first constraint equation $2x_1 + 3x_2 = 12$, the coefficient of x_1 is 2. Solve the constraint equations $2x_1 + 3x_2 = 12$ and $x_1 + x_2 = 5$ simultaneously, either by making the coefficients of x_1 or by making the coefficients of x_2 both the same size. This is done by multiplying each equation by the easiest, most appropriate multipliers.

Consider the two constraint equations intersecting in the unknown point:

$$2x_1 + 3x_2 = 12 \tag{1}$$
$$x_1 + x_2 = 5 \tag{2}$$

Equation (1) has a coefficient of 2 for x_1. Equation (2) has a coefficient of 1 for x_1. If you leave (1) as it is and multiply each term of (2) by 2, then the new equation (3) will have a coefficient of 2 for the x_1 term.

$$2x_1 + 2x_2 = 10 \qquad [2 \times (2)] \tag{3}$$

Subtracting equation (3) from equation (1) makes the x_1 terms disappear and leaves a relationship that can be solved for x_2.

$$x_2 = 2 \qquad\qquad [(1) - (3)] \tag{4}$$

Substitute the result for x_2 into one of the constraint equations, containing both x_1 and x_2, and hence find x_1. In this example the mathematics is easier for equation (2).

$$x_1 + x_2 = 5 \tag{2}$$
$$x_1 + 2 = 5$$
$$x_1 = 3$$

The simultaneous solution for $2x_1 + 3x_2 = 12$ and $x_1 + x_2 = 5$ has the value of 3 for x_1 and the value of 2 for x_2. Therefore the point of intersection is (3, 2).

Evaluate the objective function at the extreme points

Now evaluate the objective function $3000x_1 + 4000x_2$ at each of the extreme points of the feasible solution region.

Extreme point	Amount that the company receives	
(0, 0)	$3000x_1 + 4000x_2 = 0$	
(0, 4)	16 000	
(3, 2)	17 000	*** best
(5, 0)	15 000	

Choose the best value: for example, highest profit or lowest cost

The best funding result for the company is $17 000, when 3 submissions are made for government grants and 2 tenders are made to private business.

Iso-profit (iso-cost) line method

For those with a steady hand, the ruler method is a quick graphical alternative for finding the optimal point, compared with the evaluation of extreme points. This method, called the iso-profit method if maximising (or iso-cost method if minimising), involves moving a ruler across the feasible region, at the correct slope of the objective function, until you touch the last point of the feasible solution region. This point is furthest from the origin if maximising, and closest to the origin when minimising.

In this example the objective function is $3000x_1 + 4000x_2$. This has a slope of $-3000/4000$ or $-3/4$. From an arbitrary but convenient starting-point, the slope represents the amount of rise and run necessary to find another point on the line. In this case, rise -3 units vertically upwards, that is fall 3 units, and run 4 units horizontally across to the right to find another point on the line.

On figure 23.3, mark the point (0, 3) as the arbitrary starting-point since it allows room for a fall of 3 units. A fall of 3 units followed by a run of 4 units brings us to the point (4, 0). Join (0, 3) and (4, 0) together to form a line of slope $-3/4$.

Place your ruler on this line and move the ruler upwards over the feasible region until you reach the last extreme point (3, 2). This point gives the maximum amount the company will receive under the conditions of the model. Evaluate the amount by substituting (3, 2) in the objective function $3000x_1 + 4000x_2$ as before.

The previous statement about linear programming can now be extended.

Linear programming is a tool you can use to solve problems where:
1. the objective is clear;
2. there are several alternatives;
3. resources are limited;
4. the objective function and constraint inequalities are linear;
5. the constraint inequalities define a feasible solution region and the optimal solution occurs at an extreme point of this region.

23.2.3 Computer solution method

The graphical method is a useful display of the method of linear programming but it is limited to two decision variables. The **computer solution method** employs a computer package to find the solution. Stand-alone computer programs can calculate the solutions to more complex problems with many variables. There are also linear programming routines attached to some spreadsheet packages; for example Microsoft® Excel.

The computer algorithms are based on an algebraic method called the simplex tableau, devised by Dantzig in the US in 1947. This method starts from a simple solution with all decision variables set to zero. The computer then moves efficiently around the extreme points of the feasible region, using algebraic manipulation, until it finds the optimal solution. While the simplex tableau method can be worked by hand it is obviously much more efficient to use computer power. Computer programs are most useful when they use a specific model to:

- find the optimal value of the objective function;
- find the optimal point, that is the x-values that produce the optimal value;
- provide a sensitivity analysis to answer questions like: what if the model changed?

23.2.4 Using limited resources

Constraints in linear programming are imposed by lack of resources. However, the best solution may not use up all the resources. The use of resources can be checked by returning to the original constraint equations and substituting the x values for the optimal point. If both the *lefthand side (LHS)* and the *righthand side (RHS)* of a constraint equation give the same answer, then the resource has been fully utilised. Otherwise there is some slack in the system.

If a resource is fully utilised, the associated constraint is called a **binding constraint**. If a resource is not fully used, the associated constraint is called a **nonbinding constraint**. Binding constraint define the optimal point.

EXAMPLE 23.1   OPTIMISING THE PROFIT FROM SUBMISSIONS AND
TENDERS (continued)

In this example we have two limited resources. The time available for producing documents is 12 person days and no more than 5 documents can be produced in that time. Checking whether all the resources are used:

Constraint 1: Time in days $2x_1 + 3x_2 = 12$
LHS: $2x_1 + 3x_2 = 2 \times 3 + 3 \times 2 = 12$
RHS: 12

That is, the time resource is fully utilised and so $2x_1 + 3x_2 \leq 12$ is a binding constraint.

Constraint 2: Number of documents $x_1 + x_2 = 5$
LHS: $x_1 + x_2 = 3 + 2 = 5$
RHS: 5

That is, the documents resource is fully utilised and so $x_1 + x_2 \leq 5$ is a binding constraint.

23.3 Sensitivity analysis

The linear programming optimisation discussed in section 23.2, *Methods to find the optimal solution*, relies on having the correct information to formulate the model as described in section 23.1, *Formulation of the linear programming model*. This information is often derived from statistical estimation or even informed but nevertheless subjective opinion which means that the solution can vary with different sets of values.

After the first solution has been found, a **sensitivity analysis** is required. This will answer questions such as: how does changing an original value affect the solution?

One approach is to run different models through a linear programming computer package to see how the solution changes with different values. Another way is for the computer package to give tolerance limits to the original values. In this case the assumption is made that only one number is changing at a time.

The following subsections outline the steps required to achieve manually what the computer packages do. As we will investigate the effect of changing just one number at a time, the possible quantities to be changed are:

1. a resource (the righthand side of a constraint equation);
2. an objective function coefficient;
3. a constraint coefficient.

Of these, changing a constraint coefficient manually is the most difficult and is best left to a computer, so it is not discussed in this book.

23.3.1 Changing the resources

Maximise	$3000x_1 + 4000x_2$	objective function
such that	$2x_1 + 3x_2 \leq \mathbf{12}$	time constraint
	$x_1 + x_2 \leq \mathbf{5}$	documents constraint
	$x_1, x_2 \geq 0$	nonnegative constraint

A change in the amount of resource available changes the associated constraint statement and therefore produces change in the feasible region. The bold numbers in the model above are the resource amounts that can be changed. The effect of changing the amount of resource available is reflected by the shadow price or dual price and the associated resource ranges.

Shadow price or dual price

For a particular constraint, consider the change in the optimal value if one more unit of the associated resource is made available. The names **shadow price** or **dual price** are given to the increase in the optimal value for 1 unit increase in resource. However, note that some linear programming computer programs, like LINDO®, refer to the decrease in the optimal value for 1 unit decrease in the resource, in a minimisation problem, as the shadow or dual price.

EXAMPLE 23.1   OPTIMISING THE PROFIT FROM SUBMISSIONS AND TENDERS (continued)

Increasing time by one unit

If we increase time from 12 to 13 days, the time constraint becomes $2x_1 + 3x_2 \leq 13$ (RHS changes from 12 to 13). This change will affect the intersection points and hence the optimal point.

If the time was changed from 12 to 13 days, the new model would be:

Maximise	$3000x_1 + 4000x_2$	objective function
such that	$2x_1 + 3x_2 \leq \mathbf{13}$	time constraint
	$x_1 + x_2 \leq 5$	documents constraint
	$x_1, x_2 \geq 0$	nonnegative constraint

The time constraint equality becomes $2x_1 + 3x_2 = 13$ which:

- intersects the X_1 axis in the point (13/2, 0); that is, (6.5, 0);
- intersects the X_2 axis in the point (0, 13/3); that is, (0, 4.33); and
- intersects the documents equality $x_1 + x_2 = 5$ in the point (2, 3).

The revised time constraint is plotted in figure 23.4. Note that the extreme points were (6, 0), (0, 4) and (3, 2) in the original model.

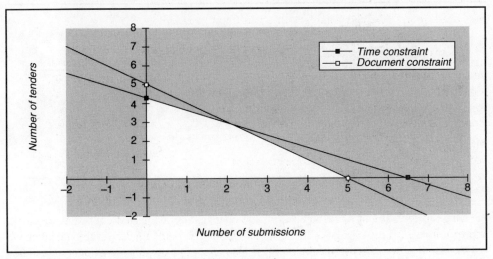

Figure 23.4   Constraints with revised time constraint

Evaluate the objective function $3000x_1 + 4000x_2$ to find the revenue received according to this model, using the extreme points of the feasible solution region:

Extreme point	$ revenue	
(0, 0)	0	
(0, 4.33)	17 333	
(2, 3)	18 000	*** best
(5, 0)	15 000	

From these calculations we can see that increasing the time constraint from 12 to 13 days, an increase of one unit, increases the best revenue from 17 000 to 18 000. Hence,

Shadow (dual) price = 18 000 – 17 000
= $1000

This means that the availability of an extra day will yield an additional $1000 revenue to the company.

Increasing documents by one unit

If we increase the number of documents from 5 to 6, the new model would be:

Maximise	$3000x_1 + 4000x_2$	objective function
such that	$2x_1 + 3x_2 \leq 12$	time constraint
	$x_1 + x_2 \leq \mathbf{6}$	documents constraint
	$x_1, x_2 \geq 0$	nonnegative constraint

The plot of the constraints, with the revised documents constraint, is given in figure 23.5.

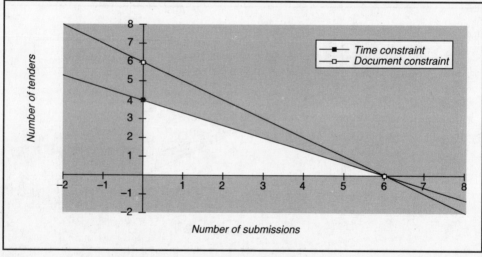

Figure 23.5   Constraints with revised documents constraint

This model defines a triangular feasible solution region with extreme points (0, 0), (0, 4) and (6, 0). As you can see, the line $x_1 + x_2 = 6$, which is the documents constraint, contributes to the feasible solution region only by intersecting at the point (6, 0). However, this is the optimal point and so documents are still contributing to the definition of the optimal point.

To find the best revenue, the objective function is evaluated at (6, 0) with the result that the best revenue is $18 000. Increasing the number of documents from 5 to 6, a difference of one unit, has increased the best revenue from $17 000 to $18 000. Hence, as long as the document constraint is involved in determining the optimal value:

Shadow (dual) price = 18 000 – 17 000
          = $1000

This means that the capacity to produce an extra document will yield an additional $1000 revenue to the company.

Although the shadow prices are the same in this example, they are not the same in every case.

Resource ranges

Obviously *resource increases* will not always yield an increase in the optimal value. The question that now arises is: how much can a resource be changed before the associated constraint no longer defines the optimal point — that is, before the constraint is no longer binding? The range over which the resource remains a binding constraint is called the **resource range**. In figure 23.5, we can see that the documents can be increased by only one unit. After that, the document constraint equation no longer plays a role in defining the optimal point, so any further changes will not affect the optimal value.

EXAMPLE 23.1   OPTIMISING THE PROFIT FROM SUBMISSIONS AND TENDERS (continued)

Time: Resource range

For the original model, the straight line associated with time, in days, is:

$2x_1 + 3x_2 = 12$

The line $2x_1 + 3x_2 = $ 'a' is a straight line parallel to $2x_1 + 3x_2 = 12$ which is associated with the time constraint. The dashed line in figure 23.6 is an example of such a line.

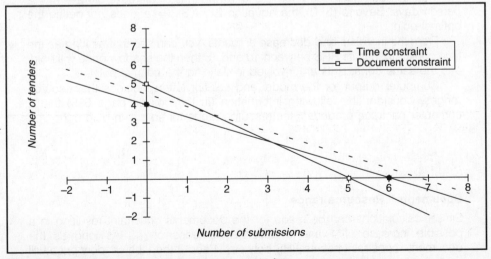

Figure 23.6   Original time and documents constraints

Move $2x_1 + 3x_2 = $ 'a' across the graph so that the RHS 'a' increases. You can do it easily with a ruler and set square. Put the ruler at right angles to the time constraint in figure 23.6. Place the set square so that one side of the right angle is on the time constraint line and the other side of the right angle is against the ruler. Move the set square upwards while keeping its side against the ruler.

Observe what happens to the optimal point as the line $2x_1 + 3x_2 = $ 'a' moves. Both constraints still define the optimal point, which is no longer (3, 2), until the point (0, 5). You can evaluate the LHS of $2x_1 + 3x_2 = 12$ at the point (0, 5) to find the value of 'a'.

$$\text{LHS} = 2x_1 + 3x_2$$
$$= 2 \times 0 + 3 \times 5$$
$$= 15$$
$$= \text{'a'}$$

That is, the line for the time constraint has become $2x_1 + 3x_2 = 15$.

The RHS has increased from 12 to 15 which is an increase of $15 - 12 = 3$ person days. Beyond (0, 5), the equation $2x_1 + 3x_2 = $ 'a' does *not* define the optimal point as the intersection point of the two (binding) constraints.

Use a similar approach to find out how much the RHS can be decreased before the inequality does not define the optimal point. Both constraints still define the optimal point until (5, 0).

$$\text{LHS} = 2x_1 + 3x_2$$
$$= 2 \times 5 + 3 \times 0$$
$$= 10$$
$$= \text{'a'}$$

That is, the line for the time constraint has become $2x_1 + 3x_2 = 10$.

The RHS has decreased from 12 to 10 which is a decrease of $12 - 10 = 2$ person days. Beyond (5, 0), the equation $2x_1 + 3x_2 = $ 'a' does *not* define the optimal point.

From the increase and decrease amounts, you can see that as long as the time constraint has its RHS between 10 and 15 then the shadow price will hold, and the same constraints are involved in defining the optimal point.

Computer output for the model and solution often includes the resource ranges. Consider the following information (in the box on page 695) that a computer package produces; the resource range for time is in bold print.

Documents: Resource range

Similar calculations can be made for the documents constraint resulting in a possible increase of 1 and a possible decrease of 1. As long as the documents constraint has its RHS between 4 and 6 then the shadow price will hold and the same constraints will be involved in defining the optimal point.

Maximise $3000x_1 + 4000x_2$ objective function
such that $2x_1 + 3x_2 \le 12$ time constraint
                   $x_1 + x_2 \le 5$ documents constraint
                   $x_1, x_2 \ge 0$ non-negative constraint

Optimal value of the objective function = 17000.000

Variable	Value
x_1	3.0000000
x_2	2.0000000

Constraint	Shadow price
Time	1000.0000
Documents	1000.0000

Resource ranges

Constraint	Value	Increase	Decrease
Time	**12.000000**	**3.0000000**	**2.0000000**
Documents	5.0000000	1.0000000	1.0000000

Objective Function Coefficients

Variable	Value	Increase	Decrease
x_1	3000.0000	1000.0000	333.33334
x_2	4000.0000	500.00000	1000.0000

Which is the best resource to increase?

Businesses are often able to increase the availability of some resources. If only one resource can be increased, both the shadow prices and the resource ranges must be considered.

EXAMPLE 23.1   OPTIMISING THE PROFIT FROM SUBMISSIONS AND TENDERS (continued)

The time constraint has a shadow price of $1000. This means that for an increase of one person day the company will gain $1000 revenue. From previous work, the number of person days can be increased by three without altering the constraints involved in defining the optimal point. This means that the maximum increase in revenue due to extra person days is 3 × 1000 = $3000.

The documents constraint has a shadow price of $1000. This means that by increasing its document handling by one the company gains $1000 revenue. From previous work, the number of documents handled can be increased by one without altering the constraints involved in defining the optimal point. This means that the maximum increase in revenue due to extra documents is 1 × 1000 = $1000.

According to these calculations, increasing the number of person days available to the maximum of three yields a greater profit than achieved by increasing the documents handled.

These quantitative calculations should not be considered in isolation. Factors such as the cost of obtaining the extra resources must also be taken into account.

23.3.2 Changing the objective function coefficients

The original linear program model, with the objective function coefficients in bold, is:

Maximise	$\mathbf{3000}x_1 + \mathbf{4000}x_2$	objective function
such that	$2x_1 + 3x_2 \leq 12$	time constraint
	$x_1 + x_2 \leq 5$	documents constraint
	$x_1, x_2 \geq 0$	nonnegative constraint

If the objective function coefficients were estimated, they would be subject to some variability. The question to ask is: how much can an objective function coefficient change without altering the linear programming optimal point? To answer this question you must consider the slope of the objective function with one changed coefficient.

Any linear form $c_1x_1 + c_2x_2$ has slope $-c_1/c_2$. This means that the slopes of the objective function and the constraints can all be expressed as a ratio like this. The solution for the optimal point will not change, even if one of the objective coefficients changes, provided the slope of the objective function lies between the slopes of the constraints defining the optimal point.

EXAMPLE 23.1   OPTIMISING THE PROFIT FROM SUBMISSIONS AND TENDERS (continued)

In this example the two constraints define the optimal point. The following are the associated slopes:

	Linear form	Slope
Maximise	$3000x_1 + 4000x_2$	$-3000/4000 = -3/4$
such that	$2x_1 + 3x_2 \leq 12$	$-2/3$
	$x_1 + x_2 \leq 5$	$-1/1$

Changing the objective function coefficient of x_1 (number of submissions)

The objective function is $3000x_1 + 4000x_2$.

Leave the coefficient of x_2 as 4000 and change the coefficient of x_1 from 3000 to c_1:

- the objective function becomes $c_1x_1 + 4000x_2$.
- this will make the slope $-c_1/4000$.

Put the slope of the objective function between those of the constraints which define the optimal point — that is, the binding constraints. The slopes of these constraints are $-2/3$ and -1 from the equations above. Of these two slopes -1 is the smaller and so the relationship between the slopes is given by $-1 \leq -c_1/4000 \leq -2/3$.

To remove the minus signs, multiply all three quantities in the expression by -1; remember that multiplying both sides of an inequality by a negative number requires that the direction of the inequality signs be changed. The expression becomes $1 \geq c1/4000 \geq 2/3$.

Multiply throughout to yield $4000 \geq c_1 \geq 8000/3$.

This means that c_1 can increase from the original value of 3000 up to 4000, an increase of 1000, without altering the optimal point (3, 2). It also means that c_1 can decrease from 3000 to 8000/3 (= 2666.67), a decrease of 333.33 without altering the optimal point (3, 2).

Refer to the following information, also presented above. The range for the coefficient of x_1 in the objective function is shown in bold.

Maximise $3000x_1 + 4000x_2$ objective function
such that $2x_1 + 3x_2 \leq 12$ time constraint
                  $x_1 + x_2 \leq 5$ documents constraint
                  $x_1, x_2 \geq 0$ nonnegative constraint

Optimal value of the objective function = 17000.000

Variable	Value
x_1	3.0000000
x_2	2.0000000

Constraint	Shadow price
Time	1000.0000
Documents	1000.0000

Resource Ranges

Constraint	Value	Increase	Decrease
Time	12.000000	3.0000000	2.0000000
Documents	5.0000000	1.0000000	1.0000000

Objective Function Coefficients

Variable	Value	Increase	Decrease
x_1	**3000.0000**	**1000.0000**	**333.33334**
x_2	4000.0000	500.00000	1000.0000

Changing the objective function coefficient of x_2 (number of documents)

The objective function is $3000x_1 + 4000x_2$.

Leave the coefficient of x_1 as 3000 and change the coefficient of x_2 from 4000 to c_2:

- the objective function becomes $3000x_1 + c_2x_2$

- the slope will be $-3000/c_2$.

Put the slope of the objective function between those of the constraints, which define the optimal point. The relationship between the slopes is $-1 \leq -3000/c_2 \leq -2/3$.

Rearranging yields $3000 \leq c_2 \leq 9000/2$. This means that c_2 can increase from the original value of 4000 up to 4500, an increase of 500, without altering the optimal point (3, 2). It also means that c_2 can decrease from 4000 to 3000, a decrease of 1000, without altering the optimal point (3, 2).

Provided a change to one of the coefficients in the objective function yields a slope that is between the slopes of the constraints defining the optimal point, then the optimal point will not change *but* the optimal value (profit or loss) will change. The optimal point should be evaluated for the new objective function to obtain the new optimal value.

EXAMPLE 23.1   OPTIMISING THE PROFIT FROM SUBMISSIONS AND TENDERS (continued)

If each submission to government yields the company \$3500 rather than \$3000, the objective function becomes $3500x_1 + 4000x_2$, since this amount falls within the allowable range for increase. If this objective function is evaluated at the optimal point (3, 2) then the optimal value is:

$$3500x_1 + 4000x_2 = 3500 \times 3 + 4000 \times 2$$
$$= \$18\,500$$

which is an increase of \$1500 to the company.

23.3.3 Coefficients of constraints

Finally, the coefficients of the constraints may be changed. The calculation to find the solution for the new model is most easily done by computer.

23.4 Chapter summary

Linear programming is a tool you can use to find the optimal solution to a problem where:
1. the objective is clear;
2. there are several alternatives;
3. resources are limited;
4. the objective function and constraint inequalities are linear;
5. the constraint inequalities define a feasible solution region and the optimal solution occurs at an extreme point of this region.

The core of linear programming is the linear programming model which is a combination of algebraic statements about the problem, including definition of the decision variables, the objective function, and the constraints.

Three methods for finding the optimal solution were discussed: the trial-and-error method; the graphical method; and the computer solution method.

Sensitivity analysis investigates the effect on the optimal solution of changing a resource, an objective function coefficient and a constraint coefficient. The effect of changing the amount of resource available is reflected by the shadow price or dual price and the associated resource ranges. You can change an objective function coefficient within the range for which the slope of the objective function remains between the slopes of the binding constraints. This change does not alter the optimal point, but it does affect the optimal value (profit or loss). Changing the constraint coefficients is most easily done by computer.

23.5   Key terms

- **binding constraint**
- **computer solution method**
- **constraint**
- **decision variable**
- **dual price**
- **extreme point**
- **feasible solution region**
- **graphical method**
- **iso-cost method**
- **iso-profit method**
- **lefthand side of a constraint**
- **linear form**
- **linear programming**
- **linear programming model**

- **nonbinding constraint**
- **objective function**
- **objective function coefficient**
- **optimal point**
- **optimal solution**
- **optimal value**
- **optimisation**
- **resource**
- **resource range**
- **righthand side of a constraint**
- **sensitivity analysis**
- **shadow price**
- **trial-and-error method**

23.6   Exercises

For exercises 23.1–23.3, answer the following:
(a) Formulate the linear programming model.
(b) Graph the feasible region.
(c) Use extreme points of the feasible solution region to find the optimal point and the value of the objective function.
(d) State the binding and nonbinding constraints, giving reasons for your answers.
(e) Compute the ranges of optimality of the objective function coefficients.
(f) Interpret the ranges in part (e).
(g) What are the shadow prices for the resources? Interpret each.
(h) Compute the range of feasibility for the righthand sides of the constraints.

23.1   A well-qualified graduate with a young family enjoys teaching and would like to work part-time in the evenings when her partner is at home to mind the family. The local tertiary institution offers her a choice of work — lectures and tutorials — and the graduate decides to take on a combination of these.

The graduate will be paid \$70 per hour for each lecture and \$42 per hour for each tutorial and the marking involved. The institution restricts the number of hours of class contact to 8. Each lecture takes 6 hours to research and prepare; each tutorial needs 2 hours total for classroom preparation and assignment marking. The graduate can spend a maximum 20 hours on preparation. Out of consideration for home commitments, the supervisor has agreed to block the work as a maximum of 4 hours per night for 2 nights. The graduate can achieve this by working from 5 pm to 9 pm.

(a) What combination of lectures and tutorials will give the graduate maximum earnings per week?

(b) What is the actual rate of pay, taking into account the total hours worked? Does this justify rejecting the offer of work or are there other noneconomic factors the graduate may be considering?

(c) What changes to the work arrangement can you suggest, and how will these changes affect the original results you obtained?

23.2   A company is planning to buy computers for its staff, and is considering two particular brands. Brand A costs $3000 and Brand B costs $4000. Although most staff are happy with either computer, three people have indicated that they won't use anything except Brand A, and five have declared that they won't use anything except model B. The company is willing to buy at least 10 computers; what brands should it order to minimise cost?

23.3   A professional person has offices in two locations. Administration requires at least an average of four hours per day at location 1 and one hour at location 2. However, it has been observed that creative productivity is three units per hour at location 2 and one unit per hour at location 1. The upper limit on the amount of time that can be spent on work per day is 12 hours. How should time be allocated to maximise creative productivity?

23.4   Use an appropriate computer package to check your answers to exercises 23.1–23.3.

For exercises 23.5 – 23.7:

(a) formulate the linear programming model; and

(b) use an appropriate computer program to provide solutions and sensitivity analysis.

23.5   An investor has decided to put $50 000 in a share investment portfolio with two components: shares in a cash management fund and shares in a listed property trust. Each share in the cash management fund currently costs $1.03 and each share in the listed property trust currently costs $2.46. The investor wants the listed property trust shares to constitute between 20% and 50% of the portfolio shares.

The degrees of risk associated with the cash management trust and with the listed property trust are rated as 20 and 37.5 respectively. The investor requires the average risk overall to be no more than 30. The cash management fund is currently returning 4.37% and the listed property trust is currently returning 8.13% of the share price.

Form a linear programming model for this question, and use an appropriate computer package to find out how to allocate the portfolio so that returns are maximised. Discuss the results of the sensitivity analysis.

23.6 A retired couple has decided to invest a lump sum of $90 000 in shares in a building society, a managed equity trust, and a general industry. These shares are selling for $3.88, $2.60 and $1.58, respectively. The building society is returning 5.52%, the equity trust is returning 4.81% and the general industrial is returning 6.96% of the listed share price. The degrees of risk are: 15 for the building society, 25 for the equity trust, and 37.5 for the general industrial share. The couple wants at least 25% of building society shares, no more than 40% in the equity trust, and 35% in the general industrial shares; the average risk overall is to be no more than 27.5.

Assuming there are no fees involved, form a linear programming model and use a computer package to find out how many shares of each type the couple should buy so that returns can be maximised. Discuss the results of the sensitivity analysis.

23.7 In personal finance money is often owed on both a house mortgage and a revolving line of credit like a Bankcard or Visacard. Optimal use should be made of money available to lessen the debt. Consider the following case.

A household has just taken out a $95 000 home mortgage loan for 20 years, with repayments based on a savings bank loan of 8.75% per annum calculated and accrued monthly. Calculate the minimum repayment the lending institution would set to amortise the loan.

On the household's Bankcard $5000 is owing, on which a minimum repayment of 3.33% is due this month, and interest is calculated at 14.45% per annum accrued monthly. The household has $1200 maximum available to lessen the debt. Form a linear programming model and use an appropriate computer package to find out how the money should be allocated to minimise interest payable over the month. Discuss the results of the sensitivity analysis.

23.8 The following are commonly referred to as examples of linear programming in business: investment portfolio selection; media mix in advertising; and staff scheduling.
(a) Investigate library sources for cases where these have been used.
(b) Select one of these and decide what data you need, and from where, to set up your model. Then collect a minimal amount to support your case.

23.9 An investor owns a 1012 m² block of land with an unimproved land valuation of $41 300.
Zoning: The land is in a local government area where medium density development is allowed under the following conditions: 2-bedroom flats must have a 165 m² minimum land allocation and 3-bedroom flats require a minimum of 260 m².

Annual rates: The general rate for a flat is $0.02593 per $1 unimproved land valuation. Water rates are $329 for the first flat and $246.40 for each flat thereafter. The sewerage rate is $429.10 per pedestal (WC).

Occupancy: Flats in the region have reasonable occupancy (average 11 months per year).

Rent: On average, 2-bedroom brick flats currently rent at $140 per week and 3-bedroom flats rent at $168 per week.

Building: The cost of building is $50 000 for 2-bedroom brick flats and $67 000 for 3-bedroom flats. The investor has a maximum of $260 000 to spend on the project at the initial stage.

Investment decision: Taking anticipated rent and annual rates into account and assuming reasonable occupancy, what combination of 2-bedroom and 3-bedroom flats will give the best return to the investor?

APPENDIX A

DATA SETS

A.1 Data on real estate sales

This appendix represents data for the residences sold over a 12-month period in three localities, the localities being three different local government areas. The variables making up the data are *Locality, Price, Number of rooms, Block area, Land use code* and *Wall type*. The *Price* is in dollars, the *Block area* is in hectares, and the limited variables coding is given in table A.1.

Table A.1 Coding for limited variables in the real estate sales survey

Locality	Code	Wall type	Code
Kensington and Norwood	15	Brick	1
St Peters	16	Iron	2
Payneham	19	Render	3
		Asbestos	4
		Freestone	5
Land use	Code	Bluestone	6
House	11	Basket Range	7
Maisonette	12	Block	8
Home unit	13		
Flat	14		
Institutional	17		

The data, which is saved in a Minitab portable worksheet file called *vgsales.mtp*, comes from the South Australian Department of Environment and Natural Resources and is reproduced here with their kind permission. It was used in examples 6.5, *Residences sold in three localities*, 8.1, *House prices in three localities*, 8.5, *House sales in two localities* and 10.1, *Prices and Block Areas in St Peters*.

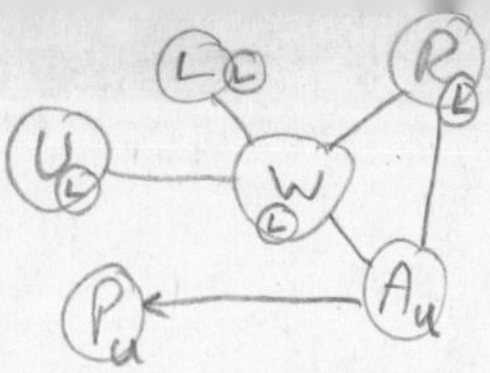

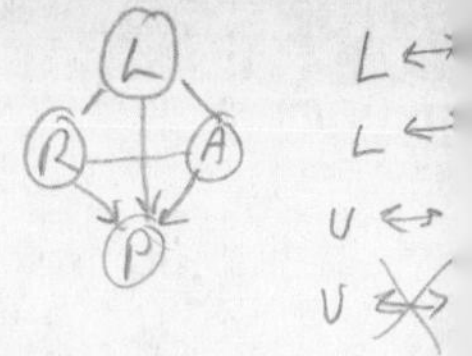

Handwritten annotations: Locality Price rooms area and use wall type

Locality	Price	rooms	area	use	walltype
15	225000	7	0.0487	11	3
15	236000	7	0.0842	11	5
15	247500	6	*	13	1
15	64500	3	*	13	1
15	157000	5	0.0465	11	1
15	127000	5	*	13	5
15	56750	3	*	13	*
15	130000	4	*	13	3
15	95000	4	*	13	1
15	190000	5	*	13	3
15	190000	5	*	13	3
15	190000	5	*	13	3
15	193000	5	*	13	3
15	193000	5	*	13	3
15	217500	6	0.0702	11	6
15	130000	4	*	13	1
15	132000	4	*	13	1
15	126000	4	*	13	1
15	135000	4	*	13	6
15	255000	5	0.0676	11	5
15	160000	5	0.0552	11	3
15	75000	5	0.0535	11	3
15	195500	5	0.0379	11	5
15	150000	6	*	13	1
15	135000	6	*	13	1
15	57500	4	0.0233	11	1
15	158000	6	0.0740	11	5
15	127000	4	*	13	1
15	126250	4	*	13	1
15	61000	3	*	13	8
15	250000	12	0.0929	11	5
15	122000	4	*	13	1
15	114000	4	*	13	1
15	100000	4	*	13	1
15	75000	3	*	13	3
15	75000	3	*	13	3
15	228000	5	0.0322	11	1
15	335000	9	0.1224	11	1
15	335000	9	0.1224	11	1
15	76000	3	*	13	7
15	127000	5	*	13	1
15	163000	2	*	13	1
15	122500	4	*	13	1
15	132000	5	*	13	1
15	135000	5	*	13	1
15	129750	5	*	13	1
15	129750	5	*	13	1
15	124000	3	*	13	6
15	128000	4	*	13	1
15	58250	3	*	13	*
15	223000	6	0.0479	11	1
15	136000	4	0.0370	11	1
15	129000	4	0.0270	11	6
15	250000	5	0.0278	11	1
15	250000	5	0.0278	11	1
15	240000	5	0.0278	11	1
15	240000	5	0.0278	11	1
15	282500	6	0.0511	11	3
15	300000	8	0.0598	11	6
15	90000	3	*	13	1
15	80000	3	*	13	1
15	74000	3	*	13	1
15	74000	3	*	13	1
15	57000	3	*	13	1
15	59000	3	*	13	1
15	83000	3	*	13	1
15	43000	2	*	13	1
15	45000	2	*	13	1
15	45000	2	*	13	1
15	146000	6	0.0557	14	8
15	84000	3	*	13	3
15	195000	5	0.0427	11	6
15	150000	5	0.0427	11	6
15	180000	5	0.0411	11	6
15	155000	4	0.0579	11	1
15	130000	5	0.0252	12	5
15	176000	5	0.0310	11	1
15	76000	4	*	13	1
15	76000	4	*	13	1
15	77000	4	*	13	1
15	79500	3	*	13	1
15	74000	3	*	13	1
15	155000	5	0.0223	12	1
15	155000	5	0.0223	12	1
15	134000	5	*	13	1
15	205000	5	0.0483	11	3
15	147500	5	0.0294	12	1
15	126750	5	0.0523	11	*
15	185500	4	0.0496	11	3
15	178000	4	0.0685	11	3
15	178000	4	0.0685	11	3
15	210000	3	0.0190	14	1
15	280000	6	0.0190	12	3
15	287500	8	*	13	3
15	285000	8	*	13	3
15	270000	8	*	13	3
15	265000	8	*	13	3
15	205000	8	*	13	1
15	250000	6	*	13	1
15	220000	6	0.0929	11	5
15	280000	8	0.0738	11	1
15	280000	8	0.0738	11	1
15	116500	5	0.0383	11	3
15	155000	6	0.0370	11	1
15	155000	6	0.0370	11	1
15	164000	4	0.0501	11	1
15	84000	3	*	13	1
15	85000	4	*	13	1
15	82000	4	*	13	1
15	77000	4	*	13	1
15	245000	7	0.0677	11	3
15	160000	4	0.0334	11	3
15	183500	7	0.0444	12	*
15	86000	3	*	12	6
15	192000	6	0.0296	11	1
15	80000	4	*	13	1
15	70500	4	*	13	1

15	106000	4	*	13	1	15	128500	4	0.0490	11	3	15	137000	5	0.0207	11	5
15	169000	5	*	13	1	15	106500	3	0.0235	11	5	15	170000	5	0.0531	11	6
15	169000	5	*	13	1	15	106500	3	0.0235	11	5	15	170000	5	0.0531	11	6
15	150000	5	*	13	1	15	112500	4	0.0348	11	1	15	170000	4	0.0371	11	5
15	49000	4	*	13	1	15	98000	4	0.0204	11	3	15	138000	6	0.0408	11	5
15	192000	5	0.0332	11	6	15	15000	4	*	13	1	15	125000	5	*	13	1
15	192000	5	0.0332	11	6	15	133000	5	0.0179	11	1	15	125000	5	*	13	1
15	88000	*	*	13	*	15	132500	4	0.0347	11	5	15	130000	4	*	13	1
15	90000	4	*	13	3	15	175000	6	0.0367	11	5	15	182000	5	*	13	1
15	153500	5	0.0189	11	6	15	235000	6	0.0548	11	6	15	79900	3	*	13	1
15	153000	5	0.0398	11	6	15	216000	5	0.0144	11	1	15	79900	3	*	13	1
15	121000	4	0.0206	11	5	15	125000	4	0.0312	12	5	15	78000	3	*	13	1
15	105000	4	0.0206	11	5	15	143500	5	*	13	1	15	75000	3	*	13	1
15	126500	4	0.0206	11	5	15	150000	5	*	13	1	15	75000	3	*	13	1
15	126500	4	0.0206	11	5	15	177500	4	*	13	1	15	74000	3	*	13	1
15	154000	4	*	13	1	15	165000	5	*	13	3	15	108000	4	*	13	1
15	158000	4	*	13	1	15	172500	5	*	13	3	15	108000	4	*	13	1
15	92500	4	0.0250	11	3	15	245000	5	0.0539	11	3	15	245000	7	0.0346	11	1
15	118000	4	*	12	3	15	245000	5	0.0539	11	3	15	105000	4	0.0305	11	3
15	125000	5	0.0309	12	3	15	200000	5	*	13	1	15	129000	3	*	13	1
15	158000	5	0.0466	12	6	15	193000	5	*	13	1	15	134000	3	*	13	1
15	175000	5	0.0418	11	1	15	171900	5	0.0557	11	1	15	134000	3	*	13	1
15	119000	4	*	13	6	15	210000	6	0.0218	12	1	15	133000	3	*	13	1
15	225000	6	0.0370	11	5	15	155000	6	*	13	1	15	146000	5	*	13	1
15	90000	5	*	13	3	15	164000	6	*	13	1	15	180000	6	0.0258	11	1
15	140000	4	0.0271	12	5	15	139000	6	0.0353	11	3	15	180000	6	0.0263	11	1
15	140000	4	0.0176	12	6	15	120000	3	0.0501	11	1	15	150000	5	0.0264	11	1
15	215000	3	0.0564	14	1	15	20000	6	0.0351	11	5	15	151500	5	0.0263	11	1
15	146000	5	0.0390	11	1	15	225000	6	0.0212	12	1	15	173000	5	0.0348	11	5
15	115000	7	0.1228	11	1	15	235000	6	0.0205	12	1	15	95000	3	0.0140	11	1
15	250000	7	0.0606	11	6	15	310000	7	0.0748	11	6	15	320000	8	0.0935	11	1
15	322000	7	0.0676	11	5	15	290000	6	0.1045	11	5	15	118000	4	*	13	1
15	72000	3	*	13	1	15	290000	6	0.1045	11	5	15	118000	4	*	13	1
15	69000	3	*	13	1	15	245000	7	0.0400	12	1	15	132000	4	*	13	1
15	146000	4	*	13	1	15	260000	6	0.0922	11	5	15	115000	3	*	13	3
15	176000	6	0.0557	11	1	15	20000	4	0.0454	12	1	15	115000	4	0.0452	12	5
15	219250	6	0.0536	11	5	15	135000	5	0.0349	11	1	15	115000	4	0.0452	12	5
15	159000	4	0.0365	11	3	15	135000	5	0.0349	11	1	15	180000	6	*	13	5
15	150000	4	*	13	1	15	205000	6	0.0466	11	5	15	135000	5	0.0196	11	5

15	120000	5	0.0636	11	5	15	231000	6	0.0288	11	1	16	148000	5	0.0476	11	6
15	165000	5	*	13	1	15	132000	4	0.0328	11	1	16	148000	5	0.0476	11	6
15	135000	4	0.0458	14	1	15	180000	5	0.0868	11	5	16	147500	4	0.0453	11	1
15	135000	4	0.0458	14	1	15	185000	5	0.0545	11	5	16	82075	5	0.0669	11	*
15	85500	4	*	13	1	15	112500	5	0.0389	11	5	16	150000	5	0.0780	11	5
15	144000	4	*	13	1	15	4000	4	0.0582	12	6	16	80000	4	*	13	1
15	144000	4	*	13	1	15	3880	4	0.0154	11	6	16	114950	4	*	13	1
15	140000	4	0.0574	11	1	15	140000	4	0.0257	11	3	16	114950	4	*	13	1
15	115500	4	0.0232	11	5	15	112000	4	*	13	1	16	76000	3	*	13	1
15	149500	5	*	13	1	15	261000	5	0.0528	11	3	16	100000	*	*	13	*
15	159000	5	0.0836	11	1	15	130000	3	0.0323	11	5	16	98000	4	*	13	1
15	66000	4	0.0510	11	3	15	85000	3	*	13	1	16	98000	4	*	13	1
15	150000	5	0.0696	11	1	15	85000	3	*	13	1	16	62000	4	*	13	1
15	77500	3	*	13	1	15	73000	3	*	13	1	16	76500	5	*	13	1
15	77500	3	*	13	1	15	62500	3	*	13	1	16	172000	6	0.0889	11	3
15	68500	3	*	13	1	15	71000	3	*	13	1	16	172000	6	0.0889	11	3
15	139500	5	0.0620	11	1	15	53000	3	*	13	1	16	97000	5	0.0529	11	3
15	330000	9	0.1137	11	3	15	160000	5	*	13	1	16	132000	4	0.0268	12	1
15	460000	10	0.1136	11	1	15	167500	5	*	13	1	16	132000	4	0.0267	12	1
15	350000	7	0.0456	12	3	15	75000	3	*	13	1	16	140500	6	0.0534	11	3
15	250000	7	0.0456	12	3	15	75000	3	*	13	1	16	145000	5	0.0534	11	3
15	216000	7	0.0657	11	1	15	74500	3	*	13	1	16	93000	5	0.0534	11	3
15	325000	8	0.0585	12	1	15	169500	5	*	13	3	16	164100	4	0.0448	11	6
15	225000	7	0.0893	11	7	16	105000	4	0.0419	11	1	16	149000	4	0.0624	11	1
15	222000	*	*	13	6	16	100000	4	0.0423	11	1	16	129300	4	0.0534	11	3
15	127500	4	*	13	1	16	106500	5	*	13	5	16	195500	6	0.1003	11	1
15	225000	6	0.1042	11	1	16	106500	5	*	13	5	16	122750	5	0.0802	11	1
15	125000	4	*	13	1	16	110000	4	0.0390	11	3	16	166500	5	0.0903	11	1
15	781000	11	0.3640	11	3	16	138000	4	0.0508	11	6	16	121000	6	0.0724	11	3
15	160000	5	0.0601	11	5	16	125000	5	0.0440	11	1	16	104000	4	0.0564	12	1
15	200000	7	0.0669	11	1	16	125000	5	0.0440	11	1	16	104000	4	0.0564	12	1
15	302000	7	0.1486	11	5	16	138000	5	0.0487	11	1	16	*	5	0.0789	11	1
15	117000	3	*	13	1	16	138000	5	0.0487	11	1	16	155000	*	0.0309	11	*
15	88000	3	*	13	1	16	122000	4	0.0471	11	1	16	157000	6	0.0728	11	1
15	117000	5	*	13	3	16	161000	6	0.0555	11	1	16	105000	4	0.0557	11	1
15	200000	6	*	13	1	16	133500	5	0.0376	11	6	16	162500	5	0.0501	11	3
15	200000	6	*	13	1	16	179500	5	0.0383	11	1	16	119500	5	0.0546	11	1
15	148000	5	*	13	1	16	138000	5	0.0481	11	1	16	180250	5	0.0546	11	1
15	155000	5	*	13	1	16	69875	5	0.0490	11	6	16	105000	4	0.0483	11	1

16	94000	5	0.0557	11	1	16	160000	5	0.1190	11	3	16	163000	7	0.0586	11	3
16	82000	4	*	11	5	16	72000	4	*	13	1	16	297000	7	0.1045	11	3
16	111000	4	*	13	1	16	72000	4	*	13	1	16	265000	8	0.1036	11	5
16	108000	4	*	13	1	16	72000	4	*	13	1	16	197500	6	0.0885	11	7
16	120000	5	0.1592	11	3	16	165100	4	0.0569	11	3	16	65000	5	0.0592	11	1
16	113000	5	*	13	1	16	340000	4	0.0406	11	3	16	52250	2	*	13	1
16	91000	4	*	13	1	16	158000	5	0.0743	11	6	16	143500	4	0.0557	11	5
16	91000	4	*	13	1	16	295000	6	0.0580	11	2	16	268000	6	0.0911	11	3
16	93000	4	*	13	1	16	206500	9	0.0731	11	6	16	320000	6	0.0818	14	1
16	96000	3	0.0237	11	1	16	96000	4	*	13	1	16	270000	7	0.0696	11	1
16	195000	4	0.0543	11	1	16	230000	5	0.0812	11	5	16	382500	7	0.1045	11	5
16	137000	4	0.0371	11	1	16	230000	5	0.0812	11	5	16	155000	5	0.0696	11	1
16	176000	6	0.0534	11	5	16	326250	6	0.0766	11	5	16	191400	10	0.1045	11	1
16	95000	3	*	11	1	16	78000	4	*	13	1	16	173000	4	0.0522	11	1
16	95000	3	*	11	1	16	76000	4	*	13	1	16	88000	3	*	13	1
16	146000	5	*	13	1	16	227000	5	0.0487	11	6	16	310000	5	0.0550	11	1
16	133000	4	*	13	1	16	244000	6	0.0696	11	5	16	194000	5	0.0966	11	1
16	134500	4	*	13	1	16	190000	6	0.0696	11	5	16	218000	6	0.0801	11	1
16	91000	4	0.0409	12	5	16	87000	4	*	13	1	16	183500	5	0.0696	11	1
16	153500	6	0.0464	11	5	16	94500	4	*	13	1	16	280000	7	0.0875	11	1
16	179000	6	0.0593	11	1	16	82000	4	*	13	1	16	267000	7	0.0892	11	3
16	137500	*	*	13	*	16	210000	6	0.0696	11	1	16	170000	4	0.1001	11	1
16	137500	*	*	13	*	16	207500	5	0.0836	11	*	16	170000	4	0.1001	11	1
16	139000	*	*	13	*	16	245000	6	0.1045	11	5	16	51840	5	0.0618	12	1
16	140000	*	*	13	*	16	344000	9	0.1045	11	6	16	431347	5	0.0616	11	3
16	208000	6	0.0627	11	5	16	20000	4	*	13	5	16	270000	6	0.0805	11	7
16	68000	4	0.0290	11	5	16	275000	7	0.0875	11	5	16	270000	6	0.0805	11	7
16	95000	4	*	13	1	16	325000	6	0.0915	11	5	16	205000	5	0.1031	11	1
16	104000	4	*	13	1	16	198000	4	0.0696	11	*	16	68000	3	*	13	1
16	152000	5	0.0445	11	3	16	560000	10	0.2071	11	6	16	56000	3	*	13	1
16	152000	5	0.0445	11	3	16	560000	10	0.2071	11	6	16	305500	6	0.1184	11	1
16	147000	5	0.0445	11	3	16	560000	10	0.1382	11	6	16	305500	6	0.1184	11	1
16	150000	4	*	13	5	16	560000	10	0.1382	11	6	16	320000	5	0.0616	11	1
16	124990	4	0.0743	11	1	16	212000	6	0.0751	11	5	16	168500	5	0.0694	11	1
16	210000	9	0.0724	11	6	16	276500	7	0.0568	11	5	16	210000	7	0.0357	11	1
16	210000	9	0.0724	11	6	16	62000	3	*	13	1	16	225000	*	0.0359	11	1
16	79750	3	*	13	1	16	235000	5	0.0696	11	3	16	265000	8	0.0696	11	5
16	84500	4	*	13	1	16	90000	3	*	13	7	16	265000	8	0.0696	11	5
16	95000	4	*	13	1	16	227500	6	0.0558	11	5	16	118000	4	*	13	1

16	185000	5	0.0282	11	5	19	144000	6	0.0581	11	5	19	100000	4	*	13	1
16	108500	4	0.0255	11	4	19	144000	6	0.0581	11	5	19	100000	4	*	13	1
16	165300	5	*	13	1	19	89000	5	0.0581	11	3	19	106000	4	*	13	1
16	146500	4	0.0278	11	3	19	130000	5	0.0581	11	5	19	260000	8	0.0890	11	6
16	148000	4	0.0278	11	3	19	146000	5	0.0581	11	5	19	117000	5	0.0418	11	1
16	72523	5	0.0389	11	5	19	180000	6	0.0581	11	5	19	130000	5	0.0750	11	5
16	320000	8	0.1303	11	6	19	155000	5	0.0581	11	5	19	130000	5	0.0750	11	5
16	200000	6	0.0526	11	3	19	84000	4	0.0781	11	1	19	133000	6	0.0802	11	3
16	114000	4	*	13	*	19	120000	5	0.0604	11	7	19	163000	7	0.0819	11	5
16	106000	4	*	13	1	19	129000	4	*	11	3	19	105000	4	0.0651	11	1
16	107500	*	*	13	*	19	145500	6	0.0785	11	1	19	58500	5	0.0748	11	1
16	114000	*	*	13	*	19	145500	6	0.0785	11	1	19	84500	4	*	13	1
16	108000	4	*	13	1	19	117000	4	0.0613	11	5	19	84500	4	*	13	1
16	106000	4	*	13	1	19	155000	5	*	13	1	19	80000	4	*	13	1
16	107000	4	*	13	1	19	100000	4	0.0613	11	1	19	136000	5	0.0665	11	5
16	111500	4	*	13	1	19	168000	6	0.0832	11	5	19	140000	5	0.0668	11	3
16	220000	6	*	13	5	19	92125	4	*	13	1	19	105000	4	*	13	1
16	305000	6	*	11	5	19	97000	4	0.0740	11	1	19	105000	4	*	13	1
16	102000	3	0.0256	12	1	19	104000	4	0.0931	11	1	19	90750	4	0.0693	11	5
16	368000	6	0.1071	11	5	19	165000	5	0.0926	11	5	19	69000	4	0.0693	11	5
16	252000	2	0.0289	14	1	19	190000	6	0.0489	12	1	19	87000	4	*	13	1
19	150000	6	0.0881	11	1	19	165000	5	0.0978	11	5	19	135000	6	0.1313	11	3
19	108000	4	*	13	1	19	130000	5	0.0931	11	1	19	63000	3	*	13	1
19	165000	4	0.0882	11	5	19	440000	15	0.1690	11	*	19	141000	4	0.0920	11	1
19	105000	4	*	13	1	19	165000	5	0.0558	11	1	19	135000	5	*	13	*
19	112500	4	0.0920	11	1	19	82000	3	*	13	1	19	130000	4	*	13	*
19	145800	5	0.0920	11	5	19	80000	3	*	13	1	19	115500	5	*	13	1
19	86500	4	*	13	1	19	79000	3	*	13	1	19	170000	5	0.1313	11	1
19	167000	5	0.0920	11	5	19	83000	3	*	13	1	19	160000	6	0.1313	11	1
19	135000	5	0.0920	11	5	19	100000	3	0.0828	11	3	19	87950	4	*	13	1
19	135000	5	0.0920	11	5	19	100000	3	*	13	1	19	180000	7	0.0920	11	1
19	140000	5	0.0920	11	1	19	100000	3	*	13	1	19	180000	7	0.0920	11	1
19	99500	4	*	13	1	19	142000	5	0.0842	11	1	19	91500	4	*	13	1
19	100000	4	*	13	1	19	150000	6	0.0890	11	5	19	94000	4	*	13	1
19	100000	4	*	13	1	19	167000	4	0.0890	11	5	19	105000	5	0.0920	11	*
19	110000	4	0.0770	11	3	19	138000	5	*	13	1	19	107000	4	0.0920	11	4
19	128000	5	0.0843	11	1	19	145000	5	0.0697	11	1	19	108000	4	*	13	1
19	89000	5	0.0581	11	4	19	255000	7	0.0976	11	5	19	130000	5	0.0920	11	3
19	106000	4	0.0581	11	3	19	165000	6	0.0651	11	5	19	130000	5	0.0920	11	3

19	109000	4	0.0775	11	3	19	125500	4	0.0489	11	6	19	126000	*	0.0588	11	*
19	109000	4	0.0775	11	3	19	135000	5	*	13	1	19	126000	*	0.0588	11	*
19	115000	5	0.0620	11	1	19	122000	5	0.0569	11	5	19	100000	5	0.0665	11	8
19	114000	5	0.0430	11	1	19	104000	4	0.0494	11	1	19	100000	5	0.0665	11	8
19	130000	5	0.0713	11	5	19	150000	6	0.0981	11	5	19	45000	4	0.0554	11	5
19	120000	5	0.1362	11	5	19	137000	5	0.0631	11	1	19	69000	6	0.0768	11	3
19	120000	5	0.1362	11	5	19	137000	5	0.0631	11	1	19	130000	8	0.0990	11	1
19	102500	4	*	13	1	19	16686	5	0.0631	11	1	19	163000	6	0.0883	11	1
19	102500	4	*	13	1	19	75000	5	0.0601	11	1	19	89000	4	*	13	1
19	120000	2	*	14	1	19	150000	6	0.1233	11	5	19	450000	8	*	14	1
19	86000	4	*	13	1	19	141000	5	*	13	6	19	141000	5	0.1134	11	1
19	105000	5	0.0712	11	1	19	140000	5	*	13	6	19	107000	5	0.0697	11	1
19	131000	6	0.0934	11	1	19	161000	6	0.0334	11	6	19	12000	5	0.0837	11	1
19	330000	9	0.2566	11	1	19	104000	4	0.0804	11	1	19	102100	4	0.0704	11	1
19	88500	4	*	13	1	19	126500	5	0.0820	11	5	19	100000	4	0.0824	11	3
19	100000	4	*	13	1	19	110000	4	0.0988	11	3	19	110000	4	*	13	1
19	75000	3	*	13	1	19	110000	4	0.0988	11	3	19	110000	4	*	13	1
19	122000	4	0.0350	12	1	19	57500	2	*	13	3	19	114000	4	*	13	1
19	122000	4	0.0350	12	1	19	55500	2	*	13	3	19	136000	5	0.0877	11	3
19	105000	4	*	13	1	19	83800	3	*	13	3	19	120000	5	0.0483	11	3
19	91500	4	*	13	1	19	83800	3	*	13	3	19	122500	5	*	13	1
19	79000	3	*	13	1	19	80000	4	*	13	1	19	135000	5	*	13	*
19	85000	3	*	13	1	19	65000	4	*	13	1	19	141000	7	0.0797	11	5
19	82000	4	*	13	1	19	93500	4	*	13	1	19	114000	5	0.0725	11	1
19	82000	4	*	13	1	19	93500	4	*	13	1	19	115000	5	0.0837	11	1
19	79500	3	*	13	1	19	110000	5	*	13	1	19	*	5	0.0778	11	1
19	79500	3	*	13	1	19	24667	3	*	13	1	19	89000	4	*	13	1
19	87000	4	*	13	1	19	93000	3	*	13	3	19	165000	7	0.0745	11	1
19	79500	4	*	13	1	19	162500	6	0.0330	11	6	19	168500	5	*	11	1
19	90000	4	*	13	1	19	153750	6	0.0324	11	6	19	120000	5	0.0539	11	1
19	90000	4	*	13	1	19	153750	6	0.0324	11	6	19	*	5	0.0603	11	1
19	86500	4	*	13	1	19	54000	3	*	13	8	19	143000	5	0.0674	11	3
19	86500	4	*	13	1	19	100000	5	0.0691	11	5	19	105000	5	*	13	1
19	78500	4	*	13	1	19	80000	5	0.0306	11	1	19	118000	5	0.0664	11	1
19	78500	4	*	13	1	19	86000	6	0.0811	11	1	19	175000	7	0.0724	11	1
19	110000	5	0.0554	11	1	19	95000	5	0.0618	11	5	19	125000	6	0.0711	11	1
19	136000	4	0.0368	11	3	19	126500	5	0.0809	11	3	19	108500	5	0.0731	11	1
19	63500	5	*	13	1	19	142000	5	0.0967	11	1	19	150000	9	0.0725	11	1
19	125500	4	0.0489	11	6	19	115100	4	0.0692	11	3	19	105000	5	0.0730	11	1

19	85000	4	*	13	1	19	56500	4	*	13	1	19	180000	5	0.0837	11	5
19	124000	5	0.1011	11	3	19	61500	4	*	13	1	19	180000	5	0.0837	11	5
19	133000	5	0.0904	11	1	19	61500	4	*	13	1	19	138250	6	0.0782	11	3
19	88000	4	0.0747	11	5	19	66000	3	*	13	1	19	138250	6	0.0782	11	3
19	29300	4	0.0747	11	4	19	30000	3	*	13	1	19	173000	5	0.0832	11	5
19	105000	7	0.0850	11	1	19	240000	4	*	14	1	19	112000	3	0.0435	11	1
19	142000	5	0.0595	11	1	19	109500	5	*	13	*	19	152000	6	0.0907	11	1
19	88600	4	0.0772	11	1	19	109500	4	*	13	*	19	130000	5	0.0523	11	3
19	99500	5	0.0699	11	1	19	109500	4	*	13	1	19	200000	6	0.0450	12	1
19	187500	6	0.1505	11	3	19	107500	*	*	13	*	19	207000	6	0.0454	12	1
19	187500	6	0.1505	11	3	19	109500	*	*	13	*	19	107500	4	*	13	1
19	205000	5	0.1934	11	5	19	1095010	5	*	13	1	19	107500	4	*	13	1
19	119200	7	0.0768	11	1	19	109500	*	*	13	*	19	135000	5	*	13	1
19	119200	7	0.0768	11	1	19	108650	5	*	13	*	19	242500	8	0.0998	11	5
19	90000	5	*	13	*	19	108500	4	*	13	*	19	161000	6	0.0784	11	3
19	90000	5	*	13	*	19	109500	4	*	13	1	19	40500	3	*	13	1
19	90000	5	*	13	*	19	109000	*	*	13	*	19	77000	3	*	13	1
19	90000	5	*	13	*	19	119500	5	*	13	*	19	180000	5	0.0948	11	5
19	104500	4	0.0797	11	5	19	119500	5	*	13	*	19	80000	3	*	13	1
19	125000	6	0.0853	11	1	19	118500	5	*	13	1	19	153000	6	0.0709	11	5
19	115000	5	0.0800	11	1	19	118000	5	*	13	*	19	300000	7	0.1467	11	*
19	86750	4	*	13	1	19	119000	*	*	13	*	19	300000	7	0.1467	11	*
19	87000	4	*	13	1	19	73500	3	*	13	1	19	156000	6	0.0837	11	1
19	115000	5	0.0746	11	1	19	148000	5	0.0655	11	5	19	45440	4	*	13	1
19	77000	5	0.0746	11	1	19	46000	5	0.0716	11	5	19	70000	2	*	13	3
19	126000	5	0.0864	11	1	19	128000	6	0.0828	11	1	19	70000	2	*	13	3
19	85500	5	0.0670	11	1	19	105000	3	*	13	1	19	80000	3	*	13	3
19	103500	6	0.0650	11	1	19	110000	4	*	13	1	19	80000	3	*	13	3
19	105000	6	0.0916	11	4	19	48000	2	*	13	1	19	171950	4	*	13	1
19	129950	5	*	13	1	19	83500	2	*	13	1	19	152500	5	*	13	1
19	129950	5	*	13	1	19	50000	2	*	13	1	19	137000	4	0.0692	11	1
19	100000	5	0.0684	11	1	19	106000	5	*	13	1	19	137000	4	0.0692	11	1
19	120500	6	0.0960	11	1	19	210000	*	0.1727	17	*	19	155000	5	0.0876	11	8
19	50000	5	0.0850	11	1	19	102000	5	0.0706	11	3	19	221000	6	0.0767	11	5
19	126500	6	0.0600	11	1	19	111000	5	0.0427	11	1	19	278000	6	0.1033	11	5
19	126500	6	0.0600	11	1	19	220000	7	0.0677	11	1	19	105000	6	0.0949	11	1
19	52500	3	*	13	1	19	200200	7	0.0877	11	5	19	490000	11	0.2460	11	1
19	70000	3	*	13	1	19	160000	*	0.0698	11	*	19	170000	5	0.0814	11	1
19	72000	4	*	13	1	19	160000	5	0.0698	11	*	19	205000	5	0.0811	11	1

19	260000	6	0.0905	11	5	19	190500	7	0.1116	11	5	19	90100	3	0.0604	11	*
19	227500	6	0.1168	11	1	19	137000	2	0.0786	14	1	19	177500	8	0.0798	11	5
19	155000	5	0.0730	11	1	19	125000	2	0.0786	14	1	19	135000	5	*	13	1
19	126000	5	0.0730	11	1	19	63000	3	*	13	1	19	70500	4	*	13	1
19	200000	7	0.0876	11	1	19	126000	4	0.0682	11	1	19	72000	3	*	13	1
19	263000	6	0.0876	11	5	19	105000	4	*	13	1	19	94500	5	0.0626	11	3
19	93500	4	*	13	1	19	107000	4	*	13	1	19	130000	5	0.0555	11	5
19	215000	6	0.0720	11	3												

SUMMARY OF MINITAB COMMANDS

This appendix gives an overview of the Minitab commands used in this book — Ryan, Joiner and Ryan (1985) give a fuller account.

B.1   General concepts

B.1.1   Data storage

When you enter data, Minitab keeps it in a worksheet.that you can modify. This is a temporary storage area in computer memory (*not* on a disk) and disappears when you stop Minitab or the power to the computer fails. Data can be saved in files on a disk as described in section B.2.11, *Save worksheet contents in file.*

B.1.2   Worksheet

In the worksheet, data are arranged in rows and columns. In general columns have different measurements; rows are for different instances of the same measurement. For example, *height* and *weight* might be the names for two different columns and rows would contain the heights and weights of different individuals.

B.1.3   Notes on subcommands

Many commands have optional subcommands. If there are several subcommands for a particular command, you can enter any one or any combination of them. To enter subcommands, you must put a semicolon (;) at the end of the original command line and after each subcommand except the last. The last subcommand line must end in a fullstop.

If you get the message:

**Subcommand does not end in . or ; (; assumed)

and you do not want to enter more subcommands, enter a fullstop (.) on a line by itself.

If you get the message:

* ERROR * Subcommand in error -- subcommand ignored

determine what the problem is and proceed as if the line producing the message had never been entered. That is, enter a legal subcommand, a fullstop (.) or, to terminate the whole command, *abort.*

B.2   Specific tasks

Minitab commands can be entered only after *MTB>*. In the following descriptions *c1, c2, c3* are used as example columns only — the number following *c* can be varied. Appendix D, *Detailed instructions for Minitab menus*, explains how to use pull-down menus to execute these commands.

B.2.1   Entering data (*set, read, end data*)

- *set data into c1* to put data in a single column. The data can be input on a single line, separated by blanks, or on several lines.
  Patterned data can be entered as abbreviations:

  set data into c1
  2(1:3),(4,5)2
  end data
  enters 1,2,3,1,2,3,4,4,5,5 into *c1*.

  A number in front of a set of bracketed numbers means repeat the set of numbers that many times. *A number following a set of bracketed numbers* means repeat each number in the set that many times.
  Two numbers separated by a colon indicate the sequence of numbers obtained by commencing with the first number and increasing the previous number by one to obtain the next number in the sequence. This is continued so that only numbers up to and including the second of the two specified numbers are included.
- *read data into c1* to enter numbers — one per line — for storage in column 1 of the worksheet.
- *read data into c1, c2* to enter pairs of numbers — a pair on each line separated by a space or comma — for storage in columns one and two of the worksheet.
- *end data* to finish entering data.

B.2.2   Naming columns (*name*)

name of c1 is 'name' (single quotes must be entered) to name column 1 *name*. For example, *incomea* or *height*.

B.2.3   Finding what data is in the worksheet (*info*)

Enter *info* to produce a summary of what is stored in the worksheet. For example:

```
COLUMN    NAME      COUNT
C1        clothes$    25
C2                    25

CONSTANTS USED: NONE
```

B.2.4   Displaying data (*print*)

To display information in columns on screen using *print* command:

print c1
print c1, c2
print c1–c4 (displays 4 columns)

B.2.5   Clearing all data (*restart, stop*)

To clear computer memory (*not files*) of all data enter *restart* or *stop*. Make sure data you want to keep has been saved in a file before using these commands.

B.2.6   Overwriting columns (*let, read, set*)

If there is already data in a column, the commands *let*, *read*, and *set* overwrite that information. For example, to overwrite a column of data, such as *c2*, with new data, just put *set data into c2* and data already in *c2* is erased.

B.2.7   Removing columns (*erase*)

To remove one or more columns use the *erase* command:

   erase c1 c10

B.2.8   Modifying columns (*data screen, code*)

Most changes can be accomplished most easily using the data screen (see Appendix D.6, *Data screen*). Either type over the number in a cell or use the Menu accessed by pressing the F10 key.

   However, some operations are better done with special purpose commands:

* To remove a column, see B.2.7, *Removing columns*.
* To remove many rows, see B.2.10, *Subsets of columns*.
* To change all instances of a particular value in some columns, use *code*. For example:
  code (1) 0 (9) 10 in c1 put c2 changes all the 1s in *c1* to 0s and all the 9s into 10s, placing the result in *c2*. Any values not specified in code command (for example, 2, 10 and so on) will be copied to *c2* unchanged.
  In *code (1:4) 1 (5:8) 2 in c1 put c1*, 1 to 4 is changed to 1, and 5 to 8 is changed to 2 in *c1*.
  In *code (0:30) 1 (31:110) 2 c1 c12*, 0 to 30 in *c1* is changed to 1 and 31 to 110 in *c1* is changed to 2, and the result placed in *c12*.

B.2.9   Subsets of columns (*copy*)

If you want to work on only some of the values in a column, you must copy the required values into the same or a new column.

   To use the first 10 out of the total of 12 values in *c1*, enter:

   copy c1 c1;
   use 1:10.

   Only the first ten values will be in *c1* after this command. The same result could be obtained by entering:

   copy c1 c1;
   omit 11,12.

   You can specify, for a column, that you want to omit or retain all rows that have specified values. For example, suppose that *c1–c5* have each got 12 values in them, with *c5* containing the values:

   1 1 1 2 2 2 3 3 3 1 1 1

To copy all those rows of *c1–c4* for which *c5* has the value 1 or 2, enter:

copy c1–c4 to c11–c14;
use c5=1,2.

As a result, all but rows 7, 8, and 9 of *c1–c4* will be in *c11–c14*.

You achieve the same result, but in addition copying the same rows of *c5* to *c15*, with the command:

copy c1–c5 to c11–c15;
omit c5=3.

B.2.10 Combining and splitting columns (*stack, unstack*)

To combine *c1*, *c2* and *c3* and put the result in *c4*, enter:

stack c1–c3 into c4

To split *c4* by putting the first 5 values from *c1* into *c11*, the next 8 into *c12* and the last 3 into *c13*, use the following commands:

set c2
5(1),8(2),3(3)
end
unstack c1 into c11–c13;
subscripts c2.

B.2.11 Save worksheet contents in file (*save*)

To save data for later use, enter (with single quotes):

save 'a:\name.mtp';
portable.

where *name* is the name to be given to the file and *a:* is the drive containing the disk on which it is to be saved. The name of the file must be no longer than 8 characters. A file can contain several pieces of data such as height, weight and so on.

B.2.12 Retrieving data in a worksheet file (*retrieve*)

To get data from a file on disk into the computer's memory enter (with single quotes):

retrieve 'a:\name.mtp';
portable.

where *name* is the name given to the file when it was saved and *a:* is the drive containing the disk on which it was saved. The name of the file must be no longer than 8 characters.

B.2.13 Reading data from a text file (*read*)

If the data has been entered into a text file (e.g. with an editor), it can be entered into Minitab. For example, suppose you have 9 measurements for each of 20 people and you have entered the 9 numbers for each person on a line, separated by blanks. The following command will enter the data:

read 'a:\name.dat' c1–c9

where *name* is the name of the file containing the data and *a:* is the drive containing the disk with the file on it. If some or all of the numbers are not separated by blanks or if the data is arranged differently, you will need different commands to read the data.

B.2.14 Executing macros (*execute*)

Some procedures that do not have Minitab commands have been implemented in macros — a **macro** is a set of Minitab commands stored in a file whose name ends with *mtb*. To run a macro involves using the *execute* command; the name of the file containing the commands is specified as part of the *execute* command. However, before running the macro, you will probably have to change to the directory containing the macro, by using the *cd* command, and have to set constants, using the *let* command. For example:

> *cd a:*
> *let k1=10*
> *let k2=0.05*
> *execute 'rtheoret.mtb'*

B.2.15 Printer output (*outfile*)

To obtain printer output, you must issue an *outfile* command before the commands whose output is required. For example:

> *outfile 'a:\ex10–3.lis'*
> *histogram of c1*
> *describe c1*
> *stop*

will store the output of the *histogram* and *describe* commands in the file *ex10-3.lis* on a disk in drive *a:*.

For a printed copy of this output, use the command to print a file for the computer you are using. Generally, the command to print a file includes the name of the file to be printed. The name must be the same as that given in the *outfile* command, *except that it is not surrounded by single quotes* (').

B.2.16 Stopping Minitab (*stop*)

Enter *stop* to exit from Minitab. Note that the worksheet in computer memory is cleared so that it will be lost if it has not been saved in a Minitab worksheet file.

B.3 Statistical calculations

This section gives a list of the Minitab commands and their subcommands used in this book for doing statistical calculations. You can get further information about them by using the Minitab *help* command. For example, *help stem* will give you information about the *stem* command, and *help stem trim* will give you information about the *stem* command's *trim* subcommand.

B.3.1 Random numbers

- *random n c1;*
  integer 1 to k.

B.3.2   Diagrams

- *histogram of c1*
- *histogram of c1;*
  by c2;
  start 75;
  increment 50.
- *stem of c1*
- *stem of c1;*
  by c2;
  trim;
  increment 50.
- *dotplot of c1*
- *dotplot of c1;*
  by c2;
  same;
  start 75 end 400.
- *boxplot of c1*
- *boxplot of c1;*
  by c2.

B.3.3   Measures of central tendency and dispersion

- *describe c1*
- *describe c1;*
  by c2.
- *mean of c1*
- *median of c1*
- *minimum of c1*
- *maximum of c1*
- *stdev of c1*
- *table c1 c2;*
  mean c3;
  median c3;
  stdev c3;
  n c3.

B.3.4   Tables of counts and proportions

- *tally c1;*
  counts;
  percents.
- *name c1 'o' c2 'e'*
  set 'o' to contain observed frequencies
  set 'e' to contain expected frequencies
  cd a:
  execute 'goodfit.mtb'
- *table c1 c2*
- *table c1 c2;*
  count;

> *colpercents;*
> *rowpercents;*
> *totpercents;*
> *chisq 2.*

- *table c1 c2;*
  frequencies;
  rowpercents;
  chisq 2.
- *set c1 to contain rows (or columns)*
  set c2 to contain columns (or rows)
  set c3 to contain observed frequencies
  cd a:
  execute 'contares.mtb'

B.3.5 Estimation procedures and hypothesis tests for an unrestricted variable

- *name c2 'zscores'*
  nscores c1 'zscores'
- *tinterval with confidence $100\gamma\%$ on c1*
- *cd a:*
  let k1 = number of data column
  let k2 = $100\gamma\%$
  execute 'predint.mtb'
- *cd a:*
  let k1 = number of data column
  let k2 = $100\gamma\%$
  let k3 = $100\pi\%$
  execute 'tolerint.mtb'
- In the following commands *c1* should contain the response variable and *c2* the variable that identifies the groups:
  name c3 'resi' c4 'fits'
  oneway c1 c2 'resi' 'fits'

B.3.6 Relationship between unrestricted variables

In the following examples *c1* contains the response variable and *c2* contains the explanatory variable.
- *plot y in c1 vs x in c2*
- *correlation between c1, c2*
- *regress c1 on 1 c2*
- *name c3 'sres' c4 'fits'*
  regress c1 on 1 c2 'sres' 'fits';
  predict 15.
- *cd a:*
  let k1 = number of column containing data
  let k2 = number of first of 2 consecutive columns to be used
  let k3 = order of moving average
  execute 'mvgavg.mtb'

- *cd a:*
  let k1= number of column containing data
  let k2= number of first of 2 consecutive columns to be used
  let k3= order of centred moving average
  execute 'cmvgavg.mtb'
- *cd a:*
  let k1= number of column containing data
  let k2= number of column to contain smoothed data
  let k3= smoothing constant
  execute 'expsmth.mtb'

B.3.7   Theoretical values

- z_T
  invcdf p;
  normal μ σ.
- t_T
  invcdf p;
  t v.
  where v is the degrees of freedom for which t_T is required.
- r_T
  cd a:
  let k1 = n
  let k2 = α
  execute 'rtheoret.mtb'
- g_T
  cd a:
  let k2 = 100γ%
  let k3 = 100π%
  let k4 = n
  execute 'gtheoret.mtb'

B.4   Troubleshooting

ERROR invalid name

The name of a column cannot be more than 8 characters. Re-enter *name* command with less characters for the name.

* ERROR * Subcommand in error -- subcommand ignored

The subcommand is in error. Determine what the problem is and proceed as if the single line producing the message had never been entered. That is, enter a legal subcommand, a fullstop (.) or, to terminate the whole command, *abort*.

* Subcommand does not end in . or ; (; assumed)

You must enter either a semicolon (;) or a fullstop (.) at the end of a subcommand. If you do not want to enter a further subcommand, enter a fullstop (.); otherwise, enter the next subcommand.

---

* ERROR * 0 is an illegal number of arguments

The command you have just entered is incorrect because it needs some argument(s) such as column(s) or constant(s) to be specified. Re-enter the command or terminate Minitab by entering *stop*.

* ERROR * Non-integers in BY column

You have included in the *by* subcommand a column that is not based on integer values.

* ERROR * values of var. 3, dimension 1not all integer

You have included in the *table* command a column that is not based on integer values. The problem is in column 3 (*c3*).

* ERROR * Values of var. 3, dimension 1 not all in range −10000 to 10000

You have included in the *table* command a column that is not based on integer values between −10 000 to 10 000. The problem is in column 3 (*c3*).

* ERROR * Error in writing file

The most likely problem is that you have no room left on the disk where you are trying to save the file. Either delete some files off the disk or use a different disk.

* ERROR * requested file does not exist

Generally this message occurs when the file named in the command is not available in the nominated directory. If it occurs while running a macro it may be because the macro requires further macro files that are not available. Make sure that you have used the *cd* command to change to the directory containing the macro files and that *all* macros files are available in this directory.

What data do I have in computer memory?

Enter command *info* and press RETURN.

What data do I have saved in Minitab Portable Worksheet (.mtp) files?

- If you have just saved a file, the data contained in the computer memory will be in the file; use *info* to find out what that data is (you must still be in Minitab, with MTB> on the screen).
- If the data is not currently in the worksheet and you know its name, retrieve the file as described above, then type in *info* and press RETURN.
- If you do not know the name of the file(s), obtain a directory listing by entering the command *dir*.

MINITAB MACROS

This appendix lists the Minitab macros that supplement the Minitab commands, and the instructions for executing them. The macros are listed in alphabetical order according to the main macro of the procedure. Some procedures require several macro files. When you execute the macros make sure that you put *all* the macros required for a procedure in the same subdirectory and that you use the *cd* command to change to this directory.

C.1   Minitab macros for computing centred moving averages

This section describes a suite of macros for computing centred moving averages, and section C.6, *Minitab macros for computing moving averages*, describes macros for computing ordinary moving averages. To compute a centred moving average, invoke the main macro *cmvgavg*, which calls other macros to output error messages and to compute the centred moving average. Before invoking *cmvgavg*, store the macros in files with the same names as the macros and the extension *.mtb*. Then set *k1*, *k2* and *k3*, as shown in table C.1. Next, change the current directory to the one containing the main macro and execute the macro with the *execute* command. For example, if you store the main macro in the file *cmvgavg.mtb* on a floppy disk in drive *a:*, the commands to execute it are as follows:

```
cd a:\
execute 'cmvgavg.mtb'
```

Table C.1   Constants to set before executing the Minitab macro *cmvgavg*

k1	number of the column containing the data
k2	number of the first of two consecutive columns for computing the centred moving average, which will be stored in the first of the two columns
k3	the order of the centred moving average

C.1.1 Main macro for computing a centred moving average

The main macro for computing the centred moving average, *cmvgavg*, is as follows. It invokes the macros *mvgaverr* and *cmvgavpr*, described in sections C.6.2, *Macro for producing an error message*, and C.1.2, *Macro for computing a centred moving average*, respectively.

```
noecho
# Macro CMVGAVG
# This macro computes a centred moving average.
# It requires k1-k3 to be set as follows:
#
#   k1 is the column number containing the data
#   k2 is the first of two consecutive columns that are used
#      for computing the centred moving average, to be
#      stored in the first of the two columns
#   k3 is the order of the centred moving average
#
#
# k4-k6 are used to store intermediate results
#
let k5=(k1=k2)
execute 'mvgaverr.mtb' k5
let k5=~k5
execute 'cmvgavpr.mtb' k5
echo
```

C.1.2 Macro for computing a centred moving average

The macro for computing the centred moving average, *cmvgavpr*, is as follows. It is called by the main macro, *cmvgavg*, and it repeatedly calls the macro *mvgtot* (see section C.6.4, *Macro for computing a total for the moving total*) to compute the moving total on which the centred moving average is based.

```
# Macro CMVGAVPR
# This macro computes the centred moving average.
#
let ck2=ck1
let k4=k3-1
let k6=k2+1
execute 'mvgtot.mtb' k4
let ck2=ck2/k3
let k5=round((k3-1)/2)
copy ck2 ck2;
omit 1:k5.
insert ck2
k5(*)
end
lag 1 ck2 ck6
let ck2=(ck2+ck6)/2
erase ck6
```

C.2 Minitab macros for computing the adjusted residuals

This section describes two macros for computing the adjusted residuals for a two-way contingency table. The main macro, *contares*, is invoked to compute the adjusted residuals; it then calls the macro *contatot* in computing row and column totals.

To run *contares*, store it and the macro it calls in files with the same names as the macros and the extension *.mtb*. Next, set up the columns *c1* to *c3* as follows:

1. Put the observed frequencies in *c3*.
2. Specify the rows of the table from which the observed frequencies come in either *c1* or *c2*.
3. Specify the columns from which the observed frequencies come in *c1* or *c2*, whichever one you left available.

Then change the current directory to the one containing the macros and execute the main macro with the *execute* command. For example, if you store the main macro in the file *contares.mtb* on a floppy disk in drive *a:*, the commands to execute the macro are as follows:

```
cd a:\
execute 'contares.mtb'
```

C.2.1 Main macro for computing the adjusted residuals

The main macro for computing the adjusted residuals, *contares*, is as follows. It invokes the macro *contatot*, described in section C.2.2, *Macro for computing totals*.

```
noecho
# Macro CONTARES
# Macro to produce adjusted residuals for a contingency table.
# It will be assumed that
#    the observed frequencies are in c3,
#    the rows of the table from which the observed frequencies
#      come is specified in one of c1 or c2, and
#    the columns from which the observed frequencies come
#      is specified in the other of c1 and c2.
# Columns c1-c3 can be named as the user pleases.
# Columns beginning at c4 will be used in computing the
#    residuals.
#
# The macro uses k1-k3
#
name c4 'exp_freq' c5 'total_1' c6 'total_2'
name c7 'st_res' c8 'adj_res'
let k1=max(c1)-min(c1)+1
let k2=k1+10
indicator c1 c11-ck2
let k3=11
execute 'contatot.mtb' k1
```

continued . . .

```
rsum c11-ck2 c5
let k1=max(c2)-min(c2)+1
let k2=k1+10
indicator c2 c11-ck2
let k3=11
execute 'contatot.mtb' k1
rsum c11-ck2 c6
let c4=c5*c6/sum(c3)
note ADJUSTED RESIDUALS FOR 2-WAY CONTINGENCY TABLE
note - use to investigate source of dependence
note - use only when variables are dependent
note - a residual whose absolute value is > zT (= 1.96 for 0.05 alpha)
note      is contributing to dependence
note
let 'st_res' = (c3 - 'exp_freq')/sqrt('exp_freq')
let 'adj_res' = (1 -'total_1'/sum(c3)) * (1 -'total_2'/sum(c3))
let 'adj_res' = 'st_res'/sqrt('adj_res')
table c1 c2;
mean 'adj_res';
noall.
echo
```

C.2.2   Macro for computing totals

The macro for computing the row and column totals, *contatot*, is as follows. It is called by the main macro, *contares*.

```
noecho
# Macro CONTATOT
# macro to produce totals of c3 corresponding to
#    indicator variable in ck3
let ck3=sum(c3*ck3)*ck3
let k3=k3+1
```

C.3   Minitab macros for exponential smoothing

This section describes the two macros for exponentially smoothing a set of data. The main macro, *expsmth*, is invoked to exponentially smooth a set of data. This macro then calls *expsmind* to exponentially smooth individual observations.

To run *expsmth*, store it and the macro it calls in files with the same names as the macros and the extension *.mtb*. Next, set $k1$, $k2$ and $k3$ as shown in table C.2. Then change the current directory to the one containing the macros and execute the main macro with the *execute* command. For example, if you store the main macro in the file *cmvgavg.mtb* on a floppy disk in drive *a:*, the commands to execute it are as follows:

```
cd a:\
execute 'expsmth.mtb'
```

Table C.2 Constants to set before executing the Minitab macro *expsmth*

k1	number of the column containing the data
k2	number of the column in which to store the exponentially smoothed data
k3	the smoothing constant

C.3.1 Main macro for exponential smoothing

The main macro for exponentially smoothing a column of data, *expsmth*, is as follows. It invokes the macro *expsmind*, described in section C.3.2, *Macro for exponentially smoothing an individual observation*.

```
noecho
# Macro EXPSMTH
# This macro exponentially smooths a set of data
# It requires k1-k3 to be set as follows:
#
#   k1 is the column number containing the data
#   k2 is the column number for storing the smoothed data
#   k3 is the smoothing constant
#
#
# k4-k6 are used to store intermediate results
#
let ck2(1)=ck1(1)
let k4=1
let k6=(count(ck1)-1)
execute 'expsmind.mtb' k6
echo
```

C.3.2 Macro for exponentially smoothing an individual observation

The macro for exponentially smoothing an individual observation, *expsmind*, is as follows. It is called by the main macro, *expsmth*.

```
# Macro EXPSMIND
# This macro provides an exponentially smoothed individual value
# It requires k1-k3 to be set as follows:
#
#   k1 is the column number containing the data
#   k2 is the column number for storing the smoothed data
#   k3 is the smoothing constant
#   k4 is the number of the observation to be smoothed
#
let k4=k4+1
let k5=k4-1
let ck2(k4)=k3*ck1(k4)+(1-k3)*ck2(k5)
```

C.4   Minitab macros for the goodness-of-fit test

This section describes a suite of macros for computing the test statistic, and its probability, for the goodness-of-fit test. The main macro, *goodfit*, is invoked to perform the goodness-of-fit test. This macro then calls *gooderr*, a macro to output an error message if an error occurs, and *goodproc*, a macro to compute the test statistic and its associated probability.

To run *goodfit*, store it and the macros it calls in files with the same names as the macros and the extension *.mtb*. Next, set up two columns: one named *o*, to contain the observed values, and the other named *e*, to contain the expected values. Then change the current directory to the one containing the macros and execute the main macro with the *execute* command. For example, if the main macro is stored in the file *goodfit.mtb* on a floppy disk in drive *a:*, the commands to execute it areas follows:

```
cd a:\
execute 'goodfit.mtb'
```

C.4.1   Main macro for the goodness-of-fit test

The main macro for performing the goodness-of-fit test, *goodfit*, is as follows. It invokes the macros *gooderr* and *goodproc* described in sections C.4.2, *Macro for producing an error message*, and C.4.3, *Macro for computing and output of the test statistic and its probability,* respectively.

```
noecho
# Macro GOODFIT
#
# This macro computes the test statistic,
# and associated probability, for the goodness of fit test.
# It require two columns set up as follows:
#
#   'o' a column containing the observed numbers
#   'e' a column containing the expected numbers
#
# k1 is set to the test statistic,
# k2 to its degrees of freedom and
# k3 to its probability.
#
let k2=sum('o')
let k3=sum('e')
let k1=k2~=k3
execute 'gooderr.mtb' k1
let k1=~k1
execute 'goodproc.mtb' k1
echo
```

C.4.2   Macro for producing an error message

The macro for displaying an error message when the sums of the values in *o* and *e* are not equal, *gooderr*, is as follows. It is called by the main macro, *goodfit*.

```
# Macro GOODERR
# macro to output illegal n error message
# for the goodness of fit test
note The sum of the observed values is:
print k2
note the sum of the expected values is:
print k3
note These are not equal and the test statistic cannot be computed.
```

C.4.3 Macro for computing and output of the test statistic and its probability

The macro for computing the test statistic and its associated probability, *goodproc*, is as following. It is called by the main macro, *goodfit*, provided there is no error.

```
# Macro GOODPROC
# macro to compute and output results
#    for the goodness of fit test.
#
let k1=sum(('o'-'e')**2/'e')
let k2=n('o')-1
cdf k1 k3;
chisq df = k2.
let k3=1-k3
note
note Goodness of fit test
note
note The chi-square test statistic is:
print k1
note and its degrees of freedom is
print k2
note The probability of the test statistic is
print k3
```

C.5 Minitab macro for a tolerance interval's theoretical value

This section describes the macro *gtheoret* that produces the theoretical value for computing the tolerance interval. To run this macro, store it in a file called *gtheoret.mtb* and set *k2–k4* as shown in table C.3. Note that if the values of *k2* or *k3* are less than 1, they are multiplied by 100 because we assume that proportions have been supplied instead of percentages. Next, change the current directory to the one containing *gtheoret.mtb* and execute the macro with the *execute* command. For example, if you store *gtheoret.mtb* on a floppy disk in drive *a:*, the commands to execute it are as follows:

```
cd a:\
execute 'gtheoret.mtb'
```

Table C.3   Constants to set before executing the Minitab macro *gtheoret*

k2	100γ%
k3	100π%
k4	*n*

```
noecho
# Macro GTHEORET
# This procedure computes gT, the theoretical value
#        used in computing the tolerance interval.
# It is based on the approximation given by Howe, W.G. (1969)
# Two-sided tolerance limits for normal populations
# - some improvements. Journal of the American Statistical
# Association, 64: 610-620.
# It requires k2-k4 to be set as follows:
#
#    k2 gamma = confidence level
#    k3 pi = proportion of the population
#    k4 n = sample of size
#
# k5 is set to the theoretical value
#
# In addition, k6-k9 are used to store intermediate results
#    k12 is set to gamma as a percentage
#    k13 is set to pi as a percentage
#
# Compute gT
#
let k5=k4-1
let k12=(k2>=1)*k2 + (k2<1)*k2*100
let k13=(k3>=1)*k3 + (k3<1)*k3*100
let k6=1-k12/100
invcdf k6 k6;
chisq k5.
let k7=(1+k12/100)/2
let k8=(1+k13/100)/2
invcdf k7 k7;
normal.
invcdf k8 k8;
normal.
let k6=k5*(1+1/k4)*k8*k8/k6*(1+(k5-2-k6)/(2*(k4+1)*(k4+1)))
let k9=1+k7*k7/k4+(3-k8*k8)*(k7**4)/6/k4/k4
let k8=k8*k8*k9*(1+(k9*(1+1/k7/k7)*k4/2/k5))
let k6=sqrt(k6)
let k8=sqrt(k8)
let k7=(1+1/k7/k7)*k4*k4
let k5=(k5<=k7)*k6 + (k5>k7)*k8
```

continued . . .

```
note THEORETICAL VALUE FOR A TOLERANCE INTERVAL
note
note The Theoretical value has been computed for
note
note a sample of size
print k4
note and the percentage of the population values to be covered being
print k13
note and the confidence level (expressed as a percentage) being
print k12
note
note The theoretical value is:
print k5
note
echo
```

C.6   Minitab macros for computing moving averages

This section describes the suite of macros for computing moving averages, and section C.1, *Minitab macros for computing centred moving averages*, describes the macros for computing centred moving averages. The main macro *mvgavg* is invoked to compute a moving average. It calls *mvgaverr*, a macro to output error messages, and *mvgavpro*, a macro to compute the moving average.

Before invoking *mvgavg*, store it and the macros it calls in files with the same names as the macros and the extension *.mtb*. Next, set *k1*, *k2* and *k3* as shown in table C.4. Then change the current directory to the one containing the macros and execute the main macro with the *execute* command. For example, if the main macro is stored in the file *mvgavg.mtb* on a floppy disk in drive *a:*, the commands to execute it are as follows:

```
cd a:\
execute 'mvgavg.mtb'
```

Table C.4   Constants to set before executing the Minitab macro *mvgavg*

k1	number of the column containing the data
k2	number of the first of two consecutive columns for computing the moving average, which will be stored in the first of the two columns
k3	the order of the moving average

C.6.1   Main macro for computing moving averages

The main macro for computing the moving average, *mvgavg*, is as follows. It invokes the macros *mvgaverr* and *mvgavpro* described in sections C.6.2, *Macro for producing an error message*, and C.6.3, *Macro for computing a moving average*, respectively.

```
noecho
#  Macro MVGAVG
#  This macro computes a moving average.
#  It requires k1-k3 to be set as follows:
#
#    k1 is the column number containing the data
#    k2 is the first of two consecutive columns to be used
#       in computing the moving average, which will be stored
#       in the first of the two columns
#    k3 is the order of the moving average
#
#
#  In addition k4-k6 are used to store intermediate results
#
let  k5=(k1=k2)
execute  'mvgaverr.mtb'  k5
let  k5=~k5
execute  'mvgavpro.mtb'  k5
echo
```

C.6.2   Macro for producing an error message

The macro, *mvgaverr*, for displaying an error message when the column specified to contain the data is the same as the column specified to store the moving average is as follows. It is called by the main macros, *mvgavg* and *cmvgavg*.

```
#  Macro MVGAVERR
#  This macro outputs same column error message
#
note The column specified to contain the data is:
print k1
note The column specified to store the moving average is:
print k2
Note: these columns cannot be the same.
```

C.6.3   Macro for computing a moving average

The macro for computing the moving average, *mvgavpro*, is as follows. It is called by the main macro, *mvgavg*, and repeatedly calls the macro *mvgtot* (see section C.6.4, *Macro for computing a total for the moving total*) to compute the moving total on which the moving average is based.

```
#  Macro MVGAVPRO
#  This macro computes the moving average.
#
let  ck2=ck1
let  k4=k3-1
let  k6=k2+1
```

continued . . .

```
execute 'mvgtot.mtb' k4
let ck2=ck2/k3
let k5=round((k3-1)/2)
copy ck2 ck2;
omit 1:k5.
insert ck2
k5(*)
end
erase ck6
```

C.6.4   Macro for computing a total for the moving total

The macro for computing the moving total on which the moving average is based, *mvgtot*, is as follows. It is called repeatedly by the main macro, *mvgavg*.

```
#  Macro MVGTOT
#  This macro is called sequentially to add one more observation
#    to a moving total.
#
#  It requires k1, k2, k5, k6 to be set as follows:
#    k1 is the column number containing the data
#    k2 is the first of two consecutive columns to be used
#       in computing the moving average
#    k6 equal to k2+1 which is the number of the working column
#    k5 is the lag to be applied in adding the next observation
#
lag k5 ck1 ck6
let ck2=ck2+ck6
let k5=k5+1
```

C.7   Minitab macro for the prediction interval for a future observation

This section describes the macro *predint* that produces a prediction interval for a future observation. To run *predint*, store it in a file called *predint.mtb*, enter the sample data into a column, and set $k1$ and $k2$ as shown in table C.5. Note that if the value of $k2$ is less than 1, it is multiplied by 100 because we assume that a proportion has been supplied instead of a percentage. Next, change the current directory to the one containing *predint.mtb* and execute the macro with the *execute* command. For example, if you store *predint.mtb* on a floppy disk in drive *a:*, the commands to execute it are as follows:

```
cd a:\
execute 'predint.mtb'
```

Table C.5   Constants to be set before executing the Minitab macro *predint*

k1	number of the column containing the data
k2	$100\gamma\%$

```
noecho
# Macro PREDINT
# This macro computes the upper and lower limits of the
#    prediction interval.
# It requires k1 and k2 to be set as follows:
#
#    k1 column containing data
#    k2 gamma = confidence level
#
# k3 is set to gamma as a percentage
# k4 and k5 are set to the upper and lower limits of the
#    prediction interval
#
# In addition, k6 is used to store intermediate results
#
let k3=(k2>=1)*k2 + (k2<1)*k2*100
let k4=n(ck1)-1
let k5=(1+k3/100)/2
invcdf k5 k6;
t k4.
let k5=stdev(ck1)
let k6=k6*k5*sqrt(1+1/(k4+1))
let k5=mean(ck1)
let k4=k5-k6
let k5=k5+k6
note
note PREDICTION INTERVAL
note
note The Prediction Interval has been computed for
note
note the confidence level (expressed as a percentage)
print k3
note from a sample whose descriptive statistics are:
describe ck1
note
note The upper and lower limits of the Prediction Interval are:
print k4,k5
note
echo
```

C.8 Minitab macros for the theoretical value for the normal probability plot correlation coefficient

This section describes a suite of macros for computing r_T, the theoretical value for the normal probability plot correlation coefficient. The main macro, *rtheoret*, is invoked to compute r_T. It then calls other macros to output warning messages, compute the theoretical value and output the theoretical value. The macro computes r_T for $n = 3 \ldots 150$ and $\alpha = 0.10, 0.05$ and 0.01.

To run *rtheoret*, store it and the macros it calls in files with the same names as the macros and the extension *.mtb*. Next, set *k1* and *k2* as shown in table C.6. Then change the current directory to the one containing the macros and execute the main macro with the *execute* command. For example, if you store the main macro in the file *rtheoret.mtb* on a floppy disk in drive *a:*, the commands to execute it are as follows:

```
cd a:\
execute 'rtheoret.mtb'
```

Table C.6 Constants to be set before executing the Minitab macro *rtheoret*

k1	n
k2	α

C.8.1 Main macro for producing r_T

The main macro for obtaining r_T, *rtheoret*, is as follows. It invokes the macros *rterrn1*, *rterrn2*, *rterralp*, *rt1*, *rt5*, *rt10* and *rtout*, described in sections C.8.2, *Macros for producing warning messages*, C.8.3, *Macros for computing r_T for different significance levels*, and C.8.4, *Macro for output of r_T*.

```
noecho
# Macro RTHEORET
# This macro computes rT, the theoretical value
#    for the normal probability correlation coefficient.
# It is based on the formula for the approximate critical
# values given by
#    Ryan, T.A. and Joiner, B.L. (1976) Normal probability
#    plots and tests for normality. Technical Report,
#    Statistics Department, The Pennsylvania State University.
#
# It requires k1 and k2 to be set as follows:
#
#    k1 n = number of observations
#    k2 alpha = significance level
#
# k3 is set to the theoretical value
#
# In addition, k4-k7 are used to store intermediate results
#
# Compute rT
#
let k4=(k1<3)
let k5=(k1 > 150)
let k6=k1
let k7=k2
execute 'rterrn1.mtb' k4
let k4=~k4
execute 'rterrn2.mtb' k5
let k5=~((k2 = 0.10) | (k2 = 0.05) | (k2 = 0.01)) & k4
execute 'rterralp.mtb' k5
let k5=(k7=0.10) & k4
execute 'rt10.mtb' k5
```

continued . . .

```
let k5=(k7=0.05) & k4
execute 'rt5.mtb' k5
let k5=(k7=0.01) & k4
execute 'rt1.mtb' k5
execute 'rtout.mtb' k4
echo
```

C.8.2   Macros for producing warning messages

The macros for displaying an error message when the values of *n* or α supplied to the macro are not equal to values for which the computations are valid, *rterrn1*, *rterrn2* and *rterralp*, are as follows. They are called by the main macro, *rtheoret*.

```
# Macro RTERRN1
# macro to output illegal n error message for rT computation
note Theoretical value cannot be computed for n less than 3
```

```
# Macro RTERRN2
# macro to output illegal n error message for rT computation
note Theoretical value can only be computed for n up to 150
note The value for n = 150 will be computed
note
let k6=150
```

```
# Macro RTERRALP
# macro to output illegal alpha error message for rT computation
note Theoretical value only available for significance levels of
note 0.10, 0.05 and 0.01. The value for 0.05 will be computed.
note
let k7=0.05
```

C.8.3   Macros for computing r_T for different significance levels

The macros for computing the theoretical value, *rt10*, *rt5* and *rt1*, are as follows. They are called by the main macro, *rtheoret*.

```
# Macro RT10
# macro to compute rT for alpha = 0.10
let k3=1.0071-0.1371/sqrt(k6)-0.3682/k6+0.7780/k6/k6
```

```
# Macro RT5
# macro to compute rT for alpha = 0.05
let k3=1.0063-0.1288/sqrt(k6)-0.6118/k6+1.3505/k6/k6
```

```
# Macro RT1
# macro to compute rT for alpha = 0.1
let k3=0.9963-0.0211/sqrt(k6)-1.4106/k6+3.1791/k6/k6
```

C.8.4   Macro for output of r_T

The macro for outputting the theoretical value, *rtout*, is as follows. It is called by the main macro, *rtheoret*.

```
#  Macro RTOUT
#  This macro outputs rT
#
NOTE  The  Theoretical value  for  the  normal  probability  plot  r
NOTE  has  been  computed  for
NOTE
NOTE  the  number  of  observations  equal  to
print k6
NOTE  and  significance  level  of
print k7
NOTE
NOTE  The  theoretical  value  is:
print k3
```

C.9   Minitab macro for the tolerance interval for population values

This section describes the macro *tolerint* for computing the tolerance interval. To run *tolerint*, store it in a file called *tolerint.mtb*, enter the data into a column, and set *k1–k3* as shown in table C.7. Note that if the values of *k2* or *k3* are less than 1, they are multiplied by 100 as we assume that proportions have been supplied instead of percentages. Next, change the current directory to the one containing *tolerint.mtb* and execute the macro with the *execute* command. For example, if you store *tolerint.mtb* on a floppy disk in drive *a:*, the commands to execute it are as follows:

```
cd a:\
execute 'tolerint.mtb'
```

Table C.7   Constants to set before executing the Minitab macro *tolerint*

k1	number of the column containing the data
k2	$100\gamma\%$
k3	$100\pi\%$

```
noecho
#  Macro TOLERINT
#  This procedure computes  the  upper  and  lower  limits  of  the
#     tolerance interval.
#  It requires k1-k3 to be set as follows:
#
```

continued . . .

735

```
#     k1 column containing data
#     k2 gamma = confidence level
#     k3 pi = percentage of the population
#
# k4 is set to the sample size
# k5 and k6 are set to the upper and lower limits of the
# tolerance interval
#
# In addition, k7-k9 are used to store intermediate results
#     k12 is set to gamma as a percentage
#     k13 is set to pi as a percentage
#
# Compute gT based on the approximation given by
#     Howe, W.G. (1969) Two-sided tolerance limits for normal
#     populations - some improvements. Journal of the American
#     Statistical Association, 64: 610-620.
#
let k12=(k2>=1)*k2 + (k2<1)*k2*100
let k13=(k3>=1)*k3 + (k3<1)*k3*100
let k4=n(ck1)
let k5=k4-1
let k6=1-k12/100
invcdf k6 k6;
chisq k5.
let k7=(1+k12/100)/2
let k8=(1+k13/100)/2
invcdf k7 k7;
normal.
invcdf k8 k8;
normal.
let k6=k5*(1+1/k4)*k8*k8/k6*(1+(k5-2-k6)/(2*(k4+1)*(k4+1)))
let k9=1+k7*k7/k4+(3-k8*k8)*(k7**4)/6/k4/k4
let k8=k8*k8*k9*(1+(k9*(1+1/k7/k7)*k4/2/k5))
let k6=sqrt(k6)
let k8=sqrt(k8)
let k7=(1+1/k7/k7)*k4*k4
let k5=(k5<=k7)*k6 + (k5>k7)*k8
#
# Compute upper and lower limits
#
let k7=mean(ck1)
let k8=stdev(ck1)
let k6=k7+k5*k8
let k5=k7-k5*k8
#
# Output tolerance interval
#
note
note TOLERANCE INTERVAL
note
note The Tolerance Interval has been computed for
```

continued . . .

```
note
note the percentage of the population values to be covered being
print k13
note and the confidence level (expressed as a percentage) being
print k12
note from a sample whose descriptive statistics are:
describe ck1
note
note The upper and lower limits of the Tolerance Interval are:
print k5,k6
note
echo
```

APPENDIX D

DETAILED INSTRUCTIONS FOR MINITAB MENUS

This appendix presents instructions for using the pull-down menus to execute the commands used in this book and listed in Appendix B, *Summary of Minitab commands*. It is ordered alphabetically according to the commands. Generally, a pull-down menu is selected by clicking on its name on the menu bar of the session window. The pull-down menus list groups of related commands; to select the required group, click on it. Table D.1 summarises the menus and options that are equivalent to the commands used in this book. However, there is no command equivalent for the data screen; it is described in section D.6, *Data screen*.

Table D.1 Menus and options for some Minitab commands

Minitab command	Menu	Option
boxplot	Graph >	Boxplot...
cd		no equivalent
cdf	Calc >	Probability Distributions >
chisq		Chisquare... > Cumulative probability
code	Calc >	Code Data Values...
copy	Calc >	Copy Columns...
omit		Omit Rows...
use		Use Rows...
correlation	Stat >	Basic Statistics > Correlation...
describe	Stat >	Basic Statistics > Descriptive Statistics...
dotplot	Graph >	Dotplot...
erase	Calc >	Erase Variables...
execute	File >	Other Files > Execute Macro...
histogram	Graph >	Histogram...
info	Edit >	Get Worksheet Info...
	(Edit >	Data Screen [Alt-D])

Table D.1 (*continued*)

Minitab command	Menu	Option
invcdf	Calc >	Probability Distributions >
normal		Normal...
t		T...
let	Calc >	Functions and Statistics > General Expressions...
mean	Calc >	Functions and Statistics > Column Statistics...
mplot	Graph >	Multiple Scatter Plot...
name	Edit >	Data Screen
nooutfile	File >	Other Files > Stop Recording Session...
nscores	Calc >	Functions and Statistics > Functions...
oneway	Stat >	ANOVA > Oneway...
outfile	File >	Other Files > Start Recording Session...
plot	Graph >	Scatter Plot...
print	Edit >	Display Data...
random	Calc >	Random Data...
discrete		Discrete...
integer		Integer...
regress	Stat >	Regression > Regression...
predict		Options...
restart	File >	Restart Minitab
retrieve	File >	Open Worksheet...
port		Minitab portable worksheet
rmean	Calc >	Functions and Statistics > Row Statistics...
save	File >	Save Worksheet As...
portable.		Minitab portable worksheet
set	Edit >	Data Screen (Alt-D)
	Edit >	Set Patterned Data...
		(for a sequence of numbers with repetitions)
sort	Calc >	Sort...
stack	Calc >	Stack...
stem	Graph >	Stem and Leaf...
stop	File >	Exit
table	Stat >	Tables > Cross Tabulation
frequencies		Frequencies
count		Counts
colpercents		Column Percents
rowpercents		Row Percents
totpercents		Total Percents
chisq 2		not available

Table D.1 *(continued)*

Minitab command	Menu	Option
table	Stat >	Tables > Cross Tabulation...
mean, median, stdev, n		Summaries...
tally	Stat >	Tables > Tally...
count		Counts
percent		Percents
tinterval	Stat >	Basic Statistics > 1-Sample t...
tsplot	Graph >	Time Series Plot...

D.1 Boxplot

Graph > Boxplot...

To use the menus to produce the box-and-whisker plot, select the *Graph* menu — this displays the menu in figure D.1.

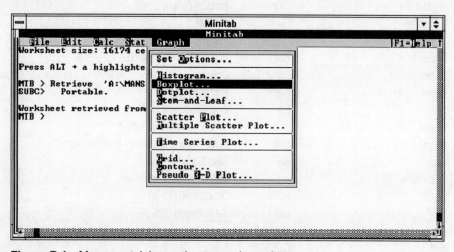

Figure D.1 Menu containing option to produce plots

Select the *Boxplot* option to display the dialog box in figure D.2, and complete the dialog box as shown in the figure. That is, specify the variable for which the box-and-whisker plot is to be produced. Also, make sure the *High resolution* option is not selected: it is selected if there is an 'X' in the option box alongside it; to make the 'X' disappear, click on it.

To use the menus to obtain the box-and-whisker plot for each value of a limited variable, complete the dialog box as in figure D.3. First, specify the variable for which the box-and-whisker plots are to be produced, in the *Variable* option box. Then put an 'X' in the *By variable* check box, and add the column containing the unrestricted variable to the *By variable* option box. Finally, make sure the *High resolution* graphics option is not selected; that is, there should not be an 'X' in the option box alongside it. Once the dialog box has been completed, click on *OK* to execute the command.

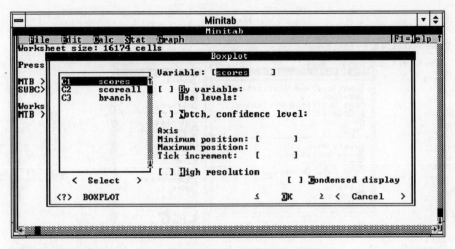

Figure D.2 Dialog box for producing box-and-whisker plots

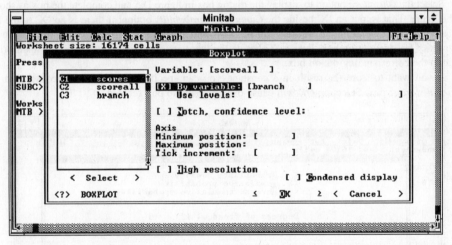

Figure D.3 Dialog box for producing box-and-whisker plot for each value of a limited variable

D.2 Cdf

The *cdf* command produces the cumulative probability, p_C, for various distributions in Minitab. For all distributions, use the *Probability Distributions* option from the *Calc* menu.

D.2.1 Chi-square distribution

Calc > Probability Distributions > Chisquare... > Cumulative probability

To use the menus to obtain the cumulative probability from the chi-square distribution, p_C, select the *Probability Distributions* option from the *Calc* menu — this displays the menu in figure D.4.

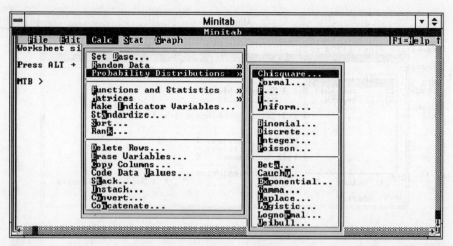

Figure D.4   Menu containing the option for obtaining p_C for the chi-square distribution

Select the *Chisquare* option to display the dialog box in figure D.5 and complete the box as shown in the figure. That is, put an 'X' beside the *Cumulative probability* option: if there is no 'X' to the left of the option, click between the brackets and an 'X' should appear. Place the degrees of freedom in the *Degrees of freedom* option box. Put an 'X' beside the *Input constant* option and place the appropriate value in the corresponding option box.

If you want to store the result in a constant, you can specify the name of the constant in the *Optional storage* box. Selecting *OK* will cause the command to be executed.

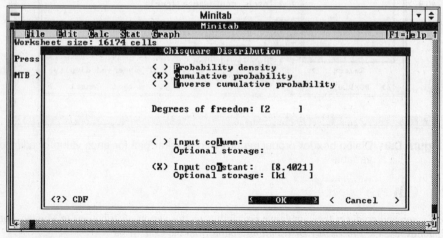

Figure D.5   Dialog box for chi-square distribution

D.3   Code

Calc > Code Data Values...

To use the menus to combine categories with the *code* command, click on *Calc* to display the menus in figure D.6.

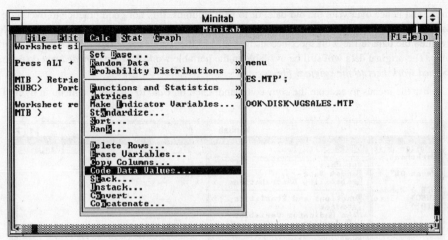

Figure D.6 Menu containing option to code values stored in a column

In this example, the values 12, 13 and 14 in the column named *landuse* are coded to become 12 and the result is placed in the column named *landuse*. In general it is not good practice to overwrite the original data. It is done in this case because the size of the worksheet is limited in some versions of Minitab.

To code the values, select the *Code Data Values* option to display the dialog box in figure D.7, and complete the box as shown in the figure. That is, enter column *landuse* as the source and destination columns and nominate 12, 13 and 14 as the original values and 12 as the new value. Click on *OK* to execute the command.

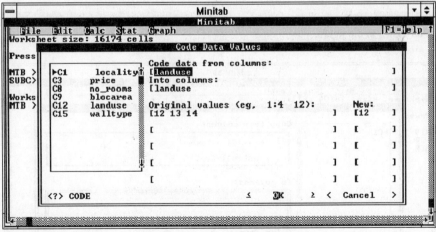

Figure D.7 Dialog box coding values stored in a column

D.4 Copy

Calc > Copy Columns...

The *copy* command is a flexible command for copying columns. You can copy entire columns to other columns, or just a subset of the rows in some columns to other columns. You can copy data to the same columns, and hence overwrite the old data, or to new columns. It is not good practice to overwrite the original data because you can lose some data altogether this way. However, sometimes we have overwritten the data in the worksheet because the size of the worksheet is limited in some versions of Minitab. The original data will still be available in the portable worksheet file *provided you do not save a modified worksheet to the original file.*

To use the menus to execute the *copy* command, click on *Calc* to display the menu in figure D.8.

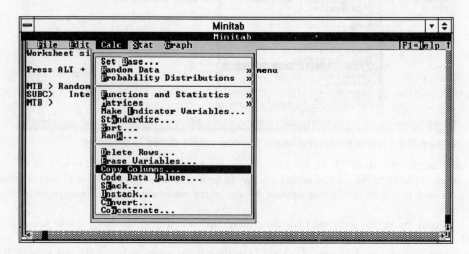

Figure D.8   Menu containing option to copy columns

To copy from *c1* to *c2*, click on *Copy Columns* to display the dialog box in figure D.9 and complete the box as shown in the figure.

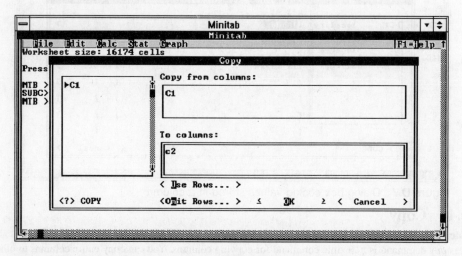

Figure D.9   Dialog box for copying a column

When you have specified the columns involved in the copy, you can copy:

1. all rows by clicking on *OK*;
2. some rows, specifying the rows to be copied by clicking on *Use Rows...*; or
3. some rows, specifying the rows to be omitted by clicking on *Omit Rows...*

You can also specify the rows by the row number or the values contained in the rows of a particular column. The examples cover these different forms.

D.4.1 Copying a subset of rows by specifying row numbers

In this example, we copy the first 300 rows from *c1*, containing 320 rows, to *c2* by specifying the row numbers of the rows to be copied. Having specified the columns as described previously, click on *Use Rows* to display the dialog box in figure D.10. Complete this box as shown to specify that only rows 1 to 300 are to be copied. Select *OK* once you have finished with this box and then select *OK* to execute the *copy* command.

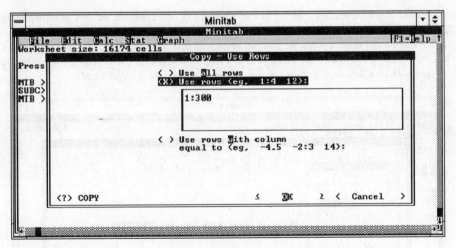

Figure D.10 Dialog box to specify which rows to use in copying columns

D.4.2 Copying a subset of rows by the values in a particular column

In this example, we copy the data in columns named *locality*, *landuse* and *walltype* back into the same columns, but omit the rows from all three columns for which the value of *walltype* is 2 or 4. To do this, first select the *Copy Columns* option from the *Calc* menu, and complete the dialog box as shown in figure D.11. That is, nominate the source and destination columns.

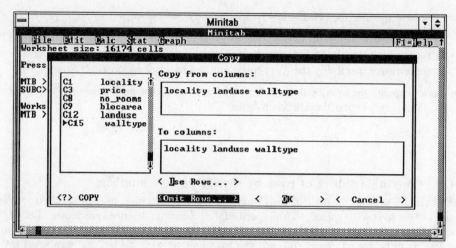

Figure D.11   Dialog box for copy command

Select the *Omit Rows* button in the dialog box in figure D.11, and complete the box as shown in figure D.12. That is, make sure the check box opposite the *Omit rows with column* option is selected. In the box at the end of this option place the column name *walltype*. Finally, place the numbers 2 and 4 in the box below the option. Once the dialog box is completed, click on *OK* to return you to the dialog box in figure D.11. Click on *OK* in this dialog box to execute the *copy* command.

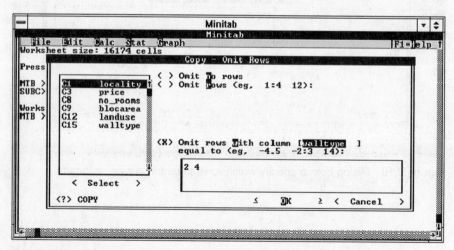

Figure D.12   Dialog box for specifying rows to be omitted

D.5   Correlation

Stat > Basic Statistics > Correlation...

To use the menus to produce the linear correlation coefficient, select the *Basic Statistics* option from the *Stat* menu — this displays the menus in figure D.13.

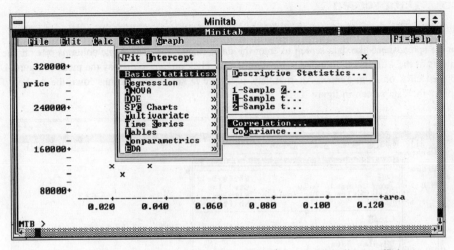

Figure D.13 Menu containing option to produce linear correlation coefficient

Select the *Correlation* option to display the dialog box in figure D.14, and complete the box as shown in the figure. That is, specify in the *Variables* box, the two variable for which the linear correlation coefficient is to be produced. Select *OK* to execute the command.

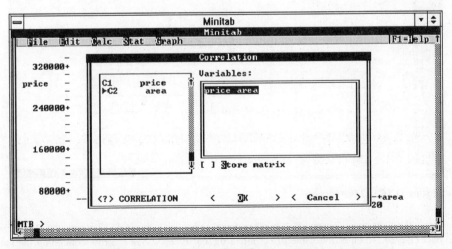

Figure D.14 Dialog box for producing the linear correlation coefficient

D.6 Data screen

Edit > Data Screen (Alt-D)

Use the spreadsheet-like data screen to enter the data, change the data, name columns or examine the contents of the worksheet. To move to the data screen, click on *Edit* to display the menu in figure D.15 and then click on *Data Screen*. Alternatively, press the *D* key while holding down the *Alt* key. This displays the data screen in figure D.16.

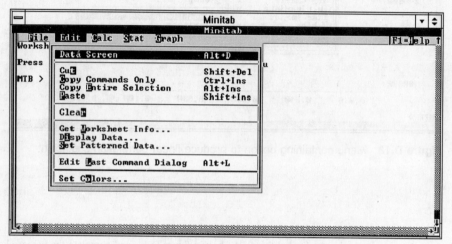

Figure D.15 Menu containing option to switch to the data screen

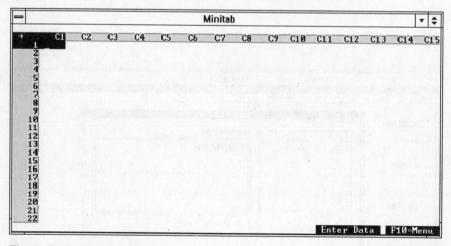

Figure D.16 Data screen

Then enter the data, using arrow keys to move from cell to cell; figure D.17 shows the *Data screen* with data entered. To enter the name *price*, move the cursor up above the row containing the list of columns and enter the name, *without the single quotation marks.*

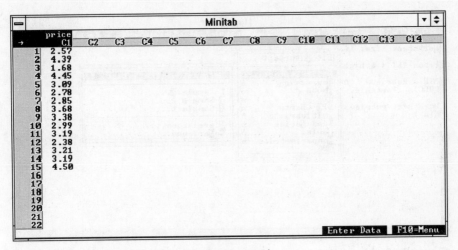

Figure D.17 Data screen showing data entered

To return to the session window, from which further Minitab commands can be executed, press the *F10* key to display the menu in figure D.18. Click on the *Go to Minitab Session* option. Alternatively, before pressing the *F10* key, press the *M* key while holding down the *Alt* key.

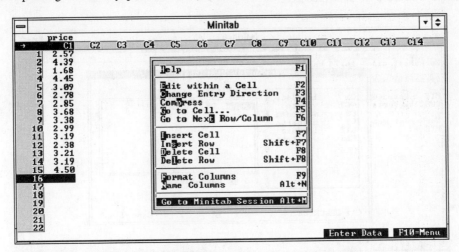

Figure D.18 Menu to exit data screen

D.7 Describe

Stat > Basic Statistics > Descriptive Statistics...

To use the menus to obtain the measures produced by the *describe* command, select the *Basic Statistics* option from the *Stat* menu — this displays the menus in figure D.19.

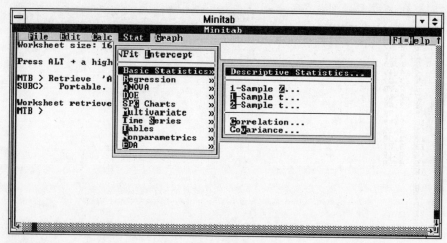

Figure D.19 Menu containing basic statistics option

Select the *Descriptive Statistics* option to display the dialog box in figure D.20, and complete the box as shown in the figure. That is, specify in the *Variables* option box the variable for which the descriptive statistics are to be produced.

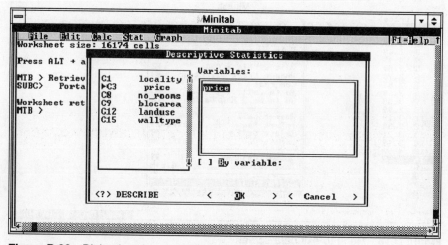

Figure D.20 Dialog box for producing descriptive statistics

If an unrestricted variable and a limited variable are involved and measures of central tendency and dispersion are required for each value of the limited variable, complete the dialog box in figure D.21. First, specify in the *Variables* option box the variable for which the descriptive statistics are to be produced. Then put an 'X' in the *By variable* check box, and add the column containing the limited variable to the *By variable* option box. Once you have completed the dialog box, select *OK* to execute the command.

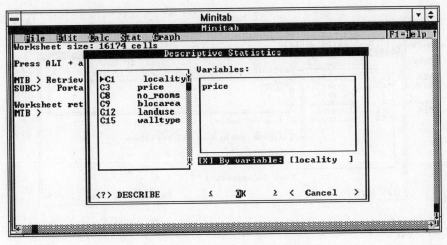

Figure D.21 Dialog box for producing descriptive statistics with the *by* subcommand

D.8 Dotplot

Graph > Dotplot...

To use the menus to produce the dotplot, click on *Graph* to display the menu in figure D.22. Select the *Dotplot* option to display the dialog box in figure D.23, and complete the box as shown in the figure. That is, specify the variable for which the dotplot is to be produced.

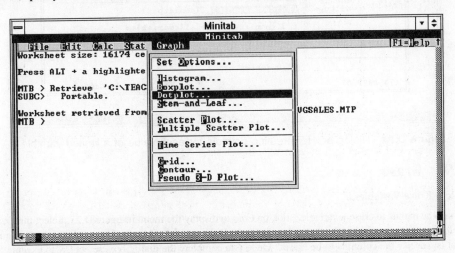

Figure D.22 Menu containing the dotplot option

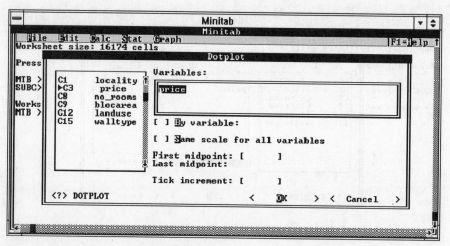

Figure D.23   Dialog box for creating dotplots

The completed dialog box for producing the dotplots, for each value of a limited variable, is shown in figure D.24. Note that the *By variable* option has been selected, and the variable has been specified as the limited variable *locality*. Once you complete the dialog box, select *OK* to execute the command.

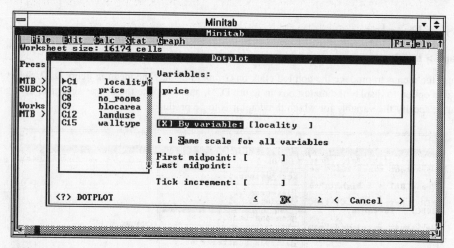

Figure D.24   Dialog box for creating dotplots for each value of a limited variable

D.9   Erase

Calc > Erase Variables...

To use the menus to erase a variable, click on *Calc* to display the menu in figure D.25. Select the *Erase Variables* option to display the dialog box in figure D.26, and complete the box as shown in the figure. That is, specify the columns to be erased. Once you complete the dialog box, select *OK* to execute the command.

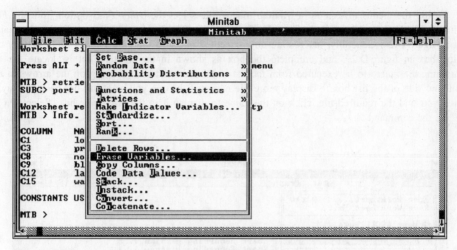

Figure D.25   Menu containing the erase variables option

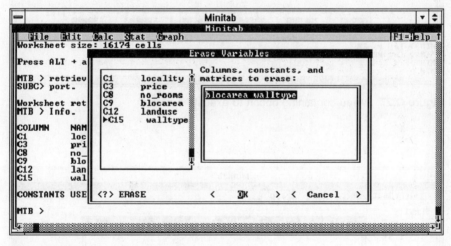

Figure D.26   Dialog box for erasing variables

D.10   Execute

File > Other Files > Execute Macro...

Some procedures that do not have Minitab commands are carried out by macros — a set of Minitab commands stored in a file whose name ends with *.mtb*. Running the set of commands that makes up a macro requires the *execute* command. However, before running the macro, you will probably have to change to the directory containing the macros and set constants.

To use the menus to execute a Minitab macro file, select the *Other Files* option from the *File* menu — this displays the menus in figure D.27. Select the *Execute Macro* option to display the dialog box in figure D.28. Generally, macros are only executed once, so click on *Select File* to display the dialog box in figure D.29, and complete the box as shown in the figure. That is, locate the file containing the macro to be executed from the list in the *Files* list box, clicking on the arrows at the righthand side of the list box to display more file names if the one you want has not been displayed. When you find the required file, click on the name to display it in the *File name* box. Select *OK* to execute the command.

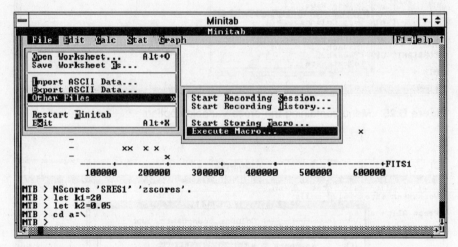

Figure D.27 Menu containing option to execute a macro

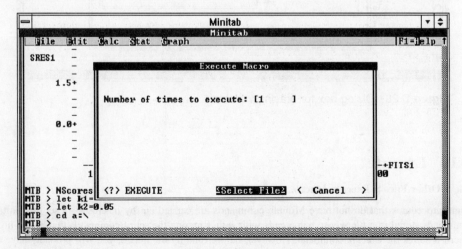

Figure D.28 Dialog box for specifying number of times to execute macro

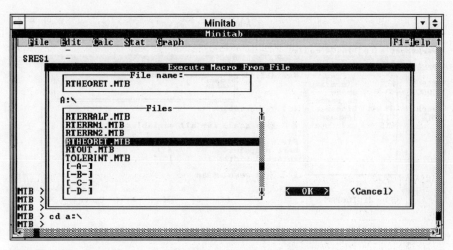

Figure D.29   Dialog box for selecting macro file to execute

D.11   Histogram

Graph > Histogram...

To use the menus to produce a frequency table and histogram, click on *Graph* to display the menu in figure D.30. Select the *Histogram* option to display the dialog box in figure D.31, and complete the box as shown in the figure. That is, specify the variable for which the histogram is to be produced, and make sure the *High resolution* option is not selected: it is selected if there is an 'X' in the option box alongside it; to make the 'X' disappear, click on it.

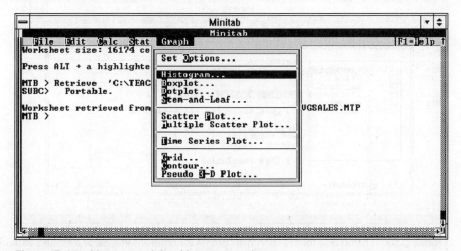

Figure D.30   Menu containing histogram option

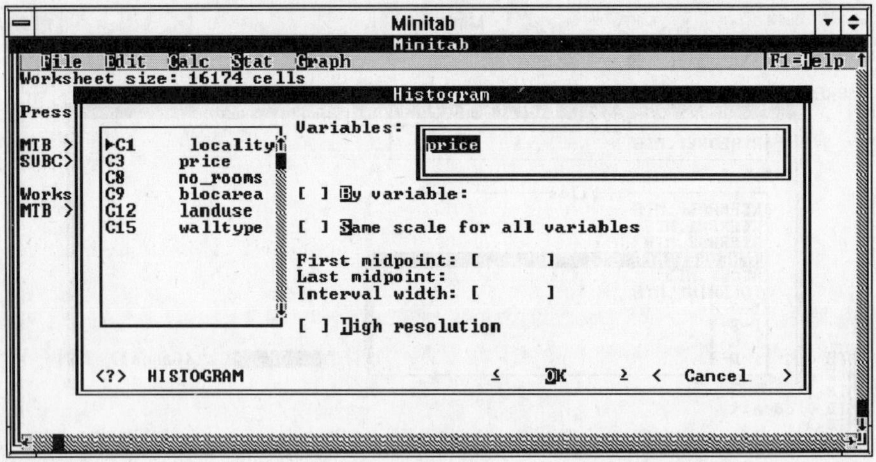

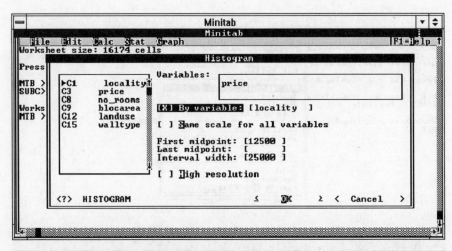

Figure D.31 Dialog box for creating histograms

If other options are required the contents of the option boxes in figure D.31 should be suitably modified. For example, to specify the class intervals, you need to specify the *First midpoint* and the *Interval width* options, as shown in figure D.32. To obtain the frequencies for each value of a limited variable, and associated frequency-based histograms, put an 'X' in the *By variable* check box and specify in the *By variable* option box the column containing a limited variable. For example, the limited variable *locality* is specified in the *By variable* box in figure D.32. Once you complete the dialog box, select *OK* to execute the command.

Figure D.32 Dialog box for creating histograms for different values of a limited variable and with specified class intervals

D.12 Info

Edit > Get Worksheet Info...

To use the menus to find out what information is stored in the worksheet, you can use either the data screen or the *Get Worksheet Info* option of the *Edit* menu. To move to the data screen, either select the *Edit* menu in figure D.15 and click on *Data Screen*, or press the *D* key while holding down the *Alt* key. To use the *Get Worksheet Info* option, first click on *Edit* to display the menu in figure D.33.

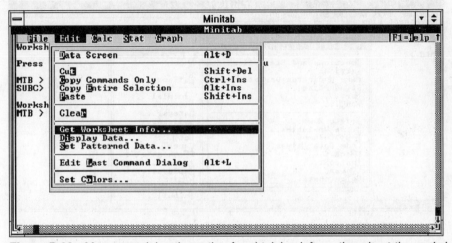

Figure D.33 Menu containing the option for obtaining information about the worksheet

Next, select the *Get Worksheet Info* option to display the dialog box in figure D.34. Click on the *OK* option button to execute the command.

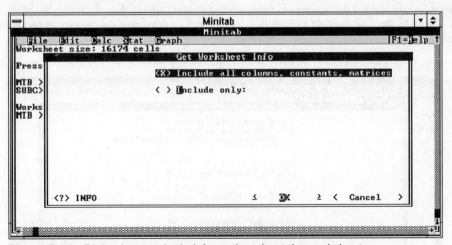

Figure D.34 Dialog box to obtain information about the worksheet

D.13 Invcdf

The *invcdf* command is used to produce theoretical values for various distributions in Minitab. For all distributions, use the *Probability Distributions* option from the *Calc* menu.

757

D.13.1 Normal distribution

Calc > Probability Distributions > Normal... > Inverse cumulative probability

To use the menus to obtain theoretical values from the normal distribution, z_T, select the *Probability Distributions* option from the *Calc* menu — this displays the menus in figure D.35.

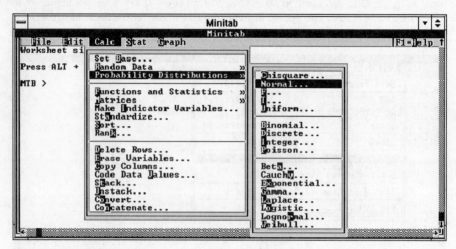

Figure D.35   Menu containing the option for obtaining z_T

Select the *Normal* option to display in the dialog box in figure D. 36, and complete the box as shown in the figure. That is, put an 'X' beside the *Inverse cumulative probability* option: if there is no 'X' to the left of the option, click between the brackets and an 'X' should appear. Put an 'X' beside the *Input constant* option and put the appropriate cumulative probability (p_C) in the corresponding option box. If you want to store the result in a constant, you can specify the name of the constant in the *Optional storage* box. Select *OK* to execute the command.

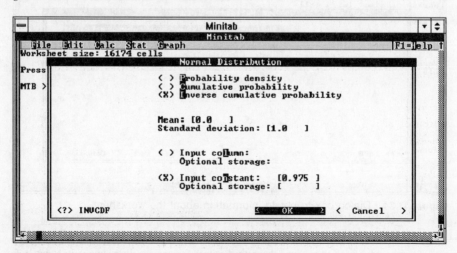

Figure D.36   Dialog box for the normal distribution

D.13.2   T distribution

Calc > Probability Distributions > T... > Inverse cumulative probability

To use the menus to obtain theoretical values from the t distribution, t_T, select the *Probability Distributions* option from the *Calc* menu — this displays the menus in figure D.37.

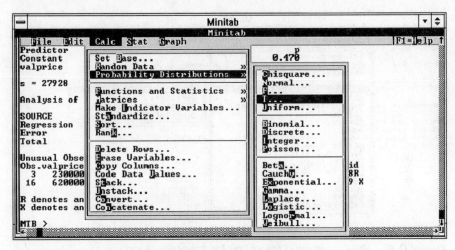

Figure D.37   Menu containing the option for obtaining t_T

Select the *T* option to display the dialog box in figure D.38, and complete the box as shown in the figure. That is, put an 'X' beside the *Inverse cumulative probability* option: if there is no 'X' to the left of the option, click between the brackets and an 'X' should appear. Put the degrees of freedom of the required t_T value in the *Degrees of freedom* option box. Put an 'X' beside the *Input constant* option and put the appropriate cumulative probability (p_C) in the corresponding option box. When you complete the dialog box, click on *OK* to execute the command.

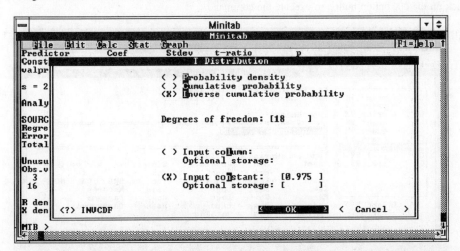

Figure D.38   Dialog box to specify the degrees of freedom and probability of required t_T

759

D.14 Let

Calc > Functions and Statistics > General Expressions...

To use the menus for calculations with the *let* command, select the *Functions and Statistics* option from the *Calc* menu — this displays the menus in figure D.39.

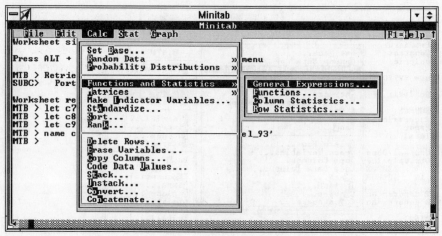

Figure D.39 Menu containing the option for specifying expressions

Select the *General Expressions* option to display the dialog box in figure D.40. Now complete the dialog box so that the expression can be calculated. The dialog box in figure D.40 has been completed appropriately for computing the mean of the data stored in a column named *prel_91* and multiplying the mean by 100. Because the calculations will yield a single value, the *New/modified variable* should be specified to be some suitable constant, such as *k1*. The expression to be evaluated has been typed into the *Expression* option box. Note that the number and positioning of the parentheses is crucial to the success of this command, and so are the single quotes (') around the name of the column *scores*. Click on the *OK* option button to execute the command.

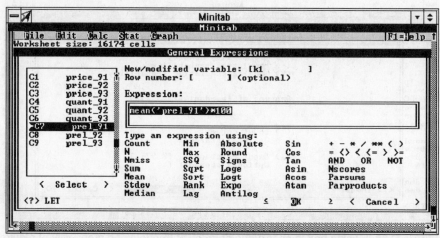

Figure D.40 Dialog box to specify the expression for a *let* command

The *let* command can also be used to perform computations on each value in a column of numbers, thereby producing a new column of numbers.

D.15   Mean

Calc > Functions and Statistics > Column Statistics...

To use the menus to compute the mean, select the *Function and Statistics* option of the *Calc* menu — this displays the menus in figure D.41.

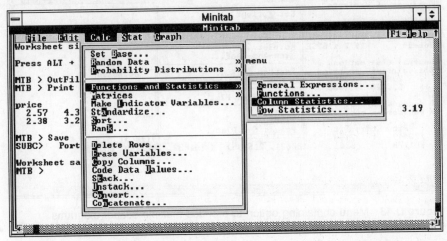

Figure D.41   Menu containing option to compute a statistic on a column

Click on the *Column Statistics* option to display the dialog box shown in figure D.42, and complete the box as shown in the figure. That is, click on the *Mean* option to choose it and specify the *Input variable* as *c1*. Finally, click on *OK* to display the mean.

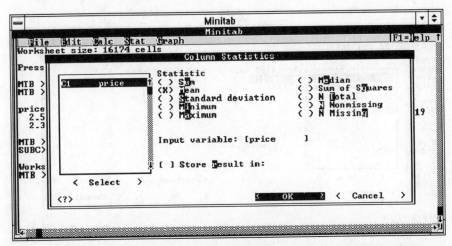

Figure D.42   Dialog box for specifying a statistic to be computed on a column

D.16 Mplot

Graph > Multiple Scatter Plot...

To use the menus to produce the scatter diagrams that contain several plots, click on *Graph* to display the menu in figure D.43.

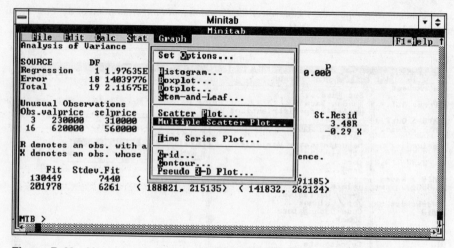

Figure D.43 Menu containing option to produce multiple scatter diagrams

Click on the *Multiple Scatter Plot* option to display the dialog box in figure D.44, and complete the box as shown in the figure. In this case two plots have been specified because each variable in the *Vertical axis* option box will be plotted against the corresponding variable in the *Horizontal axis* box. Make sure the *High resolution* option is not selected: it is selected if there is an 'X' in the option box alongside it; to make the 'X' disappear, click on it. Select *OK* to execute the command.

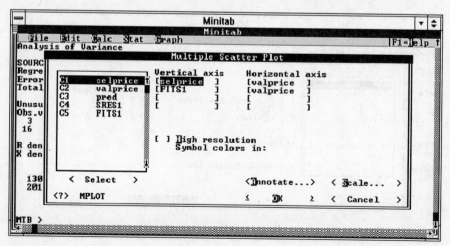

Figure D.44 Dialog box to specify the plots for a multiple scatter diagram

D.17   Name

The data screen is used to name columns. To move to the data screen, either select the *Edit* menu in figure D.15 and click on *Data Screen*, or press the *D* key while holding down the *Alt* key. To enter the name, move the cursor up above the row containing the list of columns and enter the name, *without the single quotation marks.*

D.18   Nooutfile

File > Other Files > Stop Recording Session...

When you want to stop saving output in the outfile, select the *Other Files* option of the *File* menu — this displays the menus in figure D.45. Click on *Stop Recording Session* and the *nooutfile* command will be issued. It is an optional command if it is to be followed immediately by the *stop* command, as the *stop* command also closes the file.

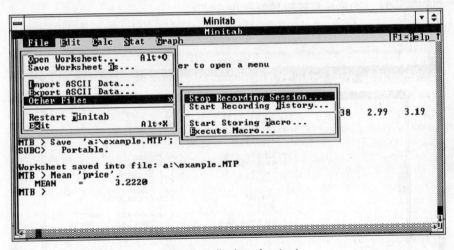

Figure D.45   Menu to stop recording displayed output

D.19   Nscores

Calc > Functions and Statistics > Functions...

To use the menus to compute the normal scores, select the *Functions and Statistics* option of the *Calc* menu — this displays the menus in figure D.46. Click on the *Functions* option to display the dialog box in figure D.47, and complete the box as shown in the figure. That is, put the column containing the data from which the normal scores are to be computed into the *Input column* option box, and place the column to contain the normal scores computed by Minitab in the *Result in* option box. Also, put an 'X' beside the *Normal scores* option. Once the dialog box is complete, click on *OK* to execute the command.

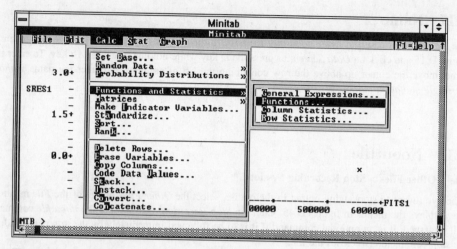

Figure D.46 Menu to access Minitab functions

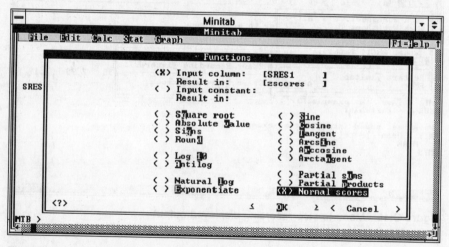

Figure D.47 Dialog box for computing normal scores

D.20 Oneway

ANOVA > Oneway...

Menus can be used to produce the one-way analysis of variance, although this method differs from directly entering the *oneway* command. With menus, the columns to contain the residuals and fitted values are not named. To use the menus to execute the *oneway* command, select the *ANOVA* option from the *Stat* menu — this displays the menus in figure D.48.

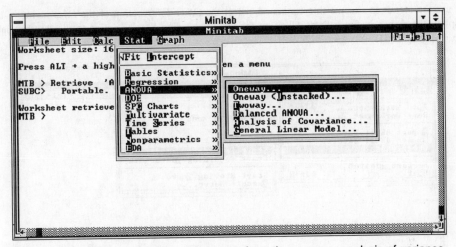

Figure D.48 Menu containing option to perform the one-way analysis of variance

Select the *Oneway* option to display the dialog box in figure D.49, and complete the box as shown in the figure. That is, enter the column containing the unrestricted variable in the *Response* option box, put the limited variable in the *Factor* option box, and put an 'X' in the *Store residuals* and *Store fits* check boxes. Note that names are not supplied for the columns to store the residuals and fitted values. Minitab automatically locates the last-used column, names the next two columns and places the residuals and fitted values in them. Select *OK* to execute the command.

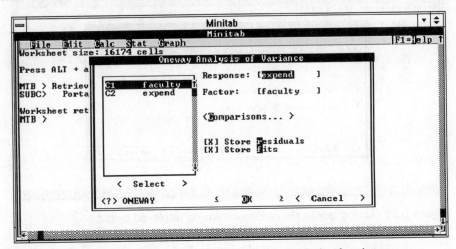

Figure D.49 Dialog box for performing a one-way analysis of variance

D.21 Outfile

Files > Other Files > Start Recording Session...

To print on paper the material that appears on the screen, you must store the information in a file that can then be printed after Minitab is stopped. To arrange for a file to be made, use the *outfile* command.

To use the menus to execute this command, select the *Other Files* option of the *Files* menu — this displays the menus in figure D.50. Click on the *Start Recording Session* option to display the dialog box in figure D.51.

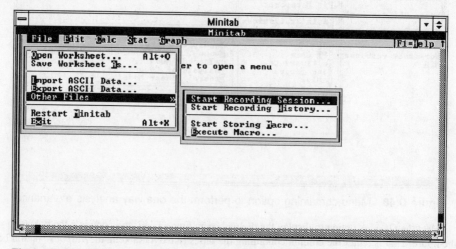

Figure D.50   Menu to start recording displayed output

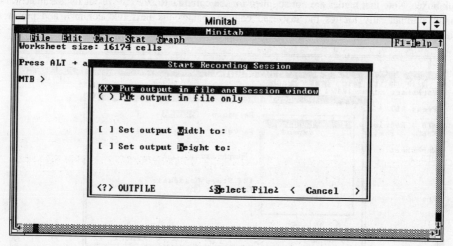

Figure D.51   Dialog box to set options for saving displayed output

Generally, the defaults will be suitable, so click on *Select File* to display the dialog box in figure D.52, and complete the box as shown in the figure. That is, enter the file name as shown.

In the example, the file to store what is displayed on the screen is called *example.lis*. The drive specification *a:* has been supplied because the disk to hold the file is in drive *a*; you might have to use a different drive as this varies from one computer system to another. The name of the file, *example*, must contain no more than 8 characters; it could not be *coffeeprice*, for instance. The extension *.lis* is supplied to indicate that it is a file containing output listing. Once you complete the dialog box, click on *OK* to execute the command.

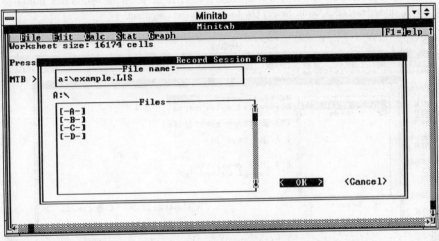

Figure D.52 Dialog box to choose file for saving displayed output

Minitab places everything that appears in the session window, *after* the *outfile* command until the *nooutfile* command, in the file *example.lis*. Note that the *outfile* command does not do the printing. It stores the displayed output so that it can be printed by using your system's command to obtain the printout of a file.

D.22 Plot

Graph > Scatter Plot...

To use the menus to produce the scatter diagram, click on *Graph* to display the menu in figure D.53.

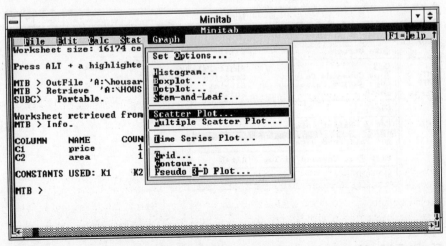

Figure D.53 Menu containing plot option

Select the *Scatter Plot* option to display the dialog box in figure D.54, and complete the box as shown in the figure. That is, specify the two variables for which the plot is to be produced and make sure the *High resolution* option is not selected: it is selected if there is an 'X' in the option box alongside it; to make the 'X' disappear, click on it. Select *OK* to execute the command.

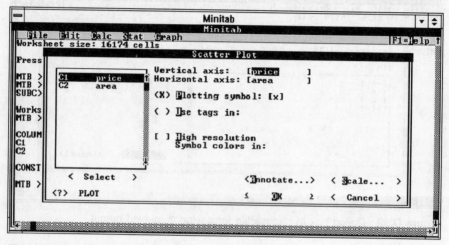

Figure D.54   Dialog box for creating scatter diagrams

D.23   Print

Edit > Display Data...

To use the menus to display the data on the screen, click on *Edit* to display the menu in figure D.55. Select the *Display data* option. Note that this print command displays data only on screen, *not* on paper.

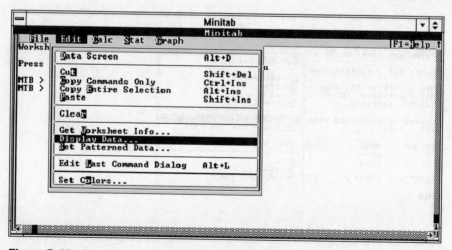

Figure D.55   Menu containing option to display data

Now, to print a column, complete the dialog box as shown in figure D.56 and select *OK* to execute the command.

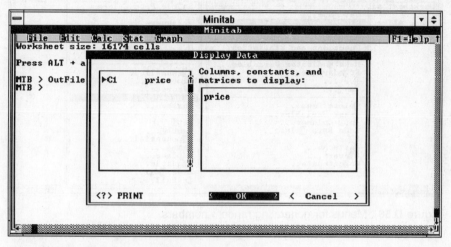

Figure D.56   Dialog box for displaying a column

On the other hand, to print constants, complete the option box of the dialog box as shown in figure D.57 and select *OK* to execute the command.

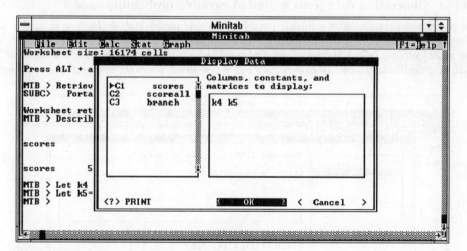

Figure D.57   Dialog box for printing constants

D.24   Random

Calc > Random Data...

To use the menus to generate the random numbers, select the *Random Data* option from the *Calc* menu — this displays the menus in figure D.58. Now select the type of random number to be generated.

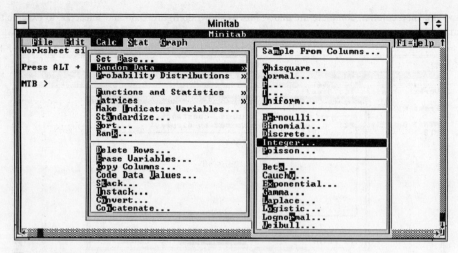

Figure D.58 Menus for generating random numbers

D.24.1 Generating data from a limited variable probability model

To generate observations from a limited variable probability model, click on *Discrete* to display the dialog box in figure D.59. Complete the box as shown in the figure to generate 200×50 numbers from the limited variable probability model specified by *c1* and *c2*; 200 of these numbers will be stored in each of the columns *c11–c60*. Once the dialog box is completed, select *OK* to execute the command.

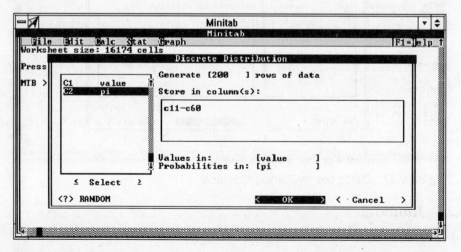

Figure D.59 Dialog box for generating numbers from a limited variable probability model

D.24.2 Generating data that consists of integers

To generate integers, click on *Integer* to display the dialog box in figure D.60. Complete the box as shown in the figure to generate 320 numbers between 1 and 25 757 and store them in *c1*. Once the dialog box is completed, select *OK* to execute the command.

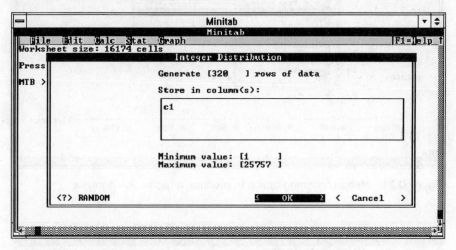

Figure D.60 Dialog box for generating integer random numbers

D.25 Regress

Stat > Regression > Regression...

When you use the menus, the specification of the *regress* command depends on what is to be produced. The major variants include:

- the basic use of the command — if, for example, you perform a regression to produce descriptive summaries;
- the use of the command to produce the basic analysis and to produce the standardised residuals and fitted values for checking the assumptions underlying the inference procedures;
- the use of the command to produce, in addition to the basic analysis and the quantities for assumption checking, the mean responses and associated intervals.

D.25.1 Basic use of the *regress* command

To use the menus to execute the *regress* command, select the *Regression* option from the *Stat* menu — this displays the menus in figure D.61. Select the second *Regression* option to display the dialog box in figure D.62, and complete the box as shown in the figure. That is, put the column containing the response variable into the *Response* option box and put the explanatory variable into the *Predictors* option box. Select *OK* to execute the command.

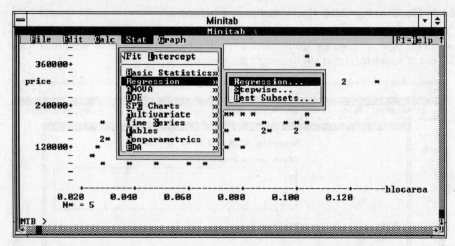

Figure D.61 Menu containing option to produce a regression analysis

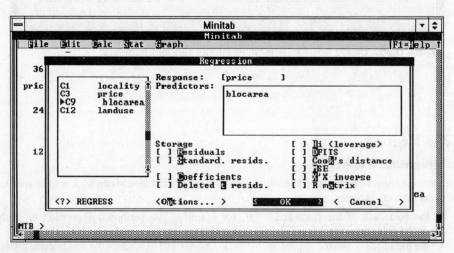

Figure D.62 Dialog box for regression

D.25.2 Regression analysis including standardised residuals and fitted values

Using menus to produce the regression analysis and the standardised residuals and fitted values differs from directly entering the *regress* command. With menus, the columns to contain the residuals and fitted values are not named. To use the menus to execute the *regress* command, select the *Regression* option from the *Stat* menu — this displays the menu in figure D.61. Select the *Regression* option on the second menu to display the dialog box in figure D.63, and complete the box as shown in the figure. That is, put the column containing the response variable into the *Response* option box and put the explanatory variable into the *Predictors* option box. Put an 'X' in the *Standard. resids.* and the *Fits* check boxes. Note that names are not supplied for the columns to store the residuals and fitted values. Minitab automatically locates the last-used column, names the next two columns and places the residuals and fitted values in them. If you do not require mean responses, select the *OK* button to execute the command. To specify values for which mean responses are required, follow the instructions in section D.25.3, *Regression analysis including mean responses and intervals.*

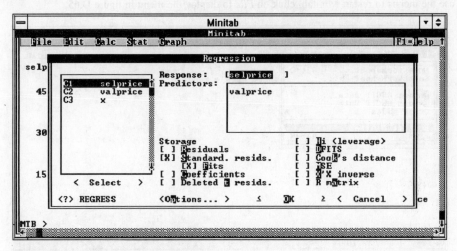

Figure D.63 Dialog box for regression

D.25.3 Regression analysis including mean responses and intervals

Select *Options* to display the *Options* dialog box in figure D.64, and complete the box as indicated in the figure. That is, put the column containing the values for which mean responses are required into the *Prediction intervals for new observations* box. Select the *OK* button, which returns you to the *Regression* dialog box in figure D.63. Select the *OK* button to execute the command.

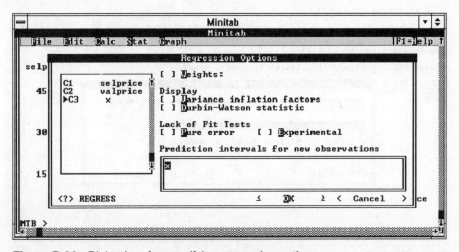

Figure D.64 Dialog box for specifying regression options

D.26   Restart

File > Restart Minitab

To use the menus to restart Minitab, click on *File* to display the menu in figure D.65.

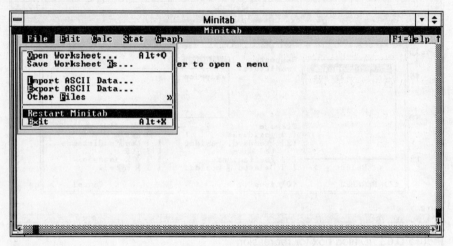

Figure D.65   Menu containing option to restart Minitab

Select the *Restart Minitab* option to display the dialog box in figure D.66. If the worksheet has just been saved, simply click on *OK* to restart Minitab without saving the worksheet. If the *save* command has not been used, click on the *Save in Minitab portable format* option, otherwise the contents of the worksheet will permanently disappear.

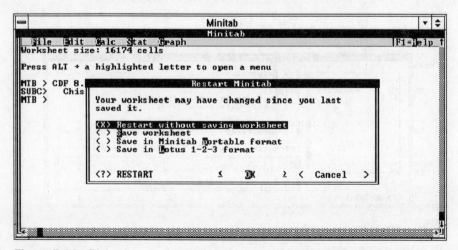

Figure D.66   Dialog box to check worksheet saved before restarting Minitab

D.27   Retrieve

Files > Open Worksheet...

To use the menus to retrieve the worksheet in a portable worksheet file, click on *File* to display the menu in figure D.67. Choose the *Open Worksheet* option to display the dialog box in figure D.68. Select *Minitab portable worksheet* and then click on *Select File*.

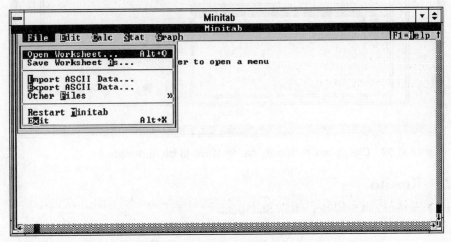

Figure D.67   Menu containing option to retrieve the worksheet in a file

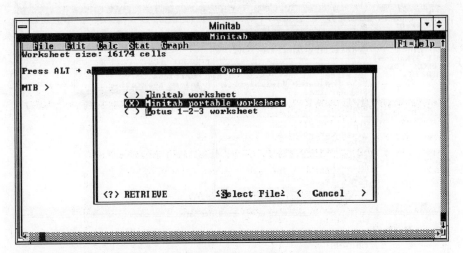

Figure D.68   Dialog box for choosing type of file to retrieve

This displays the dialog box in figure D.69; complete it as shown in the figure. That is, enter the file name as shown. When finished, click on *OK* to open the file.

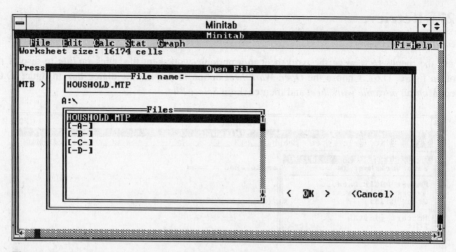

Figure D.69   Dialog box to specify name of file to be retrieved

D.28   Rmean

Calc > Functions and Statistics > Row Statistics...

To use the menus to compute the mean of each row of a set of columns, select the *Function and Statistics* option of the *Calc* menu — this displays the menus in figure D.70.

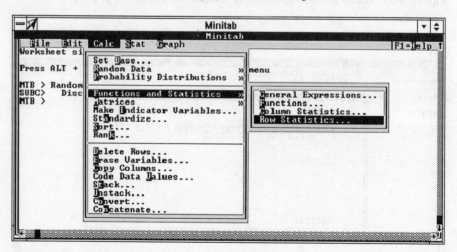

Figure D.70   Menu containing option to compute a statistic for each row of a set of columns

Click on the *Row Statistics* option to display the dialog box in figure D.71, and complete the box shown in the figure. That is, click on the *Mean* option to choose it, specify the *Input variables* as *c11–c60* and specify the *Result in* as *c61*. Finally, click on *OK* to store the means of the rows of *c11–c60* in *c61*.

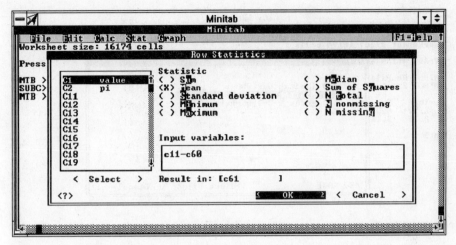

Figure D.71   Dialog box for specifying a statistic to be computed for the rows of a set of columns

D.29   Save

Files > Save Worksheet As...

To use the menus to save the worksheet in a portable worksheet file, click on *File* to display the menu in Figure D.72. Choose the *Save Worksheet As* option to display the dialog box in figure D.73. Select *Minitab portable worksheet* and then click on *Select File*.

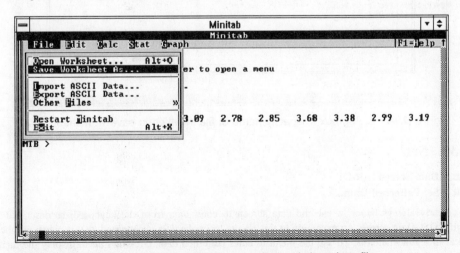

Figure D.72   Menu containing option to save the worksheet in a file

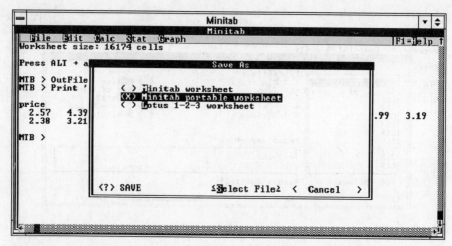

Figure D.73 Dialog box for choosing type of file for saving worksheet

This displays the dialog box in figure D.74; complete it as shown in the figure. That is, enter the file name as shown. When finished, click on *OK* to open the file.

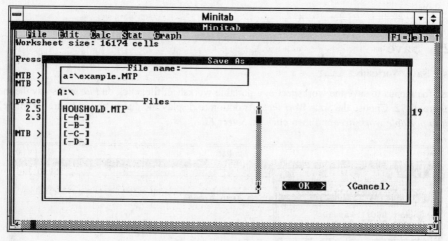

Figure D.74 Dialog box to specify name of file in which to save worksheet

D.30 Set

Edit > Data Screen (Alt-D)
Edit > Set Patterned Data...

It is nearly always better to use the data screen to enter data from the keyboard, as described in section D.6, *Data screen*. An exception to this occurs when the data is patterned, that is, when numbers repeat in regular patterns. To use the menu to enter patterned data, click on *Edit* to display the menu in figure D.75. Select the *Set Patterned Data* option to display the dialog box in figure D.76.

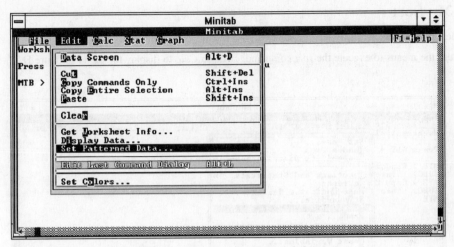

Figure D.75   Menu containing option to set patterned data

To enter the list of numbers 1, 2 and 3 twice, complete the dialog box for setting patterned data, as shown in figure D.76. That is:

- enter the column to contain the data into the *Put data into column* box;
- put an 'X' in the *Patterned sequence* check box;
- set the *Start at* box to 1;
- set the *End at* box to 3;
- set the *Repeat each value* box to 1;
- set the *Repeat the whole list* box to 2.

Select *OK* to execute the command.

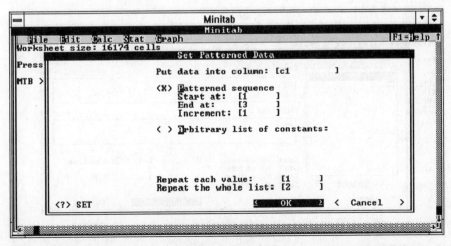

Figure D.76   Dialog box for setting patterned data

D.31 Sort

Calc > Sort...

To use the menus to execute the *sort* command, click on *Calc* to display the menu in figure D.77.

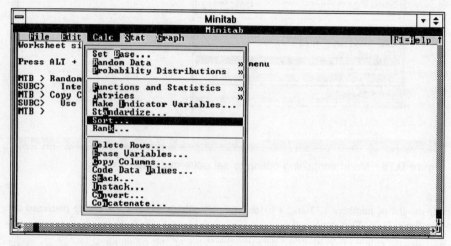

Figure D.77 Menu containing option to sort columns

Select the *Sort* option to display the dialog box in figure D.78, and complete the box as shown in the figure. Select *OK* to execute the command.

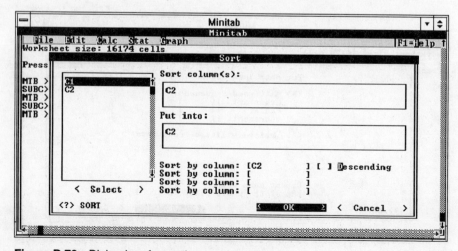

Figure D.78 Dialog box for sorting a column

D.32 Stack

Calc > Stack...

To use the menus to stack columns together, click on *Calc* to display the menu in figure D.79. Select the *Stack* option to display the dialog box in figure D.80, and complete the box as shown in the figure. That is, place one of the columns to be combined into each block — a maximum of five columns can be combined at once. Specify the column to receive the combined columns in the *And put in* box.

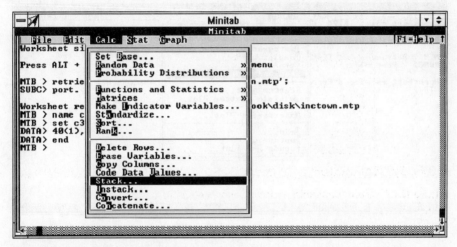

Figure D.79   Menu containing the stack option

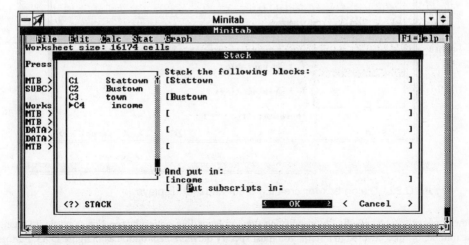

Figure D.80   Dialog box for stacking columns together

D.33 Stem

Graph > Stem-and-Leaf...

To use the menus to produce the stem-and-leaf display, click on *Graph* to display the menu in figure D.81. Select the *Stem-and-Leaf* option to display the dialog box in figure D.82, and complete the box as shown in the figure. That is, specify the variable for which the stem-and-leaf display is to be produced.

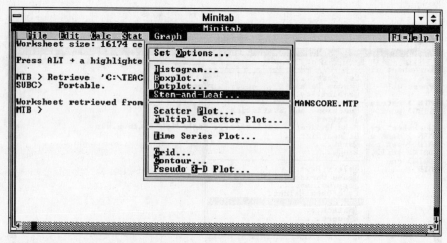

Figure D.81 Menu containing the stem-and-leaf option

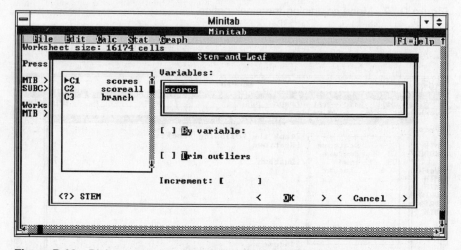

Figure D.82 Dialog box for creating stem-and-leaf displays

Other options can be specified by modifying the corresponding option boxes. For example, to change the number of lines devoted to a stem, you must specify the *Increment* option as in figure D.83. Further, to produce stem-and-leaf displays, for each value of a limited variable, you must put an 'X' in the *By variable* check box and specify a limited variable, such as *branch*, in the option box as shown in figure D.83. Once the dialog box has been completed, click on *OK* to execute the command.

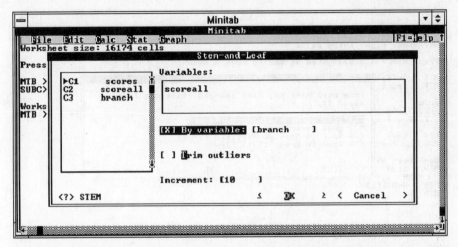

Figure D.83   Dialog box for creating a stem-and-leaf display with specified number of lines per stem and for each value of a limited variable

D.34 Stop

File > Exit

To use the menus to stop Minitab, click on *File* to display the menu in figure D.84.

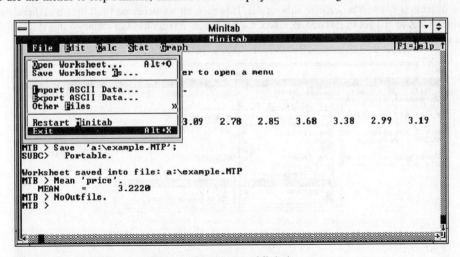

Figure D.84   Menu containing option to stop Minitab

Select the *Exit* option to display the dialog box shown in figure D.85. If the worksheet has just been saved, simply click on *OK* to stop Minitab without saving the worksheet. If the *save* command has not been used, click on the *Save in Minitab portable format* option, otherwise the contents of the worksheet will permanently disappear.

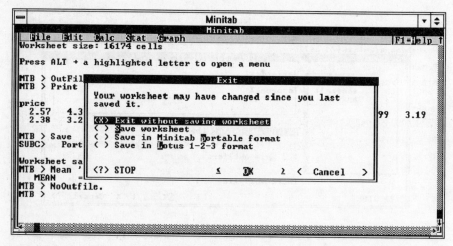

Figure D.85 Dialog box to check worksheet saved before Minitab stopped

D.35 Table

Stat > Tables > Cross Tabulation...

The *table* command can be used to produce one-way summary tables, two-way and three-way contingency tables and one-way and two-way tables of means, median and standard deviations. Each type of table is covered in separate subsections. However, all are accessed from the *Cross Tabulation* option of *Tables*. To get to this option, select the *Table* option from the *Stat* menu — this displays the menus in figure D.86.

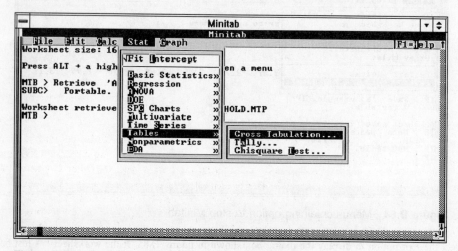

Figure D.86 Menu containing option to produce tables

D.35.1 One-way summary tables

To use the menus to obtain the one-way summary table, you can use either the *Cross Tabulation* or the *Tally* option of *Tables* from the *Stat* menu. This section describes how to use the *Cross Tabulation* option. To use *Tally*, see the separate description for the *tally* command.

To use the *Cross Tabulation* option to produce the one-way summary table, select the *Tables* option from the *Stat* menu — this displays the menus in figure D.86. Click on *Cross Tabulation* to display the dialog box in figure D.87, and to produce both counts and percentages, complete the box as shown in the figure. Click on *OK* to execute the command.

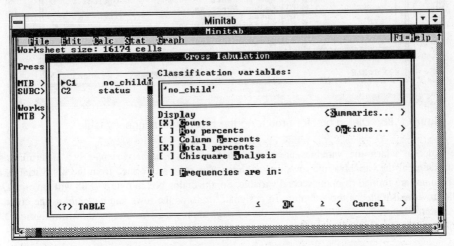

Figure D.87   Dialog box for producing the one-way summary table

D.35.2 Two-way contingency tables

To use the menus to produce the two-way contingency tables, select the *Table* option from the *Stat* menu — this displays the menus in figure D.86. Click on *Cross Tabulation* to display the dialog box in figure D.88, and complete the box as shown in the figure. That is, enter the column or names of the variables on which the contingency table is to be based and make sure that only the check box next to *Counts* is marked with an 'X'. In the dialog box shown, the variables were specified by first selecting the *no_child* column and clicking on the *Select* button, then by selecting the *status* column and clicking on the *Select* button a second time. Minitab adds the names to the *Classification variables* box, and places single quotes (') around the name that includes the underscore (_). Having finished the dialog box, click on *OK* to execute the command.

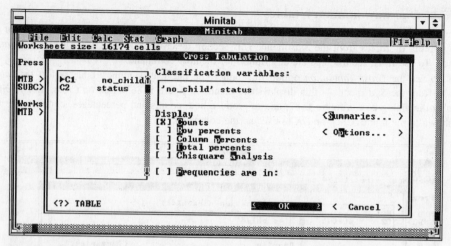

Figure D.88 Dialog box for producing the two-way contingency table

The order in which the variables are placed in the *Classification variables* box determines the organisation of the variables into rows and columns. The rows are formed from the first variable, and the columns are formed from the second variable. So, the dialog box in figure D.88 will have *no_child* as the rows and *status* as the columns. To designate *status* as the rows and *no_child* as the columns, select *status* before *no_child* to complete the *Classification variables* box as shown in figure D.89. Click on *OK* to execute the command.

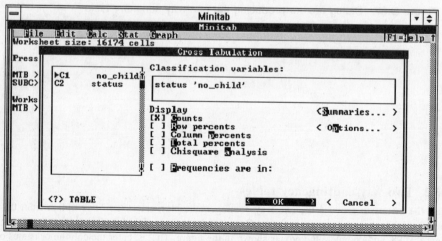

Figure D.89 Dialog box for producing the re-ordered contingency table

To use the menus to produce tables with counts and/or percentages, make sure that there are 'X's in the check boxes for the quantities that you want in the table. For example, to produce a table with both counts and column percentages, click on the check boxes next to *Counts* and *Column percents* as in figure D.90.

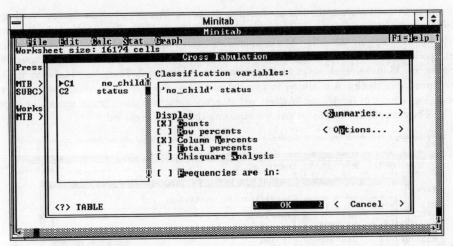

Figure D.90 Dialog box for producing a two-way contingency table with counts and column percentages

D.35.3 Three-way contingency tables

To use the menus to produce the three-way contingency tables, select the *Tables* option from the *Stat* menu — this displays the menus in figure D.86. Click on *Cross Tabulation* to display the dialog box in figure D.91, and complete the box as shown in the figure. Click on *OK* to execute the command.

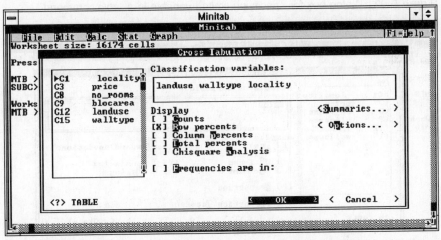

Figure D.91 Dialog box to produce a three-way contingency table

D.35.4 One-way tables of means, medians and standard deviations

To use the menus to produce the one-way tables of measures, select the *Tables* option from the *Stat* menu — this displays the menus in figure D.86. Click on *Cross Tabulations* to display the dialog box in figure D.92, and complete the box as shown in the figure. That is, select the limited variable and enter it into the *Classification variables* option box, as in figure D.92. Then click on the *Summaries* option button to display the dialog box in figure D.93, and complete the box as shown in the figure. First, specify the column containing the unrestricted variable in the *Associated variables* option box. Then put an 'X' in the check boxes for the measures to be produced. Thus, there is always an 'X' in the *N nonmissing* check box to always include the number of observations on which the measures are based. One or more of the *Means*, *Medians* and *Standard deviations* check boxes should also contain an 'X'. The example has the *Means* and *N nonmissing* check boxes selected.

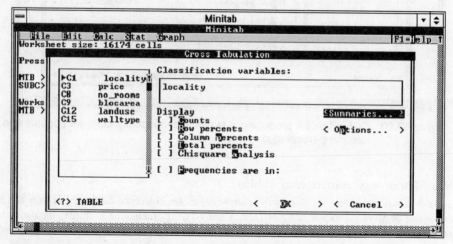

Figure D.92   Dialog box for specifying limited variable in a *table* command

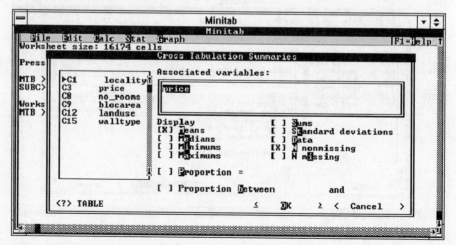

Figure D.93   Dialog box for specifying unrestricted variable and measures in subcommands of *table* command

Clicking on the *OK* button returns you to the dialog box in figure D.92, and clicking on the *OK* button a second time executes the command.

D.35.5 Two-way tables of means and medians

How to use the menus to produce the two-way tables of measures with the *table* command is illustrated for the two-way table of medians. Select the *Tables* option from the *Stat* menu — this displays the menus in figure D.86. Next, select the *Cross Tabulations* option to display the dialog box in figure D.94, and complete the box as shown in the figure. That is, specify the columns containing the two limited variables in the *Classification variables* option box.

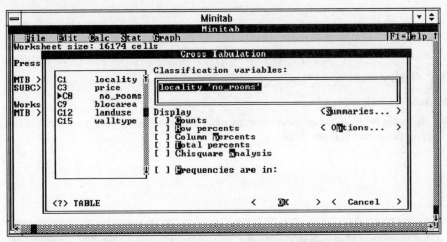

Figure D.94 Dialog box for specifying two limited variables in a *table* command

Now click on the *Summaries* option button to display the dialog box in figure D.95, and complete the box as shown in the figure. First, specify the column containing the unrestricted variable in the *Associated variables* option box. Then put an 'X' in the check boxes for the measures to be produced. We have put an 'X' in the *Medians* and *N nonmissing* check boxes.

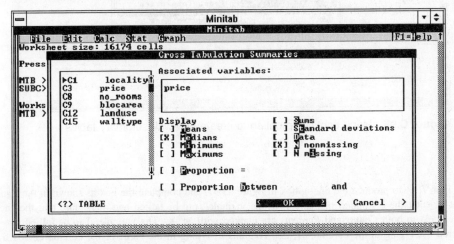

Figure D.95 Dialog box for specifying unrestricted variable and measures in subcommands of a *table* command

Clicking on the *OK* button returns you to the dialog box in figure D.94, and clicking on the *OK* button a second time executes the command.

D.36 Tally

Stat > Tables > Tally...

To use the menus to obtain the one-way summary table, select the *Table* option from the *Stat* menu — this displays the menus in figure D.96.

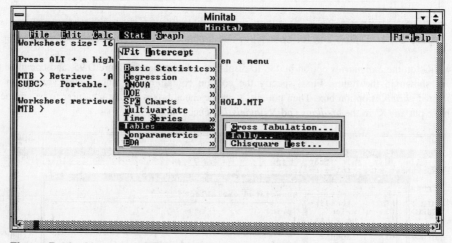

Figure D.96 Menu containing option to create one-way summary tables

Click on *Tally* to produce the dialog box in figure D.97, and complete the box as shown in the figure. That is, enter the column(s) or name(s) of the variable(s) to be tallied and make sure that the check boxes next to both *Counts* and *Percents* are marked with an 'X'. The variable(s) to be tallied can be entered by: typing in the column, $c1$, that contains it; typing in the name of the column enclosed in single quotes ('); or clicking on the desired column in the list of columns and then clicking on the *Select* button. Finally, click on *OK* to execute the command.

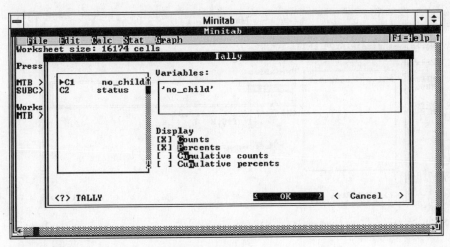

Figure D.97 Dialog box for tallying columns

D.37 Tinterval

Stat > Basic Statistics > 1-Sample t...

To use the menus to obtain the confidence interval for the population mean, select the *Basic Statistics* option from the *Stat* menu — this displays the menus in figure D.98.

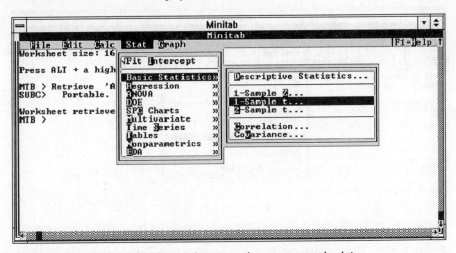

Figure D.98 Menu containing option to analyse one-sample data

Select the *1-Sample t* option to display the dialog box in figure D.99, and complete the box as shown in the figure. That is, select the column containing the data for which the confidence interval is to be calculated, make sure that the *Confidence interval* option is marked with an 'X', and enter the confidence level as a percentage into the *Level* option box. Select *OK* to execute the command.

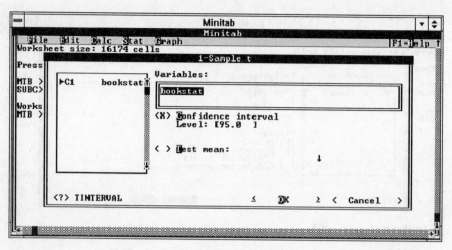

Figure D.99 Dialog box for producing the confidence interval for the population mean

D.38 Tsplot

Graph > Time Series Plot...

To use the menus to produce plots of time series, in which values from the same season are plotted with the same symbol, click on *Graph* to display the menu in figure D.100.

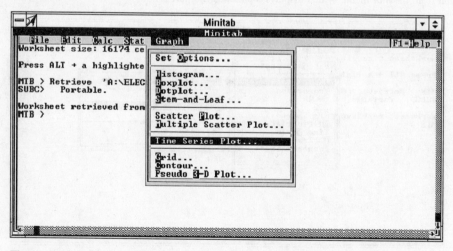

Figure D.100 Menu containing option to produce a plot of a time series

Select the *Time Series Plot* option to display the dialog box in figure D.101, and complete the box as shown in the figure. That is, specify the column containing the series in the *Series* option box, and specify the period of the seasonality in the *Period* option box. Then simply click on *OK* to produce the plot.

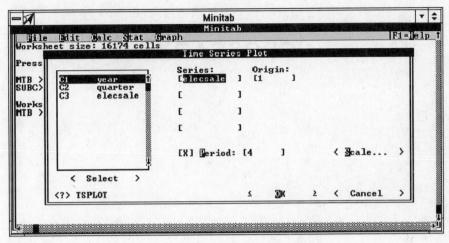

Figure D.101 Dialog box to produce a plot of a time series

GLOSSARY

For each entry, the term being defined is both bolded and italicised. Terms that form part of a definition and that are themselves defined elsewhere in the glossary are bolded but not italicised.

Accrued interest **Interest** calculated and added to the account.

Additive deseasonalisation of a **time series** Occurs when the **seasonal movement** for a season is removed by subtracting a constant amount over the whole period of the series.

Additive model for a **time series** Represents the observed **values** of the series as the sum of the four **components**.

Adjusted coefficient of determination (R^2_{adj}) A **coefficient of determination** that has been modified to take into account the **sample size**, n, and the number of **explanatory variables**, p.

Adjusted residual (R^A_{ij}) for a cell in a **two-way contingency table** Measures the difference between the **observed** and **expected frequency** for the cell, with the difference adjusted for its **variance**. Used to determine if the cell's observed frequency deviates significantly from the expected frequency.

Adjuster for cost-of-living Used to make cost-of-living adjustments to items such as wages and taxes. The **consumer price index** is commonly used for this purpose.

Aim of a **survey** Specifies the reason for conducting the survey; specific enough for the **target population** to be determined.

Alternative hypothesis for a **hypothesis test** The more general hypothesis; it allows more freedom in the possible values of each **parameter**.

Amortisation Repayment in full of an amount borrowed, plus the **accrued interest**, usually by means of equal **periodic payments**.

Analysis of variance table A table for laying out the calculations designed to compare **variances**; we take the ratio of two different variances, which are called **mean squares** in this context. The table consists of the columns for the source, **degrees of freedom** (DF), **sum of squares** (SS), mean squares (MS) and **F statistic** (F). The rows of the table consist of a total row and rows for the differing sources whose variances are to be compared.

Annuity A sequence of equal **periodic payments**.

Annuity due An **annuity** for which **periodic payments** are made at the beginning of each **time period**.

Assumptions for **statistical inference** Required for valid use of the **sampling distribution** for an **estimation procedure** or a **hypothesis test**. They can be divided as follows: a particular **probability model** represents the population **distribution of the variable**; and other validating assumptions. A set of **conditions** under which they are met can be identified.

Attitude scale in a **questionnaire** A score obtained from a series of questions designed to measure a respondent's attitude to a specific issue.

Australian Bureau of Statistics The official Commonwealth Government organisation dedicated to the collection of statistics; an important national **secondary data** source that provides an enormous amount of statistical data on various media.

Bar chart   A **distribution diagram** in which a rectangle or bar is plotted horizontally for each **value** of a **limited variable**; the length corresponds to the **frequency, proportion** or **percentage** for that value. The rectangles or bars for different values are separated to signify that the values themselves do not form, even conceptually, a continuous range.

Base period for an **index number**   The period relative to which changes in **variables** are measured. For a **fixed-base index number**, the base period is fixed at a period that is as 'normal' as possible — not in a peak or a trough of economic activity.

Basic sampling method   A **sampling method** that selects **observational units** from the whole, undivided **target population**.

Basket of commodities   The set of items for which changes in **price, value** or **quantity** are followed by using an **index number**.

Bias   The systematic deviation of sample conclusions from the actual **target population** conclusions.

Bimodal distribution   A distribution with two peaks.

Binding constraint in **linear programming**   A **constraint** defines the **optimal point** and is associated with a fully utilised **resource**.

Box-and-whisker plot (or **boxplot**)   A diagram particularly useful for illustrating the **central tendency** and **dispersion** for **unrestricted variables**. Constructed using the five measures: the minimum and maximum **values**, the **first** and **third quartiles** and the **median**.

Categorical variable   Its **values** are thought of as a set of possible categories for describing **observational units**.

Category rating scale in a **questionnaire**   A special type of **multiple choice question** used in **rating scale questions**. It consists of a set of ordered categories and respondents must mark the category that best describes their opinion. **Coding** a catetory rating scale question for input into the computer consists of assigning numeric values to repondents' answers.

Census   A study that observes every individual in the **population**.

Central tendency   The common tendency of the **values** of a **variable** to cluster about a typical value.

Centred moving average of order k [*CMA*(*k*)]   Obtained by computing a **moving average of order** k and then computing, from this moving average, the arithmetic **means** of successive pairs of **values**. Used when k is even.

Chain-base index number   An **index number** for which the increase for one period is expressed as a percentage of the previous period.

Chi-square distribution ($\chi^2_{degrees\ of\ freedom}$) with specified **degrees of freedom**   The **sampling distribution** of **Pearson's chi-square statistic**, the **test statistic** for the **goodness-of-fit test** and the **contingency table analysis**. The exact form of the distribution varies with its degrees of freedom — the peak of the distribution is always less than its degrees of freedom.

Class intervals in a frequency table   The divisions in the table which correspond to continuous, nonoverlapping ranges of the **values** of the **unrestricted variable** on which the table is based.

Class midpoint in a frequency table   The **mean** of the two values that define a **class interval**.

Classes in a one-way summary table   The divisions in the table which correspond to the **values** of the **limited variable** on which the table is based.

Classical time series analysis   Involves identifying and separating out the four **components** or types of movements in a **time series**: **long-term trend**; **cyclic movements**; **seasonal movements**; **irregular movements**.

Classification question in a **questionnaire**. A **factual question** that is asked chiefly to classify a respondent.

Closed question in a **questionnaire**   Offers the respondent a set of possible answers from which to choose.

Cluster of a **target population**   A group formed by **subdividing the population** before sampling and then selecting only some of the groups for observation.

Cluster sampling   The **target population** is subdivided into groups before sampling and the groups are then randomly selected; all units in the selected **clusters** are observed. Each cluster, and therefore each **observation unit** in a cluster, has the same chance of being selected.

Coding frame   The set of numeric values (usually 1, 2, 3 and so on) that are associated with the answers to a particular **questionnaire** question; used in **data coding**.

Coding the time period   Replacing the **values** of a time **variable** with convenient numeric values; 1, 2, 3 and so on are usually used when the times are equally spaced.

Coefficient of determination (R^2)   A **measure of association** that measures the **linear association** between two **unrestricted variables**, but with the direction of the **linear relationship** eliminated. Obtained by squaring the **linear correlation coefficient** and multiplying by 100. In the context of **regression**, it can be interpreted as the percentage of the total variation in the **response variable** that can be explained by the **explanatory variable**.

Coefficient of variation (*CV*)   A **measure of dispersion** that measures the spread in a set of numbers, as a percentage of the mean. Its formula is $CV = s/\bar{y} \times 100$ where s is the **standard deviation** and $\bar{y}$ is the **mean**.

Collapsed contingency table   Obtained by omitting and/or combining the rows and/or columns in the table. To combine rows, add the **frequencies** in the same column from the rows to be combined and recompute any percentages; do likewise for combining columns.

Collectively exhaustive values   A set of **values** for a **variable** whereby all **observational units** have values in the set. That is, a set of collectively exhaustive values covers all possible observed values.

Column chart   A **distribution diagram** in which a rectangle or bar is plotted vertically for each **value** of a **limited variable**; the height corresponds to the **frequency, proportion** or **percentage** for that value. The rectangles or bars for different values are separated to signify that the values themselves do not form, even conceptually, a continuous range.

Column percentage for a cell in the **main body of a contingency table**   The cell's **frequency**, divided by the total for the column in which the cell lies, and then multiplied by 100.

Column total in a **contingency table**   The total of the **frequencies** in a column of the table.

Component of a time series   A type of movement in the series.   In **classical time series analysis**, the components are: **long-term trend; cyclic movements; seasonal movements; irregular movements**.

Composite index number   An **index number** that measures changes in the **prices, values** or **quantities** of more than one item; the set of items is referred to as the **basket of commodities**.

Computer prompt   The set of characters at the lefthand edge of a line that a computer outputs to indicate that it is waiting for a response from you.

Computer solution method in **linear programming**   This finds the **optimal solution** by using a computer package like LINDO or EXCEL.

Compound interest   **Interest** calculated for both the original amount and the interest that has accrued to that time.

Conditions for **statistical inference**   These specify the circumstances that must apply to a situation, when an **estimation procedure** or **hypothesis test** is being employed, so that the **assumptions** required to use the **sampling distribution** for the procedure or test can be met.

Confidence interval bound   The value that defines the limits of a **confidence interval** and is equal to half the width of the confidence interval. It indicates the **precision** with which a **statistic** estimates the corresponding **parameter**.

Confidence interval (100γ%) for a parameter   The interval we can be 100γ% confident includes the **parameter** because it includes the parameter 100γ% of the time. The general form of a confidence interval is:

(**statistic** – theoretical value × variability of statistic,

statistic + theoretical value × variability of statistic)

where the theoretical value comes from a **sampling distribution** and is obtained by using a computer.

Confidence level (100γ%) for a **confidence interval**   The **probability** that the confidence interval will include the **parameter** being estimated.

Constraint in **linear programming**   A restriction that limited **resources** impose on the solution of the problem. Usually written as inequalities in terms of the **decision variables**.

Consumer price index in Australia   A **Laspeyres** type **index number** designed to measure quarterly variation in retail **prices** of goods and services that represent a high proportion of the expenditure of metropolitan employee households.

Contingency table   A **distribution table** presenting the **frequencies, proportions** or **percentages** for each possible combination of the **values** of the **limited variables** on which it is based.

Contingency table analysis   A **hypothesis test** that applies when the data consists of the **values** of two **limited variables** and when the **question to be investigated** is: are the two limited variables **dependent**?

Continuous variable   One for which the underlying **variable** measures a characteristic that, conceptually at least, varies continuously and so *potentially* the **values** form a continuum over the observed range.

Convenience sampling   The selection of **observational units** that are most easily obtained from the **target population**.

Count   The number of times a **value** or a **range of values** occurs; also called a **frequency**.

Cumulative probability (p_C)   The proportion of values below a specified value of a particular quantity, when the quantity is distributed according to a nominated **probability distribution function**.

Curvilinear association between two **unrestricted variables** Occurs when the **scatter diagram** for the two variables displays a curved trend.

Cyclic movements (*C*) in a **time series** The medium-term oscillations and swings that are of unequal length; each swing usually takes several years.

Data coding of a **questionnaire** Establisng the **coding frame** for each question and using these to choose numeric codes for each respondent's answers.

Data collection procedures Procedures for collecting data that maximise the validity of the collected information.

Data entry Entering data into the computer for analysis.

Data screen A spreadsheet-like screen in **Minitab**, for entering or modifying data.

Decision variable in **linear programming** This variable defines one of the alternatives you have to choose from to solve an **optimisation** problem. Decision variables are denoted by x_1, x_2 and so on.

Degrees of freedom for a **statistic** The number of independent values that are summed in obtaining the statistic.

Dependent limited variables Occur in **two-way contingency tables** and **two-way tables of a central tendency measure**.
  - In a two-way contingency table, the **limited variables** are dependent if there is a difference between the **column (row) percentages** in different columns (rows) of the **contingency table**. That is, the pattern of percentages in a column (row) depends on which column (row) is being examined.
  - In a two-way table of a central tendency measure, the limited variables are dependent in their effect on the **unrestricted variable** if the differences between the values of the measure in a row (column) of the table are not the same for all rows (columns) of the table. That is, the pattern in the values of the measure computed from the unrestricted variable depends on which row (column) is being examined.

Descriptive summaries Statistical procedures for summarising aspects of the behaviour of just the data being analysed.

Deseasonalisation The removal of the **seasonal movements** from an observed **time series** to produce a **deseasonalised series**.

Deseasonalised series The series formed after removing the **seasonal movements** from an observed **time series**.

Deviation from the mean $(y_i - \bar{y})$ The difference between an observed **value** and the **mean** of all the observed values of a **variable**.

Discrete variable The underlying **variable** measures a characteristic that is, conceptually, discontinuous, either because it is **nominal** or because its **values** are separated and so *potentially* cannot form a continuum over the observed range.

Dispersion The spread exhibited by the observed **values** of a **variable**.

Distribution Short form of *distribution of variables*.

Distribution attributes The aspects of the **distribution of variables** that are commonly examined: the **general shape**, **central tendency**, and **dispersion** of the distribution and the presence of **outliers**.

Distribution diagram A diagrammatic presentation of the **frequencies, relative frequencies (proportions)** or **percentages** from a **distribution table**.

Distribution of variables The pattern of observed **values** for a **variable** or observed combination of values of several variables; it reflects how frequently the various values or combinations occur.

Distribution table Summarises the **distribution** of one or more **variables**. It contains, for the **values** of a variable or combinations of values of several variables, the **frequencies, relative frequencies (proportions)** or **percentages** or some mix of these three.

Dotplot A **distribution diagram** constructed by drawing a line with a scale that covers the observed range of the data. Individual observations are plotted above this line as dots (or crosses), and coincident values have dots placed one above the other.

Dual price in **linear programming** The increase (decrease) in the **optimal solution** if one more (less) unit of **resource** is available for a **binding constraint**. Also called the **shadow price**.

Effective annual interest rate (*r*) for **compound interest** The **nominal interest rate** for a year obtained from the **interest rate for the time period**; it is the **interest** rate such that the **accrued interest** over the year computed using simple interest with it is the same as that computed using compound interest with the interest rate for the time period.

Equation for a straight line $(Y = b_0 + b_1 X)$ (or $Y = \beta_0 + \beta_1 X$)   The mathematical expression that specifies the position of the line on a **scatter diagram**. In the equation for the straight line: Y and X are the names of the variables; b_0 (or β_0) is the **intercept** and b_1 (or β_1) is the **slope**. The computed intercept and slope are collectively known as the **regression coefficients**.

Error checking   Checking data stored in the computer, for the inevitable errors that occur in **data coding** and **data-entry**.

Estimation procedures   Statistical procedures for estimating **population** quantities using a **sample**.

Expected frequency (E_{cell}) for a cell in a **one-way summary** or **contingency table**   The **frequency** that exactly conforms to an hypothesis about the population **proportions** for the cells of the table.

Experimental data   Obtained when the investigator manipulates the situation and the response to the manipulations is observed. That is, the investigator intervenes.

Explanatory variable (X) in **regression**   The **values** of this **variable** are to be specified in obtaining computed quantities. Quantities that might be computed are the **mean response**, the **intercept**, the **slope** or an **interval estimate**. In all these, the value of one variable is specified and the quantity computed for the other variable.

Exponential smoothing of a **time series**   The smoothed value at a particular time is the **weighted mean** of all previous **values** in the series; the **weights** decrease exponentially as you go back in the series. How much the previous observation contributes to a smoothed value is determined by the **smoothing constant**.

Extrapolation in **regression**   The computation of the **mean response** for **values** of the **explanatory variable** outside the observed range.

Extreme point in **linear programming**   The point of intersection of the **constraints**. The set of extreme points define the **feasible solution region** and are used to find the **optimal solution** for the problem.

F distribution $(F_{degrees\ of\ freedom_1,\ degrees\ of\ freedom_2})$ with *degrees of freedom$_1$ and degrees of freedom$_2$*   The **sampling distribution** for the **F statistic**, the **test statistic** for the **one-way analysis of variance** and the **F-test for the slope**. It is the sampling distribution of a test statistic that is the ratio of two **mean squares**. The exact form of the distribution varies with the degrees of freedom of the two mean squares in the observed F statistic.

F statistic $(F_{degrees\ of\ freedom_1,\ degrees\ of\ freedom_2})$ with *degrees of freedom$_1$ and degrees of freedom$_2$*   The **test statistic** for the **one-way analysis of variance** and the **F-test for the slope**. It is the ratio of two **mean squares** and is calculated using an **analysis of variance table**. The F statistic measures how far the data are from what would be expected under the **null hypothesis** for the **hypothesis test**.

F-test for the slope   The **hypothesis test** that applies when the data consists of the **values** of two **unrestricted variables** and when the **question to be investigated** is: is there a **linear relationship** between the two unrestricted variables?

Factual question in a **questionnaire**   Used to ascertain facts.

Feasible solution region in **linear programming**   The region where all **constraints** are satisfied.

Field-coded open question in a **questionnaire**   The interviewer asks an **open question** and records a **code** for the response; the interviewer determines the code from her or his private list.

Filter question in a **questionnaire**   Used to direct respondents to answer different sets of questions depending on their response to a previous question.

Finance mode   The mode that business calculators, such as the Sharp EL-735 calculator, use for financial calculations.

Financial mathematics   A set of rules for computing financial quantities. An understanding of these rules allows both business and individuals to obtain optimal results from their financial affairs.

Financial mathematics keys   The keys of a business calculator, such as the Sharp EL-735 calculator, which are important in **financial mathematics**. For the Sharp EL-735, they are $\boxed{n}$, $\boxed{i}$, $\boxed{PV}$, $\boxed{FV}$, $\boxed{PMT}$.

Finite population   In practice, one that is not very much larger than the **sample**. As a guide, the **population** is regarded as finite if its size is less than or equal to 20 times the **sample size** $(N \leq 20n)$.

Finite population correction factor   The factor that must be applied to the **confidence interval** when a **finite population** has been observed.

First quartile $(Q1)$ The **value** that has 25% of the observations below it; the $\left(\dfrac{n+1}{4}\right)$ th value in an ordered list of the observed values.

Fitted line   A line fitted to the pairs of **values** of two **unrestricted variables**; it summarises the trend in the relationship between two unrestricted variables.

Fitted values   A value obtained by replacing an observed **value** of the **unrestricted** (response) **variable** by the value of this variable that fits the **probability model** assumption. In **simple linear regression**, the probability model assumption is that of a **normal probability model with a linear relationship**. A fitted value for an **observational unit** ($\hat{y}_i$) is the value of the **response variable**, Y, for the point on the fitted line corresponding to the observed value of the **explanatory variable**, X, for that unit. In **one-way analysis of variance**, the probability model assumption is that of a **normal probability model with different group means**. A fitted value for an observational unit ($\bar{G}_i$) is the **mean** of the unrestricted variable for the group to which the unit belongs.

Fixed-base index number   An **index number** for which the increase over time is expressed as a percentage of the period nominated to be the **base period**.

Fixed numbers from the groups in a **survey**   Occurs when a predetermined, possibly unequal, number of **observational units** is selected from each group of the **target population** for inclusion in the **sample**.

Forecast   The value obtained in **forecasting** from a **time series**.

Forecasting for a **time series**   The prediction of future values for the **variable** on which the series is based. The value obtained is referred to as the **forecast**.

Frequency   The number of times a **value** or a **range of values** occurs; also called a **count**.

Frequency table   A **distribution table** that may contain either the **frequencies, proportions** or **percentages**, or some combination of these for the **class intervals** in the table.

Future value (S_n or FV)   The total amount, including **accrued interest**, at the end of the nth **time period**.

General level at a particular time in a **time series**   The value, at that time, with the **seasonal** and **irregular movements** removed; for an additive time series it is the value of $T_i + C_i$ and for a multiplicative time series it is the value of T_iC_i.

General shape of the **distribution of variables**   The type of pattern in which the observed **values** of a **variable** are distributed across the observed range.

Goodness-of-fit test   A **hypothesis test** used when the data consists of the **values** of one **limited variable** and when the **question to be investigated** is: are the population **proportions** for the values of the limited variable different from those hypothesised?

Grand total   The total number of observed **values**.

Graphic rating scale in a **questionnaire**   Used in **rating scale questions**. A standard length line (say 10 cm) is provided for the respondents to mark where they believe they fit between two extremes at either end of the line. The answer is recorded as the numeric **value** obtained by measuring the distance from one end of the line to the respondent's mark.

Graphical method in **linear programming**   The use of a diagram to find the **feasible solution region** for the **constraints** and, therefore, the **optimal solution**.

Gross annual rate of return   The amount of return on an investment, not taking account of expenses incurred in obtaining the return.

Grouped chart   A **bar** or **column chart** for two or more **limited variables** in which there is a rectangle for each combination of the **values** of the variables and the rectangles are grouped. A group of rectangles is formed by placing side-by-side those that have the same combination of values of all the variables, except one. That is, one variable is selected to have its values differ between the rectangles in any group.

Halo effect in a **questionnaire**   Occurs when the respondent gives a similar response to each of a series of questions without considering each question independently.

Histogram   A **distribution diagram** for an **unrestricted variable**; it consists of a set of joined boxes, each covering that part of axis corresponding to a **class interval**. For equal class intervals, the height of a box or length of a rectangular column is proportional to the **frequency, proportion** or **percentage**, whichever is being plotted.

Homogeneity of variance   Means equal **variance**. This term is used with **statistical inference** procedures in which the **normal probability model** involves more than one **normal distribution**. It is a condition for these procedures that all the normal distributions have the same variance, or equivalently the same **standard deviation**.

Hypothesis tests   Statistical procedures for answering yes/no questions about the **population** using a **sample**.

Independence condition   Requires that the outcome of any observation is not influenced by the outcome of any other observation.

Independent limited variables   Occur in **two-way contingency tables** and **two-way tables of a central tendency measure**.

- In a two-way contingency table, the limited variables are independent if there is no difference between the **column (row) percentages** in different columns (rows) of the **contingency table**. That is, the pattern of percentages in a column (row) is independent of which column (row) is being examined.

- In a two-way table of a central tendency measure, the limited variables are independent in their effect on the **unrestricted variable** if the differences between the values of the measure in a row (column) of the table are the same for all rows (columns) of the table. That is, the pattern in the values of the measure computed from the unrestricted variable is independent of which row (column) is being examined.

Index number   A **statistic** that measures the change in **variables** over time, or between different locations, relative to a **base period**. Conventionally expressed as a percentage with the value for the base period being 100%.

Infinite population   In practice, one that is very much larger than the **sample**. As a guide, the **population** size should be at least 20 times the **sample size** ($N > 20n$).

Influential outlier in **regression**   An observation that has a large influence on the value of the **slope** of the **fitted line**. It is separated, in the horizontal direction, from most points in the **standardised-residuals-versus-fitted-values plot**.

Intercept (b_0 or β_0) from the **equation for a straight line**   The position at which the line crosses the vertical (Y) axis; the value of the response variable (Y) when the explanatory variable (X) is zero.

Interest   The financial reward for lending or the price paid for borrowing money over a length of time.

Interest rate for the time period   The rate at which **interest** is to be accrued for the **time period** that applies to a particular interest calculation.

Interpolation in **regression**   The computation of the **mean response** for **values** of the **explanatory variable** within the observed range.

Interquartile range (*IQR*)   A **measure of dispersion** that is the difference between the **first** and **third quartile**; it gives the range covered by the middle 50% of the observed **values**.

Interval estimate   A continuous range of feasible values for a **parameter**.

Interval/ratio variable   One whose **values** can be ordered; also, numerically equal differences between values represent the same difference in the characteristic being observed.

Inventory question in a **questionnaire**   Based on a list that the respondents are asked to check or mark in some way; they are generally asked to mark several responses. The essential difference between an inventory question and other types of **closed questions** is that the list is not intended to be exhaustive.

Inverse cumulative probability distribution function   Yields the value of a quantity that is distributed according to a nominated **probability distribution function**, such as the **standard normal distribution** function. The value produced corresponds to a specified **cumulative probability**.

Irregular movement (*I*) in a **time series**   The transitory movement in a single observation, caused by chance events; that is, the outcome of events that will not occur again.

Iso-cost method in **linear programming**   The method of finding a minimum by moving a ruler, at the angle of the slope of the **objective function**, across the **feasible solution region** to the **extreme point** which is closest to the origin. This extreme point is called the **optimal point**.

Iso-profit method in **linear programming**   The method of finding a maximum by moving a ruler, at the angle of the slope of the **objective function**, across the **feasible solution region** to the **extreme point** which is furthest from the origin. This extreme point is called the **optimal point**.

Judgement sampling   The selection of certain **observational units** from the **target population**, chosen because the selector believes them to be representative.

Large-number condition   Requires a minimum size for certain frequencies in **one-way summary** or **contingency tables** — usually 5 or more. This requirement must be fulfilled by the **observed frequencies** for **confidence intervals** and by the **expected frequencies** for **hypothesis tests**.

Large-residual outlier in **regression**   An observation that deviates more than most from the **fitted line**. It is separated, in the vertical direction, from most points in the **standardised-residuals-versus-fitted-values plot**.

Laspeyres index number (*Index number$_L$*)   Both a **weighted** and a **prices index number**, it is computed using **base period** (year) **weights**, where the weights are the **quantities** of the commodities sold. The index number is the ratio, expressed as a percentage, of the total cost of the quantities of the commodities sold in the base period, at current period **prices**, to the total cost of the quantities of the commodities sold in the base period, at the base period prices.

Leaf of a number   The first digit to the right of the **split-point** for a **stem-and-leaf display**.

Leaf unit for a **stem-and-leaf display**   The unit of a number's **leaf** — it might be 100, 10, 1, 0.1, and so on.

Least significant difference [*LSD*(α)]   The smallest difference between a pair of **means** required to declare them to be **significantly** different. Computed after an **analysis of variance** when the **null hypothesis** of no **population** group mean differences has been rejected.

Lefthand side of a constraint in **linear programming**   The algebraic statement about the **resources** required.

Limited variable   One for which only a few (≤ 10, say) **values** are obtained. Its crucial feature is that a particular value is likely to be observed repeatedly.

Limited-variable probability model   The **variable** has k possible **values**, the ith value occurring in the **population** with **probability** π_i where $0 \leq \pi_i \leq 1$ and $\Sigma_{i=1}^{k} \pi_i = 1$.

Line diagram   Has two **variables** plotted and a line drawn between points with consecutive values on the horizontal axis.

Linear association between two **unrestricted variables**   Occurs when the **scatter diagram** for the two variables displays a straight line trend. Linearly associated variables are also said to have a **linear relationship**.

Linear correlation coefficient (r or ρ)   A **measure of association** that measures the extent to which two **unrestricted variables** are **linearly related**.

Linear form in **linear programming**   An equation in which every term is a constant times one **decision variable**. There are no terms with powers like $2x^2$ or products of variables like $3x_1x_2$.

Linear programming   A mathematical technique that provides the **optimal solution** for a problem involving several variables subject to **constraints**. There must be a clear objective, several alternatives, limited **resources**, an **objective function** and constraint inequalities that are **linear forms**. The constraint inequalities may define a **feasible solution region**, and the optimal solution usually occurs at an **extreme point** of this region.

Linear programming model   A combination of algebraic statements about the problem, including definition of the **decision variables**, the **objective function**, and the **constraints**.

Linear relationship between two **unrestricted variables**   Occurs when the **scatter diagram** for the two variables displays a straight line trend. Variables displaying a linear relationship are said to be **linearly associated**.

Long-term trend (T) in a **time series**   The general direction of the series over a long period of time. Usually at least 30 observations are required for any persistent pattern to emerge.

Main body of a contingency table   The cells of the table containing the **frequencies, proportions** or **percentages** corresponding to each possible combination of the **values** of the **limited variables** on which the table is based.

Main body of a two-way table of a central tendency measure   The cells of the table containing the **means** or **medians** for each possible combination of the **values** of the two **limited variables** on which the table is based.

Major category of financial mathematics   One of the four different areas of financial situations covered in this book: **simple interest; compound interest; ordinary annuity; annuity due.**

Major category of statistical procedures   One of the four basic subdivisions of statistical procedures: **data collection procedures; descriptive summaries; estimation procedures; hypothesis tests.** Each major category has the same broad objective.

Margins of a contingency table   The row and column added to the **main body** of the table; they contain **frequencies** or **percentages** computed from the main body.

Maximum tolerable error (e)   The **precision** to be achieved in estimating a **parameter**.

Mean ($\bar{y}$ or μ)   A **measure of central tendency**, calculated as the sum of the observed **values** divided by the number of observations. Can be described as the balance point of the data.

Mean response ($\bar{\bar{y}}$ or μ_Y) in **regression**   The typical or average **value** of the **response variable** (Y) for a specified value (x) of the **explanatory variable** (X). It is the value of Y that lies on the **fitted line** at the position that corresponds to the specified value, x, of X.

Mean square   An alternative name for a **variance**, used primarily in the context of an **analysis of variance** table. A **sum of squares** of some quantity divided by the **degrees of freedom** of the sum of squares.

Measure of association   A number that measures the extent to which the **values** for two **unrestricted variables** are related.

Measure of central tendency   A number calculated from a set of **values** for a **variable** to represent the value about which they tend to cluster or their typical value.

Measure of dispersion   A number calculated from a set of **values** for a **variable** to represent the amount of spread exhibited by them.

Median (M)   A **measure of central tendency**; the **value** that has as many values below it as above it — the middle value for the data.

Menu bar   The strip across the top of the session window that contains a list of the **pull-down menus** available in **Minitab**: File, Edit, Calc, Stat, Graph and Help.

Method of least squares   The procedure used in **regression** to fit the straight line or curve to the observed data. In this method, the sum of the squared distances of the observations from the **fitted line** is made as small as possible.

Method of smoothing   Dampens down the fluctuations in a **time series** to produce a **smoothed series**. Methods of smoothing include **regression, moving averages** and **exponential smoothing**.

Minitab   A statistical package with a wide range of statistical procedures; relatively easy to use and available on a wide range of computers.

Minitab command   A line of information that begins with the name of the command and specifies an operation to be performed.

Minitab prompt   MTB > which is placed at the bottom of the screen or window by Minitab to indicate that it is waiting for you to enter a **Minitab command**.

Minitab subcommand   An additional line of information that begins with the name of the subcommand and specifies additional information to be taken into account in carrying out the **Minitab command**.

Missing value in a **questionnaire**   Occurs when a respondent does not answer a question. A code for missing values must be included in the **coding frame** for a question.

Mode   The **value** of a **variable** that occurs most frequently because it has the highest **frequency**.

Mode of response   The method of obtaining a response.

Moving average [$MA(k)$]   The set of **means** formed from consecutive, overlapping subsets of the observations. The number of observations in each subset is the same and is called the **order of the moving average** (k). Computing the moving average for a set of data is a **method of smoothing** it.

Multiple choice question in a **questionnaire**   Respondents are given a set of possible answers; these answers are exhaustive.

Multiplicative deseasonalisation of a **time series**   Occurs when the **seasonal movement** for a season is removed by dividing by a constant proportion over the whole period of the series. Achieved by applying **additive deseasonalisation** to the logarithms of the observed series.

Multiplicative model for a **time series**   Represents the observed **values** of the series as the product of the four **components**.

Multistage sampling   Involves more than a single **subdivision of the population** before sampling. Can involve combinations of **stratified, cluster** and **quota sampling**.

Mutually exclusive values   A set of **values** for a **variable** whereby an **observational unit** can take only one value. That is, there is no ambiguity in the value taken by an observational unit.

Negative cashflow   Money paid out.

Negative linear relationship between two **unrestricted variables**   A **linear relationship** for which larger **values** of one **variable** are associated with smaller values of the other variable.

Nominal interest rate (j)   Usually the quoted interest rate per annum.

Nominal variable   Its **values** are names and they have no implicit order as far as the characteristic being observed is concerned.

Nonbinding constraint in **linear programming**   A **constraint** that does not define the **optimal point** and is associated with a **resource** that is not fully utilised.

Nonlinear association between two **unrestricted variables**   Another name for **curvilinear association**.

Nonprobability sampling   A **sampling method** in which the probability of selecting an **observational unit** is unknown.

Nonresponse bias in a **survey**   Occurs when selected **observational units** fail to provide a response.

Normal distribution   A **symmetric distribution** that is bell-shaped. The only possible difference between two normal distributions is in their **mean** and **standard deviation**.

Normal probability model   The **variable** is **continuous** and its **values** in the **population** follow the **normal distribution**.

Normal probability model with a linear relationship   Used in **simple linear regression**; has the following properties:
- the population **distribution** of the **response variable**, for a particular **value** of the **explanatory variable**, is approximated by the **normal distribution**;
- there is a **linear relationship** between the population **means** of these normal distributions and the values of the explanatory variable;
- all normal distributions have the same population **standard deviations**.

Normal probability model with different group population means   Used in **one-way analysis of variance**; has the following properties:
- the population **distribution** of the **unrestricted variable**, for a particular group, is approximated by the **normal distribution**.
- the population **means** of the groups may be different;
- the population **standard deviations** are the same for all groups.

Normal probability plot   Produced by plotting a set of numbers against their **normal scores**.

Normal probability plot correlation coefficient (r_N)   The **linear correlation coefficient** between the observed **values** and the values that would be expected for a **sample** of the same size from a **population** whose distribution is normal; that is, between the data and their **normal scores**.

Normal score   Approximates the average value that would be expected for the ith smallest observation in a **sample** of n observations of a **variable** whose **population** distribution is normal. For example, the normal score for the smallest of n numbers is the value expected for the smallest observation in a sample of n observations of a **normally distributed variable**.

Normally distributed variable   One for which the relative frequency distribution for the **values** of the **variable** for all **observational units** from the **population** is approximately **symmetric** and bell-shaped. Hence, the population **distribution of the variable** can be approximated by the **normal distribution**.

Null hypothesis (H_0), for a **hypothesis test**   Generally the hypothesis that postulates specific conditions on the values of the **parameters**; the hypothesis that is presumed true in carrying out a hypothesis test.

Numbers out of the head   Numbers written down just as they come to mind.

Objective function in **linear programming**   A **linear form** that defines the profit (cost) in terms of **decision variables**; the function to be maximised (minimised) to obtain the **optimal solution**.

Objective function coefficient in **linear programming**   The profit (cost) for each unit of a **decision variable**.

Observational data   Collected to examine things as they are.

Observational study   Collects **observational data**; might be a **census** or a **survey**.

Observational unit   The unit to be observed as a single entity; for example, responses might be obtained from a company or household as a whole or from an individual.

Observed frequency (O_{cell}) for a cell in a **one-way summary** or **contingency table**   The **frequency** with which a **value** of a **limited variable**, or a combination of the values of two or more limited variables, occur in a set of data.

One-way analysis of variance (one-way ANOVA)   The **hypothesis test** that applies when the data consists of the **values** of one **unrestricted** and one **limited variable** and when the **question to be investigated** is: is there a difference between the population **means** of the unrestricted variable for the different values of the limited variable?

One-way summary table   A **distribution table** that contains classes corresponding to the **values** of the **limited variable** and, for each class, the **frequency**, **relative frequency** or **percentage** or some combination of these three. It is a one-way table because it is classified by one limited variable.

One-way table of a central tendency measure   Consists of the values of a **measure of central tendency** such as the **mean** or **median**. Each value in the table corresponds to a **value** of the **limited variable** and is computed from the values of the **unrestricted variable** for the **observational units** that have that value of the limited variable. Called a *one-way table* because it contains data for the different values of only one limited variable.

One-way table of a dispersion measure   Consists of the values of a **measure of dispersion** such as the **standard deviation** or **interquartile range**. Each value in the table corresponds to a **value** of the **limited variable** and is computed from the values of the **unrestricted variable** for the **observational units** that have that value of the limited variable. Called a *one-way table* because it contains data for the different values of only one limited variable.

Open question in a **questionnaire**   The only restriction that is placed on the respondent's reply is the space provided for it.

Opinion question in a **questionnaire**   Used to find out about people's opinions and attitudes.

Optimal allocation of numbers from the groups in a **survey**   Choosing the number of **observational units** sampled from each group of the **target population** to obtain the most precise estimates.

Optimal point in **linear programming**   A combination of the values of the **decision variables** which will give the **optimal value** within the limits of the **resources**. It is found by evaluating the **objective function** for each of the **extreme points** and choosing the one(s) that produces the largest (smallest) value.

Optimal solution in **linear programming**   The set of **optimal points**. In the problems presented in this book, the optimal solution has consisted of only a single optimal point.

Optimal value in **linear programming**   The maximum profit (minimum cost) achievable under the **constraints**. It is the combination of the **decision variables** that gives the largest (smallest) value of the **objective function**; found by evaluating the objective function for each of the **extreme points** and choosing the largest (smallest) value.

Optimisation   A method of finding the **optimal solution**.

Order of the moving average (k)   The number of observations in each subset of the data for which a **mean** is computed.

Ordinal variable   Its **values** can be ordered, but it can not be determined how far apart they are.

Ordinary annuity   An **annuity** for which **periodic payments** are made at the end of each **time period**.

Outlier   An extreme **value** of a **variable** that is either much smaller or much larger than nearly all the other observed values of the variable.

Paasche index number (*Index number$_p$*)   Both a **weighted** and a **prices index number**, it is computed using current period (year) **weights**, where the weights are the **quantities** of the commodities sold. It is the ratio, expressed as a percentage, of the total cost of the quantities of the commodities sold in the current period, at current period **prices**, to the total cost of the quantities of the commodities sold in the current period, at **base period** prices.

Parameter   A quantity calculated from the **values** of one or more **variables** for all **observational units** in the **population**. Represented by Greek letters.

Pearson's chi-square statistic ($X^2_{degrees\ of\ freedom}$) with the specified **degrees of freedom**   The **test statistic** for the **goodness-of-fit test** and the **contingency table analysis**. It measures the difference between a set of **observed frequencies** and a set of **expected frequencies**.

Pearson's product moment correlation coefficient (r or ρ)   Another name for the **linear correlation coefficient**.

Percentage   Just a **proportion** multiplied by 100.

Periodic payment (p)   The name given to a regular payment or savings amount in an **annuity**.

Pie chart   A **distribution diagram** for a **limited variable** in which a circle is divided into arcs, one for each **value** of the limited variable, so that the angle defining each arc is proportional to the **relative frequency** for that value.

Pilot survey   A small **sample** taken to test timing and **questionnaire** design prior to conducting the main **survey**.

Physical device for random selection   One of many devices designed for doing random selection; for example, coins that are tossed, a pack of playing cards, a dice, a container with numbered tickets or a set of numbered balls.

Point estimate of a **parameter**   A **statistic** that provides a single value estimate.

Polygon   A **distribution diagram** for an **unrestricted variable**; the **frequency**, **proportion** or **percentage** is plotted against the **class midpoint** as points and the points are joined with lines. It is a special type of **line diagram**.

Pooled standard deviation (s_{pooled}) from a **one-way analysis of variance**   The value obtained by combining the **standard deviations** from the different groups. It is equal to the square root of the error **mean square** from the **analysis of variance table**.

Population for a **question to be investigated**   The set of all **observational units** about which conclusions are to be drawn as a result of the statistical procedure used to analyse a set of data.

Population frame   The complete listing of a **target population**.

Positive cashflow   Money received.

Positive linear relationship between two **unrestricted variables**   A **linear relationship** for which larger **values** of one **variable** are associated with larger values of the other variable.

Possible outlier   An observation that the distance below the **first quartile** or above the **third quartile** is more than 1.5 times the **interquartile** range.

Precision with which a **statistic** estimates a **parameter**   The maximum discrepancy between the statistic and the parameter in $100\gamma\%$ of **samples**. Hence, it is the maximum error that is likely to be made in estimating the parameter. It is equal to the **confidence interval bound** and is half the width of the **confidence interval**.

Precoded questionnaire   Includes on the **questionnaire** form the **codes** for the answers to the **closed questions**.

Prediction interval (100γ%) for a future observation   The interval we can be 100γ% confident includes the **single value** of the **unrestricted variable** for a future observation from the same **population** as the **sample**. That is, an **interval estimate** of a single value is obtained.

Present value (P or PV)   The original amount lent or borrowed; also called the **principal**.

Price of a good or service   The amount to be paid to purchase the good or service.

Price index number   An **index number** that measures the change in the **prices** of goods and services.

Price relative   The proportion obtained by taking the ratio of the **price** of a single commodity in a period (year) to the price of that item in the **base period** (year).

Primary data   Data used by an investigator that made, or was responsible for, the original observations.

Principal (P or PV)   The original amount lent or borrowed; also called the **present value**.

Probability   The **relative frequency** of the **values** of a **variable** for a very large **population**.

Probability distribution function   A mathematical equation for computing **probabilities** for a **distribution**. **Probability models** and **sampling distributions** are specified in terms of probability distribution functions.

Probability model   A representation of the **relative frequencies** with which the **values** of the **variable** occur in the **population**. Hence, it represents the population **distribution**.

Probability of the test statistic (p_T) The **probability** of obtaining the observed value, and more extreme values, of the **test statistic**, assuming the **null hypothesis** is true and the **assumptions** are met. This probability is computed from the **sampling distribution** of the test statistic.

Probability sampling   A **sampling method** in which the probability of selecting an **observational unit** is known .

Probable outlier   An observation that the distance below the **first quartile** or above the **third quartile** is more than three times the **interquartile range**.

Problem-solving tool   A tool for solving the problem of answering **questions to be investigated**.

Processed data   Tables and diagrams summarising the information contained in the original **raw data**.

Proportion   Generally obtained as the ratio of two numbers. The **relative frequency** (p or π) is a proportion commonly used in statistics that can be presented in a **distribution table**.

Proportional numbers from the groups in a **survey**   Occur when the proportion of **observational units** to be selected from the **target population** is decided. Then, the proportion of observational units to be selected from each group for inclusion in the **sample** is the same as for the whole population.

Pull-down menu   A list of groups of related **Minitab commands** that Minitab displays when the menu name is selected on the **menu bar**.

Qualitative variable   Its **values** describe the *attributes* of the characteristic on which the **variable** is based.

Quantitative variable   Its **values** measure the *quantity* of the characteristic on which the **variable** is based.

Quantity of a good or service   The total volume or mass of the good or service sold or produced over a period of time.

Quantity index number   An **index number** that measures the change in the **quantities** of goods and services produced or sold.

Question to be investigated   A specific question that is answered by collecting data and applying a statistical procedure to the data; this way the investigator may solve a problem.

Questionnaire   A set of questions for ascertaining facts and opinions from a group of people.

Quota sampling   Before sampling, the **target population** is subdivided into groups and the quota, or number of **observational units** to be sampled, is specified for each group; units are then selected from the whole target population by **convenience sampling**, and units from a particular group are rejected once the quota for that group has been filled.

Random numbers   Numbers tested for randomness, obtained from computer software or a textbook table.

Range (R)   A **measure of dispersion** that is the maximum observed **value** minus the minimum observed value.

Range of values   A continuous range specified by an upper and lower limit. Some **estimation procedures** estimate the range of values covered by a specified **proportion** of **observational units** in the **population**.

Rating scale question in a **questionnaire**   An **opinion question** that asks the respondent to give a rating for the subject of the question.

Raw data   The recorded **values** of the **variables** for the **observational units**.

Registers of a calculator   The memories of a calculator, such as the Sharp EL-735, used to store numbers in calculations for **finance** and **statistics modes**.

Regression   The fitting of straight lines and curves to describe the relationship between **unrestricted variables**.

Regression coefficients The computed quantities from the fitted equation for the line or curve obtained when **regression** is used to do the fitting. In **simple linear regression**, the regression coefficients are the **intercept** and **slope**.

Relative frequency (p or π) Computed by dividing the **frequency** of a **value**, or a **range of values**, by the total number of observations. It is also called the **proportion** and can be presented in a **distribution table**.

Representative sample An unbiased fraction of the **observational units** in the **target population**. The fraction will be **biased** if you systematically exclude from the **sample**, segments of the population whose observation would alter the **survey's** conclusions.

Residual (e_i or e_{ij}) The difference between an observed value of the **unrestricted** (response) **variable** and its **fitted value**.

Residual-versus-fitted-values plot Produced by plotting the **residuals** on the vertical (Y) axis against the **fitted values** on the horizontal (X) axis.

Resource in **linear programming** Material available in limited quantities as described by the **constraints**.

Resource range in **linear programming** The amount by which a **resource** may be changed before a **binding constraint** becomes **nonbinding**.

Response bias A systematic error in the response given to a question in a **survey**.

Response variable (Y) **in regression** The **variable** for which quantities are to be computed for specified **values** of the **explanatory variable**. Quantities that might be computed are the **mean response**, the **intercept**, the **slope** or an **interval estimate**. In all of these, the value of one variable is specified and the quantity computed for the other variable.

Righthand side of a constraint in **linear programming** Usually the amount of the **resource** which is available.

Row percentage for a cell in the **main body of a contingency table** The cell's **frequency** divided by the total for the row in which the cell lies and then multiplied by 100.

Row total in a **contingency table** The total of the **frequencies** in a row of the table.

Sample The fraction of the **population** that is observed in a **survey**.

Sample size (n) The number of **observational units** to be observed in a **survey**.

Sampling distribution of a **statistic** Gives the probability with which values of the statistic will occur when a **population** is repeatedly sampled, the statistic being computed, for each **sample**, from the **values** of the **variable** being observed.

Sampling distribution for the sample proportion The **normal distribution** centred on π and with the **standard deviation** given by $\sigma_p = \sqrt{\pi(1 - \pi)/n}$.

Sampling distribution of a test statistic The **sampling distribution** that applies to the **test statistic** from a **hypothesis test**. It gives the **probability** with which values of the test statistic will occur when a **population** is repeatedly sampled, *if* the **null hypothesis** is true. The two distributions used in this book for sampling distributions of test statistics are the **chi-square** and **F distributions**.

Sampling method A strategy for selecting **observational units** in a **survey**.

Scatter diagram Displays the relationship between two **unrestricted variables**. A point is plotted for each pair of **values** of the unrestricted variables.

Seasonal index for a single season Measures the discrepancy between the **general level** and the value expected for that season. A seasonal index, computed as part of **additive deseasonalisation**, indicates the amount that the value for that season can be expected to be above or below the general level. A seasonal index, computed as part of **multiplicative deseasonalisation**, indicates the proportion of the general level that can be expected for that season.

Seasonal movements (S) in a **time series** The short-term patterns that recur repeatedly. The time period over which a complete pattern occurs is always the same and is usually no more than a year.

Secondary data Data used by an investigator who neither made, nor was responsible for, the original observations; usually obtained from a publication.

Selection bias Caused by systematic inclusion or exclusion of segments of the **target population** when selecting **observational units** for a **sample**.

Self-selected sample The **observational units** sampled are those who volunteer in response to a widely broadcast invitation to take part in the **survey**.

Sensitivity analysis in **linear programming** A method of investigating how the **optimal solution** changes under different conditions.

Session window An area of the computer screen set up by **Minitab** to display the **Minitab commands** that have been executed, along with the output produced by these commands.

Shadow price in **linear programming**   The increase (decrease) in the **optimal value** if one more (less) unit of **resource** is available for a **binding constraint**. Also called the **dual price**.

Significance level (α) for a **hypothesis test**   Specifies the **probability** that will be classified as unlikely enough to consider that the evidence against the **null hypothesis** is overwhelming. Another interpretation: the level of risk we are prepared to take in making a **type I error**, the mistake of rejecting the null hypothesis when it is true.

Significant   The term for describing the result of a **hypothesis test** when the **null hypothesis** is rejected.

Simple index number (*Index number$_s$*)   An **index number** calculated from a single item; the ratio of the **prices, values** or **quantities** in a period (year) to the prices, values or quantities in the **base period** (year), multiplied by 100.

Simple interest   **Interest** calculated for the agreed **time period** and paid on the original sum of money borrowed or invested.

Simple linear regression   Fitting a straight line to the trend exhibited by two **unrestricted variables**.

Simple random sampling   The independent selection of **observational units** from a complete list of the **target population** so that each unit has the same chance of being selected.

Single value   The **value** of a **variable** for a single **observational unit**. Some **estimation procedures** estimate a single value.

Sinking fund   A special fund into which **periodic payments** are made for a specific purpose such as buying a car.   As it involves periodic payments it is an **annuity**.

Skew-to-the-left distribution   A **unimodal distribution** characterised by having a few **values** that are much smaller than most of the values.

Skew-to-the-right distribution   A **unimodal distribution** characterised by having a few **values** that are much larger than most of the values.

Slope (b_1 or β_1) from the **equation for a straight line**   The rate of change in the **variable** on the vertical axis (Y) for each unit change in the variable on the horizontal axis (X).

Smoothed series   Produced from a **time series** by using a **method of smoothing**; has less fluctuations than the observed series.

Smoothing constant for **exponential smoothing**   The number that controls the extent to which the previous observation contributes to a smoothed value. The smoothing constant must be between zero and one.

Split-point for a **steam-and-leaf display**   The position before which the numbers are to be split. They might be split before the hundreds, tens, units, first decimal place, second decimal place or some other point.

Stable population proportions condition   The **proportion** of the **population** taking a particular **value** of the limited **variable** must remain constant throughout the period of data collection and to which the inferences are to apply.

Stacked chart   A **bar** or **column chart** for two or more **limited variables** in which there is a rectangle for each combination of the **values** of the variables and the rectangles are stacked. A stack of rectangles is formed by placing end-to-end those that have the same combination of the values of all the variables, except one; that is, one variable is selected to have its values differ between the rectangles in any stack.

Standard deviation (s or σ)   A **measure of dispersion** that can be interpreted loosely as the 'average' absolute **deviation from the mean**; that is, the typical distance from the mean, ignoring whether the observations are above or below the mean. It is computed as the square root of the **variance**. It can be proven that at *least* 75% of observations fall within two standard deviations of the mean, irrespective of the **distribution** of the data.

Standard deviation about the regression line (s_y)   Measures the spread of the original observations around the **fitted line**. Compare this to the ordinary **standard deviation** that measures the spread of the observations around the **mean**.

Standard error of a **statistic** ($s_{statistic}$)   Measures the variability of the statistic under repeated sampling from the **population**. Standard errors encountered in this book include those for the **proportion** (s_p), the **mean** (s_y), the **intercept** (s_{b_0}), the **slope** (s_{b_1}) and the **mean response** ($s_{\bar{y}}$).

Standard normal distribution   A **normal distribution** with a **mean** zero and a **standard deviation** of one. This distribution is a special normal distribution that applies to a **normally distributed variable** that has been **standardised**.

Standardise a set of **values**   Subtract the **mean** of all values from each **value** and divide the result by their **standard deviation**.

Standardised residuals   Obtained by **standardising** the **residuals**; as the residuals already have a **mean** of zero, each residual is standardised by dividing it by its **standard deviation**.

Standardised-residuals-versus-fitted-values plot Produced by plotting the **standardised residuals** on the vertical (Y) axis against the **fitted values** on the horizontal (X) axis.

Standardised score (z) The number of **standard deviations** by which a **value** deviates from the **mean**.

Statistic Colloquially, a quantity computed from the **values** of one or more **variables**. In **statistics**, a quantity computed from the values of one or more variables that come from a **sample** only. Represented by roman letters.

Statistical inference Uses information from a **sample** to draw conclusions about the **population**; comprised of two branches of **statistics** — **estimation procedures** and **hypothesis tests**.

Statistics The science that deals with the collection, classification, and use of numerical facts or data, bearing on a subject or matter.

Statistics mode The mode that calculators, such as the Sharp EL-735 calculator, use for statistics calculations.

Stem of number The value formed from the digits to the left of the **split-point** being used in forming a **stem-and-leaf display**.

Stem-and-leaf display A combined **distribution table** and **distribution diagram** in which the **leaves** for the observations are grouped according to their **stems**.

Stratified random sampling The **target population** is subdivided into groups before sampling and **observational units** are randomly sampled from each group. Each unit in a group has the same chance of being selected.

Stratum (plural **strata**) of a **target population** A group formed by **subdividing the population** before sampling and then observing **observational units** from all groups.

Subdividing the population Dividing the **population** into groups before selection, then using the **basic sampling methods** to sample from them. The basis of several **sampling methods**.

Sum of products of a set of pairs of numbers The result of multiplying each pair of numbers together and summing the products.

Sum of squares of a set of numbers The result of squaring each number and summing the squared values.

Survey An **observational study** that observes only a fraction of the **observational units** in the **target population**.

Symmetric distribution A **unimodal distribution** for which the shape to the left of the peak is a mirror image of the shape to the right. Put another way, if you folded the distribution along the centre line, its left side would fit exactly onto its right side.

Systematic sampling The selection of **observational units** from a complete list of the **target population** and only the first unit is selected at random; then the other units are obtained by taking every kth unit, where k is suitably chosen.

Target population for a **survey** The set of all **observational units** about which the investigator **aims** to draw conclusions.

Term deposit Money lent for a fixed length of time, after which it is returned as **principal** and **accrued interest**.

Test statistic for a **hypothesis test** Measures how far the observed data is from what would be expected if the **null hypothesis** were true; quantifies the evidence against the null hypothesis.

Theoretical value for computing the tolerance interval (g_T) corresponding to n, $100\pi\%$ and $100\gamma\%$ The value that has been theoretically derived for computing the **tolerance interval ($100\pi\%$, $100\gamma\%$) for the middle $100\pi\%$ of population values**.

Theoretical value for the normal probability plot correlation coefficient (r_T) corresponding to n and α The value such that in only $100\alpha\%$ of samples will the value of the **normal probability plot correlation coefficient** be less than it.

Theoretical value for the standard normal distribution (z_T), corresponding to $100\gamma\%$ The value such that $100\gamma\%$ of the **values** for a **standard normal distribution** are between $-z_T$ and z_T.

Theoretical value for the t distribution (t_T) corresponding to $100\gamma\%$ and the specified **degrees of freedom** The value such that $100\gamma\%$ of the values for a t distribution with these degrees of freedom are between $-t_T$ and t_T.

Third quartile ($Q3$) The **value** that has 75% of the observations below it; the $\left(\dfrac{3(n+1)}{4}\right)$th value in an ordered list of the observed values.

Three-way contingency table A **contingency table** based on three **limited variables**.

Time period in **interest** calculations The length of time over which interest is calculated or accrued on a single amount of money such as the balance in an account. For **simple interest**, it corresponds to the period over which the money is lent or borrowed. For **compound interest**, it is the period for which it is agreed that interest will be accrued. For an **annuity**, it corresponds to the time between successive **periodic payments**.

Time series   The history of a **variable**; that is, the recorded **values** of the variable over a particular period of time.

Toggling on a calculator   Switching between alternative states by pushing a single key.

Tolerance interval (100π%, 100γ%) for the middle 100π% of population values   The interval we can be $100γ\%$ confident includes the range containing the middle $100π\%$ of the values, of the **unrestricted variable**, in the **population**. It is an **interval estimate** of a **range of values**.

Total interest (I_T) The interest accumulated over the total time of a loan. It is the difference between the final **future value** and the original **principal** or **present value**.

Total percentage for a cell in the **main body of a contingency table**   The cell's **frequency**, divided by the **grand total** and then multiplied by 100.

Trial-and-error method in **linear programming**   It finds the **optimal solution** by substituting a series of values for the **decision variables**.

Two-stage cluster sampling   Involves not only the **simple random sampling** of **clusters**, but the random sampling of **observational units** from the selected clusters.

Two-way contingency table   A **contingency table** based on two **limited variables**.

Two-way table of a central tendency measure   Consists of the values of a **measure of central tendency** such as the **mean** or **median**. Each value in the table corresponds to a combination of the **values** of two **limited variables** and is computed from the values of the **unrestricted variable** for the **observational units** that have that combination of the values of the two limited variables. Called a *two-way table* because it contains data for the different values of two limited variables.

Type I error in a **hypothesis test**   The **null hypothesis** is true and it is rejected; analogous to convicting an innocent person. The **probability** of making a type I error is equal to the **significance level**, $α$.

Type II error in a **hypothesis test**   The **null hypothesis** is false and it is not rejected; analogous to failing to convict a guilty person.

Type of statistic   A class of **statistics** that have a common property: they all measure the same aspect of the behaviour in a set of data.

Unimodal distribution   A **distribution** with a single peak.

Unpaired t-test   The **hypothesis test** that applies when the data consists of an **unrestricted variable** and a two-valued, **limited variable** and the **question to be investigated** is: is there a difference between the two population **means** of the unrestricted variable, for the different values of the limited variable? This test is equivalent to the **one-way analysis of variance** in that, for the same hypotheses, the **probability of the test statistics** from the two tests are equal.

Unrestricted variable   One for which many (>10, say) **values** are obtained. Its crucial feature is that a particular value does not recur very often.

Unweighted aggregative index number (*Index number$_{UA}$*)   Measures the change in the **prices** of a set of commodities by taking the ratio of the sum of the prices in a period (year) to the sum of the prices in the **base period** (year), multiplied by 100. Unweighted aggregative index numbers can be similarly computed for **values** or **quantities**.

Unweighted relatives index number (*Index number$_{UR}$*)   Measures the change in the **prices** of a set of commodities as the **mean** of the **price relatives**, multiplied by 100. Unweighted relatives index numbers can be similarly computed for **values** or **quantities**.

Value of a good or service   The amount paid for the total **quantity** of the good or service sold or produced over a period of time.

Value of a **variable**   The number or category representing the amount or state of the characteristic associated with the variable.

Value index number   An **index number** that measures the change in the monetary **value** of goods and services.

Variable   A characteristic that varies from one **observational unit** to another.

Variance   **Sum of squares** of some quantity, such as the **deviations from the mean**, divided by the **degrees of freedom** of the sum of squares.

Weight (w_i) A quantity that reflects the importance of the number with which it is associated.

Weighted index number   Measures the change in the **prices**, **values** or **quantities** of a set of commodities, taking into account the relative importance of the different items as reflected in a set of **weights**. Usually the changes in the prices are measured and the weights are the quantities of the items sold.

Weighted mean ($\bar{y}_w$ or $μ_w$)   The **mean** of a set of numbers that takes into account a set of **weights**. The **sum of products** of the weights and the numbers divided by the sum of the weights.

Well-defined limited variable   One for which the **values** are **mutually exclusive** and **collectively exhaustive**. Consequently, each **observational unit** in the **population** can be unambiguously classified as taking one of the possible values for the variable.

X is known without error   Means that there is no error in the **values** recorded for the **explanatory variable**, *X*, in **regression**.

z-test for a proportion   The **hypothesis test** that applies when the data consists of one two-valued **limited variable** and when the **question to be investigated** is: are the population **proportions** for the **values** of the limited variable different from those hypothesised? This test is equivalent to the **goodness-of-fit test** in that, for the same hypotheses, the **probability of the test statistics** from the two tests are equal.

z-test for a proportion difference   The **hypothesis test** that applies when the data consists of two two-valued, **limited variables** and the **question to be investigated** is: are the two variables **dependent**? This test is equivalent to the **contingency table analysis** in that, for the same hypotheses, the **probability of the test statistics** from the two tests are equal.

REFERENCES

Australian Bureau of Statistics (1983–92) *Monthly summary of statistics, Australia.* ABS Catalogue No. 1304.0, Canberra.

Australian Bureau of Statistics (1984, 1986, 1991) *Apparent consumption of selected foodstuffs and nutrients, Australia.* ABS Catalogue No. 4306.0, Canberra.

Australian Bureau of Statistics (1988) *The Australian Consumer Price Index: Concepts, Sources and Methods.* ABS Catalogue No. 6461.0, Canberra.

Australian Bureau of Statistics (1989–93) *Tourist Accommodation, Australia, Quarterly.* ABS Catalogue No. 8635.0, Canberra.

Australian Bureau of Statistics (1992) *Consumer Price Index.* ABS Cat. No. 6401.0, Canberra.

Australian Bureau of Statistics (1993a) *Measuring Australia's economy: a student guide.* ABS Catalogue No. 1360.0, Canberra.

Australian Bureau of Statistics (1993b) *A guide to the consumer price index.* ABS Catalogue No. 6440.0, Canberra.

Australian Bureau of Statistics (1994a) *Catalogue of Publications and Products.* ABS Catalogue Number 1101.0, Canberra.

Australian Bureau of Statistics. (1994b) *Year Book Australia 1994, No. 76.* ABS Catalogue No. 1301.0, Canberra.

Australian Guarantee Corporation Limited (1993) AGC investment rates. (Advertisement.) *The Australian*, 10 December 1993, 21.

Bankers Trust Australia Group (1993) This is Perhaps the Most Infuriating Ad You Will Ever Read. Unless You are 21. *The Persxonal Financial Review* in *The Weekend Australian*, 23–24 October 1993, p. 16.

Baum, P., and Scheuer, E. M. (1976) *Statistics made relevant: a casebook of real life examples.* Wiley, New York.

Choice (1991) Interest rates, where do they come from? Vol. 32 (6), pp. 18–20.

Cody, R. P., and Smith, J. K. (1985) *Applied Statistics and the SAS Programming Language.* North Holland, New York.

Delbridge, A., Bernard, J. R. L., Blair, D., Peters, P., and Butler, S. (1991) *Macquarie Dictionary.* 2nd edn. The Macquarie Library, Sydney, NSW.

Dilmore, G. and Wilson, A. R. (1992) Investment return and risk. *The Appraisal Journal*, 60, pp. 532–48.

Elliot, K. and Christopher, M. (1973) *Research Methods in Marketing*. Holt, Rinehart and Winston, London.

Farr, J. E. (1993) Late starters end up with more. (Business: Letters to the Editor) *The Australian*, 23 November 1993, p. 43.

Graduate Careers Council of Australia. (1993) *Graduate Destination Survey 1992*. Graduate Careers Council of Australia, Melbourne.

Guthrie, F. (1993) Bankers trust alchemy sounds fantastic. (Business: Letters to the Editor) *The Australian*, 11 November 1993, p. 23.

Hahn, G. J. and Meeker, W. Q. (1991) *Statistical intervals: a guide for practitioners*. Wiley, New York.

Halper, S. D., Davis, G. C., O'Neil-Dunne, P. J., Pfau, P. R. (1985) *Handbook of EDP Auditing*. Warren, Gorham & Lamont, Boston, pp. 14.13–14.14.

Hely, S. (1989) *Women and Money: Financial Strategies for Women*. Allen and Unwin, Sydney.

Hider, J. (1994) Local crime rate slashed by 10pc. *The Eastern Courier Messenger*, 20 July 1994, Messenger Press, Adelaide.

Hillier, F. S. and Lieverman, G. J. (1990) *Introduction to Operations Research*. 5th edn. McGraw-Hill, Sydney.

Howe, W. G. (1969) Two-sided tolerance limits for normal populations — some improvements. *Journal of the American Statistical Association*, 64, pp. 610–20.

Hruby, H. F. and Panton, D. M. (1993) Scheduling transfer champagne production. *OMEGA International Journal of Management Science*, 21, pp. 691–7.

Maher, C. and Burke, T. (1991) *Informed Decision Making*. Longman-Cheshire, Melbourne.

Martin, P. and Burrow, M. (1991) *Applied Financial Mathematics*. Prentice-Hall, Sydney.

Mellor, J. and Best, P. (1993) Smart package a boost for private buyers. *The Australian*, 2 November 1993, Number 9108.

Moser, C. A. and Kalton, G. (1971) *Survey Methods in Social Investigation*. 2nd edn. Heinmann Educational Books, London.

Oppenheim, A. N. (1966) *Questionnaire Design and Attitude Measurement*. Heinemann Educational Books, London.

Reserve Bank of Australia (1980–93) *Reserve Bank of Australia Bulletin*. Sydney.

Ryan, T. A. & Joiner, B. L. (1976) Normal probability plots and tests for normality. Technical Report, Statistics Department, The Pennsylvania State University.

Ryan, B. F., Joiner, B. L. & Ryan Jr., T. A. (1985) *Minitab Handbook*. 2nd edn. PWS-Kent, Boston.

Sharp EL-735 Instruction Guide and Application Manual. Sharp Corporation, Japan.

South Australian Department of Labour, Commissioner for Public Employment. (1992) *1991/92 Annual Report*. South Australian Department of Labour, Adelaide.

South Australian Commissioner of Police (1993) *Statistical Review — Annual Report 1992–93*. South Australian Police Department, Adelaide.

The Advertiser (1990) National Trading Stocks: Property Trusts. (Business) 6–9 October 1990.

The Advertiser (1993a) National Trading Stocks: Industrials. (Business) 13 November 1993, p. 49.

The Advertiser (1993b) Labour closing the gap, poll finds. 27 November 1993, pp. 1–2.

Watson, R. T. (1989) Key issues in information systems management: an Australian perspective — 1988. *The Australian Computer Journal*, 21, pp. 118–29.

INDEX

Senario : (Q1-Q3) (28%)

Des summa[?] : Doesnt have a clear point

Estimation : estimate, £, Proportion

Hypothesis test : If, whether, claim (Yes/non answer)

statistics (Q4 - Q6) 48%

Regression : 1. forecast, Price = 2.82 + 1.81 ba

Index numbers

Time series — trend, cyclic, seasonal, irregularities
  - add / mult model
  - Period (7 day etc quartly)
  - moving averages / centre averages
      (odd)   (even)